Teaching Special
Students in
General Education

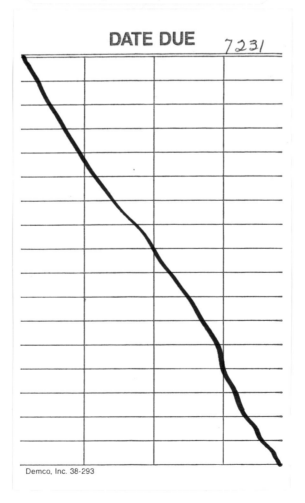

FIFTH EDITION

Teaching Special Students in General Education Classrooms

Rena B. Lewis
San Diego State University

Donald H. Doorlag
San Diego State University

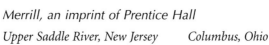

Merrill, an imprint of Prentice Hall

Upper Saddle River, New Jersey   Columbus, Ohio

Library of Congress Cataloging-in-Publication Data

Lewis, Rena B.

Teaching special students in general education classrooms / Rena B. Lewis, Donald H. Doorlag — 5th ed.

p.   cm.

Rev. ed. of: Teaching special students in the mainstream. 4th ed. c1995.

Includes bibliographical references and index.

ISBN 0-13-095307-5

1. Inclusive education—United States.   2. Special education—United States.   3. Mainstreaming in education—United States.   I. Lewis, Rena B. Teaching special students in the mainstream.   II. Doorlag, Donald H.   III. Title.

LC1201L48 1999

371.9—dc21   98-4433

CIP

Cover Photo: © Uniphoto, Inc.
Editor: Ann C. Davis
Production Editor: Julie Peters
Production Buyer: Laura Messerly
Production Coordination and Text Design: Elm Street Publishing Services, Inc.
Photo Researcher: Nancy Ritz
Cover Designer: Dan Eckel
Director of Marketing: Kevin Flanagan
Marketing Manager: Suzanne Stanton
Advertising/Marketing Coordinator: Krista Groshong

This book was set in Minion by The Clarinda Company and was printed and bound by R. R. Donnelley & Sons Company. The cover was printed by Phoenix Color Corp.

Photo Credits: Tony Freeman/Photo Edit, p. 3; Kevin Fitzsimmons/Merrill, p. 6; Larry Hamill/Merrill, pp. 12, 38, 95, 99, 101, 132, 183, 239, 311; Scott Cunningham/Merrill, pp. 23, 63, 147, 233, 258, 267, 295, 359, 374, 393, 427, 437, 465; Tom Watson/Merrill, pp. 27, 150, 202, 395, 399, 429; Michael Newman/Photo Edit, pp. 28, 323; James L. Shaffer, pp. 35, 370, 377, 415; David Napravnik/Merrill, p. 69; Richard Hutchings/Photo Edit, pp. 77, 343; Todd Yarrington/Merrill, pp. 87, 152, 176, 235, 304, 406; Jeff Greenberg/Photo Edit, pp. 117, 199; Tom Hutchinson/Merrill, p. 123; Elena Rooraid/Photo Edit, p. 141; Mary Kate Denny/Photo Edit, pp. 161, 424; Bonnie Kamin/Photo Edit, p. 173; Bill Aron/Photo Edit, p. 188; Courtesy of Intellitools, p. 220; Courtesy of Sunburst Communications, p. 222 (top left); Courtesy of Edmark Corporation, p. 222 (top right); Courtesy of Don Johnston, Inc., p. 222 (bottom left); Courtesy of Dragon Systems, p. 222 (bottom right); Courtesy of Prentke Romich Company, p. 223; Courtesy of TeleSensory Company, p. 224; A Ramey/Photo Edit, p. 227; Anthony Magnacca/Merrill, p. 278; Paul Conklin/Photo Edit, p. 286; Barbara Schwartz/Merrill, pp. 331, 442; Courtesy of Ablenet, pp. 334, 361; Courtesy of Sentient Systems Technology Inc., p. 335; Frank Siteman/Photo Edit, p. 352; T. Hubbard/Merrill, p. 360; Robin Sachs/Photo Edit, p. 367; Courtesy of Phonic Ear, Inc., pp. 384, 385; Nancy Sheehan/Photo Edit, p. 410; David Young-Wolff/Photo Edit, p. 420; Courtesy of The Learning Company, p. 428; Courtesy of Intelligent Peripheral Devices, p. 441; Anne Vega/Merrill, p. 452; Mary Hagler/Merrill, p. 454.

Printed in the United States of America

10 9 8 7 6 5 4 3 2 1

ISBN: 0-13-095307-5

Prentice-Hall International (UK) Limited, *London*
Prentice-Hall of Australia Pty. Limited, *Sydney*
Prentice-Hall of Canada, Inc., *Toronto*
Prentice-Hall Hispanoamericana, S.A., *Mexico*
Prentice-Hall of India Private Limited, *New Delhi*
Prentice-Hall of Japan, Inc., *Tokyo*
Simon & Schuster Asia Pte. Ltd., *Singapore*
Editora Prentice-Hall do Brasil, Ltda., *Rio de Janeiro*

With thanks for your support and encouragement
through the years:

Jim Lewis

Deanne Doorlag

Wayne and Florence Douglas

With the highest hopes for the years ahead:

Dylan Lewis

Kristi Doorlag

Scott Doorlag

Preface

This book is about two things: special students and teaching. It is designed to prepare the professional educator to effectively teach the range of students found in the typical elementary or secondary classroom. It provides information about four groups of students with special needs: students with disabilities, gifted and talented learners, culturally and linguistically diverse individuals, and students at risk for school failure. In addition, it presents practical strategies for adapting standard instruction to meet the learning needs of all students in general education classrooms.

THE FIFTH EDITION

The fifth edition has been thoroughly updated with the addition of several new topics and expanded coverage of others. Included are discussions of important areas such as:

- The Individuals with Disabilities Education Act (IDEA) Amendments of 1997, including new provisions for the development of IEPs and new discipline procedures
- Inclusion, full inclusion, and least restrictive environment
- Collaboration and the team approach
- Instructional adaptations for students with attention deficit hyperactivity disorder (ADHD) and those with traumatic brain injury
- Strategies for the inclusion of students with severe disabilities
- Classroom modifications for students with autism
- The World Wide Web and other technology resources for general educators

The fifth edition reflects current research in the fields of special and general education (more than 150 new references have been added), and there is information on the newest technologies available for use with special students in general education classrooms. Several of the "Spotlight on Technology" sections now feature software and assistive devices recommended for students with special needs.

A new feature, "Window on the Web," introduces readers to websites that offer valuable information about special education, general education, or the teaching-learning process.

ORGANIZATION AND CONTENT

In organizing this book, we have attempted to maintain a noncategorical approach to instruction while acknowledging the differential impact of student characteristics on school performance. To accomplish this, the first eight chapters of the book (and the Epilogue) address the needs of all special students and their teachers. The chapters dealing with instructional methods (Chapters 9 to 17), in contrast, are tied to specific populations of students and the types of school problems they most often encounter. However, the instructional strategies discussed in these chapters are relevant for any student with the same difficulties. For example, because students with learning disabilities are characterized by the problems they experience with mastering basic skills, the chapter focusing on this group includes techniques for teaching reading, written language, and mathematics skills. These techniques can and should be used with other students facing similar skill acquisition problems.

The 17 chapters of this book are divided into four major sections. The first part, "Introduction," identifies the purposes of inclusion, provides a rationale for a team approach to the solution of educational problems, and describes the major instructional needs of special students.

The second part, "Skills for the General Education Teacher," addresses the needs of the educator. Strategies are provided for achieving four basic instructional goals: adapting instruction, managing classroom behavior, promoting social acceptance, and coordinating the classroom learning environment. Also, information is provided on the effective use of computers and other technologies in the general education classroom.

In the third part, "Methods for Teaching Students with Disabilities in General Education," teaching strategies are suggested for a variety of different types of special students. These include students with learning disabilities, mild retardation, behavioral disorders, communication disorders, physical and health impairments, and visual and hearing impairments. This part also discusses interventions for individuals with four other types of disabilities: students with attention deficit hyperactivity disorders (ADHD) (Chapter 9), severe disabilities (Chapter 10), autism (Chapter 12), and traumatic brain injuries (Chapter 13).

The fourth part, "Methods for Teaching Students with Other Special Needs in General Education," recommends instructional techniques for three other groups of students: gifted and talented individuals, culturally and linguistically diverse students, and students at risk for school failure.

A brief Epilogue, "Inclusion Today . . . and Tomorrow," ends the book. It examines past mistakes, current practices, and some of the promising approaches that will give new direction to the inclusion of special students in school and society.

SPECIAL FEATURES

You will notice several types of special features boxed throughout this book.

- "Inclusion Tips for the Teacher" answers some of the questions teachers most often ask about inclusion.

- "For Your Information" boxes highlight important facts teachers should know about the field or their students.

- "Spotlight on Technology" boxes provide information about the use of new technologies with students with special needs.

- "Window on the Web," a feature new to this edition, describes sites on the World Wide Web of interest to teachers of special students.

- "Things to Remember" boxes end each chapter and provide a brief summary of major points in each chapter.

In addition to these special feature boxes, key terms are highlighted in the text in **bold** print and are correspondingly defined in the glossary at the end of the book. At the end of each chapter are activities which extend the information presented in the

chapter by providing opportunities for school observations, interviews with practicing professionals, perusal of the special and general education literature, and exploration of the World Wide Web.

 SUPPORT MATERIAL FOR STUDENTS AND INSTRUCTORS

The fifth edition has an enhanced instructor support package, including a Student Study Guide, an Instructor's Manual, Computerized Test Banks in both Macintosh and Windows formats, Companion Website for both the professor and student, and an ABC Video Library. The following are descriptions of each of these support materials.

Student Study Guide

A new addition to the package for this text is a Student Study Guide. The guide provides students with information and activities to extend learning. It is organized by chapter and students can check their understanding of major concepts through guided reviews and self-tests.

Instructor's Manual

The Instructor's Manual, also organized by chapter, contains objectives, terminology, a detailed outline, a set of questions appropriate for class discussions, and essay assignments. Also within the manual are over 1,000 objective test questions (multiple-choice, true-false, and completion) as well as questions that may be used for essay examinations.

Computerized Test Bank

In addition to the printed test bank of questions found in the Instructor's Manual, the *Prentice Hall Custom Test* is available in either Macintosh or Windows format. This software is available upon request from your Prentice Hall sales representative.

Companion Website

A companion website is available for both students and professors. Students can take self-quizzes and submit their responses online to the professor as well as view their scores and obtain page references in the text for answers to questions marked incorrectly. Students also have access to chat rooms and bulletin boards for peer discussions. Professors will have a syllabus builder which allows them to develop and customize a syllabus for their course.

ABC Video Library

Free to professors is a video library containing 14 video segments from ABC News. Of varying lengths and covering a variety of topics, these segments give students a poignant picture of students with disabilities, their families, and their teachers. The full list of segments, including their source and time, is noted below.

ABC Video	Programming and Length
Common Miracles: The New American Revolution in Learning, Part I	ABC Special Parts I and II 42:45
Bill Cosby's Dyslexia Crusade: Cosby's Tribute to Ennis	Good Morning America 5:47
Almost Home	Primetime Live (approx. 13:10)
Teacher's Little Helper	20/20 13:25
Gee Whiz, Whiz Kids	Turning Point 42:14
Building Brains: The Sooner, the Better	Nightline 7:51
Race for a Miracle: Brad and Vicki Marqus Story	Turning Point 42:24
Stephen's World	20/20 12:40
Children's Legacy	Primetime Live 14:19
My Child	Primetime Live 14:20
Billy Golfus	Person of the Week 4:31
Ebonics and the Teaching of Standard English	Nightline 6:47
Maggie Lee Sayre	Person of the Week 4:16
Marla Runyon	Person of the Week 3:43

ACKNOWLEDGMENTS

Our greatest debt is owed to our students and the special and general educators and educators-in-training who asked the difficult questions that prompted the writing of this book. We also wish to thank Dr. Kris English for her contributions in the area of inclusion strategies for students with hearing impairments and Dr. Tamarah Ashton for her assistance with the development of a model IEP form and her preparation of the student study guide, instructor's manual, and test bank for this edition. Thanks also to our editors, Ann Castel Davis and Carol Sykes. We'd also like to thank the following reviewers: Robert J. Evans, Marshall University; Christine Givner, California State University, Los Angeles; Nancy Lahmhuber, Eastern Michigan University; Jennifer E. Miederhoff, Murray State University; Robert G. Monahan, Lander University; RaeLynne Rein, UCLA; Colleen Shea Stump, San Francisco State University; Qaisar Sultana, Eastern Kentucky University; and Carolyn Talbert-Johnson, The University of Dayton.

Last, but never least, we say thanks one more time to our partners, Jim and Deanne, for continuing their support and understanding through yet another edition.

Rena B. Lewis
Donald H. Doorlag

Contents

Chapter 8

Using Computers and Other Technologies in the Classroom 198

PART III
Methods for Teaching Students with Disabilities in General Education 231

Chapter 9

Teaching Students with Learning Disabilities and Attention Deficit Hyperactivity Disorders 232

PART 1

Introduction

chapter 1

Success for All Students in the General Education Classroom

Behind each classroom door lies a world of diversity. In a typical class of students, there is a wide range of abilities. Some students learn easily; others require much assistance. Some are well behaved; others, mischievous. Some are friendly; others, ill at ease with their peers. In addition, students perform differently at various times and under different circumstances. The class leader may be overcome with shyness when asked to speak at a school assembly. The student who excels in science may write and spell poorly. Addition and subtraction problems may be easy for a student, but multiplication may be extremely difficult. Such variations contribute to the wonder of individuality.

When students with special needs are members of a class, the range of diversity increases. Students with disabilities, gifted and talented students, and culturally and linguistically diverse students are indistinguishable from their peers in most ways. However, their learning needs may be more serious or more compelling. Such students are individuals with different personalities, preferences, skills, and needs. Like all students, they present a challenge to the teacher.

This book is for teachers who wish to learn more about students with special needs. It is also about good teaching. All students, particularly those with special learning needs, deserve special care and special teaching. This book provides teachers with the skills needed to deal with the complex and often perplexing diversity that lies behind the classroom door.

CHANGING TERMINOLOGY: FROM MAINSTREAMING TO INCLUSION

Many different terms have been used to describe the practice of educating students with special needs in the general education classroom. In the 1970s and 1980s, most professionals called this approach *mainstreaming*. In the 1990s, the terms *full inclusion* and *inclusion* became more popular. However, these terms differ somewhat in meaning, and it is important to understand those differences.

Mainstreaming* refers to the inclusion of special students in the general educational process. Students are considered mainstreamed if they spend any part of the school day with general education class peers. In a typical mainstreaming program, special students in general education classrooms participate in instructional and social activities side by side with their classmates. Often they receive additional instruction and support from a special educator such as a resource teacher. That instruction may take place within the general education classroom or outside of it in a setting such as a resource room.

Special students are those with special learning needs. Because of these needs, they require instructional adaptations in order to learn successfully. This book considers four types of students special: pupils with disabilities, gifted and talented individuals, culturally and linguistically diverse students, and students at risk for school failure. Because of physical, cognitive, or emotional disabilities, some children and adolescents receive special education services in addition to (or, in some cases, in place of) the general educational program. Other special students may not be offered special programs in their schools, but their special learning needs soon become apparent to the general education teacher.

Integration of special students into the mainstream of education differs according to the needs of the individual. The amount of time special students participate in regular class activities varies from student to student. For some, the mainstream is their full-time permanent placement; for others, mainstreaming occurs only for a portion of the school day. The activities in which mainstreamed students take part also vary. Some interact with typical peers primarily on a social basis; others are included in both social activities and classroom instruction. In the area of instruction, many participate in most of the general education curriculum, whereas others are mainstreamed only for selected subjects.

Mainstreaming is an educational program that varies with the needs and abilities of the student. It is characterized by the meaningful interaction of special and typical students in social activities and/or classroom instruction. Mainstreaming has been defined in many ways. In one early definition, mainstreaming is described as "temporal, instructional, and social integration" (Kaufman, Gottlieb, Agard, & Kukic, 1975, p. 5). Not only are students with special needs placed in an educational environment with typical peers for some specified amount of time (temporal integration), they participate meaningfully in the academic activities of the general educa-

---

*Words appearing in **boldface** in the text are defined in the Glossary.

tion class (instructional integration) and are accepted as members of that class by their teacher and classmates (social integration). Integration to this extent is a real possibility for many special students, particularly those with mild learning and behavior problems. However, severe disabilities may prevent some students from full participation in all instructional aspects of the general education class.

Full inclusion, a newer term than *mainstreaming,* was introduced by professionals interested in students with severe disabilities. The full inclusion movement calls for reform of practices that exclude and segregate individuals with disabilities (Stainback & Stainback, 1985; Thousand & Villa, 1990). Advocates of full inclusion maintain that the general education classroom is the most appropriate full-time placement for all students with disabilities—not only those with mild learning and behavior problems, but also those with more severe disabilities. In the purest form of this model, students do not leave the mainstream to receive special services; instead, support is provided within the regular classroom setting.

Many special education professionals disagree with the assumption that full-time mainstreaming is the only appropriate placement for students with disabilities. They argue that other options, such as resource rooms, should be available so that educational programs can be tailored to the specific needs of individual students. This is the position of the Council for Exceptional Children (CEC), the major professional organization in special education. According to the *CEC Policy on Inclusive Schools and Community Settings* (1993b),

> CEC believes that a continuum of services must be available for all children, youth, and young adults. CEC also believes that the concept of inclusion is a meaningful goal to be pursued in our schools and communities. In addition, CEC believes children, youth, and young adults with disabilities should be served *whenever possible* in general education classrooms in inclusive neighborhood schools and community settings [italics added].

As discussed later in this chapter, this position is consistent with current federal laws and their requirements for placement of students with disabilities in the "Least Restrictive Environment."

Inclusion is the term most often used today to describe the placement of students with special needs in general education. *Inclusion* is a more modern term than *mainstreaming,* but unfortunately its meaning is imprecise. Sometimes *inclusion* is used as shorthand for *full inclusion;* at other times, it is a synonym for *mainstreaming.* It is important to determine what each speaker and writer means by the term *inclusion* because there are basic philosophical differences between the approaches of full inclusion and mainstreaming.

In this book, we use the term *inclusion* to refer to the meaningful participation of students with disabilities and other special needs in general education classrooms and programs. Although we believe that all students should be participants in the general education process, we also contend that the nature and extent of their participation should be determined on an individual basis. No one program, placement, or service arrangement meets the needs of all students.

Including students with special needs in general education programs is not a new idea. In the early days of education in the United States, classrooms served a wide variety of individuals, including some students with disabilities. The one-room schoolhouse with its range of ages and skills is an example. Kirk and Gallagher (1979) describe an inclusion program that began in 1913 for students with vision losses. Students spent part of their day in the regular classroom and part in a special "sight saving class."

Today, most special students begin school in general education and receive the majority of their education there. Many never leave the general education classroom. If their learning problems become apparent, some are identified as disabled and receive special education services. Of these, few are served in special classes and special schools. Those who do attend special classes often join their regular class peers for social activities and for instruction in nonacademic subjects such as art, music, and physical education. However, most students with disabilities are educated in general education classes with part-time special services provided if necessary. In the 1994–1995 school year, for example, the general education classroom was the primary educational placement for 73% of this nation's children and youth with disabilities ages 6 to 21 (U.S. Department of Education, 1997a). Consider the stories of Tiffany and Josh that follow. Tiffany and Josh are students with disabilities who participate fully in general education while receiving special assistance in problem areas. They are examples of successfully included students.

Tiffany is 8 years old and likes to swim, roller-skate, and eat hot dogs. She and her two best friends, Jennifer and Sarah, walk to school together each morning. They are all in Ms. Cole's second grade class. Tiffany likes school this year, but last year was very different. Tiffany is a student with special needs; she has learning problems. In first grade Tiffany had great difficulty with reading. This year she works with the resource teacher for a half hour each day, and she's beginning to make progress in reading. In her second grade class she does well in math and handwriting, and she can keep up with her classmates in spelling. Tiffany is successfully included.

Josh is a high school student who is planning to attend college when he graduates. He wants to study chemistry or physics. This year he's taking English, American history, biology, and geometry. Josh is a student with special needs; he has a physical disability and travels by wheelchair. Josh rides a special bus to school and attends an adapted physical education class. Josh writes and types slowly, so he sometimes needs extra time to complete tests and assignments. His grades in all his classes are excellent, and he has many friends. Josh is successfully included.

Later in the chapter we will take a look at portions of the Individualized Education Programs for Tiffany and Josh.

STUDENTS WITH SPECIAL NEEDS

Most discussions of inclusion concentrate on only one type of special student: children and adolescents with disabilities. Students who have a disability that negatively affects their school performance are served by special education, and federal laws uphold their right to a free, appropriate, public education. In this book, however, we have expanded the concept of special students to include three other groups with learning needs significant enough to warrant special consideration. These are gifted and talented students (often served by special education but not protected by the laws for learners with disabilities), culturally and linguistically diverse students, and students at risk for school failure. The special needs of these students, like those of many students with disabilities, can often be ac-commodated within the general education classroom.

Special students are a heterogeneous group. They may learn quickly and easily or with great difficulty. Their school behavior may be beyond reproach or frequently inappropriate. Some have sensory or physical disabilities. Others stand out because of their speech, language, or culture. Despite their special needs, such students can and do learn. However, more than most students, they require good teaching to succeed in general education classrooms.

Students with disabilities may have special learning needs because of a cognitive, physical, sensory, language, or emotional disability. According to Public Law 105-17, the Individuals with Disabilities Education Act Amendments of 1997, students with disabilities include those with

> mental retardation, hearing impairments (including deafness), speech or language impairments, visual impairments (including blindness), serious emotional disturbance (hereinafter referred to as 'emotional disturbance'), orthopedic impairments, autism, traumatic brain injury, other health impairments, or specific learning disabilities. [Sec. 602(3)(A)(i)]

Another disability, attention deficit disorder (ADD), is covered under other federal legislation.

Some of the terms that describe disabilities in federal laws are replaced or changed in common usage. For example, most special educators prefer *behavioral disorders* to *emotional disturbance.* Also, *orthopedic impairments* are often called *physical impairments,* and the term *ADD* may be changed to *ADHD* to include students with attention deficit hyperactivity disorder.

Students with learning disabilities have adequate general intelligence and are able to succeed in many school tasks. However, because of specific disabilities in areas such as attention, perception, and memory, they experience difficulty in school. They may encounter learning problems in one or more, although usually not all, academic subjects. In contrast, students with mental retardation generally are delayed in most, if not all, academic subject areas. They are characterized by a slower rate of learning and difficulty with reasoning tasks.

Students with behavioral disorders may have adequate academic achievement despite poor classroom behavior, or their behavior problems may interfere with learning. Such students may be disruptive or withdrawn, they may experience difficulty controlling their own behavior, or they may lack the skills necessary for building and maintaining interpersonal relationships with peers and adults.

Communication problems are primary in students with speech and language impairments. A student's speech may be difficult for others to understand, or language development may be delayed. Students with autism experience difficulty in socialization as well as in communication. With visual and hearing impairments, the disability is sensory. Individuals with visual impairments may be blind or partially sighted; those with hearing impairments may be deaf or hard of hearing. In either case, learning takes place through the senses still available to the student.

Students with physical and health impairments may participate fully in regular class activities. However, those with limited physical mobility, such as those who travel by wheelchair, may take a less active role. Some with chronic health problems may have special needs because of prolonged school absences. In general, students with physical and health needs can learn successfully in general education. For many of these special students, their physical problems have little effect on their ability to learn.

Two other groups of individuals with disabilities are often members of general education classes: students with traumatic brain injury (TBI) and those with attention deficit hyperactivity disorder

(ADHD). Most students with TBI are members of general education classes when the accident or other trauma that causes the injury to the brain occurs, and most return to that setting after hospitalization and rehabilitation. Students with ADHD typically remain in the general education setting while receiving assistance for problems in attention, impulsivity, and hyperactivity.

Like learners with disabilities, **gifted and talented students** are exceptional. Although they usually do not encounter school failure, their special abilities require special teaching. Gifted students are unusually bright; they may learn quickly and excel in all areas. They may be far ahead of their peers and thus require special attention and instruction. Some gifted students are creative; others may have special abilities in specific areas such as art, music, drama, and leadership. Opportunities for expression of creativity and talents can be provided within the general education classroom.

Culturally and linguistically diverse students present a different type of challenge. Although many students from diverse groups do not need special assistance to succeed in general education, some do. The customs, traditions, and values of their culture may set them apart from their peers and hinder their acceptance. Some students may be fluent speakers of English; others may be bilingual, speaking English and another language; and still others may be just beginning to acquire English language skills. If communication is difficult, learning problems may result.

Also posing a challenge to the teacher are **students at risk for school failure.** Although these students are not considered disabled under the law, their current performance and future welfare are threatened by a host of complex societal problems: poverty, homelessness, child abuse, and drug and alcohol abuse. They are the potential school dropouts, potential or actual delinquents, runaways, teenage parents, and suicide risks. Like other special students, students at risk have very real educational needs that must be addressed if the likelihood for school failure is to be reduced.

Students with special needs come to the attention of their teachers when they require instructional assistance in order to succeed in school. Their needs, however, are similar to those of their peers, although probably more serious and long-standing. Every class, no matter how homogeneous, has its bright and not-so-bright students, its troublemaker

For Your Information

Special Students

- Although students with special needs differ in the extent of instructional adaptation they require, most have mild learning problems. Only a small proportion have severe disabilities.
- Approximately 10.5% of the population aged 6 to 17 is identified as disabled (U.S. Department of Education, 1997a). In a typical classroom of 30 students, there may be 3 students with disabilities.
- Many people think of physical problems when they hear the term *disability*. However, physical, visual, and hearing impairments are the least common types of disabilities. Most frequent are learning disabilities, speech and language impairments, behavioral disorders, and mental retardation.
- It is usually not possible to tell whether students are special from their physical appearance. Typical students may be indistinguishable from gifted students, students with learning disabilities, and those with speech impairments.
- It is possible for a student to have more than one special need. A young child with mental retardation may have poor speech and language skills, a talented adolescent may have a learning disability, and a student who is blind may be gifted.

---

or behavior problem, and its student with a transitory physical impairment in the form of a broken arm or leg. Special students only enhance the range of skills and abilities within the general education classroom. To learn more about students with special needs, see "For Your Information" above. Boxes such as these, placed throughout the book, present facts of interest to teachers.

HISTORICAL PERSPECTIVES AND CURRENT PRACTICES

Today, most students with special needs are educated in general education classrooms. If identified as disabled, gifted, or in need of English language instruction, they may also receive part-time services from a trained specialist such as a special education teacher. In some cases, that professional provides support to students (or to the teacher) within the general education classroom; in others, students leave the classroom for brief periods to receive instruction in a resource room or other setting. In either case, students with special needs remain with their peers for all general education activities in which they can successfully participate.

Not all students with special needs spend the majority of the school day in the general education classroom. Special classes (and, in some locations, special schools) are available for students with severe disabilities whose instructional needs are different from and more intense than those of their age peers. Although educated in separate programs, these students are included in general education nonacademic and social activities whenever feasible. Also, they may increase their level of participation in the general education program as they acquire new skills and/or as professionals become more proficient at providing them the support they need to succeed in the regular classroom. The door to the general education classroom remains open to all students with special needs. This has not always been so. Inclusion, as it is known today, has had a long developmental period.

The Past

In the early days of education in the United States, special students were placed in general education classes because this was the only placement available. Special services were virtually nonexistent. Students with special needs did not receive assistance from trained specialists; classroom teachers were left to cope with special students as best they could. Students considered difficult to teach, such as those with severe disabilities, were often excluded from public education.

With the growth of special education and other such services, changes occurred. Children and adolescents with severe disabilities, who had been denied an education, were provided with special schools. Regular class students with learning and behavior problems were removed from general education and placed in separate special classes. Because those students were having difficulty meeting the demands of the general education classroom, intensive full-time special education services were seen as the remedy. It was thought that the needs of students with disabilities could best be served by specially trained teachers in special situations, far from the general education mainstream.

Although the idea of providing special services to students with special needs was a worthwhile notion, serious problems grew out of the special class movement. It was soon discovered that full-time special education was not the answer for most students with disabilities. Many special students did not require full-day services. Many were able to participate in at least some general education activities; all could benefit from contact with their peers. But students in special classes were removed from the mainstream of education; special classes were often located in obscure places in the school building. Special class students were also segregated from their peers and often excluded from typical school activities such as assemblies. In addition, the labeling process set special students further apart from their peers. In order for students to qualify for special services, it was necessary to determine the existence of a disability. Students were tested and, often on the basis of inadequate assessments, were labeled brain injured, mentally retarded, or emotionally disturbed. Labels such as these did not provide useful educational information for the classroom teacher or the special educator; worse, they attached a stigma to special students.

Another major problem was the inappropriate placement of students in special classes. Students who spoke little or no English were tested in English and labeled retarded. Students from diverse cultures were compared with middle-class, Anglo American peers and were found different, therefore inferior. Such students were placed in special classes side by side with students with disabilities. And once removed from general education, a student had little chance to return. Special class placement was virtually permanent.

These practices were soon recognized as problems. Parent groups, such as the Association for Retarded Citizens and the Learning Disabilities Association of America (formerly the Association for Children with Learning Disabilities), became active in support of appropriate services for all special students. Leaders in special education began to speak out against special class abuses; the article "Special Education for the Mildly Retarded—Is Much of It Justifiable?" by Lloyd Dunn (1968) is an example. Researchers like Jane Mercer (1973) accumulated evidence that students from diverse groups were vastly overrepresented in special classes. *The Six Hour Retarded Child,* by the President's Committee on Mental Retardation (1969), found that many students acted disabled only in the school situation. Court cases were filed. The *Diana* suit (1970, 1973) attacked testing abuses with students who did not speak English; the *Larry P.* case (1972, 1979, 1984) pointed up abuses with students from diverse cultures.

As more and more information became available, the prevailing educational philosophy began to shift. With the report of the Project on Classification of Exceptional Children by Hobbs (1975, 1976), the disadvantages of labeling became apparent. Normalization, or the belief that individuals with disabilities have the right to as normal an existence as possible, became an accepted goal of special services (Nirje, 1969; Wolfensberger, 1972). The pendulum swung away from segregation of special students in separate special schools and classes and toward inclusion in the mainstream of education. This viewpoint was endorsed not only by parents and professional educators but also by state and federal laws such as Public Law 94-142, the Education for All Handicapped Children Act of 1975.

As "For Your Information" on page 10 explains, PL 94-142 expanded the idea of normalization and applied it to school programs by requiring that students with disabilities be educated in the least restrictive environment—that is, alongside their peers without disabilities—whenever feasible. Congress enacted this law in 1975 for several reasons. At that time, one million children with disabilities had been excluded from the public school system. Also, large numbers of students in general education classes were experiencing failure because their disabilities had not been detected. Congress concluded that less than half of the students with disabilities in the United States were receiving appropriate educational services (PL 105-17, 1997). PL 94-142 has been updated several times since its passage in 1975. It was given a new name in 1990, the Individuals with Disabilities Education Act (IDEA), and the most recent version is PL 105-17, the Individuals with Disabilities Education Act Amendments of

For Your Information

Landmark Legislation for Persons with Disabilities

Two federal laws passed in the 1970s have had a dramatic impact on the lives of individuals with disabilities in the United States. Two newer laws, passed in the 1990s, follow the same tradition as earlier legislation and extend the rights guaranteed to persons with disabilities.

Legislation Related to Education

Public Law 94-142, the Education for All Handicapped Children Act of 1975, had as its major provision the guarantee of appropriate educational services to all school-aged students with disabilities. It also required that students with disabilities be educated with general education peers to the maximum extent appropriate. Listed here are the major provisions of PL 94-142:

- All students with disabilities are guaranteed a free, appropriate public education.
- An Individualized Education Program (IEP) must be developed for each student with disabilities.
- Parents have the right to participate in planning their child's educational program.
- Students with disabilities are to be educated in the least restrictive environment, that is, with students not identified as disabled, whenever possible.
- Tests and other assessment procedures used with students with disabilities must not discriminate on the basis of race, culture, or disability.
- Due process procedures must be in place to protect the rights of students with disabilities and their parents.
- The federal government provides some funding to states to help offset the costs involved in educating students with disabilities.

Public Law 105-17, the Individuals with Disabilities Education Act Amendments of 1997, the current update to PL 94-142, introduced several modifications. Known as the IDEA Amendments of 1997, this law:

- allowed states to serve youngsters ages 3 to 9 as children experiencing developmental delays

(rather than requiring identification of a specific disability);
- required that students with disabilities participate in state- and district-wide assessments, with accommodations as necessary, or in alternative assessments;
- mandated that charter schools serve students with disabilities;
- expanded IEP teams to include both special and general education teachers, when appropriate;
- revised IEP requirements to include consideration of students' involvement with and progress in the general education curriculum;
- added provisions related to discipline of students with disabilities for weapons, drugs, alcohol, and injury to self or others.

Civil Rights Legislation

Section 504 of the Vocational Rehabilitation Act of 1973 applies to people of all ages. Known as the civil rights act for persons with disabilities, it provides that:

> no otherwise qualified handicapped individual in the United States . . . shall, solely by reason of his handicap, be excluded from the participation in, be denied the benefits of, or be subjected to discrimination under any program or activity receiving federal financial assistance.

Section 504 forbids discrimination in employment, in admissions to institutions of higher education, and in the provision of health, welfare, and other social services (Berdine & Blackhurst, 1985). Also, it entitles school-aged children with disabilities to a free, appropriate public education.

Public Law 101-336, the Americans with Disabilities Act of 1990, or ADA, is a comprehensive law designed to "provide a clear and comprehensive national mandate for the elimination of discrimination against individuals with disabilities." To this end, ADA prohibits discrimination in employment, public accommodations (e.g., restaurants, hotels, theaters, and medical offices), services provided by state or local governments, public transportation, and telecommunications.

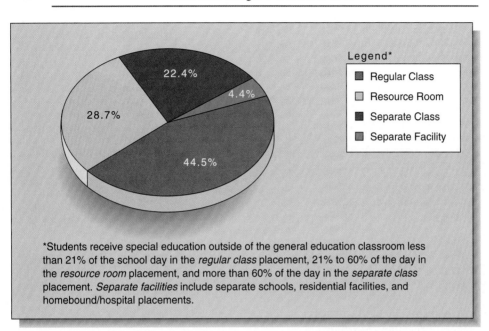

FIGURE 1-1   **Educational Environments for Students with Disabilities, Ages 3–21, 1994–1995**

Legend*
- ■ Regular Class
- □ Resource Room
- ■ Separate Class
- ■ Separate Facility

22.4%
4.4%
28.7%
44.5%

*Students receive special education outside of the general education classroom less than 21% of the school day in the *regular class* placement, 21% to 60% of the day in the *resource room* placement, and more than 60% of the day in the *separate class* placement. *Separate facilities* include separate schools, residential facilities, and homebound/hospital placements.

Note. From data provided in *Nineteenth Annual Report to Congress on the Implementation of the Individuals with Disabilities Education Act* by U.S. Department of Education, 1997, Washington, DC: Author.

1997. The "For Your Information" section also describes two other pieces of federal legislation considered to be landmark civil rights laws for persons with disabilities.

The Present

Today, the inclusion of special students in general education is a reality. As Figure 1–1 shows, more than 95% of students with disabilities are educated in regular schools (U.S. Department of Education, 1997a). These students receive instruction in general education classes, resource rooms, and separate classes. The majority (more than 70%) are placed in general education and receive special education services for some portion of the school day (the regular class and resource room options). Less than one-fourth are educated in separate classes within regular schools, and less than 5% are educated in separate facilities.

There are several important differences between current practices and those of several decades ago. First, today the general education classroom is not the only service available to students with special needs, although it is viewed as the most appropriate option for many. Second, rather than being allowed to flounder and fail in the mainstream, students with disabilities are provided with aid and assistance including, when necessary, individualized instruction from a specialist.

Third, general education teachers also receive assistance from specialists. Professionals such as resource teachers or special education consultants may aid in planning educational programs for students with special needs, provide suggestions for modification of general education classroom activities, and supply special materials and equipment. As part of the team that serves students with special needs, the general educator contributes by sharing information and ideas with parents and specialists.

According to federal law, alternative placements must be available for students with disabilities whose educational needs cannot be met in general education classes. However, such students are encouraged to interact with general education peers in any way feasible. For example, in many districts students once placed in special schools are now members of special classes located within regular schools. This greatly enhances their opportunities to interact with age peers. In addition, special classes are not viewed as permanent placements; students may reenter the mainstream at some time in the future if they are able to benefit from the general educational program.

Although school districts typically offer a range of special education services for students with disabilities, services for other types of special students are less common. If available, programs for students who are gifted, talented, bilingual, or at risk for school failure are similar to those offered by special education. That is, students are educated in regular classes for a portion of their school day and receive individualized services from specialists as necessary. Most programs also provide assistance and support to the general education teacher.

 ## BENEFITS OF INCLUDING SPECIAL STUDENTS

There are many benefits when students with special needs are members of general education classrooms. Special students remain with their peers; they are not segregated from the normal activities of the school. Labeling is deemphasized. Students leave the classroom for special help, not to see the teacher of students with mental retardation or emotional disturbance. Resource room services have aided in decreasing the stigma attached to special education because resource teachers often serve students with many different types of special needs. In addition, research indicates that students with disabilities can achieve academic success in mainstream classrooms. Success is most likely when general education instruction is individualized and when support is available not only to students with special needs but also to their teachers (Leinhardt & Pallay, 1982; Madden & Slavin, 1983; Schulte, Osborne, & McKinney, 1990).

Current practices safeguard against the inappropriate placement of students in special education programs. Every effort is made to keep special students in general education situations, and those students in separate special programs are encouraged to participate in as many of the school's regular activities as feasible. For example, they should attend school assemblies, use the playground with other classes, and eat at the regular lunchtime.

General education students benefit from association with their peers with special needs. The inclusion of individuals with disabilities in school activities is a realistic introduction to U.S. society. As "For Your Information" on page 13 shows, typical students learn about those different from themselves and have the opportunity to learn that the differences are unimportant.

Teachers and specialists also gain when students with special needs are included in general education. Special educators are able to serve more students. Special classes usually contain only 10 to 15 individuals, whereas resource programs may serve as many as 25 to 30 students. Also, specialists are able to concentrate on the special learning needs of the student and are not forced to duplicate the efforts of the general education classroom. General educators benefit, too, from collaboration with other professionals and in the support they receive in the team approach. Specialists provide special students with individualized help and are available to assist the teacher in meeting the needs of students placed in the general education classroom.

Of course, difficulties may occur in the inclusion process. General education teachers who have little experience with special students may be reluctant to participate. Both typical and special students and their parents may be apprehensive. These problems are exacerbated when financial and personnel

For Your Information

Students' Perceptions of Inclusion

Until quite recently, Jessica Rose attended a special school for students with multiple disabilities. Last fall, however, Jessica became a fifth grader; with support from a special education teacher, Jessica was included as a member of a grade 5 general education classroom located in a regular neighborhood school. Jessica's parents, Peggy and Tim, describe Jessica as a beautiful 9-year-old who is nonverbal, nonambulatory, and unable to feed, dress, or care for herself. Her fifth grade classmates have a somewhat different perspective. Read a sample of their responses (presented here in their original form) when they were asked at the end of the year to describe what it was like to have Jessica in their class:

- I feel that Jessica has changed my life. How I feel and see handicapped people has really changed. My friends used to make fun of handicaped children. When I saw Jessica I was scared and I didn't know what of. I used to think about handicaped people being really weak and if I would touch her I would hurt her but now I think diffrently.

- Whenever I'm around Jessica I feel very special. I feel lucky to be able to interact with her. When I look at Jesse and then look at myself I look back at how I used to be. I never used to look at a disabled person without staring at them. I've learned alot from Jesse. She taught me how to accept peopl's differences. Jessica is very special to me. She's a pleasure to be around.

- I feel like she is just a normal person. I though that I would not ever have a eperence with a handycaped but I do now. I feel lucky to have this experience. I use to feel unconferble but now I do not. I like her in our room now.

- I think it is great that Jessica is in our room. Jessica is very fun. She laughs and smiles a lot. Sometimes she crys but that is OK. I have learned that Handicapped people are just like the others. I used to say "ooh" look at that person but now I don't I have a big heart for handicapped because they are interesting they can do things that other people can't do. I think Jessica has changed because she is with lots of other kids.

- I like Jessica a lot and I enjoy it a lot when I hear her giggle. I feel just because she is in a wheelchair that doesn't mean she is bad. I have learned a lot about Jessica. Jessica will allways be my friend.

- I really like having Jessica in my class. Before she came I always had thought people in wheelchairs were real weak. I was wrong. Jessica is really quite strong. I never really thought that she could have feelings because she was handicapped. She can have feelings too. She can paint with guided help. I never thought she could paint. Having Jessi in my class has taught me stuff others might never know.

- I think that I used to be scared of handy caped people but now that Jessica came in I am not scared anymore. Because I think we should be treated equally. Because we are all the same.

- I really like Jessica in my class. Befor I met her I never really cared about handycapt people. Jessie is really nice and I like her alot. Jessica is almost like a sister to me. I like to spend my recess playing with her. I thought a handycapt kid would never be part of my life but now one and alot more are.

resources are reduced; there may be fewer services for special students and less assistance to teachers. Such difficulties are minimized when general education teachers are skilled in dealing with special students. One purpose of this book is to help teachers develop the necessary skills. See "Inclusion Tips for the Teacher" on page 14 to learn about meeting the needs of special students as well as those of the other pupils in the classroom.

THE ROLE OF SPECIAL EDUCATION

According to federal laws, **special education** is instruction specially designed to meet the unique needs of students. That instruction can take place in a variety of settings (such as classrooms, homes, and hospitals), and it includes instruction in physical education.

Inclusion Tips for the Teacher

Teaching Special Students and All the Others

As the teacher of a regular classroom, you are responsible for the education of your students. Each of the children or adolescents in your charge has specific learning needs; each is an individual. When students with special needs are members of your class, you may feel overwhelmed. Don't! Special students have specific learning needs, just like the other students in your class. They are individuals, just like their peers. Their differentness comes from the severity of their needs. They require more help in some areas than typical students do. In these areas they receive special education. In your classroom they participate in general education. Some adaptations of instructional procedures or the classroom environment may be necessary, but many "regular" students also need such changes.

Shortly after the passage of PL 94-142, Mills (1979) made several suggestions for teachers of general education classrooms. These suggestions are still good ones, and, although they deal specifically with students with disabilities, they are equally applicable to all types of students.

- Develop the necessary skills.
- Think positively.
- Know your own strengths and weaknesses.
- Insist on in-service.
- Seek assistance.
- Utilize parents.
- Prepare your class.
- Smile.

This last suggestion deserves more explanation. Mills elaborates:

> These are kids, too. They need the same love and warmth as do all children and may need a little assurance of the mainstream's desire to have them there. The other children won't accept the child with problems if the teacher isn't ready to do so. Be a leader in your own class; set the stage for a positive learning environment for all children. (p. 16)

In his definition, Heward (1996) describes the type of instruction involved and its purposes:

> *Special education* is individually planned, systematically implemented, and carefully evaluated instruction to help exceptional children achieve the greatest possible personal self-sufficiency and success in present and future environments. (p. 47)

Special educators serve students identified as having disabilities: students with learning disabilities, behavioral disorders and emotional disturbances, mental retardation, speech and language impairments, autism, physical and health impairments, traumatic brain injury, and visual and hearing impairments. Many states also provide special education services to gifted and talented students. Unless they are also disabled or gifted, culturally and linguistically diverse students are not eligible for special education; instead, they may receive services from specialists in bilingual education or from teachers of English for speakers of other languages.

Special education services are available to both special students and their teachers. These services range from special consultation provided to the teacher of a student with disabilities, to special instruction delivered to a special student a few minutes per day by a special education resource teacher within the general education classroom or in the resource room, to full-day special classes for students with severe and comprehensive disabilities.

Several other **related services** may be provided to special students if necessary. These include psychological services for assessment and counseling, transportation, speech and language services, special physical education, rehabilitation counseling, and physical and occupational therapy. Auxiliary services such as these are available to help students with special needs derive the maximum benefit from special education.

Supplementary aids and services, in contrast, are supports provided to students with special needs to help them succeed in general education classes and other settings. Examples are special materials such as taped textbooks, equipment such as computer adaptations, and services such as peer tutors.

Many different professionals may provide service to the same student with disabilities. For example,

Tiffany, the 8-year-old student introduced earlier in this chapter, receives instruction from her second grade teacher, Ms. Cole, and from the resource teacher. Josh, the high school student, attends four different subject matter classes, sees the adapted physical education teacher, and receives special transportation services. The resource teacher coordinates his program and provides assistance to his general education teachers as necessary. In addition, the assistive technology specialist will be working with Josh to find a computer adaptation to help increase his writing speed.

A team approach is used to plan and deliver the educational programs of students such as Tiffany and Josh. That team is made up of the student's classroom teacher (or teachers), any specialists who work with the student, the parents of the student, and, when appropriate, the special student. Each of these individuals has an important role in planning and executing the inclusion experience. The team approach is critical in fostering communication, cooperation, and collaboration among those interested in the education of the special student.

One of the functions of the team is to plan the student's educational program. As soon as a student is found to be eligible for special educational services, the team meets to make several important instructional decisions. After the student's present level of performance in important educational areas is identified, the team plans the student's program for the next year, and annual goals and short-term objectives (or benchmarks) are established. The next decisions concern placement and services. The extent to which the student is able to participate in the general education program is determined, along with any supplementary aids and services needed to support the student's participation in general education. Special education and related services are provided to meet the remaining educational needs. In this way the student's needs determine the amount and kind of services and supports to be provided. Placement outside the general education class occurs only when absolutely necessary.

The educational plan devised by the team is called the **Individualized Education Program,** or IEP. It is a written plan agreed upon by a team that includes the student's parents and often the student. An IEP is prepared for each student who receives special education services. The IEP is available to all team members and must be reviewed at least once a year, and more often if necessary.

A sample IEP form is shown in Figure 1–2. On this form, the team records information about the student's present performance and lists annual goals

FIGURE 1-2 IEP Form

Date ____________
❒ Initial IEP
❒ Annual Review
❒ Three-year Review
❒ Other ________

Orchard County Public Schools
Individualized Education Program (IEP)

Student Information

Name ______________________________ Birth Date __-__-__
Male ❒ Female ❒ Age ______ Grade ______ Ethnicity ____________
Social Security Number _____-___-_____ LEP Yes ❒ No ❒
Home Language ________________ Interpreter Required Yes ❒ No ❒
Address ____
School of Residence ____________________________________
School of Attendance ___________________________________
Rationale for placement, if other than student's school of residence:
____

continued

FIGURE 1-2 Continued

Parent/Guardian Information
Name _____
Address _____
Home phone _____ Work phone _____
Interpreter Required Yes ❑ No ❑

Assessment Information
Present Levels of Performance (include how disability affects involvement and progress in general curriculum)
_____
_____
_____
_____

Modifications needed in State and districtwide assessment _____
_____
Why needed _____

IEP Information
Date of Next IEP _____ Date of 3-year Review _____
Primary Disability Category _____
Primary Placement _____
P.E. Type _____
Transportation _____

Special Education & Related Services; Supplementary Aids & Services; Program Modifications	Start Date	Duration	Frequency	Location

Extent to which student will not participate with nondisabled students in regular class _____
_____
Explanation _____
Annual Goals, Short-term Objectives/Benchmarks, Progress Measures
_____
_____
_____
_____
_____
_____
_____
_____
_____
_____
_____
_____

Parents/guardians will be informed of student's progress via _____
_____

continued

FIGURE 1-2   **Continued**

As appropriate, the following factors were considered in the development of this IEP:
- ❐ for students whose behavior impedes learning, positive behavioral interventions, strategies, and supports
- ❐ for students with limited English proficiency, language needs
- ❐ for students who are blind or visually impaired, instruction in and use of Braille and appropriate reading and writing media
- ❐ communication needs of the students
- ❐ for students who are deaf or hard of hearing, language and communication needs
- ❐ assistive technology devices and services

Transition Services
- ❐ Transition service needs included in this IEP
- ❐ Transition service needs described in attached Individualized Transition Plan
- ❐ Student has been informed of his or her rights

Signatures

My due process rights have been explained to me.
- ❐ I consent to the IEP.
- ❐ I consent to portions of the IEP as described on the attached form.
- ❐ I do not consent to the IEP.

Parent/Guardian's Signature   Date

Student's Signature   Date

Signature of Administrator/Designee   Date

Signature of General Education Teacher   Date

Signature of Special Education Teacher/Specialist   Date

Signature/Title of Additional Participant   Date

Signature/Title of Additional Participant   Date

Signature of Interpreter   Date

Note. Developed by Tamarah M. Ashton, Ph.D., Assistant Director of the Enhancing Writing Skills Project and Project LITT, San Diego State University.

and short-term objectives. Special education services are described, and the extent to which the student will participate in the general education program is noted. At the bottom of the form is a space for parents to indicate their approval of the educational program and placement.

Portions of the IEPs for Tiffany and Josh appear in Figure 1–3. Included for each student are present levels of educational performance, annual goals, and the persons responsible for achieving those goals. After that come descriptions of the educational services to be provided. Note that both special education services and the amount of general education participation are specified.

General education placement is considered optimal for students with disabilities if they are capable of making progress in the standard school curriculum. As Figure 1–4 on page 19 illustrates, a range of special

FIGURE 1-3   Portions of the IEPs for Tiffany and Josh

Tiffany
Current Grade: 2
Present Levels of Educational Performance
* Tiffany is in good health with normal vision, hearing, and motor abilities. She is well adjusted and gets along well with her peers.
* Tiffany's listening and speaking skills are age-appropriate. She performs at grade level in math and handwriting.
* Tiffany is able to say the alphabet and identify all letters. She knows most of the consonant sounds and the short sound of *a*. Her sight vocabulary is approximately 70 words. Tiffany reads on the primer level.
* Tiffany is able to spell most of the words in the first grade spelling text (although she cannot read them all). She receives passing grades in spelling in her second grade classroom.

Annual Goals
1. By the end of the school year, Tiffany will read at a beginning second grade level with 90% accuracy in word recognition and comprehension.
   Person responsible: Resource teacher
2. By the end of the school year, Tiffany will increase her sight vocabulary to 150 words.
   Person responsible: Resource teacher
3. By the end of the school year, Tiffany will know the short and long sounds of the vowels.
   Person responsible: Resource teacher
4. By the end of the school year, Tiffany will read and spell at least 70% of the second grade spelling words.
   Person responsible: Second grade teacher
5. By the end of the school year, Tiffany will successfully complete second grade requirements in math, handwriting, science, social studies, art, music, and physical education.
   Person responsible: Second grade teacher

Amount of Participation in General Education
* Tiffany will participate in the second grade class for all subjects except reading.

Special Education and Related Services
* Tiffany will receive special instruction in reading (Annual Goals 1, 2, and 3) from the resource teacher for 30 minutes daily.

Josh
Current Grade: 10
Present Levels of Educational Performance
* Josh is unable to move his legs and has difficulty with fine-motor tasks involving eye-hand coordination. He is able to travel independently by wheelchair.
* Josh's general health is good. His hearing and vision are within normal limits. He is well adjusted and friendly and appears to get along well with his peers.
* No academic problems are apparent. Josh received As and Bs in Grade 9 classes and scored well above average in group academic achievement tests.
* Josh communicates better orally than in writing because of motor difficulties. His handwriting and typing are slow and require much effort.

Annual Goals
1. By June, Josh will successfully complete all 10th grade requirements, including physical education.
   Persons responsible: General education teachers, resource teacher, adapted physical education teacher
2. By June, Josh will increase his writing speed by using a computer with an adaptation such as word prediction or voice input.
   Persons responsible: Resource teacher, assistive technology specialist

Amount of Participation in General Education
* Josh will participate in regular 10th grade classes four out of five periods per day.

continued

FIGURE 1-3   Continued

Special Education and Related Services
• Josh will receive special transportation services between his home and the school.
• Josh will attend an adapted physical education class one period per day.
• The assistive technology specialist will assess Josh to determine an effective computer adaptation.
• The resource teacher will provide consultation as needed to Josh's regular class teachers.

FIGURE 1-4   Placement in the Least Restrictive Environment

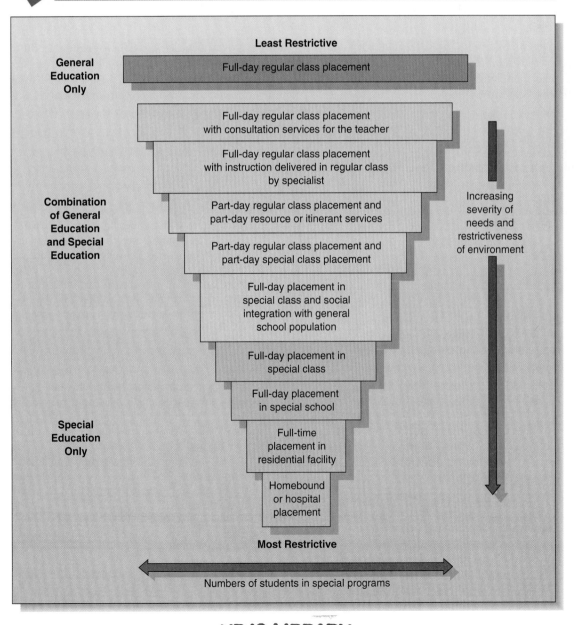

sevices is available, and many of these include at least part-time placement in the general education classroom. For example, a special educator may collaborate with the classroom teacher to identify appropriate instructional adaptations for one or more students or assist in the general education classroom by teaching lessons to a small group that includes a student with special needs. The array of special education service options is sometimes viewed as a continuum. The continuum extends from placement in general education with no special services or supports to options that serve small numbers of students with very severe needs, such as a school within a hospital for young children receiving treatment for cancer.

In selecting placements for students with special needs, it is necessary to follow the principle of **Least Restrictive Environment,** or LRE. The LRE for a student with disabilities is believed to be the appropriate placement closest to the general education classroom. As PL 105-17 states:

> To the maximum extent appropriate, children with disabilities . . . are educated with children who are not disabled, and special classes, separate schooling, or other removal of children with disabilities from the regular educational environment occurs only when the nature or severity of the disability of a child is such that education in regular classes with the use of supplementary aids and services cannot be achieved satisfactorily. [Sec. 612 (a) (5) (A)]

For students unable to function successfully in a general education class, placement in a special class within a public school is less restrictive (i.e., closer to the mainstream) than placement in a separate school or residential facility. This concept does not imply that students should be placed in less intensive settings simply to bring them closer to the mainstream. Their placement must be feasible; they must have a good chance of successful performance. The goal is the least restrictive *and* most appropriate placement possible. For most students with disabilities, this means the general education classroom with special services for the student and teacher.

CURRENT ISSUES AND TRENDS

Several important factors have begun to influence general education, special education, and their collaboration in the provision of services to students with special needs. The educational reform movement is one major trend. The 1980s produced a se-

ries of commission reports and recommendations aimed at improving the quality of U.S. schools. Best known among these is *A Nation at Risk: The Imperative for Educational Reform* (National Commission on Excellence in Education, 1983). This report and others calling for educational reform led to the excellence in education movement. Among the results of this movement were an increased emphasis on content area subjects (as opposed to basic skills), longer school days and years, higher expectations and grading standards, and more stringent discipline requirements.

The next wave of reforms led to the school restructuring movement and efforts to increase the decision-making powers of educators through site-based management models. At the same time, the nation's governors led by then-President Bush agreed on six national educational goals (*America 2000,* 1990). Modified slightly, these goals became the framework for President Clinton's Goals 2000: Educate America Act of 1994. By the year 2000:

- All children in America will start school ready to learn.
- The high school graduation rate will increase to at least 90 percent.
- American students will leave grades 4, 8, and 12 having demonstrated competency over challenging subject matter including English, mathematics, science, foreign languages, civics and government, economics, arts, history, and geography, and every school in America will ensure that all students learn to use their minds well, so they may be prepared for responsible citizenship, further learning, and productive employment in our modern economy.
- The Nation's teaching force will have access to programs for the continued improvement of their professional skills and the opportunity to acquire the knowledge and skills needed to instruct and prepare all American students for the next century.
- United States students will be first in the world in mathematics and science achievement.
- Every adult American will be literate and will possess the knowledge and skills necessary to compete in a global economy and exercise the rights and responsibilities of citizenship.
- Every school in America will be free of drugs, violence, and the unauthorized presence of firearms and alcohol, and will offer a disciplined environment conducive to learning.
- Every school will promote partnerships that will increase parental involvement and participation in

promoting the social, emotional, and academic growth of children. (National Education Goals Panel, 1997)

Goals 2000 calls for a number of reforms such as drug-free schools and improved high school graduation rates. Math and science achievement is stressed, but attention is also given to universal literacy and readiness for school. In addition, *all students* is defined as including not only typical students and those who are academically talented but also students with disabilities, those from diverse cultural and ethnic groups, those with limited proficiency in English, and those who are disadvantaged. Progress is being made toward some goals, but it is unlikely all will be met by the turn of the century (Manzo, 1996).

Other recent trends are the standards movement and voluntary national tests. Several national professional organizations have established student performance indicators or standards in subjects such as mathematics, science, history, and English-language arts. In addition, almost all states have developed or are developing common academic standards for their students, and most states intend to link student assessment to standards (American Federation of Teachers, 1996). The standards movement has not been without controversy as groups have attempted to achieve consensus about appropriate educational outcomes for students. There also remain many questions about how best to ensure that students with disabilities participate in standards-based assessments with appropriate accommodations and modifications (National Research Council, 1997).

Voluntary national tests, proposed by President Clinton in 1997, will assess reading skills in grade 4 and mathematics achievement in grade 8. According to the U.S. Department of Education (1997b), "These tests will, for the first time in history, provide parents and teachers with information about how their students are progressing compared to other states, the nation, and other countries."

Another major trend is the changing nature of the school-aged population in the United States. As reform movements lead to more rigorous educational standards, the student population is becoming more diverse and in some ways less able. Children under 18 are now the poorest segment of the national population; in 1995, 20.8% of this group fell below the poverty line (U.S. Census Bureau, 1996). Several general population trends will have

dramatic effects on the needs of students entering general education classrooms. The population of the United States continues to increase and with it the number of school-aged children. School enrollment set a record high in 1996–1997, and it is expected to increase each year until it reaches 54.6 million in 2006 (Hendrie, 1996). The racial and ethnic composition of the United States is also changing, and it is estimated that by the start of the twenty-first century almost one-third of the country's population will be African American, Hispanic, Asian American, or American Indian (PL 105-17, 1997). The U.S. Census Bureau (1997) reports that more than one-fourth of the children born in 1994 were born to unmarried mothers, and the number of single parents tripled between 1970 and 1994. In addition, the fastest-growing segment of the U.S. population is persons with limited proficiency in English language skills (PL 105-17, 1997).

Changes such as these are likely to increase the number of students at risk for school failure. This suggests that educational reform efforts that divert funds away from remedial programs may be moving in the wrong direction. There is a need for more support for low-performing students and their teachers, not less (McLoughlin & Lewis, 1994).

Within special education, there has been much debate about full inclusion, the movement that calls for increased integration of students with severe disabilities. Leaders such as Stainback and Stainback (1985, 1990b, 1992) and Thousand and Villa (1990) advocate the full-time inclusion of all students, including those with severe disabilities, in general education classrooms in neighborhood schools. Others disagree. Groups such as the Council for Exceptional Children (1993b), the Division for Learning Disabilities (1993), the National Joint Committee on Learning Disabilities (1993), and the Learning Disabilities Association of America (1993) maintain that one educational option is not sufficient. Instead, a variety of special education programs should be available to serve the diverse needs of students with disabilities. For example, in its position statement, the Learning Disabilities Association of America (1993) emphasizes the need for individualization:

The Learning Disabilities Association of America does not support "full inclusion" or any policies that mandate the same placement, instruction, or treatment for ALL students with learning disabilities. Many students with learning disabilities benefit from being served in the

For Your Information

People First Language

Language is a powerful tool. When talking or writing about people with disabilities, professionals should make every effort to use language that reflects positive attitudes, not negative stereotypes. One important consideration is putting the person first, not the disability. Consider these examples from the California Governor's Committee for Employment of Disabled Persons (1990):

DON'T SAY . . . "Mr. Lee is a *crippled teacher* and *confined to a wheelchair*. All of his students are *normal*."

BUT INSTEAD SAY . . . "Mr. Lee is a *teacher with a disability*. He is a *wheelchair-user*. All of his students are *nondisabled*."

The Research and Training Center on Independent Living (1990) provides several suggestions in its pamphlet *Guidelines for Reporting and Writing about People with Disabilities*. Here are examples:

* Do not use generic labels for disability groups, such as "the retarded," "the deaf." Emphasize people not labels. Say *people with mental retardation* or *people who are deaf*.
* Put people first, not their disability. Say *woman with arthritis, children who are deaf, people with disabilities*. This puts the focus on the individual, not the particular functional limitation. . . .
* Emphasize abilities not limitations. Consider: *uses a wheelchair/braces, walks with crutches*, rather than confined to a wheelchair, wheelchair-bound, or is crippled. Similarly, do not use emotional descriptors such as unfortunate, pitiful, and so forth.

The *Guidelines* are updated periodically. To obtain a copy of the latest version, send a stamped, self-addressed envelope to Research and Training Center in Independent Living Publications, University of Kansas, 4089 Dole Building, Lawrence, KS 66045. Or visit the Center on the World Wide Web at **www.lsi.ukans.edu/rtcil/write.htm**

regular classroom. However, the regular classroom is not the appropriate placement for a number of students with learning disabilities who may need alternative instructional environments, teaching strategies, and/or materials that cannot or will not be provided within the context of a regular classroom placement. (p. 594)

Another trend in special education is increased interest in preschool and postsecondary age groups. Federal laws such as the 1997 IDEA Amendments focus attention on young children with disabilities and their families. States may offer programs for infants and toddlers with disabilities; with very young children, an Individualized Family Service Plan (IFSP) guides the delivery of services instead of an IEP. Federal special education laws also address the needs of adolescents and young adults with disabilities. For example, the IDEA Amendments of 1997 require a transition plan for students with disabilities beginning at age 14 in order to ensure coordination between school programs and postschool options such as vocational training, postsecondary education, employment, and adult services.

At present, the effects of educational reform movements and the changes in student demographics are becoming apparent in general education. Special education is directing some of its efforts to the early childhood years in an attempt to reverse or at least slow the effects of disabilities on young children's readiness for school. There is also debate about the relationship of special and general education and the most effective ways of promoting the social and instructional integration of students with disabilities. As this debate continues, it will become increasingly important for general and special educators to collaborate in the search for solutions to the educational problems facing all types of special students, not only those with identified disabilities.

GENERAL EDUCATION TEACHERS AND SPECIAL STUDENTS

General education teachers make several contributions to the success of special students. The teacher is often the first professional to identify the special needs of students and to initiate the referral process. The classroom teacher is also a source of valuable information about current school performance when students are assessed for possible special education services. As part of the inclusion team, the teacher participates in planning the student's educational program and in developing the IEP.

The teacher's most important role is implementation of the special student's general education program. This process sometimes requires adaptation of classroom procedures, methods, and/or materials to guarantee success for the student with special needs. Classroom activities should be coordinated with the special services received by the student. And communication between parents and professionals is crucial.

In addition, the classroom teacher may help to evaluate the student's progress not only in the general education program but also in the areas served by specialists. Evaluation is a critical step in the educational process because it helps determine program modifications. Figure 1–5 presents the educational process, including the final step of evaluation. This diagram also provides a summary of the general education teacher's roles.

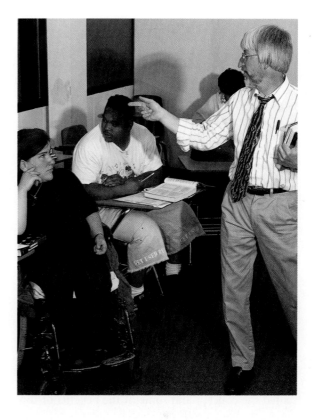

FIGURE 1-5   **The Special Education Process**

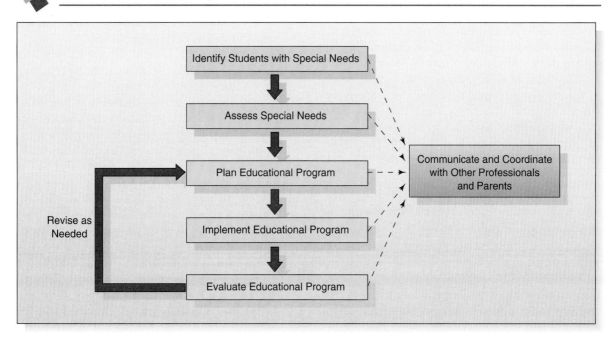

Things to Remember

- Most students with special needs can succeed in general education classrooms.
- Inclusion is the meaningful participation of students with special needs in the general educational process.
- Special students include students with disabilities (students with learning disabilities, behavioral disorders, mental retardation, speech and language impairments, autism, physical and health impairments, traumatic brain injury, and visual and hearing impairments), gifted and talented students, culturally and linguistically diverse students, and students at risk for school failure.
- Inclusion in general education allows special students to interact with typical peers. It also reduces the effects of labeling.
- Most special students receive the majority of their education in general education. These students and their teachers are provided with aid and assistance to ensure their success.
- The general education teacher contributes to the success of students with special needs by participating in assessment, program planning and IEP development, placement decisions, and most important, implementation of students' general education program.

Even though these roles are not new ones for the teacher, special students may require special teaching skills. The first part of this book provides basic information about inclusion. Chapter 1 has presented the concept and some of the benefits of this approach, has introduced special students and special education, and has briefly described the roles of the general education teacher. Chapter 2 will acquaint the teacher with the team approach and the collaboration process. In chapter 3 the special needs of special students will be explored.

Part II focuses on the teacher's role in helping students with special needs to succeed in the general education classroom. Each of the chapters in that section deals with an important skill area: adapting instruction, managing behavior, promoting social acceptance, coordinating the classroom learning environment, and integrating computers and other technologies into classroom learning activities. In the third and fourth parts of this book, these skills are applied to each type of special learner.

Before turning to chapter 2 to meet the team, check your understanding of this chapter by consulting the section entitled "Things to Remember."

ACTIVITIES

Here are several activities that will help increase your understanding of the concepts presented in this chapter. Some are designed to acquaint you with the literature or resources on the World Wide Web. Others are explorations of current programs and practices in your local schools and community. You will find activities such as these at the end of each chapter.

1. Arrange a visit to an elementary, middle, or high school. Talk with the principal or one of the staff members about the special services at the school. What types of programs are available? Is there a resource teacher who provides part-time special services to students with disabilities? If possible, visit a general education class and observe the students carefully. Can you tell which are identified as having special needs?

2. Interview several general education teachers about their perceptions of inclusion. Have they taught students with special needs in their classrooms? If so, what special learning needs did these students have? What do the teachers believe are the advantages and disadvantages of inclusion?

3. Select one or two of the major educational journals in your field. Look for articles that present useful suggestions for adapting instruction for students with special needs. You may also wish to look at some of the journals in special education. Two that feature practical articles about educating students with disabilities are *Intervention in School and Clinic* and *Teaching Exceptional Children*. Despite its title, *Teaching Exceptional Children* includes suggestions for both elementary and secondary teachers.

Window on the Web

The Council for Exceptional Children

http://www.cec.sped.org

The national headquarters of CEC maintains this website to provide information to its members and others interested in special education, students with disabilities, and gifted and talented students. The Public Policy and Legislative Information section is a good source to consult to learn about bills now in Congress and recently passed laws. The ERIC Clearinghouse on Disabilities and Gifted Education offers a host of resources for teachers, including databases, fact sheets, digests, and links to other useful websites.

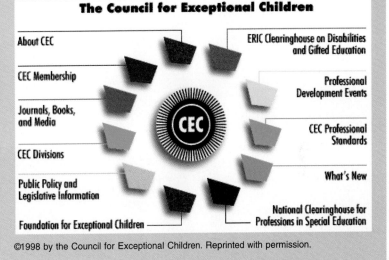

©1998 by the Council for Exceptional Children. Reprinted with permission.

4. Search the World Wide Web for information on mainstreaming. Then search for inclusion. (If you're unfamiliar with the World Wide Web or search techniques, consult chapter 8 for an introduction.) Which search term produced the most results? Visit some of the sites to get an idea of what people are saying. Are any of the sites sponsored by elementary or secondary schools?

5. The major professional organization in special education is the Council for Exceptional Children, or CEC. Many communities have local CEC chapters, and student chapters are often found at colleges and universities. The national CEC office is located at 1920 Association Drive, Reston, VA 22091. Get in touch with your local or state CEC, or contact the national headquarters to learn more about this organization. (See the "Window on the Web" above for its World Wide Web location.) Is CEC concerned with all types of special students? Are all its members special education teachers? How does it attempt to improve educational services for students with disabilities?

chapter 2

Collaboration and the Team Approach

The team approach is not new in education. Most professionals are aware of individuals who work together as a team to accomplish some common goal. Teams can be established at different levels within the educational system for a variety of purposes, such as selection of instructional materials, development of curriculum, and evaluation of educational programs. These school teams work to plan, evaluate, or improve various aspects of the educational system.

In special education, the team approach has traditionally been used to decide whether students should receive special services. Groups of specialists, often called placement or child study teams, have met to determine whether students were eligible for special education services and, if so, to select the special educational placement of most benefit to the student.

Today, not only special educators but also general education teachers and parents assist in making important decisions about the education of students with special needs. Moreover, the purpose of the team approach to serving special students goes beyond that of placement. Team members collaborate to plan and evaluate the general education experience for students with special needs, and the educators on the team work to implement the plan in the classroom.

It is important to remember that not all students with educational problems need special education services. Often problems can be resolved by modifying the student's current instructional program. The team approach can help here, too, when professionals work together to adapt instructional strategies to meet the student's educational needs within the general education classroom.

TEAMS SERVING STUDENTS WITH SPECIAL NEEDS

Teams serving students with special needs are established within a school to initiate, facilitate, supervise, and evaluate the participation of students with special needs in the general and special education programs. Teams are found at all levels of education, from infant programs through high school. Teams serving students with special needs serve one or more of the following purposes: (a) assisting teachers in meeting the educational needs of students with special needs within the general education classroom; (b) determining whether students are eligible for services such as special education; and (c) planning, monitoring, and evaluating the provision of special services.

Although the team approach is required by federal special education legislation, there is much variation from district to district and from state to state in the names given to different teams and the

For Your Information

Important Provisions of PL 105-17, the Individuals with Disabilities Education Act (IDEA) Amendments of 1997

Public Law 105-17, the Individuals with Disabilities Education Act (IDEA), is the 1997 amendments of the federal law that provides guidelines for many of the activities and procedures that take place in special education, including requirements for the assessment and IEP teams. IDEA is the current version of the original legislation, Public Law 94-142, the Education for All Handicapped Children Act of 1975 that was initiated to ensure that children with disabilities and the families of such children have access to a free, appropriate public education and to improved educational results. Check the explanations of the following terms to further your understanding of federal special education laws:

- **Assessment team.** The **local education agency** (LEA) or district is responsible for providing an assessment team composed of professionals who possess the appropriate training and experience to evaluate students referred for consideration for special education services. Although the professionals involved in each evaluation may vary according to the needs of the student, it is the responsibility of the team to consider referral information, develop a plan for the evaluation, obtain the permission of the parent(s) to conduct the evaluation, and then evaluate the student to determine (a) whether the student has a disability and (b) his or her educational needs. Upon completion of the evaluation the professionals and the parents determine if the student has a disability, and the parents receive a copy of the evaluation and documentation that eligibility has been determined.
- **IEP team.** This group develops, reviews, and revises the IEP. Individualized Education Programs are written for all students with disabilities who receive special education services, and they must be reviewed and revised as necessary, but at least annually. The IEP team is composed of the following members: (a) the parents of the student with a disability; (b) at least one of the student's general education teachers (if the student is, or may be, participating in the general education program); (c) at least one special edu-

cation teacher or special educator who provides service to students with the type of disability being considered; (d) a representative of the LEA who is qualified to provide or supervise the provision of special education and is knowledgeable about the general curriculum and the availability of the LEA's resources; (e) an individual who can interpret the evaluation results if one is not already represented on the team; (f) at the discretion of the parent or the LEA, others with expertise regarding the student; and (g) the student with a disability, when appropriate.

- **Due process hearing.** If the school or the parents of a student with disabilities are not satisfied that the student is receiving an appropriate educational program, an impartial due process hearing can be requested. Hearings attempt to resolve disagreements regarding issues such as identification, evaluation, and educational programs and placements. When a hearing is requested, the student remains in the current placement until the disagreement is resolved.
- **Child find.** Active programs are maintained by state and local education agencies to identify unserved students in need of special education.
- **Nondiscriminatory assessment.** Assessment is nondiscriminatory when it does not penalize students for their native language, race, culture, or disability.
- **Confidentiality.** The provisions of IDEA guarantee "confidentiality in the disclosure of information that may unnecessarily identify a student as having a disability" (Strickland & Turnbull, 1993, p. 261). Parents of students with disabilities must be informed of the confidentiality requirements for personally identifiable information (e.g., name, address) and must give consent before this information can be released to anyone outside the school district. The district must maintain confidential records of each student, and these records must be accessible to parents. Legally responsible parents and guardians have the right to examine all records maintained on their child by the school and to participate in meetings with respect to identification, evaluation, and

continued

placement. In addition, they can request (a) explanation or interpretation of information, (b) amendments to records, (c) deletions of information in the records, and (d) a due process hearing to resolve disagreements regarding proposed modifications in the records.

- **Surrogate parent.** If a parent of a student with disabilities is not available to work with the school, a surrogate parent can be appointed. The surrogate parent approves the student's placement, works on the IEP team, and serves as an advocate for the student.

- **Transition services.** Under IDEA, these services must be provided according to the individual needs of each student with disabilities. Transition services are a coordinated set of activities for a student with a disability that: "(A) is designed within an outcome-oriented process, which promotes movement from school to post-school activities, including post-secondary education, vocational training, integrated employ-

ment (including supported employment), continuing and adult education, adult services, independent living, or community participation; (B) is based upon the individual student's needs, taking into account the student's preferences and interests; and (C) includes instruction, related services, community experiences, the development of employment and other post-school adult living objectives, and when appropriate, acquisition of daily living skills and functional vocational evaluation" [PL 105-17, Sec. 602 (30)]. By the age of 14, the student's IEP must include an annually updated statement of the needed transition services that focuses on his or her courses of study (e.g., vocational education program). At the age of 16 (or younger if considered appropriate by the IEP team), the student's IEP must include a statement of needed transition services, and any required coordination or linkages between the school and other agencies.

responsibilities that these teams assume. As described in the "For Your Information" section on the 1997 Individuals with Disabilities Education Act, two types of teams are mandatory: the assessment team and the Individualized Education Program (IEP) team. When an educator or a parent submits a referral for a student who is a potential candidate for special education services, the assessment team is responsible for developing a plan for evaluating the student to determine whether he or she is eligible for special education services; it is sometimes called the *special services committee, special education committee,* or *placement committee.* Once a student is found eligible, the IEP team is charged with planning and monitoring that student's IEP. The IEP team may be called the *IEP committee* or the *educational planning team.* In some districts, one team assumes both the duties of the assessment team and those of the IEP team.

The third type of team for students with special needs is designed to assist teachers to solve problems in the general education classroom, before referrals are made to special education or other types of special services. This prereferral team may be called the *student study team,* the *prereferral committee,* or the *teacher assistance team.* Although not required by federal laws, such teams are mandatory in some states and districts.

This book advocates that general and special educators work together as a team when making educational decisions about all students with special needs, particularly those who are served in the general education program. The team should be concerned with not only students identified as having disabilities but also students being considered for special education and similar services. For students with disabilities, state and federal laws and regulations describe the purpose, responsibilities, and membership of the teams that make educational decisions. For other students with special needs such as gifted and talented individuals, culturally and linguistically diverse students, and students at risk for school failure, there may be no laws or regulations that require the team approach. However, this book will stress the importance of the role of prereferral, assessment, and educational planning teams in helping all students with special needs succeed in the general education program.

Teams serving students with special needs are composed of individuals directly involved with some aspect of delivering or supporting instruction. Included are general and special educators, some of whom may provide direct service to the student. Other professionals such as school psychologists, speech-language pathologists, and school nurses are involved as necessary. School administrators serve as resources to the team, and the parents of the student are an important addition. Although typically not professional educators, parents are able to provide information about the student and thus play a significant role in the educational decision-making process. If appropriate, the special student should be encouraged to participate.

Teams serving students with special needs are multipurpose in nature. Major duties are the planning, implementation, and evaluation of educational programs for students with special needs who are enrolled in general education classes. A prereferral team considers students experiencing difficulty in school and determines, first, whether the general education program can be modified to meet student needs. If these modifications are appropriate, they work to plan the modification, monitor its implementation, and evaluate its effectiveness. If this cannot be accomplished, students are referred to the assessment team to be evaluated to decide whether they are eligible for special education or another type of special service. For students determined to have a disability, an IEP team then works to plan a specific educational program. Several IEP team members may be responsible for implementation of that program. For example, the special education resource teacher may assist the general education teacher in adapting classroom instruction for the student. Or the special teacher may provide the student with part-time instruction in mathematics while the general education teacher takes responsibility for all other subject matter areas. At regular intervals (at least yearly), the IEP team evaluates the student's progress and makes any needed programmatic changes.

Teams provide a vehicle for general and special educators to effectively carry out their shared responsibility for the education of students with special needs. They provide the opportunity for parents and professionals, sharing a common concern for the education of students with special needs, to work together to share information and expertise.

In effective teams, there is open communication and cooperation among members. Communication is the sharing of information that will assist in providing a more appropriate education for students. Formal meetings establish a working relationship among team members that can then be continued and solidified in informal contacts. For example, team members may compare notes about a student's

progress by chatting in the teacher's lounge, by telephone, or in a home visit with the family. The team works together, with each team member contributing a different viewpoint. Parents, teachers, and other professionals collaborate to provide the best education possible for the student with special needs. See Figure 2–1 for a glimpse of such teams in action.

Three features set teams serving students with special needs apart from other typical education teams. First, these teams consider each student individually. When recommendations are made, they are specific in nature and have direct application to the student's educational program. This practice is different from the operation of many educational teams that consider the needs of groups of students. For example, teams may make general recommendations about all the third grade classes in the district or all the basic freshman English classes at a certain high school. The teams serving students with special needs, however, focus their attention on one student at a time.

Second, teams serving students with special needs are composed of both general and special educators, other professionals as needed, and the student's parents. Team composition is truly multidisciplinary. In the past, each of these disciplines often worked separately to provide instructional services, and there was a minimum of communication with others. This approach frequently led to poor coordination of educational programs, with overlap in some areas of the curriculum and neglect of others. Frequently the instructional strategies or other interventions used from setting to setting were inconsistent. The multidisciplinary team approach can reduce or eliminate this problem by developing an educational plan that clearly specifies the responsibilities of each team member and coordinates the activities of all individuals involved in its implementation.

Third, membership of teams serving students with special needs varies according to the role of the team and the special needs of the student under consideration. Although a different special education teacher (or consultant) may be required for students with different needs, the same professional responsible for interpreting the evaluation results and the administrative designee may serve on all of the teams serving students with special needs within a school. The parents and general education teachers who participate will change as each new student is considered. Other professionals may become a

FIGURE 2-1   The Team Approach to Serving Special Students

Marvin and Jake

Marvin and Jake are 15-year-old freshmen at Jefferson High. They have always been somewhat less-than-average students with minor problems in school, but they have never been considered for special education services. This year Mr. Morse, the boys' English teacher, has decided to ask that their cases be reviewed. In English class Marvin is disruptive and uncooperative; he fails to complete most of his writing assignments. Those that are finished are usually late and of poor quality (Marvin's average grade on writing assignments is 38%). In addition, when bothered by Marvin's outbursts, the other students in the class retaliate by commenting on his poor progress, which leads to arguments in class and in the hall after class. Jake also is doing poorly on his assignments, often turning them in late (Jake's average grade on assignments is 59%). He is late to class several times a week and appears to be confused about assignments; he seldom asks questions and never participates in class discussions.

The prereferral team at Jefferson High reviewed Mr. Morse's request for assistance and decided that they would like additional information about both students. Mr. Morse was asked to collect data on their academic performance and classroom behavior. He carefully recorded their daily grades and collected samples of their work. He also collected information on the frequency of Marvin's classroom disturbances and arguments and the occurrence of Jake's tardiness and classroom participation. The special education resource teacher observed both of the students during their English classes and carefully reviewed samples of their work.

After the prereferral team's review of this information, it was decided that it was most appropriate for Mr. Morse to attempt to meet Jake's educational needs without referral to special education. The team suggested that Mr. Morse establish a reinforcement system to encourage Jake's arriving in class on time, writing down directions for his English assignments and their due dates, completing the assignments, and participating in class. Mr. Morse was to continue to collect data on Jake's performance. The remedial English resource teacher was contacted for information about appropriate instructional materials for a student such as Jake. In addition, the special education resource teacher offered to provide periodic consultation services to Mr. Morse.

The review of Marvin's case led to the determination that a formal referral should be submitted to the assessment team and a full-scale evaluation conducted. An assessment plan was developed by the team, the parents' approval obtained, and the assessments carried out. Mr. Morse collected additional data on Marvin's in-class performance. The school psychologist and the special education resource teacher assessed Marvin's overall academic performance and his general ability. The school counselor visited Marvin's parents to discuss home performance.

part of the team as students with different needs are studied. For example, the school nurse may be a necessary team member for a student with a physical impairment but not for a student with learning disabilities.

In addition, one of the teams serving students with special needs, the IEP team, must include not only professionals but also the parents of the student with special needs and, if appropriate, the student as well. This is a radical departure from past practices. The parents and student now have the right to be active members of the IEP team and to provide input regarding instructional needs, goals, and programs. They have access to the information concerning the student and participate in making important decisions about edu-

cational placement and programming. Figure 2–2 on page 34 summarizes the responsibilities of the different teams that typically serve students with special needs.

ROLES OF TEAM MEMBERS

Teams serving students with special needs are made up of a variety of different members. Both special education and general education are represented. Teachers and administrators are included as well as specialists such as psychologists, physical therapists, and counselors. In addition, parents and special students themselves may participate in team deliberations. Each of these individuals plays an important role.

FIGURE 2-1   Continued

The counselor also contacted Marvin's math, science, and history teachers to determine how he was doing in those classes. The assessment team then met with the parent to review the assessment data. Results indicated that Marvin has good general ability and is able to read at grade level. His grades in subjects other than English are passing but low. Marvin's writing skills are very poor, particularly in the areas of spelling, grammar, punctuation, and capitalization. In addition, he lacks the social skills necessary for establishing interpersonal relationships; he experiences particular difficulty relating to peers. From these results the team concluded that Marvin was qualified for special education services, and his case was forwarded to the IEP team.

An IEP team—composed of the vice principal, the counselor, Mr. Morse, the special education resource teacher, the school psychologist, Marvin, and Marvin's mother—then met to develop the IEP. According to the plan agreed on by the IEP team, Marvin will continue to attend his regular academic classes, including English. He will also see the resource teacher one period per day for special instruction in written expression. In addition, the resource teacher will meet at least once a week with Mr. Morse to assist in adapting Marvin's writing assignments. The school counselor will work with Marvin to develop the skills Marvin needs to get along with other students. The counselor, resource teacher, and Mr. Morse will meet with Marvin to establish a contract system to reward successful completion of classroom assignments and appropriate classroom behavior.

The IEP is to be evaluated in 6 months. In the interim the school counselor will monitor Marvin's progress in all of his ninth grade classes. Marvin and his mother agree with the IEP goals and the special services to be provided. Optimistic about Marvin's future, they believe that with help Marvin will succeed in the general education program.

The three teams involved in developing and implementing Marvin's educational program at Jefferson High were all teams serving students with special needs. The teams shared members, and the primary goal of each was to match Marvin's specific needs with an appropriate educational program directed at improving his ability to function in the general education program. The prereferral team examined his current performance and considered whether modifications could be made in Marvin's current general education classes. After it had been determined that his needs could not be fully met in his current program, they referred his case to the assessment team. The assessment team designed an evaluation plan for Marvin, evaluated him, and considered his eligibility for special education. After the determination that he was eligible for special education services, the IEP team identified appropriate educational goals for Marvin, decided who was going to provide the services needed to meet those goals, and then decided what modifications were to be made in his current placement.

Building Principals

School principals or vice principals serve as key members of teams serving students with special needs. As administrators, they are responsible for the general education programs and often the special education programs housed within their buildings. In large elementary or secondary schools, the vice principal with supervisory responsibilities for the special education program may represent the principal on the team.

The principal often schedules and chairs the team's formal meetings. Although usually not directly responsible for implementing any portion of the student's IEP, administrators do influence the operation and effectiveness of the effort. They are the educational leaders of the school and, as such, are aware of the school's program and personnel resources. Their activities, the attitudes they convey, and the support they provide can help establish the necessary school climate for developing educational programs that serve a wide variety of learners and for building successful programs that provide appropriate services for students with special needs.

Special Education Administrators

Special education directors are responsible for supervising the provision of appropriate educational programs for all students with disabilities within a district. Their primary activities include the direction of intensive special education programs (such

---

FIGURE 2-2   **Responsibilities of Teams Serving Students with Special Needs**

Prereferral Team
• Identify possible problem.
• Consider previous interventions.
• Design data collection.
• Design prereferral interventions.
• Identify needed support/services to implement intervention plan.
• Coordinate implementation of prereferral interventions.
• Evaluate prereferral interventions.
• Modify interventions as needed.
• Initiate special education referral if general education interventions not successful.

Assessment Team
• Review referral for special education.
• Review data on prereferral interventions.
• Identify team members needed to develop assessment plan.
• Design assessment plan.
• Provide assessment plan to parents and review plan.
• Obtain parents' permission to conduct assessment.
• Conduct assessment.
• Summarize assessment results.
• Conduct meeting with parents to determine eligibility.

Individualized Education Program (IEP) Team
• Identify IEP team membership needed for specific student.
• Review assessment results.
• Establish present levels of educational performance.
• Identify and select appropriate annual goals and objectives.
• Designate the appropriate placement in the Least Restrictive Environment (LRE).
• Develop plan for implementation of the IEP.
• Develop evaluation plan.
• Identify process for reporting student's progress to parents.
• Establish and monitor reevaluation plan.

---

as special schools) as well as the provision of support services to special classes, resource programs, and consultants to general education teachers within regular school buildings. Frequently they are responsible for developing in-service training programs to help general education teachers work more effectively with students with disabilities.

On assessment and IEP teams, special education administrators assist in the review of assessment information and help the team examine appropriate special education placement options. In some districts, these professionals serve on the team only when students are likely to require placement in separate special classes or schools.

General Education Teachers

The involvement of general education teachers is critical because they have firsthand experience with students with special needs in their classrooms. They share ideas with parents and other professionals, and they assist in devising strategies for successful programs to serve special students included in the general education program. If these teachers do not participate on the team, the effectiveness of the effort to include students with special needs in general education classes is compromised.

At the secondary level, students are served by a number of general education teachers, and the

school counselor may be designated as the teachers' representative on teams serving students with special needs. The counselor collects information from each teacher about a student's classroom performance and reports to the team. The counselor is then responsible for conveying team decisions and recommendations to each of the student's teachers. Of course, it is possible (and often desirable) for secondary teachers to serve as members of the team, as in the example of Mr. Morse, Marvin's and Jake's ninth grade English teacher (Figure 2–1).

General education teachers who have worked with students being considered for special education services can provide the team with much information. They are aware of special strengths students may have, students' past responses to various instructional programs and procedures, and specific areas in which students may require the most assistance. The presence of these teachers on the team can assure that all important classroom information is considered. In addition, their experience with individual students may temper the interpretation of assessment results or the recommendations made by the team.

General education teachers responsible for implementing a portion of the IEP should be involved in the team's discussion of assessment results and any other relevant information gathered by professionals or provided by parents. Teachers can de-scribe their classroom programs and their perceptions of a student's ability to participate in activities in the general education class. They can also benefit from the team's discussion of ways to adapt the general education program. As soon as the modified classroom program or the IEP is initiated, the classroom teacher can inform the team of the student's progress in the general education class. This input helps the team evaluate the current program in order to make any necessary changes needed to enable the student to meet the goals established by the prereferral or IEP team.

Special Educators

In addition to general education teachers, **special educators** also provide instructional services to students with disabilities. The special educators most likely to serve on the teams serving students with special needs are those assigned to a classroom or office within the student's school. The special educator may be a teacher-consultant who provides assistance to general education teachers with students with special needs in their classes. Or the special educator may be a resource room teacher who provides direct service to special students as well as consultation to their teachers. The special class teacher also may participate as a member of the team; this teacher serves students who require more intensive special education but who may be included in the general education program for selected activities.

Itinerant special education teachers who work with students with disabilities participating in the general education program also serve on the team as necessary. **Itinerant teachers,** who travel from school to school, may be specialists in the education of students with speech or language impairments, visual impairments, hearing impairments, physical or health impairments, or other special needs. One of the most common itinerant specialists is the **speech-language pathologist,** who serves students with communication disorders. These and other specialists serve on the team when a student likely to receive their specific services is being considered.

Special educators fulfill a variety of roles on the team. Often they are responsible for organizing the teams serving students with special needs, conducting the meetings, and monitoring the services provided to students with disabilities. They may observe a student in the general education class and conduct much of the educational assessment. Special education teachers explain the different types of available special services and describe in detail the support services for general education teachers. Also, these professionals help interpret assessment results and assist the team in formulating the educational plan. In the implementation of the IEP, they typically provide direct services to special students and consultant services to general education teachers.

The special educator most likely to provide instruction to a specific student should serve on the IEP team when that student's educational program is being planned. This involvement provides the special educator with the opportunity to meet the student and his or her parents and teacher(s). The special educator thus becomes familiar with the student's current performance and specific educational needs, as well as with the views of the student's general education teacher(s), the student's parents, and other professionals concerned with the student's education.

Parents and Students

At first, parents may be reluctant to participate in the activities of teams serving students with special needs, particularly if past contacts with the school have been primarily negative. They may also be apprehensive about becoming a member of a team composed mainly of professionals. Team members may need to give them a great deal of reassurance regarding the importance of their involvement.

Programs are more effective for students when parents are active participants. Parents can provide the team with information about the performance of the student with special needs outside the school setting. They are also able to assist in establishing appropriate educational goals. In addition, parents contribute to the team effort by specifying which aspects of the educational program can be supported or supplemented within the home. The parents' awareness of the specific program designed for their child and the resultant coordination between home and school can make an important difference for many students. Moreover, the team's concern for the needs of their child may win parental support for the effort to meet the child's educational needs. See "Window on the Web" for information about Family Village, a site on the World Wide Web with many resources for families that include a student with disabilities.

The team should make every effort to include the special student's parents as fully participating team members. If possible, conflicts between parents and professionals should be resolved at the team level. However, if parents do not agree with the recommendations made by the team, they may request a hearing to appeal the team's decisions. The school district also has the right to appeal if it believes that the parents are not acting in the student's best interests.

Students with special needs participate in the activities of the team when appropriate. As a general rule, students who have reached adolescence are the most likely to be included. Students attending team meetings should be encouraged to discuss their reactions and perceptions regarding possible educational goals and placements.

School Psychologists

School psychologists typically assist the assessment team in evaluating students referred for special education services. In addition to administering tests and other assessments, psychologists may observe the student in the general education classroom, interview the parents, or consult with other professionals who have information about the student's recent performance. Their participation on the assessment and IEP teams also involves explanation or interpretation of assessment results.

School psychologists generally have training in counseling and classroom management. However, their responsibilities for assessing students, writing reports, and serving on several prereferral, assessment, or IEP teams throughout the district often consume most of their time. Because they are usually required to serve more than one school, they may not be available for consultation with a teacher who has an immediate concern.

School Social Workers

School social workers assist in collecting information from parents, coordinating the efforts of the prereferral or IEP teams with community agencies, and observing the student's interactions in settings outside the classroom. They are able to provide consultative services to parents, teachers, and students themselves.

School Counselors

Although counselors are most likely to be found at the secondary level, in some districts they are available for students of all ages. Counselors serve

Window on the Web

Family Village

http://www.familyvillage.wisc.edu

The Family Village website provides resources for persons with disabilities and their families. The site is organized like a village. Visit the Library to find information about all types of disabilities; visit the Shopping Mall to learn about assistive technology and adaptive products. The Coffee Shop is the place to make connections with other families; it includes the Family Village discussion boards and chat rooms as well as information about Internet mailing lists and newsgroups. The Post Office features parent-to-parent web boards organized by topic; for example, persons interested in ADHD, Down syndrome, or learning disabilities can read messages written by others and leave their own messages with questions or comments. Other locations in the Family Village include the Hospital (for health-related information), House of Worship, School, Recreation and Leisure, Community Center (for family resources), Bookstore, and University (for links to sites related to disability research).

in a number of roles on teams serving students with special needs and also provide direct services to these students. They assist in gathering information from teachers, school records, parents, and community agencies (particularly when school social workers are not available). Students with special needs may receive counseling or educational guidance from these professionals. Counselors at the secondary level often coordinate the educational programs for students with special needs and assume responsibility for communicating each student's progress to teachers, parents, and the student.

School Nurses

The school nurse may collect appropriate medical information regarding special students; for example, nurses can screen students for possible vision or hearing problems. As team members, nurses assist in interpreting a student's medical records and reports and in explaining the educational implications of medical information. They may provide services to students with physical impairments, those with chronic illnesses, or others needing continual medical attention. In addition, they assist parents in obtaining medical services for their children.

Other Team Members

Other persons join teams serving students with special needs when their special expertise is needed. For instance, for students with physical impairments, professionals such as **physical therapists, occupational therapists,** and **adapted physical education teachers** are important team members. When young students with disabilities enter school, it is important to obtain information from the **early interventionist** familiar with their progress in infant and toddler or preschool programs to facilitate their transition into the school program. For secondary students, **vocational rehabilitation counselors** may be an important addition. **Audiologists** contribute to the team's understanding of hearing losses, and medical personnel may assist when students with health impairments are considered. **Assistive technology specialists** can advise the team regarding the selection, acquisition, and use of technological devices to increase, maintain, or improve the functional capabilities of students with a disability. Another possible addition is the instructional aide who has worked closely with the special student.

Although these professionals are included as team members as needed, the effective team involves only those individuals who are necessary for careful and complete consideration of the student's special needs. Large teams of more than five to seven members become unwieldy, and productivity declines. At the minimum, however, every team should include the student's parents and his or her general and special education teachers.

◆ COLLABORATION IN THE IDENTIFICATION AND PREREFERRAL STAGES

A primary function of prereferral teams is identification of students with special needs. When students are located, adjustments must be made in the general education program to respond to their needs. If classroom modifications do not improve student performance, the student is formally referred for special education services. The assessment team then plans and conducts an assessment to determine whether the student is eligible for special education services. Although this may not appear to be a complex task, a number of important factors must be taken into account.

Identification

Federal and state laws and regulations specify procedures for educational agencies to follow in the identification process. Team members must fully understand these legal requirements. (Usually the administrators or special educators on the team take primary responsibility for keeping abreast of rules and regulations.) For example, it is the responsibility of each school district to locate all students with disabilities in need of special education and then to provide appropriate services. Each state also has specific regulations regarding district responsibilities in this and other areas, such as notification of parents, due process procedures, and confidentiality of student records.

Many classroom teachers may be unaware of the types of special education services offered within their districts (or even within their school build-

ings). Also, they may not know the specific criteria or standards used to determine whether students are eligible for special education services. Teams serving students with special needs should make sure that this information is available to all educators and other interested parties, such as parents and appropriate community agencies.

Anyone within the school community can refer students for consideration for possible special education services. Most **referrals** originate with general education teachers, but many come from parents, counselors, social welfare agencies, and physicians. Teams serving students with special needs should set up clear referral procedures; the steps in the process should then be communicated to all teachers and staff within the building as well as to parents and others who may initiate referrals. However, it is important to consider other possible options within the general education program before beginning referral procedures. Research indicates that, once students are referred for special education services, they are likely to be assessed (92%) and ultimately placed (73%) in special education (Algozzine, Christenson, & Ysseldyke, 1982).

Prereferral Interventions

Classroom teachers refer students for special education and other types of support services for many reasons. In one recent study, the most common reasons were general academic problems, difficulty in reading, and behavioral problems such as inattentiveness (Lloyd, Kauffman, Landrum, & Roe, 1991). However, before a referral is made, the teacher can try several strategies to solve the instructional problem. Because of *when* they occur, these strategies are often called **prereferral interventions.**

Interventions undertaken during the prereferral stage often eliminate the need to refer students for special education or other special services. For example, a change in instructional strategies or an adaptation of the classroom learning environment may lead to improved student performance. Although not mandated by federal special education laws, prereferral interventions are required or recommended by more than half the states (Safran & Safran, 1996). In many states, school personnel must document that all possible general education interventions have been attempted before a student can be formally referred for special education services.

Data Collection. When students experience difficulty with some aspect of the general education program, one of the first steps teachers should take is the collection of data to describe the instructional problem. This information allows the teacher to verify the existence of the problem, describe its characteristics, and determine its severity. For example, if a teacher is concerned about a student's off-task behavior during the time set aside for journal writing, the teacher could conduct an observation to determine how often the student is off-task. If results indicate that the student is writing in his or her journal only about half the time and talking with peers the other half, the teacher would likely conclude that the problem is severe enough to warrant intervention.

Collaboration with Parents and Colleagues. Once the instructional problem is described, it is often useful to confer with other professionals familiar with the student in question. The student's former teachers may be able to describe interventions that they have found effective for similar problems; current teachers can share their experiences with the student and their observations of his or her ability to cope with classroom demands. Parents, too, can provide information about the student. In some cases, simply making parents aware of the problem is an effective intervention. For example, if the

problem concerns homework, parents may decide to increase their supervision of the student's study sessions or make a valued activity (such as watching television) contingent upon the completion of all assignments.

In some districts, special educators such as resource teachers or teacher-consultants work with general educators to help them modify classroom programs to meet the needs of students not yet referred for special education services (Idol, 1993; Sugai & Tindal, 1993). In many schools, teachers can also seek assistance from teams of colleagues. These teams are known by several different names: *teacher assistance teams, student study teams, prereferral assistance teams,* and so on. They are typically composed of several general educators representing different grade levels or subject areas; other members may include an administrator such as the principal, a specialist such as a special educator, and parents. Their major role is to collaborate with teachers in solving instructional problems. The research on teacher assistance teams (Chalfant & Pysh, 1989) and consultation services (Doorlag, 1989a; Graden, Casey, & Christenson, 1985; Idol, 1993) indicates that these approaches are quite successful in solving problems at the classroom level, thereby reducing the number of referrals to special education (Hocutt, 1996; Safran & Safran, 1996).

Idol and West (1991) emphasize the collaborative nature of the team approach. The teacher seeking assistance becomes a member of the team and participates fully in the problem-solving process. This process involves six steps:

- Step 1: Entry/Goal Setting
- Step 2: Problem Identification
- Step 3: Intervention Recommendations
- Step 4: Implementation of Recommendations
- Step 5: Evaluation of the Action Plan and the Team Process
- Step 6: Follow-Up/Redesign (pp. 77–78)

For example, in step 3, the entire team (including the student's classroom teacher) brainstorms possible solutions to the instructional problem, evaluates the advantages and disadvantages of each solution, and then selects the most appropriate one. Consult "Inclusion Tips for the Teacher" to learn more about collaborating with prereferral or teacher assistance teams and special education consultants.

Inclusion Tips for the Teacher

Collaborating with Other Professionals During Prereferral

Special education consultants and prereferral or teacher assistance teams provide prereferral services to general educators in order to resolve educational problems within the general education classroom. To make the best use of these services, consider the following suggestions:

1. The job of the consultant or team is to assist you in developing a plan for working with the "target" student. The consultant or team is not there to dictate what should be done for the student or to "take over" the student's educational program.

2. The student continues to be your responsibility and you are in charge of his or her educational program.

3. Establish an agreement as to your role and that of the team or consultant. It may not be necessary to have this agreement in writing, but it is important that everyone be aware of each other's expectations.

4. It is important that you and the consultant or team work together collaboratively. While your training and experience may be different from that of special education professionals, you are responsible for the quality of the program in your classroom, you are aware of the needs of your students, and you can describe their history in your classroom. The team or consultant is there to assist you.

5. Try to keep the focus of the discussions on the problems the "target" student has experienced. Be as specific as you can in your statements, and don't digress regarding other problems.

6. Provide specific information on the behaviors of the student and on the interventions you have tried. Data on the number of times a behavior occurs or how long it persists, the performance of the student in problem academic or social areas, or the success of an intervention can assist the team or consultant in providing feedback to you. You may be asked some questions regarding this information to clarify the team's understanding of the problem.

7. The team or consultant may suggest that additional data on the problem behavior be collected. Attempt to collect these data, but if you are not comfortable with the type of data to be collected, how the data should be collected, or how much of your time will be required, share these concerns and resolve the specifics of the data collection process. Some teams or consultants can assist with the initial collection of data on students.

8. The team or consultant should help you develop more than one possible intervention for the problem behavior. Don't expect "one magic solution." Do expect to be actively involved in providing suggestions and developing possible interventions.

9. Implement the interventions in the way they were developed by you and the team or consultant. If you are not comfortable with the intervention or are unsure of the specifics, ask for clarification or assistance. The consultant or a team member may be able to demonstrate the intervention or inform you of other teachers using similar techniques you could observe.

10. Be sure that a plan is devised to evaluate the effectiveness of the intervention(s). This plan should specify the type of data needed for evaluation. It should also include the length of time the intervention should be attempted and the alternative interventions that should be attempted if the initial one fails. Set a date for you and the team or consultant to review the progress of the intervention and to consider next steps. If it later becomes necessary to refer the student for special education services, be sure to share the information you have collected on the student and the interventions attempted.

11. Consider your work with the team or consultant an opportunity to gain new skills in working with students with special needs. Once these skills are mastered, they will help you work with other students with similar problems.

12. Provide feedback to the team or consultant. This feedback will help improve the prereferral services provided to you and other teachers.

Team deliberations are most fruitful when the teacher is able to clearly describe the student's problem and any attempts to remedy it. The student intervention checklist shown in Figure 2–3 is one method for recording this information. The teacher begins by noting the area or areas of concern (e.g., academic achievement, classroom behavior) and the steps already taken to solve the problem (e.g., student or parent conference). He or she then describes the student's present performance and current classroom procedures. At the end of the checklist, the teacher identifies the type of assistance he or she is seeking, and there is space for the team to record the results of its deliberations and the outcomes of any interventions.

Classroom Modifications. A number of prereferral intervention strategies involve changes in the instructional program of the general education class. To improve student performance, modifications can be made in any aspect of the program: the classroom curriculum, how instruction is delivered, the learning activities in which students participate, how students are graded, the physical arrangement of the classroom, and strategies for managing student behavior.

Curricular adaptations are changes in the body of knowledge and skills taught to students. One option is to retain the standard grade-level curriculum but teach only a portion of it—those areas determined to be the most important. Another option is the substitution of an alternative curriculum. In the general education classroom, this usually involves teaching the prerequisite skills that students lack and/or using curricular materials from a lower grade level. For example, a fifth grade teacher might use fourth grade reading materials for some students in the class.

Instructional adaptations are the most common type of classroom modification. These changes may involve any part of the teaching-learning process: the teacher's instructional methods and strategies, learning activities and instructional materials, performance requirements for students, testing and grading procedures, and grouping arrangements. Examples are as follows:

- Providing additional instruction in areas where students experience difficulty
- Structuring practice activities so that students have ample time to master one set of skills before moving on to the next

- Modifying task requirements so that students can listen rather than read or give answers orally rather than write
- Giving students extra time to complete exams and assignments
- Allowing students to use aids such as calculators and dictionaries
- Reducing the number of problems students are required to solve or the number of paragraphs they must write
- Grouping students with similar needs for instruction and changing the composition of the groups, as needed

Management adaptations are changes in the classroom behavior management system. The teacher may need to provide additional instruction to all students on the rules for classroom conduct. Or he or she may need to modify the standard classroom management system if several students begin to display inappropriate behaviors. In some cases, it may be necessary to begin a systematic behavior change program for one or more students with more severe behavioral problems. For example, the teacher and student might negotiate a behavioral contract in which the student agrees to reduce his or her inappropriate behavior, and in exchange the teacher promises to provide a suitable reward.

Environmental adaptations are changes in the physical environment of the classroom. For example, a teacher may modify the arrangement of student desks and the location of learning materials in order to make classroom activities accessible to a student who uses a wheelchair. Students with visual and hearing impairments may be seated near the front of the room, if that is where instruction typically occurs. Students who act out and those who have difficulty focusing their attention may also be seated near the teacher. The classroom itself may be arranged so that there are areas for several different activities including large- and small-group instruction, independent study, work at the computer, and so on.

According to recent research, general education teachers use several different techniques to modify instruction for students with special needs. However, although teachers consider many kinds of classroom modifications valuable, they are less positive about their feasibility (Johnson & Pugach, 1990; Ysseldyke, Thurlow, Wotruba, & Nania, 1990). In general, teachers are most likely to introduce

F I G U R E   2 - 3   **Student Intervention Checklist**

Name ——————————————— Age ——— Date ————
Teacher ——————————————— Grade ———

1. **Area(s) of Concern**
   ——— academic   ——— language   ——— gross motor   ——— hearing
   ——— behavior   ——— speech   ——— fine motor
   ——— emotional   ——— physical   ——— vision
2. What kinds of strategies have been employed to resolve this problem?
   A. **Records Review and Conference**
      ——— student conference(s)   ——— review of educational records
      ——— parent conference(s)   ——— vision   ——— medical   ——— hearing
   B. **Environmental Modifications**
      ——— class seating arrangement   ——— group change   ——— other
      ——— individual seating   ——— teacher change
      ——— schedule modification   ——— teacher position in class
   C. **Instructional**
      ——— modifications in methods used with group or class
      ——— modifications in learning aids used with group or class
      ——— individual methods with regular materials
      ——— individual learning aids with regular materials
      ——— individual methods and materials different from group or class
   D. **Management**
      ——— modification in classroom management system
      ——— use of systematic group management techniques
      ——— use of individual behavior management techniques
3. What methods are currently employed to address the concern?

4. Where does this student stand in relationship to others in class, group or grade regarding systemwide tests, class average behavior, completion of work, etc.?

Student Behavior	Class or Group or Grade Behavior

5. Is the concern generally associated with a particular time, subject, or person?

6. In what areas, under what conditions, does this student do best?

7. Assistance requested (observation, materials, ideas, etc.):
   ————————————————————————————————————
   ————————————————————————————————————
   ————————————————————————————————————
   ————————————————————————————————————

continued

FIGURE 2-3   Continued

Assistance provided:

Dates	Nature of Assistance	Individuals Responsible	Outcome

Permission granted by the publisher for noncommercial reproduction.

Note. Reprinted with the permission of Prentice-Hall, Inc., from *Developing and Implementing Individualized Education Programs* (3rd ed.) by Bonnie B. Strickland and Ann P. Turnbull. Copyright © 1993 by Prentice-Hall, Inc.

interventions that they themselves can accomplish quickly and easily within their own classrooms (El-lett, 1993; Johnson & Pugach). Some of the most common strategies are modifying assignments so they are shorter or less difficult, allowing students to respond orally on tests, and offering preferential seating (Bacon & Schulz, 1991; Munson, 1986).

General Education and Community Resources. In addition to making modifications in their own classrooms, teachers can draw upon the resources of the general education program to assist students with school problems. Although there will be differences among schools in the types of resources available, all teachers have access to some level of support within their school, district, and community.

The use of students as instructional assistants is one example. Students act as tutors to other students, which thereby increases the amount of individualized instruction that takes place within the classroom. Peer tutoring programs are inexpensive in terms of both time and money, and research supports their effectiveness for increasing the skill levels of students with school achievement problems (Lloyd, Crowley, Kohler, & Strain, 1988). Parents, other family members, and community volunteers can also act as assistants within the classroom.

The general education program may offer a number of resources: schoolwide peer tutoring and/or peer counseling programs, academic assistance in the computer lab, remedial programs for low-income students, reading and math labs or tutorial services, programs for students learning English, bilingual education, enrichment opportunities for students with special gifts and talents, and so on. The community may offer additional resources such as after school programs with homework assistance, big brother and big sister programs, sports activities and clubs, or a homework hotline with telephone tutors. School and community resources such as these are one set of options that teachers should consider when they select prereferral interventions for students with special needs.

COLLABORATION IN REFERRAL AND ASSESSMENT

In some cases, prereferral interventions do not solve the problems that students with special needs are experiencing in the general education classroom. When this happens, the next step is a referral to determine if the student has a disability and is eligible for special education services. An assessment team considers the referral information, including the data collected during the prereferral stage, and designs a plan for evaluating the student to determine his or her eligibility and educational needs.

Referral

When students are formally referred, specific time lines and notification procedures are followed, assuring that each student is evaluated in a timely manner as required by state and federal laws. Good educational practice dictates that any identified need be considered promptly, without relegating the student to a waiting list (as often occurred in the past). Delays deny the student access to appropriate services and also frustrate the individual making the referral.

Many different individuals can refer students for consideration for special education. The general education teacher, however, is the primary referral source because classroom teachers observe students daily in the school setting, constantly monitoring their physical status, academic performance, classroom behavior, and social interactions. Classroom teachers are able to compare the performance of one student with that of current classmates as well as students from previous school years.

Classroom teachers differ in the number and type of referrals they make to special education. Some teachers refer a high percentage of their students; others refer none. This discrepancy may occur for a number of reasons. Teachers may not have a clear understanding of how serious a student's problems should be before special education services are considered. Some teachers may not be aware of the special programs or consultation services available; others may already be capable of adapting their classroom program to meet the needs of a wide range of students. Still others may be unfamiliar with the appropriate referral procedures, or they may feel that referrals reflect negatively on their ability as a teacher and classroom manager. Most classroom teachers fall somewhere between the two extremes. Generally, the more teachers know about dealing with students with unique needs—and about the special services available, criteria for special education, and referral procedures—the more accurate and appropriate their referrals.

The exact procedure for making referrals varies greatly from school to school and from district to district. It can involve completing a short form with a minimal amount of information, an elaborate checklist, or a report requiring detailed data on the student's current and past performance. As part of the referral process in many districts, teachers must document the steps they have taken to meet the student's educational needs within the general education classroom. Figure 2–4 provides an example of a prereferral intervention checklist that a teacher might be asked to complete.

Students are referred for special education if they have special needs that interfere with their school performance *and* if these needs cannot be adequately met within the general educational pro-

gram. Blankenship and Lilly (1981) provide the following guidelines:

> As a basic principle teachers should refer students when two conditions exist: (1) the student is experiencing significant difficulty in the classroom, and (2) the teacher is unsuccessful in solving the problem as it exists. Many students experience difficulty in learning and not all should be referred for special education. Individual teachers have strengths in dealing with certain types of learning and behavior problems, and are confident that they can handle these problems as they occur. *If the teacher is handling a problem successfully, the student should not be referred.* (p. 36)

Although students with special needs may exhibit a variety of problems, their needs generally cluster into one or more of the following areas:

- *Physical needs*—difficulty with one or more of the senses, with mobility or motor coordination, or with physical activities requiring strength and stamina.
- *Academic needs*—poor performance in relation to peers in one or more areas of the curriculum. These needs may be evident in the communication skills of listening and speaking, academic areas such as reading and mathematics, and/or content areas such as science and history.
- *Classroom behavior needs*—difficulty in controlling inappropriate behaviors that interfere with other students, the instruction of the classroom, or the student's own study activities. Either acting-out or withdrawn behaviors may be considered inappropriate.
- *Social needs*—poor ability to establish and maintain interpersonal relationships, either with peers or with adults.

Information on special needs such as these is reported in a referral form such as that illustrated in Figure 2–5. This sample form asks for specific information about the student's current performance and his or her reactions to any instructional adjustments made by the teacher. Members of assessment and IEP teams work hard to make careful eligibility and placement decisions and provide educators and parents with specific programmatic recommendations. To accomplish these tasks, specific, accurate, and objective data are needed. It is difficult for teams to provide assistance when given only general information, such as "the student is

FIGURE 2-4   Prereferral Intervention Checklist

Appropriate activities on this checklist must be completed before referring a student for assessment for special education services. Place the date that activities were completed in the space next to the activity. This form must accompany the referral form.

1. _____ Reviewed student educational records to determine longevity of concern and previous interventions.
2. _____ Established that student has passed vision and hearing screening or referred student for vision and hearing screening.
3. _____ Met with student to discuss concerns and possible solutions.
4. _____ Met with parents to discuss concerns and possible solutions.
5. _____ Collected and analyzed recent examples of student's classwork.
6. _____ Collected specific information from records and performance regarding student's academic skills.
7. _____ Collected specific information from the record and class regarding student's behavior.
8. _____ Brainstormed with co-teachers to obtain strategies that have worked in other similar cases.
9. _____ Identified in writing the student's specific educational problem.
10. _____ Consulted with counselor regarding student's behavior.
11. _____ Consulted with resource teachers in school to discuss concerns and obtain strategies.
12. _____ Obtained observation by another teacher or school resource to obtain information regarding concern.
13. _____ Developed and implemented instructional strategies with assistance of other educators.
14. _____ Developed and implemented a behavior management plan with other educators.
15. _____ Obtained or developed instructional learning aids to address this student's problem.
16. _____ List any other modifications, interventions, or strategies you have attempted to maintain this student in the classroom.

_____

_____

_____

Teacher Signature _____ Date _____

Permission granted by the publisher for noncommercial reproduction.

Note. Reprinted with the permission of Prentice-Hall, Inc., from *Developing and Implementing Individualized Education Programs* (3rd ed.) by Bonnie B. Strickland and Ann P. Turnbull. Copyright © 1993 by Prentice-Hall, Inc.

slow," "acts out in class," "never talks," or "works below grade level."

Specific statements that describe the current status of the student are much more helpful. Examples of pertinent information to include on referral forms are

• correct and error rates on academic assignments and the level of academic performance as compared with that of other students in the classroom,
• the frequency with which inappropriate behaviors occur during the class period or school day, or

• the number of assignments completed by the student and an analysis of the student's errors.

Specific information on the success or failure of changes in classroom instruction or management is also extremely helpful. The more objective and complete the data provided in the referral, the more accurately the assessment and IEP teams will be able to determine what additional assessment information is needed, what types of special education services should be considered, and which educational recommendations are appropriate.

FIGURE 2-5   Referral for Special Education Services

Directions: Teachers or other individuals referring a student for special education services should complete all sections of this form. The completed form should be sent to the principal's office for processing. Complete and specific information will assist the assessment and IEP teams in determining the student's eligibility for special education and specific educational needs. Use behavioral descriptions whenever possible.

Teacher _____ Grade/Class _____ Report Date _____
Student _____ Age _____ Birth Date _____

1. What is the student's problem? How does it affect his or her ability to participate in classroom activities?

2. How frequently does the problem occur? (For example, once a week? Six times a week?)

3. What changes have occurred in the behavior during this school year?

4. What changes in classroom activities, assignments, procedures, and so on, have you made to try to solve the problem? What are the results of these changes?

5. What are the student's major strengths and talents?

6. What special interests, hobbies, or skills does the student have?

Assessment

When the assessment team has determined that a referred student may be in need of special education services because adaptations of the general education program have not resolved the student's problems, the team designs a complete plan for evaluating the student and presents it to the student's parents for their approval. The assessment plan indicates which tests and other assessment procedures will be used in the evaluation of the student. This process is designed to gather relevant functional and developmental information to de-termine whether the student has a disability and to determine the student's educational needs.

The assessments used with students suspected of having a disability must meet several criteria. They must not be discriminatory on a racial or cultural basis and they must be administered in the student's native language (when feasible) or other mode of communication (e.g., sign language). They must be validated for the purpose for which they are used, and they must be administered by trained personnel in conformance with the instructions provided by the producers of the assessment instruments. No single instrument can serve as the sole criterion for determining an appropriate educational placement for a student. Tests and other evaluations should assess specific areas of educational need for each student; typical concerns are academic performance, classroom behavior, and social skills. The student should be assessed in all areas that are related to the suspected disability. In addition, the general education teacher can assist by providing curriculum-based assessment information relating to the student's past performance in the classroom setting. The student shall not be determined to have a disability if this decision is based upon the lack of instruction in reading or math or limited English proficiency.

The assessment information, collected from various sources by the team and presented in a written report, indicates the student's present levels of performance. This information is used to determine whether the student has a disability and is eligible for special education services; if so, it serves as the basis for the IEP team to design an individualized educational program and determine the appropriate educational placement for the student.

Under federal laws, eligibility for special education services is determined by two criteria: it must be established that the student has a disability, *and* there must be evidence that the disability in some way adversely affects the student's educational performance. Satisfying one criterion but not the other is not sufficient. For example, many students with school problems do not meet eligibility requirements because they do not have a disability. Similarly, a student with a mild disability (e.g., a mild vision loss or physical impairment) would not qualify for special education services if he or she were not experiencing educational difficulties.

COLLABORATION IN DESIGNING THE INDIVIDUALIZED EDUCATION PROGRAM

Once it has been determined that a student is eligible for special education, the next step is design of the Individualized Education Program or IEP. This written plan must be developed prior to the start of special education services. The IEP, which must be reviewed and modified at least annually, must include several specific components (see "For Your Information" for an explanation of the legal requirements).

A review of the student's present levels of performance may indicate a variety of educational needs. It may not be appropriate, or possible, to deal with each of these areas in the IEP. Possible measurable annual goals should be determined by the team and then ranked in priority order. When the goals have been selected, specific instructional objectives are prepared. Objectives should be stated in observable terms for each of the IEP goals; the criteria for successful performance of each objective are then specified.

The sample IEP presented in Figure 2–6 on pages 49–51 outlines the student's present levels of performance and provides goals and objectives in the curriculum areas of spelling and written expression. Although the format used to present information may vary from district to district, the essential components should be present in all IEPs written for special students.

The IEP team is responsible for assuring that the student's educational program is implemented as specified in the IEP. Instructional recommendations and service provisions called for in the IEP are to be followed unless the plan is modified by the team and the changes are approved by the student's parents.

An annual evaluation of the IEP is required, but it may be necessary to determine the appropriateness of the IEP well before it is a year old. The IEP team should be open to reconsidering the special educational needs of a student if one of the team members believes that the IEP is in need of revision. Data should be systematically collected and presented to the team for their review prior to the actual team meeting. Any changes made in the IEP must be approved by the student's parents prior to implementation.

The annual evaluation of the student's progress can be conducted in the same manner as that used for the initial assessment of the student. However, this is neither practical nor necessary with the majority of special students. The annual evaluation is much more specific; it is concerned with the student's progress toward the goals and objectives stated in the IEP. Much of the evaluation information required will have been collected on an ongoing basis during the school year by the general and special educators providing service to the student. The continuous collection of data allows teachers to make immediate modifications in the student's instructional program. Also, continuous data are

For Your Information

Required Components of the Individualized Education Program (IEP)

PL 105-17, the Individuals with Disabilities Education Act (IDEA) Amendments of 1997, mandates the components of the IEP. Because the requirements are very specific, it is important that educators carefully review the requirements of PL 105-17 in the following excerpt from the law:

Section 614 (d) (1) (A) INDIVIDUALIZED EDUCATION PROGRAM—The term 'individualized education program' or 'IEP' means a written statement for each child with a disability that is developed, reviewed, and revised in accordance with this section and that includes—

(i) a statement of the child's present levels of educational performance, including—

  (I) how the child's disability affects the child's involvement and progress in the general curriculum; or

  (II) for preschool children, as appropriate, how the disability affects the child's participation in appropriate activities;

(ii) a statement of measurable annual goals, including benchmarks or short-term objectives, related to—

  (I) meeting the child's needs that result from the child's disability to enable the child to be involved in and progress in the general curriculum; and

  (II) meeting each of the child's other educational needs that result from the child's disability;

(iii) a statement of the special education and related services and supplementary aids and services to be provided to the child, or on behalf of the child, and a statement of the program modifications or supports for school personnel that will be provided for the child—

  (I) to advance appropriately toward attaining the annual goals;

  (II) to be involved and progress in the general curriculum in accordance with clause (i) and to participate in extracurricular and other nonacademic activities; and

  (III) to be educated and participate with other children with disabilities and nondisabled children in the activities described in this paragraph;

(iv) an explanation of the extent, if any, to which the child will not participate with nondisabled children in the regular class and in the activities described in clause (iii);

(v) (I) a statement of any individual modifications in the administration of State or districtwide assessments of student achievement that are needed in order for the child to participate in such assessment; and

  (II) if the IEP Team determines that the child will not participate in a particular State or districtwide assessment of student achievement (or part of such an assessment), a statement of—

   (aa) why that assessment is not appropriate for the child; and

   (bb) how the child will be assessed;

(vi) the projected date for the beginning of the services and modifications described in clause (iii), and the anticipated frequency, location, and duration of those services and modifications;

(vii) (I) beginning at age 14, and updated annually, a statement of the transition service needs of the child under the applicable components of the child's IEP that focuses on the child's courses of study (such as participation in advanced-placement courses or a vocational education program);

  (II) beginning at age 16 (or younger, if determined appropriate by the IEP Team), a statement of needed transition services for the child, including, when appropriate, a statement of the interagency responsibilities or any needed linkages; and

  (III) beginning at least one year before the child reaches the age of majority under State law, a statement that the child has been informed of his or her rights under this title, if any, that will transfer to the child on reaching the age of majority under section 615(m); and

(viii) a statement of—

  (I) how the child's progress toward the annual goals described in clause (ii) will be measured; and

  (II) how the child's parents will be regularly informed (by such means as periodic report cards), at least as often as parents are informed of their nondisabled children's progress, of—

   (aa) their child's progress toward the annual goals described in clause (ii); and

   (bb) the extent to which that progress is sufficient to enable the child to achieve the goals by the end of the year.

In addition, several other factors must be considered when applicable to individual students:

Section 614 (d) (1) (B) CONSIDERATION OF SPECIAL FACTORS—The IEP Team shall—

(i) in the case of a child whose behavior impedes his or her learning or that of others, consider, when appropriate, strategies, including positive behavioral interventions, strategies, and supports to address that behavior;

(ii) in the case of a child with limited English proficiency, consider the language needs of the child as such needs relate to the child's IEP;

(iii) in the case of a child who is blind or visually impaired, provide for instruction in Braille and the use of Braille unless the IEP Team determines, after an evaluation of the child's reading and writing skills, needs, and appropriate reading and writing media (including an evaluation of the child's future needs for instruction in Braille or the use of Braille), that instruction in Braille or the use of Braille is not appropriate for the child;

(iv) consider the communication needs of the child, and in the case of a child who is deaf or hard of hearing, consider the child's language and communication needs, opportunities for direct communications with peers and professional personnel in the child's language and communication mode, academic level, and full range of needs, including opportunities for direct instruction in the child's language and communication mode; and

(v) consider whether the child requires assistive technology devices and services.

FIGURE 2-6   Sample IEP

Date 11/18/98
☐ Initial IEP
☒ Annual Review
☐ Three-year Review
☐ Other _____

Orchard County Public Schools
Individualized Education Program (IEP)

Student Information
Name ___Steven Cooper___ Birth Date ___7-23-87___
Male ☒ Female ☐ Age __11-4__ Grade __6__ Ethnicity __white, nonHispanic__
Social Security Number _000-00-000_ LEP Yes ☐ No ☒
Home Language __English__ Interpreter Required Yes ☐ No ☒
Address __1400 Lilac Rd. Blanchard 00000__
School of Residence ___Piper Middle School___
School of Attendance ___Piper Middle School___
Rationale for placement, if other than student's school of residence:
N/A

Parent/Guardian Information
Name _Bob Cooper and Helen Downing-Cooper_
Address ___same___
Home phone _555-5555_ Work phone _555-0000_
Interpreter Required Yes ☐ No ☒

Assessment Information
Present Levels of Performance (include how disability affects involvement and progress in general curriculum)
Steven has average performance in all areas except written language. He scores in the below average to low average range in spelling and written expression. Steven should be able to function well in general education with support in written language.

Modifications needed in State and districtwide assessment _in assessments requiring written expression, use of dictionary and thesaurus; time and a half to complete essays_

continued

FIGURE 2-6 **Continued**

Why needed <u>student requires support in written expression</u>

IEP Information
Date of Next IEP <u>11/99</u>   Date of Three-year Review <u>11/00</u>
Primary Disability Category <u>specific learning disability</u>
Primary Placement <u>regular class & resource room</u>
P.E. Type <u>regular</u>
Transportation <u>N/A</u>

Special Education & Related Services; Supplementary Aids & Services; Program Modifications	Start Date	Duration	Frequency	Location
Resource Room	11/98	1 year	1 hour, 5 days/week	Rm. 5
Consultation to general education teacher	11/98	1 year	as needed	Rm. 7
Testing accommodations in regular class, State/district assessments	11/98	1 year	as needed	Rm. 7
Assistive technology assessment	11/98	as needed	as needed	Rm. 5, Rm. 7

Extent to which student will not participate with nondisabled students in regular class <u>one hour per day</u>
Explanation <u>Steven will participate in spelling activities in the regular classroom and receive additional spelling</u>
<u>instruction in the resource room. He will begin written expression assignments in the regular class and receive</u>
<u>support in editing and revising in the resource room.</u>

Annual Goals, Short-term Objectives/Benchmarks, Progress Measures
1.   WRITTEN LANGUAGE. Steven will write a 5-sentence paragraph.
     (a). Steven will be assessed by the assistive technology specialist to determine the need for word processing or other adaptations. (b). When writing sentences, Steven will begin all sentences with a capital and end sentences with the appropriate punctuation with 95% accuracy. (c). Steven will write a paragraph with a topic sentence and two or more supporting sentences with 95% accuracy. (d). Steven will write a 5-sentence paragraph with topic, supporting, and concluding sentences with 95% accuracy.
2.   SPELLING. Steven's spelling skills will improve.
     (a). Steven will score 70% or higher in weekly spelling tests in the regular classroom. (b). Steven will score 90% or higher in weekly spelling tests in the regular classroom.
     EVALUATION. Portfolio assessment of Steven's work samples. All writing assignments and spelling tests will be graded with the criteria used for general education students.

Parents/guardians will be informed of student's progress via <u>monthly progress reports and regular report cards</u>

continued

FIGURE 2-6   **Continued**

As appropriate, the following factors were considered in the development of this IEP:
❏ for students whose behavior impedes learning, positive behavioral interventions, strategies and supports
❏ for students with limited English proficiency, language needs
❏ for students who are blind or visually impaired, instruction in and use of Braille and appropriate reading and writing media
☒ communication needs of the student
❏ for students who are deaf or hard of hearing, language and communication needs
☒ assistive technology devices and services

Transition Services
❏ Transition service needs included in this IEP
❏ Transition service needs described in attached Individualized Transition Plan
❏ Student has been informed of his or her rights

Signatures
My due process rights have been explained to me.
☒ I consent to the IEP.
❏ I consent to portions of the IEP as described on the attached form.
❏ I do not consent to the IEP.

Helen Downing-Cooper	*11/18/98*
Parent/Guardian's Signature	Date
Steven Cooper	*11/18/98*
Student's Signature	Date
Marianne Kemp	*11/18/98*
Signature of Administrator/Designee	Date
Connie Hernandez	*11/18/98*
Signature of General Education Teacher	Date
Edward Johnson	*11/18/98*
Signature of Special Education Teacher/Specialist	Date
Marsha Humphries, Advocate	*11/18/98*
Signature/Title of Additional Participant	Date
Signature/Title of Additional Participant	Date
Signature of Interpreter	Date

Note. Developed by Tamarah M. Ashton, Ph.D., Assistant Director of the Enhancing Writing Skills Project and Project LITT, San Diego State University.

more sensitive to the small incremental changes in performance often observed with students with special needs.

Information should also be collected on a regular basis from the parents of students with special needs. It is important to continue their involvement with the team and elicit their perceptions of their child's progress in school and at home. When data

are collected from parents, it is appropriate to share information with them about the school performance of the student.

The IEP is a formal instructional plan designed for and based upon the specific individual educational needs of each student with disabilities. It should clearly communicate to all team members the exact nature of the student's educational program.

Inclusion Tips for the Teacher

IEP Responsibilities of General Educators

General education teachers have many questions about IEPs and their responsibilities in the IEP process. Some of the most commonly asked questions (and their answers) appear here.

- *Does the classroom teacher participate in the development and review of IEPs?* Under current federal law, general education teachers are required to serve on the IEP team when students they are (or will be) teaching are being considered for special education services or when their IEP is being reviewed. When students with disabilities receive both general and special education services, the teacher in the general education classroom is expected to aid in the development of the IEP. At the elementary level, the classroom teacher is required to participate because he or she is probably the only general education teacher working with the student. At the secondary level, however, a staff member such as the school counselor is often selected to serve as the classroom teachers' representative on the IEP team.

- *Is the IEP a contract? Are teachers legally responsible for meeting each of the goals on the IEP?* The IEP is a contract because schools and agencies are legally responsible for providing the services indicated on the IEP. However, teachers are not held legally accountable for accomplishing IEP goals and objectives. Nevertheless, teachers do have the responsibility for making good-faith efforts to assist the students in accomplishing the goals and objectives stated in the IEP (Strickland & Turnbull, 1993).

- *Do IEPs cover both special education and general education programs?* The IEP must state an explanation of the extent, if any, to which the student will not participate in the general education program. Goals and objectives are written for only those portions of the school day in which students require specialized services. The IEP must also include information about supplementary aids and services and other supports that will be provided in general education classes or other education-related settings to enable children with disabilities to be educated with nondisabled children to the maximum extent appropriate. If major adaptations are made in general education classroom procedures, then those will be reflected in IEP goals and objectives. However, for most students with special needs, general education goals are not needed.

- *Who is responsible for implementing the IEP?* The IEP states who is responsible for implementing the special education program to meet each of the annual goals. In most cases this will be the special educator. However, if the IEP contains general education class or even home goals, then the general education teacher or the parent may be named as one of the persons responsible.

- *Who may see the IEP?* Copies of the IEP are available to the student's parents and each of the persons responsible for implementing portions of the IEP. Many districts do not distribute copies of the IEP to all teachers working with the student because of the cost of copying and because IEPs are considered confidential documents that must be stored securely. To see the IEPs of students included in the general education program, teachers should contact the special educator or their school principal.

The IEP coordinates the efforts of the team by specifying what the team is attempting to accomplish, who is responsible for implementing each component of the plan, which evaluation procedures will be used to determine the student's progress, and how parents will be regularly informed of progress. Development of the IEP requires the team to carefully review each student's needs. The time spent in this analysis helps to improve the quality and appropriateness of the educational experiences provided for each student with special needs. See the "Inclusion Tips for the Teacher" section to learn more about the responsibilities of general educators in the IEP process.

SPECIAL EDUCATION PROGRAM OPTIONS

Special education programs vary in the opportunities afforded to students with special needs for participation in the general education program. Some programs permit students with disabilities to spend their entire school day in the general education classroom (least restrictive), whereas other programs exclude the students from any interaction with their general education class peers (most restrictive). The remainder of the programs fall between these two extremes. Each type of program is designed to serve students with disabilities with a specific type or intensity of educational need.

The IEP team is responsible for assuring that each student receives educational services in the most appropriate setting that is also the Least Restrictive Environment (LRE). While current federal law requires that the IEP attempt to meet the needs in a way that enables the student "to be involved in and progress in the general curriculum" with their "nondisabled" peers, the general education classroom is not the LRE for all students. If the educational needs of a student with disabilities cannot be fully met in the general education program, the IEP team is responsible for considering the appropriateness of other placement options. For some students with special needs, the special class or the special school is the LRE. The majority of special students, however, can benefit from spending at least part of their school day in the general education classroom.

Professionals and advocates interested in specific disability groups often have divergent perspectives regarding the educational needs of students with disabilities. They also have different views regarding the services that general and special education programs should provide to meet these educational needs. For example, advocates for students with severe disabilities are most concerned about the social outcomes for these students rather than their academic performance (Hocutt, 1996). They have much less of a concern regarding the students' meeting the academic expectations of the general curriculum and are primarily interested in improvements in (a) the social skills of the students with disabilities, (b) the attitudes of the nondisabled students toward those with disabilities, and (c) the development of positive relationships and friendships between students with disabilities and their nondisabled peers (Machado, Belew, Jans, & Cunha, 1996). These groups propose that the educational needs of students with disabilities can be met while they are fully included in the general education program.

On the other hand, advocates for students with learning disabilities have a somewhat different outlook. They are concerned with the ability of these students to perform academic tasks and the need for access to a continuum of special education services that provides the IEP team with placement options to ensure that students develop their academic skills (e.g., Zigmond, Jenkins, Fuchs, Deno, & Fuchs, 1995). It is important that IEP teams consider these different perspectives in identifying specific goals for students with disabilities, choosing the appropriate education services and placements for these students, and evaluating their progress. It is also important to note that the different perspectives present quite different instructional demands on the general education teacher (i.e., arranging and supervising socialization activities versus providing specific individualized academic instruction) that may influence the implementation of the IEP.

When the IEP team considers the appropriate placement for each student with special needs, it generally has a number of special education program or placement options available at the school or within the district. Options may vary from district to district, but those noted in chapter 1 (Figure 1–4) are typical for students in the K–12 school levels. They range in intensity from residential schools to full-time participation in the general education class. Other programs, such as home-based programs in which special educators work directly with parents, are available for infants and toddlers or preschool students; community-based vocational programs may be offered for older students with severe disabilities.

As Figure 2–7 illustrates, three major categories of placement options are available for students with disabilities. In the first, general education programs, students with special needs are members of general education classes and the general education teacher takes primary responsibility for their instruction. These programs serve the greatest number of students with disabilities. In the second option, special class programs, students are members of special education classes, and the special education teacher takes primary responsibility for their educational program. The third option, more restrictive programs, serves the smallest

FIGURE 2-7 Program Options

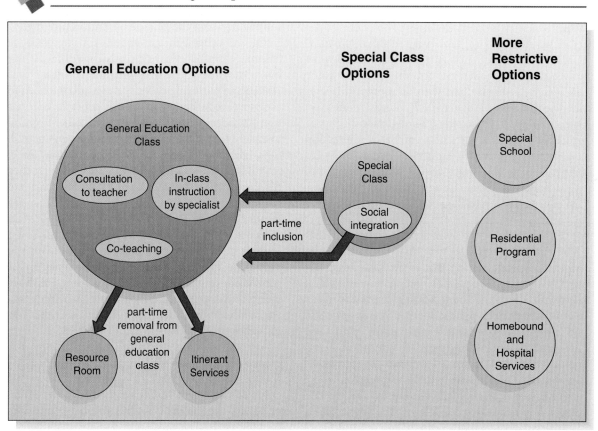

number of students with disabilities. It is designed for the students with the most severe, comprehensive, and specialized needs.

General Education Class Options

General Education Class. The general education classroom is the least restrictive of all the educational placement options. Students not currently identified as having special needs spend their entire school day in the regular classroom; neither the students nor their teachers receive any direct special education services. The majority of students with special needs begin their educational careers in this setting. For most students identified as having disabilities, the goal is to provide appropriate educational programs to assist in developing the skills necessary for returning to the general education classroom. For some students with more severe disabilities, this goal may not be realistic.

Indirect services that do not relate to any particular student with special needs may be provided to general education teachers and their classes. For example, in-service training opportunities may be offered to teachers by the special education staff in areas such as special education legislation, referral procedures, or techniques for working with students with learning or behavioral problems. Students enrolled in general education classes may participate in special assemblies that explain various types of disabilities and encourage the acceptance of all individuals, regardless of their unique needs. Special education teachers may visit elementary or secondary classes to discuss alternative communication systems, such as Braille, sign language, or electronic communication devices. Students in the general education class may be trained by special educators to serve as classroom assistants or cross-age tutors in general or special education classrooms.

Students placed in the general education class may have received special education services at one time but now be able to function appropriately without special services. For instance, a student with a hearing impairment may have received special education services in the past but now be fitted with an appropriate hearing aid, trained to use and care for it properly, and able to supplement the information received via the hearing aid with speechreading skills. A student with a visual impairment may now have appropriate glasses, magnification devices, or other devices or skills that permit independent functioning in the general education classroom. Students who have been identified as having special needs at one time do not necessarily require special services throughout their entire educational careers. Many acquire the skills needed to function in the general education program without special support.

General Education Class with Consultation to the Teacher. In this placement option, the student with special needs spends the entire school day in the general education classroom and receives no direct special education services. Instead, the general education teacher receives services; a special educator provides consultation on the needs of special education students included in the teacher's classroom.

Consultation services can take a number of forms. A specialist, such as a special education consultant or a school psychologist, may assist the teacher in designing and implementing a behavior management program for a student with classroom behavior problems. An itinerant teacher of students with visual impairments may furnish the teacher with large-print, Braille, or tape-recorded versions of class textbooks and provide information on how these materials can best be used. The special education resource teacher may help the teacher modify the regular reading or math program for a student with learning disabilities.

Specialists who provide consultation services typically have extensive experience in both general and special education settings. They are aware of the needs of general education teachers and special students. Their goal is to assist the teacher in gaining access to appropriate materials and developing the skills and confidence required to meet the students' educational needs, not to evaluate classroom instruction or management. General education teachers should feel free to call on special education consul-

tants for aid in adapting instruction, managing behavior problems, and promoting social acceptance of students with special needs. Whereas the general education teacher has the primary instructional responsibility for students with special needs, the consultant can help ensure their successful inclusion in the general education program.

General Education Class with Instruction Delivered by the Specialist. This type of service is a relatively recent innovation in most schools and districts. In this option, students with disabilities receive special education services within the general education classroom. Instead of leaving their classroom to visit a specialist, students remain where they are. The specialist comes to the students' class and delivers services there.

The special education services are provided in the general education classroom by a special educator working alone or with a trained assistant. These staff members "can support integrated special students in many ways, including (a) making adaptations when needed; (b) assisting the classroom teacher in working with a student; (c) coaching nondisabled peers; (d) providing direct instruction; and (e) facilitating positive interactions among students" (Hamre-Nietupski, McDonald, & Nietupski, 1992, p. 8).

The amount of support provided by specialists to students who are included full time in general education classrooms depends on the needs of each individual student. For students with mild learning problems, the specialist may visit the classroom for a brief period each day to deliver specialized instruction to target students and perhaps some of their peers with similar needs. For students with more severe disabilities, it may be necessary to provide support throughout the entire school day. In many cases, the amount and nature of services required will change over the course of the school year. For example, the specialist may be able to reduce time spent in the classroom once a cadre of peer tutors or other volunteers has been trained to assist the special student. Or the general education teacher may feel that he or she has developed the skills necessary to work with the students with special needs, thereby reducing the need for specialist support.

The advantages of this program option have been described by educators concerned with a range of students with special needs, from those with milder disabilities (e.g., Wiedmeyer & Lehman, 1991) to those with more severe disabilities (Hamre-Nietupski et al., 1992). Benefits include the opportunity for students with disabilities to have continuous interactions with their general education peers, reduction of the stigma associated with having a disability and receiving special education services, increased opportunities for exposure to the general education curriculum, and greater probability that the skills learned will be useful in other "normalized" settings. These educators also note that the success of this type of program is dependent on continuous cooperative planning between general and special educators to assure that the educational needs of all students in the classroom are met.

General Education Class with Co-teaching. A variation of the specialist teaching in a general education class is the co-teaching model. In this option, a general educator and a special educator co-teach a class composed of students with and without disabilities. For example, if the class includes 30 students, 20 may be typical students and 10, students with identified disabilities. The teachers share responsibility for all the students in the class, with the special educator providing specialized interventions for students with special needs, as required.

General Education Class and Resource Room or Itinerant Services. In this service option, special education services are generally provided to special students in a setting outside the general education classroom. However, the students continue to spend the majority of their school day in the general education class.

The **resource room** is usually located within the student's regular neighborhood school. At a regularly scheduled time each day (or several times a week), students leave their general education classroom to participate in special instruction in the resource room. Resource programs, common in both elementary and secondary schools, may serve several types of special students (e.g., those with learning disabilities, physical impairments, mild mental retardation), or they may limit service to only students with one particular disability.

A trend exists for resource room programs to include different types of students with special needs. In these cross-categorical or multicategorical resource rooms, there is no longer a reliance on the idea that the student's disability determines the ed-

ucational needs of that student. One resource teacher may provide educational programs for several groups of students, including those identified as having physical impairments, learning disabilities, behavioral disorders, and mild mental retardation. This capability exists because the educational needs of these students are often quite similar despite their different disabilities.

Consultation services, such as those described earlier, are often provided for the general education teachers of the students with special needs enrolled in a resource room program. These services can assist the teacher and help coordinate regular class and resource instructional activities.

The services provided by itinerant special education teachers, who travel from school to school, are managed in somewhat the same way as those of resource programs. Students with special needs may spend the majority of their day in the general education classroom but leave the classroom daily (or several times a week) to receive the services of itinerant teachers, such as speech and language clinicians. Whereas resource room teachers generally serve only students with disabilities who spend the majority of their day in the general education class, itinerant teachers may also serve students enrolled in a special class.

Resource and itinerant teachers serve the majority of the students with disabilities receiving special education services today. They supplement and support the general education program by providing assistance to students with disabilities and their general education classroom teachers. Although students with special needs usually leave their general education classrooms to receive special education services, special educators (or their instructional aides) occasionally teach small instructional groups within the general education classroom. As noted in the previous section, in this service arrangement, the special student is considered to be fully included and receives all instruction, both general and special education, within the general education classroom.

Special Class Options

Special Class and General Education Class. **Special classes** are located within regular elementary or secondary schools. Students receiving service in this placement option spend the majority of their school day in the special class and some time each day in the general education classroom. Participation in the general education class can vary from approximately half a day to only a few minutes. This is the most restrictive of the educational environments in which the student still spends time in the general education program.

Students with disabilities placed in this program option need intensive special education services. The student's involvement in the general education program is planned in curriculum areas in which success is fairly certain. Participation in general education for such students is limited to the period of time in which they can function successfully without becoming frustrated or creating a disruption.

Special classes can be operated for students in any of the categories of special education (e.g., students identified as having mental retardation, physical impairments, or behavioral disorders). General education teachers working with students in this option generally have consultation services available to assist them in designing and implementing appropriate instructional programs.

Full-Time Special Class and Social Integration. An increasing number of students with severe disabilities are being educated on regular school campuses at all levels of education. This trend provides educators with the opportunity to integrate these individuals with their typical age peers whenever it is appropriate. While many of these students may never attend regular academic classes, it is possible for them to participate in social activities such as lunch periods, assemblies, or recreational activities. Such activities offer students with severe disabilities the opportunity to interact with other students and gain the skills needed to function independently. Some schools have a reverse inclusion program in which general education students participate in activities in the special class. These programs are particularly appropriate for preschool and early elementary students.

Full-Time Special Class. Students placed in this program option are no longer included in the general education program, for they spend their entire school day in the special class. Special class programs are generally available at both elementary and secondary levels for students with different types of disabilities. Special classes may have different focuses, but the main goal of all such classes is to provide an intensive program to de-

velop skills that will prepare students for adulthood and, if possible, inclusion in the general education program.

Special classes for students with physical, language, visual, and hearing impairments may be concentrated at the lower elementary level. These students are readily identified at an early age, and providing intensive instruction in preschool or as soon as the students enter the elementary grades can enable their inclusion in the general education program at an earlier age. Special classes for these students at the secondary level are somewhat less common; by this time students have either acquired the necessary skills to function effectively in the general education program, or they have been placed in special school programs.

Special classes for students with behavioral disorders, mental retardation, and learning disabilities are most typically found at the upper elementary, junior high, and high school levels. As these students progress through school, the discrepancy between their performance and that of their peers becomes apparent, particularly if they do not receive appropriate educational services. The special class provides intensive services to students with serious educational needs that cannot be successfully met in the general education classroom.

At one time, special classes served as the primary special education program option between the general education class and the special school options. Their use has diminished as other less restrictive programs, such as the resource room and teacher consultants, have become popular.

More Restrictive Options

Special School. Special schools are generally the most restrictive placement option regularly offered by the public school system. Students are placed in this option on the premise that they cannot presently benefit from inclusion in the general education program. This program typically serves students with more severe disabilities (e.g., those with multiple disabilities, severe behavioral disorders, severe mental retardation). In the past, one justification for the concentration of students in one special school was the centralization of specialized services. It was thought that when psychologists, social workers, and physical and occupational therapists were housed in one building, they would be available to assist special education teachers in meeting the educational needs of the students. However, concerns over the segregation of these students from their age peers have led to the mandated closing of many special schools and the distribution of the students onto integrated regular school campuses (Pumpian, 1988; Sailor, Gee, & Karasoff, 1993).

Residential Program. Residential programs primarily serve two groups of students with disabilities. The first includes those who need intensive services that cannot be provided in less restrictive special education settings within the general education program. Students in this group may be those with severe behavioral disorders, severe or profound mental retardation, and severe multiple disabilities. These students may require specialized educational services and medical care that cannot be provided either in public schools or by their parents at home. In the residential setting, the 24-hour program permits the coordination of medical, psychological, educational, and other services.

The other students served in residential facilities are those who reside in a sparsely populated area that cannot practically offer a special program to serve their educational needs. When schools are so far from home that students cannot travel to school on a daily basis, the placement becomes residential. Placements of this type are becoming much less frequent as communities continue to expand the special education services offered locally.

As school districts have assumed more responsibility for offering appropriate educational programs to all students with disabilities, the role of the residential school has changed. For example, a few years ago a residential school may have served all the students with visual impairments in a state. Today, the majority of these students attend local school programs. Fewer students live at a residential facility, and those who do have severe or multiple disabilities.

The residential setting is the most restrictive special education setting because the students do not have regular contact with typical peers. In many cases they are also restricted from normal community and home contacts. However, for some students with very special needs, this is the least restrictive placement in which they can function successfully.

Homebound and Hospital Services. A relatively small number of students are provided their education at home or in a hospital setting. This arrangement is generally not permanent, but it may occur for various periods of time each year depending on the needs of the particular students. These students may have physical impairments, health impairments, or emotional or behavioral disorders that interfere with their attendance in classes at school. Typically a teacher visits the student several times a week to provide instruction and furnish the educational materials needed by the student. If the students have been included in the general education program or are capable of completing regular class assignments, the general education teacher may be asked to assist in providing assignments and materials to the teacher of homebound or hospitalized students.

Programs for Infants and Preschoolers with Disabilities

Public Law 105-17, the Individuals with Disabilities Education Act Amendments of 1997, includes provisions designed to assure appropriate special education services for preschoolers (ages 3 through 5) and to encourage similar services for infants and toddlers (birth through age 2). These services typically involve a multidisciplinary, interagency program that coordinates a wide variety of services for young children with or at risk for disabilities and their families. Each state is expected to design a program in which various education and human service agencies collaborate to provide services such as medical and educational assessment, speech and language intervention, physical therapy, and parent counseling and training. The early intervention services are identified and implemented according to an Individualized Family Services Plan (IFSP) that is developed by a multidisciplinary team that includes the child's parents. Key elements of these programs are (a) the early identification and resolution of problems that may contribute to developmental delays in order to maximize the child's potential for independent living in society and (b) the coordination of these efforts with the programs for school-age students to improve the transition of the young children from early childhood to school programs.

Many program options are available to students with special needs. Districts provide a continuum of services ranging from the general education class-

Things To Remember

- The goal of the various teams serving students with special needs is to assure that students are provided an appropriate education based on their individual abilities and needs.
- Teams serving students with special needs are composed of school administrators, general and special education teachers, parents, students with special needs (when appropriate), and other professionals whose expertise relates to the needs of the student.
- Teams serving students with special needs identify and evaluate students with disabilities, develop the IEP, determine an appropriate placement, and periodically evaluate student progress. Teams also assist the general education teacher in meeting the educational needs of other students with special needs who may be experiencing difficulty within the general education classroom.
- Placement of the student with special needs must be in the LRE for that student.
- Individualized Education Programs include information about the student's current performance, the goals and objectives of the educational program, necessary special services and placement, an explanation of the amount of time they will not participate in the general education classroom, and procedures for evaluating and reporting student progress.

- The IEP, including the student's placement, must be evaluated at least annually. No placement should be considered permanent.
- The special student's disability does not indicate the appropriate program or placement. Each student's placement must be based on his or her special needs in the areas of academics, classroom behavior, and social performance.
- Consultation is generally available to teachers working with students with special needs in the general education program. Teachers should request this service if it is needed.
- Special education consultants and teacher assistance teams can help teachers develop the skills needed to provide interventions for students with problems; if the prereferral interventions are successful, these students may not require special education services.
- Prereferral interventions include the collection of data to describe the learning problem, collaboration with colleagues and parents, classroom modifications, and use of available general education and community resources. The most common types of classroom modifications are curricular, instructional, management, and environmental adaptations.
- General and special educators share responsibility for the education of students with special needs included in the general education program.

room to more intense separate programs. Most students with disabilities, however, are able to succeed in the general education program if provided with appropriate support services.

In chapter 3, we will look more closely at students with special needs, their learning needs, and the challenges they provide to general education teachers when they are included in their classrooms.

ACTIVITIES

1. Visit a local elementary or secondary school that provides services for students with disabilities. What are the school's teams serving students with special needs called? Who serves on the teams? How often do they meet? Do they consider only students with disabilities? Gather information that will help you explain the operation of these teams to another educator. If possible, obtain permission to observe a team meeting.

2. Interview two individuals from a local school who serve on the same team serving students with special needs. Select persons who represent different roles—for example, a parent and a special educator, a general education teacher and a psychologist, or a speech-language clinician and a counselor. Compare their opinions of the operation and effectiveness of the team. You may

want to ask questions such as these: What is the purpose of the team? Are all team members encouraged to participate in deliberations? Are assessment results explained so that all members can understand them? Are the IEPs that are developed appropriate to the needs of students with special needs? Is each student's progress reviewed periodically? Summarize your findings, noting whether there is agreement between the perceptions of the two team members.

3. Read two journal articles on collaboration, the team approach, or consultation as it relates to the education of special students. *Exceptional Children* and *Remedial and Special Education* are journals that often address these topics. Write a brief summary and evaluation of each article you read.

4. Contact a local school district to find out what types of special education programs are offered. Are resource rooms, special classes, and all the programs described in this chapter available? How have program options changed in the past 5 years? Compare your findings with those of someone who has investigated another district. Explain why programs may vary from district to district.

5. Several organizations are designed to serve parents of special students. Two of the most prominent are the Learning Disabilities Association of America (LDA), whose national headquarters is at 4156 Library Road, Pittsburgh, PA 15234, and the Arc (formerly the Association for Retarded Citizens), located at 500 East Border Street, Suite 300, Arlington, Texas 76010. Are there local chapters of these organizations in your community? Contact a local or national office of LDA or the Arc to learn the purpose of these groups. Do they provide information about special students? Serve as advocates for parents? Work for better special education legislation? What should classroom teachers know about these organizations?

6. There have been several studies of general educators' views on classroom modifications for students with special needs. Examples are the articles by Ellett (1993), Johnson and Pugach (1990), and Ysseldyke, Thurlow, Wotruba, and Nania (1990). Read one of these articles to find out which modifications teachers feel are most valuable. Are the most valuable interventions the ones that teachers consider most feasible?

chapter 3

Special Students, Special Needs

Cases

Jody's vision is limited; her textbooks, worksheets, and other reading materials are in large print.

Luis has diabetes; he takes medication and must carefully monitor his diet and physical activity.

George has poor reading skills; he uses taped textbooks for reading assignments, and he is learning to "take notes" in class with a tape recorder.

Tom is impulsive and often leaves his seat, speaks out in class, and interrupts the work of other students; he and his teacher have set up a program to help Tom control these behaviors.

Annette is very bright and academically far ahead of her peers; she works on special assignments in subjects that interest and challenge her.

Special students such as these can succeed in the general education classroom with the assistance of the teacher and other members of the team. Because the educational needs of these students are not radically different from those of their peers, they can participate in many aspects of the general education program without special educational interventions. In areas where adaptations are necessary, support services are available to the student and to the classroom teacher. Special materials and equipment are provided, such as the large-print books needed by students with visual impairments and the tape recorders and taped texts needed by students with reading problems. The school nurse assists students with physical and health needs. The resource teacher works with the classroom teacher to set up behavior change programs for disruptive students and enrichment activities for advanced students. In this way the members of the team collaborate to meet the needs of special students within the general education classroom.

SPECIAL STUDENTS

Special students include those with disabilities, gifted and talented students, culturally and linguistically diverse individuals, and students at risk for school failure. Most special students have relatively mild learning problems and are thus able to succeed in the general education classroom.

Students with special needs make up a sizable portion of the school community. In a collection of 100 students, there may be 9 or 10 with disabilities and 3 to 5 who are gifted; depending on the community, any number of students may be from diverse groups. Learning disabilities, mild retardation, behavioral disorders, and speech and language impairments are the most common disabilities; physical, health, visual, and hearing impairments are relatively rare. Mild disabilities are much more frequent than severe disabilities. It is likely that at least 75% of the special education population has mild learning needs that can be met, at least in part, in general education.

It is important to note that not all disabilities are equally represented in the general education classroom. As Figure 3–1 illustrates, students with more severe and comprehensive disabilities (such as mental retardation and multiple disabilities) are more likely to be placed in separate classes and other separate environments. In addition, even for groups such as students with learning disabilities and those with speech or language impairments for whom inclusion is the most common practice, some students require the more intensive, specialized services available in settings such as special classes.

Students with Learning Disabilities

Teachers often use the word *puzzling* to describe students with **learning disabilities.** These students are average, even bright, learners who encounter difficulties in specific school subjects. Because they seem capable and do learn some things quickly and easily, their failure to learn in other areas is perplexing.

Students with learning disabilities have adequate intelligence. Their learning problem is not due to hearing or visual impairments, physical or health impairments, or emotional disturbance. The reason for their poor school performance is much more subtle and elusive: they have difficulty processing information. **Information processing** (sometimes called *psychological processing*) refers to the way in which persons receive, store, and express information. Students with learning disabilities may have difficulty receiving information because of attention or perception problems, their memory may be poor,

FIGURE 3-1 Special Education Services for Students with Different Disabilities

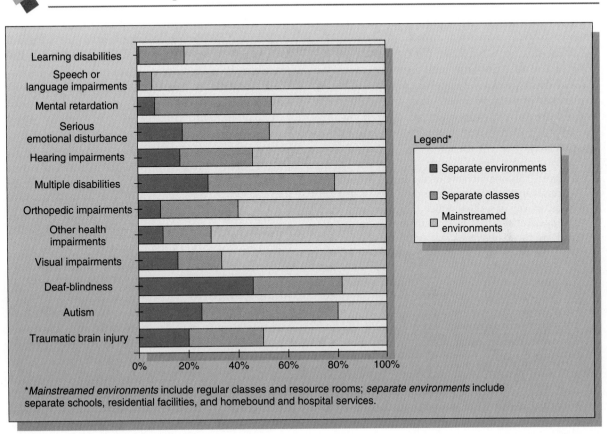

Mainstreamed environments include regular classes and resource rooms; *separate environments* include separate schools, residential facilities, and homebound and hospital services.

Note: From data provided in *Nineteenth Annual Report to Congress on the Implementation of The Individuals with Disabilities Education Act* by U.S. Department of Education, 1997, Washington, DC: Author.

or they may have difficulty communicating information to others because of expressive language problems. Students with learning disabilities may use poor strategies for learning (Robinson & Deshler, 1995; Swanson & Cooney, 1996); for example, such students may be passive learners who fail to become actively involved in the learning task (Torgesen, 1977). When given a list of spelling words to learn or a textbook chapter to read, such students may simply stare at the page, or read and reread it, without actively studying its content.

Despite adequate general ability, students with learning disabilities experience school learning problems. They appear able to achieve, but their performance in school falls short of expectations. Even more perplexing than this discrepancy between expected and actual achievement is the variability of performance that characterizes individuals

with learning disabilities. They are successful in some areas while having great difficulty in others. In addition, their performance may vary from day to day; teachers often comment that students with learning disabilities appear to know something one day but forget it the next.

Many different labels have been used to describe students with learning disabilities. Although the emphasis today is on educational terminology, it is still possible to encounter medical terms. For example, students with learning disabilities may be called *brain injured, brain damaged, neurologically impaired,* or *perceptually handicapped;* these labels refer to the theory that learning disabilities are due to some type of damage to the central nervous system. There are also medical terms for common academic problems: *dyslexia* (difficulty in reading), *dyscalculia* (difficulty in math), and *dysgraphia* (difficulty in writing). More recent additions to the medical terminology associated with learning disabilities (and with behavioral disorders) are *attention deficit disorder* (ADD) and *attention deficit hyperactivity disorder* (ADHD).

There has been much debate over what constitutes a learning disability and how the condition should be defined. One widely accepted definition, which has been incorporated into several state and federal special education laws, is that of the National Advisory Committee on Handicapped Children (1968):

> A disorder in one or more of the basic psychological processes involved in understanding or in using language, spoken or written, which may manifest itself in an imperfect ability to listen, think, speak, read, write, spell, or to do mathematical calculations. . . . The term does not include children who have learning problems which are primarily the result of visual, hearing, or motor handicaps, of mental retardation, or of environmental, cultural, or economic disadvantage.

This definition, like most definitions of learning disabilities, excludes other disabilities and points to information-processing deficits as the reason for poor school performance. In the general education classroom, students with learning disabilities may have special needs in the areas of academic, behavioral, social, and physical performance.

Academic Needs. Students with learning disabilities typically experience difficulty in one or more of the basic school subjects. Young children may enter school with poor listening or speaking skills. In the early grades, acquisition of language arts skills such as reading and spelling may prove difficult. For most elementary-aged students with learning disabilities, reading is the major stumbling block in academic achievement. However, some fare well in this area yet have specific disabilities in other subjects such as math or handwriting.

The basic skill problems of students with learning disabilities persist into middle school and high school (and beyond). These students may fail to acquire reading, writing, and perhaps math skills equal to those of their peers. Although able to cope with the content of secondary-level courses, many students with learning disabilities achieve poorly because of their inability to read texts and complete written assignments. Those with poor listening skills find lecture presentations a serious problem.

Behavioral Needs. Some students with learning disabilities, particularly in the elementary grades, are characterized by a high activity level. Such students may be constantly in motion and, as a result, may have difficulty paying attention to school tasks. Others, not overactive, may be impulsive and distractible; they, too, may have difficulty focusing their attention on appropriate aspects of the learning environment.

Older students with learning disabilities often have behavioral needs in the areas of classroom conduct and study skills. They may be unable to work independently (at least in part because of poor academic skills). Their attention span may continue to be a problem, and their organizational skills may be poor. In addition, there is some evidence of a link between juvenile delinquency and learning disabilities in adolescents (Leone et al., 1991).

Social Needs. The social arena is another area in which students with learning disabilities may perform poorly. Research indicates that some children and adolescents with learning disabilities have social perception deficits (Bryan, 1997; Bryan, Pearl, Donahue, Bryan, & Pflaum, 1983). That is, they may lack the skills needed for understanding and communicating appropriate social messages. Social communication requires not only speech but also an understanding of more subtle cues such as facial expression, vocal inflection, and body language; it becomes particularly important when students enter the peer-conscious world of the adolescent (Lerner, 1997).

Physical Needs. Students with learning disabilities do not have obvious physical needs; in appearance they are indistinguishable from their peers. However, some students with learning disabilities have motor coordination problems. They may appear clumsy and may perform gross-motor skills, such as running and jumping, poorly. Fine-motor skills such as cutting, manipulating small objects, and mastering the use of pencils and pens may also be troublesome areas. In school, motor problems such as these become evident in physical education and art activities and in academic tasks requiring handwriting.

Special Services. For students with disabilities severe and comprehensive enough to warrant placement in separate programs, many districts offer special classes. However, the majority of students with learning disabilities remain in general education throughout their educational careers and receive special services on a part-time basis from professionals such as resource teachers. Because students with learning disabilities have average ability and are able to perform as well as general education students in some areas, they are excellent candidates for inclusion.

Students with Behavioral Disorders

Behavioral disorders are a more obvious disability than learning disabilities. Students with behavioral disorders are often described by teachers as behavior problems or troublemakers. They may be rowdy, unruly, disruptive, and even aggressive. Some, whose behavior does not call attention to itself as readily, may appear withdrawn or depressed. All are characterized by inappropriate school behavior. Although most students with behavioral disorders have adequate intelligence as well as acceptable hearing, vision, and physical abilities, they often show poor achievement in academic skills. Some students, however, achieve satisfactorily despite inappropriate classroom behavior.

The term *behavioral disorders* includes a wide range of disabilities. The most severe are seen in students with serious emotional disturbance, such as individuals with psychotic behavior and childhood schizophrenia; such students generally require intensive special education services and are not included in regular class instructional programs. However, most students with behavioral disorders have relatively mild problems that can be dealt with successfully in general education. In fact, the special needs of many of these students are virtually identical to those of the problem student found in every classroom.

Even though apparently obvious, the disability of behavioral disorders is difficult to describe and define. It is necessary to decide which behaviors are appropriate and which are not. The problem is further complicated by the fact that all students behave inappropriately at one time or another in their school careers. Kauffman (1977) sidesteps some of these problems by defining students with behavioral disorders as

> those who chronically and markedly respond to their environment in socially unacceptable and/or person-

ally unsatisfying ways but who can be taught more socially acceptable and personally gratifying behavior. (p. 23)

This definition contains several important points. First, behavioral disorders are chronic and severe. The student's behavior must be inappropriate over time, not a one-time occurrence. The student's behavior problem must also be serious; it must in some way impair the student's ability to function in the school environment. Second, behaviors are judged to be inappropriate by either social or personal standards. This allows not only teachers and parents but also students themselves to determine problem behaviors. It also provides for inclusion of behaviors such as withdrawal that may be socially acceptable but are detrimental to the student. Third, Kauffman's definition recognizes that behavior is learned and that students with behavioral disorders are able to acquire more acceptable responses to their environment. This point is crucial for teachers who seek to change the behavior of their students.

The definition proposed by Bower (1969) is included in many special education laws. It describes students with behavioral disorders as those who show at least one of the following characteristics "to a marked extent" and "over a period of time":

1. An inability to learn which cannot be explained by intellectual, sensory, or health factors. . . .
2. An inability to build or maintain satisfactory interpersonal relationships with peers and teachers. . . .
3. Inappropriate types of behaviors or feelings under normal conditions. . . .
4. A general, pervasive mood of unhappiness or depression. . . .
5. A tendency to develop physical symptoms, pains, or fears associated with personal or school problems. (pp. 22–23)

A student need not exhibit all five of these characteristics to be identified as having a behavioral disorder; only one is necessary, although students may meet several of the criteria. This definition stresses the educational aspects of behavioral disorders by focusing on learning problems, student-teacher relationships, and school phobia problems. Like the definition of learning disabilities proposed by the National Advisory Committee on Handicapped Children, the Bower definition contains an exclusion clause: The learning problems of students with behavioral disorders must not be due to retardation, visual or hearing impairments, or health impairments.

The Council for Exceptional Children (1998) is critical of the definition found in current laws and recommends this revision:

> Emotional disturbance refers to a condition in which behavioral or emotional responses of an individual in school are so different from his/her generally accepted, age-appropriate, ethnic, or cultural norms that they affect educational performance in such areas as self-care, social relationships, personal adjustment, academic progress, classroom behavior, or work adjustment.

According to CEC, this definition reflects current professional knowledge and research and is endorsed by mental health and education organizations, including CEC's Council for Children with Behavioral Disorders.

As Heward (1996) remarks, definitions of behavioral disorders "require a child's behavior, in order to be considered disordered, to differ markedly (extremely) and chronically (over time) from current social or cultural norms" (p. 286). In the general education classroom, this means that students with behavioral disorders may have special needs in the areas of social and academic, as well as behavioral, performance.

Behavioral Needs. Children and adolescents with behavioral disorders are a heterogeneous group who exhibit a wide range of inappropriate classroom behaviors. These students may be disobedient, aggressive, or overly shy and retiring. One way to conceptualize this array of possible problem behaviors has been suggested by Quay (1979), who describes four typical patterns or dimensions of disordered behavior: conduct disorder, socialized aggression, immaturity, and anxiety-withdrawal.

Students with conduct disorders are aggressive, defiant, uncooperative, disobedient, and disruptive. Their behavior is judged socially unacceptable by teachers and others in authority. Students falling under the socialized aggression dimension also are perceived as behaving inappropriately. They are socialized in that they belong to gangs, but they participate in delinquent activities such as truancy and theft. Less obvious dimensions are immaturity and anxiety-withdrawal. Immature students appear delayed in development; they may be passive, have a short attention span, appear preoccupied, and daydream. Students characterized by anxiety and withdrawal appear fearful, timid, depressed, and lacking in self-confidence.

Students with behavioral disorders may have difficulty following classroom rules and meeting teachers' expectations for appropriate school conduct. Although aggressive students are the ones most easily and quickly identified by teachers, withdrawn and immature students also require special help. In middle school and high school, the truancy problems of pre-delinquent and delinquent students complicate their difficulties in meeting school demands.

Social Needs. Students with behavioral disorders often have trouble establishing interpersonal relationships. Their inappropriate behaviors may make them unattractive to peers and to teachers. They may lack the social skills necessary to make and keep friends. In addition, the self-concept of students with behavioral disorders is often low, especially in individuals who are anxious and withdrawn. And the problem perpetuates itself. Students with poor social skills remain friendless, and their self-esteem suffers; students with low self-esteem are unwilling to risk interpersonal relationships.

Academic Needs. Students with behavioral disorders, like those with learning disabilities, often experience difficulty with basic school skills (Whelan, 1995). Most studies of the academic achievement of students with behavioral disorders find poor performance in reading, math, and other subjects such as spelling and language (e.g., Rubin & Balow, 1978). Some evidence suggests that math achievement problems may be more serious than reading problems (Bower, 1969). The precise relationship between academic underachievement and inappropriate classroom behavior, however, is difficult to assess. Students may act out or withdraw as a reaction to school failure, or problem behaviors may interfere with successful school learning. In either case, most students with behavioral disorders require instruction in both behavioral and academic skills.

Special Services. Some students with behavioral disorders require intensive special education services in special classes, special schools, and even residential facilities. Most, however, are able to participate in at least some aspects of regular classroom instruction. Some may spend part of their day in a special class and part in general education. Others take part more fully in regular class activities and receive only part-time special services. The general education classroom is generally the most appropriate placement for students with mild behavioral disorders, provided, of course, that necessary support services are available to students and teachers.

Students with Mild Mental Retardation

Students with mental retardation have comprehensive learning problems. Because of below-average intellectual ability, they may learn slowly and may appear delayed in most areas of school performance when compared with their age peers. Tasks requiring reasoning and abstract thinking may be particularly difficult for them.

Mental retardation is one of the oldest areas of study within the field of special education, and there is general agreement regarding the definition of this disability. According to the American Association on Mental Retardation (1992),

> *Mental retardation* refers to substantial limitations in present functioning. It is characterized by significantly subaverage intellectual functioning, existing concurrently with related limitations in two or more of the following applicable adaptive skill areas: communication, self-care, home living, social skills, community use, self-direction, health and safety, functional academics, leisure, and work. Mental retardation manifests before age 18. (p. 1)

Less-than-average intelligence is central to the concept of mental retardation. Individuals considered retarded are those whose general aptitude for learning is impaired. Intellectual functioning is assessed by intelligence or IQ tests; these measures typically contain several types of verbal and nonverbal reasoning and problem-solving tasks. General ability level is established by comparing the performance of one student with that of others of the same age. Individuals who fall within the lowest 2% to 3% are considered retarded; that is, their intellectual performance is significantly subaverage in comparison to that of their peers. However, as Heward (1996) points out, measurement of intelligence is not an exact science, and it is possible for IQ scores to change significantly over time.

In addition to poor intellectual performance, students must show impaired **adaptive behavior** in order to be considered mentally retarded. Adaptive behavior, sometimes referred to as social competence, is "the effectiveness or degree with which individuals meet the standards of personal independence and social responsibility expected for their age and cultural group" (Grossman, 1983, p. 1). It is the way in which students meet the expectations of the total social environment, not merely those of the school. Expectations for adaptive behavior vary with the age of the student. Parents expect preschool youngsters to learn to walk, talk, and interact with family members; teachers expect school-aged children to learn to read, write, do math, and interact with peers; society expects adults to be gainfully employed and get along in the community. Expectations also vary across cultures. For example, while American teachers expect their students to ask questions and participate in discussions, Asian parents may expect their children to be quiet and obedient and listen to adults without asking questions or challenging their authority (Cheng, 1991).

Thus, students with mental retardation are characterized by both below-average intellectual ability and deficits in adaptive behavior. A low IQ score alone is not sufficient to determine retardation; the student's learning problem must be substantiated in the home, neighborhood, and community. The problem must also become apparent during the developmental period (i.e., before age 18). Older persons whose intellectual abilities are impaired by an injury, accident, or illness are not considered mentally retarded.

Within the group of students considered mentally retarded are several levels of abilities. Students with mild retardation, as the term is used in this book, are those who are able to learn basic academic skills. The special needs of students with severe retardation are more serious and comprehensive. Students with severe disabilities may be educated in a full-day special class; such classes are typically located on regular school campuses to facilitate social interactions between students with severe disabilities and typical students. In some cases, however, students with severe disabilities are fully included in general education classes with support from special education personnel. Severe disabilities are discussed more fully in a later section of this chapter.

Many students with mild retardation are able to participate in at least some of the instructional activities of the regular classroom. The special needs of this group, which makes up approximately 80% of the population identified as retarded, are in the areas of academic, behavioral, social, and physical performance.

Academic Needs. Students with mild retardation generally master academic skills at a slower rate than regular class students of the same age. Because they enter school somewhat behind their peers, they may not be ready to begin formal academic instruction immediately. Individuals with mild retardation are able to acquire basic school skills, but their achievement is below grade-level expectations. Nonetheless, most individuals with mild retardation acquire upper-elementary-level reading and math skills by the completion of their school career (Kirk & Gallagher, 1979).

Some aspects of school learning are especially troublesome for students with mild retardation. They may have difficulty focusing attention, remembering, and transferring information and skills learned in one setting to another situation. Tasks involving abstract reasoning, problem solving, and creativity pose special problems. For example, students with mild retardation perform less well on arithmetic reasoning tasks than on straightforward computational problems.

In the elementary years, the discrepancy between the age of students with mild retardation and their achievement level is not great. In adolescence, the gap widens. At the secondary level, such students often participate in special programs that stress vocational training. Despite their evident learning needs, students with mild intellectual disabilities may be identified as retarded only during their school years. Outside the school environment, with its academic demands, many individuals with mild retardation do not have obvious needs.

Behavioral Needs. As a group, students with mild retardation display more problem behaviors than their general education peers, perhaps because of their slower rate of learning. Their repertoire of classroom behavioral skills may be appropriate for their developmental level but not for their age group. Another possible factor is the low frustration tolerance of many students with mild retardation. Repeated failure in school and social situations contributes to this decreased capacity for handling frustration.

Social Needs. Students with mild retardation may not be socially accepted by their age peers. Lacking social skills, they may be rejected or ignored. This difficulty in establishing interpersonal relationships may be due to the apparent immaturity of students with mild retardation. Their social skills are not well developed in comparison with those of their age peers, and their problem behaviors may make them unattractive. Also, the play and leisure interests of students with mild retardation may be inappropriate for their age.

Physical Needs. Not all individuals with mild retardation have special physical needs; indeed, some excel in the physical area. However, as a group, these students are somewhat deficient in motor skills. When compared with their age peers, they perform less well in tasks requiring agility, coordination, strength, and dexterity (Bruininks, 1977). In addition, youngsters with mild retardation show visual problems and hearing losses more frequently than do typical students.

Special Services. Students with mild retardation are educated in a range of settings. Some are placed

Window on the Web

National Information Center for Children and Youth with Disabilities

http://www.nichcy.org

The website of the National Information Center for Children and Youth with Disabilities provides information on "disabilities and disability-related issues for families, educators, and other professionals." Visit this site to learn about NICHCY publications (y publicaciones en español), resource sheets for each state, links to other information centers, and conferences related to disability issues.

Note. Courtesy of National Information Center for Children and Youth with Disabilities.

in a special class but may attend general education programs for nonacademic activities. Others are members of general education classes for the majority of the day while receiving part-time special education services. As with all special students, decisions regarding the amount of inclusion for pupils with mild retardation must be made on an individual basis.

Students with Other Disabilities

Many general education classrooms include students with disabilities other than learning disabilities, behavioral disorders, and mild mental retardation. Among these are speech and language impairments, physical and health impairments (including traumatic brain injury), and visual and hearing impairments. Students with attention deficit hyperactivity disorder are also frequently served in general education settings. Students with autism and those with other types of severe disabilities participate in general education programs in some districts; in others, they receive more comprehensive special education services.

Communication Disorders. Among the most common of all disabilities are **speech and language impairments.** According to Van Riper (1978), speech is

considered abnormal "when it deviates so far from the speech of other people that it calls attention to itself, interferes with communication, or causes the speaker or his listeners to be distressed" (p. 43). Articulation disorders, or difficulty with the production of sounds, are the most typical speech problem, especially in young children. Other possible trouble areas include voice problems and disorders of fluency, such as stuttering.

Speech is the production of sounds for the communication of oral language. Oral language includes not only the expression of messages by speaking but also the reception of messages by listening. Students with language impairments may experience difficulty in either or both areas. Some students show an overall delay in language development. Others have particular difficulty with a specific component, such as grammatical structure (syntax) or the meaningful aspects of language (semantics).

In the general education classroom, students with speech and language impairments have special academic and social needs. In addition to receiving special help from speech-language pathologists, they may require instruction in listening skills, vocabulary, grammar, and oral expression. In the social area, students with communication problems may find interpersonal encounters stressful. Such students may need assistance in order to become full participants in classroom social interactions.

Physical and Health Impairments. This group of students is relatively small (less than 1% of the school-aged population) but extremely diverse. **Physical and health impairments** encompass a multitude of different conditions and disabilities that range from mild to severe and from invisible to obvious. According to Sirvis (1982), this group includes individuals with *functional limitations* "related to physical skills such as hand use, trunk control, mobility" (p. 384) and individuals with *medical conditions* that affect strength and stamina.

Students with physical impairments include those with missing limbs, spinal cord injuries causing paralysis, and conditions such as muscular dystrophy. Two of the most common physical problems are cerebral palsy and epilepsy. Cerebral palsy is a motor impairment caused by damage to the brain; it results in difficulty with coordination. Epilepsy is a convulsive disorder; students with epilepsy may have seizures during which they lose consciousness and motor control. Examples of health problems that may affect school performance are diabetes, cardiac conditions, asthma, hemophilia, and cancer.

In the general education classroom, students with physical and health impairments may encounter few difficulties; if special needs do arise, they are likely to be in the areas of physical, academic, and social performance. Special services may be provided by adapted physical education teachers or other motor specialists; school nurses help with students needing special diets, medication, or activity restrictions. For students with physical mobility problems (such as individuals who walk with crutches or those who travel in wheelchairs), it may be necessary to modify the physical environment of the school to allow access. Instructional materials are adapted for students whose physical problems make writing difficult. Although students with physical and health impairments are not poor achievers as a group, those with chronic medical conditions may miss much school and may fall behind their peers as a result. Social acceptance is another possible problem area, particularly for students with conspicuous disabilities.

Traumatic brain injury was recognized as a separate disability by the Individuals with Disabilities Education Act of 1990. The National Head Injury Foundation Task Force defines traumatic brain injury as

> an insult to the brain, not of a degenerative or congenital nature, but caused by an external physical force that may produce a diminished or altered state of consciousness which results in impairment of cognitive abilities. (as cited in Tucker & Colson, 1992, p. 198)

The most common causes of head injuries in school-aged individuals are motor vehicle accidents, falls, sports injuries, and, in some parts of the country, assaults (Mira & Tyler, 1991). Students with traumatic brain injury often have physical, academic, and social-behavioral needs. Such students receive educational services in hospital settings, at home, and in a variety of school placements, including general education classrooms.

Sensory Disorders. Another small group of students with disabilities includes those with **visual impairments** and **hearing impairments.** Many school-aged individuals are able to see and hear normally despite visual and hearing problems; their difficulties either have responded to medical treatment or are corrected by eyeglasses or hearing aids. Such students are not considered disabled. Only those whose senses remain impaired after treatment and correction are identified as having a visual or hearing impairment.

Students with visual impairments may be **blind** or may have **low vision.** Individuals who are blind receive so little information through the eyes that they must learn through their other senses; for example, they use the sense of touch to read Braille. Students with low vision, although visually impaired, are able to use their residual vision to learn. In the general education class, students with visual problems may have physical, academic, and social needs. They may require assistance in learning to move about the school and classroom environments; itinerant or resource teachers assist by teaching students basic orientation and mobility skills. These specialists also locate and provide any special materials and equipment needed for academic instruction; some examples are large-print books, Braille materials, raised or embossed maps, tape recorders and taped textbooks, magnification devices, and computers with "talking" word processing programs. In the social area, students with visual impairments may need encouragement to interact with sighted peers.

Students with hearing impairments may be **deaf** or **hard of hearing.** Individuals who are hard of hearing hear well enough to understand speech, usually with the assistance of a hearing aid. Students who are deaf, however, receive so little information through the ears that the sense of hearing is not useful for speech comprehension. In the general education classroom, students with hearing impairments may have special physical, academic, and social needs. Difficulty in speech and language development is one of the major educational problems associated with hearing loss. Students with hearing impairments may require classroom adaptations in order to use the skills taught by special educators. For example, sitting near the front of the classroom helps in hearing or speechreading the verbal instructions of the teacher.

Some students with hearing impairments communicate with speech; others use a manual communication system such as sign language. Interpreters may accompany some students who are deaf to the classroom, particularly at the secondary level; interpreters are hearing individuals who translate the spoken word into manual signs and vice versa. Students with hearing losses may be academically delayed in subjects related to language, such as reading, spelling, and written expression; they may receive special instruction from a resource or itinerant teacher in these areas. Speech and language problems may also inhibit the social interaction of students with hearing losses. If they communicate via speech, articulation problems may make them difficult to understand; those who use manual communication may be isolated from peers unless they, too, have acquired basic signing skills.

Attention Deficit Hyperactivity Disorder. Lerner, Lowenthal, and Lerner (1995) describe this disorder as a "condition characterized by developmentally inappropriate attention skills, impulsivity, and, in some cases, hyperactivity" (p. 4). In its recent definition of ADHD, the American Psychiatric Association (1994) differentiated three subgroups: predominantly inattentive, predominantly hyperactive-impulsive, and combined (i.e., showing inattentiveness, hyperactivity, and impulsivity). ADHD appears to be quite common; a 1991 policy memorandum of the U.S. Department of Education estimated that 3% to 5% of the school-aged population has significant educational problems related to ADHD. Students with ADHD may experience difficulty in academic achievement in addition to their behavioral problems.

Many students with ADHD are served in general education programs. Although this disorder is not included as a disability under current federal special education laws, some students may meet eligibility qualifications for other disabilities such as learning disabilities, emotional disturbance, or health impairments. In addition, the U.S. Department of Education (1991) has ruled that students with ADHD are eligible for services under Section 504 of the Rehabilitation Act of 1973. Under this law, students with ADHD may receive special education services, related services, and/or adjustments in the general education program.

Autism. Kauffman (1997) calls autism a "pervasive developmental disorder" because it affects all areas of functioning and is identified before a child reaches 3 years of age. Individuals with autism have difficulty engaging in interactions with other people; experience marked delays in language development; may use echolalic speech (i.e., instead of responding to a question, the person with autism echoes or repeats the question); and engage in behaviors such as tantrums, self-stimulatory repetitive activities, and self-mutilatory acts (Kauffman; Lovaas & Newsom, 1976).

Experts often disagree about autism. Some maintain it is a severe behavioral disorder; others suggest it is a severe disorder of language or a type of health impairment (Heward & Orlansky, 1992). Because of this controversy, autism was designated as a separate disability under the Individuals with Disabilities Education Act of 1990. Clearly, students with autism have special needs in all areas: behavioral, social, academic, and physical performance. These students are often served in special schools or classes. In recent years, some students with autism have been placed in general education classes as part of the full inclusion movement. When that occurs, special education personnel must provide comprehensive support services in the regular classroom to assist the general education teacher and increase the probability that the student with autism will benefit from the inclusion experience.

Severe Disabilities. Students with severe disabilities have the most serious and comprehensive needs of all the individuals served by special education. Such students have severe mental retardation and/or show significant developmental delays; their cognitive disabilities are often accompanied by physical, health, communication, and sensory impairments. The U.S. Department of Education describes students with severe disabilities as those

> who because of the intensity of their physical, mental, or emotional problems, or a combination of such problems, need highly specialized educational, social, psychological, and medical services beyond those which are traditionally offered by regular and special education programs, in order to maximize their potential for useful and meaningful participation in society and for self-fulfillment. (*Federal Register,* 1988, p. 118, as cited in Heward, 1996)

In the past, students with severe disabilities were served in special schools and residential programs. Today, however, these students typically attend special classes in regular schools. Like students with autism, students with severe disabilities are fully included in general education classes in some districts.

In working with special educators and others who serve students with disabilities, one of the first things that most general educators notice is terminology. Because special education is a technical field, many terms are used to describe disabilities. Abbreviations, designed as shortcuts in communication, are also used abundantly. However, statements like "Joel has a BD and an LD, and his IEP says the RR is the LRE for him" certainly do not further communication. Translations of some of the common abbreviations used in special education are listed in "For Your Information" on page 75.

Other Special Students

In addition to typical students, general education classrooms usually contain not only students with disabilities but also individuals with special gifts and talents. In many towns and cities, culturally and linguistically diverse students may also be class members. In addition, classrooms often include students at risk for school failure. Members of these three groups of students may have special learning needs.

Gifted and Talented Students. These students, who are estimated to make up 3% to 5% of the school-aged population, may be exceptionally bright (i.e.,

gifted), have special talents in areas such as art or music, or be both gifted and talented. One definition of this group is found in federal law.

> The term *gifted and talented children* means children and, whenever applicable, youth who are identified at the preschool, elementary, or secondary level as possessing demonstrated or potential abilities that give evidence of high performance capabilities in areas such as intellectual, creative, specific academic, or leadership ability, or in the performing and visual arts. . . . (Section 902, PL 95-561, Gifted and Talented Children's Act of 1978)

Gifted students are characterized by above-average performance on measures of intellectual performance; they may excel academically in all subjects or be particularly advanced in one. Some have creative ability that allows them to produce unusual or novel solutions to problems. Talented students may excel in leadership, drama, art, music, dance, or other areas.

Many states provide special educational opportunities for this diverse group of students. Some gifted individuals are allowed to enter school early and accelerate quickly through the curriculum, perhaps skipping one or several grades. Others attend special schools or classes. Most common, however, is regular class placement with part-time special services either in a resource setting or through special enrichment activities such as seminars or after-school programs.

In the general education classroom, gifted and talented students may have special academic and social needs. Those who are advanced academically benefit from special learning projects and assignments to help them continue their development. Some, however, although bright, may achieve poorly in relation to their potential; for example, they may be unmotivated, lack prerequisite skills, become bored with what they perceive as elementary-level instruction, or fail to achieve because a disability interferes with their performance. Students who are creative and talented may be academically advanced or typical of individuals their age; whatever their academic ability, they require guidance to develop their talents. Some gifted and talented students have excellent social skills; others, especially those with extraordinary abilities, may need assistance in relating to their age peers. It is also possible for special populations to overlap. A culturally diverse student with a disability

For Your Information

Making Sense of Special Education Abbreviations

Special educators are sometimes accused of speaking in jargon and "alphabet soup." Here are some of the abbreviations commonly used in discussions of students with disabilities. If you hear one that is not on this list and you fail to understand its meaning, stop the speaker and ask for an explanation. Remember that communication can occur only if the listener is able to comprehend the speaker's message.

ADA	The Americans with Disabilities Act of 1990
ADD	Attention deficit disorder
ADHD	Attention deficit hyperactivity disorder
BD	Behavioral disorder; often used synonymously with emotional disturbance (ED) or serious emotional disturbance (SED)
COHI	Crippled and other health impairment; an older term sometimes applied to physical and health disorders (Note: The term *crippled* is considered pejorative.)
DHH	Deaf and hard of hearing
ED	Emotional disturbance
EMR	Educable mental retardation; an older term that refers to mild mental retardation (MMR)
FAPE	Free and appropriate public education; refers to the basic guarantee of federal laws such PL 94-142, the Education for All Handicapped Children Act, and the Individuals with Disabilities Education Act (IDEA) and its amendments
HH	Hard of hearing
HI	Hearing impairment

IDEA	The Individuals with Disabilities Education Act of 1990
IDEA-97	The Individuals with Disabilities Education Act Amendments of 1997
IEP	Individualized Education Program
LD	Learning disability; also called specific learning disability (SLD) and language and learning disability (LLD)
LRE	Least Restrictive Environment
MMR	Mild mental retardation
MR	Mental retardation
OHI	Other health impairment; refers to health disorders
OI	Orthopedic impairment; refers to a physical impairment involving the skeletal system
PH	Physical handicap; an older term that refers to physical impairment
PL	Public Law, as in PL 94-142
POHI	Physical and other health impairment
RR	Resource room
SC	Special class, also called special day class (SDC)
SED	Serious emotional disturbance; used in federal law to refer to emotional disturbance (ED)/behavioral disorders (BD)
SH	Severely handicapped; often used to describe individuals with severe retardation and/or multiple serious disabilities
TBI	Traumatic brain injury
TMR	Trainable mental retardation; an older term that refers to moderate and severe retardation
VI	Visual impairment

may also be identified as gifted, and some gifted youngsters may be at risk for school failure.

Culturally and Linguistically Diverse Students. Culturally diverse individuals are those reared in a culture that is at variance with that found in the school or different from the dominant culture in the United States. These students face at least two sets of expectations—those of the home and those of the school—and many times these expectations are discrepant. Included within this group are linguistically diverse students; these youngsters may speak languages other than English or be bilingual, speaking English and the language of the home. Some culturally and linguistically diverse students have special learning needs; others do not.

Students who speak little or no English are likely to be members of minority cultures. They are at an extreme disadvantage in school if both their language and experiential backgrounds set them apart from their peers. Many schools offer such students bilingual education, in which they develop English language skills while learning more about their own culture and the dominant culture of the United States. Minority students include Native Americans and Alaskan natives, Asians and Pacific Islanders, African Americans, and Hispanics. African Americans and Hispanics are the two most prevalent minority groups in the United States today. Within the Hispanic group are individuals of Mexican, Cuban, Puerto Rican, or other Spanish culture or origin. Some minority students are bilingual, some may be considered culturally diverse, but many are English-speaking members of the dominant American culture.

Culturally diverse students are those whose background and experiences differ from those of their peers. Cultural differences must be defined in terms of local norms. For instance, a Christian student may be perceived as culturally different in a predominantly Jewish community; a student who speaks with a Boston accent may appear out of place among residents of the Deep South.

Students with ethnic, linguistic, and cultural backgrounds different from those of their peers add diversity and variety to the general education classroom. However, they may have special academic and social needs. Those still developing skills in understanding and speaking English may experience difficulty with academic instruction. Others may fail to meet teacher expectations because of different entry-level skills or different cultural values and motivational systems. Social acceptance may be withheld by peers unaccustomed to cultural variations.

Students at Risk for School Failure. Students can be at risk for many reasons. They may live in an impoverished family with inadequate housing, poor nutrition, and little or no medical care; with their basic needs in jeopardy, such students often have few resources left to devote to school learning. Others may be slow learners who, although they do not have disabilities, learn at a pace that falls somewhat below grade level expectations. Some students are unmotivated to achieve in school, and as a result their academic performance is less than satisfactory. Older students with a history of poor school

achievement may become truant or contemplate leaving school. According to the National Coalition of Advocates for Students (1985), one of every four students who enters the ninth grade drops out before graduating from high school.

Every classroom contains students at risk for school failure, although it is difficult to determine precisely how many general education students fit within this category. Many types of students can be considered at risk. Among these are potential school dropouts, students with suicidal behaviors, those who use or abuse alcohol or other drugs, teenage mothers, victims of child abuse or neglect, those with eating disorders, and delinquents.

At-risk students often have needs in the area of academic performance; they may fail to achieve, show little interest in instructional activities, or achieve at levels far below their potential. Some students may also show special needs in the area of behavior; they may exhibit inappropriate behavior in the classroom or begin to develop very serious problems such as drug and alcohol abuse, gang activity, and delinquency. Social acceptance may be a problem particularly for students who fail to meet the school's expectations for achievement and the peer group's expectations for behavior.

SPECIAL NEEDS

It is common practice to divide students with special needs into separate groups or categories such as students with learning disabilities, those with mental retardation, and so on. In the classroom, however, the special needs of these students are often so similar that distinctions among categories become blurred. It also becomes difficult to differentiate between students with identified disabilities and some of their peers with similar learning problems.

Academic needs are common. The acquisition, mastery, and application of school skills proves difficult for many special students and for many of their classmates. Children are expected to enter school with listening, speaking, and other readiness skills. In the primary years (grades 1, 2, and 3), the basic skills of reading, writing, and mathematics are taught; at the intermediate level (grades 4, 5, and sometimes 6), students learn to use these skills to acquire information in content areas such as science and social studies. In middle school and high

For Your Information

Special Needs

- A student may have a disability without being handicapped. A disability is some sort of impairment. It becomes a handicap only when it interferes with performance in some important area.
- Male students with special needs are more common than female students. No one knows exactly why this is so. It may be that males are more susceptible to the inheritance of learning problems and disabilities. Or it may be related to the cultural expectations for students of different genders.
- There is no relationship between physical impairments and intelligence. People with severe physical problems may be bright, and individuals with mental retardation may have no physical impairments.
- Most special students are not identified as disabled until they encounter difficulty in school. Children identified in the preschool years have serious or obvious disabilities or conditions that place them at risk for developmental delays.
- Given the right circumstances, any student could be considered culturally different. For example, a student who moves from Texas to New England will encounter new speech patterns, foods, social customs, and even sports activities.

school, the focus of the curriculum shifts to these content areas; mastery of basic skills is assumed. For many students, this assumption is unwarranted; they are not able to read, write, and calculate at the level expected in the secondary grades. Those who have acquired rudimentary basic skills may fail to acquire content area knowledge and concepts. Still others may require alternatives to the general education curriculum; their major educational need may be career education with an emphasis on vocational training.

Classroom behavior needs frequently occur among special students and their general education peers. Elementary school students are expected to obey their teacher and others in authority, adhere to the rules of classroom conduct, and get along with their peers during instruction and in less structured situations such as lunch and recess. These expectations are also true for secondary students. In addition, however, it is assumed that they have developed the study skills and work habits necessary for independent learning. Many students require assistance in meeting these expectations for classroom behavior.

Students may also have special *physical needs*. Children are expected to enter school with intact visual, hearing, and physical abilities. Those with sensory losses cannot participate in many classroom activities designed for sighted and hearing students. Many students, including those with physical and health impairments, cannot walk, run, or play games and sports as well as their regular class peers. They have special needs in the area of physical development.

Special students and others often have *social needs*. Young children are expected to know how

TABLE 3-1 Typical Needs of Special Students

Special Students	Special Needs			
	Academic	Classroom Behavior	Physical	Social
Learning disabilities	X	X	X	X
Behavioral disorders	X	X		X
Mental retardation	X	X	X	X
Speech/language impairments	X			X
Physical/health impairments	X		X	X
Visual/hearing impairments	X		X	X
ADHD	X	X		X
Autism	X	X	X	X
Severe disabilities	X	X	X	X
Gifted/talented students	X			X
Diverse students	X			X
Students at risk	X	X	X	X

to make friends with their classmates. Instruction is often presented in group situations that require students to interact with both their teacher and peers. Many school activities are at least partly social in nature; personal interactions take place during lunch, recess, assemblies, and field trips and in clubs, organizations, and sports teams. Social skills become increasingly important as individuals approach adulthood; secondary students are expected to build and maintain friendships and begin establishing interpersonal relationships as preparation for courtship and marriage. Because they may appear to be different in some ways, special students may have difficulty gaining acceptance from their regular class peers. Students with poor social skills (whether they are identified as special or not) need instruction and training in this area.

Most students require assistance in one or more of these areas at some time during their school careers. Special students are no exception. However, with special students it is possible to predict some of the areas in which they are likely to encounter difficulty. As shown in Table 3–1, it is probable that all will have special academic and social needs. Some may also have needs in the areas of classroom behavior and physical development. This diagram depicts only the typical needs of groups of students; it is certainly possible for students with speech and language impairments to display problem behaviors or for students with physical impairments to require no special academic assistance.

There are many similarities among special students and between special students and their regular class peers. This is particularly true in relation to students with mild disabilities: learning disabilities, behavioral disorders, and mild retardation. These students make up perhaps 5% to 7% of the school population. They are physically indistinguishable from their regular class peers and are usually not identified as special until they experience failure in school. They begin school in general education classes and receive the majority of their education in mainstreamed situations. According to Hallahan and Kauffman (1976), students with mild disabilities cannot be differentiated by the causes of their learning problems, the methods found effective in their instruction, or their behavioral characteristics. All have academic, behavioral, and social needs that may require adaptations in general education classrooms.

When adaptations are made for special students, general education teachers often wonder how to explain these changes to the rest of the class. Students may wonder why others are receiving special treatment. Ideas for handling this situation are listed in "Inclusion Tips for the Teacher."

Inclusion Tips for the Teacher

Explaining Classroom Modifications to Peers

It is sometimes necessary to make changes in classroom activities so that students with special needs can succeed. For example, students with academic needs may be given special assignments or may be required to complete only part of the work assigned to the rest of the class. Those with behavioral needs may earn special rewards for good behavior. The rest of the class may become curious about why these students rate special treatment from the teacher.

Teachers can prevent problems from occurring by following these suggestions:

- Don't call undue attention to students with special needs. Treat them as you would any other student in your class.
- When special assignments are necessary, give them privately. Then, when the class is working on individual assignments, the student with special needs will not be conspicuous.
- Group students with similar learning needs together. If a student with a disability requires extra instruction in reading, set up a small group that includes peers with similar needs. If students with special needs have difficulty following class rules, consider beginning a behavior program for the entire class.
- When class members have questions, answer them promptly and honestly. Acknowledge that you are individualizing assignments and activities so that everyone in the class can learn successfully. A matter-of-fact response will usually satisfy curiosity and allay any feelings of resentment.

CAUSES OF LEARNING PROBLEMS

For most special students, the cause, or **etiology,** of their learning problem is unknown. Although a host of causative agents has been identified, it is often impossible to state with certainty which was responsible for the disability of a particular student.

Causes can be classified according to when they occurred in the life of the individual: prenatal (before birth), perinatal (during the birth process), or postnatal (after birth). An example of a prenatal cause is rubella or German measles. If contracted by a woman during the first three months of her pregnancy, rubella can lead to hearing, visual, physical, and cognitive impairments in the fetus as it develops. Oxygen deprivation during the birth process is a perinatal cause, whereas a head injury sustained in an auto accident at 3 years of age is a postnatal cause.

Another view of etiology is the dichotomy of hereditary and environmental factors. Some types of deafness are inherited, and there is some indication that reading problems tend to run in families. Environmental causes of learning problems include poor nutrition, lack of sensory stimulation, and inadequate instruction.

The causes of learning problems are of interest for two reasons: treatment and prevention. Medical research has developed treatments for some known etiologies and preventive techniques for others. For example, the Salk vaccine has virtually eliminated the crippling disease of polio in the United States, and progress is being made in use of gene therapy for conditions such as muscular dystrophy. In education, the emphasis is on environmental causes of learning problems. Research indicates that providing appropriate early educational experiences for children with special needs may lessen or prevent later learning problems (Casto & Mastropieri, 1986; White, Bush, & Casto, 1986). Education itself is one of the environmental influences on students, one that can precipitate learning problems. Poor or inappropriate instruction has been cited as a major factor in the development of school problems. Reynolds and Birch (1982) contend that "most pupil behaviors called learning disabilities and behavior disorders are best acknowledged as the consequences of failure to provide enough high quality individualized instruction" (p. 237).

ASSESSMENT OF SPECIAL LEARNING NEEDS

Assessment is the process of gathering information about students to make important educational decisions (McLoughlin & Lewis, 1994). In special education and other supplementary school services, it is necessary to determine whether students meet certain legal requirements before services can begin. In special education, for example, students are considered eligible for services only if they are disabled and if their disability has a negative effect on school performance. That is, students must experience difficulty in school, and that difficulty must be attributable to a disability.

Classroom Assessment

General educators play many roles in the assessment process. As discussed in chapter 2, it is typically the classroom teacher who refers students for special education and other types of assessment. In addition, teachers collect all sorts of information about their students. Some of the assessment strategies that classroom teachers use most often are

- observation of students as they engage in academic activities and social interactions;
- analysis of students' errors and correct responses on work samples such as homework assignments, tests, essays, and math papers;
- administration of quizzes and exams to assess student progress toward instructional goals; and
- interviews with students to learn more about their attitudes, viewpoints, and the strategies they use to interact with classroom tasks.

These techniques are **informal assessment** strategies. Unlike the formal, norm-referenced tests often used in special education, their purpose is not to compare one student's performance to that of others of the same age or grade. Instead, they are considered **curriculum-based assessments** because they focus on students' mastery of the instructional goals addressed in the general education classroom.

Informal curriculum-based techniques fit well with the current move toward alternative assessment in general education. This approach is also known as authentic assessment, outcome-based assessment, and performance assessment (Worthen,

1993). Its proponents call for less reliance on traditional achievement tests, particularly those made up of multiple-choice questions, and more emphasis on authentic tasks that require students to demonstrate problem-solving abilities rather than rote memory skills.

At present, **portfolio assessment** is the most popular tool for alternative assessment (McLoughlin & Lewis, 1994). Portfolios are simply collections of student work gathered over time; however, students are responsible for selecting their best work for inclusion in the portfolio and for evaluating their own progress (Grady, 1992). Teachers evaluate the contents of a portfolio with the same informal techniques used to analyze other types of student work samples.

One major reason for the collection of data is to evaluate the effectiveness of instruction. When done systematically, this is called **clinical teaching** (McLoughlin & Lewis, 1994). First, the teacher gathers data about student performance on the task in question. Then, an intervention is introduced and data collection continues. Any of the informal assessment strategies described earlier can be used in clinical teaching: observation, analysis of student work samples, quizzes, and so on. The intervention is considered successful if results indicate that student performance has improved.

Curriculum-based measurement (CBM) is an informal assessment strategy used in special education to monitor student progress (Deno, 1985, 1987; Shinn & Hubbard, 1993). It is easy to use and sensitive to small changes in students' skill levels, which makes it a useful measurement technique for clinical teaching. In CBM, the teacher collects very brief samples of important student behaviors. For example, to assess oral reading skills, students read aloud for 1 minute while the teacher (or an assistant) records the number of words read correctly. This "probe" is administered frequently (e.g., two or three times each week), and results are graphed to provide a visual record of the student's progress. In clinical teaching, this graph is inspected to determine whether desired changes occurred when the new intervention was introduced.

Assessment for Program Eligibility

When students are referred for special education assessment, a multidisciplinary team is formed to plan the process of gathering information about the need for extraordinary services. **Norm-**

> ### FIGURE 3-2   Measures Used in Special Education
>
> **Measures of Intellectual Performance**
>
> *Wechsler Intelligence Scale for Children-Third Edition*—Contains 13 tests that assess verbal and nonverbal reasoning in students ages 6 to 16; results include global IQ scores (Verbal, Performance, and Full Scale IQ) as well as scores for four cognitive factors: Verbal Comprehension, Perceptual Organization, Freedom from Distractibility, and Processing Speed. Called the WISC-III, this is the most commonly used measure of intellectual performance in schools.
>
> *Woodcock-Johnson Psycho-Educational Battery-Revised, Tests of Cognitive Ability*—Estimates overall intellectual performance and provides measures of seven cognitive factors: Long-Term Retrieval, Short-Term Memory, Processing Speed, Auditory Processing, Visual Processing, Comprehension-Knowledge, and Fluid Processing; designed for ages 2 to 90+.
>
> *Stanford-Binet Intelligence Scale: Fourth Edition*—Assesses four areas of intellectual performance in persons from age 2 to adulthood: Verbal Reasoning, Abstract/Visual Reasoning, Quantitative Reasoning, and Short-Term Memory. This test is the current version of the original IQ test devised in the early 1900s by Binet and Simon.
>
> **Measures of Overall Academic Achievement**
>
> *Peabody Individual Achievement Test-Revised*—Includes tests of General Information, Reading Recognition, Reading Comprehension, Mathematics, Spelling, and Written Expression for students in grades K through 12.
>
> *Wechsler Individual Achievement Test*—A newer measure with 8 subtests that assess reading, mathematics, and written language as well as listening and speaking skills; designed for grades K through 12.
>
> *Woodcock-Johnson Psycho-Educational Battery-Revised, Tests of Achievement*—Contains 14 tests to assess Reading, Mathematics, Written Language, and Knowledge (science, social studies, and humanities) for ages 2 to adulthood.
>
> *Wide Range Achievement Test 3*—More limited in scope, the WRAT3 assesses spelling, arithmetic, and reading recognition skills in students ages 5 through adulthood.
>
> **Measures of Specific Academic Skills**
>
> *Woodcock Reading Mastery Tests-Revised*—Used to identify strengths and weaknesses in Word Identification, Word Attack, Word Comprehension, Passage Comprehension, and reading readiness skills in K–12 and college students.
>
> *KeyMath Revised*—Offers 13 subtests to assess mathematics skills in Basic Concepts, Operations, and Applications; normed for grades K through 9.
>
> *Test of Written Spelling-3*—A dictation spelling test of Predictable and Unpredictable Words for ages 6 to 19.
>
> *Test of Written Language-3*—Identifies strengths and weaknesses in areas of written language such as vocabulary, spelling, and mechanics (e.g., capitalization and punctuation) in students ages 7 to 18; one part of the TOWL-3 requires students to write a story describing a picture.

referenced tests are typically used for this type of assessment. These tests provide information about a student's status in relation to other students of the same age or grade; this type of comparison is needed to determine whether a student's problem is severe enough to warrant special educational intervention.

The tests are administered by trained specialists to one student at a time. Group administration procedures are not used because they can depress the performance of students with special learning needs. Group tests require students to read, write, and attend to test tasks for a relatively long period of time. On individually administered tests, a student's knowledge of science can be separated from his or her reading skills because the tester reads the questions to the student; also, if the student's attention wavers, the professional can help the student refocus on the task at hand.

No matter what disability is suspected, the team will collect information on three major areas of functioning:

1. *Intellectual performance.* Tests of intellectual performance, sometimes called intelligence or IQ (intelligence quotient) tests, are used to assess the student's skills in reasoning and problem-solving tasks. These measures do not determine innate potential; instead, they assess a student's aptitude for academic tasks (McLoughlin & Lewis, 1994).
2. *Academic achievement.* At the beginning of assessment, tests that include several academic subjects (e.g., reading, spelling, composition, mathematics, content area knowledge) are administered to identify broad areas of need. Then, more specific measures (e.g., a test of reading skills) are used to pinpoint areas of difficulty.
3. *Area of disability.* In special education assessment, it is necessary to establish the existence of a disability. For instance, in mental retardation, the team will study intellectual performance and adaptive behavior. In learning disabilities, the focus is information processing, and in behavioral disorders, severe and long-standing conduct disorders. Federal laws provide regulations for determining eligibility, and states and school districts supplement these with additional guidelines.

Figure 3–2 (page 81) lists and describes some of the individually administered norm-referenced tests used most often in special education assessment. Included are measures of intellectual performance as well as academic achievement tests.

Although classroom teachers do not administer tests such as these, test results are often discussed in the deliberations of the team. To help teachers become better acquainted with the tests and other data collection procedures used in special education, common assessment tools and techniques are discussed throughout this book. However, this book places most emphasis on the types of assessment tools that teachers find useful in the classroom. These are typically informal assessments—measures and strategies devised by teachers to answer specific questions about the academic, social, physical, and behavioral needs of their students. The measures also tend to be curriculum-based rather than norm-referenced; that is, their purpose is to compare a student's performance to the demands of the local curriculum and the expectations in a particular classroom.

SKILLS FOR THE GENERAL EDUCATION TEACHER

General education teachers play an important role in the prevention and treatment of school learning problems. With appropriate instruction, students with disabilities and others with special learning needs can experience success in the general education classroom. The next chapters of this book focus on the major skills needed by teachers to adapt instruction, manage behavior, promote social acceptance, and coordinate the learning environment of the classroom. These skills are simply good teaching procedures; they can be used with any student, special or not. Good teaching skills focus on the needs of the student (rather than any particular disability), and they are based on the following four assumptions about special students and the teaching-learning process.

All students can learn. Despite any special needs they may have, all individuals are able to acquire new skills and absorb new information and attitudes. Students learn at different rates, and the same person may learn some things more quickly than other things. Although much is known about different types of special students and their disabilities, it is impossible to accurately predict the specific areas in which they will experience difficulty. However, we do know that they *can* and, with proper instruction, *will* learn.

Learning is determined by changes in behavior. Learning is a process of change. Students acquire new skills, become more proficient in previously learned skills, and learn to perform in certain ways. Teachers evaluate students' progress by their behavior; that is, they observe students' overt responses and infer that learning has occurred. Students demonstrate that they have learned academic, classroom conduct, and social skills in many ways; they may display new behaviors, a greater number of appropriate behaviors, or fewer inappropriate behaviors. Teachers monitor the learning process by noting what students say in class discussions, what they write on assignments and exams, and how they act in the many situations of the school day.

Teaching involves manipulation of the environment. If learning is the change of student behaviors, then teaching is the arrangement of the learning environment to maximize the chance that desired behaviors will occur. In instruction, teachers have control over two important factors: the **antecedents** and **consequences** of student behaviors.

Things To Remember

- Both special students and their regular class peers may have special learning needs. Special needs occur in the areas of academic, classroom behavioral, physical, and social performance.
- Special students, as a group, typically experience difficulty in academic and social areas; some students also have special behavioral and physical needs.
- Information about special needs is more useful to the teacher than knowledge of the student's categorical label.

- Causes of learning problems are important if they help in treatment or prevention.
- Teachers use informal assessment tools to gather information for instructional decisions.
- Appropriate instruction can prevent some learning problems and help to overcome others.
- Teachers manipulate the learning environment to produce changes in the behavior of students.
- Data-based instruction is efficient and effective in teaching special students the behaviors needed to succeed in the general education classroom.

An antecedent is anything that precedes or comes before a behavior; typical teaching activities such as lectures, small-group discussions, text readings, and written assignments are all instructional antecedents that can be manipulated to enhance learning. Consequences, or events that follow behaviors, include grades, teacher praise or scolding, and rewards (remember gold stars?) and punishments; these, too, are powerful tools that can be used to facilitate learning. Just as students learn at different rates, they also respond differently to instructional antecedents and consequences. Although there is no one sure-fire teaching method, material, or reward system, empirical evidence suggests that some instructional procedures are more effective than others. For example, direct instruction methods that focus on skill development have been found useful for teaching basic academic skills (Stevens & Rosenshine, 1981).

Data collection increases teaching efficiency. Because there are almost unlimited options to choose from in setting up an instructional system of antecedents and consequences, it is important to approach the task systematically. After the desired student behavior is stated as precisely as possible, the most simple and straightforward strategy for teaching that behavior is tried. The teacher collects information about the behavior before instruction and also during the instructional intervention. If the behavior changes in the desired way, the intervention is considered successful; if it does not, the

teacher proceeds to a more complex or intensive instructional strategy. In this way, instructional decisions are made on the basis of data rather than on guesses or hunches; teaching becomes more efficient, with the end result that students learn more. This data-based approach to instruction is particularly beneficial for special students and others who encounter difficulty in learning.

Turn to the next chapter to see how these assumptions about the teaching-learning process can be applied to the adaptation of instruction for special students and others in the general education classroom.

ACTIVITIES

1. Disabilities are not the same as handicaps. However, some disabilities interfere with the performance of tasks required by certain professions. For example, consider blindness for a painter or deafness for a musician. Are there any disabilities that would interfere in the profession of teaching? If so, what are they? What disabilities would a teacher be able to overcome? Be prepared to discuss your answers to these questions.
2. Interview two or more general educators about the students they teach. How many students with disabilities are included in their classrooms? What types of special needs do these

students have? Are there others in the classroom with similar needs? What kinds of classroom modifications have the teachers made to accommodate the special needs of these students?

3. Many special education journals concentrate on one disability. For instance, the Council for Exceptional Children publishes *Behavioral Disorders, Education and Training in Mental Retardation and Developmental Disabilities,* and *Learning Disabilities Research and Practice.* Select one or two of these journals, and look at several recent issues. Did you find any articles on the inclusion of students with special needs in general education?

4. Search the World Wide Web for information about one of the disabilities discussed in this chapter. What kinds of sites did you locate? Are they sponsored by professional organizations? parent groups? districts or schools? individuals?

5. A person's culture affects many perceptions. Talk with someone from a culture different from yours, and compare your experiences. You might discuss foods, dress, manners, or traditional celebrations or holidays. Also, compare the ways in which different cultures view the birth of a child with a disability. Are persons with disabilities treated differently by different cultures?

PART II

Skills for the General Education Teacher

Adapting Instruction

Eleanor, a fourth grader, reads at the beginning third grade level.

Patrick can solve math computation problems with ease, but he has trouble with word problems.

Erin's handwriting is barely legible, and the assignments she turns in are wrinkled, messy, and full of crossed-out words.

Although Patty seems to understand the information presented in chemistry class, she has failed every quiz this semester.

Ian's essays contain excellent ideas, but his spelling, grammar, and punctuation are atrocious.

Billy is habitually late to class, and he often forgets to do his homework.

Dan's vocational skills are good, but he'll have difficulty completing job applications.

Students such as these have special needs in the area of academic performance. For them to succeed in the general education classroom, it may be necessary to adapt instructional procedures. In order to do this, teachers should be familiar with the typical **academic problems** of students with special needs and their peers, methods for gathering data about academic performance, and strategies for adapting **instruction** to meet the needs of all students.

ACADEMIC PROBLEMS IN THE CLASSROOM

Students can experience difficulty with academic instruction at any age and in any subject. Such students come to the attention of their teacher when their classroom performance does not meet teacher expectations. Elementary teachers often describe students with academic problems as "achieving below grade level" in one or more subjects. Secondary teachers, on the other hand, take note of students who receive poor or failing grades in specific courses, such as English 9, biology, American history, or woodshop.

School learning involves the acquisition of both information and skills. Students are expected to absorb vast amounts of information in academic subjects and to develop and sharpen their thinking and learning skills. Problems can occur in any one of the three stages of learning: acquisition, maintenance, and generalization. **Acquisition** is initial learning, **maintenance** is the recall of previously learned material, and **generalization** is the application or transfer of learned material to similar situations and problems. Students may require more time to learn new information and skills, have difficulty sustaining performance over time, or fail to apply old learning to new situations.

Teachers evaluate student responses to determine whether learning is occurring as expected. Students respond in the classroom in a number of ways: oral answers to teacher questions, participation in class discussions, in-class assignments and homework, and quizzes and examinations. Academic problems are suspected if one (or more) of the following response patterns is evident:

- *High number of incorrect responses.* The majority of the student's responses are incorrect, or the student's accuracy rate falls below the criterion set by the teacher. For example, George solves only 6 out of 10 subtraction problems correctly; the teacher's criterion is 90% accuracy.
- *Low number of responses.* The student fails to respond to a significant number of questions, problems, or activities. For example, Jack answers only 7 of the 15 questions at the end of the chapter.
- *Inconsistent responses.* The student's responses to the same question, problem, or activity vary in correctness from time to time. For example, Thelma writes all 20 spelling words correctly on the Wednesday practice quiz but scores only 40% on the test on Friday.

Of course, if many students show response patterns such as these, the first step would be to evaluate classroom instructional procedures.

Inappropriate response patterns can be seen in any school subject. One typical trouble spot is **basic skills;** listening, speaking, reading, writing, and mathematics often are difficult for students to acquire, maintain, and generalize. The written language skills of reading and writing are built on the oral language skills of listening and speaking. Students may have trouble with the reception of information (listening and reading), the expression of information (speaking and writing), or all aspects of the communication process. The development of

Window on the Web

AskERIC

http://www.askeric.org

AskERIC is an online education information service. It is part of the federally funded ERIC (Educational Resources Information Center) system. Among the features of this website are the Virtual Library and the Question and Answer Service, where users can ask questions and receive online responses from AskERIC Information Specialists within 48 hours.

As the menu in the lower graphic shows, the Virtual Library contains a number of resources, including AskERIC InfoGuides on a variety of topics, lesson plans in major cirriculum areas, and instructional materials to accompany television series such as those shown on A & E, CNN, C-Span, the Discovery Channel, and PBS.

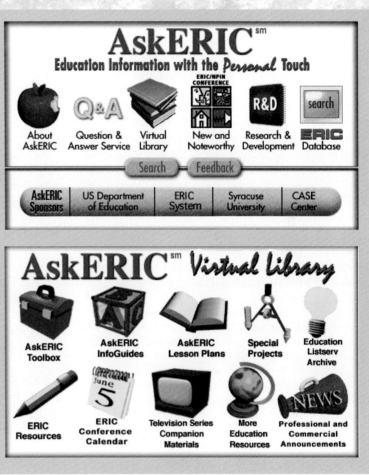

basic skills is a high-priority instructional goal in the elementary grades. Special students may experience difficulty with the rote aspects of these skills (e.g., word recognition, handwriting, spelling, mathematics facts and computation) or with the more conceptual aspects (e.g., reading comprehension, written expression, mathematical problem solving).

At the secondary level, instruction centers on **content area subjects** rather than basic skills. The academic curriculum is organized according to bodies of knowledge: English (including both composition and literature) and other languages; science (biology, chemistry, physics); higher math (algebra, geometry, trigonometry); the social sciences (history, social studies, geography); and other areas such as art, music, and physical education. However, academic problems in basic skills may persist; students

may not have acquired (or maintained) adequate reading, writing, and mathematics skills, or they may be unable to apply these skills to the acquisition of new information. Students may also have difficulty learning the skills, information, concepts, and principles of particular content areas. Poor organizational and study skills may also interfere with student performance.

Preparation for the transition from adolescence to adulthood is another aspect of school learning in which academic problems can arise. Hasazi, Furney, and Hull (1995) define **transition** as a "series of purposeful activities designed to ensure that students have the skills, opportunities, and supports needed to locate and maintain employment, to pursue postsecondary education and training, to participate in the social fabric of the community, and to make decisions about their lives" (p. 420). Transition planning is required by federal law for students with disabilities; it is also an important concern for many other students with special needs. One aspect of transition planning is specific vocational training experience at the secondary level. Another is the application of basic skills and content area information to the solution of daily life problems, such as reading menus, making change, and selecting appropriate items to purchase. Students may have difficulty in the acquisition of specific vocational skills, such as typing, mechanical drawing, or welding. They may also have difficulty in the generalization of basic work habits, such as punctuality and task completion, and the application of school learning to job and community situations.

Because academic instruction is one of the major goals of U.S. education, academic problems are a concern to classroom teachers at all levels. However, as Montgomery (1978) points out, not all variations in student performance are learning problems.

> Johnny reads with his book turned sideways, or kneels instead of sitting on his chair, or wears his jacket in class. Do we "fix" him or let him be? Before we can answer that question realistically we must ask, "Is it a problem for Johnny—or for us?" Does it hamper Johnny's learning, or do we see it as a problem because of our own preoccupation with things being normal, with Johnny acting like everyone else? (p. 112)

PRINCIPLES OF INSTRUCTION

Students with special needs have the necessary skills to participate in many classroom activities. They may take part in all instructional aspects of the general education program, or they may be included only for selected subjects. The decision is made on the basis of three factors: the student's skills in the subject area, the amount of instructional support required to ensure the student's active participation, and the usefulness or functionality of the academic subject for the student. When students are included only for those subjects that are useful to them and in which successful performance is probable, the general education curriculum is appropriate; that is, *what* is taught need not be modified by the classroom teacher. However, it is often necessary to alter instructional procedures, that is, *how* skills and information are taught to special students.

Much is known today about what teachers can do to have positive effects on student performance. This knowledge comes from a large body of research on teaching behaviors, sometimes known as the teacher effectiveness literature (Brophy & Good, 1986; Medley, 1982; Rieth & Evertson, 1988; Rosenshine & Stevens, 1986; Weil & Murphy, 1982). The major factors found to have a positive influence on student achievement are listed here (Weil & Murphy, 1982):

- Teachers maintain an *academic focus* in selecting classroom activities and directing classroom work.
- Teachers maintain *direction and control* in the management of the classroom learning environment.
- Teachers hold *high expectations* for the academic progress of their students.
- *Students are accountable* for the satisfactory completion of classroom work.
- Students work together, showing *cooperation* rather than competition.
- The affective climate of the classroom learning environment is *not negative.*

Among the most critical concerns in fostering student achievement are the quantity and pace of instruction (Brophy & Good, 1986). Both concerns are related to an opportunity to learn. Learning increases when more time is devoted to academic pursuits and when students are actually engaged in learning during that time. Learning also increases when students move through the curriculum at a brisk pace, provided that students maintain a high rate of successful performance.

Both quantity and pace of instruction can be enhanced by active teaching. According to Brophy and Good (1986), in active teaching "the teacher carries the content to the students personally rather than depending on the curriculum materials to do so" (p. 361). The teacher directs the learning experience, and students "spend most of their time being taught or supervised by their teachers rather than working on their own (or not working at all)" (p. 361). Active teaching has also been called **direct teaching** (or *direct instruction*). In direct teaching, the teacher demonstrates appropriate strategies for the performance of the learning task, allows maximum opportunity for students to respond, and provides systematic and frequent feedback on their task performance (Archer,

⬥ **F I G U R E   4 - 1   Instruction**

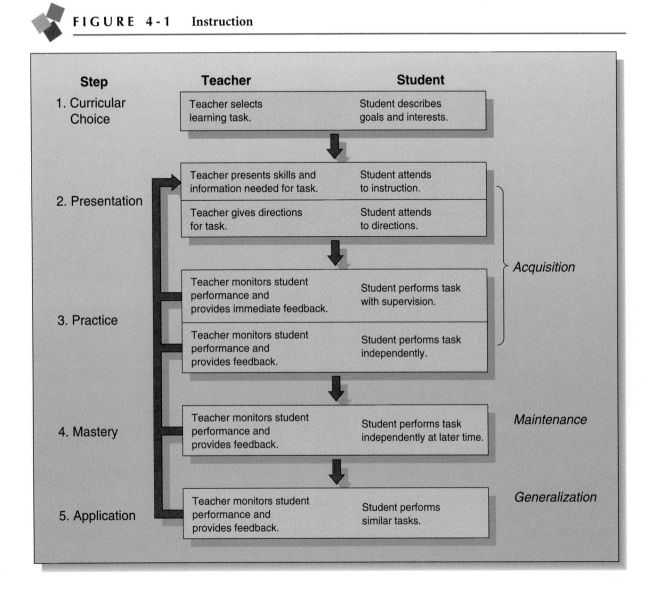

Gleason, Englert, & Isaacson, 1995; Archer, Gleason, & Isaacson, 1995; Lewis, 1983).

Lloyd and Carnine (1981) call this *structured instruction,* or the "carefully organized manipulation of environmental events designed to bring about prespecified changes in learners' performance in skill areas of functional importance" (p. viii). It is **individualized instruction,** designed to meet the needs of each student. This does not mean that instruction must be individual, delivered by one teacher to one student. Stevens and Rosenshinc (1981) view instruction as individualized when a high proportion of student responses is correct. Good instruction can

occur in large groups, small groups, or one-to-one; the criterion is student success.

As shown in Figure 4–1, instruction takes place in a series of steps involving both teacher and student(s) and progressing from the active direction of the teacher (teaching) to the active involvement of the student(s) (learning). There are five steps: curricular choice, presentation, practice, mastery, and application.

1. *Selection of the learning task.* To make this curricular decision, the teacher considers the scope and sequence of the general education curriculum,

the skills and information already acquired by the student, and the student's current interests and learning needs. The learning task represents the goal of instruction, and successful performance of this task is the desired student behavior.

2. *Presentation to the student of the material necessary for task performance.* The teacher uses procedures such as lectures, in-class activities, and reading assignments to provide the student with the skills and information required for the task. The teacher may model or demonstrate the skill or explain new information by presenting rules, principles, and examples. Then the teacher gives directions for the performance of the task. The student's role at this stage is to give adequate attention to instruction and feedback to the teacher if instruction is unclear.

3. *Practice of the learning task.* The student first performs the task under the close supervision of the teacher (guided practice); gradually the teacher's guidance is withdrawn, and the student performs independently (independent practice). The teacher's role is to monitor student performance and provide feedback to the student regarding the adequacy of task performance. In guided practice, feedback is immediate, whereas in independent practice, it is delayed. If a high proportion of student responses is incorrect, the teacher returns to the presentation step. Presentation and practice lead to acquisition of skills and information.

4. *Mastery of the learning task.* At some later time, the student performs the task independently, and the teacher monitors student responses. If performance is not adequate, it may be necessary to return to the practice steps or even to the presentation steps. Mastery is determined by maintenance of previously acquired learning.

5. *Application of previous learning.* The student performs tasks similar to the original learning task. If the teacher notes poor performance at this step, it may be necessary to reteach the original task through presentation and practice or to devise a new instructional sequence in which generalization of skills or information is taught directly. Application generalizes previous learning.

The teacher directs instruction by selecting the desired student behavior, arranging instructional antecedents, and providing consequences such as feedback regarding performance accuracy. Even though the teacher is the instructional manager, student factors that influence learning must also be considered. Several of these are described in Table 4–1. In addition, the principles of teaching discussed in the following sections should guide the instructional process.

Before proceeding, it is important to differentiate between direct instruction and an alternative approach, **discovery learning.** In discovery learning, information and skills are not taught directly. Instead, the teacher arranges the learning environment and students explore that environment as they attempt to discover the facts, concepts, principles, and skills that make up the school curriculum. Discovery approaches are considered *constructivist* because students are expected to construct their own knowledge by building upon the prior knowledge they bring to the learning task (Cegelka, 1995a). For example, many proponents of the whole language approach to reading and writing instruction recommend discovery learning (Gersten & Dimino, 1993; Keefe & Keefe, 1993; Mather, 1992). Students are expected to become proficient readers and writers by "exposure to and participation in many experiences involving written language" (Richeck in Lerner, Cousin, & Richeck, 1992, p. 227), not through direct teaching.

Unfortunately, some students do not succeed in programs in which discovery learning is the norm (Gersten & Dimino, 1993). Students with mild disabilities and others at risk for academic learning problems are more likely to succeed when instruction is presented using the principles of direct teaching (King-Sears, 1997; Vergason & Anderegg, 1991). As Morsink and Lenk (1992) point out, effective instruction of students with special needs can take place in any setting, general education or special, if teachers "(a) engage in teacher-directed instruction, (b) provide students with opportunities for active academic responding, (c) use high rates of contingent reinforcement, and (d) adapt teaching strategies to accommodate individual differences" (p. 36).

Select Appropriate Learning Tasks

Selection of the learning task is a critical instructional decision. No matter how excellent the teaching procedures, instruction will not be effective if the task selected is inappropriate for the learner. Task selection is even more critical for students with special needs because they may learn new informa-

TABLE 4-1   **Facilitating Learning**

Factor	Principle
Meaningfulness	A student is more likely to be motivated to learn things that are meaningful to him or her.
Prerequisites	A student is more likely to learn something new if he or she has all the prerequisites.
Modeling	A student is more likely to acquire a new behavior if he or she is presented with a model performance to watch and imitate.
Open communication	A student is more likely to learn if the medium used in the learning situation is structured so that the teacher's messages are open to the learner's inspection.
Novelty	A student is more likely to learn if his or her attention is attracted by relatively novel presentations.
Active appropriate practice	A student is more likely to learn if he or she takes an active part in practice geared to reach an instructional objective.
Distributing practice	A student is more likely to learn if practice is done in short periods over time.
Fading	A student is more likely to learn if instructional prompts are withdrawn gradually.
Pleasant conditions and consequences	A student is more likely to learn if the instructional conditions are pleasant.

Note. From "General Principles of Learning and Motivation" by N. A. Carlson, 1980, *Teaching Exceptional Children, 12,* pp. 60–62. Copyright 1980 by The Council for Exceptional Children. Adapted by permission.

tion and skills more slowly than their peers. The teacher should select the most important portions of the general education curriculum as target behaviors. In making these decisions, priority should be given to skills and information that are useful both now and in the future. Special educators often use the term *functional* to refer to such learning tasks, whereas general educators talk about *authentic* tasks.

In addition, tasks should be described as precisely as possible. Some, such as Mager (1984), advocate the use of instructional objectives, which are statements of the desired student behavior in specific, observable terms. They spell out the conditions under which the behavior should occur and the criterion for successful performance of the behavior. Objectives help clarify the goals of instruction. Unlike broad goals such as "Students will become better readers," instructional objectives are stated with precision: "When presented with a 100-word passage from a book or story written at the grade 3 level, students will read the passage aloud with no more than 5 word recognition errors."

After the desired student behavior is identified, the teacher chooses instructional activities to pre-

sent the skills and information required for task performance. Most teachers use commercial programs and supplement them with teacher-made materials and activities. The teacher must be sure that ready-made programs present all necessary skills and information and do not include extraneous or irrelevant material. The teacher must also consider current performance level when placing a student in a program sequence. For example, grade 9 texts may not be appropriate for ninth graders who read at the seventh grade level. Students should be placed in educational programs at a level at which they can succeed, that is, their instructional level.

Break the Learning Task into Teachable Subcomponents

Tasks often require several skills or many different kinds of information for successful performance. Sometimes, particularly with commercial education programs, **task analysis**—the breaking down of tasks into smaller subtasks—is necessary. When the components of the task are identified, they can be presented to students in a systematic fashion. First,

Inclusion Tips for the Teacher

Writing Instructional Objectives

An objective, according to *Webster's New Collegiate Dictionary,* is "something toward which effort is directed; an aim, goal, or end of action." In education, objectives clearly state the aim of instruction. Their purpose is to direct the teacher in the selection of instructional activities.

Writing clear and useful instructional objectives is not an easy task. One common mistake is confusing objectives with goals. Goal statements are less specific than objectives; they generally describe only the behavior of interest and the direction in which the behavior should change.

Goal: By the end of the school year, Jaime will increase his sight word vocabulary.

Goal: Next semester Susie will be absent from school fewer days.

Instructional objectives, in contrast, are much more detailed. They include specific information about the exact behavior in question, the conditions under which the behavior should occur, and the criterion for successful performance of the behavior (Mager, 1984).

Objective: When given a simple job application form,
(conditions)
Jack will write his complete name and address
(behavior)

in legible handwriting with no errors in spelling.
(mastery criterion)

One of the most important (and most difficult) steps in writing objectives is stating student behaviors in observable and measurable terms. The statement "Louise will write her name" is observable, but "Henry will know the meaning of all new vocabulary words" is not. Look at the lists of words below. The "observables" are action verbs; you can easily see whether someone is writing or walking. The "nonobservables" cannot be seen; it is not possible to see whether someone is understanding, knowing, or appreciating.

Observables	Nonobservables
Write a letter	Understand subtraction
Point to the answer	Know state geography
Say the alphabet	Appreciate sculpture
Read aloud from the text	Realize the importance of budgeting
Raise a hand to volunteer	Differentiate hand tools
Look at the teacher	Attend to class lectures
Name the U.S. presidents	Perceive the main idea
Draw a triangle	Draw conclusions

the prerequisites for learning the task should be considered. For example, students who have not learned to solve multiplication problems will encounter difficulty in calculating the area of a room. If necessary prerequisite skills are not present, instruction should begin with them. Next, the learning task is divided into subtasks. The subtasks may be a series of sequential steps or a collection of important subskills. An example of a task that can be broken into steps is addition of three-digit numbers; first the numbers in the ones column are added, then the numbers in the tens column, and finally the numbers in the hundreds column. Other tasks made up of a sequence of subtasks are building a model and locating a reference in the library.

Writing a friendly letter is a task that can be divided into component subskills: handwriting (or keyboarding), spelling, capitalization, punctuation, and paragraph writing. Other such tasks are telling time, making change, and reading with comprehension.

The identification of subtasks and subskills allows the teacher to make decisions about the order in which skills and information will be presented. With tasks that are sequential in nature, subtasks are generally taught in the order in which they occur. With tasks made up of several components, the easier subskills are presented first. For example, in cursive writing instruction, simpler letters, such as lowercase *a* and *o,* are taught before more difficult letters, such as uppercase *F* and *G.*

Use Systematic Instructional Procedures

Effective instruction follows the demonstration-prompt-practice model. After the teacher presents a demonstration or explanation of the skills and information necessary for performance of the learning task, students attempt to perform the task with prompts or assistance from the teacher. Students then **practice** the task independently. In other words, presentation is followed by guided practice, then independent practice.

In **demonstration,** the teacher may model the performance of new skills. If factual information is being presented, the teacher may simply tell students the new material. For example, in mathematics instruction, teachers can model appropriate performance by stating a fact or a rule, performing a task as students watch and listen, or asking one student a question while others observe (Lloyd & Keller, 1989). When information is conceptual, principles and examples are used to aid in explanation (Kameenui & Simmons, 1990). In one method (Close, Irvin, Taylor, & Agosta, 1981), the teacher presents new concepts directly, then cites relevant examples; guided practice is provided when students answer direct questions, and then the teacher repeats and summarizes the original presentation.

In the prompt or **guided practice** stage, students are given opportunities to perform the task under the supervision of the teacher. This should occur before independent practice to ensure that students do not practice incorrect responses. In guided practice, the teacher gives immediate feedback to students regarding the accuracy of their responses; correct responses are confirmed, and incorrect responses are corrected. This step can be done individually, with small groups, or with the entire class. For example, the teacher can present new material to the class and then conduct a short question-and-answer session with all students. Stevens and Rosenshine (1981) recommend this technique and advocate the use of factual questions and whole-group unison responses.

In **independent practice,** the teacher continues to provide students with feedback or knowledge of results. Because this form of practice usually takes place in individual work sessions in class or as homework assignments, the time delay between student performance and feedback from the teacher is greater.

Direct teaching is another important feature of effective instruction. Skills are taught directly, and teaching activities are designed to be as close to the instructional goal as possible. For example, if the goal is for students to read words aloud, the teacher does not include activities such as matching words with pictures, looking up words in the dictionary, or writing sentences using the words. Instead, the teacher models, and students practice, reading words aloud.

Two other major considerations are maximizing the number of student responses and monitoring the accuracy of student performance. First, because students learn by responding, it is important to maximize the number of response opportunities available to each student. The goal is as many student responses as possible within given time limits. Second, because students learn by receiving information about the quality of their responses, it is important to monitor student performance by the frequent collection of data. Teachers (and students themselves) should collect information about the number and accuracy of student responses; this should occur frequently, even daily, but at the minimum once a week. This information provides feedback to both students and teachers. If the total number of student responses

Inclusion Tips for the Teacher

Direct Teaching

If you wish to teach spelling skills, here is one direct instruction method you can use. Be sure to select words that the students know the meaning of and can read. Then teach spelling.

Teacher:	Let's spell the word *avalanche.* Watch me. (Teacher writes a word on board and says letter names.) *A-v-a-l-a-n-c-h-e, avalanche.* Everyone say that with me.
Teacher and students:	*A-v-a-l-a-n-c-h-e, avalanche.*
Teacher:	Right. *Avalanche is* spelled *a-v-a-l-a-n-c-h-e.* Now, everyone, write *avalanche* on your paper.
Students:	(Students write word.)
Teacher:	Did you write *a-v-a-l-a-n-c-h-e, avalanche?* Good! Everyone say it with me.
Teacher and students:	*A-v-a-l-a-n-c-h-e, avalanche.*
Teacher:	*Avalanche* is spelled *a-v-a-l-a-n-c-h-e.* Now, turn your paper over and write *avalanche.*
Students:	(Students write word.)
Teacher:	*Did you write a-v-a-l-a-n-c-h-e, avalanche?* Good spelling.

This presentation requires only 2 or 3 minutes. In this short time the teacher has modeled the spelling of the word for the class once by writing it and five times orally. Students have spelled the word twice orally, have written it twice, and have been provided with immediate feedback each time. In just a few minutes each student in the class can be provided with several response opportunities.

---

or the proportion of correct responses becomes low, the teacher can modify the instructional procedures.

Effective instructional strategies can be incorporated into any type of teaching situation for any age learner. Rosenshine and Stevens (1986) suggest that there are six fundamental steps that teachers should follow in the instructional sequence:

1. Review, check previous day's work (and reteach, if necessary)
2. Present new content/skills
3. Guide student practice (and check for understanding)
4. Feedback and correctives (and reteach, if necessary)
5. Independent student practice
6. Weekly and monthly reviews (p. 379)

This sequence is based on the demonstration-prompt-practice model; it is easily adapted to any subject matter area and is equally appropriate for elementary and secondary students. For more infor-

mation about the specific procedures for each step, consult Figure 4–2.

Archer and Gleason (1989a) suggest that lessons based on the demonstration-prompt-practice model be divided into three important components:

1. *Opening of the lesson.* The teacher gains the attention of the students and reviews any skills or knowledge areas critical to the content of the lesson. Then, he or she states the goal of the lesson and tells why the skill to be learned is important and when and where it will be used.
2. *Body of the lesson.* The teacher models the new skill and provides two types of guided practice: prompt and check. First, the teacher uses prompting to assist students in performing the new skill. Second, the teacher checks the students' progress by having them perform the new skill without assistance. According to Archer and Gleason (1989a), with simpler skills, "MODEL, PROMPT and CHECK can occur in

FIGURE 4-2   **Steps in Instruction**

1. **Daily Review and Checking Homework**
   Checking homework (routines for students to check each other's papers)
   Reteaching when necessary
   Reviewing relevant past learning (may include questioning)
   Review prerequisite skills (if applicable)
2. **Presentation**
   Provide short statement of objectives
   Provide overview and structuring
   Proceed in small steps but at a rapid pace
   Intersperse questions within the demonstration to check for understanding
   Highlight main points
   Provide sufficient illustrations and concrete examples
   Provide demonstrations and models
   When necessary, give detailed and redundant instructions and examples
3. **Guided Practice**
   Initial student practice takes place with teacher guidance
   High frequency of questions and overt student practice (from teacher and/or materials)
   Questions are directly relevant to the new content or skill
   Teacher checks for understanding (CFU) by evaluating student responses
   During CFU teacher gives additional explanation, process feedback, or repeats explanation—
   where necessary
   All students have a chance to respond and receive feedback; teacher insures that all students participate
   Prompts are provided during guided practice (where appropriate)
   Initial student practice is *sufficient* so that students can work independently
   Guided practice continues until students are firm
   Guided practice is continued (usually) until a success rate of 80% is achieved
4. **Correctives and Feedback**
   Quick, firm, and correct responses can be followed by another question or a short acknowledgment of cor-
   rectness (i.e., "That's right")
   Hesitant correct answers might be followed by process feedback (i.e., "Yes, Linda, that's right because . . .")
   Student errors indicate a need for more practice
   Monitor students for systematic errors
   Try to obtain a substantive response to each question
   Corrections can include sustaining feedback (i.e., simplifying the question, giving clues), explaining or re-
   viewing steps, giving process feedback, or reteaching the last steps
   Try to elicit an improved response when the first one is incorrect
   Guided practice and corrections continue until the teacher feels that the group can meet the objectives of
   the lesson
   Praise should be used in moderation, and specific praise is more effective than general praise
5. **Independent Practice (Seatwork)**
   Sufficient practice
   Practice is directly relevant to skills/content taught
   Practice to overlearning
   Practice until responses are firm, quick, and automatic
   Ninety-five percent correct rate during independent practice
   Students alerted that seatwork will be checked
   Students held accountable for seatwork
   Actively supervise students, when possible

continued

FIGURE 4-2   Continued

6. Weekly and Monthly Reviews
Systematic review of previously learned material
Include review in homework
Frequent tests
Reteaching of material missed in tests
Note: With older, more mature learners, or learners with more knowledge of the subject, the following adjustments can be made: (1) the size of the step in presentation can be larger (more material is presented at one time), (2) there is less time spent on teacher-guided practice and (3) the amount of overt practice can be decreased, replacing it with covert rehearsal, restating and reviewing.

Note. From B. Rosenshine and R. Stevens, "Teaching Functions," from *Handbook of Research on Teaching,* Third Edition, Merlin C. Wittrock, Editor, pp. 376–391. Copyright © 1986 by the American Educational Research Association. Reprinted by permission of the publisher.

---

quick succession (e.g., '*This word is* against. *Say the word with me. What word?*')" (p. 5).

3. *Close of the lesson.* The teacher ends the lesson by reviewing the critical information presented and providing a preview of the next lesson. Then students are assigned work for independent practice.

Consider Both Speed and Accuracy

In selecting and describing learning tasks, teachers should determine whether the instructional goal is rapid or accurate performance. This decision influences both presentation and practice.

For most learning tasks, particularly those that involve skills, both speed and accuracy are desired. The teacher demonstrates rapid, accurate performance; students practice for accuracy first and then speed. It is imperative in skill acquisition to provide practice that ensures that students acquire both accuracy and speed. If skills such as reading and writing are performed slowly, their usefulness decreases.

In skill acquisition, initial practice activities emphasize accuracy. Research suggests that students should achieve a 70% to 90% success rate during guided practice and at least a 90% success rate during independent practice (Englert, 1984; Rieth & Evertson, 1988; Rosenshine & Stevens, 1986). However, instruction should not stop with achievement of accuracy; further guided practice stressing speed should be given. This approach helps develop automatic responses that are both quick and accurate and also helps prevent students from acquiring slow response habits.

Maximize Engaged Time

Engaged time refers to the minutes and hours during which students are actively involved and participating in instruction. During that time they are "on task," whether that means listening to the teacher, watching a science experiment, answering the teacher's questions, reading, or writing. As engaged time increases, learning increases.

Students are engaged in learning for only certain portions of the school day because many noninstructional activities intrude. Even during time allocated for instruction, student attention may be directed elsewhere (Bulgren & Carta, 1992). In one study (Karweit & Slavin, 1981), actual instruction in elementary mathematics classes accounted for only 81% of the scheduled instructional time, and students were found to be engaged during only 68% of the time scheduled for instruction. Student inattention accounted for the greatest loss of learning time.

Similar results are reported by other researchers. In a study of general education classrooms, although 78% of class time was allocated to instruction, students with special needs were actively engaged only 63% of that time (Rich & Ross, 1989). Christenson and Ysseldyke (1986) compared regular classes and resource rooms and found that, regardless of the setting, students with learning disabilities and their peers spent less than 30 minutes of a 95-minute instructional period actively responding to academic tasks.

Student engagement can be increased in several ways. First, teachers should make full use of scheduled instructional time. Other activities such as cler-

Group responding is one way to increase the number of active student responses. In **choral responding,** all of the students in the group respond in unison to questions posed by the teacher. Heward, Courson, and Narayan (1989) recommend including several brief (5- to 10-minute) choral response sessions throughout the school day for different academic subjects. The questions asked should require short answers (no more than three words), and only one correct response should be possible.

Response cards are another method to promote group responding (Heward et al., 1996). Instead of answering orally, students hold up a card with the response they believe to be correct; for example, students might choose between a *true* card and a *false* card or among cards saying *carnivore, herbivore,* and *omnivore.* A variation is the "pinch card" (Heward et al., 1996, p. 5). The card contains several responses (e.g., *25%, 50%, 75%,* and *100%*), and the student pinches or points to the location of one of those responses. A third technique is group writing. The teacher asks a question or poses a problem (e.g., "What does the word *democracy* mean?"), and each student writes his or her response. Class members then discuss their answers and make corrections, as needed.

Englert (1984) presents several suggested ways to increase the amount of class time allocated to learning and methods for promoting student engagement during allocated learning time. The teacher checklist in Figure 4–3 summarizes these suggestions. For instance, teachers should spend at least 80% of class time in instructional activities and interact with 70% or more of their students each hour.

ical and housekeeping chores should not be done during the time allotted to teaching and learning. Make every minute count!

Second, teachers should emphasize instruction rather than independent practice. Research indicates that students show much higher engagement rates in teacher-led activities than in seatwork tasks (Rieth & Evertson, 1988).

Third, instruction should be designed to engage student attention. Materials and activities should be selected so that they are attractive, interesting to students, and at an appropriate level of difficulty. The length of the lesson should be neither too short nor too long; if the lesson is too long, student interest and attention may decline. The pace of instruction should be brisk. While not rushing students, the teacher should ensure that instruction proceeds at an energetic tempo with few pauses, hesitations, interruptions, or opportunities for boredom.

Fourth, engagement increases when students are required to respond. Students should be provided with as many response opportunities as possible; students actively involved in asking and answering lesson-related questions are engaged in learning. Maximum response opportunities that result in high proportions of correct responses are basic to successful instruction.

Give Clear Task Directions

For students to succeed, the directions for the learning task must be clearly stated and understandable. Before giving directions, the teacher should be sure that students are paying attention. Directions can be presented orally, in written form, or both. If directions are complicated and contain a number of steps, they should be broken down into subsets. For example, teachers who say, "Get out your math book and a sheet of paper, turn to page 46, do the even-numbered problems in Section A, the odd-numbered problems in Section C, and the first three story problems at the top of page 47" will likely find that their directions are not followed.

FIGURE 4-3   Are You Making Optimal Use of Class Time?

Respond to each item in terms of the extent to which it describes yourself: (1) not at all descriptive, (2) descriptive to a small extent, (3) descriptive to a moderate extent, (4) descriptive to a large extent, (5) descriptive to an extremely large extent.

Competencies

Allocated Time

		Performance Evaluation
1.1	Maximizes time in instruction by continually scheduling students in direct instruction (e.g., interacts with 70% or more of the students per hour).	1 2 3 4 5
1.2	Minimizes time in non-instructional activities (e.g., spends 80% or more of class time in instructional activities).	1 2 3 4 5
1.3	Keeps transition time between lessons short (e.g., no more than 3 minutes between change of students and activity; no more than 30 seconds when a change of activity only).	1 2 3 4 5
1.4	Established procedures for lessons that signal a clear beginning and end.	1 2 3 4 5
1.5	Gains all students' attention at the beginning of the lesson and maintains student attention during lesson at 90% level.	1 2 3 4 5
1.6	Prepares students for transitions in advance by stating behavioral expectations and informing students that lesson is drawing to a close.	1 2 3 4 5

Engaged Time

2.1	Maintains students' attention during seatwork at 80% levels or higher.	1 2 3 4 5
2.2	Monitors seatwork students continuously through eye scanning.	1 2 3 4 5
2.3	Circulates among seatwork students between lessons to assist students and to monitor progress.	1 2 3 4 5
2.4	Maintains seatwork accuracy at 90% level or higher.	1 2 3 4 5
2.5	Tells rationale for seatwork and communicates the importance of the assignment.	1 2 3 4 5
2.6	Provides active forms of seatwork practice clearly related to academic goals.	1 2 3 4 5
2.7	Sets seatwork and assignment standards (neatness, accuracy, due dates).	1 2 3 4 5
2.8	Uses tutoring (e.g., peer, volunteers, aides) and other specialized instructional technology to increase opportunity for active academic responding during seatwork.	1 2 3 4 5
2.9	Establishes procedures for early finishers, students who are stalled, and those seeking help.	1 2 3 4 5
2.10	Schedules time to review seatwork.	1 2 3 4 5
2.11	Requires that students correct work and make up missed or unfinished work.	1 2 3 4 5
2.12	Gives informative feedback to students in making written or verbal corrections.	1 2 3 4 5

Note. From "Measuring Teacher Effectiveness from the Teacher's Point of View" by C. S. Englert, 1984, *Focus on Exceptional Children, 17*(2), p. 9. Copyright 1984 by Love. Reprinted by permission.

Directions can be simplified by presenting only one portion at a time and by writing each portion on the chalkboard as well as stating it orally. When using written directions, the teacher must be sure that students are able to read and understand the words and comprehend the meaning of the sentences. Also, directions should be presented immediately preceding the learning task (Rosenkoetter & Fowler, 1986). Students beginning an assignment at 10 a.m. are not likely to recall or follow the directions given by the teacher at 9:30 a.m.

Teachers can determine whether directions are clear by attending to feedback from students. Puzzled expressions and failure to follow the directions are immediate cues that directions are unclear. If students are asked to repeat the directions to the teacher, misunderstandings become apparent. Clear directions are an important part of effective instruction, and clarity is one of the teacher characteristics most valued by students. Figure 4–4 on page 102 presents a checklist for students to use in assessing their teachers' clarity.

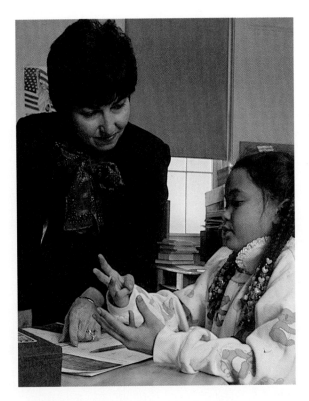

task performance with attention, praise, and compliments; with letter or number grades; with recognition of the student's accomplishment before peers or parents; and with awards, privileges, and special activities.

Consequences, like instructional antecedents, are powerful tools for promoting successful classroom performance, and their use will be described in more depth in the next chapter. However, consequences must be used systematically. They should follow behaviors as closely in time as possible, especially when students are in the acquisition stage of learning. Consequences should also be used consistently. Behaviors confirmed as correct and rewarded on one day should receive the same consequences on the next day.

Check for Maintenance and Generalization

The majority of the time spent in instruction is devoted to acquisition of skills and information. However, if students are to use what they have learned in later school and life situations, maintenance and generalization are also important. It cannot be assumed that tasks performed successfully today will also be performed successfully next week, next month, or next semester. Acquisition does not guarantee maintenance. Skills and information, particularly those that are verbal in nature, are forgotten if not practiced. To enhance maintenance, task performance should be monitored over time, and practice should be provided when necessary.

Generalization cannot be assumed, either. Students may perform quite well on one task but be unable to transfer their learning to a similar task. For example, words spelled correctly on a spelling test may be misspelled in a book report or essay. Generalization is crucial because there is insufficient time to teach all the possible situations in which particular skills and information may be needed. Teachers can promote transfer by evaluating its occurrence; if necessary, the teacher can demonstrate how skills and information are used in many different situations and then provide students with practice in generalization.

Provide Consequences for Successful Task Performance

In most classrooms, a variety of consequences are available for the teacher's use. Successful task performance may be followed by teacher attention, praise, special privileges, or awards. Unsuccessful performance, on the other hand, may result in the loss of teacher attention and praise or other unpleasant consequences. Because behaviors followed by pleasant consequences are more likely to occur again, teachers should make a systematic effort to reward successful task performance.

One powerful consequence is feedback to the student or **knowledge of results.** The student responds, and the teacher comments about the accuracy of the response; correct answers are confirmed, and incorrect answers are corrected. Students provided with information about the acceptability of their responses tend to modify their performances to increase the number of correct responses. Eventually they begin monitoring their own performances rather than relying on teacher feedback. Suggested ways of providing feedback are listed in "Inclusion Tips for the Teacher" on page 103.

In addition to knowledge of results, other consequences can be used. Teachers can reward successful

If Change Is Needed, Try the Least Intrusive Intervention First

Data on student performance may indicate the need for a change in instructional procedures. Student responses may be infrequent, inconsistent, or less

As your teacher I hope I am clear. In order to improve my ability to be clear I need your help. Below are 28 statements that describe what clear teachers do. Read each statement and place a check mark in the column that tells how often I perform the behavior that is described. In that way I'll know what I do well and what I need to improve.

(Put a check ✔ in one box after each statement.)

As our teacher, you:

	All of the time	Most of the time	Some of the time	Never	Doesn't apply to our class
1. Explain things simply.					
2. Give explanations we understand.					
3. Teach at a pace that is not too fast and not too slow.					
4. Stay with a topic until we understand.					
5. Try to find out when we don't understand and then you repeat things.					
6. Teach things step-by-step.					
7. Describe the work to be done and how to do it.					
8. Ask if we know what to do and how to do it.					
9. Repeat things when we don't understand.					
10. Explain something and then work an example.					
11. Explain something and then stop so we can ask questions.					
12. Prepare us for what we will be doing next.					
13. Give specific details when teaching.					
14. Repeat things that are hard to understand.					
15. Work examples and explain them.					
16. Give us a chance to think about what's being taught.					
17. Explain something and then stop so we can think about it.					
18. Show us how to do the work.					
19. Explain the assignment and the materials we need to do it.					
20. Stress difficult points.					
21. Show examples of how to do classwork and homework.					
22. Give us enough time for practice.					
23. Answer our questions.					
24. Ask questions to find out if we understand.					
25. Go over difficult homework problems.					
26. Show us how to remember things.					
27. Explain how to do assignments by using examples.					
28. Show us the difference between things.					

"The Clear Teacher Checklist" is based substantially on research findings contained in the article by Kennedy et al. in *Journal of Educational Research*, Sept./Oct. 1978.

Inclusion Tips for the Teacher

Providing Students with Feedback

- When students respond correctly, tell them! A simple "Yes," "Right," "Good," or "Correct" lets a learner know that the answer was on target.
- If a student's response is correct but hesitant, the teacher should provide process feedback. The response is confirmed and the teacher explains why it was correct. For example, the teacher might say, "Yes, John, that's correct. The first word in every sentence begins with a capital."
- If students give incorrect responses, again they should be told. The teacher can say "No" or "Not quite." If the teacher believes a student answered incorrectly because he or she did not understand the question or was not paying attention, the question should be repeated.
- The next step is the use of a correction procedure. After making the student aware that the response was incorrect, the teacher should help the student produce the correct answer. The teacher can model the correct response.

Teacher: Spell *this.*
Student: T-h-e-s.
Teacher: No, *this* is spelled *t-h-i-s.* Spell *this.*
Student: T-h-i-s.
Teacher: Right!

With some learning tasks a prompt can be given.

Teacher: Read this word: *shut.*
Student: Cut.
Teacher: Not quite. The first sound is *sh.* Read it again.
Student: Shut.
Teacher: Good reading.

Or the task can be made easier.

Teacher: Who was the first president of the United States?
Student: Lincoln.
Teacher: No. Was it George Washington or Thomas Jefferson?
Student: Washington.
Teacher: Correct.

Knowledge of results is a powerful tool for helping students learn. However, when students make errors, feedback alone is not sufficient. To help students learn the correct response, correction procedures must also be used.

---

accurate than desired. To increase the likelihood of successful performance, the learning task is made easier—by changing teaching procedures, modifying materials and activities, or altering task requirements. Several ways of accomplishing this are described later in this chapter.

However, unsuccessful performance should not result in the immediate substitution of an alternate task. First, the original task should be modified in an attempt to increase response accuracy. The simplest, least dramatic changes should be tried first; for instance, task failure may be due to insufficient practice or poor understanding of the directions. Intense interventions such as radically different instructional procedures, new materials and activities, or abandonment of the original task should be used only when all other options have been exhausted.

The principles of instruction presented here apply to learners of all ages and all ability levels. The instructional technique used to help you learn these principles has been direct presentation with occasional examples. Another appropriate technique is the use of nonexemplars, or examples of noninstances. In teaching colors, we show students several examples of red and then introduce the concept of nonred by showing blue, yellow, green, and pink objects. See Figure 4–5 for nonexemplars of effective instructional strategies.

It is possible for teachers to use effective instructional techniques but to apply these techniques unequally with different groups of students. Research indicates that teachers treat high achievers and low achievers quite differently. For example, in one study (Alves & Gottlieb, 1986), general education teachers interacted less frequently with students

FIGURE 4-5   **Common Mistakes in Instruction**

Inappropriate Instructional Strategy	Example
Instructional content is presented sporadically, rather than sequentially and systematically over time.	The teacher presents an exercise demonstrating syllabication of words. He provides a verbal description of the process and written exercises which he scores. The next day a different concept is taught. Observation shows that syllabication activities are taught again 2 weeks later; the same procedure is used.
Well-written instructional activities are followed by nonspecific evaluation.	Although the teacher develops written lesson plans complete with behavioral objectives and teaching procedures, the evaluation component generally consists of such global statements as "It seems to go pretty well" or "I should make the material more relevant."
Conditions for independent seatwork are not stated clearly.	The teacher initiates and leads a group. Five minutes later Ruthie approaches the teacher and asks for help with her seatwork. The teacher excuses herself to help Ruthie. An observer notes that reading is resumed but is interrupted five more times in the 15-minute reading session.
Reading activities are geared to frustration rather than to comprehension level.	The teacher asks Dotty to read a three-paragraph (64-word) selection during an individual instruction session in a resource room. An observer's record shows that the teacher supplied (read) 22 words that Dotty failed to read.
Children's error rates are consistently high.	Tommy hands in a math exercise, and the teacher says, "OK." Observation reveals that he made 7 errors in the set of 15 problems. A question elicits this response: "Oh, he knows that; it's just sloppy work." No data are available to confirm or deny the statement.
Additional learning trials are presented after criterion has been met.	Mark, a 10-year-old member of a [special] class . . ., proudly reads his primer to an observer. A question reveals that he has been reading it without error for the last 2 weeks.

Note. From "A Teacher's Guide to Instructional Programming" by J. W. Tawney, C. G. Kruse, P. T. Cegelka, and D. L. Kelly, 1977, *Teaching Exceptional Children, 10,* pp. 2–6. Copyright 1977 by The Council for Exceptional Children. Adapted by permission.

with disabilities than with their classmates without disabilities. Students with disabilities also were asked fewer questions by their teachers and received less feedback on their performance. For instruction to be truly effective, it must address the needs of all students within the classroom.

METHODS FOR GATHERING DATA

Information about student performance helps the teacher make instructional decisions. For example, data are gathered to determine the student's current level of academic performance before instruction begins. Such information aids in planning the educational program and placing the student in the correct portion of the instructional sequence. During instruction, data are used to evaluate student progress and to explore reasons for poor performance; this information helps to determine whether instructional adaptations should be made.

Although many types of assessment techniques are available, in most cases informal assessment rather than formal testing is the method of choice for gathering information about a student's classroom performance. One approach to informal assessment is **curriculum-based assessment** (CBA), which Gickling and Thompson (1985) define as "a procedure for determining the instructional needs of students based on the student's ongoing performance in existing course content" (p. 206). That is, the curriculum of the student's classroom is used as the yardstick by which to measure educational progress. Results of such assessments have immediate instructional applications. Skills that the student has not yet mastered become the next goals in the instructional sequence. The sections that follow provide principles for gathering useful information about student performance.

Determine the Student's Current Levels of Performance

Before beginning instruction, teachers are interested in determining what skills have already been acquired by the student. The group achievement tests given routinely to students in many school districts are one source of this information. Measures such as the *Comprehensive Tests of Basic Skills,* the *Metropolitan Achievement Tests,* and the *Stanford Achievement Tests* provide information about the level of performance in basic skills such as reading and mathematics. For example, results may indicate that a sixth grade student is performing at a fifth grade level in reading comprehension, a sixth grade level in mathematics, and a fourth grade level in written language.

Stone, Cundick, and Swanson (1988) suggest that results of group achievement tests can be used to identify students who may need interventions such as special education. They recommend using the 5th percentile as a cutoff point. Percentile rank scores indicate the percentage of a test's norm group that a particular student's performance equals or exceeds. Thus, a student scoring at the 5th percentile would show achievement equal to or better than 5% of norm group peers (and worse than 95% of that group).

Reynolds, Zetlin, and Wang (1993) recommend a somewhat different procedure, "20/20 Analysis." Results of group achievement tests are studied to identify two groups of students who benefit from adaptations of the general education program: (a) students with learning problems, defined as students who fall in the lowest 20% (i.e., below the 20th percentile), and (b) high achievers, defined as students who fall in the highest 20% (above the 80th percentile).

Because student achievement levels change over time, only recent achievement test results are of interest. However, even recent test data should be considered with caution because test tasks may differ from classroom learning tasks. Also, some students do not perform to the best of their ability on tests administered in group settings. In general, standardized measures such as group achievement tests are not the best source of information about current levels of performance; instead, more informal measures such as placement tests, inventories, and criterion-referenced tests should be used.

Measures of current student performance are provided in many commercial educational programs and textbook series. These placement tests assess the student's skill levels and provide information about where in the educational program the student should begin. If these measures are not available, the teacher can devise informal assessments such as inventories and criterion-referenced tests.

Inventories are measures that sample a variety of different skills and information within a subject matter area. They are designed to estimate the approximate level of student functioning. For instance, an informal math inventory would not assess all aspects of a mathematics curriculum. However, it might include a range of problems sampling knowledge of basic number facts, skills in basic operations (addition, subtraction, multiplication, and division), and ability to solve problems requiring regrouping. Student performance on this inventory would give the teacher some information about which skills have been acquired and which have not. An informal handwriting inventory appears in Figure 4–6; this measure provides general information about current levels of performance in the skill area of handwriting.

For more specific data, more precise measures are necessary. **Criterion-referenced tests** assess whether students have mastered the educational goals stated in instructional objectives. The teacher selects an objective, sets up the necessary conditions, and sees whether students are able to perform well enough to meet the criterion for acceptable performance. For example, to determine mastery of the objective "Students will write the names of at least 45 of the states with no errors in spelling," the teacher simply directs students to write the names of each of the states. Responses are acceptable if

FIGURE 4-6   Handwriting Inventory

Print your name on the line below.

_____

- -

Fill in the missing letters.

_____

a   cd   fg   ij   l   no   qr   tu   w   y

Print the uppercase (capital) letter that goes with each of the lowercase (small) letters below.

a A

b _____   f _____   d _____

g _____   r _____

Copy this sentence in your best printing.

Foxes and rabbits are quick, but turtles are slow.

_____

Write your name in cursive on the line below.

_____

- -

Finish writing the cursive alphabet.

a b c _____

Write the following words in cursive.

dog _____   like _____   and _____   the _____

Write this sentence in your best cursive handwriting.

At the zoo you can see lions and tigers, elephants, bears, and monkeys.

_____

_____

they are state names and if they are spelled correctly. Students with fewer than 45 correct responses have not yet met the objective and should receive further instruction.

Evaluate Progress

Information about student performance during instruction provides the teacher with feedback about the effectiveness of teaching procedures. Before in-

FIGURE 4-7   Observations of Academic Performance

Day	Number of Questions	Number of Responses	Number of Correct Responses	Percentage of Correct Responses
Monday	7	7	3	43%
Tuesday	9	9	4	44%
Wednesday	6	6	3	50%
Thursday	10	10	5	50%
Friday	8	8	3	38%

Student: ___Juan___
Subject: ___Science 9___
Task: ___Homework Assignments___

struction begins, it is important to pretest students to establish a performance baseline. This initial performance then becomes the reference point for evaluating progress in the instructional program.

Systematic observation is a useful technique for monitoring pupil progress. As chapter 5 will explain, observation is a flexible technique that can be used with a variety of student behaviors. In academic instruction, observation generally focuses on the number of responses made by the student and the proportion (or percentage) of correct responses. Figure 4–7 presents an example in which the teacher observed Juan's performance on science assignments for a 1-week period. Although Juan answered all the questions, the proportion of correct responses never rose above 50%. Thus, the teacher will modify instruction in an attempt to increase response accuracy.

As discussed in chapter 3, curriculum-based measurement is an effective strategy for monitoring student progress (Deno, 1985, 1987; Fuchs, 1986, 1987; Howell, Fox, & Morehead, 1993). Deno and Fuchs (1987) describe the procedures needed to establish a system of curriculum-based measurement in the classroom. The teacher decides what to measure and how to measure it, then formulates a specific instructional goal and objective. In the example provided by Deno and Fuchs (1987), the goal is

> In 19 weeks, when presented with stories for 1 minute from Level 2-SRA series, Michael will read aloud 80 words with no more than 6 errors. (p. 13)

The accompanying objective is to increase the number of words Michael reads correctly by an average of 2.6 words per week.

The teacher assesses this student's progress by having him read randomly selected passages from his reading text for 1-minute periods. These data are collected frequently, at least twice a week. The student's performance is graphed (see Figure 4–8), and his progress is compared with the aimline, a diagonal line extending from his baseline performance to the instructional goal (marked with an *X* on the graph).

Analyze Reasons for Task Failure

When task performance is unsatisfactory, the student's responses can be analyzed to help locate problem areas. Called **error analysis,** this technique involves scoring each response as correct or incorrect and then looking for error patterns. For example, a student may solve only 8 of 22 addition problems correctly; by systematically analyzing the student's responses, the teacher may find that all errors involved problems requiring regrouping and that the student was using an inappropriate strategy, such as failing to carry:

$$\begin{array}{r} 42 \\ + \ 39 \\ \hline 711 \end{array}$$

Use the essay in Figure 4–9, which was written by a ninth grade student, to practice your error

FIGURE 4-8   Curriculum-Based Measurement

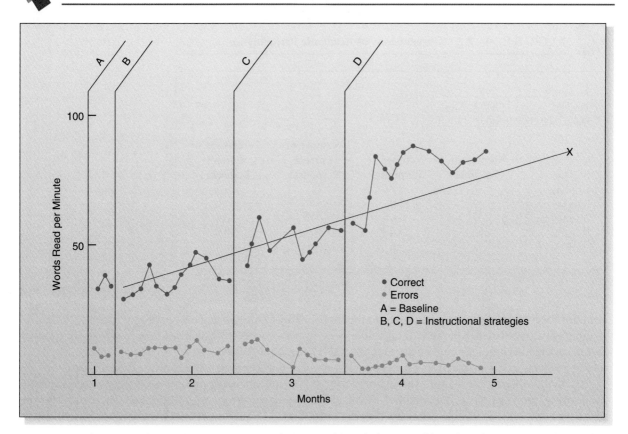

Note. From "Developing Curriculum-Based Measurement Systems for Data-Based Special Education Problem Solving" by S. L. Deno and L. S. Fuchs, 1987, *Focus on Exceptional Children, 19*(8), p. 15. Copyright 1987 by Love. Reprinted by permission.

FIGURE 4-9   Writing Sample for Error Analysis

Essay

last year I was in the musical "Annie get your gun" that gat me started in the preforming arts. I have tryed out for the teater to be in "annie get your gun, kismit, and music man but I didn't make it today I am trying out for a choir at the high shcool I tryed out for the wizerd of oz

Error Analysis

Punctuation

Number of periods needed in the essay _____5_____

Number of correct responses made by the student _____1_____

Percentage of correct responses made by the student _____20%_____

Capitalization

Number of capital letters needed in the essay _____

Number of correct responses made by the student _____

Percentage of correct responses made by the student _____

Spelling

Number of words written by the student _____

Number of correct responses made by the student _____

Percentage of correct responses made by the student _____

analysis skills. The punctuation errors have been analyzed for you; consider the capitalization mistakes and then the misspellings. Do you see any patterns in the errors?

If student performance is poor (few responses are made, or most of the responses are incorrect), analyzing the task rather than the specific student errors may be helpful. With task analysis, the task is broken down into component parts, and then students are asked to perform each of the parts. In this way, the subtasks that are causing the most difficulty can be identified, and instruction can begin with those areas.

STRATEGIES FOR ADAPTING INSTRUCTION

When students have difficulty acquiring skills and information, the teacher adapts instruction to better meet the students' needs. Teachers can modify instructional materials and activities, change teaching procedures, or alter the requirements of the learning task. Several of the specific strategies for instructional adaptations appear in Figure 4–10. These should be used in an attempt to improve student performance before more involved modifications are made. Note that the strategies are arranged in numerical order from 1 to 10. Number 1 should be tried before number 2, number 2 before number 3, and so

on. Of course, before these methods are used, teachers should be sure that the learning task is at an appropriate level of difficulty for the student.

Modify Materials and Activities

The first type of adaptation to try is modification of instructional materials and activities. The learning task remains the same; what is changed is the way in which the necessary skills and information are presented to the student. Three possible strategies are the clarification of task directions, addition of prompts to the learning task, and correction of specific student errors (items 1, 2, and 3 in Figure 4–10).

Clarify Task Directions. Students may perform tasks poorly if the directions for the task are unclear. Several changes can make directions more understandable:

- Give directions both orally and in writing.
- Restate oral directions in simpler language.
- Give only one or two oral directions at a time.
- Be sure students are able to see directions written on the chalkboard.
- Keep written directions on the student's reading level.
- Explain any new or unfamiliar terms.

FIGURE 4 - 1 0   Adapting Instruction

IF students experience difficulty in task performance,
TRY these adaptations of . . .
Materials and activities:
  1. Clarify task directions
  2. Add prompts to the learning task
  3. Teach to specific student errors
Teaching procedures:
  4. Give additional presentation of skills and information
  5. Provide additional guided practice
  6. Make consequences for successful performance more attractive
  7. Slow the pace of instruction
Task requirements:
  8. Change the criteria for successful performance
  9. Change task characteristics
  10. Break each task into smaller subtasks
BEFORE selecting an alternate task.
IF NECESSARY, substitute a similar but easier task or a prerequisite task.

After giving directions, the teacher should demonstrate task performance and then answer any questions students may have.

Add Prompts. *Prompts* or *cues* are any features added to learning tasks that assist students in task performance. Prompts can be verbal, visual, or physical and can either call attention to the cues already available in the learning task or introduce an artificial cue system.

Prompts are often used to make critical features of the learning task more noticeable. For example, if students confuse addition and subtraction symbols, teachers might circle the symbols, make them larger, write them in red, or remind students to "check each problem to see whether you add or subtract." If students read aloud without attending to punctuation, punctuation marks can be underlined, highlighted, or color-coded to make them stand out.

Artificial prompts can also be added to learning tasks. In handwriting instruction, for instance, guidelines are provided to assist beginning writers. Another example is the use of underlining; teachers who underline important words and phrases on the board are providing prompts. Teachers can also give verbal prompts or reminders; for example, before students begin to write a paragraph, the teacher might say, "Remember to begin each sentence with a capital letter."

Any learning task can be made easier by the use of prompts. However, as students learn, it is important to withdraw the prompts from the task, fading them gradually (as shown in Figure 4–11) to maintain successful student performance.

Teach to Specific Student Errors. If students make consistent errors that affect overall task performance, the teacher should focus on the correction of those errors. This approach is effective if a few types of errors account for the majority of incorrect responses. For example, if a student writes the cursive alphabet correctly with the exception of the letters *m* and *n*, these letters should be singled out and taught directly. Or if oral reading is characterized by frequent repetitions ("I want . . . I want to go to the . . . I want to go to the store . . . I want to go to the store to buy . . ."), the teacher should attempt to correct this error. However, if task failure is due to several types of errors (or too few responses), it is probably necessary to modify the procedures used in teaching.

Change Teaching Procedures

If modification of instructional activities and materials does not result in successful performance, the next step is to adapt the teaching procedures. Strategies include additional presentation, additional practice, changing the consequences, and slowing the pace of instruction (items 4, 5, 6, and 7 in Figure 4–10).

Give Additional Presentation of Skills and Information. An additional presentation of the skills and information necessary for task performance may be appropriate. With this strategy, the teacher demonstrates skills and explains information. A repetition of the original presentation may produce the desired results. However, the teacher must usually provide a more complete (or simpler) explanation, additional examples, or several instances in which the skill is modeled.

Provide Additional Guided Practice. Poor task performance may be improved by additional guided practice. The teacher can increase the amount of practice by requiring more student responses, lengthening practice sessions (although not to the point of student fatigue), or scheduling extra sessions throughout the school day. To make practice more effective, teachers can increase both the amount and the quality of their feedback to students. To increase the amount, feedback can be given after every response rather than after every third or fifth answer. To increase the quality of feedback, the teacher can describe important features of the student's behavior in addition to telling the student whether the task was performed correctly. The statement "That's right. You remembered to put a period at the end of the sentence" tells the student that the response was accurate and points out the specific behavior for which praise is given.

Make Consequences for Successful Performance More Attractive. This strategy involves changing the consequences of the behavior rather than its antecedents. Consequences for successful performance include knowledge of results and rewards supplied by the teacher. To increase the effect of knowledge of results, teachers can improve the quality of feedback, as previously described. In addition, students become more aware of their performance if they are

FIGURE 4-11 Fading Prompts from the Learning Task

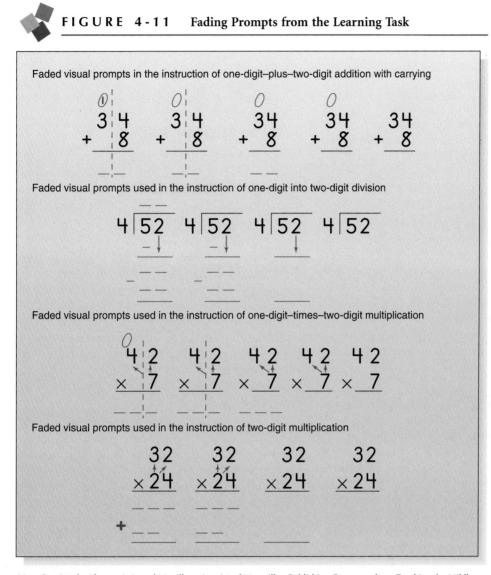

Note. Reprinted with permission of Merrill, an imprint of Macmillan Publishing Company, from *Teaching the Mildly Handicapped in the Regular Classroom* (2nd ed., p. 107) by J. Affleck, S. Lowenbraun, and A. Archer. Copyright © 1980 Merrill Publishing Company, Columbus, Ohio.

involved in data collection procedures. They can place an *X* or a check mark beside each correct response on their assigned papers and then plot their performance on a graph.

The reward system in use in the classroom may also need to be altered. Students may require incentives to begin or complete a task. And teachers may need to reward approximations toward successful task performance (e.g., 60% accuracy, then 70%, etc., until the criterion is achieved). The nature of the rewards used by the teacher may also require

modification; things perceived by teachers as rewards may be less attractive to students.

Slow the Pace of Instruction. If changes in antecedents and consequences do not produce acceptable performance, slowing the pace of instruction may be necessary. The learning task and the time allotted for instruction remain the same, but less material is presented and practiced. For example, the teacher may demonstrate telling time to the hour and to the half hour in two separate sessions rather than one. If this strategy is unsuccessful, the teacher should consider altering the requirements of the learning task.

Alter Task Requirements

The learning task itself can be modified to enhance student success. Possible strategies are changing task criteria, changing task characteristics, and breaking the task into smaller subtasks (items 8, 9, and 10 in Figure 4–10).

Change the Criteria for Successful Performance. The criteria for successful performance generally address three aspects of the task: quantity, speed, and accuracy. The requirements for each can be reduced. The number of questions, problems, or activities to be performed can be lessened. The time limits imposed can be increased so that speed demands are relaxed. Or a lower accuracy rate can be accepted. However, the teacher should maintain reasonable accuracy requirements to ensure that the student is learning the task.

Change Task Characteristics. Task characteristics include the conditions under which the task is performed and the nature of the behavior itself. If the task requires students to perform from memory without aids and assistance, the teacher might allow the use of aids. For example, students may be able to solve multiplication problems if they can use an aid such as a multiplication table or a pocket calculator. Presentation and response modes can also be changed. A task's presentation mode is the way it presents information; for example, many classroom tasks require reading skills. Instead of reading, students might listen to lectures and tapes or watch television and videos. Response modes can also be modified. Instead of writing, students might type, answer orally, tape-record their responses, or dictate them to a peer.

Break Tasks into Smaller Subtasks. If alteration of task characteristics and criteria does not produce success, the task is probably too complex and should be broken into smaller subtasks. For example, if writing (or dictating or tape-recording) an essay is overwhelming to a student, the teacher can set up a series of smaller tasks: selection of a

topic, preparation of an outline or organizational map, writing the title, formulation of the topic sentence for the first paragraph, and so on. This strategy is the last in a series of instructional modifications; the next step is to substitute an alternate task.

Select an Alternate Task

When student performance remains poor despite instructional adaptations, the teacher should consider replacing the learning task with an alternate task. Two choices are possible: a similar but easier task or a prerequisite task.

Substitute a Similar but Easier Task. The teacher can select an alternate task similar in nature to the original task but easier for students to perform. For example, if students are unable to cope with the history textbook (even in taped form), the teacher can substitute another text that covers the same material but in less depth and at a lower reading level. This allows students to proceed at their own levels and rates while remaining in the same general subject area as their peers.

Substitute a Prerequisite Task. The most drastic intervention available to the general education teacher is replacement of the original learning task with a prerequisite task. For example, if students with poor basic skills are unable to solve algebraic equations (even with the aid of a calculator), the teacher may substitute instruction in math facts and the operations of addition, subtraction, multiplication, and division. This strategy should be the last employed in the general education classroom because it involves the most radical change from typical classroom procedures. Students whose needs cannot be met with this strategy are candidates for special education services.

The most comprehensive instructional modification that can be made is change of the curriculum. This often occurs when students with severe disabilities are included in general education classes as part of their special education program. In most cases, the educational goals for students with serious learning needs address areas such as socialization and communication skills, rather than academic performance. For students such as these, instruc-

Things To Remember

- Students may experience difficulty in the acquisition, maintenance, and generalization of basic skills, content area information, and transition training.
- Academic problems are indicated by a high number of incorrect responses, a low number of responses, or an inconsistent response pattern.
- Instruction is individualized when a high proportion of student responses is correct.
- In systematic instruction the learning task is selected, material necessary for task performance is presented, and practice is provided; skills are taught directly and the demonstration-prompt-practice technique is used.
- Increasing student engagement by increasing response rate accelerates learning.
- Student performance data provide information about current levels of functioning, rate of progress, and reasons for task failure.

- When student performance is unsatisfactory, teachers introduce the least intrusive instructional modification first.
- Materials and activities are modified by clarifying task directions, adding prompts, and correcting specific student errors.
- Teaching procedures are changed by providing additional presentations and practice, making consequences more attractive, and slowing the pace of instruction.
- Task requirements are altered by changing the criteria for successful performance, changing task characteristics, and breaking the task into smaller subtasks.
- Substitution of an alternate learning task, the most drastic instructional change, is used only as a last resort.

tional adaptations usually include the substitution of an alternative curriculum. For example, a student with severe disabilities might participate in the same lesson on volcanoes as others in the class, although the instructional goal for that student relates to learning to work with others, rather than science. Chapter 10 provides more information about instructional and curricular adaptations for students with serious learning needs.

The next chapter discusses typical behavior problems and presents strategies for managing the classroom behavior of regular class students, including those with special needs.

ACTIVITIES

1. Visit the AskERIC website to find out more about adapting classroom instruction for students with special needs. "Window on the Web" on page 89 describes the site. Look for information in AskERIC's Virtual Library or use the Question and Answer Service to receive an online response to a specific question.

2. Arrange to observe in a special or general education classroom. Explain to the teacher that you are interested in seeing how much of the school day is actually spent in instruction. Observe and keep a log of the teacher's activities for an hour or so. How much time is spent in large-group instruction? Small-group instruction? Supervision of students' independent work? Noninstructional duties?

3. Task analysis is used to break tasks into teachable subcomponents. Select one of the tasks that follow, and list all of the steps necessary to complete the task. Check your analysis by trying to do the task using only the steps you have listed.
   - Brushing your teeth
   - Looking up a number in the phone book
   - Frying an egg
   - Making a bed
   - Writing a check

4. Ways of adapting instruction include changing the characteristics of the task and the performance criteria. Try your hand at modifying this objective:

> When given a page of 25 math problems, the student will write the correct answers to at least 20 problems within 5 minutes.

Describe how you would alter the task for each of the modifications listed here; the first one is done for you.

Modification	Altered Task
Reduce quantity	Give student only 20 problems
Reduce speed	
Reduce accuracy	
Change presentation mode	
Change response mode	

5. Explain why substitution of an alternate learning task should be the last instructional modification attempted.

chapter 5

Managing Classroom Behavior

Cases

Henry is late for class at least 2 days each week.

Maxine hasn't completed an assignment this semester.

Several times each day, John interrupts the teacher's lecture by talking and making noises.

Pablo argues and fights with other students in the classroom.

During independent study time, Lisa looks around the room and watches other students or writes notes to her friends.

Sue doesn't ask questions in class; in fact, the only talking she does is at lunch with her two close friends.

Willie is seldom in his seat; he seems to be constantly on the move, and he holds the class record for the longest round-trip to the pencil sharpener.

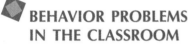

Classroom behavior problems such as these are not rare occurrences. They are a sampling of the problem behaviors that teachers face daily in a general education classroom.

BEHAVIOR PROBLEMS IN THE CLASSROOM

Behavior problems are exhibited by typical students and students with special needs of all ages and at every grade level. Some students call attention to themselves only in the classroom; others also experience difficulty on the playground, in the school cafeteria, on the way to and from school, at home, and in the neighborhood.

The behavior problems of students frequently contribute to their placement in special education programs. When students with special needs return to the mainstream, teachers in general education are often concerned that their problem behaviors will interfere with the operation of the classroom. In addition, such behaviors may hinder the special students' academic achievement and may have a negative effect on their acceptance by others.

Two major types of behavior problems are of concern to the teacher: inappropriate classroom behavior and poor study skills. Behaviors that interfere with classroom instruction, impede social interaction with teacher and peers, or endanger others are considered **classroom conduct problems.** Examples of inappropriate classroom behaviors are talking out, fighting, arguing, being out of one's seat, swearing, and avoiding interactions with others. Immature and withdrawn behaviors also fall under this category. Behaviors that interfere with the special student's academic performance and/or the teacher's ability to assess academic progress are considered **study skill problems.** Typical study skill problems are failure to complete assignments, poor attention during lectures or class discussion, failure to follow directions, and poor management of study time.

Problem behaviors are exhibited in one of three ways: low rate of appropriate behaviors, high rate of inappropriate behaviors, or absence of the appropriate behavior from the student's repertoire. Different management strategies are linked to each type of problem behavior.

- *Low rate of appropriate behaviors.* Students exhibit appropriate behaviors but not as frequently as expected or required. For example, a student may be able to complete homework assignments but chooses to do so only 10% to 20% of the time. Also, students may behave appropriately in one setting but not in another. For instance, a student with disabilities may work well in the resource room but may find it difficult to work in a small-group setting in the general education classroom. To alleviate these problems, the teacher sets up a systematic program to increase the occurrence of appropriate behaviors or to help students generalize behaviors from one situation to another.
- *High rate of inappropriate behaviors.* Inappropriate behaviors that are troublesome to teachers occur frequently or for long periods of time. Examples include students who are out of their seats 30 to 40 times per day, those who talk during 50% to 60% of the class lecture, and those who use profanity 5 to 10 times in one class period. To overcome these high rates of inappropriate behavior, teachers attempt to decrease the frequency or duration of the undesired behavior by increasing appropriate behaviors that are incompatible. For instance, to decrease running in the classroom, the teacher can work to increase the frequency of walking.
- *Absence of the appropriate behavior from the student's repertoire.* Students may not yet have learned the appropriate behavior for social interaction or classroom functioning. The age or grade

For Your Information

Behavior Problems

- According to a 1997 nationwide study, the general public believed that the most important problem in public schools was lack of discipline. In 1996, lack of discipline was second only to the use of drugs (Rose, Gallup, & Elam, 1997).
- The National Education Association (NEA) surveyed teachers and found that 54% believe that "student behavior interferes with teaching" ("NEA Survey," 1980, p. 49).
- One major study reported that 60% of elementary school children are identified by at least one of their teachers as having a behavior problem (Rubin & Balow, 1978).
- In effective classrooms, the teacher's classroom management program maximizes the time students spend on learning tasks, and student achievement increases (Smith, Finn, & Dowdy, 1993).
- Students with poor social behaviors do not achieve as well academically as peers with appropriate social skills. Improving performance in personal interactions and task-related social skills increases both academic performance and social acceptance (Cartledge & Milburn, 1986; Gresham, 1984; Zirpoli & Melloy, 1997).
- The behaviors that are appropriate in the classroom are determined by the teacher, the policies of the school, and the beliefs of the community. An inappropriate behavior for one teacher may be totally acceptable to another.

level of a student is not an accurate predictor of behavioral competence; it is necessary to consider each student individually. For instance, sixth graders may not know how to start a conversation or how to organize their time to ensure completion of assignments. To remedy this, the effective teacher directly teaches the new behavior (conversation skills or time management), provides instruction on when and how the behavior is to take place, and carefully builds practice and review opportunities into the instructional sequence (Emmer, 1981; Olson & Platt, 1996).

Behavior problems do not occur in isolation. The way in which the classroom learning environment is arranged and the actions of others can promote, initiate, or reinforce inappropriate behaviors. If classroom behavior problems are to be understood and managed, not only the behavior of the target student but also that of the teacher and peers must be examined. For example, a sarcastic comment from a teacher can initiate a verbal retort from the student. Classmates who laugh at clowning or wisecracks assure that similar behaviors will recur.

Students show inappropriate behavior when they have not learned correct responses or have found that acting inappropriately is more rewarding than acting appropriately. Such behavior problems do respond to instruction. According to one point of view within the education community, behavior problems belong to the teacher, not the student. This viewpoint holds that it is not the students who fail; instead, educators have failed to develop acceptable student behaviors. Opinions on and results of research into student behavior in the schools are presented in "For Your Information" above. Figures 5–1 and 5–2 provide checklists of both teacher and student behaviors to consider as possible factors contributing to student misbehavior in the classroom.

PRINCIPLES OF MANAGING BEHAVIOR

Students who exhibit inappropriate behaviors require a classroom management system that is systematic, consistent, and concerned with both the prevention and cure of problem behaviors. This system should provide for group management yet be flexible enough to allow individualization for the problems of one specific student.

Behavior management follows many of the same principles used in adapting academic instruction. Teachers state precise goals, break behaviors into teachable subcomponents, institute systematic management procedures, and collect data to monitor student progress. Whereas instruction (as discussed in chapter 4) deals primarily with academic skills, behavior management is concerned with classroom conduct and study skills; in both, the teacher arranges the classroom environment to produce

FIGURE 5-1   Possible Contributions to Misbehavior: A Checklist of Teacher Behavior

- *Am I consistent in responding to children's behavior?* If your response to children's conduct—good or bad—is unpredictable, children will have difficulty learning how they are to behave. Your students should know what the consequences of appropriate behavior and misbehavior will be. Give clear directions; hold firm to your expectations; and be consistent in following through with rewards and punishment.

- *Am I rewarding the right behavior?* Children who present difficult management problems often are ignored when they are behaving appropriately. Often, about the only time they receive attention is when they are criticized or reprimanded for misbehavior. Sometimes teachers make the mistake of praising them (for something else) or making physical contact with them (in attempts to offer loving correction) when they misbehave. Make sure that children are receiving your attention primarily when they are behaving appropriately. You must make certain that desirable conduct receives a hefty amount of recognition and the misbehavior does not.

- *Are my expectations and demands appropriate for children's abilities?* When expectations are too high, children feel too much pressure and experience too much failure. When expectations are too low, children become bored and may feel resentful. Make certain that your expectations fit each child's ability level so that the child is challenged while his or her progress is obvious.

- *Am I tolerant enough of children's individuality?* Children have as much right as adults to express their individuality. Many children rebel against teachers who demand strict uniformity and regimentation or are unwilling to encourage appropriate individuality. Make certain that your rules and expectations allow sufficient room for harmless preferences and idiosyncrasies.

- *Am I providing instruction that is useful to children?* People do not learn quickly or happily when they see no point in what they are doing. First, you must make sure that you have chosen the most important things to teach. When children do not see the importance of what you are teaching, you must point out to them the value of what they are learning. If they still do not understand, you must find a way to make the material interesting or worth their while—perhaps by offering meaningful rewards or privileges for learning.

- *Are children seeing desirable models?* Children are great imitators of their teachers and their high-status peers. Make certain that if children are imitating you, they are behaving appropriately. Monitor your own behavior, and change it if necessary. Call attention to the desirable conduct of children's peers. Point out the kind of behavior you want to see.

- *Am I generally irritable and overreliant on punishment as a control technique?* Teachers set a tone in their classrooms by their general attitudes toward persons and events. A teacher who is easily upset, frequently short-tempered, quick to punish minor misbehavior, and hesitant in expressing approval is virtually certain to foster irritability and defiance in students. General irritability and a focus on punishment suggest depression; and a teacher's depression may contribute to children's depressive behavior.

- *Am I willing to try a different tack on the problem or to seek the help of colleagues or consultants?* A teacher who resists the suggestions of others, who insists on "going it alone," or who discards any different approach as useless or doomed to failure is not likely to be successful for long. Teaching today presents complex behavior management problems for which even the most competent teacher needs consultation. An attitude of openness and a willingness to look outside oneself are essential to success.

Note. From "Classroom Management: Teacher-Child-Peer Relationships" by J. M. Kauffman, P. L. Pullen, and E. Akers, 1986, *Focus on Exceptional Children, 19*(1), p. 3. Copyright 1986 by Love. Reprinted by permission.

changes in student behavior. The following paragraphs present principles to follow in setting up a systematic behavior management program.

Remember That Behavior Is Learned

Problem behaviors are learned behaviors that have developed from the student's experiences and reinforcement history. Sometimes called **operant be-** **haviors,** they are under the voluntary control of the individual. Because behavior is learned, students can acquire new ways of acting; present behaviors can be replaced or supplemented. The learning of new behaviors occurs at different rates for different students, and instructional procedures affect individuals differently. This individuality is particularly important with students with special needs, who may require extra time or additional

---

FIGURE 5-2   **Possible Contributions to Misbehavior: A Checklist of Student Behavior**

- *Is the child overdependent on you?* Children who cannot work independently are a constant source of interruption of the teacher's work and their peers' concentration. Their frequent demands for help, or their refusal to work without the teacher's constant oversight, are wearing on the teacher and may trigger rivalry from peers.
- *Does the child have difficulty concentrating and paying attention?* Learning requires focused attention. A child's lack of attention to task requires additional teacher effort, provides an inappropriate model for peers, raises the probability of disruptive behavior, and lowers the probability of academic success.
- *Does the child become easily upset under pressure to achieve?* The world contains many sources of pressure for productive activity and achievement. Therefore, a classroom without any pressure whatsoever for achievement is an unrealistic and debilitating environment. Children's resistance to expectations for performance is a source of frustration for the teacher and for peers who are striving to achieve.
- *Is the child's work sloppy?* Reflective, careful work is needed in the workplace, and it should be expected in the classroom. Teachers are justified in requiring reasonably neat, thoughtful responses. Teaching is difficult and progress is slow when the child has not learned good work habits and impulse control.
- *Does the child tease, annoy, or interfere with the work of other students?* Annoyance or hassle by neighbors or coworkers is a common and sometimes serious source of stress for adults and children. A child who interferes with the lives of others becomes a source of bad feelings and a sinkhole for the energies of teachers and peers.
- *Is the child negative toward schoolwork, self, teachers, or peers?* Faultfinding, whining, and criticism—whether directed toward others or oneself—induce negative responses in others. These characteristics often are indicative of depression, and they tend to make others feel depressed.
- *Does the child have poor personal hygiene or habits of self-care?* People, young or old, who are dirty or smelly are less likely to be approached socially or to be befriended by others than are those who maintain good hygiene and self-care. Teachers will have difficulty being positive toward children whose odor or appearance is offensive.
- *Is the child usually withdrawn or reticent?* A withdrawn or reticent child is easily overlooked by teachers and peers. A child with those characteristics is unlikely to be drawn into positive, reciprocal social exchanges without special intervention.
- *Does the child engage in self-stimulation or self-injury?* Excessive or socially inappropriate self-stimulation is incompatible with learning and social acceptance. Self-stimulation and self-injury usually are off-putting to others and inhibit normal psychological and physical development.
- *Is the child aggressive toward teachers or peers?* Aggression in the form of verbal threats, intimidation, extortion, or physical attack heightens anxiety and stress in all parties involved. An aggressive child can be expected to induce hostility and counter-aggression in others.

Note. From "Classroom Management: Teacher-Child-Peer Relationships" by J. M. Kauffman, P. L. Pullen, and E. Akers, 1986, *Focus on Exceptional Children, 19*(1), p. 5. Copyright 1986 by Love. Reprinted by permission.

practice. They are certainly capable of acquiring new behaviors but may need a more systematic management program than their typical general education peers.

Consider Both the Antecedents and the Consequences of Behavior

As suggested earlier, behaviors do not happen in isolation. The occurrence of a behavior is affected by the events that precede it and the consequences that follow it. Antecedents and consequences are both important in the management of behavior. New skills can be taught, or current behaviors can be modified, by either altering antecedent events or conditions and/or by manipulating consequences. As a general rule, if antecedents are contributing to the behavior, teachers should first alter the antecedent conditions and then consider changing the consequences. For example, if students fail to follow directions, the first step may be to alter the directions. A change from "Get back to your seat!" to "Would you please return to your seat?" may produce the desired behavior.

It is also possible to modify both antecedents and consequences at the same time. According to Walker (1995),

> Simultaneous manipulation of antecedent(s) and consequences is probably the most effective method for changing behavior. A simple example of the manipulation of both an antecedent and consequences would be in the case where a teacher carefully defines classroom rules and then allows children to accumulate minutes of free time for following them. (p. 59)

Reduce Behavior Management Problems with Careful Organization of the Classroom

The physical organization of the classroom, the procedures established for movement within the classroom, and the quality of the instructional program all play important roles in determining the frequency of behavior problems. Careful arrangement of such things as physical space, student seating, storage of instructional materials, and student traffic patterns can greatly reduce the potential for disruptions of instructional activities and the occurrence of behavioral problems. Appropriate instructional programs and streamlined classroom procedures are also likely to reduce behavior problems. Chapters 4 and 7 provide specific suggestions for adapting instruction and coordinating the classroom learning environment.

Increase the Occurrence of Behaviors by Reinforcement

Behaviors followed by reinforcers are more likely to occur again. A student who receives praise from the teacher for raising her hand to speak in class is more likely to raise her hand the next time she wishes to contribute something. This is an example of **positive reinforcement;** the behavior is followed by the presentation of a pleasant (or positive) event that makes the behavior more likely to recur. This is a constructive procedure that helps students feel better about themselves. Examples of positive reinforcers are praise, special privileges, positive notes to students and parents, early dismissal for lunch, and special awards. Positive reinforcement is a powerful tool for managing and changing behavior.

Although less favored, negative reinforcers also increase the probability that behaviors will recur. In **negative reinforcement,** the behavior is followed by the removal of an aversive (unpleasant or punishing) event or condition. A student who completes his homework to stop the nagging of his teacher and parents is being negatively reinforced; that is, the desired behavior, finishing the assignment, is followed by the removal of the aversive event, nagging, and is thus more apt to recur in the future. The student who stops talking to classmates and begins working to stop the frown of the teacher is also being negatively reinforced. Negative reinforcement should not be confused with punishment; negative reinforcers increase the occurrence of a behavior by removing something that is aversive. However, because it is a negative approach, negative reinforcement may produce avoidance, escape, or aggressive behaviors on the part of the student (Zirpoli & Melloy, 1997).

Reinforcement is most effective when the reinforcer is clearly associated with the specific behavior and is presented closely following that behavior. The effect of reinforcing a student with immediate praise for entering class on time is much greater than complimenting the student at the end of the day. Reinforcement should be immediate, systematic, realistic, and meaningful to students in order to be effective. Table 5–1 gives examples of reinforcement procedures that influence the strength of a behavior.

Decrease the Occurrence of Behaviors by Removing Reinforcers or Introducing Aversive Events

The strength of a behavior decreases when it is followed by an aversive event or when it stops being followed by a reinforcer. The student who no longer receives laughs and snickers from peers for muttering profanities will generally decrease this activity. Tardiness will decrease if students lose privileges (such as time in the game center) for each minute they are late; the same is true for students who lose the use of the family car for coming home after curfew.

Extinction is the removal of reinforcers that have previously followed the behavior. If the objective is to decrease an inappropriate behavior that has been reinforced in the past, the reinforcer is withheld. For example, the teacher may wish to decrease the number of times Mike talks out in class. If the teacher has been reinforcing Mike's out-of-turn responses by attending to them, this positive reinforcer must be withdrawn; the teacher should ignore Mike's comments until he raises his hand. Although extinction procedures will reduce and eliminate a behavior,

TABLE 5-1 Procedures to Change Behaviors

Learning Concepts	Educational Procedures	Effects on Behavior	Examples of Positive or Aversive Events Presented or Removed
Positive reinforcement	Behavior is followed by positive event	Increase in strength of behavior	Smile, approval, affection, task completion, money, special privileges, recognition, passing grade
Negative reinforcement	Behavior is followed by removal of aversive event	Increase in strength of behavior	Frown, criticism, poor grade, threat of restriction of use of car, rejection, nonattention
Extinction (of behavior previously strengthened by positive reinforcement)	Behavior is not followed by positive event associated with previous occurrence	Decrease in strength of behavior	Smile, approval, affection, peer attention, bonus, special privilege
Extinction (of behavior previously strengthened by negative reinforcement)	Behavior is not followed by removal of aversive event associated with previous occurrence	Decrease in strength of behavior	Criticism, rejection, threat of loss of privileges, poor grade
Punishment: Presentation of aversive events	Behavior is followed by aversive event	Decrease in strength of behavior which results in the aversive event	Criticism, poor grade, rejection by peers, threat of dismissal from club
Punishment: Removal of positive events through time-out or response cost	Behavior is followed by temporary or permanent loss of positive events	Decrease in strength of behavior which results in loss of positive events	Smile, approval, affection, money, privilege, group membership

Note. From *Learning and Behavior Characteristics of Exceptional Children and Youth: A Humanistic Behavioral Approach* (p. 210) by William I. Gardner, 1977, Boston: Allyn and Bacon. Copyright 1977 by Allyn and Bacon. Reprinted by permission.

their use may be somewhat frustrating. A teacher may be unable to identify or control all the classroom reinforcers. In addition, the effect of extinction procedures is not always immediate; there may even be a temporary increase in the student's undesirable behavior before it decreases. For example, the frequency of Ann's tantrums might increase until she realizes the teacher's attention can be gained only by exhibiting appropriate behaviors.

Some inappropriate behaviors should be ignored from the outset (e.g., occasional call-outs, brief whisperings). Behaviors falling into this category are (a) those of short duration that are not likely to spread or persist, (b) minor deviations from classroom rules, and (c) behaviors where a reaction from the teacher would interrupt a lesson or draw undue attention to the behavior. Procedures that decrease behaviors more rapidly (such as punishment or overcorrection) should be considered if the behavior to be reduced is harmful to others (such as fighting) or if it causes a major disruption of the classroom (such as yelling or stealing).

The presentation of an aversive event following a behavior is called **punishment.** Examples of punishers are verbal reprimands, criticism, and low grades. Two of the milder punishment procedures often used in the general education classroom are

response cost and time-out. In **response cost,** an inappropriate behavior is followed by the loss or withdrawal of earned reinforcers or privileges. In **time-out,** the student is removed from an event that is reinforcing, or reinforcement is withdrawn for a specified period of time. Time-out may involve **contingent observation** (viewing from the "sidelines"), exclusion time-out (excluding students from observing or participating in activities without leaving the room by, for example, turning their chair toward the wall or placing it behind a screen), or temporary removal from the room. Time-out is effective only if it is carefully planned and systematically implemented and if its effects are carefully evaluated and documented (Cuenin & Harris, 1986).

Punishment is a negative procedure that can rapidly decrease a behavior. However, it should be used only if more positive approaches are not appropriate or feasible. Before punishment is used with students with special needs, teachers should carefully check district and state policies and regulations regarding its use in a school setting as there is an increasing concern about the potential misuse of many negative procedures. In addition, the permission of their parents should always be obtained because punishment can harm students' self-concept and can produce avoidance, escape, or aggressive behaviors.

Punishment is most effective if it is combined with positive reinforcement. This combination will bring about more rapid and effective changes than the use of either procedure alone (Walker, 1995). For example, a student who runs in the classroom will learn appropriate behavior more quickly if he or she receives both positive reinforcers (such as praise and extra recess time) for walking and also punishers (such as loss of earned free time or verbal reprimands) for running.

Identify Consequences That Are Meaningful to Students

To have the desired effect on behavior, consequences must be meaningful to the student. This is true for both positive and negative consequences. A consequence that is positive for one person may be negative for another. For example, going to the library is positive for the book lover but not necessarily so for the sports addict; watching a football game may be a negative activity for those who like to play tennis or visit museums. In addition, the effect of a specific consequence on an individual can change under different conditions. Earning a dessert for completing classwork is reinforcing to a student under most conditions; however, an offer of a banana split for doing the dishes would not be appealing even to the most avid dessert lover who had just eaten a huge meal.

Educators often assume that students are motivated by grades; however, for many students with special needs, grades are aversive. They have received poor grades that resulted in ridicule from their peers and negative feedback from their parents and teachers. For them grades are no longer positive consequences, and other reinforcers must be found.

It is possible to misinterpret the potential effects of a consequence. A teacher may use verbal reprimands as an aversive consequence for inappropriate behavior. However, the teacher's attention may be a positive reinforcer for the student, regardless of the nature of the attention. On the other hand, verbal praise from a teacher may have the effect of a punisher; for instance, to adolescents, praise from a teacher may be distasteful if given in front of their peers.

Consequences must have meaning to their recipients. For instance, most teachers would soon tire of receiving grades instead of paychecks for their work. Pay is not bribery; it is the presentation of a meaningful reinforcer for hard work. Because the paycheck is negotiable, teachers can choose which secondary reinforcers they wish to purchase.

Beware of Noneducational Interventions

Periodically, methods that claim to bring about dramatic changes in the behavior of students appear in the field of education. Many of these are noneducational treatments and interventions. For example, special diets, medication, and therapies (e.g., relaxation therapy) may claim to solve academic and social problems. Teachers should exercise extreme caution in considering such approaches. Most are medical-type interventions; many have little empirical evidence to support their usefulness (Silver, 1987). Information about the use of drugs to manage hyperactivity and other behavior problems is presented in "Inclusion Tips for the Teacher."

Inclusion Tips for the Teacher

The Use of Drugs in Managing Hyperactivity

Authors such as Axelrod and Bailey (1979), Kauffman (1997), and Walker (1995) have discussed the concerns frequently raised about the effectiveness of drugs in managing hyperactivity and other inappropriate student behaviors. These experts have noted the need for continuing research in this area and indicate that teachers should approach the medical management of behavioral problems with due caution. Axelrod and Bailey suggest the following guidelines for the use of drug treatment in school settings:

1. Physical examinations should be prerequisites to commencing and continuing drug treatment. This is necessary not only to monitor possible physiological problems, but also to determine whether physical anomalies might be causing problem behaviors.
2. Drugs should be considered only when there is a demonstration of inordinately inappropriate behavior. . . . The mere claim from a parent or teacher that a child's behavior warrants drug treatment is insufficient.
3. Before drug treatment is implemented, behavior modification procedures or other remedial techniques should be attempted.
4. Children who receive drugs should be exposed to two different dosage levels, a baseline phase, and a placebo condition. Whenever possible,

drug and placebo conditions should be conducted in a double blind manner.
5. A continual, preferably daily, record of a child's behavior should be maintained. This should be done not only when attempting to determine a child's appropriate drug treatment, but throughout treatment.
6. The effects on at least one behavior that should increase and one behavior that should decrease should be monitored.
7. Minimal goals for each behavior of interest should be specified in advance. Only when drug treatment meets the prespecified goals should the treatment be continued.
8. During the course of drug treatment, the child should periodically be drug free. If the child's behavior again becomes disorderly, it may be concluded that the drugs were responsible for the previously noted improvement. If the child's behavior remains appropriate, it may be possible to permanently discontinue drug use.
9. Drug treatment should not be considered a permanent solution to a youngster's problems. When drug therapy is considered necessary, it might be combined with more standard educational procedures. As the package of techniques improves a student's behavior, it may be possible to wean the student from drug treatment. (pp. 547–548)

If questions arise, the teacher can consult the school nurse, counselor, special educator, or principal. Noneducational procedures should not be used with students with special needs unless the use of a particular procedure for a particular student has received the full endorsement of the team of professionals working with the student and the parents have given their informed consent.

METHODS FOR GATHERING DATA

Gathering data on the classroom behavior and study skills of students is an essential component of a behavior management program. Many special educators now use the term **functional analysis** to describe the systematic process used to collect data

that will help educators to (a) understand the factors contributing to the problem behavior and (b) develop effective methods for modifying the behavior (Walker, 1995). The problem behaviors exhibited by many students continue to persist because they "serve one of two purposes: (1) to obtain something or to produce a desired effect, or (2) to escape or avoid something" (Walker, p. 78).

General education teachers can collect information through informal techniques such as direct observation of behavior and behavior inventories. Teachers use such data to determine students' current levels of performance, identify antecedents and consequences that may influence behavior, determine the effectiveness of the intervention program, and communicate progress to students and parents.

Knowledge of progress can be a strong reinforcer for students.

Direct Observation of Behavior

The most useful method for gathering information on classroom behavior and study skills is the direct observation of student behavior. Observations are usually conducted in the classroom setting by the teacher, an aide, or a trained volunteer; in some cases, students can be trained to collect information on other students or on their own performances.

Although teachers observe students every day, such observations are usually not systematic or precise; general impressions do not provide enough information for planning intervention programs. Instead, direct observations should be carefully planned and should follow the steps outlined in the following paragraphs.

Specify the Behavior to Be Observed. The first task is to specify the behavior of interest to the teacher. This behavior must be described as specifically as possible. If it is stated clearly, two or more observers will be able to agree on whether the student has produced the behavior. Imprecise descriptions of behaviors make them difficult to observe and measure. The statements "Jack is hyperactive," "Mark is nasty," "Judy is restless," and "Sam has poor study habits" lack specificity and leave much to the interpretation of the observer. Descriptions such as "Louis hits other students," "Wen-Chi leaves her seat frequently," "Candy talks out without raising her hand," and "José doesn't turn in his homework assignments" are more precise.

At times, teachers may wish to collect data on the overall performance of a student in order to identify specific problem behaviors. Sulzer-Azaroff and Mayer (1977) suggest narrative recording or sequence analysis for this purpose. In **narrative recording,** the observer describes all the behaviors displayed by the student during the observation period; this record is then analyzed to determine whether there is any pattern in the student's behaviors. **Sequence analysis** is more systematic; the observer describes each behavior and attempts to identify its antecedent and consequence. Table 5–2 presents a portion of a sequence analysis of John's behavior during instruction. Examination of the events that precede and follow a behavior yields much more information than is obtained in a simple observation.

TABLE 5-2   Example of a Sequence Analysis

Time	Antecedent	Behavior	Consequence
9:05	Teacher asks the class a question.	John raises hand.	Teacher calls on Bill.
9:07	Teacher asks question.	John yells answer.	Teacher reprimands John.
9:11	Teacher asks question and reminds students to raise hands.	John raises hand.	Teacher calls on John and compliments him for raising his hand.

However, narrative recording and sequence analysis may not be practical ways for the general education teacher to collect data. The teacher may be unable to undertake a detailed observation such as this while managing all of the activities of a regular classroom. One solution is to have someone other than the classroom teacher conduct the observation; this person could be an instructional aide, an adult volunteer, a special education teacher or consultant, or even a peer tutor. Another technique is to develop a simpler observation system. In any event, when the task is to identify problem behaviors, it is important to consider not only the behavior itself but also the effect of antecedents and consequences on it.

Select a Measurement System. As soon as a behavior has been identified and specifically described, the system to observe and measure the behavior can be selected. There are several different types of behaviors, and their nature influences the kind of measurement system chosen. One type is that of permanent products such as completed assignments, worksheets, and essays, which are available for review at a later time. Other behaviors are more transitory; they must be observed at the time of the occurrence. Examples include fighting, verbal outbursts, stealing, and being out of one's seat. These behaviors may be discrete (i.e., like writing and talking, they have a definite beginning and ending), or they may be continuous (e.g., studying). Some transitory behaviors can be converted into permanent products if they are audio- or videotaped for later study.

Several methods of recording data are possible during an observation:

1. *Permanent product or work sample analysis.* A sample of the student's work is evaluated, and information such as the number of problems correct is recorded.
2. *Event recording.* The number of times a behavior occurs within a time interval is noted; for example, the teacher counts the number of times a student leaves her seat during one class period.
3. *Duration recording.* The length of time a behavior occurs is recorded; for example, the teacher times how long a student takes to complete an assignment.
4. *Interval recording.* The occurrence or nonoccurrence of a behavior is noted within a specific time interval; for example, the teacher might observe that Bill was reading his science book dur-

ing only two of the five 3-minute observation periods.

Which method to use depends on the type of behavior and the kind of data that will be most useful to the teacher. Also, the system must be easily implemented by the observer. Table 5–3 describes several kinds of information that result from the different recording systems: percentage, frequency, duration, and interval data.

Permanent product recording and **event recording** produce frequency data that can be converted into percentage data. Percentages and frequencies are appropriate measures for academic, classroom, and study skills behaviors. A teacher might be interested in the percentage of words read correctly or the percentage of time students spent on a task. Frequency data indicate the number of occurrences of a behavior. In order to compare

TABLE 5-3   Measures of Behavior

Measure	Derived From	Example	Application
Percent	Number of units correct out of number of total units recorded	8 math problems correct out of 10 total math problems: $\frac{8}{10} \times 100 = 80\%$ accuracy	When a measure of accuracy is of concern without regard for time or proficiency
Frequency	$\frac{\text{Count of behavior}}{\text{Observation time}}$	12 handraises in a 6-minute observation period: $\frac{12}{6} = 2$ handraises per minute	When it is desired to know how often a distinct behavior occurs within a period of time
Duration	Direct measures of length of time	A child tantrums for 15 minutes	When the total length of time a continuous behavior occurs is desired
Intervals	Number of fixed time units in which behavior occurred or didn't occur	Children are observed for 30 seconds, then the observer records whether or not behavior occurred during the interval. Observers then repeat the process. Usually data is expressed in terms of percentage of intervals during which behavior occurred. $\frac{5 \text{ intervals}}{10 \text{ intervals total}} \times 100 = 50\%$ of intervals	When total duration is not possible and an estimation of the occurrence of continuous behavior is desired

frequencies, the teacher should be sure that observation periods are equal in length and that the student has the same opportunity to produce the behavior during each observation period. For example, results would be misleading if a student's questioning behavior during the teacher's lecture were compared with that student's questioning behavior during a discussion period. Frequency data gathered during unequal observation periods can be more easily compared if they are transformed into rate information, which is simply the number of times a behavior occurs within a certain period (e.g., 8 times per minute; 17 times per hour). Examples of rate data are the number of math problems completed correctly per minute or the number of tantrums per day. Rate and percentage data are easy to compare. For instance, it is possible to compare the percentage of correct responses or the rate of reading words from one day to the next even if the student does not read the same number of words per day.

Duration recording is useful if the length of time the student engages in a behavior is of interest. For example, teachers might note the amount of time students require to line up for lunch or the time a student takes to begin work after the teacher gives directions. Duration can be reported in actual time units (e.g., Katie cried for 14 minutes; Elijah now starts his work within 15 seconds after the teacher gives his group the assignment) or as a percentage (e.g., Ralph was out of his seat 10% of the school day).

Interval recording is particularly useful for the teacher of a general education class because it does not require that students be observed continuously. McLoughlin and Lewis (1994) describe several of the different interval recording systems:

> With these techniques, the observer determines whether a behavior occurs during a specified time period. The class day, period, or activity is broken down into short intervals of a few minutes or even a few seconds, and a record of the presence or absence of the target behavior is kept for each interval. These techniques can also be used with discrete behaviors if a complete record of every occurrence is not necessary.
>
> Several variations of interval recording and time sampling are available.
>
> • *Whole-interval recording.* The student is observed for the entire interval, and the observer notes if the target behavior occurs continuously throughout the interval. Observation intervals are very brief, usually only a few seconds.
> • *Partial-interval time recording.* The student is observed for the entire interval, but the observer notes

only if the behavior occurred at least once during the interval. Again, time intervals are very brief.
> • *Momentary time sampling.* The student is observed only at the end of each interval; at that time, the observer checks to see if the behavior is occurring. Intervals are usually longer—3, 5, or even 15 minutes—making this a more convenient method for classroom teachers. However, it is less accurate than [whole- or partial-] interval recording techniques because much of the student's behavior goes unobserved. (p. 99)

Figure 5–3 provides an example of the use of momentary time sampling with an entire class. In this example, the teacher was interested in determining what percentage of the class was on-task during reading instruction. The same observation system could also be used with individual students or small groups.

Decide Who Will Observe and How Often Observations Will Occur. Observers must be able to record data accurately and consistently. If the teacher is the only adult in the classroom, the kind and frequency of observations that are possible may be limited. However, the teacher can record data while conducting instruction or while assisting students; devices such as clipboards, data sheets, stopwatches, and counters are helpful. Some behaviors can be self-recorded if students are monitored by the teacher and reinforced for accurate recording. For more information about conducting observations in the general education classroom, see "Inclusion Tips for the Teacher" on page 130.

The frequency of observations depends on several factors, including the availability of the student, the type of behavior being observed, the observation system, and the availability of the observer. Data collection should occur frequently, but observations usually require only a short period each day. The observation must be long enough to obtain an accurate picture of the student's behavior. The time of day or the length of the observation should be adjusted if the teacher believes that this sample of behavior is not typical. Observations that occur for shorter periods over several days provide more accurate data concerning student behavior than monitoring efforts that occur over one or two longer time periods (Walker, 1995).

Collect and Graph Baseline Data. Before any intervention is begun **baseline data** are collected under the natural conditions of the classroom.

FIGURE 5-3   Observation Using Momentary Time Sampling

Student(s) observed:	Entire class
Behavior observed:	Number of students on-task, working on independent assignment or actively partici-pating in assigned group activity
Measurement system:	Momentary time sampling (observer determines the number of students on-task at the end of each interval)
Length of interval:	5 minutes
Time of measurement:	Reading instruction time (9:00–9:52 a.m.)
Data recorded:	Number of students on-task/Number of students in class (percentage can be calculated for each observation or for the entire period)
Results:	Over the entire time scheduled for reading instruction, 62% of the students in the class were on-task. However, the percentage of students on-task decreased as the class pro-gressed.

Observation Time	Data	Observation Time	Data
9:05	24/30 = 80%	9:30	18/30 = 60%
9:10	27/30 = 90%	9:35	15/30 = 50%
9:15	24/30 = 80%	9:40	12/30 = 40%
9:20	21/30 = 70%	9:45	15/30 = 50%
9:25	21/30 = 70%	9:50	9/30 = 30%

Class totals: 186/300 = 62%

Baseline data are generally gathered for at least 5 days to ensure that the extremes of the behavior have been established. These data, recorded on a graph, are used to determine the rate or magnitude of the problem, to suggest possible interventions, and later to set the standard for evaluating the effectiveness of instruction. Baseline data may indicate that the behavior believed inappropriate is not as frequent or intense as hypothesized; if so, a behavior change program is not necessary. When the teacher is sure that the desired behavior is not part of the student's repertoire or when a behavior is injurious to the student or others, baseline data need not be collected.

Graphing data permits the teacher and student to easily see the behavior and its rate of occurrence. Graphs can present baseline data, progress during intervention, and later the maintenance of behavior after intervention has been discontinued. Graphs are an excellent way to communicate progress to parents and other educators. Figure 5–4 presents an example of a graph that could be used in the classroom.

Collect Data During Interventions. Data collected during the intervention phase help the teacher determine whether the intervention is having the desired effect on behavior. The teacher can then decide whether the intervention program should continue as originally developed or be modified to improve its effectiveness.

Intervention data should be gathered for a minimum of 5 days. Longer data collection periods permit a more careful evaluation of the program's effectiveness. Figure 5–4 shows information collected by the teacher about Elsie's completion of assignments. During the intervention phase, Elsie was rewarded with 3 minutes in the game center for each assignment she finished on time; this was the only way Elsie could earn time in the game center, an activity she enjoyed very much. After 1 week, Elsie's teacher decided that the intervention was working and that it should be continued.

Informal Assessment

Informal behavioral assessment is another method of gathering data about student performance. Teacher-made or commercially prepared behavior rating scales and inventories designed to provide information about the student's present level of functioning are used to identify potential target behaviors that may need modification. They are most useful as screening devices, suggesting areas for further assessment by direct observation of behavior.

Inclusion Tips for the Teacher

Techniques for Conducting Observations in the General Education Classroom

One typical concern of general education teachers is that they do not have time to set up and run behavior management programs. They are busy teaching 30 or more students and cannot drop everything to systematically observe the behavior of a specific pupil. However, several techniques allow the teacher to conduct observations while carrying on regular instructional activities. It is not necessary to stop teaching to observe; in fact, it is almost impossible to teach without observing! Try the following suggestions for integrating observations into your classroom procedures:

1. Carry a small card such as an index card; on it list the names of one or two target students and the problem behaviors you wish to observe (e.g., hitting, being out-of-seat, talking to others). Place a tally mark on the card (and possibly the time of the behavior) each time the behavior occurs. Start this system with one or two students and gradually expand it as your skills improve.
2. Require students to record on their in-class work their starting and finishing time. This approach permits the calculation of rate as well as frequency and accuracy data. Students can also note the times they leave and return to their desks; then the total amount of time in-seat each day or each period can be calculated.
3. Carry a stopwatch to measure the duration of behaviors. For example, start the watch each time Maynard leaves his seat, and stop it when he returns. Continue this (without resetting the watch) and time each occurrence of the behavior. At the end of the observation period, note the total amount of time recorded.
4. To count behaviors without interfering with the operation of the class, use wrist counters (golf counters), supermarket counters, paper clips moved from one pocket to another, navy beans in a cup, and other inexpensive devices.
5. Have a seating chart in front of you as you talk to the class. Place a tally mark by a student's name for each target behavior, such as asking a question, talking out, or answering a question correctly.
6. Recruit volunteers to observe in the classroom. Older students, parents, senior citizens, college students, or other students in the class can be excellent observers. If the teacher has developed a method to record the data and clearly stated the behavior to be observed, a nonprofessional should be able to conduct the observation.

FIGURE 5-4
Graphing Baseline and Intervention Data

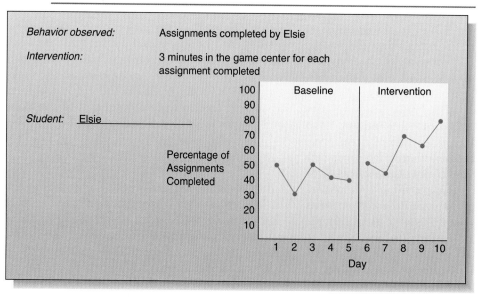

Behavior observed: Assignments completed by Elsie

Intervention: 3 minutes in the game center for each assignment completed

Student: Elsie

FIGURE 5-5 Behavior Inventory

	Rating
Cooperation	
Continually disrupts classroom; unable to inhibit responses	1
Frequently demands attention; often speaks out of turn	2
Waits his/her turn; average for age and grade	3
Above average; cooperates well	4
Excellent ability; cooperates well without adult encouragement	5
Attention	
Never attentive; very distractible	1
Rarely listens; attention frequently wanders	2
Attention adequate for age and grade	3
Above average in attention; almost always attends	4
Always attends to important aspects; long attention span	5
Organization	
Highly disorganized; very slovenly	1
Often disorganized in manner of working; inexact, careless	2
Maintains average organization of work; careful	3
Above-average organization; organizes and completes work	4
Highly organized; completes assignments in meticulous manner	5
Completion of Assignments	
Never finishes even with guidance	1
Seldom finishes even with guidance	2
Average performance; follows through on assignments	3
Above-average performance; completes assignments without urging	4
Always completes assignments without supervision	5
Tactfulness	
Always rude	1
Usually disregards feelings of others	2
Average tact; behavior occasionally inappropriate socially	3
Above average in tactfulness; behavior rarely inappropriate socially	4
Always tactful; behavior never socially inappropriate	5

Note. From *The Pupil Rating Scale Revised* by H. R. Myklebust, 1981, New York: Grune & Stratton. Copyright 1981 by Grune & Stratton. Reprinted by permission.

Informal measures should reflect the behavioral expectations of the teacher. Rating scales and inventories, like task analyses, generally break broad categories of behavior into smaller subcomponents. In constructing or selecting an inventory, the teacher should be sure that all important aspects of classroom behavior are included. Figure 5–5 shows a portion of the personal-social behavior section of the *Pupil Rating Scale Revised* (Myklebust, 1981), with which the teacher (or other educators or the parents) can rate each student on behaviors such as cooperation, attention, and organization. Because measures such as these rely somewhat upon the in-

terpretation of their users, results may be less objective and less precise than those obtained with direct observation of behavior.

POSITIVE STRATEGIES FOR MANAGING AND IMPROVING BEHAVIOR

Teachers can use several strategies in the management of classroom behavior and the development of study skills. Most effective are intervention programs based on student performance data; these programs help students learn new behaviors, increase or maintain appropriate behaviors, and decrease inappropriate behaviors. Because classroom and study skills are learned behaviors, many of the principles of instruction presented in chapter 4 remain applicable.

The goal in behavior management is to establish a learning environment in which students are accepted as individuals but in which there are definite guidelines for acceptable classroom conduct. This goal is communicated most effectively to students by positive behavior change approaches. Students understand the need for guidelines and accept them if they are applied fairly, equally, and consistently. However, questions may arise when behavior change programs are used with some students but not with others. See "Inclusion Tips for the Teacher" on page 133 for ideas on how to handle this situation.

Managing and improving classroom behavior is a systematic process of identifying expected student behaviors, analyzing student performance to see whether it meets expectations, and implementing interventions when necessary. Figure 5–6 presents the step-by-step process followed by the teacher to plan, develop, implement, evaluate, and revise interventions.

The need for intervention can be reduced through preventive planning. Expectations for behavior should be communicated to students; students who meet expectations should receive positive reinforce-

ment. If intervention is needed, the least intrusive approach should be attempted first; often a change in seating, a careful explanation of class rules, a demonstration of the expected behavior, or a mild reprimand in private can eliminate the problem. Intensive behavior change programs should be used only when less dramatic methods have proven to be unsuccessful.

FIGURE 5-6   Systematic Behavior Management Model

1. State the behavioral expectations for all students.
2. Determine whether students meeting expectations are receiving reinforcement to encourage maintenance of these behaviors.
3. Determine whether some students do not meet expectations. If so, do they know and understand the expectations? Do they have the prerequisite skills for the behaviors?
4. For students with inappropriate behaviors, identify target behaviors to be achieved.
5. Select an observation system, and collect baseline data on each behavior.
6. Analyze data to determine the need for an intervention program.
7. If data indicate the need for an intervention, determine whether the target behavior needs to be learned, increased, or decreased.
8. Select (or design) the intervention that uses the most positive approach.
9. Implement the intervention.
10. Collect data on student performance.
11. Analyze the data to determine the need to continue, modify, or terminate the intervention. Take required action.
12. When the behavior is at the desired level and is no longer dependent on the intervention, continue to collect maintenance data and return to step 4.

Inclusion Tips for the Teacher

Explaining Special Behavior Programs to General Education Peers

Differential treatment of students is often a concern to teachers. However, no teacher is able to treat all students exactly alike, and students themselves realize that some may require a different type of instruction or additional attention from the teacher. In an individualized classroom, special interventions designed to improve the behavior of one or two target students should draw little attention. Try the following suggestions when implementing behavior change programs in the classroom:

1. If questions do arise, explain that each student has different needs, and some may need special help, special reinforcers, or other program modifications to enable them to learn appropriate social and academic skills.
2. Do not expect to place every student on a different special program. Instead, design programs for the entire class. For example, class members might earn points for assignments completed, books read, and so on. This type of system can be easily adjusted so that one or

two students can earn additional reinforcers for accomplishment of special target behaviors.
3. An intervention program should interfere as little as possible with the operation of the class. Teachers can provide students with reinforcers without interrupting classroom activities and without calling attention to the student in question. However, it is essential that the student being reinforced knows it! The teacher can make a mark on the chalkboard, give the student a silent signal, write on a card at the student's desk, or place poker chips or other tokens in a jar.
4. Include other students in the program. Rewarding nearby classmates when the target student is successful often contributes to the effectiveness of the program and the classmates' attitudes toward the special student.
5. Teachers using programs that base decisions on data and careful manipulation of antecedents and consequences find that the benefits of the approach far outweigh its disadvantages.

Establish Behavioral Expectations and Communicate Them to Students

Students are often unaware of the behavioral expectations for a specific classroom situation. Although more able students are capable of interpreting expectations from environmental cues (e.g., teacher signals, behavior of other students), students with behavior problems often do not interpret these cues. They need specific direction and instruction to know how they are expected to act. Effective classroom managers have been found to be particularly skilled in establishing classroom rules and procedures that communicate behavioral expectations to students (Doyle, 1986). Research results suggest that effective teachers take the following measures:

1. *Establish classroom rules and procedures at the start of the year.* Effective managers do not wait until problems occur; they anticipate potential problems prior to the beginning of school.

2. *Introduce rules and procedures on the first day of the class.* When rules and procedures are communicated to students immediately (from the beginning of the first day of school), they need not guess what the expectations are. Information overload is avoided by introducing the most essential rules and procedures first and presenting others as they are needed. The rules are posted or given to students as a handout, and new students are immediately oriented to the classroom expectations when they arrive in class.
3. *Explain rules and procedures clearly and teach them deliberately to students as part of a system for classroom operation.* A rationale is provided and instruction continues until the students have the rules and procedures mastered.
4. *Make rules and procedures concrete, functional, and explicit so that they contribute to the accomplishment of work and the order of the classroom.* The statements should be few, clear, and plainly stated. They should indicate the desired

behavior (e.g., "Work quietly at your desk," "Respect other people's property") rather than all the undesired behaviors (e.g., "Don't talk when you are working at your desk," "Don't write on the desks").

5. *Associate rules and procedures with clear signals that indicate when students are to carry out or stop specific behaviors or activities.* For instance, the teacher may use a specific phrase (e.g., "Please close your books and straighten your materials") to indicate that it is time to stop the current activity and quietly prepare to move to the next class or activity. In addition, the teacher may need to remind students about acceptable conduct prior to activities that are likely to elicit inappropriate behaviors (e.g., "You may sharpen your pencil but remember not to talk to others").

6. *Demonstrate or model rules and procedures and then allow students to rehearse them.* The teacher demonstrates both the correct and incorrect forms of the behavior (e.g., sitting at a desk, getting to the pencil sharpener). The demonstration enables the students to discriminate the dimensions of the behavior. Students are then given an opportunity to practice the required behavior. Mastering rules and procedures is similar to learning academics; it requires teacher instruction and feedback combined with student practice.

7. *Design rules and procedures to anticipate possible classroom interruptions or problems and to manage these situations.* For example, students may be expected to continue working when classroom visitors enter the room or to stop all activities immediately and line up quickly and quietly when there is a fire drill. Although these events may occur infrequently, expectations should be established and practiced.

8. *Monitor closely how well students follow rules and procedures.* Appropriate behavior is reinforced, and inappropriate behavior is stopped promptly. The teacher must be able to enforce the rules and procedures that are specified; failure to do so diminishes or eliminates their effectiveness. Rules should be modified or eliminated if they prove to be ineffective, unenforceable, or no longer needed. Specific teacher practices for monitoring and enforcing rules and classroom behaviors are presented throughout this chapter.

Prevent Inappropriate Conduct by Monitoring Behavior and Providing Feedback

To prevent behavior problems from occurring, teachers must be constantly aware of the behavior of their students and provide them with feedback regarding their performance. This process is as important in developing and maintaining appropriate classroom conduct and study skills as it is in providing academic instruction.

Two important skills related to preventing behavior problems have been identified by the research on effective teaching. These are (a) the ability to simultaneously monitor one or more groups while directing the activities of another and (b) the ability to direct the activities of those students who are not involved in the lesson being conducted by the teacher (Englert, 1984). The first skill requires that teachers position themselves to permit a continual visual scanning of the entire class so that they can observe and make eye contact with students not involved in the lesson. The second skill involves more than observation; it requires that the teacher respond to the observed behavior with verbal or nonverbal signals (e.g., frown, finger point, head nod) that will redirect the student to the assigned task. Effective managers do this without interrupting the lesson they are conducting.

The combination of providing positive attention for appropriate behavior and ignoring inappropriate behavior is frequently advocated for decreasing behavior problems. However, it is more effective to use positive attention for appropriate behavior together with the careful use of **negative attention** (i.e., a verbal or nonverbal response indicating disapproval) for inappropriate behavior (Jones & Eimers, 1975; Jones & Miller, 1974). This combination can be implemented without interfering with the activities of the classroom if teachers follow certain guidelines:

1. *Identify potentially disruptive behaviors at an early stage.* The teacher anticipates the need to act by observing student actions that are likely to lead to inappropriate behaviors.

2. *Develop a repertoire of quick, low-intensity gestures and verbalizations that signify that a student is not following the accepted guidelines.* For example, the teacher may say "John" (student's name)

or "That's all" to get the student's attention and identify the current activity as inappropriate.

3. *Establish physical proximity to the disruptive student and orient yourself toward the student.* This strategy may involve the teacher's moving closer to the student and facing him or her to signal that the teacher is aware of, and does not approve of, the student's behavior. At the same time, the teacher maintains direction of an instructional group. Teacher movement around the room and a tight horseshoe arrangement of desks facilitate the use of this procedure.

4. *Promptly respond to inappropriate student behavior.* The teacher uses negative attention to interrupt the student's disruptiveness before it can produce approval or attention from peers.

5. *With negative attention, use a facial expression and tone of voice that is consistent with disapproval.* It is important to communicate to the offending student that the teacher is registering disapproval.

6. *After negative attention, provide immediate reinforcement and attention when the student displays the appropriate behavior.* This identifies the accepted behavior and reaffirms that appropriate behaviors are reinforced and inappropriate behaviors are punished.

7. *If necessary, use prompting to elicit the desired behavior, and then reinforce the student immediately.* Effective teachers actually require misbehaving students to practice the appropriate behavior until they have exhibited it at the established criterion level; these teachers often drill students until they perform the behavior automatically.

Reinforce Appropriate Behavior

It would be wonderful if all students behaved appropriately in school because their teachers expected them to or because it was intrinsically rewarding. However, this expectation is simply not realistic for many students. Teachers need to help students learn that accomplishments themselves can be rewarding. To do this, a powerful tool—reinforcement—is available.

When appropriate behaviors occur, they should be rewarded. To be effective, the reinforcer should follow the desired behavior. Rewards should not be provided when students promise to exhibit the behavior at some time in the future. Only performance is rewarded. *If* the student behaves appropriately, *then* the reward will occur. Appropriate behaviors should also be reinforced immediately. Reinforcers are most effective when delivered immediately after the occurrence of the behavior. For example, if the target behavior is completion of assignments, the student should be reinforced when handing in his or her paper. The reinforcer would lose its effect if it were delivered several hours later, after the teacher had corrected the paper.

When students are learning new behaviors, each occurrence should be reinforced. Continuous reinforcement rewards an appropriate behavior every time it happens. This is the most effective schedule for establishing a new behavior or for increasing the occurrence of an infrequent behavior. As soon as the behavior has become established, the reinforcers can be delivered according to one of the intermittent schedules described in Table 5–4; intermittent reinforcement requires less attention than the continuous schedule. If reduction in reinforcement is gradual, the student will eventually maintain the desired behavior with little reinforcement. Schedules of reinforcement should move from continuous to fixed interval/ratio and then to variable interval/ratio. With variable schedules, students are less able to predict when reinforcement will occur because reinforcers are given after an average period of time (interval) or after an average number of responses (ratio). For example, a variable ratio of 1:10 may deliver the reinforcer after 8 responses, then 7, then 13, as long as the *average* is 1 reinforcer for every 10 responses.

Provide Reinforcers That Are Valued by Students

Reinforcers of little value to students soon lose their effect. The simplest method of finding out what students perceive as rewarding is to ask them. Figure 5–7 on page 137 is an example of an inventory that can be used to discover students' reinforcement preferences. Another method of gaining this information is to observe how students use their free time.

It is also important to use a variety of reinforcers. Of the many types available, those that have strong effects on behavior are preferred. Following are several types of reinforcers found to be useful in the classroom:

TABLE 5-4 Properties of Four Types of Intermittent Schedules of Reinforcement

Name of Schedule	Definition of Schedule	Effects on Behavior	
		Schedule in Effect	Schedule Terminated (Extinction)
Fixed Ratio (FR)	Reinforcer is given after each X responses.	High response rate.	Irregular burst of responding. More responses than in continuous reinforcement, less than in variable ratio.
Variable Ratio (VR)	Reinforcer is given after X responses on the average.	Very high response rates; the higher the ratio the higher the rate.	Very resistant to extinction; maximum number of responses before extinction.
Fixed Interval (FI)	Reinforcer is given for first response to occur after each X minutes.	Stops working after reinforcement; works hard just prior to time for next reinforcement.	Slow, gradual decrease in responding.
Variable Interval (VI)	Reinforcer is given for first response after each X minutes, on the average.	Steady rate of responding.	Very resistant to extinction; maximum time to extinction.

Note. From *The Acting-Out Child: Coping with Classroom Disruption* (2nd ed., p. 127) by Hill M. Walker, 1995, Longmont, CO: Sopris West. Copyright 1995 by Hill M. Walker. Reprinted by permission.

1. *Social reinforcement.* Social attention or interaction with teachers and peers is a strong reinforcer for most students. It is easy to deliver and is naturally available in the school environment. It can be provided immediately after the occurrence of the desired behavior, and the effects can be generalized to other settings. When social reinforcement is provided, the teacher should tell the student the reason for the reward. The teacher can say (or write on the student's paper), "Good reading," "Nice job on the assignment," "I like the way you lined up for recess," or "Your handwriting is very easy to read." The teacher can also try smiles and, for younger students, hugs; these and other forms of positive attention are easy to give, free, and the supply is unlimited.

2. *Activity reinforcers.* Activities are also strong reinforcers. Any activity that the student enjoys can serve as a reward for the performance of a less desired task. This approach is known as the **Premack Principle.** If Joe finishes his math, then he can feed the gerbil; or if the class works quietly all morning, then they will see a movie after lunch. Other examples of activity reinforcers are spending time in the listening center, watching television, reading comics or magazines, helping the teacher, and watching filmstrips. These reinforcers are readily available in the school and involve minimal cost.

3. *Tangible reinforcers.* Objects such as certificates, notes to parents, toys, and school supplies can also serve as reinforcers for students. However, tangible reinforcers should be used only after social and activity reinforcers have proved too weak to support the occurrence of the behavior. When tangible reinforcers are delivered, they should always be accompanied by a social reinforcer; over time, the tangible reinforcer can be gradually faded so that it is replaced by just the use of the social reward. Disadvantages of tangible reinforcers include their cost (in terms of money or time to prepare) and a possible loss of effectiveness if they are provided too frequently. In addition, many parents and educators disagree with their use. Because they are not universally available, their effects may not generalize to other school settings.

4. *Edible reinforcers.* The use of edibles should be considered only if social, activity, and tangible reinforcers have been found ineffective. Edibles have disadvantages similar to those of tangible reinforcers. If edibles are used, their presentation should always be paired with the delivery of a social reinforcer.

F I G U R E   5 - 7   Reinforcement Inventory

1. If you could do anything you wanted to do this afternoon, how would you spend your time?_____
_____

2. Name your three favorite television shows:_____
_____
_____

3. What is your favorite thing to do in each of these seasons:
summer _____   fall _____
winter _____   spring _____

4. If someone gave you $5 today, how would you spend it? _____

5. What is the best movie you ever saw? _____

6. Who is the adult you like the best? _____

7. Name your three favorite foods:_____
_____
_____

8. If you could play a quiet game with anybody in this school, who would you play with? _____
_____

9. What are your three wishes?_____
_____
_____

10. What do you like to read about?_____

Finish these sentences:

11. When I'm alone, I like to_____

12. It makes me really happy when my teacher_____
_____

13. When I grow up, I_____

14. The most fun at home is when_____

15. If I could take home something from school, I would take home_____
_____

16. If I were the teacher in this room, I would
_____

Note. Reprinted with permission of Merrill, an imprint of Macmillan Publishing Company, from *The Resource Room* (p. 62) by M. F. Hawisher and M. L. Calhoun. Copyright 1978 Merrill Publishing Company, Columbus, Ohio.

5. *Negative reinforcers.* Unlike other forms of reinforcement, negative reinforcers are removed when the desired behavior occurs. For example, the teacher can eliminate 2 math problems for each 10 that are completed correctly. Or the teacher's frown can disappear when students begin working. Like the more positive reinforcers, these have a place in the classroom. When negative reinforcers produce the desired behavior, the student should be rewarded. For example, when the student begins to work, the teacher can stop frowning *and* praise the student for working.

The variety of reinforcers available in the classroom is limited only by the teacher's imagination. Additional examples are listed in "Inclusion Tips for the Teacher" on page 138. Remember, though, that social, activity, tangible, and edible reinforcers are rewards only if they are valued by the student.

Use Token Economies to Deliver Reinforcers

In a **token economy,** students are presented with tokens rather than reinforcers after the occurrence of a desired behavior. Such a system can be used with

Inclusion Tips for the Teacher

Classroom Reinforcers

Here are several examples of different types of reinforcers appropriate for use in school settings. Social and activity reinforcers have special appeal since they are usually available at no cost to the teacher.

	Social	Activity	Tangible	Edible
Elementary-aged students	Hug Positive comments: "Good job," "I like the way you raised your hand," "You really pay attention" Pat on the back	Helping teacher Popcorn party Being team leader Reading with a friend Time in the computer center Choosing game for P.E. Extra minutes of recess X minutes of free time Cleaning the chalkboard Eating lunch with teacher	Toys Crayons Pencils Erasers Paper Art materials Books Stars Good note to parents	Cereal Fruit Cake Nuts Popcorn Ice cream Sandwich Milk
Adolescents	Signal or gesture of approval Handshake Positive comment on appearance Positive comments: "Great job," "Best work I've seen," "Great to see you working so well"	Field trip Free time Early lunch Choosing class activity Listening to tape for X minutes Attending a concert	Pens Paper Rental of tapes/CDs School supplies Sports equipment Magazines Posters Positive note home	Teacher buys lunch Popcorn Chips Juice Candy Fruit Soft drinks

one student, small groups, or the entire class. Students collect the tokens—such as poker chips, gold stars, or points—and later trade them for backup reinforcers listed on a **reinforcement menu.** Tokens should be delivered as soon as the desired behavior has occurred and should always be paired with a social reinforcer. In setting up a token economy, the teacher should

• specify and define the behaviors that earn tokens;
• use tokens that are appropriate for the students;

• develop and post a menu that includes a variety of reinforcers and a wide range of costs—students should be able to "cash in" for either high- or low-cost reinforcers;
• allow students to help in developing the menu;
• revise the menu regularly to ensure variety;
• use a record system that is clear and cannot be sabotaged by students (who might add points or take the tokens of others);
• give students frequent opportunities to cash in (daily or at least several times per week);

FIGURE 5-8 Reinforcement Menu

Reinforcers	Points
Apple	10
Cookie	10
Pencil	10
Popcorn	10
Small candies	15
Large candies	45
Gum	45
Viewing educational videotape (10 minutes)	50
Viewing entertainment videotape (10 minutes)	100
Pen	100
Grab bag	100
Cassette tape recorder (rental)	100
Cassette tape or CD rental	150
Tokens for video games	150
Hamburger at fast-food restaurant	500
Free time	500
Time with the computer	500
Shampoo and set	500
Time for game with a friend	700
Lunch with the teacher	750
Blank cassette tapes or computer disks	1,000
Music tapes	1,500
CDs	2,500
Price as marked:	
Paperbacks of your choice	——
Magazines (Motorcycle, Car, Autocross, etc.)	——
Movie tickets/passes	——
Models	——
Computer software	——
Field trip	——

• set up a cash-in system that takes a minimal amount of time and does not disrupt the operation of the class;
• provide clear rules to staff for distribution of tokens; and
• gradually reduce the value of the tokens to increase reliance on more natural reinforcers.

Token systems have been shown to be effective with general education students and students with special needs (Smith, Finn, & Dowdy, 1993), and they are easily understood by teachers and students. The menu allows students to select their own rewards. Also, token systems accommodate students who have difficulty waiting for their reinforcers;

they can cash in when they want to. When the token economy is first set up, students tend to cash in frequently; however, as they grow accustomed to this system, they are able to wait for longer periods. Figure 5–8 presents a reinforcement menu that can be used in a token economy.

With Older Students, Use Contingency Contracts

Contingency contracts are written agreements between the student and teacher that indicate what the student must do to earn a specific reward. These agreements, like most contracts, are negotiated; both parties must accept the terms. Because they in-

FIGURE 5-9   Contingency Contract

Official Contract

Effective Dates: From _____ to _____
This contract involves an agreement between _____ and
                                        (Teacher/Parent)
_____. This agreement will be reviewed on the following
       (Student)
date(s) _____ and can be renegotiated at any time by
agreement of both parties.
When _____ (Student) does the following: _____
_____
_____
then _____ (Teacher/Parent) will: _____
_____
_____

According to this agreement the teacher/parent will provide the agreed-upon
reinforcers to the student only if he or she fulfills his or her part of the contract. If the student does not fulfill his or her part of the agreement, the reinforcers will be withheld.

Teacher/Parent Signature _____ Date _____
Student Signature _____ Date _____

---

volve negotiation and require students to assume responsibility for fulfilling their part of the bargain, contracts are probably best for older students.

Homme, Csanyi, Gonzales, and Rechs (cited in Blankenship & Lilly, 1981) provide the following rules for developing contracts in the classroom:

1. The contract payoff (reward) should be immediate.
2. Initial contracts should call for and reward small approximations.
3. Reward frequently with small amounts.
4. The contract should call for and reward accomplishment rather than obedience.
5. Reward the behavior after it occurs.
6. The contract must be fair.
7. The terms of the contract must be clear.
8. The contract must be honest.
9. The contract must be positive.
10. Contracting as a method must be used systematically. (p. 235)

A sample contract form, providing space for recording the agreement that has been negotiated between the student and the teacher, is shown in Figure 5–9. A good contract identifies the responsibilities of both parties and the consequences if the terms are not fulfilled.

Teach Behaviors by Shaping

Shaping involves the reinforcement of successive approximations or small, progressive steps toward the desired behavior. The technique of shaping is used to teach new behaviors or increase the occurrence of behaviors exhibited infrequently. For example, shaping can be used with a student who completes only one or two assignments per week, when the desired behavior is eight assignments per day. First, a target of one completed assignment per day is established. This is reinforced until the student regularly finishes the daily work. Then the target is raised to two, then three assignments, and so on, as the student progresses toward the ultimate goal of eight assignments per day. For the student who completes no assignments, the beginning target might be a few problems or items of each assignment; this goal would be gradually increased toward the classroom goal of eight completed assignments per day.

Use Modeling to Improve Student Behavior

Modeling involves the reinforcement of another individual, the model, for exhibiting the desired behavior in the presence of the target student. The target student is then reinforced when he or she imitates the modeled behavior. For example, the model seated near the target student might be reinforced for studying; the teacher clearly identifies the reason for the reinforcement by saying, "I like the way you are working quietly in your seat." When this behavior is imitated by the target student, he or she is also rewarded.

Consider Involving Peers in Behavioral Programs

Involving class members in implementing programs designed to improve student behavior can be effective. Students can often provide strong reinforcers for the behavior of their peers, and in many cases they are able to monitor and respond to behaviors that the teacher might miss. The use of peers can involve either individual or group programs.

Group contingencies involve establishing a criterion level for the entire group, and the distribution of reinforcement to individual class members is based on the performance of the entire group. For example, a teacher concerned with the high number of talk-outs (average of 45 per day) could establish a system in which the entire class earns 5 minutes of extra recess if there were no more than 20 talk-outs the previous day. As the students improve, the teacher can gradually reduce the number of talk-outs accepted (e.g., they might be reduced by 1 each week).

Team-based contingencies involve grouping students into teams that compete against each other. As with group contingencies, individual students can help or hurt their team. A teacher wishing to increase the amount of homework completed might establish a prize based on the percentage of assign-

ments completed for the week. The prize (i.e., consequence) could be awarded in one of several different ways: (a) only the team with the highest percentage wins, (b) each team wins that reaches a percentage higher than a preset criterion (e.g., 95%), or (c) the prize earned by each team is based on the percentage of assignments completed by that team (e.g., a team completing 50% of the assignments earns 30 minutes in the computer area, whereas the team that completes 100% earns 1 hour). Greater changes are usually achieved by dividing groups into teams than by concentrating on whole groups.

Another way of involving peers is to have group members share in the consequences earned by a particular student. A rather withdrawn student in a general education class might earn points for each social interaction with a peer. Peers might seek to increase their interactions with that student if the entire class receives an extra minute of recess for every 10 points earned by the student. Similarly, a student who is easily distracted might experience fewer interruptions from classmates if they are all earning reinforcers for increases in the student's on-task behavior.

Peers can be trained to reinforce students such as the withdrawn or distractible students described above. They might provide the reinforcement for such students, especially if they earn reinforcers for the other student's performance. They might also be used to record the other student's performance (e.g., actual interactions or the amount of on-task behavior); these data may be more accurate than teacher-collected data.

Although such programs can be effective, teachers must consider several factors before involving peers in interventions. First, all the students involved must be able to perform the desired behavior. Otherwise, students may be subjected to potential physical or verbal abuse. Second, individual students should not be able to subvert the efforts of the group. Third, students should not be able to do the work required of others in order to improve the performance of their group. The interactions resulting from these programs can be very reinforcing to the students involved, and they often lead to improved transfer of behaviors and to positive interactions outside the typical classroom setting. As with other interventions, careful planning increases the likelihood of success.

Involve Students in Managing Their Own Behavior

Students can be directly involved in managing their own behavior by (a) participating in setting goals, (b) self-monitoring, or (c) assisting in the intervention itself by evaluating their own performance and rewarding themselves for appropriate behavior (Graham, Harris, & Reid, 1998; Prater, 1994; Reid, 1996). If they learn techniques that help improve their behavior in one setting, they can often transfer those skills to other settings.

Teachers can identify several areas in which students need to improve their behavior. The students themselves, especially those at the secondary level, can help to set goals for improvement in these areas, or they can choose other areas of need. Assisting in identifying goals increases students' active involvement in improving their own behavior.

Self-monitoring can take a number of forms. Students may simply be required to judge whether they are "working" at the end of each 5- to 10-minute segment of the class period or at the time a teacher-set buzzer rings. They might also record and graph their daily spelling performance, the number of times they leave their desk, or the length of time they are away from their desk each day. In addition, the number of talk-outs or the number of social interactions they initiate can be recorded by the students. Self-monitoring needs to be supervised by the teacher, with reinforcement provided for accu-

racy; reinstruction should be provided if the data are not consistent with those collected by the teacher. Self-monitoring decreases the demands on the teacher for collecting data, and it also makes students acutely aware of their own behavior.

A variety of interventions can be self-administered by students. They can learn to evaluate and self-reinforce their own performance in class. For example, they might give themselves points or check marks for improving their spelling performance or for reducing the amount of time they are out of their seats during a day. Self-punishment might involve deducting points for talking out in class or failing to complete a homework assignment. Other approaches might involve teaching students a strategy to use in resolving various kinds of problems they encounter. Students might be taught to ask specific questions or to make specific self-statements (i.e., **self-instruction**) to help themselves develop problem-solving skills (e.g., "What am I supposed to do? What is my plan? How do I do it?"). A combination of these various approaches (e.g., self-instruction followed by self-reinforcement) can actively involve students in improving their own behavior. It also increases the chance of the intervention's success and the generalization of newly learned skills to other situations.

Involve Parents in Behavior Management Programs

Parents are often willing and helpful participants in behavior management programs. They can provide continuation of the intervention program at home; for instance, parents can reinforce students for time spent doing homework. They can also assist by providing reinforcers for the school behavior of their children. For example, if students earn a certain number of points in school, parents can provide a special activity, such as a camping trip, or a gift, like a baseball glove or doll.

Positive notes to parents from teachers can be reinforcing both for students and for parents. Many parents of special students have received few good reports from school. A note from a teacher praising the accomplishments of a student can increase the level of praise that the student receives at home.

Before involving parents in intervention programs, teachers should be sure that the parents are willing and able to implement procedures consistently. If home and school programs are not well

FIGURE 5-10   **Are You Managing the Classroom Effectively?**

Respond to each item in terms of the extent to which it describes yourself: (1) not at all descriptive, (2) descriptive to a small extent, (3) descriptive to a moderate extent, (4) descriptive to a large extent, (5) descriptive to an extremely large extent.

Competencies

Classroom Set-up and Organization

1.1	Arranges physical space and instructional materials to minimize disruptive movement around classroom and to facilitate easy access to high-use materials.	1 2 3 4 5
1.2	Establishes and implements minimally disruptive traffic patterns and procedures.	1 2 3 4 5
1.3	Establishes and implements procedures for nonacademic class business (e.g., tardiness, material use, movement in and out of room, distributing materials, talk among students, bathroom breaks).	1 2 3 4 5
1.4	Establishes and implements procedures for academic business (e.g., seatwork procedures, obtaining help, volunteer behavior during small group, learning centers, set-up and takedown of lessons).	1 2 3 4 5

Teaching Rules and Procedures

2.1	Communicates clearly what behavior will be tolerated and what will not.	1 2 3 4 5
2.2	Gives behavior reminders and statements of desired behavior in advance of activity.	1 2 3 4 5
2.3	Clearly introduces rules, procedures, and consequences at beginning of school year and whenever needed.	1 2 3 4 5
2.4	States rules, posts rules, and provides discussion of rules at the time of their introduction.	1 2 3 4 5
2.5	Presents examples and non-examples of rules and procedures.	1 2 3 4 5
2.6	Requires student rehearsal of rules and procedures.	1 2 3 4 5
2.7	Monitors rule compliance and provides specific behavioral feedback.	1 2 3 4 5
2.8	Consequates rule noncompliance by stopping inappropriate behavior immediately and requiring students to practice the procedure until it is performed automatically.	1 2 3 4 5

Maintaining Rules and Procedures

3.1	Positions self in the room to provide high degree of visibility (e.g., can make eye contact with all students).	1 2 3 4 5
3.2	Scans constantly and makes eye contact with all students on an equal basis.	1 2 3 4 5
3.3	Detects disruptive behavior early and cites rule or procedure in responding to disruptive behavior.	1 2 3 4 5
3.4	Reinforces appropriate performance through specific praise statements (e.g., states specific behaviors).	1 2 3 4 5
3.5	Administers praise contingently.	1 2 3 4 5
3.6	Includes students in the management of their own behavior.	1 2 3 4 5
3.7	Uses nonverbal signals to direct students when teaching other groups of students.	1 2 3 4 5

Note. From "Measuring Teacher Effectiveness from the Teacher's Point of View" by C. S. Englert, 1984, *Focus on Exceptional Children, 17*(2), p. 5. Copyright 1984 by Love. Reprinted by permission.

coordinated, the effectiveness of both may decrease. Consistency can be improved by providing some parent training or with frequent communication between parents and teachers. Englert (1984) provides several suggestions for improving classroom behavior management techniques. The checklist in Figure 5–10 summarizes these suggestions.

Techniques for promoting the social acceptance of students with special needs included in the general education classroom are discussed in the next chapter. Thank you for reading to the end of this chapter. When you complete your review of "Things to Remember" and the activities that follow, you may want to reward yourself with a short break or a favorite beverage.

Things to Remember

- To function successfully in the general education classroom, students may need to increase some behaviors, decrease others, and learn new ways of acting.
- Classroom behavior problems interfere with instruction and social interactions; study skills problems affect a student's academic performance.
- Intervention may be necessary if there is a low rate of appropriate behavior, a high rate of inappropriate behavior, or an absence of the appropriate behavior from the student's repertoire.
- Behavior is learned and can be taught; it is increased by reinforcement and decreased by the removal of reinforcers or the introduction of aversive events.
- Behaviors do not occur in isolation; their antecedents and consequences must be considered.
- Direct observation of student behavior provides the most useful data for classroom teachers.
- Class rules and procedures make students aware of the expectations for behavior.
- Methods of using reinforcers to change behavior include token economies, contingency contracts, and group contingencies.
- Preventing behavior problems involves careful monitoring of students, reinforcement of appropriate behaviors, and use of negative teacher attention for potentially disruptive behavior.
- Students can participate in self-management of behavior by setting goals, monitoring their own performance, or implementing interventions such as self-reinforcement or self-instruction.
- Effective reinforcers are those valued by the students.

ACTIVITIES

1. Collect observation data on an individual (friend, student, teacher) during five separate observation periods. Be sure you have identified a specific behavior to observe (such as being on-task). Record and graph the data using a format similar to the one presented in this chapter. When you are finished, show your graph to another individual; can that person interpret your data? Can you speculate about what antecedents and consequences contribute to the observed occurrence of the behavior? Describe an intervention you might use if you wished to change the behavior.

2. Interview both a special educator and a general education teacher. Obtain information about the approaches they advocate for managing students in the general education classroom. What do they consider to be problem behaviors? According to the teachers, are special techniques needed for students with special needs, or are the behavior problems of all students managed in generally the same way? Ask the teachers to describe how they use student performance data in behavior change programs. Do they collect data before beginning a program? During the program? How do they decide when a program is working? When it needs to be changed?

3. Develop a set of rules for a classroom you have recently observed. Describe the class and establish five to eight rules using the guidelines stated in the chapter. Explain specifically how you would implement these rules at the beginning of a school year. Identify potential problems you might experience in implementing your rules, and describe how you would deal with these problems.

4. Read and summarize two articles that discuss token economies, contracting, or one of the other techniques described in this chapter. Journals such as *Psychology in the Schools, Journal of Applied Behavior Analysis, Education and Treatment of Children,* and *Behavior Modification* often feature articles on these topics.

5. Consider different viewpoints on classroom discipline. Contact local school districts to learn about their policies. Also, get in touch with a national teachers' organization, such as the American Federation of Teachers or the National Education Association (see "Window on the Web"). Compare the policies of local districts with those of the professional organization you con-

Window on the Web

American Federation of Teachers and National Education Association

The American Federation of Teachers (AFT) and the National Education Association (NEA) are national professional organizations for teachers, and each sponsors a website with information for educators and others interested in education.

http://www.aft.org
The AFT website provides information about the organization, a weekly online newsletter, articles about current projects and initiatives, legislative and lobbying updates, links to related sites, and news tailored for specific groups of professionals (e.g., K–12 teachers). In addition, it is possible to search the AFT website for information about specific topics.

http://www.nea.org
NEA's website contains Homeroom (the site's home page with current news); helpfrom.nea.org (ideas for improving teaching and learning); What's New?; Good Schools, Good Students (links to schools with model programs); Resource Room (information about innovative educational approaches); NEA Info Center; and Recess! (classroom humor). Also available is a search feature where teachers can search the website for information on specific subjects.

Note. Courtesy of American Federation of Teachers and National Education Association.

tact. What changes would you make in these policies? Why would you make these changes?

6. Develop a reinforcement menu for a school-aged student. Begin by interviewing the student using the inventory presented in Figure 5–7. You may want to add questions and observe the stu-

dent in different situations. Then develop a menu that includes at least 10 items, ranging in cost (points) from cheap to expensive. Describe how a general education teacher could use this menu when implementing a behavior change program.

chapter 6

Promoting Social Acceptance

Cases

Juan has been included in a general education class for a month and still eats lunch alone.

Jackie, who travels by wheelchair, is the only girl in her fifth grade class who hasn't been invited to a birthday party yet this year.

June dislikes talking in class because the other students make fun of her speech.

Even though Matt's classroom behavior has improved, his teacher is reluctant to have him join the class for assemblies and field trips.

Maria's American history teacher wants her to read the text like everyone else rather than listen to special tapes.

The school janitor is irritated because Hank's crutches leave marks on the floors of the classroom, halls, and bathroom.

Mike attends a class for students with severe disabilities that was moved to the campus of the neighborhood school last month. Although members of his class eat in the lunchroom, attend assemblies, and use the playing fields and the gym for physical education, students in the general education program avoid social or verbal interactions with Mike and his classmates.

Several of the parents of Tim's classmates are concerned about his mild seizures; they wonder whether Tim's condition is contagious.

Students with special needs participating in general education programs often suffer rejection during their school years. They have often been rejected by their general education peers, their teachers, or the parents of their classmates. This lack of acceptance has a negative effect on not only their self-concept but also their school performance (Heron & Harris, 1993; Schumaker & Hazel, 1984). To be effective, a general education program that includes students with special needs must make provisions for improving the social skills of these students and enhancing their social integration (Maag & Webber, 1995). This requirement holds true both for students with disabilities who enter the general education class from a special program and for those who have never left the mainstream setting.

SOCIAL PROBLEMS IN THE CLASSROOM

Many special students encounter difficulty in social interactions with general education peers and teachers. One source of this difficulty can be the behavior of the special student. At least equally important are the attitudes and feelings of the general population. Many people have little accurate information about students with special needs, and this lack of knowledge can create fear and prejudice.

Students with special needs may fail to conform to the expectations of school and society. They may not look or act the same as other students. For teachers and peers unfamiliar with special students, these differences can create apprehension, distrust, and even hostility. The abilities, talents, and needs of the special student are frequently overlooked.

Some special students can be easily identified; their appearance or their actions are visibly different. One example is the student who travels by wheelchair. Others have no observable signs but stand out when their performance falls below expectations. For instance, students with learning disabilities are indistinguishable from their peers until they are asked to read or write or do math.

Throughout their school careers, students with special needs encounter failure. When placed in the general education classroom, they may be apprehensive about attempting activities. This fear of failure and feeling of incompetence may cause them to withdraw. This withdrawal can contribute to their rejection and make it difficult for even the most effective and creative teacher to provide an appropriate learning situation (Gresham, 1984; Meisgeier, 1981).

Students with special needs can be as delayed in their social development as they are in other areas (Odom, McConnell, & Chandler, 1994). Thus, poor social skills can be another factor in their rejection (Hollinger, 1987). Many special students are not as capable as their general education peers of initiating and sustaining appropriate social relationships. For example, the research of Bryan and Pflaum (1978) found students with learning disabilities lacking in the language skills necessary for effective social communication. Students with disabilities may fail to develop appropriate social skills because they have fewer friends and are rated significantly lower in sociometric status than their peers (Asher & Taylor, 1981; Drabman & Patterson, 1981; McIntosh, Vaughn, & Zaragoza, 1991; Ray, 1985). Or it may be that they have difficulty using social cues; some misperceive their social standing and feel that they are better accepted by peers than they actually are (Heron & Harris, 1993). According to Bryan and Bryan (1977), students with learning disabilities exhibit more aggressive or negative behaviors, are less accurate in interpreting nonverbal communications, and "emit a lot [of] nasty statements to their peers" (p. 142). Drabman and Patterson describe students with special needs as "opposing peers, displaying disruptive behavior and exhibiting withdrawal behavior" (p. 48). It is difficult to determine the cause of the problem: Friendless students have little opportunity to develop social skills, and those with poor skills are unlikely to form friendships.

At the secondary level, these problems may increase. In adolescence, social interaction with peers becomes extremely important. For students with disabilities who have spent the majority of their educational careers segregated from age peers, the transition to the general education environment can be hazardous. Students with disabilities not only may lack a common experiential background with general education students but also may be delayed in the acquisition of important social skills. These obstacles, combined with the barriers to acceptance in the general education class, magnify the difficulty of promoting the social acceptance of secondary students with special needs.

Research indicates that general education students and teachers do not consistently accept the student with disabilities (e.g., Bryan, 1997; Drabman & Patterson, 1981; Gans, 1985; Sabornie & Kauffman, 1985; Sale & Carey, 1995). Teachers and peers are more likely to ignore social interactions initiated by special students. And teachers are more critical of their behavior, provide fewer praise statements, and consider them less desirable as students (Heron & Harris, 1993); this is especially apparent if the students are boys (e.g., Schlosser & Algozzine, 1980; Slate & Saudargas, 1986; Stitt et al., 1988).

One factor that influences teacher attitudes is labeling. When students are identified by a negatively perceived label (e.g., learning disabilities, mental retardation), teachers are less able to objectively observe, rate, and plan appropriate interventions for their behavior (Campbell, Dodson, & Bost, 1985). Although the effects of labeling on social acceptance have not been consistently supported by research (Gottlieb & Leyser, 1981), evidence is adequate to caution against reliance on labels for educational information. For instance, Gillung and Rucker (1977) found that teachers expected less from students who

were labeled than from unlabeled students with identical behaviors. Alves and Gottlieb (1986) reported that teachers involved students with disabilities in fewer academic exchanges; these students were asked fewer questions and were given less feedback than their peers without disabilities. In a study conducted by Reschly and Lamprecht (1979), students' labels lowered the initial expectations of teachers; however, as teachers spent more time with special students and observed their behavior, expectations became more realistic. Thus, labels can be misleading and can have a negative effect, at least on the initial acceptance of special students by their teachers.

Another factor that can contribute to the rejection of students with disabilities by general education teachers and administrators is a lack of special training and experience (Heron & Harris, 1993; Maag & Webber, 1995; Martin, 1974). Some teachers are afraid that they do not have the skills necessary for teaching students with special needs. Others may feel that working with these students is not as gratifying as working with typical individuals. Teachers with negative attitudes toward special students can convey these feelings to all the individuals in the class and thereby further reduce the chance for successful programs that include students with disabilities (e.g., Garrett & Crump, 1980; Heron & Harris).

A portion of the problem related to the attitudes toward students with special needs can be attributed to former special education practices. For some time, special classes were virtually the only special education service available for students with disabilities. Special educators advocated that these students be removed from the mainstream and entrusted to the care of a specialist in a separate class setting. As a result, general education teachers were not encouraged to attempt to meet the needs of students with disabilities within the mainstream setting. At present, however, a variety of part-time special education services are available for both the special students and their general education teachers. In addition, mainstreaming and inclusion are now common practices, and training programs for general education teachers currently require some level of preparation in dealing with the needs of students with disabilities. One important aspect of effective special education programs is ensuring that the collaboration and consulting role of the special educator helps teachers in general education classes realize that students with disabilities can successfully participate in general education settings for a portion of the school day that is appropriate for each student.

The parents of students with disabilities can also contribute to the social problems of their children. Parents can be overly protective and restrict a student's involvement in normal social activities, which thereby reduces the opportunities for acquiring friends and fosters a limited experience base. Parents reluctant to allow their child to experience failure can actually be increasing the probability that failure will occur in future social interactions. In addition, the parents of general education students can influence the acceptance of special students. Some may resist inclusion in the general education program if they believe that it will reduce the quality of their children's education. Other parents may discourage their children from interacting with the students with disabilities in the class. These negative attitudes are often based on limited information about, and limited experience with, students with special needs.

PRINCIPLES FOR ENHANCING SOCIAL ACCEPTANCE

When rejected by general education teachers and peers, students with special needs may perform more poorly, both socially and academically. The self-concept of rejected students can be affected. In addition, because they are not encouraged to participate in classroom activities, rejected students may fall further behind in all skill areas. Simply including students with disabilities in general education classes does not guarantee their social acceptance or their acquisition of improved social skills (Sale & Carey, 1995; Vaughn, 1995). In most cases, the general education teacher must participate in developing and implementing a systematic program designed to improve the students' social skills and to increase their social integration. Effective mainstreaming and inclusion programs require that educators pay attention to the social needs as well as to the academic, behavioral, and physical needs of their students (Gresham, 1984; York, Vandercook, MacDonald, Heise-Neff, & Caughey, 1992). The principles described in the following paragraphs assist in planning and implementing a successful program for social acceptance.

Change Attitudes with Information

Attitudes are extremely important. The attitudes of the teacher have a significant effect on the attitudes of the students within the class; negative feelings toward students with disabilities can be communicated by

Inclusion Tips for the Teacher

How to Get to Know People with Disabilities

Have you ever wondered about how to interact with a person with disabilities? Here are several suggestions:

- Converse with an individual with disabilities in spirit, content, and approach as you would with anyone else.
- When you think someone with a disability may need assistance, ask, "Do you need help? How should I help you?"
- Do not shout at blind persons. They have lost their *vision* not their hearing.
- Do not "talk over" or provide the words for someone who stutters or speaks with difficulty. Be patient and listen, and let the person speak for himself.
- *Always FACE* a person with a hearing impairment. Be sure the person can see your lips; speak clearly without exaggerating lip movements.
- Speak directly to a person with disabilities. Do not direct your conversation to an attendant, assistant, or nearby companion as if she did not exist.
- Do not call special attention to a person with disabilities. Approach her as another person who happens to have a disability—*not* as a disability that belongs to a person.

Note. From "Some Social Tips for Non-Disabled Folks," *Report from Closer Look,* Spring 1981, p. 5. Adapted by permission.

the teacher (Cartledge, Frew, & Zaharias, 1985; Garrett & Crump, 1980; Simpson, 1980). Teachers should realize that their words and actions provide a model for students; they should attempt to convey a positive attitude that encourages acceptance of the student with special needs. Attitudes are affected by information. When students and adults increase their knowledge about special students, their attitudes improve (Donaldson & Martinson, 1977; Handlers & Austin, 1980; Simpson). Information dispels misconceptions and clarifies misunderstandings; prejudice and fear decrease. Teachers and peers in the general education class become more accepting as they learn more about the abilities and problems of special students (Fiedler & Simpson, 1987; Simpson).

Knowledge about students with disabilities can be gained in many ways. Students and teachers can read or view films, videotapes, and television programs about special students. Also, simulations of disabilities can be used to increase understanding. Visits to special education settings can be arranged, or students and adults with disabilities can be interviewed or invited to the general education classroom. Even higher levels of exposure can be gained if teachers volunteer to accept students with special needs in their classes or general education students are encouraged to work as peer tutors with special students. As more is learned about individuals with

disabilities, they appear less different, more familiar, and more acceptable. See "Inclusion Tips for the Teacher" for some suggestions on how to get to know individuals with disabilities.

Recognize the Similarities Between Special and General Education Students

Teachers and students may form opinions about the abilities of a student with special needs solely on the basis of physical appearance, labels, or occasional behaviors. Assumptions made by teachers are extremely important because they may influence instructional expectations for the student. A student's looks or assigned label is an insufficient database for programming decisions or for predicting the characteristics of his or her personality. Although it is easy to jump to conclusions, more information is necessary before educational plans and predictions can be made. What is needed is specific assessment information about the student's skills and abilities and an opportunity to observe the student in the classroom. Knowledge that a student has a visual impairment, for example, raises the anxiety level of the teacher. More pertinent is information that, although the student reads Braille materials, she is able to participate in class discussions, benefit from lectures, and interact socially with her classmates.

When the team determines that students are able to benefit from placement in the general education classroom, those students do not need to be protected by the teacher. They should be included in as many activities as feasible and treated like any other student in the classroom—that is, as individuals.

Teachers often talk about the behaviors and characteristics of the students with disabilities in their classrooms. However, in most cases the academic problems and inappropriate behaviors of students with special needs are also evident in many of their "normal" peers. If teachers were to list the typical behaviors, traits, and concerns of general education students, they would find that these are also typical of students with special needs. Special students are children and adolescents with identified needs; despite these needs, however, they remain individuals. As Turnbull and Schulz (1979) state, "A difference is only a difference when it makes a difference. . . . [C]hildren [with disabilities] have far more similarities than differences with the [children without disabilities]" (p. 48).

Prepare Students in the General Education Class for the Inclusion of Students with Disabilities

Students in the general education program are often isolated from any contact with students with disabilities. Consequently, general education students may never have met a person with a disability unless an individual with special needs is among their family, friends, or neighbors. This limited knowledge and experience can lead to the development of prejudice and nonaccepting attitudes and a natural discrimination against individuals who are different. Evidence suggests that "discriminatory responses may exist as relatively normal patterns of behavior" (Simpson, 1980, p. 2).

The attitudes of students in the general education class can be improved and their acceptance of students with disabilities increased (Donaldson, 1980; Fox, 1989; Guralnick, 1981; Johnson & Johnson, 1984; York et al., 1992). Before students with disabilities are placed in the general education class, activities should be conducted to provide information and skills to general education students. For example, students can learn about disabilities and gain skills in assisting students with special needs in the classroom. Such experiences also benefit students with disabilities who never leave the general education classroom. This training can be provided by general educators or general and special educators working together.

Prepare Special Students for Inclusion

One of the reasons for rejection of students with disabilities is their frequent lack of social skills. In most cases, students with disabilities should be provided with specific training in the social skills needed to function successfully in school and the community (Brady & McEvoy, 1989; Cartledge, Frew, & Zaharias, 1985; Gresham, 1984; Hollinger, 1987; Schumaker & Hazel, 1984; Weiner & Harris, 1997). Students with special needs are able to acquire appropriate social behaviors; however, this is not likely to occur if students are only provided with opportunities to interact with peers and adults. Specific instruction, including modeling, imitating, coaching, and practice, is usually necessary (Elliot & Gresham, 1993) and can be provided in either the special or the general education classroom. In fact, the most successful social skills interventions are those that are structured for individuals or small groups and designed to be conducted over long-term periods (McIntosh et al., 1991).

Prepare Parents for the Inclusion of Students with Disabilities

Parents of both typical students and those with disabilities can make important contributions to the social acceptance program. The attitudes they convey to their children influence their children's viewpoints, the teacher's efforts, and the school program. Parents often have concerns about students with disabilities being involved in the general education program because they are uncertain about the effects on their children. Informing parents about the needs of students with disabilities, the purpose of the program, and the impact on their children will help gain their support. It is important that parents realize that after students leave school, they will all be intermingling in the community. The school program helps prepare them for this involvement.

METHODS FOR GATHERING DATA

Data collection is just as important in promoting social acceptance as it is in instruction and management of classroom behavior. Assessment information can determine the current attitudes and social behaviors of students and teachers. If the effectiveness of a social acceptance program is to be evaluated, data should be collected both before and after the program is implemented. In addition, continuous monitoring of progress is necessary so that program modifications can be made.

Information about social skills and acceptance can be gathered from many sources: general education students and those with special needs, general and special education teachers, other professionals, and parents. Various methods are used in assessment. **Sociometric measures** provide information about how special students are perceived by general education peers. Teacher opinions can be obtained in interviews or teacher ratings or rankings of class members. Self-concept measures, such as those in Figure 6–1, are used to see how special students feel about themselves. In addition, the observational techniques described in chapter 5 assist in identifying the types of social behaviors exhibited by students with special needs and their social interactions with teachers and peers. McLoughlin and Lewis (1994) describe a variety of assessment devices useful in a social acceptance program. These include measures of self-concept, attitudes toward school, interactions with teachers, and peer relationships.

One of the most popular methods for gathering data about acceptance and rejection of special students is the sociometric measure. Sociometric devices, which measure the attitudes of group members toward one another, are often recommended for determining how well students with special needs are accepted by peers (Kauffman, 1997; Polloway & Patton, 1993). Results can serve as an overall index of the social skill development of students with disabilities (Cartledge & Milburn, 1995;

FIGURE 6-1   **Assessing Self-Concept**

Adjective Check List
Directions: Put an X by each word that describes you.

_____ 1. smart	_____ 7. quarrelsome	_____ 13. bothersome
_____ 2. funny	_____ 8. fidgety	_____ 14. cranky
_____ 3. tired	_____ 9. energetic	_____ 15. eager
_____ 4. happy	_____ 10. friendly	_____ 16. honest
_____ 5. blue	_____ 11. shy	_____ 17. lazy
_____ 6. busy	_____ 12. sad	_____ 18. selfish

Behavioral Check List
Directions: Put an X by each description that fits you.

_____ 1. makes friends easily	_____ 6. seems to lack confidence
_____ 2. not as smart as most kids	_____ 7. is a good leader
_____ 3. likes to be alone	_____ 8. enjoys school
_____ 4. is fun to be with	_____ 9. feelings are easily hurt
_____ 5. laughs a lot	_____ 10. daydreams a lot

Note. Reprinted with permission of Merrill, an imprint of Macmillan Publishing Company, from *Teacher Diagnosis of Educational Difficulties* (2nd ed.) by R. M. Smith, Copyright © 1982 Merrill Publishing Company, Columbus, Ohio.

TABLE 6-1   Sociometric Methods

Method	Description	Example	Scoring	Comments
Nomination	Requires students to name classmates who fit a particular sociometric criterion. Can be based upon positive or negative criteria.	Name three classmates whom you would like to have sitting near you (positive). Name three classmates whom you do not like to have sitting near you (negative).	A student's score is the total number of nominations received from classmates. (Tally those with positive and negative criteria separately.)	Scores are generally stable over time. Not as stable for very young children. Ratings are obtained on only those students nominated.

Rating scale	All students in the class are listed, and a rating scale (e.g., 1 = low and 5 = high) is provided. Each student in the class is rated.	Circle the number which best indicates your opinion. I would like to study with . . .
		
		        Not A
		        at all lot
		Joe 1 2 3 4 5
		Mary 1 2 3 4 5
			Each student's score is an average of [his or her] ratings from all students.	All students are rated by all other students in the class. Has high test-retest reliability.

Paired-comparison	The most preferred classmate is chosen from all possible pairings of students in the class.	Circle the classmate in each pair with whom you would most like to study.
		  1. John or Martha
		  2. John or Sam
		     .
		     .
		     .
		40. Martha or Sue
			A student's score is the number of times he or she was chosen by other students in all the possible pairings.	All students are rated by all other students. Has high test-retest reliability. Administration and scoring take more time than other methods.

Note. From "Social Outcomes of Mainstreaming: Sociometric Assessment and Beyond" by S. R. Asher and A. R. Taylor, 1981, *Exceptional Education Quarterly, 1*(4), pp. 13–30. Copyright 1981 by PRO-ED, Inc. Adapted by permission.

Luftig, 1989). These devices are relatively simple, quick to administer, and easy to interpret. However, it is important to note that while they provide an overall measure of the acceptance of students, they do not identify specific behaviors or skills that require intervention (Foster, Inderbitzen, & Nangle, 1993).

As shown in Table 6–1, several different types of sociometric measures are used. Students can be asked to nominate favorite peers, rate their classmates, or choose between pairs of students. The nomination method tends to be a measure of friendship, whereas rating scales tend to assess the student's level of acceptance. General acceptance of special students by their peers is probably a more appropriate instructional goal than an increase in the students' number of friendships. This point

should be considered when selecting a sociometric device (Asher & Taylor, 1981).

Before using sociometric methods to gather data about social acceptance, teachers should consider district and school policies. These methods involve the collection of confidential information, and some schools allow their use only with parental permission. Results should be treated with caution; when students are asked to rate other students, they should be encouraged to keep the nature of their responses confidential. Also, it is important that teachers not share overall ratings with students, particularly those who may already have a poor self-concept (McLoughlin & Lewis, 1994). Sociometric devices also tend to lose their sensitivity to changes in the behavior of children over 10 years old. Finally, they provide little diagnostic information regarding

FIGURE 6-2   Social Environment Checklist

Teacher's Behavior

Direct Influence

- Can the teacher specifically state both appropriate and inappropriate student classroom behaviors he/she would like to increase or decrease?
- Does the teacher frequently follow appropriate behavior with encouragement and praise?
- Does the teacher refrain from punishing and criticizing students and rather consistently withdraw his/her attention following inappropriate behaviors?
- Does the teacher objectively record (tally, tape-record, use counter) and evaluate the frequency and consequences of his/her behaviors to document the effects they have on student behavior?
- Does the teacher clearly specify the classroom guidelines, responsibilities, and limitations for students?

Indirect Influence

- Has the teacher continued to grow by adapting teaching plans to meet the needs of each group of students?
- Is the teacher aware of any personal, social, racial, or mental prejudices and does she/he attempt to overcome these through objective teaching and evaluation methods?
- Has the teacher devised a method of getting the students' perceptions and feedback on the teacher and the class (questionnaire, suggestion box)?
- Does the teacher encourage and reinforce self-expression and participation from all the members of the class?

Peer Behavior

- Can the teacher identify the classroom leaders, followers, and isolates?
- Can the teacher identify the peer-group norm base and stereotypes that are held by the class?
- Can the teacher identify and redirect inappropriate peer attention (laughing at a class clown, picking on a . . . child [with a disability]) to promote more constructive activities?
- Does the teacher attend to the problems of the quiet, withdrawn children as much as to the acting-out problem children?
- Does the teacher use concrete activities and arrangements to maximize the social acceptance and participation of all the children?
- Do the classroom physical arrangements (seating plan) and group activities consider both the elimination of behavior problems and enhancement of social relationships?

Curriculum

- Does the curriculum encourage high levels of student independence and initiative?
- Does the curriculum present a balanced emphasis on students' personal social development and academic skill development?
- Does the curriculum provide challenging new ideas that require students to develop skills in analytic and evaluative thinking?
- Is the curriculum enhanced with a motivational system that guarantees that each child will have a successful learning experience?
- Does the curriculum require participation and interaction from the teacher and students?
- Does the curriculum encourage interaction and cooperation among the students?
- Is the subject content relevant to the interests and backgrounds of the students?
- Is an effort made to meaningfully relate the concepts covered in class to everyday experiences?
- Does the curriculum provide ample opportunity for student enrichment by frequently introducing new and different ideas and problems?
- Is motivation enhanced through liberal use of teacher praise and encouragement?
- Are students with special skills allowed or encouraged to share their expertise with their classmates?
- Is an attempt made to incorporate student ideas and suggestions into the instructional program?

Note. Reprinted with permission of Merrill, an imprint of Macmillan Publishing Company, from *Evaluating Educational Environments* (pp. 120–125) by R. M. Smith, J. T. Neisworth, and J. G. Greer, Copyright © 1978 Merrill Publishing Company, Columbus, Ohio.

which social skills should be taught, and, if used too frequently, they may actually contribute to the rejection of some students (Schumaker & Hazel, 1984).

Direct observation techniques are helpful in assessing and monitoring the specific social skills exhibited by students with special needs (e.g., Prasad, 1994) and the behaviors of teachers and peers toward these students. Direct observation can take place in analogue settings (i.e., simulated situations, such as role playing or a contrived play setting) or a natural environment. This functional assessment attempts to identify factors that predict, trigger, or maintain particular behaviors by examining what is occurring in the setting and the antecedent and consequent factors that contribute to the occurrence of the behavior. This information is essential in developing appropriate interventions (Sugai & Lewis, 1996). Frequent data collection is important to ensure that the initial assessment is valid and to evaluate interventions to provide a measure of the timeliness of program modifications. Data can be recorded on a graph to allow analysis of behavioral changes over time. Examples of appropriate targets for direct observation include the frequency of positive statements made by the teacher to the student with special needs or the number of social interactions between the student with disabilities and a peer in general education.

Rating scales and checklists are also useful in collecting information about a student's performance. Typically, these measures list specific behaviors that are likely to occur in a particular setting. The teacher completes the checklist or rating scale following an observation of the student. For example, a student may be observed participating in an instructional group and then rated on a number of classroom behaviors (e.g., "The student attends to the teacher's instructions? The student raises his or her hand before responding? The student maintains eye contact when talking with the teacher?"). The teacher can simply check the items that describe the student's behavior or rate the quality of the behaviors observed (i.e., from Inappropriate to Appropriate on a 5-point scale).

Behavioral rating scales may also offer a broader set of items that provide more general descriptions of behaviors (e.g., "The student participates appropriately in an instructional group"). A person who knows the student well (a teacher, parent, peer, or even the student in question) reads each description and then rates the student on a numerical scale (e.g., from 1 to 7). Checklists and rating scales permit the collection of consistent information from several different observers to assess the skill level of the student, identify problem behaviors, or assess the student's progress.

Parents can aid in gathering data by reporting on the special student's social interactions in the home, neighborhood, and community. They can also keep a record of the comments the student makes about school or self. This information can reflect changes in the student's self-concept or attitudes toward school.

Figure 6–2 presents a checklist for evaluating the social environment of the classroom. It can be used to assess not only teacher behavior but also peer behavior and the curriculum. Use this measure to find out about the social climate of your classroom.

STRATEGIES FOR PROMOTING ACCEPTANCE OF SPECIAL STUDENTS

Teachers can use several methods to increase the likelihood that students with disabilities will be socially accepted. These methods are directed toward students and teachers in general education, parents, and students with special needs themselves. Whereas general educators are typically responsible for implementing these strategies, special educators are available to provide necessary assistance.

Inform General Education Students About Disabilities

Increasing their knowledge about individuals with disabilities improves the attitudes of general education students and teachers (e.g., Donaldson, 1980; Fiedler & Simpson, 1987; Handlers & Austin, 1980; Schultz & Torrie, 1984). Students should be informed about disabilities, preferably before students with special needs enter the general education classroom. Instruction can take many forms. Teachers can present information directly to younger students; more advanced classes can conduct some of their own research. Some teachers may develop texts and workbooks to use with their students (Schultz & Torrie); others may use commercially developed materials. Special educators such as the resource teacher can direct general education teachers and students to other sources of information about disabilities. For example, many books, films, instructional materials, and even television programs discuss various types of disabilities.

The goal of instruction is to increase awareness of both the abilities and the problems of students with disabilities. The teacher can introduce the concept of individual differences and point out that each person is unique, with a distinct array of strengths and weaknesses. At the same time, the similarities between general education students and students with special needs should be emphasized (Schulz & Turnbull, 1983). Typical disabilities should be identified and discussed; students should learn why some individuals require special assistance. It is also possible to describe typical special education services and compare these with the general education program. The lives of famous people with disabilities, such as Helen Keller and Franklin D. Roosevelt, can be studied. Class discussions provide the opportunity for students to exchange information, experiences, and feelings about people with disabilities. Teachers should direct these discussions and clarify or correct any misperceptions or misinformation.

Provide General Education Students with Experiences with Individuals with Disabilities

Attitudes of general education students are also affected by meeting and interacting with individuals with disabilities. One way to provide this experience is to invite adults with special needs to the classroom; students can listen to the viewpoint of the person with disabilities and then ask questions. Another method is to visit special education programs such as the resource room or special class located within the school. Older students can also be given assignments to interview an adult with disabilities. The teacher should guide all of these experiences by ensuring that students prepare appropriate questions prior to visits, interviews, and discussions.

Simulation is another way of experiencing disabilities. Simulations assist general education students in understanding the problems experienced by individuals with special needs and thereby improve the general education students' level of acceptance (Aiello, 1979; Handlers & Austin, 1980; Israelson, 1980). Some possible simulation activities are traveling around the school in a wheelchair,

wearing a blindfold during lunch or art, using earplugs to limit hearing, and attempting to communicate without speaking. For younger children, puppets with various disabilities provide a type of simulation; students can talk with the puppets or become the puppeteers (Binkard, 1985). See "Window on the Web" for a description of an innovative approach to disability awareness using puppetry. All simulations should be carried out in a businesslike manner. Following the activities, students should write or talk about their experiences to ensure that they have no misconceptions.

Literature can also be used to provide experience with people with special needs. A wealth of fiction, biography, and autobiography about individuals with special needs is available; much is appropriate for students to read or listen to. "Inclusion Tips for the Teacher" on page 159 provides several suggestions.

Structure Interactions Between Typical Students and Students with Disabilities

Classroom and other interactions between general education students and students with disabilities have a greater chance for success if teachers provide guidelines. If the general education student's initial contact with a peer with disabilities is purposeful and occurs in a well-structured situation, positive attitudes are more likely to develop. Four techniques for structuring interactions are cooperative learning experiences, group rewards, special friendship programs, and peer or cross-age tutoring programs.

In **cooperative learning,** general education students and students with special needs work together as a team to complete activities or assignments (Maag & Webber, 1995). These teams, which operate in mainstream settings, are small groups of students with a range of abilities (i.e., low-, moderate-, and high-achieving individuals). According to the research reviewed by Gottlieb and Leyser (1981) and Johnson and Johnson (1980), cooperative learning is superior to both competitive learning and individualistic learning. In competitive situations, students attempt to outdo each other; in individualistic situations, the achievement of each student is unrelated to that of any other student. Cooperative learning increases the special student's opportunity to experience success (Slavin, 1990; Snell & Brown, 1993), it provides practice in school skills (Foyle & Lyman, 1990), and the social interactions involved promote the development of the social skills of the student

Window on the Web

Kids on the Block

http://www.kotb.com

Kids on the Block is a disability awareness organization that began in 1977, shortly after the passage of the Education for All Handicapped Children's Act. It develops programs for children and adults related to disabilities, medical and educational differences, and social and safety concerns. Among the topics are cerebral palsy, leukemia, learning disabilities, gifted and talented children, sexual abuse prevention, and children of divorced parents. These programs are brought to life by large puppets, the "Kids." Community groups, schools, hospitals, and other organizations form puppet troupes that bring the Kids to audiences across the United States and in several other countries.

Visit the Kids on the Block website to learn more about this organization, the puppets it creates, and its programs. The site also

provides links to Kids on the Block puppet troupes and a newsletter, *Keeping Up with the Kids.*

Note. Courtesy of The Kids on the Block, Inc.

with disabilities (Andersen, Nelson, Fox, & Gruber, 1988; Fad, Ross, & Boston, 1995; Johnson & Johnson, 1989) and their acceptance by peers in general education (Slavin, 1987; Slavin, Madden, & Leavey, 1984).

The teacher plays an important role in establishing and guiding the cooperative learning approach. Gottlieb and Leyser (1981) outline the following steps:

a. teacher specifies the instructional objectives;
b. selects the group size most appropriate for the lesson;
c. assigns students to groups and assures that the small groups are heterogeneous with students [with and without disabilities] in the same group;

d. specifies a structured role within the cooperative groups for the . . . students [with disabilities];
e. makes the requirements for the . . . child [with disabilities] reasonable;
f. provides appropriate materials to the groups;
g. explains the task and the cooperative goal structure;
h. trains . . . [all students] in helping, tutoring, teaching, and sharing skills; and
i. observes interactions. (p. 67)

It is important to consider that learners with disabilities may require some additional special preparation or support to allow them to participate effectively in cooperative learning activities (Johnson &

Inclusion Tips for the Teacher

Children's Literature About Disabilities

Children's literature is one way for students to learn more about disabilities and other special needs. The books listed below are organized by general disability areas, and recommended ages appear at the end of each brief description. For more suggestions, see Ashton-Coombs and James (1995) and Orr and others (1997).

Learning Disabilities, Learning Differences, and Attention Problems

The Don't-Give-Up Kid and Learning Differences by J. Gehret (Fairport, NY: Verbal Images Press, 1990). The story of Alex, a young boy with reading problems who wants to become an inventor. (primary grades)

Little Monster at School by M. Mayer (Green Frog Publishers, 1978). Little Monster has school friends including Yally. Yally isn't good at reading or math but he can draw better than anyone else. (primary grades)

Shelley, the Hyperactive Turtle by D. M. Moss (Rockville, MD: Woodbine House, 1989). Shelley, unlike other young turtles, cannot sit still. (primary grades)

Eagle Eyes by J. Gehret (Fairport, NY: Verbal Images Press, 1991). Ben's attention problems interfere with his life at school and home. (primary grades)

Josh, a Boy with Dyslexia by C. Janover (Burlington, VT: Waterfront Books, 1988). Josh, a boy with a learning disability, begins fifth grade in a new school. (intermediate grades)

Trouble with School: A Family Story about Learning Disabilities by K. B. Dunn and A. B. Dunn (Rockville, MD: Woodbine House, 1993). Allison and Allison's mother take turns telling the story of how Allison's learning disability was identified in second grade. (primary/intermediate grades)

When Learning Is Tough: Kids Talk about Their Learning Disabilities by C. Roby (Morton Grove, IL: Albert Whitman & Company, 1994). Eight young people discuss their lives, learning disabilities, and triumphs. (intermediate grades)

What Do You Mean I Have a Learning Disability? by K. M. Dwyer (New York: Walker, 1991). Jimmy, a 10-year-old, learns that he is not stupid and that he can succeed in school. (intermediate grades)

Mental Retardation and Severe Disabilities

Charlsie's Chuckles by C. W. Berkus (Rockville, MD: Woodbine House, 1992). The adventures of Charlsie, a 7-year-old boy with Down syndrome. (primary grades)

Where's Chimpy? by B. Rabe (Niles, IL: Albert Whitman & Company, 1988). Misty, a young girl with Down syndrome, has lost her favorite toy, her stuffed monkey. (primary grades)

Making Room for Uncle Joe by A. B. Litchfield (Niles, IL: Albert Whitman & Company, 1984). Uncle Joe, an adult with Down syndrome, comes to live with Amy, Beth, and Dan. (intermediate grades)

I'm the Big Sister Now by M. Emmert (Niles, IL: Albert Whitman & Company, 1989). Michelle Emmert tells the story of her older sister Amy, a teenager with severe disabilities. (intermediate grades)

Physical and Health Problems

Books featuring heroes and heroines who travel by wheelchair:

- *Nick Joins In* by J. Lasker (Chicago: Albert Whitman & Company, 1980). (primary grades)
- *Howie Helps Himself* by J. Fassler (Chicago: Albert Whitman & Company, 1975). (primary grades)

continued

- *Arnie and the New Kid* by N. Carlson (New York: Viking, 1990). (primary grades)
- *Princess Pooh* by K. M. Muldoon (Chicago: Albert Whitman & Company, 1989). (primary grades)
- *Grandma's Wheelchair* by L. Henrod (Chicago: Albert Whitman & Company, 1982). (primary grades)
- *Our Teacher's in a Wheelchair* by M. E. Powers (Chicago: Albert Whitman & Company, 1986). (primary grades)
- *Special Parents, Special Children* by J. E. Bernstein and B. J. Fireside (Chicago: Albert Whitman & Company, 1991). (primary/intermediate grades)

Books about specific disorders:

- *Even Little Kids Get Diabetes* by C. W. Pirner (Chicago: Albert Whitman & Company, 1991). (primary grades)
- *David Has Aids* by D. Sanford (Portland, OR: Multnomah, 1989). (primary grades)
- *Alex, the Kid with AIDS* by L. W. Girard (Chicago: Albert Whitman & Company, 1991). (primary/intermediate grades)
- *All about Asthma* by W. Ostrow and V. Ostrow (Chicago: Albert Whitman & Company, 1989). (intermediate grades)
- *There's a Little Bit of Me in Jamey* by D. M. Amadeo (Chicago: Albert Whitman & Company, 1989). The story of Jamey, a young boy with leukemia. (intermediate grades)
- *How It Feels to Live with a Physical Disability* by J. Krementz (New York: Simon & Schuster, 1992). (intermediate grades/middle school)

Visual and Hearing Impairments

Handtalk Birthday by R. Charlip, M. B. Miller, and G. Ancona (New York: Aladdin Books, 1991). A storybook in words, photos, and sign language that includes the signs for numbers. (primary grades and up)

A Cane in Her Hand by A. B. Litchfield (Chicago: Albert Whitman & Company, 1977). The story of Valerie, a young girl with low vision who learns to use a cane to help her travel from place to place. (primary/intermediate grades)

I'm Deaf and It's Okay by L. Aseltine, E. Mueller, and N. Tait (Chicago: Albert Whitman & Company, 1986). A young boy tells about his life and the problems he experiences because he is deaf. (primary/intermediate grades)

Words in Our Hands by A. B. Litchfield (Chicago: Albert Whitman & Company, 1980). Michael, Gina, and Diane's mother and father are deaf. Michael tells about the family's move to a new town. (intermediate grades)

Special Parents, Special Children by J. E. Bernstein and B. J. Fireside (Chicago: Albert Whitman & Company, 1991). Includes the story of Lisa, whose father is blind, and that of Angela, Vanessa, and Ryan, whose mother and father are deaf. (primary/intermediate grades)

Johnson, 1989). The student with special needs may require preparatory coaching or instruction in the social or academic skills required to participate in a group. Other students may need instruction on how to best teach or encourage their group member with disabilities. Descriptions of various methods of using cooperative learning in the classroom, plus highlights of research findings, are provided in Figure 6-3 on page 162.

A second method of structuring interactions is the use of group rewards (discussed in chapter 5). The teacher sets up a system in which students can earn classroom reinforcers when (a) general education students interact positively with students with disabilities, (b) a student with special needs per-

forms a desired behavior, (c) class members reinforce a student with behavior problems for an appropriate behavior, or (d) class members ignore a student's inappropriate behaviors. Class members pool their earnings, and the entire class is rewarded. These approaches lead to an increase in the number of positive interactions with students with special needs and thereby help to improve the attitudes of general education students (Heron & Harris, 1993; Salend, 1987).

A third technique is to encourage the development of friendships through communication, social interactions, and recreational activities involving typical students and students with disabilities (Searcy, 1996). As friends, students are encouraged

to provide support and assistance to others. For example, this support may involve assisting students with physical or visual impairments in their travels around school or providing a student with severe disabilities the opportunity to learn and practice age-appropriate skills while participating in games or verbal interactions with others (Falvey, Grenot-Scheyer, & Bishop, 1989).

Programs designed to promote friendships vary greatly in their structure. Teachers may reinforce natural interactions, provide students with information or skills related to their interactions, or establish more structured programs that actually provide training for general education students in how to assist and develop interactions with students with disabilities (Campbell, 1989; Perske & Perske, 1988). These programs may build peer support by (a) fostering proximity of students with disabilities with their general education peers, (b) encouraging the development of support and friendship, (c) teaching support and friendship skills, (d) fostering respect for individual differences, and (e) providing a positive model for appropriate interactions (Searcy, 1996; Stainback, Stainback, & Wilkinson, 1992). The implementation of programs that encourage friendships becomes especially important as more stu-

dents with disabilities spend increasing amounts of time in general education programs.

The use of students as tutors is a fourth approach. General education students can help students with disabilities as peer tutors (working with agemates or classmates) or cross-age tutors (working with younger tutees). General education students gain in experience and information by working with students with special needs, and students with disabilities benefit from the instruction and the model provided by the general education tutor. Tutoring programs have demonstrated their effectiveness in many situations (Heron & Harris, 1993; Jenkins & Jenkins, 1985; Krouse, Gerber, & Kauffman, 1981; Maag & Webber, 1996; Maheady, Sacca, & Harper, 1988; Strain, 1981a, 1981b). Students have been found to be effective teachers with individuals who are withdrawn, students with acting-out behaviors, and those with academic needs. Tutors should receive specific training prior to their service, be provided with structured and carefully prescribed lessons, meet frequently with their tutee, and be continually monitored with needed reinforcement and reinstruction provided by the teacher. In addition, peer tutors should be warned that they may be rejected at first but that this response will

Cooperative learning methods are aimed at reducing student isolation and perceived hostile climates that exist in highly competitive classrooms, and at increasing students' ability to interact and work with other students toward common goals.

The most widely used cooperative learning methods include

- **Student Teams-Achievement Divisions** (STAD)—Students assemble in teams of four or five members mixed according to achievement level, gender, and ethnicity to master the material covered in a lesson just presented by the teacher. Subsequently, they individually take a quiz on that material. The team's overall score is determined by the extent to which each student *improved* over his or her past performance. The team demonstrating the greatest improvement is recognized in a weekly class newsletter.

- **Teams-Games-Tournament** (TGT)—The procedure in TGT is the same as that used in STAD, but instead of taking quizzes, the students play academic games in tournaments with other members in the class whose past performance was similar to their own. The team score is also based on individual improvement. The balance[s] of the groups involved in the tournament are maintained by weekly adjustment of group members based on their performance.

- **Team Assisted Individualization** (TAI)—Teams of elementary or middle school math students are established and evaluated in the same manner as in STAD and TGT. This procedure uses placement tests to determine each student's individualized level and they proceed at their own rate. Teammates check each other's instructional work and help each other with problems. Student performance is based on individual tests and team rewards are based on the number and accuracy of units completed each week. TAI is based on a specific set of materials and its individualized features make it very appropriate for heterogeneous groups.

- **Cooperative Integrated Reading and Composition** (CIRC)—A comprehensive program for teaching reading and writing that involves pairs of students from different reading groups using basal readers and working on decoding, vocabulary, writing, spelling, and comprehension activities. Teacher instruction is provided to a team while others are working on individual activities and is usually followed by team practice, preassessments for the team, and tests. Tests are not taken until the team members determine their teammate is ready.

- **Jigsaw**—Students meet in five- or six-member teams. The teacher gives each student an item of information which the student must "teach" to the team. Students are then individually tested for their mastery of the material. **Jigsaw II** is the same, except that students obtain their information from textbooks, narrative material, short stories, or biographies. The class is then quizzed for individual and team scores.

- **Learning Together**—After the teacher has presented a lesson, students work together in small groups on a single worksheet. The team as a whole receives praise and recognition for mastering the worksheet.

- **Group-Investigation**—This is a more complex method, requiring students to accept greater responsibility for deciding what they will learn, how they will organize themselves to master the material, and how they will communicate what they have learned to their classmates.

These methods share four positive characteristics. (1) The cooperation required among students prevents one student from doing most of the work for the others. (2) In spite of the cooperative nature of the groups, each student must learn the material in order to improve his or her own score and the team score. (3) Even low achievers who may not contribute greatly can receive recognition since scores are based on individual improvement, however small, over past performance. (4) Students are motivated to cooperate since they receive not just a grade on a piece of paper, but public recognition from the teacher and the class.

Cooperative learning methods have positive effects in several areas. They contribute significantly to student achievement—to an equal extent in both elementary and secondary schools; in urban, suburban, and rural schools; and in diverse subject matter areas.

Schools with racially or ethnically mixed populations do not necessarily have better intergroup relations based solely on student proximity. However, when dissimilar students work together in small groups toward a common goal and are allowed to contribute equally, they will learn to like and respect one another.

Cooperative learning methods also increase acceptance and understanding among students with disabilities and their nondisabled classmates. They also have a positive effect on student self-esteem.

Students who participate in cooperative learning like school more than their peers who are not allowed to work together; they are better able to interact appropriately with others and to understand another person's point of view.

Note. From Slavin, R. E. (1981). "Synthesis of Research on Cooperative Learning," *Educational Leadership, 38,* p. 659. Used by permission of the Association for Supervision and Curriculum Development. Copyright 1981 by ASCD. All rights reserved. Adaptations based on *Cooperative Learning: Theory, Research, and Practice* by R. E. Slavin, 1990, Englewood Cliffs, NJ: Prentice-Hall. Copyright 1990 by Prentice-Hall, Inc.

Inclusion Tips for the Teacher

Enhancing Social Acceptance

- Be open and honest with your students. Don't avoid answering questions.
- Discuss disabilities with your class.
- Invite guest speakers—parents of children with disabilities or adults with disabilities.
- Read books to your class about people with disabilities.
- Hold class discussions. Allow students to ask questions and explore feelings.
- Emphasize how much alike we are, rather than how different we are.
- Take the mystery away from adaptive aids such as wheelchairs, braces, and hearing aids by exposing children to them and providing explanations of how they work.

- Try simulation exercises such as a blind walk or a soundless movie.
- Encourage a buddy system.
- Arrange for students without disabilities to work with special students as helpers or tutors.
- Look for ways to capitalize on the strengths of the student with disabilities and provide status and recognition through athletics, drama, the school newspaper, chorus, or as peer tutors.
- Locate and view media—filmstrips and films—on individuals with disabilities.

Note. From *Teaching Handicapped Students in the Mainstream,* 2/e, by A. L. Pasanella and C. B. Volkmor. Copyright © 1981 by the University of Southern California and by Macmillan College Publishing Company, Inc.

most likely diminish as instruction proceeds (Doorlag, 1989a; Gable, Strain, & Hendrickson, 1979).

Students with disabilities can also serve as peer or cross-age tutors. These experiences can provide the student with special needs with new status, increased acceptance by other students in the school, opportunities to develop social skills, and practice and improved performance in academic skill areas (Cochran, Feng, Cartledge, & Hamilton, 1993). For instance, a student with special needs may help a classmate practice spelling words, or a sixth grade student with learning disabilities may enjoy practicing third grade math if this occurs during the tutoring of a third grade student. Students with disabilities serving as tutors should be provided the same type of training and assistance suggested for other tutors. These students often benefit more than their tutees from this educational experience (Osguthorpe & Scruggs, 1986). See "Inclusion Tips for the Teacher" above for more ideas about how teachers can help general education students accept their peers with special needs.

Improve the Social Skills of Students with Disabilities

For many students with special needs, the development of appropriate social skills improves their

chances of gaining social acceptance and succeeding when they are included in the general education program (Heron & Harris, 1993; Maag & Webber, 1995; Nelson, 1988; Sugai & Lewis, 1996; Zaragoza, Vaughn, & McIntosh, 1991). Drabman and Patterson (1981) say that "it is important that integrated exceptional children display as many positive characteristics as they can to facilitate acceptance by nonexceptional peers" (p. 54). Social skills are best developed through direct instructional procedures, following the same principles as academic instruction and provided as a regularly planned component of the instructional day (Maag & Webber; Sugai & Lewis; Sugai & Tindal, 1993). Initially, the teacher describes why the skill is needed, how the skill is performed, when it is to be used, and what its specific components are. Appropriate social behaviors are modeled for the student with special needs by the teacher and peers or by videotapes and films. The student is then questioned about the skill and the steps involved in it and is provided with the opportunity to practice the new behaviors. It is important that the teacher make use of prompts, praise, and corrective feedback during each of the steps of instruction. Providing multiple examples of how the skill is used and opportunities to practice in other settings improves the chance that the skills learned in the classroom will generalize to other settings (Cartledge & Milburn, 1995; Doorlag, 1989b; Elliott & Gresham, 1993; Maag & Webber; Sugai & Lewis; Winget & Kirk, 1991).

Instructional materials are available to assist in the teaching of social skills. Examples of programs designed for elementary grade students are listed here:

- *Skillstreaming the Elementary School Child* by McGinnis and Goldstein (1984)
- *DUSO-Revised: Developing Understanding of Self and Others* by Dinkmeyer and Dinkmeyer (1982)
- *ACCEPTS* (A Curriculum for Children's Effective Peer and Teacher Skills) *Social Skills Curriculum* by Walker and others (1983)
- *Getting Along with Others: Teaching Social Effectiveness to Children* by Jackson, Jackson, and Monroe (1983)
- *Social Skills in the Classroom* by Stephens (1978)

Meisgeier (1981) describes a program for students with special needs who are included in general education classes in the secondary grades. Designed for adolescents, *The Social/Behavioral Curriculum* covers four major areas: responsibility, communication, assertiveness, and problem solving. Other programs designed for older students—*Skillstreaming the Adolescent* (Goldstein, Sprafkin, Gershaw, & Klein, 1980), *Life Skills Counseling with Adolescents* (Schinke & Gilchrist, 1984), and *The ACCESS* (Adolescent Curriculum for Communication and Effective Social Skills) *Program* (Walker, Todis, Holmes, & Horton, 1988)—provide teachers with guidelines and activities for teaching social skills at the middle and high school levels.

Programs such as these typically cover several social skill areas. They often include checklists or rating scales designed to assess student behavior and identify appropriate areas in which to begin social skills instruction. For example, the *ACCEPTS* program offers a placement test that is designed to assess the five areas covered in the program: classroom skills (e.g., attending to teachers, following rules), basic interaction skills (e.g., maintaining eye contact, speaking in a moderate tone), getting along skills (e.g., sharing, assisting others), making friends skills (e.g., being clean and neat, complimenting others), and coping skills (e.g., appropriately expressing anger, ignoring teasing). This program includes specific lesson plans and scripts for the teacher to follow for each of the skill areas

taught. Optional videotapes provide both positive and negative examples of the student behavior taught in each lesson, or the teacher can reenact these scenes from the description provided. The advantages of programs such as *ACCEPTS* and *ACCESS* are that their structured lessons permit them to be implemented readily by the teacher with a minimal amount of preparation because the lessons have been designed and field-tested by individuals with experience in teaching social skills. Others, such as the *Skillstreaming* programs, are more flexible; they provide less structured guidelines for lessons, behavioral steps for each skill, a general lesson format, and suggested learning and homework activities.

Another method for developing social skills is the use of **cognitive training** approaches. These methods focus on improving behavior by changing the thinking strategies of the student in order to develop skills that can be used in a variety of settings with a minimum of external support. Students are involved as active participants in the program—they are aware of the behaviors targeted for change, receive training in how the change program will operate, and are actively involved in the intervention (Graham, Harris, & Reid, 1998; Henker, Whalen, & Hinshaw, 1980). Cognitive training programs teach students strategies such as how to (a) use a sequence of steps to deal with a problem (self-instruction), (b) consider several solutions to a situation (problem solving), (c) collect and record data on their performance and evaluate the consequences of each alternative used (self-monitoring/self-evaluation), or (d) reinforce themselves for acceptable performance (self-reinforcement). It is important that the students are provided adequate instruction and practice in the use of cognitive training approaches; implementation of this type of program requires that teachers reward students for accurate evaluation of their own behaviors (Zirpoli & Melloy, 1997).

Cognitive training is an efficient approach because it allows teachers to train students to become responsible for portions of their instructional program; the teacher then assumes a monitoring role. A typical cognitive training program to teach social problem solving includes

- problem definition (specifically define the problem),
- goal statement (identify what you want to accomplish),

- delay response (determine ways to stop and think before you act),
- determine alternatives (identify as many solutions to the problem as possible),
- consider consequences (evaluate the different consequences that may follow each alternative solution),
- decision making/implementation (implement the alternative selected as most appropriate),
- review results (provide a self-evaluation and correct errors in strategies used in order to improve results in future), and
- provide reinforcement (provide yourself a "pat on the back" for improving).

Introduce Students with Disabilities to the General Education Program According to Their Individual Needs

Adjustment can be made easier for the student with special needs who is entering the mainstream (and for the teacher and students in the general education class) if inclusion is carefully planned and occurs gradually. For instance, the first step can be an informal meeting between the student with disabilities and the general education teacher. Then the student can visit the classroom when general education students are not present. The next approximation can be participation in a nonacademic activity, such as music or art. These first steps are important because they allow the student to become acquainted with the new teacher, students, and classroom before academic demands are made. They also help the teacher learn about the new student and begin to plan effective instructional and social acceptance programs. It is important to note that not all students with disabilities require a gradual introduction into the general education program; this must be determined on an individual basis as part of the planning for the implementation of the student's IEP.

Upgrade the Teacher's Information and Skills

At present, about 80% of the states require teachers to complete coursework related to the inclusion of students with disabilities before they receive a teaching certificate or credential (Allinder & Peterson, 1992). However, some teachers have limited knowledge of and experience with students with special needs. Their teacher preparation program may have provided only a minimal amount of training in working with these students, and they may not have had the opportunity to learn about students with special needs through in-service training.

Because of the strong relationship between attitudes and information, teachers should be sure they have adequate knowledge about students with disabilities and the appropriateness of different educational interventions (Gable, Laycock, Maroney, & Smith, 1991). The strategies recommended for informing general education students about disabilities (e.g., visitations, simulations, readings, films, discussions) are also appropriate for teachers. For example, several recent films feature characters with disabilities: *Scent of a Woman, My Left Foot, Forrest Gump, Lorenzo's Oil, Philadelphia,* and *Rainman* (Smith, Polloway, Patton, & Dowdy, 1998). Educators can direct their own study or request assistance in getting this information and training from resources available in their district or region.

While teachers often have support available from special educators, it is "essential that the [general education] teacher assume primary 'ownership' and accept responsibility for the education of a student with disabilities, just as he/she does for all students on the class list" (Putnam, 1992, p. 132). In order to carry out this responsibility effectively, teachers should strive to upgrade their own skill levels. For example, research indicates that teachers make more negative comments to students with disabilities, ask them fewer questions, and provide them with less feedback. This affects the attitudes of students in the general education class as well as the self-concept and achievement of the student with special needs. Because it is important to provide positive support for the appropriate behaviors of students with disabilities, teachers should assess their own behavior. They can count the different types of statements they make (e.g., positive, negative, instructional) and determine which are made most frequently to students with special needs. Teachers can collect these data by self-recording while the class is in progress or by using observers or tape recorders.

Communicate with and Involve Parents

Parents should be informed of the purpose of implementing inclusion programs and the effects these programs will have on their child's education. Parents of students with disabilities may be concerned that their child will be rejected by students and teachers in the general education program. They also may regret the loss of the special attention and services provided in the special education program. In addition, they may fear that their child will experience failure when included in the mainstream. On the other hand, parents of typical students in the general education class often believe that students with disabilities require a great deal of the teacher's attention and that the amount of instruction their children receive will be reduced. They may also be concerned that the behavior of a student with special needs will have a negative effect on the behavior of their children.

Many of the apprehensions of parents can be eliminated if they are provided with accurate information concerning the inclusion of students with disabilities in the general education program. For example, the PTA can feature programs on the needs of special learners, pamphlets explaining inclusion can be sent to all parents, and the acceptance of students with special needs can be a topic of discussion at parent-teacher conferences. Parents of students with disabilities will receive specific information at the meeting of the IEP team. Students in the general education class can assist by communicating accurate information about students with special needs to their parents.

Teachers should communicate regularly with parents to ensure that they remain informed. Parents of students with disabilities often hear from the school only when their children behave inappropriately; they receive limited information about accomplishments and successes. In addition, students with special needs may convey distorted reports of classroom occurrences to their parents; for example, they may say that "all" the students in the general education class pick on them. Parents of general education students also need direct communication from the teacher; they may have misconceptions about inclusion because their children talk about only the negative acts of students with special needs. Parents of all students should be informed that they are important to their children's program and should be encouraged to visit the classroom if they have questions (Heron & Harris, 1993).

According to Kroth (1981), parents should be recognized as their children's major teachers and professionals as consultants to parents. The Mirror Model of Parental Involvement advocated by Kroth (see Figure 6–4) suggests that, even though professionals may provide parents of students with disabilities with information and skills, those parents also are able to aid professionals and other parents. With appropriate assistance, parents can improve their skills in working with their children, help professionals assist the students at school, and aid students and other parents in understanding and working with their special children (Binkard, 1985).

Edgar and Davidson (1979) recommend that communication with parents include information about specific events and activities. Professional terms such as *inclusion, mainstreaming,* and *Least Restrictive Environment* should be avoided; educators should use words everyone understands. Communication should occur on a regular basis so that parents keep in touch with the program, are informed of current events, and begin to accept and support the inclusion of students with disabilities. Figure 6–5 presents the opinions of the parent of a student with special needs about issues that teachers should consider when working with parents. Although the original statement was directed to special education teachers (Roland, 1989), it contains information that all individuals working with the parents of students with special needs should contemplate.

In this chapter, several techniques for promoting the social acceptance of students with disabilities in the general education classroom have been described. Consult the checklist in Figure 6–6 to review factors important in preparing to serve students with special needs. Next, you will learn about coordination skills for management of the total learning environment. Before proceeding, however, check "Things to Remember" to review ways to enhance social acceptance.

◆ ACTIVITIES

1. Visit a general education classroom that includes students with disabilities. Select one student with special needs and one general education peer to observe. Watch each of these students for approximately 30 minutes, and collect information about the number of times each of the following interactions occurs: the student talks to

FIGURE 6-4   Mirror Model of Parental Involvement

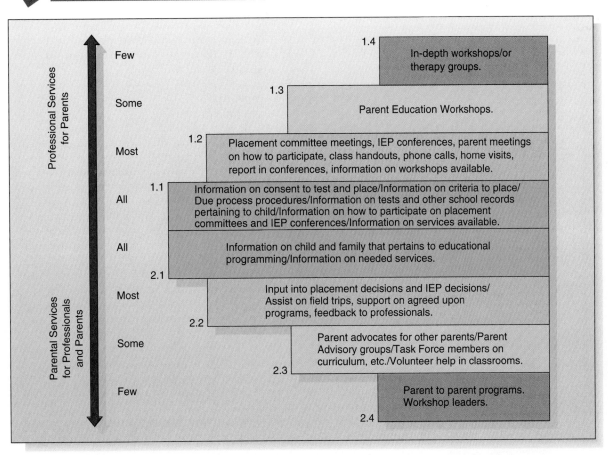

Note. Reprinted with permission of Merrill, an imprint of Macmillan Publishing Company, from "Involvement with Parents of Behaviorally Disordered Adolescents" by R. Kroth. In *Educating Adolescents with Behavior Disorders* (p. 129) by G. Brown, R. L. McDowell, and J. Smith (Eds.). Copyright © 1981 Merrill Publishing Company, Columbus, Ohio.

other students, the student talks to the teacher, other students talk to the student, the teacher talks to the student. Compare your results for the two students. Do you find any differences? Does one seem to be better accepted by the peers and teacher than the other?

2. Interview a student with disabilities who spends part of the school day in a general education setting. How does the student feel about the inclusion experience? Does he or she feel comfortable in the general education class setting? How positive does the student perceive the attitudes of the teacher and general education class peers to be? Does he or she feel accepted or rejected?

Summarize your findings, and use them to prepare a list of questions you might use to interview another student.

3. Select two articles that discuss social acceptance of special students. Journals such as *The Exceptional Parent, Journal of Special Education,* and *Teaching Exceptional Children* would be good places to look. Read the articles to find suggestions for promoting the social acceptance of students with disabilities within the general education classroom.

4. Talk with special and general education teachers from two different schools about ways to improve the social acceptance of students with

---

FIGURE 6-5　A Parent of a Special Student Speaks to Educators

The following recommendations to teachers about working with parents of students with special needs were written by Peggy Roland, who is "the mother of a 12-year-old daughter with education difficulties" (Roland, 1989, p. 3). While the statement was originally directed to special education teachers, it contains concerns and advice that should be considered by others working with special students and their parents.

I'd like to express a few thoughts on behalf of the parents of your students.

Please by frank and *honest* with us. We need the information you have to share and we respect your professional advice and expertise. It may be painful for us to listen to what you have to say but inside we feel relief just hearing something. Our path has been, and always will be, long, but knowing you are there helps.

Please respect us, our children, our families, but above all, the feelings and thoughts that we have shared with you. You may believe we are unrealistic, opinionated, or guilty of ignoring the obvious, but it is probably the best we can manage at the moment. Tomorrow, perhaps even an hour from now, we may express very different feelings.

"They laugh so as not to cry." Such true words! Tears come easily and frequently and they are as much a surprise to us as they are to you. Don't be embarrassed or feel guilty when we cry. Take it as a sign of our humanness and feelings of safety that we react so when we're with you. Many people in the outside world understand neither our laughter nor our tears.

The same is true when we lash out or act defensive. Anger comes with the pain. That anger has no focal point so you may bear its brunt very undeservedly. For that we apologize. Do try to understand that it is usually not directed at you personally but rather at a situation which makes us feel very helpless and, often, very alone. Lashing out may be our overreaction to knowing we can't change the way things are.

Your work and continuing efforts on behalf of our disabled children mean more to us than we can ever explain. Without you, our children would not have achieved the sense of self-worth, the academic and physical success, the societal acceptance they have achieved. Without you, our families would be in more upheaval and distress. Please try to understand that our lives may be just a little different from the average; we have learned to take life one day, sometimes one hour at a time and to be aware and appreciative of the smallest steps while still maintaining our sense of humor and balance.

We are part of this vast thing called life and you are a most important and integral part of our lives. Thank you for being there and helping us establish and maintain a quality of life appropriate for *all* the members of our family.

We look forward to another year of working together!

Note. From "A Parent Speaks to Special Educators" by P. Roland, August 1989, *Exceptional Times,* p. 3.

---

disabilities. What suggestions can they offer? What have they tried in the past that has worked? Ask about activities for teachers, students, parents, and staff members such as secretaries, custodians, and bus drivers.

5. Design a classroom activity that you could use to help general education students be more accepting of students with special needs. First, decide on a specific goal, and then describe the methods you would use to reach this goal. Include ideas about how you would go about implementing this program in your classroom and how you would evaluate its effectiveness.

6. Locate one of the social skills training programs mentioned in the chapter (e.g., *AC-CEPTS, Skillstreaming the Adolescent*) and use the program to teach a lesson on a specific skill to one or more of your friends, colleagues, or students. Write a short report on your experience, and describe specifically how you would use the lesson (or its techniques) with a student with disabilities included in a general education classroom.

FIGURE 6-6 **A Checklist to Evaluate the Readiness of the Mainstream for a Special Student**

Teachers and parents must be committed to carrying out the least restrictive alternative concept for children with disabilities. If individuals with disabilities are ever to be fully accepted in our society, this integration should occur as early and widely as possible. Educators should be willing to put forth their best efforts to make a general education class experience rewarding and enriching for students with disabilities. Special class teachers can do much to make these successes happen when students are included in the mainstream program.

The key to a successful experience in the mainstream is preparation. The checklist below can serve as a guide for the special class teacher in preparing not only the students with disabilities, but also the other people who must support the effort to include these students in the mainstream. Before placing each student with disabilities in a mainstreamed setting, the teacher should examine and work on each element of the checklist, until most, if not all, of the "yes" boxes can be checked.

1. Student with disabilities:

   Yes   No

   ____ ____   Is familiar with rules and routine of the general education classroom?

   ____ ____   Follows verbal and written directions used in the general education classroom?

   ____ ____   Remains on-task for adequate time periods?

   ____ ____   Has expressed a desire to participate in the general education class setting?

   ____ ____   Reacts appropriately to teasing, questions, criticism, etc.?

   ____ ____   Student's IEP objectives match instructional objectives in the general education class?

2. General education teacher:

   Yes   No

   ____ ____   Has been given rationale for activities related to including student with disabilities in the mainstream and asked to cooperate?

   ____ ____   Has information about the needs, present skills, and current learning objectives of the student with disabilities?

   ____ ____   Has been provided with special materials and/or support services as needed?

   ____ ____   Has prepared class for including student with disabilities in the mainstream?

   ____ ____   Has acquired special helping skills if necessary?

   ____ ____   Will be monitored regularly to identify any problems that arise?

3. Typical general education peers:

   Yes   No

   ____ ____   Have been informed about the participation of the student with disabilities and about his/her disability(ies) (if appropriate) with the opportunity to ask questions?

   ____ ____   Have been asked for their cooperation and friendship toward the student with disabilities?

   ____ ____   Have learned helping skills and praising behaviors?

continued

FIGURE 6-6   Continued

---

4. Parents of the student with disabilities:

   Yes   No

   ____ ____   Have received verbal or written information about plan to include student with disabilities in the mainstream?

   ____ ____   Have been asked to praise and encourage child's progress in the general education and special education class(es)?

5. Parents of the typical general education peers:

   Yes   No

   ____ ____   Have been informed about the plan to include student with disabilities in the mainstream at PTA meeting, conferences, or through other vehicle, and asked for their cooperation?

6. School administrator:

   Yes   No

   ____ ____   Has been informed about specifics of plan to include student with disabilities in the mainstream?

   ____ ____   Has indicated specific steps she or he will take to encourage and support these activities?

Note. From "Helping Teachers Integrate Handicapped Students into the Regular Classroom" by J. C. Dardig, 1981, *Educational Horizons, 59,* pp. 124–130. Copyright 1981 by *Educational Horizons.* Adapted by permission.

Things to Remember

- Programs designed to include students with disabilities in general education should emphasize the social acceptance of these students because rejection can damage both self-concept and academic performance.
- Students with special needs may be rejected if they do not look or act like their peers; another contributing factor is that some students with disabilities have poor social skills.
- Attitudes are very important; the attitudes of teachers influence the attitudes of their students.
- Attitudes are affected by information; the more teachers and peers know about students with disabilities, the more likely they are to accept them.
- General education students, students with special needs, and parents should be prepared for programs that include students with disabilities in the mainstream.
- Sociometric measures are often used to find out how students with special needs are perceived by their peers.

- Functional assessment and behavioral rating scales and checklists are used to help assess a student's social skill performance, identify problem areas that may require instruction, or assess the student's progress.
- Instruction about disabilities, experiences with people with special needs, and structured interactions with students with disabilities can be provided to help general education students (and teachers) gain information.
- Students with special needs can learn appropriate social skills; however, it is usually necessary to provide specific instruction in this area.
- Parental support for the inclusion program can be increased by explaining the purpose of the program, letting parents know how it will affect their children, encouraging parents to participate, and keeping parents informed through frequent communication.

chapter 7

Coordinating the Classroom Learning Environment

Coordination Skills for the Teacher

Arranging the Physical Environment

Organizing the Instructional Environment

- *Inclusion Tips for the Teacher:* Self-Correcting Instructional Materials

Using Educational Technologies

- *Spotlight on Technology:* Tape Recorders

Managing Time and Other Resources

- *Inclusion Tips for the Teacher:* Time Management

- *Inclusion Tips for the Teacher:* Peer Tutors and Adult Volunteers

Activities

- *Things to Remember*

- *Window on the Web: Electronic Learning,* an Online Magazine

In general education classrooms, teachers adapt instruction, manage behavior, and promote the social acceptance of students with special needs. In addition, the teacher is responsible for the arrangement, management, and coordination of the total learning environment.

◆ COORDINATION SKILLS FOR THE TEACHER

As managers, teachers structure the physical environment in which learning takes place and within these physical surroundings set up the instructional environment. To do this, teachers coordinate many different resources: time, people (including both students and instructional personnel), and educational materials and equipment. Management skills aid in the successful coordination of the general education classroom.

Classroom management is "what teachers do to help make student life in the classroom pleasant, meaningful, safe, and orderly" (Stephens, 1980). Stephens outlines 6 classroom management elements that teachers should consider:

> *Demographics,* the group's composition
> *Physical environment,* the use of the room and its furnishings
> *Time,* the amount of time available in the class and the teacher's and students' use of it
> *Student encouragement,* ways that students are reinforced for performance
> *Provisions for interacting,* among the students and with teachers
> *Differentiating instruction,* the extent to which and how the instruction is individualized (p. 4)

The management skills of the teacher have been found to be related to the amount of student learning; good managers are more able to adapt instruction to student needs, particularly in heterogeneous classes (Evertson, Sanford, & Emmer, 1981). This chapter describes several of the factors to consider in managing the total learning environment. Included are principles for arranging the physical environment, organizing the instructional environment, using educational technologies, and coordinating time and other resources.

The teacher can structure the learning situation in many different ways. He or she receives a room, students, curriculum guidelines, and some standard instructional materials (such as grade level textbooks); all other factors are under the teacher's control. Because there is a great deal of freedom in the selection of options, teachers should be aware of the reasons underlying their choices.

Figure 7–1 is a learning style questionnaire based on the work of several persons (Dunn & Dunn, 1978, 1979; Gartner & Riessman, 1977; Lewis, 1980; Pasanella & Volkmor, 1981; Renzulli & Smith, 1978; Schubert, Glick, & Bauer, 1979). Read this survey and determine which conditions *you* favor for learning. Consider your tolerance for environmental variations (noise, distractions, physical surroundings), your personal work habits (time of day, attention span, closure, rate), and your favorite learning methods (other learners, structure, presentation and response modes, activities, reinforcement). Then compare your preferred learning style with your present teaching style.

Many teachers, in arranging the physical and instructional environments, select options that reflect their own preferences as learners. Depending on the needs of the students in the classroom, this approach may or may not be successful. Teachers should be familiar with many different ways to structure the learning environment so that management decisions can take into account not only the preferences of the teacher but also those of the students.

◆ ARRANGING THE PHYSICAL ENVIRONMENT

The **physical environment** is made up of the classroom and its furnishings. The nature of the physical environment and its arrangement have an effect on the behavior of both teachers and students (Smith, Neisworth, & Greer, 1978). For example, environmental constraints make it difficult to teach running skills in a closet, demonstrate cooking and food preparation techniques in a gymnasium, or supervise small-group discussions in a large auditorium with fixed seats. Environment exerts the greatest influence on the nonacademic performance of students. Reviews of research (Doyle, 1986; Weinstein, 1979) conclude that classroom characteristics affect attitudes and social behavior but have little impact (with the exception of seating arrangements) on student achievement. In the following paragraphs are several principles to consider in arranging the physical environment of your classroom. Keep in mind that some aspects of the physical environment, such as classroom seating arrangements, are easy to modify; others, such as the size of the classroom and the colors of its walls, are less amenable to change.

FIGURE 7-1   What Is Your Learning Style?

When do you work best? What type of learning environment do you prefer? Is the learning environment that *you* prefer the one you provide for students? If so, please reconsider. Your goal as a teacher is to meet the needs of the students!

Factor	Preference
Noise	Do you work best in absolute silence? in a quiet room? with music playing? with television on? with others talking?
Distractions	Are you able to work with many visual distractions (e.g., interesting pictures, bulletin boards, objects)? Can you work near a window? with people moving about? Do you work best with your desk or table clear?
Physical surroundings	Do you work best sitting upright in a straight-backed chair? an easy chair? on the floor? Do you prefer a desk or table for writing? Can you work anywhere at all? Do you work best if it is warm? cool? Are the best conditions those where you can eat? drink? move about at will?
Time of day	Is early morning the best time for you to learn? midmorning? midday? afternoon? evening? late at night? When are you most alert?
Attention span	Are you able to concentrate only a few minutes? a half hour? for long periods of time? until the work is done? How often do you need to take a break? Are you able to get back to work immediately after a break?
Closure	Do you want to finish a task once you've started it, or can you stop working at any point in the task? Do you like to take breaks in the middle of tasks? have work interrupted before it's completed? have to stop before you have finished?
Rate	Are you a fast or slow worker? Do you spend the most time planning? doing the task? checking your work?
Other learners	Do you like to work alone or with others? with peers or adults? If you work one-to-one, should the other person be the teacher? another student? Do you enjoy working in small groups? teams? committees? large groups?
Structure	Are you most comfortable when all task requirements are clearly spelled out for you? when you can make some choices? when you have complete freedom?
Presentation mode	In learning about something new, would you rather read about it? hear someone talk about it? see it in pictures? watch a videotape? listen to an audiotape? interact with a computer program? watch someone demonstrate it? try it yourself? try explaining it to someone else?
Activities	Which of the following instructional activities help you learn: lecture? discussion? projects? drill? peer teaching? independent study? games? programmed instruction? simulation? role playing?
Response mode	Do you like to show what you've learned by writing reports? taking exams? telling others? demonstrating how to do it? expressing it artistically?
Reinforcement	Do you need incentives to do a good job? peer approval? praise and recognition from the teacher? tangible rewards? grades? pay? satisfaction that you did your best?

Ensure a Safe and Barrier-Free Environment

A primary concern with any environment is the safety of its inhabitants. Although this is important for all students, students with physical and sensory impairments require special precautions. For example, books, other objects, and clutter on the classroom floor are hazards for students with balance problems or poor eyesight. Students with limited mobility may need help to move out of the school quickly during fire drills; students who are deaf may need visual cues in order to react in emergency situations.

Another major consideration is **access** to the school and classroom. Many of the newer school buildings are designed to be barrier-free; that is, **architectural barriers** are avoided, to allow individuals with disabilities entry to and use of the facility.

Buildings have elevators and ramps, stairs have handrails for persons with crutches or canes, doorways are wide enough to allow wheelchairs to pass through, and bathroom facilities are specially designed. Drinking fountains, lockers, vending machines, trash cans, towel dispensers, and telephones are installed so that they can be easily reached by a person in a wheelchair. In older schools that do not have these features, it may be necessary to make modifications to allow access to students with disabilities.

The environment of the classroom should also be barrier-free. The room should be arranged to allow easy travel between desks and tables. Instructional materials should be placed within reach, and storage space should be provided for special equipment such as magnification devices, crutches, and adapted keyboards for computers. In addition, bookshelves, chalkboards, and bulletin boards should be conveniently located and low enough to permit their use by students in wheelchairs.

Make the Working Conditions Pleasant

A pleasant physical environment is one that is both comfortable and attractive. The comfort of students and teachers depends on factors such as temperature, ventilation, lighting, and noise level. Classroom temperature should be moderate; hot or cold environments may hinder performance. Ventilation should be adequate so that the room is not stuffy. All work areas should be well lighted and free from glare; some students with visual impairments may require special lighting. Windows permit natural illumination but may offer distractions to students; these distractions can be avoided by building windows above eye level or by temporarily drawing the drapes. Noise can also distract students from their work or interfere with their ability to hear others speak. Soundproofed walls, carpeting, acoustical ceiling tiles, and drapes all help to decrease unwanted environmental sounds (D'Alonzo, D'Alonzo, & Mauser, 1979). Although some aspects of the physical environment are difficult to change (e.g., a poor heating or cooling system), it is possible to make classrooms more comfortable by additions such as heaters, fans, and lamps for additional lighting (Murdick & Petch-Hogan, 1996).

The attractiveness of the learning environment is important. Attractive classrooms help improve attendance, participation, and attitudes toward instruction (Weinstein, 1979). One aspect of aesthetic appeal is the use of color. Smith, Neisworth, and Greer (1978) caution against dark or bright colors for classroom walls; they say that "wall surfaces should be light in tone and subdued though not drab in hue, so that they can better function as a pleasant background for whatever is placed on them or occurs in front of them" (p. 134). The room decor also affects its attractiveness. Furnishings, bulletin boards, pictures, posters, mobiles, and displays of educational materials and equipment all contribute to visual appeal. These stimuli should be interesting and enjoyable to look at without being sources of distraction.

Obtain Appropriate Furniture and Special Equipment

Classroom furniture should be comfortable, attractive, durable, and functional. The primary furnishings of most classrooms (with the exception of specialized classes such as shop and home economics) are chairs and tables or desks. Chairs should be the correct size; students should be able to sit comfortably with their backs supported and their feet on the floor. Tables and desks should be level and should provide adequate writing space and leg room. Special tables and desks may be needed by persons in braces or wheelchairs.

Students with visual, hearing, and physical impairments often require special classroom equipment. Students may bring with them some types of special equipment: wheelchairs, canes, braces,

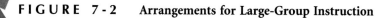

FIGURE 7-2   Arrangements for Large-Group Instruction

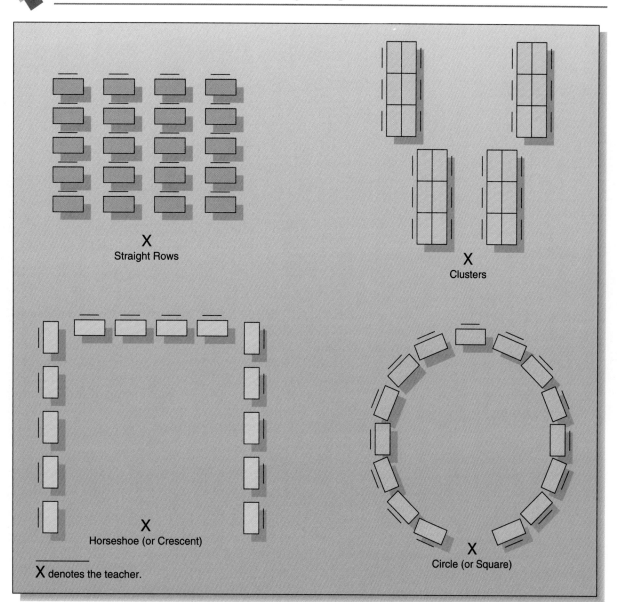

crutches, hearing aids, and eyeglasses. Other types are furnished by the special education teacher. For example, students with visual impairments may use a Braille notetaker or a slate and stylus to write, an abacus or talking calculator for math, and optical aids and magnification devices. Those with hearing losses may need amplification equipment. Students with physical impairments may require lapboards for writing, automatic page turners for reading, or special standing tables. Chapters 13 and 14 describe the special equipment needs of students with sensory and physical impairments.

Arrange Space Functionally

Classroom space should be divided into performance areas or zones to accommodate routine activities and tasks (Berdine & Cegelka, 1980; Mercer

FIGURE 7-3 **Small-Group Arrangements**

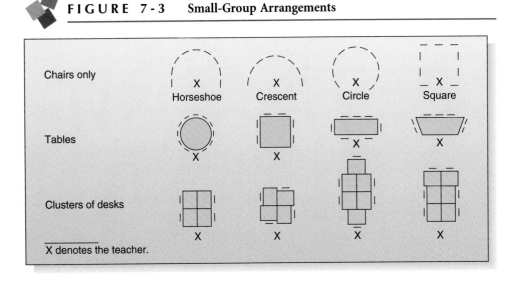

& Mercer, 1998). Stowitschek, Gable, and Hendrickson (1980) suggest that, in planning the room arrangement, teachers consider typical student groupings, storage needs for materials and equipment, and procedures for distribution and collection of materials and student work.

When the room is divided into separate areas, one essential consideration is space for instruction. Usually at least two areas are needed: one for large-group instruction and another for small-group instruction. As shown in Figure 7–2, desks and chairs can be arranged in many different ways for large-group instruction. Typical patterns are straight rows, clusters of desks, and configurations in the shape of horseshoes, crescents, circles, and squares. Some arrangements for small-group instruction are shown in Figure 7–3. Arrangements can use chairs only, both tables and chairs, or clusters of desks.

In some classrooms, small-group instructional areas are set up for specific subjects or activities. For example, in classrooms that use learning centers or stations, there may be separate areas for math, language arts, and science. These areas can be used by the teacher for direct instruction or by students for independent study or self-instructional activities. Mercer and Mercer (1998) recommend a separate area for each subject, even at the secondary level; for example, a classroom in which English is taught could be divided into writing, literature, free reading, and listening areas.

In addition to instructional areas, each student should have an individual work space. Usually the student's desk is the space where he or she works independently and takes part in large-group instruction. Students should have storage space in their desks or, if tables are used instead of desks, in cupboards, cabinets, or bookcases. Care should be taken to ensure that individual work areas are relatively quiet and private. Some students may benefit from separate work areas. Cubicles, carrels, booths, and partitions can be used to set up private office areas for students who are highly distractible or who have difficulty sustaining attention.

Teachers also need a work and storage area, which is usually the teacher's desk. Some teachers do not use their desks as a work area during school hours; they may move from place to place throughout the classroom or station themselves in one of the small-group instructional areas. The classroom should be arranged so that the teacher can visually monitor students' activities throughout the school day. Stainback, Stainback, and Froyen (1987) say that "the teacher should be able to make a visual sweep of the room and detect when students need assistance and what social interactions are occurring" (p. 12).

Other areas can be incorporated into the classroom if desired. A separate storage location may be needed if materials and equipment are not housed in learning centers. Some teachers set up a specific location at which students pick up their work for the day and return completed assignments. The classroom computer may be placed at the back or side of the room, so that students can interact with instructional programs without disturbing the work of others. Another option is a free time or recreational area with games, tapes, books, and other types of reading materials. Time in this area can be used as reinforcement for appropriate behavior, completed work, or accurate performance.

The plan for an elementary grade classroom in Figure 7–4 includes areas for several types of activities. Student desks are clustered for either large- or small-group instruction. There are listening centers and study carrels, a partitioned area for quiet study or games, and a small carpeted area with beanbag chairs. Three tables are available for small-group work, and storage space is ample and conveniently located. There are also many possibilities for flexibility; the placement of desks and tables can be easily changed and the portable chalkboard can serve as a temporary partition.

The relationship among the different areas within the classroom should be carefully planned. According to Doyle (1986), the major concerns are provision of separate areas for different instructional purposes, careful design of classroom traffic patterns, and minimization of density. It is also important to arrange classroom space to encourage smooth and quick transitions between instructional activities (Rieth & Evertson, 1988). Among the factors to consider are these:

1. *Sound.* Separate quiet areas from noisy areas.
2. *Convenience.* Store equipment, supplies, and materials near where they are used; locate instructional groups near the chalkboard.
3. *Student traffic patterns.* Make traffic patterns direct; discourage routes that lead to disruptions (e.g., students distracting others when turning in assignments or moving to new activities). Also, make sure that traffic areas are uncluttered and wide enough to accommodate the flow of student traffic, particularly during transitions from one activity to another (Stainback, Stainback, & Froyen, 1987).
4. *Teacher mobility.* Use an open room arrangement so that the teacher can move quickly and easily to any location. This allows the teacher to "respond to student needs as well as to potential behavior problems" (Cegelka, 1995b, p. 139).

5. *Flexibility.* Ensure that all classroom activities can be accomplished; make areas multipurpose or use different arrangements for different tasks. Stainback, Stainback, and Slavin (1989) recommend classrooms with "areas that can be opened, closed, or screened off depending on the needs of students when working on different tasks" (p. 140).
6. *Density.* Arrange student seating so that personal space is preserved; avoid crowding. High density can reduce attentiveness and increase dissatisfaction and aggressiveness (Doyle, 1986; Zentall, 1983).

When arranging classroom space, the teacher should not consider it permanent. New arrangements should be tried as often as necessary to increase the effectiveness of the learning environment. As Polloway and Patton (1993) comment, "every teacher should periodically review why the room is arranged as it is. There is no one best way to arrange a classroom, but some ways are clearly superior to others" (p. 59).

Consider Educational Goals in Making Seating Arrangements

How students are arranged in relationship to each other can affect their academic performance, classroom behavior, and social interactions. Weinstein (1979) concludes from a review of research studies that achievement is related to seat position: In classrooms arranged in rows, students sitting in the front center seats participate more, are more attentive, and spend more time on task. This finding may be due to the availability of more cues from the teacher (e.g., increased eye contact, better reception of nonverbal messages) (Doyle, 1986). It may also be due to self-selection if students choose their own seats or to the tendency of teachers to seat low achievers farther away from the teacher's desk than high achievers (Alves & Gottlieb, 1986). However, according to Heron and Harris (1993), low achievers improve academically as their seats are moved from the back to the front of the classroom. This improvement is attributed to closer proximity to the teacher and the stimuli to which they should attend.

Seating also influences classroom behavior. Axelrod, Hall, and Tams (1972) found that study behaviors improved when students were seated in rows rather than in groups around tables. To prevent behavior problems, inattentive or disruptive students

FIGURE 7-4 Classroom Plan

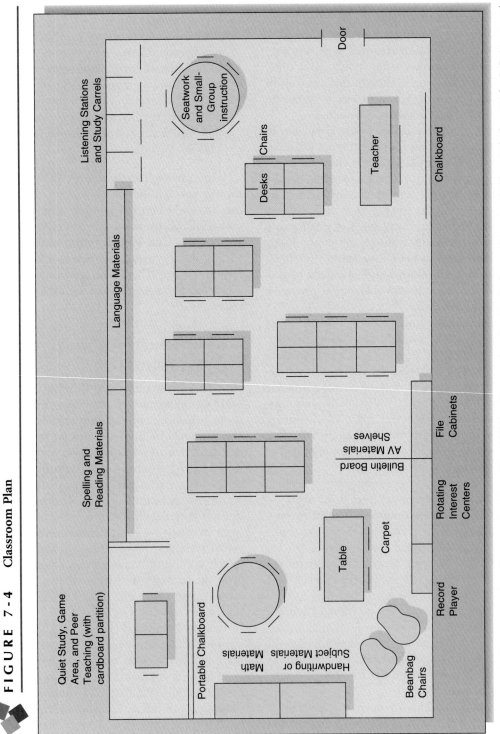

Note. Reprinted with permission of Merrill, an imprint of Macmillan Publishing Company, from *Teaching Students with Learning Problems* (3rd ed., p. 85) by C. D. Mercer and A. R. Mercer. Copyright © 1989 Merrill Publishing Company, Columbus, Ohio.

are placed near the teacher; those who argue or fight are separated. Disruptive students improve their behavior when grouped with well-behaved students (Stainback, Stainback, & Froyen, 1987). In some cases, teachers may move students to separate areas, away from their peers. Students who act out or display serious inappropriate behaviors may be removed to a time-out area. Those who are highly distractible can be seated in individual study carrels or booths. However, teachers should consider all possible alternatives before physically isolating students from others in the classroom.

Social interaction can be facilitated by seating arrangements. Smith, Neisworth, and Greer (1978) note that interaction increases when students are seated close to each other or opposite one another. Heron and Harris (1993) observe that verbal communication tends to move across tables rather than around them. They recommend seating a low-verbal student across from a high-verbal student to enhance performance. In this arrangement, the low-verbal student is better able to receive the verbal messages and the facial and gestural cues of the peer model.

The physical environment of the classroom can be arranged in many ways to promote successful student performance. The environmental checklist in Figure 7–5 summarizes several important concerns.

ORGANIZING THE INSTRUCTIONAL ENVIRONMENT

The **instructional environment** of the classroom includes the procedures, routines, materials, and equipment used by the teacher to increase student performance. The teacher organizes the curriculum, groups students, and sets up delivery systems for the presentation and practice of skills and information. This structure directly affects nonacademic performance as well as student achievement. Students actively involved in appropriate instruction are less likely to exhibit problem behaviors and more likely to feel good about their competence. Several principles are important to consider in arranging the instructional environment.

Organize Curricular Skills and Information

Although the scope and sequence of the general education curriculum are usually well specified for the teacher, there is opportunity to arrange the skills and information in different ways. The traditional organization follows academic subjects; this is most apparent at the secondary level, where the curriculum is broken down into separate courses. At the elementary level, skills and information can also be divided into different subjects, such as language arts, mathematics, social studies, and science.

An alternate way of organizing the curriculum is the **unit approach,** which cuts across subject matter areas (Polloway & Patton, 1993). Meyen (1981) describes unit teaching as a generic instructional approach that integrates instruction "on academic and social skills, with information structured around a common theme building on the previous experience of students" (p. 3). Topics of interest and importance to students become the vehicle for teaching academic skills. For instance, Meyen (1981) suggests experiential themes, such as transportation, the community, leisure time, and the newspaper. The teacher organizes the unit around a central theme and includes activities in each of the core areas: communication skills, math, social competencies, safety, health, and vocation.

Many teachers use thematic units as a supplement to the standard curriculum. While continuing instruction in specific academic subjects, they also introduce activities related to a special topic or interest area. Examples are space travel, February holidays, contributions of African Americans, and endangered species. This approach is more common at the elementary level but can also be adapted for secondary-aged students.

If units are carefully planned to ensure the inclusion of several important academic skills, they are a valuable addition to the instructional environment. Units include a variety of different activities, and the teacher can tailor instruction to the needs of the individual students within the classroom. In addition, the use of themes that interest and motivate students can increase their willingness to participate in academic activities.

Another method of organizing curriculum is the blending or integration of academic subjects. For example, at the elementary level, the whole language approach integrates the language arts of listening, speaking, reading, and writing (Lapp & Flood, 1992). Skills are taught in the context of authentic communication tasks, not as separate (and isolated) subjects (Westby, 1992). Writing across the curriculum is another example. In this approach, secondary

FIGURE 7-5   Physical Environment Checklist

Physiological Effects

Illumination
- Is there adequate light for reading and other demanding visual tasks?
- Is the lighting throughout the classroom varied and home-like?
- Is lighting used to help define the different activity areas of the room?
- Is the lighting warm yet not glaring?

Temperature
- Can adequate air movement be obtained when needed?
- Is there an adequate supply of fresh air?
- Are temperatures controlled within a comfortable range (68–74°)?
- Are children assisted in making necessary clothing adjustments for the room temperature?
- Is humidity adequate year round?

Noise
- Can windows be opened without interference from outside noise?
- Is the noise level of each classroom controlled so that the activities of the other classrooms are not disturbed?
- Is the teacher rarely asked to repeat what he/she has said?

Color
- Are the colors in the classroom pleasantly varied?
- Is color used to define areas of the room and to attract attention to important educational displays?
- Are the colors in the room subdued, mellow, and pleasing?

Materials
- Does the classroom contain furnishings, materials, and displays in addition to typical institutional furnishings?
- Do teachers and students bring in a variety of materials and displays related to current assignments?
- Are learning materials and displays well organized by topics or learning area?
- Have excessive, unorganized materials been removed to eliminate confusion or distraction?

Spatial Effects
- Are related compatible activities arranged together and unrelated, incompatible activities separated within the classroom?
- Have an appropriate time and place been designated and assigned for all activities?
- Is there a variety of places where different-sized groups can meet and work?
- Are there special places that individual children can go (a) for isolation, (b) for rest and quiet, (c) to let off steam, (d) to reward themselves, (e) for private instruction, (f) to work independently, (g) to be disciplined privately?
- Can children enter, leave, clean up, and dress, etc. without disturbing others?
- Can children space themselves as they need or desire?
- Do the relative amounts of space allocated to various activities reflect their importance in the teaching program?

Physical Effects
- Is the environment kept clean?
- Are the furnishings (desks, displays, etc.) moveable to provide a variety of groupings and areas within the room for different learning tasks?
- Can the teacher control visual distractions between groups of children (by separating groups, raising room dividers, etc.)?
- Are storage facilities accessible to the students for getting out and putting away materials which they are allowed access to?
- Have high physical barriers been eliminated so that the teacher has visual access to the entire room?

Setting Effects
- Can the teacher identify an "overcommitted" setting (one in which most children are observers rather than performers and leaders) and then attempt to create new, smaller work or activity groups?
- Have physical barriers to children with disabilities been removed?
- Does the teacher periodically change the environment to improve the teaching program?
- Does the teacher systematically observe and evaluate the effects of the environment on the social behaviors and learning of the class?

Note. Reprinted with the permission of Macmillan College Publishing from *Evaluating Educational Environments* by R. M. Smith, J. T. Neisworth, and J. G. Greer. Copyright © 1978 Macmillan College Publishing Company, Inc.

students are expected to practice their writing skills in all subjects, not just in English classes.

Group Students for Instruction

Before presentation of skills and information can begin, the teacher must decide how to group students. Two factors must be determined: group size and group type. The number of students per group can vary from one (in a tutoring situation) to the entire class. Class size is a factor in instruction; it has been noted that student achievement increases as the number of students in the class decreases (Glass & Smith, 1978). However, this does not necessarily mean that classes of 30 or more students should always be broken into several groups for instruction. Using the whole class as a group is an efficient way of presenting new material, if that material is appropriate for all of the students (Brophy & Good, 1986). Also, providing guided practice for the entire class at once is an effective use of time. For instance, if the time allotted for mathematics is 1 hour, the teacher can spend only 2 minutes with each of 30 individual students or can devote the entire period to the class as a whole.

When it is necessary to present different material to different students, small groups are appropriate. According to Brophy and Good (1986), small groups are necessary in beginning reading instruction and in highly heterogeneous classes. Also, smaller groups can lead to greater student participation (Mercer & Mercer, 1998). Small groups generally range in size from 3 to 7 or 8 individuals. For some students, individual instruction is needed; this can be presented by the teacher or other instructional personnel, such as peers, aides, and volunteers.

The criterion used to group students together often determines the size of the group. The most typical criterion is homogeneity: students of similar ability, at similar levels, or with similar skills are placed in one group. For example, a placement test might be given to pinpoint each student's current instructional level and the results used to form instructional groups. A **skill-specific group** is made up of students requiring instruction in the same skill area. This type of homogeneous grouping, although temporary because skill needs change, is the most effective means of individualizing instruction.

Heterogeneous grouping can also be used for instruction. In this type of group, lower-functioning students are provided with models (Smith, Neis-

worth, & Greer, 1978); for example, students with articulation problems can benefit from hearing the more appropriate speech of their peers. Also, heterogeneous grouping can be used to promote the development of social skills (Bossert & Barnett, 1981). In groups with a range of skills represented, Affleck, Lowenbraun, and Archer (1980) recommend individualizing by using the same task to develop different skills. For example, having students read a short story can be used for instruction in several types and levels of comprehension skills.

Flexible grouping is the practice of using several kinds of grouping formats at different times; this allows all students to interact with one another (Schubert, Glick, & Bauer, 1979). Although skill-specific grouping remains the most effective for the purpose of instruction, several of the other methods suggested by these authors may be appropriate for nonacademic and social activities. Examples are grouping by common interests, grouping by choice, proximity grouping, alphabetical grouping, and grouping by counting off.

Set Up Systems for Monitoring Practice

Opportunities for practice are provided after new material is presented. During practice, student performance is monitored, either directly by the

Inclusion Tips for the Teacher

Self-Correcting Instructional Materials

With instructional materials that are self-correcting, students receive immediate feedback on the accuracy of their response. Some of the most common teaching tools contain self-correcting features. For example, at the end of many textbooks are the answers to all or some of the questions and problems.

Teachers can also design self-correcting materials to meet the needs of specific students. One example of an easy-to-make device that can be used for almost any school subject is suggested by Mercer and Mercer (1998):

Strips are cut in one side of a manila folder, which then is laminated. Worksheets containing problems and answers are inserted into the folder so that only the problem is presented. The student uses a grease pencil or a felt-tip pen to write the responses under each problem. Then the worksheet is pulled upward, and the answers appear in the strip.

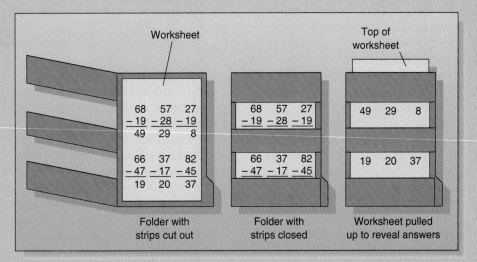

Note. Reprinted with the permission of Merrill from *Teaching Students with Learning Problems*, 5th ed., by Cecil D. Mercer and Ann R. Mercer (p. 72). Copyright © 1998 Prentice-Hall, Inc.

Flashcards are another example of a self-correcting material. The question or problem appears on one side of the card and the other side contains the answer. Like the folder device, flashcards are easy to make and can be adapted for many different subjects. Also, students can use flashcards for independent practice or for review with a peer.

When students use self-correcting materials for class assignments, teachers often ask how to prevent them from merely copying down the correct answers. Here are three ways to avoid this problem:

• Within each activity or assignment, include a few questions or problems for which the answer is not provided. These items serve as probes to determine whether students can transfer skills to questions for which the answers are not supplied.
• Have students correct each other's work. Students can trade assignments, or one or two indi-

viduals can be selected to be graders for the period or the day.
- Distribute answer keys only after students have completed their work; be sure, however, that the

feedback occurs as soon after completion of the assignment as possible.

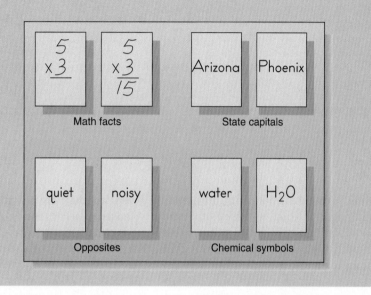

| Math facts | State capitals |
| Opposites | Chemical symbols |

teacher or through the use of **self-instructional learning materials.** With self-instructional materials, students receive feedback from the materials themselves and thus are able to practice independently without the assistance of the teacher. This approach frees the teacher for other activities, such as direct instruction.

Among the different forms of self-instruction are self-correcting materials, programmed learning, and mediated instruction. **Self-correcting materials** are those that provide the student with the correct answer so that responses can be checked for accuracy. For example, math fact flashcards with the problem on one side and the answer on the other allow immediate feedback. Teachers can also prepare answer keys for independent practice activities and encourage students to check and correct their responses. Mercer and Mercer (1998) point out that this works well with students who have a history of academic failure because they are able to make (and correct) mistakes privately. See "Inclusion Tips for the Teacher" for more information about self-correcting materials.

Programmed instruction is another method that allows students to monitor their own practice.

Figure 7–6 describes and illustrates this approach. The learner covers the answers on the right-hand side of the page and attempts to answer the questions; each response can then be checked immediately. Heron and Harris (1993) note that programmed instruction allows learners to progress at their own rate through small, incremental steps that build on previous learning.

Mediated instruction is any procedure that includes the use of media. For example, many computer software programs provide programmed instruction or practice activities with immediate feedback and correction of errors. Another example is the use of audiotapes for self-instruction. As de Grandpre and Messier (1979) suggest, teachers can develop self-instructional tapes to aid secondary students in reviewing material before exams. The student listens to a tape-recorded question, stops the tape, writes an answer, and then continues the tape to find out whether the response is correct. The tape directs the student to correct any errors immediately.

A **learning center** is a common way to organize self-instructional materials for independent classroom practice. According to Berdine and Cegelka

---

> ◆ **FIGURE 7-6**   **Programmed Instruction**
>
> ---
>
> Programmed instruction does three things:
>   *First*, it breaks learning tasks down into small steps. These small _____ help learners   steps
> avoid making mistakes. That, then, is the first purpose of programmed instruction—to break
> material into small steps to help learners avoid making _____.   mistakes
>   *Second*, programmed instruction requires that students make active responses while they
> work. These active _____ are often made by filling in blanks in the programmed material.   responses
>   *Third*, as you respond actively by filling in each _____, you can check immediately to   blank
> see whether you made a correct response. This immediate knowledge of correct response is
> the reinforcement built into the program. When you see that you gave the correct response,
> that knowledge is your _____.   reinforcement

Note. From *Individualizing Instruction* (2nd ed., p. 241) by C. M. Charles, 1980, St. Louis, MO: C. V. Mosby. Copyright 1980 by C. V. Mosby. Reprinted by permission.

(1980), a learning or interest center is "an area especially designed for auto-instructional use by the student" (p. 212). Centers provide independent work for one or several students in one or several skill areas. A typical arrangement is by academic subject; for example, many elementary classrooms contain centers for language arts, mathematics, science, and social studies.

Learning centers should be based on specific instructional objectives, house all necessary media and materials, and provide clear and simple directions for student activities. Pretests allow students to select appropriate activities; several kinds and levels of activities should be included in each center. Another important component is a record-keeping system; for example, checklists can be used to note which activities each student has completed. Student progress is measured by posttests or other evaluation devices.

Learning centers can be constructed so that practice activities are individualized. Centers promote independence, free the teacher for other duties, and encourage students to work cooperatively. Like other types of self-instructional systems, they also provide students with immediate feedback on the adequacy of their performance during practice.

Provide Guidelines for Student Behavior

Classroom rules and routines help structure the learning environment. Many students need guidelines for behavior and benefit from consistently enforced rules. As noted in chapter 5, rules for classroom conduct are helpful for students of any age. Madsen, Becker, and Thomas (1968) recommend that classroom rules be short and to the point, few in number, and phrased positively (e.g., "Keep your hands to yourself" rather than "Don't hit others"). Affleck, Lowenbraun, and Archer (1980) add that rules should be simple, clearly stated, and directly enforceable by the teacher. Classroom rules should be explained to students and reviewed frequently.

Structure can also help the academic performance of students. When consistent classroom routines are established, students are aware of what they should do, where they should be, and how they should act. For example, there may be a specific time and place in the classroom for turning in assignments. Some teachers provide each student with a daily assignment card that spells out each of the activities that must be completed. Secondary teachers can establish a routine pattern of assignments (e.g., quiz on Wednesdays, essay due on Fridays) and provide students with a weekly assignment sheet (Raison, 1979). It is also possible to use student work folders that contain the schedule for the day, assignments to be completed, answer keys, and check-off sheets to record finished tasks (Eaton & Hansen, 1978).

Another way to provide structure is the use of prompts and models. Somewhere in most elementary classrooms is a model of the alphabet for students to consult if they have difficulty remembering how to form letters. This technique can be used in most other subjects. For example, procedures for long division, alphabetizing, or constructing a para-

FIGURE 7-7   **Daily Assignment Sheet**

Work for	Monday		
Name	George		
MATH	Do page 68, numbers 1 through 12.	I did it _____ I scored it _____ I corrected it _____	My score was _____ right.
SPELLING	Do page 42, numbers 4, 6, 8, 9, 10, 11, and 15.	I did it _____ I scored it _____ I corrected it _____	My score was _____ right.
READING	Read pages 6 and 7. Do worksheet 17A.	I did it _____ I scored it _____ I corrected it _____	My score was _____ right.

graph can be written on the board. These prompts help students to function independently.

Use Systematic Record-Keeping Procedures

A great many sources of data are available to the teacher in the general education classroom, and it is easy to become overwhelmed by masses of information. However, by using systematic record-keeping procedures, the teacher can collect sufficient information to make informed instructional decisions.

Teachers generally collect and record two types of data: activities completed (e.g., math workbook, pages 32–34) and actual measures of student performance on tests, quizzes, and other achievement indices (e.g., science test, 75%). Keeping detailed records of every activity completed by every student is probably not necessary. However, student performance should be measured in each major subject area at least once per week and more often if students are encountering difficulty.

One way to make data collection simpler is to enlist the aid of students. After correcting their academic work, they can record their scores or the number of correct responses. For example, Figure 7-7 shows George's daily assignment sheet for Monday. After completing an activity, he checks his answers with the key provided, records his score, and then corrects his mistakes. George can also learn to graph his scores so that he and his teacher can easily see his progress from day to day.

Smith, Neisworth, and Greer (1978) recommend that the following information be collected and recorded for each instructional objective: the date instruction began, the date the objective was achieved, and the student's performance level at completion. For groups of students working on the same skill, the teacher can simply record the starting and ending dates of instruction and the individual scores of each student.

Systematic record keeping requires consistency. Teachers should decide what data will be collected, how frequently, and what methods will be used for recording. It is best to begin gradually, perhaps with one or two subjects per week. The record-keeping system should be one with which the teacher is comfortable. Some teachers use computer programs such as grade books. Others favor loose-leaf notebooks divided into sections by academic subjects, a file folder for each instructional group, or a 5 × 8 index card for each student. The most important factor is that data are collected regularly, recorded in a systematic fashion, and then utilized to determine whether instructional modifications should be made.

USING EDUCATIONAL TECHNOLOGIES

In a broad sense, the technology of education includes all types of instructional strategies and approaches; thus, systematic instruction and behavior management techniques could be considered educational technologies. More common, however, is the

use of the term *educational technology* to refer to equipment and media with potential for contributing to the instructional process: computers, television and radio, audio- and videotapes, and so on. As Norris commented in 1977, technologies such as these have the capability to "revolutionize the quality, productivity, and availability of education" (p. 451).

In the general education classroom, both modern and traditional technologies can aid the teacher in providing individualized instruction and enhancing the standard curriculum. Several breakthroughs in the development of **assistive technology** make this particularly true for students with disabilities. For example, assistive technologies allow students who cannot see to hear the words that appear on a computer screen. Other students, unable to type on a computer keyboard, can write by speaking into a microphone. Special educational applications of technology are described throughout the rest of this book in sections entitled "Spotlight on Technology." The "Spotlight" in this chapter focuses on a very common technology, the tape recorder, and how this device can be used to enhance instruction for students with special needs and their peers.

Be Aware of Available Technologies

To use technology wisely, teachers must be aware of the resources available in their school and community and must keep informed about new developments. A vast array of technologies is currently available, and many are valuable tools for the presentation and practice of skills and information.

One way of classifying educational technologies is by their communication mode: visual, auditory, or multisensory. Visual media and equipment include photographs and cameras, slides and slide projectors, filmstrips and filmstrip projectors, and transparencies and overhead projectors. Visual technologies are often used with students with hearing losses. For example, with captioned films and television programs, the audio portion of the show is presented on the screen in text; the student reads the print captions, just as an English speaker would read the subtitles in a foreign film.

Records and record players, audiotapes and tape recorders, audio compact discs (CDs) and CD players, and radios are auditory technologies. They can be used by an entire class or selected individuals who listen through headphones. Students with vi-

Spotlight on Technology

Tape Recorders

Audiotape recorders and players are one of the most common technologies available today. Tape players, particularly personal stereos, are popular with students of all ages. According to Mercer and Mercer (1998), these devices have several advantages for classroom use. They are inexpensive, easy to operate, small in size, and portable. When used with headphones, they are quiet. Only the student wearing the headphones hears the tape so that others in the classroom are not distracted.

Teachers can use tape recorders as part of instruction in several ways. Mercer and Mercer (1998) provide several suggestions:

1. A tape can be made of reading material (e.g., literature, stories, and magazines). The student can read along with the tape to practice reading. Thus, the tape can provide feedback, increase speed, and help the student identify and practice difficult words.
2. In a language activity, the student can use a tape recorder to make a tape of a story. Later, the student can write the story from the tape with a peer, aide, or teacher.
3. Oral directions can be put on tape to accompany seatwork activities. The student who has difficulty with oral directions can play the tape until the directions are understood.
4. Spelling tapes are useful for practice and taking tests. One commonly used format gives the spelling word; the word used in a sentence; and a pause, a beep, and the word spelled correctly. The pause can be eliminated by having the student stop the tape recorder to write the word and then start it to check the spelling.
5. Stories, facts, or a report of an event can be recorded. News programs, commercials, telephone messages, weather reports, and teacher-made content can be used. The student listens and then responds to comprehension questions. For example, a weather report is taped and the student is required to answer the following questions: High temperature? Low temperature? Any rain? Forecast for tomorrow? What season is it?
6. One-minute samples of instrumental music can be taped for students to use in conducting timings. These tapes usually begin with the word "start" and end with the word "stop." The teacher may prefer to use only the words and omit the music. In place of a kitchen timer, tapes of different time spans can be used to mark the end of any timed activity.
7. Correction tapes can be used to provide feedback to students who have completed math seatwork.
8. Music can be recorded on tapes for students to listen to when they have completed an assignment. Also, pleasant background music can be played while students are engaged in activities such as cleaning up, settling down after recess, free-choice, seatwork, or art.
9. At the secondary level, class lectures and discussions can be taped. These tapes can be used to help the students review or understand the material.

Note. Reprinted with the permission of Merrill from *Teaching Students with Learning Problems*, 5th ed., by Cecil D. Mercer and Ann R. Mercer (p. 88). Copyright © 1998 Prentice-Hall, Inc.

---

sion losses benefit from auditory devices such as the talking calculator.

Multisensory technologies are common; these include language masters, films, videotapes, television, computers, and interactive videodisc technology. The language master, an adaptation of the tape recorder, uses a card with an audiotape affixed to the bottom. As the card with its printed message moves through the machine, the audiotape plays.

An important trend is the increased use of computers for classroom instruction and other educational purposes. **Computer-assisted instruction,** or the direct delivery of instruction to learners via computers, has proved effective with several types of learners, including students with disabilities. In addition, computers are useful tools for students and for teachers. As Lewis (1993) points out, "technology can increase teachers' professional productivity and reduce the amount of time that must be spent in noninstructional classroom duties" (p. 126). The next chapter in this book focuses on strategies for using computers and other technologies in the general education classroom.

Match Technologies with Educational Goals

Educational technologies can be used for many instructional goals. It is important, however, to analyze the purpose of instruction and ensure that the medium selected is the most appropriate one available. The use of sophisticated technology, when a simple explanation from the teacher would suffice, is not effective management of instructional resources.

Technologies serve 5 major instructional functions in the classroom. They aid in the presentation of new material, provide practice opportunities, serve as rewards for appropriate behavior, and promote the development of social skills. In addition, assistive technologies allow students with special needs to bypass disabilities so that they can participate in the same types of classroom learning activities as their peers.

Almost any type of technology can be used to present new information: films, filmstrips, television, video- and audiotapes, overhead transparencies, computer and interactive videodisc programs, and so on. Likewise, several types of media offer opportunities for practice. For example, many computer programs provide students with immediate feedback so that they can monitor their own performance during independent practice.

Technology activities can also serve as rewards. For example, some teachers set up classroom management programs in which students can earn time to listen to radios or tapes, work with the computer, or watch videos. Production activities can also be reinforcers; students might take photos, make an audio recording of something they have written, or produce a videotape.

In the social area, technology can be used for both instruction and practice. For instance, students might view videotapes of interpersonal interactions that model appropriate skills. Or, the teacher (or a peer assistant) could videotape students as they participate in role plays of typical social situations; the tapes could then be used for discussion and feedback. To promote social acceptance, many teachers take photographs of class members for a bulletin board or class book. This approach helps acquaint

students with one another at the start of the school year and can also be used to teach about individual differences and similarities.

MANAGING TIME AND OTHER RESOURCES

When the physical and instructional environments have been arranged and the teacher begins to implement the classroom educational program, coordination skills become crucial. The teacher, as manager of the total learning environment, supervises the allocation, organization, and use of essential learning resources: time, educational materials and equipment, and instructional personnel. Principles for coordination of these resources appear in the following sections.

Manage Instructional Time Effectively

Time is a valuable and irreplaceable resource; its effective use is essential in the classroom and in other areas of a teacher's busy life. **Time management,** however, is a skill that most teachers and other professionals need to improve. Several key time management points appear in "Inclusion Tips for the Teacher."

In the classroom, teachers manage time by establishing a daily schedule. A schedule divides the day into segments and allots specific amounts of time to different activities. Time should be scheduled so that student engagement in important learning tasks is maximized (Englert, 1984). The highest-priority tasks should be given the most time, and noninstructional activities should be kept to a minimum.

Several suggestions for scheduling, presented by Mercer and Mercer (1998), are appropriate for both the elementary grade teacher, who schedules the entire school day, and the secondary grade teacher, who schedules several different class periods. Among these suggestions are the following recommendations:

Schedule for maximum instructional time.
Proceed from short work assignments to longer ones.
Alternate highly preferred with less preferred tasks.
Provide a daily schedule for each student.
Schedule assignments that can be completed in one school day.
Provide time cues.
Plan a variety of activities. (pp. 83–84)

Inclusion Tips for the Teacher

Time Management

1. *Set goals.* What are your long-term goals? What are your goals for the next semester? Consider all aspects of your life: professional, personal, social, family, and community.
2. *Establish priorities.* Which of your goals are most important? Separate your goals into those of high value, moderate value, and low value.
3. *Analyze present time use.* Are you using your time to reach your high-priority goals? Keep a log or diary for a few days and see.
4. *Eliminate time wasters.* Spend your time on priority tasks that lead to high-priority goals.
5. *Recognize the difference between "urgent" and "important."* Urgent tasks are those that demand immediate attention; they may or may not be important tasks that lead to your high-priority goals.
6. *Don't procrastinate.* Instead, break large tasks into smaller, manageable tasks. Begin a smaller task immediately.
7. *Make a daily list of things to do.* Make one list and update it daily; be sure to assign a priority to every item on the list.
8. *Begin with high-priority tasks.* Completion of these tasks will reap the most benefit; low-priority tasks can be postponed.
9. *Ask yourself, Is this the best use of my time right now?*

Note. Suggestions from *Getting Things Done* by E. C. Bliss, 1978, New York: Bantam Books; *Get it All Done and Still Be Human* by T. and R. Fanning, 1979, New York: Ballantine Books; *How to Get Control of Your Time and Your Life* by A. Lakein, 1974, New York: New American Library; *Working Smart* by M. LeBoeuf, 1980, New York: Warner Books; and *How to Put More Time in Your Life* by D. Scott, 1981, New York: New American Library.

The Premack principle is also important to consider when designing an instructional schedule. According to Polloway and Patton (1993), "It is often called 'grandma's law' because it is reminiscent of the traditional dinner table remark, 'If you eat your vegetables, then you can have dessert' " (p. 102). Thus, schedule highly preferred activities after less preferred activities. For example, *if* students finish their assignments, *then* they can select a free time activity.

It is usually best to begin with a structured schedule that includes several short activities. As students progress, the activities can become longer, and more choices can be offered. The schedule should be shared with students and remain consistent from day to day, providing a guideline to help students know what they should be doing at any time during the day. Figure 7–8 shows a schedule for a 55-minute secondary class; times are allocated

FIGURE 7-8   Sample Schedule for a Secondary Class

Time	Amount	Activity
9:00	5 minutes	Opening: Welcome, collection of assignments, directions for today's activities
9:05	15 minutes	Group A: Small-group instruction with teacher Group B: Independent seatwork Group C: Small-group work at center
9:20	15 minutes	Group A: Independent seatwork Group B: Small-group work at center Group C: Small-group instruction with teacher
9:35	15 minutes	Group A: Small-group work at center Group B: Small-group instruction with teacher Group C: Independent seatwork
9:50	5 minutes	Closing: Feedback on today's activities, directions for tomorrow's assignments

FIGURE 7-9 Checklist for Evaluating Instructional Materials

Instruction
1. Are instruction procedures for each lesson clearly specified?
2. Does the material provide a maximum amount of direct teacher instruction on the skills/concepts presented?
3. Does the direct teacher instruction provide for active student involvement and responses?
4. Are the direct instructional lessons adaptable to small-group/individual instruction?
5. Is a variety of cueing and prompting techniques used to elicit correct child responses?
6. When using verbal instruction, does the instruction proceed in a clear, logical fashion?
7. Does the teacher use modeling and demonstration when appropriate to the skills being taught?
8. Does the material specify correction and feedback procedures for use during instruction?

Practice
1. Does the material contain appropriate practice activities that contribute to mastery of the skills/concepts?
2. Are the practice activities directly related to the desired outcome behaviors?
3. Does the material provide enough practice for the . . . learner [with special needs]?
4. Does the material provide for feedback on responses during practice?
5. Can the learner complete practice activities independently?
6. Does the material reduce the probability of error in independent practice activities?

Sequence of Instruction
1. Are the scope and sequence of the material clearly specified?
2. Are facts/concepts/skills ordered in a logical manner from simple to complex?
3. Does the sequence proceed in small steps, easily attainable by the . . . learner [with special needs]?

Content
1. Does the selection of the concepts and skills adequately represent the content area?
2. Is the content consistent with the stated objectives?
3. Is the information presented in the material accurate?
4. Is the information presented in the material current?
5. Are various points of view concerning treatment of minorities and . . . people [with disabilities], ideologies, social values, sex roles, socioeconomic class, etc., objectively represented?
6. Are the content and topic of the material relevant to the needs of . . . students [with special needs] as well as to the other students in the regular classroom?

Behavioral Objectives
1. Are objectives clearly stated for the material?
2. Are the objectives consistent with the goals for the classroom?
3. Are the objectives stated in behavioral terms including the desired child behavior, the criteria for measurement of the behavior, and the desired standard of performance?

Entry Behaviors
1. Does the material specify the prerequisite student skills needed to work with ease in the material?
2. Are the prerequisite student skills compatible with the objectives of the material?

Initial Assessment/Placement
1. Does the material provide a method to determine initial placement into the material?
2. Does the initial placement tool contain enough items to accurately place the learner into the material?

Ongoing Assessment/Evaluation
1. Does the material provide evaluation procedures for measuring progress and mastery of objectives?
2. Are there sufficient evaluative items to accurately measure learner progress?
3. Are procedures and/or materials for ongoing record keeping provided?

FIGURE 7-9   Continued

Review/Maintenance
1. Are practice and review of content material provided?
2. Are review and maintenance activities systematically and appropriately spaced?
3. Are adequate review and maintenance activities provided for the . . . learner [with special needs]?

Motivation/Interest
1. Are reinforcement procedures built in or suggested for use in the program?
2. Are procedures specified for providing feedback to the student on his/her progress?
3. Has the program been designed to motivate and appeal to students?

Adaptability to Individual Differences
1. Can the pace be adapted to variations in learner rate of mastery?
2. Can the method of response be adapted to the individual needs of the learner?
3. Can the method of instruction be adapted to the individual needs of the learner?
4. Can the child advance to subsequent tasks when he has demonstrated proficiency?
5. Can the learner be placed in the material at his own level?
6. Does the material offer alternative teaching strategies for students who are failing to master an objective?

Physical Characteristics of the Material
1. Is the format uncluttered?
2. Is the format grammatically correct and free of typographical errors?
3. Are photographs and illustrations clear, attractive, and consistent with the content?
4. Are the type size and style appropriate to the students?
5. Are auditory components of adequate clarity and amplification?
6. Are the materials durable?
7. Can the materials be easily stored and organized for classroom use?

Teacher Considerations
1. Is a teacher's manual or set of teacher guidelines provided?
2. Are teacher instructions clear, complete, and unambiguous?
3. Does the material specify the skills and abilities needed by the instructor to work effectively with the material?

Note. Adapted with permission of Merrill, an imprint of Macmillan Publishing Company, from *Teaching the Mildly Handicapped in the Regular Classroom* (2nd ed., pp. 125–127) by J. Affleck, S. Lowenbraun, and A. Archer. Copyright © 1980 Merrill Publishing Company, Columbus, Ohio.

for a class opening and closing, direct instruction, center activities for small groups, and independent seatwork.

Select Learning Materials Wisely

Instructional materials, media, and equipment are other resources that teachers manage. A major consideration is their selection. Few teachers have unlimited funds, and budgets for materials must be used wisely. Smith, Neisworth, and Greer (1978) recommend the evaluation of both the technical and practical aspects of instructional materials. One important technical factor is whether the material has been validated, that is, proven to be effective for its recommended use. Practical considerations include the cost of the material, the number of students with whom it can be used, the strength of its physical construction, and its portability. According to Goodman (1978), characteristics such as difficulty level, presentation sequence, input modes, and modes of response should also be considered. The checklist in Figure 7–9 contains several important factors to take into account when evaluating instructional materials.

Teachers often design their own teaching materials if commercial ones are unavailable or too costly. When time and effort are devoted to the production of new instructional tools, the teacher should be sure to make materials that will last. Cohen and Hart-Hester (1987) say, "Never make a material twice; make it durable from the start" (p. 57). For example, elementary grade teachers can laminate supplementary math problem worksheets; secondary grade teachers may wish to keep a file, notebook, or computer disk with class handouts or directions for homework assignments. In addition, teacher-designed materials should be saved for several years. A worksheet or activity from last year, although not useful this year, may be just the thing that is needed *next* year.

Commercial materials as well as those made by teachers should be stored within the classroom so that they can be easily located and retrieved by students and teachers alike. Mercer and Mercer (1998) recommend the use of a filing system for organization; materials are organized by subject area (e.g., reading) and then by skill (e.g., comprehension). Another possibility is a skill file system designed for student use, with practice materials sequenced according to skills and skill tests included (Stowitschek, Gable, & Hendrickson, 1980). In addition, the books *Getting Organized* (Winston, 1991) and *Taming the Paper Tiger* (Hemphill, 1997), although not written specifically for educators, give several suggestions that can be used in establishing a management system for classroom materials.

Recruit, Train, and Supervise Instructional Personnel

In many cases, teachers do not have instructional aides, and they may view themselves as the only human instructional resource in their classrooms. However, two excellent sources of assistance are available to every teacher: peer tutors and adult volunteers.

Peer tutors are students who assist by teaching other students. They can come from the same class or can be older, more advanced students (usually called cross-age tutors). Students can learn to perform many instructional duties: they can be scoring monitors and check others' assignments; teach specific skills to individuals in need of extra help; or deliver reinforcers such as points, verbal praise, and feedback (Jenkins & Jenkins, 1985; Stowitschek, Gable, & Hendrickson, 1980). Ehly and Larsen (1980) and Utley, Mortweet, and Greenwood (1997) conclude from reviews of research that peer tutoring produces learning gains not only for the learner but also for the tutor. Thus, while tutoring is generally used to provide extra assistance to low-functioning students, such students also can improve their skills by becoming tutors. For instance, a sixth grader with special needs might be assigned as a cross-age tutor in a second grade classroom. This experience could provide motivation and recognition to the older student while benefitting both individuals academically. Krouse, Gerber, and Kauffman (1981) caution that tutoring programs should ensure that the student who is tutored is not stigmatized.

Adult **volunteers** can also provide instructional assistance. Platt and Platt (1980) describe a program that recruited parents and retired persons to help in the schools. Each volunteer was asked to specify areas of interest; choices included working with students on a one-to-one basis, working with small groups, performing clerical duties, and supervising activities outside the classroom.

Training must be provided for instructional personnel, whether they be adults or students. In one program (Heron, Heward, & Cooke, 1980; Parson & Heward, 1979), tutors were taught four skills: preparing learning materials, prompting student responses, praising correct answers, and plotting the results of the tutoring session. Teachers must also supervise and monitor the performance of tutors and volunteers. They can meet with their assistants before instruction or provide written directions. Each assistant should be observed frequently, and further training should be provided as needed. Consult "Inclusion Tips for the Teacher" for additional information about peer tutors and adult volunteers.

This chapter has presented several principles for the arrangement, management, and coordination of the classroom learning environment. The next chapter describes techniques for the effective use of one important type of instructional resource: computers and other technologies. Before going on, check "Things to Remember" to review coordination skills.

Inclusion Tips for the Teacher

Peer Tutors and Adult Volunteers

Peer tutors and adult volunteers are valuable instructional resources. They assist the teacher by taking responsibility for some of the more routine duties in the classroom. One of the first steps in beginning a peer tutoring or adult volunteer program is specification of the duties that these assistants will assume. Remember when choosing tasks that it will be necessary to train tutors and volunteers to perform them.

Student tutors can be trained to
- provide students with feedback about response accuracy,
- correct written assignments,
- deliver reinforcers such as verbal praise and points in a token economy,
- teach specific skills to individuals or small groups of students,
- supervise independent activities such as learning centers, and
- administer simple assessments.

Adult volunteers can be trained to perform any of the duties suggested for student tutors. They can also learn to
- supervise small groups of students in the classroom, at lunch, during assemblies, and so on;
- collect and record data on student performance;
- assist in the preparation of instructional materials;
- perform routine clerical duties; and
- help with classroom housekeeping chores.

When selecting duties for peer tutors, keep in mind that they are students. Choose tasks that relate directly to school learning; save clerical and housekeeping chores for adult volunteers.

Another important consideration is the system that the teacher will use to communicate with tutors and volunteers after these classroom assistants are trained. Hammill and Bartel (1986) suggest using a notebook that contains three different forms:

- *Tutor's Lesson Plan*—a description of the instructional activities, procedures, and amount of time to be spent on each
- *Tutor's Log Sheet*—a reporting form for the tutor to record student performance data and any observations about the tutoring session
- *Teacher's Note*—a page for the teacher to give feedback to the tutor, praise good performance, and suggest ideas for changes

ACTIVITIES

1. Several educational journals offer suggestions to teachers about coordination of the classroom learning environment. Examples are *Teaching Exceptional Children, Focus on Exceptional Children,* and *Intervention in School and Clinic.* Find an article that interests you and summarize its recommendations.
2. Visit a school, university, shopping mall, or library to check its accessibility. Are there architectural barriers that would deny access to some individuals with disabilities? Watch for curbs, stairs, and steep inclines. If ramps are provided for wheelchairs, try traveling by this route. Is it less direct? Are information signs (e.g., signs on restrooms, elevators, telephones) in raised print and Braille?
3. Check the library, educational materials center, and catalogues from school supply houses for self-correcting materials. You might also want to consult the book *Self-Correcting Learning Materials for the Classroom* by Mercer, Mercer, and Bott (1984). Are such materials available for subjects you teach? Are they more or less expensive than other materials? In your opinion, could students use them independently? What self-correcting materials could you design and make yourself?
4. Talk with teachers who have used peer tutors or adult volunteers in their classrooms. How were the classroom assistants selected or recruited? Were they provided with a training program?

Things to Remember

- Teachers arrange, manage, and coordinate the learning environment.
- The physical environment of the classroom affects students' attitudes and social behavior; it should be safe, barrier-free, comfortable, and attractive.
- Arranging classroom space by functions helps structure the environment for students with special needs and other class members.
- The instructional environment of the classroom affects both achievement and nonacademic performance.
- The class-as-a-group is an effective use of time; homogeneous skill-specific groups are optimal for individualized instruction.

- Self-instructional learning materials are used to monitor the independent practice of students.
- Educational technologies can present new material, provide practice opportunities, serve as rewards, promote socialization, and help students with special needs bypass disabilities.
- Time, educational materials and equipment, and instructional personnel are essential learning resources that are managed by the teacher.
- Daily schedules assist in time management; time should be scheduled to maximize student involvement in important learning tasks.
- Peer tutors and adult volunteers can be effective classroom assistants.

How did the teacher communicate with these helpers? Ask the teachers to discuss the advantages of tutors and volunteers. Are there any disadvantages?

5. One of the most exciting areas in education today is technology. Try to discover some of the latest technological innovations designed for use in education. You might contact a local school district, browse through a recent professional journal or magazine, or consult an online publication such as *Electronic Learning* (see "Window on the Web"). Consider how the new technologies you identify could be used to improve instruction for students with special needs.

Window on the Web

Electronic Learning, an Online Magazine

http://scholastic.com/EL

Electronic Learning is a magazine for educators that is published in both a standard print version and an online version. Both contain articles about the classroom uses of technology, product reviews, reports on research and emerging technologies, and information about grants and references. The Scholastic Website (scholastic.com) also offers an online version of *Instructor Magazine,* a well-known publication for elementary teachers.

chapter 8

Using Computers and Other Technologies in the Classroom

Today, computers are a common feature of schools and classrooms in the United States. In the early 1980s, however, less than 40% of school districts owned computers (Quality Education Data, Inc., 1985). Numbers grew dramatically and by the late 1980s, almost every public school in the United States owned at least one computer (Office of Technology Assessment, 1988; Scrogan, 1988). By the early 1990s, more than 2.5 million computers were being used for public school instruction, with a national average of one computer for every 19 students (Market Data Retrieval, as cited in Kinnaman, 1992). Today, there are 6 million computers in U.S. public schools and that number is expected to increase to 10 million or more by 2000 (Wujcik & Associates, as cited in Salpeter, 1997). In 1996–1997, the national average was less than 10 students per school computer (Market Data Retrieval, as cited in Salpeter, 1997).

Computer technology has great potential for assisting teachers in the delivery of quality instructional programs, particularly for students with special needs. As Lance (1977) observed, "If a truly appropriate education is to be provided for each child, teachers must be supported by a technology that will permit them to deal with a vast range of individual differences" (p. 94). That technology is now available: computers, CD-ROMs, the World Wide Web, more traditional educational technologies such as audio- and videotape players and recorders, and assistive technologies such as electronic communication aids and talking calculators designed specifically for persons with disabilities. When used appropriately, these technologies can help teachers individualize instruction in the general education classroom.

Computers and other technologies represent only one of the many types of instructional tools available to teachers, however. They are not a panacea for the ills of education. What they do offer is an additional medium for instruction, another way for teachers to attempt to meet student needs.

CLASSROOM USES OF COMPUTERS

According to Taylor (1981), a classroom computer can be a tutor, tool, or tutee. The *tutor* role is the most traditional; the computer acts as a teaching assistant and delivers instruction to students. This application is called **computer-assisted instruction** (CAI). When the computer is used as a *tool,* it assists the student (or other user) in accomplishing some task. For example, a student writing a term paper might compose the paper at the computer, using a word processing program. The computer acts as a *tutee* when the student becomes the tutor and teaches the computer something, as when a student programs a computer with a computer language such as Logo or creates a personal home page on the World Wide Web. Computers serve all three of these purposes in schools today; Figure 8–1 summarizes the research findings regarding computer use by both typical learners and those with special needs.

Computers are versatile tools that can be used for a variety of educational purposes. They offer several potential advantages as a medium for instruction:

- *Computers allow individualization of instruction.* Computers are also called personal computers (PCs) because they are intended for use by one person. They are a technology for individuals. If there were 30 students in a classroom, each sitting at a computer, these students could be learning or practicing skills in 30 different content areas. Or they could all be working on the same content, but each at the skill level appropriate for his or her level of learning. In addition, most computer programs allow learners to proceed at their own pace. Some programs also let teachers (or students) make choices about how instruction will take place. For example, the teacher might be able to choose how many times a question or problem will be repeated before the student is presented with the correct answer.

- *Computers motivate students.* Novelty is an important factor in motivation, and computers are still a new enough instructional medium to excite students' interest. In addition, many computer programs use a game format so that learning activities seem more like play than work. Some programs also personalize instruction by addressing the student by name. Another motivating feature, particularly for students with learning needs, is that many programs provide feedback to the learner in a nonjudgmental manner. If the student makes an error, the program simply says, "Not quite, Olivia. Try again."

- *Computers allow new types of learning and new ways of accomplishing old tasks.* With computers,

> ### FIGURE 8-1   Research Findings Regarding Computer Use
>
> - When computers are used, students tend to learn the material in less time.
> - The use of computers seems to result in increased attention, motivation, and time on task.
> - The general effects of computer instruction are similar regardless of the type of software used. This does not imply that the quality of individual software is not a factor, but rather that one category of software has not consistently been found to be superior to others.
> - Exceptional as well as nonexceptional learners tend to view the computer in the instructional setting quite positively.
> - Drill-and-practice is the most frequent type of program used. This type of program is most useful with lower-ability students but has been found to be effective overall.
> - Higher-ability students appear to benefit the most from the use of computers in terms of the amount and diversity of learning attained. This would appear consistent with the learning characteristics of this group.
> - Using computers appears to more easily provide education to students who have typically been difficult to reach and teach.
> - Computers are helpful in reviewing previously learned material. This may be a very significant factor in mainstreamed settings.
> - The most effective use of computers is when they are used to supplement other instruction.
> - Use of computers leads to better social interaction when students work jointly than when they work in isolation or when they work in traditional ways with traditional instruction.
> - Computers do not stifle creativity nor do they dehumanize education.
> - The benefits of computers are not inherent. The environment in which they are used and the way in which they are used are the determining factors.
> - Teachers remain excited about the technology but do not spend much time actually using computers in the instructional process. Computers continue to be used in ways that are isolated from the instructional mainstream.

Note. From "Computers and Exceptional Individuals" (p. 12) by A. E. Hannaford, in J. D. Lindsey (Ed.), *Computers and Exceptional Individuals* (2nd ed.), 1993, Austin, TX: PRO-ED. Copyright 1993 by PRO-ED, Inc. Reprinted by permission.

teachers can provide students with a variety of learning experiences not usually possible in a traditional classroom setting. For example, using computer programs called **simulations,** students might learn to manage a small business, command troops in a Civil War battle, conduct a series of chemistry experiments, or travel to Jupiter. By interacting with the **World Wide Web,** students can move beyond classroom walls to visit the White House, see NASA's latest expedition, learn about current exhibits at the Smithsonian, check the status of the stock market, and interact with students in classrooms throughout the world. Computers also provide new ways of doing old tasks. With **word processing programs,** for example, writing becomes a somewhat different process. As soon as the writer has entered text into the program, that text can be modified and manipulated quickly and easily. The writer can add or delete words or phrases, change the order of sentences or paragraphs, for-

mat the text in many different ways, and even add graphics. This flexibility makes writing an easier task for students because errors are less difficult to correct.

- *Computers help students with special needs bypass or compensate for disabilities.* Computers permit many special students to bypass physical or sensory limitations so that they can take part in general education classroom activities. For example, a student who is paralyzed and able only to nod his head can "type" on a computer by using a special switch mounted on the headrest of his wheelchair. Or a student who is blind can use a computer to translate her Braille essay into regular print that her teacher can read. Computers can also help students compensate for their difficulties in basic academic skills. Students who spell poorly, for example, can write with a word processor, then use a spelling checker program to help locate and correct misspelled words.

There are also potential disadvantages to classroom computer use. Computers are only as good as the computer programs they run, so the selection of instructionally sound software is critical. Not all computer programs are based on sound principles of instruction; and although a wide selection of educational software is now available, it may not be possible to find a program that fits the content, level, and interest needs of a particular student. In addition, although research shows that computers can improve student performance (Sivin-Kachala & Bialo, 1996), most programs do not provide field-test data to support their effectiveness.

Another potential area of difficulty is access to computer equipment. There may be only a few computers in the school; teachers may need to share a computer across several classrooms or schedule their students in a central computer lab for a limited time each week. In addition, computers become outmoded as new versions are introduced, and software designed to run on newer systems may not work on older ones.

COMPUTERS AND OTHER TECHNOLOGIES

Two types of technology are important to consider in relation to students with special needs: instructional technology and assistive technology. **Instructional technology** is any type of device with the capacity to support the teaching-learning process. Common classroom examples are computers, VCRs, and televisions. **Assistive technology,** in contrast, is technology specially designed to aid individuals with disabilities. For example, one type of assistive technology for persons who are blind is a device that scans the pages of a book and reads them aloud. The paragraphs that follow describe computers and other typical instructional technologies. Assistive technology is discussed in a later section of the chapter.

Computers

Several different types of computers are found in schools today, but the most common are DOS/Windows, Macintosh, and Apple computers. According to Salpeter (1997), 1996–1997 studies of computer ownership in U.S. schools found that 45% of computers were DOS/Windows machines, 34% were Macintoshes, and 20% were Apples. Despite the variety in computer brands and models, all computer systems share the same basic components: input and output devices, the central processing unit, memory, and storage.

First, there must be some way for the person who uses the computer system (the user) to send information to the computer. The most common input device is the computer keyboard. This resembles a typewriter keyboard with a few additional keys; it can be built into the computer or can be a separate (but connected) unit. The mouse, another common input device, sits on the desk next to the computer. The computer also must be able to send information to the user. The monitor, which looks like a television screen, is the output device used for this purpose. Most computers today have color monitors, a nice feature for many educational programs. Most computers also contain one or more speakers to transmit auditory information to the user.

The central processing unit, or CPU, is the "brain" of the computer. It directs the flow of information through the computer and controls all operations. Memory is where information is stored within the computer. Memory in today's computers is measured in units such as megabytes and gigabytes. One megabyte (1 MB) is equal to about 1,000,000 bytes of information; one gigabyte (1GB) is 1,000 megabytes. Computers are described by the amount of memory they contain, and the more memory available, the better.

The most usual way of storing information for later use is to record it on a computer disk. Disks (sometimes called *floppy disks* or *diskettes*) are used with computers just as film is with cameras. Disks store data that the user creates and, in many cases, when a program is purchased it is stored on one or more disks. Disks are placed in the disk drive so that the information they store can be sent to the computer. Hard drives are large-capacity storage units that are often built into computers. They are used to store copies of frequently used programs; when a program is on the computer's hard drive, the user does not need to load that program from a floppy disk. Most modern computers also contain CD-ROM devices that allow the use of CD-ROM discs. Most new commercial software programs for education are sold on CD-ROM.

CD-ROM discs resemble the audio CDs on which music is stored. *CD* stands for compact disc; *ROM* means read-only memory. In contrast to floppy disks, CD-ROM discs can only be "read"; the user cannot alter them or "write" new information on them. One CD-ROM disc can store a tremendous amount of information: approximately 250,000 pages of text, 15 hours of recorded audio, or 15,000 color photos (Holzberg, 1991; Oehring, 1992; Salpeter, 1988). For instance, one CD-ROM disc can hold the complete works of Shakespeare or an entire encyclopedia.

CD-ROM technology is likely to be replaced by a new medium, DVD (sometimes called digital video disc or digital versatile disc). According to Shatz-Akin (1997), the advantages of DVD include "huge capacity, backward compatibility with CD technology, the potential for video quality that surpasses that of laserdisc, multichannel sound quality far better than that of audio CD, and great interactive-multimedia capabilities" (p. 74).

Multimedia and Hypermedia

Multimedia is one of the hallmarks of modern educational computing. Today's computers and software programs typically present information to users through a combination of several different media. While traditional programs are typically limited to text and graphics, multimedia software may offer animation, video, audio (e.g., music, sound effects, and voice), and high quality photos and artwork. For example, in addition to reading a text description of elephants and seeing a drawing, the student may be able to look at color photos of different types of elephants, see a map showing where elephants live, hear a recording of an elephant's call, and watch a video of a mother elephant interacting with her calf. One drawback of multimedia programs is the amount of storage space they require. Because of this, multimedia programs are generally stored on CD-ROMs instead of traditional computer disks.

Many multimedia programs are designed as **hypermedia** rather than traditional, linear software. In traditional software, the program controls the sequence of events and the way in which the user moves from one activity to another. In most cases, the progression is linear: activity 1, activity 2, and so on. Hypermedia applications are quite different. The user is presented with choices so that he or she can take greater control over the flow of interactions with the program. It is possible to choose all or none of the options available, and it is up to the user in which order the selections are made. One good example is how users interact with websites on the World Wide Web. Most webpages contain links that users can choose to move to different parts of the website or to different sites. For instance, at the website for the San Diego Zoological Society, students can move from the introductory page to pages that feature new natural habitats at the zoo such as the Polar Plunge, videos of the pandas visiting from China, or information for visitors. At the website for the Smithsonian Institution in Washington, DC, it is possible to link to the many museums that the Smithsonian sponsors as well as to affiliated organizations such as the John F. Kennedy Center for the Performing Arts and the National Gallery of Art.

Connections: Networks, Modems, and the Internet

Although computers are designed for individual users, they can also be linked or networked together. Networks within a single classroom or school are called *local area networks* or *LANs*. For example, all the computers in a school computer lab can be networked together so that they share a printer. Or, the entire school can be networked so that computers in various classrooms, offices, and the library/media center can share software and communicate with each other. When a school is networked, students may be able to access encyclopedias or other reference software in the library/media center from their classroom computer; in addition, students in different classrooms may be able to work collaboratively on projects such as a school newspaper.

Telecommunications is another method for linking computers. Specifically, it "is the process of transferring information over a distance via a conduit such as telephone lines" (Lewis, 1993, p. 365). Two computers located far from each other can communicate over phone lines if each is equipped with a device called a **modem.** More commonly, computers equipped with modems use telephone lines to connect to a commercial information service (e.g., America Online) or to gain access to the Internet, the international information highway.

The **Internet** is a worldwide computer network. Begun in the 1970s as a U.S. military research project (Posth, 1997), it has evolved into a communication system that today reaches literally millions of people across the globe. The World Wide Web (WWW) is a relatively new addition to the Internet. It differs from other parts of the Internet because it contains not only text but also graphics. Some sites on the Web also offer multimedia features such as audio and video. The range of information available on the Web is truly astounding. Information can be found on almost any subject, and it is possible to use the Web for a variety of purposes including online shopping; "visiting" another state, another country, or even another planet; communication with family, friends, and professional colleagues; and getting up-to-the-minute news and weather, to name but a few possibilities. America Online and other commercial Internet service providers are not part of the Web. They are open only to their members, although members can use the service to gain access to the Web.

THE WORLD WIDE WEB

The World Wide Web and other parts of the Internet can provide valuable instructional resources for general education teachers who serve students with disabilities and other special needs. Today, most colleges, universities, and school districts provide Web access to their students and teachers. If an educational service is not available, it is always possible to purchase a membership in a commercial service.

Browsing the Web

Web addresses are everywhere. Turn on the TV, read a newspaper or magazine, pick up a catalog, or listen to the radio and you'll find something like:

http://www.anyschool.edu

This is the address of a site on the World Wide Web. It is called a URL (pronounced "U-R-L") or Uniform Resource Locator. The first part of the address is a command. The letters *http* stand for HyperText Transfer Protocol. The letters *www* stand for the World Wide Web, and the middle portion of the address ("anyschool" in the example above) is a short name for the website. The last three letters indicate the type of site. Education sites are designated *edu,* government sites *gov,* sites of organizations *org,* and commercial sites *com.* When a URL is read aloud, a period in the address is read as "dot."

Sometimes a URL will be longer. That indicates that it is the address of a specific portion of a website. For example, in the website for an educational publisher, there may be a separate section for instructional software. To reach that section, the URL might be:

http://www.anypublisher.com/software/index.html

The last letters of the address, *html* (or sometimes *htm*), stand for HyperText Markup Language, the computer language of the Web.

When the URL for a website is known, it is easy to access that site. The user logs onto the Web, starts up a web browser software program (e.g., Netscape Navigator or Internet Explorer), and opens a website. Usually that involves typing the URL in its entirety.

It is often possible to determine a URL of a company or organization by making an educated guess. For example, the URL for the software publisher GT Interactive is www.gtinteractive.com. However, sometimes the guessing strategy does not work. For example, the web address for the Council for Exceptional Children is not www.cec.org, as would be predicted. Instead, it's www.cec.sped.org. When a URL is not available or predictable, it is necessary to search the Web, a procedure that will be explained in a later section.

Navigation Techniques

When a user first starts up a web browser software program, that program goes directly to a home page. A home page can be any website. Programs, when first purchased, are typically set to the website of their publisher. This can be changed to any other site. For example, a teacher might want the school's website to be his or her home page.

Most webpages contain links that allow movement to other locations, either within the same website or to other sites. When text is underlined, that signals that it is linked to something else. Consider this excerpt from a student's webpage:

I like all kinds of animals but especially cats. I used to live in Chicago but now I live in San Diego.

Three links are available: cats, Chicago, and San Diego. Clicking on the word cats could move the user to a photo of the student's cats (within the same page) or to an article on cats in an online encyclopedia (in a different website). Clicking on a city name might bring up the website sponsored by that city's tourist bureau.

Links are also found in graphics. In many websites, the first page contains a graphical menu that allows users to go to the section of the site in which they're interested. That graphical menu could be a menu bar with words describing the parts of the website, a drawing depicting the site, or a series of photos. In most cases where there are graphical links, text links are also provided, although these may be in very small print.

In a typical session on the Web, a user begins with one website, selects links within that site, and then moves to another site either by selecting a link in the first site or by typing in another URL. This process is usually repeated several times. For example:

Exemplary Art Museum (first website)
Modern Art (part of first site)
Impressionism (part of first site)
Renoir (part of first site)
France (second website)
Paris (part of second site)

At some point in the session, the user may want to return to one of the pages visited previously. To return to the last page visited, the Back command is used. In the example above, if the user is on the Paris page, using the Back command would move him or her to the France page. The Forward command moves the user forward. Choosing forward from the France page would move the user to the Paris page. Another method is to use the special history menu in the Web browser program (e.g., the Go menu in Netscape Navigator). That menu lists the sites visited in the session and any one can be selected. It also lists Home as an option, if the user wants to return to the home page.

Bookmarks are another important feature of most web browsers. A bookmark records the URL of a website so that it can easily be accessed in the future. Whenever users find an interesting website, they should go to the Bookmark menu and choose the command to add a bookmark. The name of the website will then be listed on the Bookmark menu, and selecting that name will move the user to the website. The bookmark file can be edited, and it can be saved so that it can be shared with others.

Search Strategies

One of the most powerful features of the World Wide Web is the ability to search all of its websites. With just a few keystrokes, users have the ability to shift through literally millions of webpages to locate information on a specific topic. That topic can be very broad (e.g., educational reform) or quite narrow (e.g., hearing ear dogs for persons with hearing impairments). It can be professional in nature or relate to more personal concerns (e.g., Hawaiian vacations, clogged toilets, the care and feeding of gerbils).

To search the Web, the user goes to one of the many sites that provide search services. Examples are Yahoo, AltaVista, and Lycos. The basic procedure is quite simple. The user types in a descriptor (e.g., disability), clicks on "search," and the search service generates a list of hits, that is, websites that match the descriptor. That list contains links to each of the matching sites and usually brief descriptions of them. In most cases, the most relevant sites (the ones with the closest match to the descriptor) appear first in the list.

The search engine in each service works a bit differently, and this results in varying numbers of hits from one service to another. For example, on a recent search for *disability,* AltaVista reported 66,364 hits, Lycos 33,867 hits, and Yahoo 1,464 site hits and 48 category hits (e.g., Society and Culture: Disabilities). Search services typically provide information on the way in which they go about searching the Web so that users can make informed choices about which service to select for a specific purpose.

One of the problems that often occurs is that a search produces too many hits. Search services offer different ways of handling this problem, but most allow users to modify their search terms to narrow the scope of their search. For example, if the topic of interest is hearing ear dogs, it is usually possible to tell the search engine to treat those words as a unit, rather than individual words. That narrows the search so that the results do not include all of the Web documents on the topics of hearing, ears, and dogs. In a recent AltaVista search, just typing the words *hearing ear dogs* produced 937,050 hits; when those words were enclosed in quotation marks (the convention for grouping words in this search service), 157 hits resulted.

Most search services also allow the user to specify that a specific term must be included in documents—or that a term must not be included. For example, if a person is looking for seafood restaurants in Boston, he or she might want to make sure that the term *lobster* is included in any Web documents located in the search; to get that result, on some search services the user would type: Boston restaurants +lobster. If a person wants information about San Diego but does not want to locate webpages about the Carmen Sandiego software and television series, he or she might type: San Diego –Carmen.

E-Mail

E-mail or electronic mail, is a quick, easy way to communicate with others who have access to the Internet. E-mail is provided as part of most educational and commercial Internet services. E-mail addresses take this format:

username@anyschool.edu

The first part of the address specifies the person. This person can be found at (signified by the symbol @) a particular school or district, and this location is an educational institution. Thus, a teacher's address might be

pqsmith@longhornelem.edu

Like URLs, e-mail addresses from businesses or commercial Internet providers end in *com* (e.g., mrchips@aol.com). E-mail addresses from other countries end in a country code such as *ca* for Canada, *jp* for Japan, *se* for Sweden, and *uk* for the United Kingdom.

Sending e-mail is quite simple. Using an e-mail program such as Eudora (or the e-mail section of a commercial Internet service), the user chooses "New Message." In most e-mail systems, the user will be asked to provide three types of information: the e-mail address of the person to whom the message should be sent, the subject of the message, and the message itself. A teacher might see something like this:

To:
From: myname@myschool.edu
Subject:
Message:

After "To:" the teacher types in the e-mail address of the recipient. It is usually possible to type more than one address here so that the same message can be sent to several recipients. This is a very useful feature when it is necessary to share information across a group of individuals. The "From" space is often filled in automatically by the e-mail program. "Subject" typically is a brief description of the content of the message, and the "Message" area is where the electronic communication is typed. In many e-mail systems, it is also possible to attach computer files to e-mail messages. All sorts of files can be attached, including documents created on word processors. For example, at many universities, students turn in their written assignments via e-mail.

When users open their e-mail program, they learn whether or not they have received any mail. Usually this information is provided in a list or table that indicates who sent the message, when the message was sent, and the subject. This allows users to scan their incoming mail and decide whether or not to read it. Once a message has been opened and read, the user typically has several options: replying to the message, sending a copy of the message to someone else, printing a copy of the message, and saving or discarding the message. In addition, most e-mail systems provide an electronic address book where users can record the e-mail addresses of persons with whom they correspond.

Other Resources

Newsgroups are electronic bulletin boards where individuals can post messages and read and respond to the messages that others leave. There are separate newsgroups for a very wide variety of topics including educational research, Star Trek, chinchillas, Elvis, urban planning, and Apple II computers. The names of newsgroups begin with an abbreviation that indicates their type. For example, those beginning with *alt* are alternative groups, those beginning with *comp* relate to computers, and those beginning with *k12* are designed for educators.

In most systems, the user enters the News portion of the Internet service and chooses a specific newsgroup. In a program such as Netscape Naviga-

For Your Information

Listservs on Disability Topics

Marfilius and Roznakski (1997) describe dozens of Internet mailing lists or listservs for teachers and others interested in disability. Here are several examples:

Name of Listserv	Subject	E-mail Address to Subscribe
ADDKIDS	Attention Deficit Hyperactivity Disorder	listserv@sjuvm.stjohns.edu
AUTISM	Autism and developmental disabilities	listserv@sjuvm.stjohns.edu
BEHAVIOR	Behavioral/emotional disorders	listserv@asuvm.inre.asu.edu
BLIND-L	Computer use for persons who are blind	listserv@uafsysb.uark.edu
DOWN-SYN	Down syndrome	listserv@vm1.nodak.edu
EDUDEAF	Deaf education	listserv@ukcc.uky.edu
ld-list	Learning disabilities	majordomo@curry.edu
SPEDTALK	Topics in special education	majordomo@virginia.edu

tor, it is also possible to select "Open" and type the name of the newsgroup in a format like this:

news:k12.ed.special

The command *news* moves the user to the News portion of the Internet and then to one of the k12 newsgroups, the special education newsgroup.

Within a newsgroup, the titles and dates of each posted message appear, and messages that are responses to other messages are indented. For example, recent postings on a newsgroup related to education might look like this:

Subject	Sender	Date
Zero Tolerance for School Violence	ajones	Wed 8:11 AM
Re: Zero Tolerance for School	bsmith	Wed 1:15 PM
Re: Zero Tolerance for School	cgarcia	Wed 7:30 PM
Nominations due for Teacher of Year	dgov	Thu 9:02 AM

Note that the first message, Zero Tolerance for School Violence, provoked two responses (the two indented messages).

Real-time conferencing with other Internet users is also possible. For example, commercial service providers such as America Online offer conference or chat rooms organized by topic. Users "enter" the chat room, then listen and perhaps contribute to the discussion. Electronic discussion groups may also be set up for specific purposes. For instance, a network news site on the Web may offer the opportunity for persons to chat with an important news figure. Or, a university professor might set up an online discussion between his or her students and a prominent expert in the field.

Newsgroups and online discussions can be considered *pull technologies* (Fonner & Zabala, 1997). That is, the user must go to the information source and pull relevant material from it. Browsing the Web and using search services would also be examples of pull technologies. In contrast, *push technologies* push relevant information directly to the user. The user specifies the types of information desired and that information is automatically forwarded to him or her.

Listservs are one type of push technology. A listserv is an e-mail mailing list to which a user subscribes. Like other resources on the Internet, there are listservs available for a wide variety of topics including education. See "For Your Information" for several examples. To subscribe, the user sends an e-mail message to the listserv. The "subject" portion of the e-mail is left blank. In the message area are three entries: the word *SUBSCRIBE,* the name of the listserv, and the user's first and last names. The first message to be delivered by the listserv will be a notification that the subscription has been received. Then, messages will flow to the user as they are posted to the listserv.

Some listservs do not accept messages from individuals, but most do. It is important to remember when posting a message that it will likely reach all persons who subscribe to that listserv. In some cases, that means hundreds or thousands of persons. Some listservs are moderated, and the moderator deletes inappropriate messages before they are transmitted to the entire readership. It is easy to be removed from a listserv. The procedure for subscribing is followed except that the message reads *UNSUB* followed by the name of the listserv.

Another web resource available to teachers is distance learning. As Witherspoon (1996) comments, virtual universities are now a reality. Individuals can enroll in online courses, communicate with instructors and classmates via e-mail, and participate in teleconferences and online discussions. Of course, learning is not limited to formal university education, even on the Internet. Organizations and agencies also sponsor learning opportunities. For example, the National Center to Improve Practice in Special Education (NCIP) features online workshops and regular opportunities to interact with authors of articles that appear in the journal *Teaching Exceptional Children*. The URL for NCIP is:

http://www.edc.org/FSC/NCIP

Safeguarding Students

One of the primary advantages of the Internet, the variety of the resources it offers, is also its major disadvantage. There are numerous websites and newsgroups that address topics that parents and teachers find objectionable for school-aged children and adolescents. And, it is possible for students to come upon these sites accidentally as they browse the Web or conduct a search. Gregor (1997), writing in *HOMEPC*, provides this example:

> Recently, I typed the word *girl* into the AltaVista search engine to find some fun sites for my daughter. I received almost half a million references—but thousands of them interpreted the word *girl* in a less-than-innocent manner. The lesson? At its best, the Internet offers an unprecedented opportunity for children to learn about the people and places around them; at its worst, it displays a world filled with pornography and violence. (p. 243)

It is important to decide how best to supervise students when they have access to the Internet. One method is for teachers to observe and monitor students' online activities; however, this can be difficult if several students are accessing the Internet at the same time. Another method is the use of software programs that block entry to portions of the Internet. These filtering programs monitor the information coming from the Internet and search for words and addresses that signal objectionable material (Gregor, 1997). If a target word or address is detected, access to that site is denied. However, filtering programs are not infallible. Although they can provide assistance in the classroom, teachers must also continue to supervise their students' online interactions.

EDUCATIONAL SOFTWARE

Educational software was once a scarce commodity, but that is certainly not the case today. According to a 1988 report of the Office of Technology Assessment, more than 10,000 educational programs have been produced by approximately 900 commercial firms. Today thousands of instructional software programs are available. Most current programs are technically excellent, many are educationally sound, and the number and variety of instructional programs continue to increase.

Instructional programs are available for most areas of the school curriculum, including basic skills subjects such as reading, spelling, writing, and mathematics as well as content area subjects such as science, social studies, and history. There is instructional software for preschool children, programs to teach computer literacy and programming skills, and programs that address the development of prevocational and vocational skills.

Software can also be classified by the type of instructional mode used to present the content. The most common types are tutorials, drill-and-practice programs, simulations, problem-solving programs, discovery programs, educational games, software tools such as word processors and data management programs, and programs for teacher use.

Tutorials

Tutorials are designed to present content that is new to the learner. They introduce and explain new skills or information and then supervise the student's first attempts to practice and apply this new material. Although tutorials assume no prior experience with the content to be presented, the learner may need prerequisite skills or information to take full advantage of instruction. For instance, basic math skills would be needed to benefit from a tutorial on adding fractions.

Of course, for any tutorial (or any other type of instructional program), students must have sufficient computer skills to operate the program. And in many cases students must also be able to read and interpret the information that appears on the screen. Typing and spelling skills may also be needed for the learner to respond to questions in the program.

Drill-and-Practice Programs

Drill-and-practice programs, one of the most common types of academic software, provide learners with the opportunity to practice material to which they have already been exposed. Drill programs do not present new material or attempt to teach new skills or explain new concepts. Instead, they review material introduced previously, giving students practice so that performance can improve. Most drill programs provide students with immediate feedback on the accuracy of their responses, and many impose speed demands to encourage students to respond both quickly and accurately.

One variation of drill-and-practice software is arcade-type instructional programs. Their purpose is the same as that of any drill program, but they incorporate the features of arcade games in an attempt to motivate learners. For example, in one early program, the student piloted a helicopter and spelled words by shooting the letters in order. In other programs, the student might work against the clock trying to answer questions or problems correctly in order to prevent a spaceship from crashing or extraterrestrials from launching their missiles. Arcade-type programs often incorporate animation and sound effects to enhance their appeal to young learners.

Simulations

Often used for enrichment activities in content area subjects, these programs provide students with experience in situations difficult or impossible to duplicate in the classroom. For instance, students might command troops in a Revolutionary War battle, manage a household budget, or travel to the Moon. One of the most popular social studies programs is *The Oregon Trail,* in which students simulate the pioneers' journey across the United States.

Simulations provide students with information about the situations they will encounter and then ask them to make decisions. The student space travelers, for example, might need to select provisions for their journey and chart the route they will follow. When the simulation begins, events unfold and more choices must be made; in many simulations, there is an element of chance so that students may be unsuccessful despite careful planning and prudent decisions. Simulations, unlike tutorials and drills, are discovery learning activities. Students are expected to learn through experience by perceiving the consequences of the decisions they make.

Programs to Teach Problem-Solving Skills

Problem-solving programs are not tied to any one curriculum area; instead, their purpose is to set up a learning environment in which students can practice critical thinking and acquire skills in problem analysis and solution. A good example of this type of software is Logo, a programming language designed for children. It is essentially content-free, and, as Seymour Papert (1980) explains in *Mindstorms,* it places the child in control of the computer, rather than letting the computer control the child. Papert suggests that "in teaching the computer how to think, children embark on an exploration about how they themselves think" (p. 19).

Although Logo is perhaps the most comprehensive system for teaching thinking skills, several other programs are available that attempt to achieve the same end. These programs pose a problem and then allow students to gather information about the problem, suggest alternative solutions, and evaluate the effectiveness of each. For example, in *The Factory,* students are provided with a set of machines with which to manufacture a product that matches the model presented by the program. The order in which the machines are used affects the outcome, so students must experiment in order to come up with the right product.

Discovery Programs

Discovery programs provide students with a rich learning environment to explore. There is no attempt to teach specific skills or information, and there are no drill activities with certain answers correct and others clearly incorrect. Perhaps the best example of this type of software is the talking storybook program. These programs are children's books on CD-ROM; the text in the story is read aloud and students can interact with both text and graphics. For instance, the Living Books series contains several talking storybooks including *Arthur's Teacher Trouble, Just Grandma and Me,* and *Stellaluna.* Although the intent of such programs is to expose students to children's literature in the expectation that they will enhance their reading skills, the software provides opportunities for learning, rather than instruction.

Educational Games

There is a plentiful supply of games software, and some of these programs are of value in the classroom. Games can be used to teach thinking skills, provide practice in the application of academic skills, and serve as a leisure activity rewarding appropriate classroom behavior. Most of the traditional board games, such as Monopoly and Scrabble, are available as computer programs, as are card games and word games such as hangman. Another variety, adventure games, is quite similar to simulations, except that the situations that are portrayed are selected for their entertainment value rather than their educational value. In adventure games, participants often engage in role playing, and decisions made by the player alter the course of the adventure. Arcade-type computer games are perhaps the most popular games outside the classroom; players earn points by skillful maneuvering and careful aim while they do battle with some opponent, make their way through a maze or labyrinth, or play the electronic version of some sport or conventional arcade game.

Software Tools

The most widely used software tool in school settings is the word processing program. Word processors present the user with the computer equivalent of a blank sheet of paper—an empty screen—and then provide a system for entering text onto that screen. Their main value, however, is the ease with which that text can be changed and manipulated. The writer can correct errors quickly and easily, alter the sequence and format of the text, and then store what has been written for later use.

There are many popular word processors designed for classroom use. Most contain spelling checkers to help students identify and correct spelling errors. Some programs also provide a thesaurus and a few offer a grammar checker. Word processors for younger students offer features such as simple operation and large-sized text. Others have the capacity to talk so that students can hear the text they have written read aloud.

A **desktop publishing program** is a special type of software tool that allows students to add graphics to their text. In some desktop publishers, the emphasis is on graphics. For example, with the classic *Print Shop* program, students (and their teachers) create posters and signs, banners, greeting cards, letterheads, and calendars. Other desktop publishing programs are word processors with the capacity to include graphics within written products. One well-known example is *The Writing Center.* This program has been updated several times, and the current versions include the *Student Writing Center, Student Writing & Research Center,* and *Ultimate Writing & Creativity Center.*

Database management programs are a popular type of software tool with teachers, and students use them in some content area subjects. Integrated programs such as *ClarisWorks* and *Microsoft Works* contain both a word processor and a database management system (as well as other features such as spreadsheets for manipulating numerical information). Database programs assist in the organization and management of large bodies of information; in effect, they create a computer-based filing system. The user determines the type of information to be stored and the exact data to be included in each record. The major value of such a record-keeping system is that, once the information has been stored, it can be sorted and retrieved quickly and easily. For example, in social studies students might search a database on countries of the world to find all the nations with Spanish as an official language or all that are democracies. See "Inclusion Tips for the Teacher" for a sample lesson plan to introduce students to database management programs.

Reference programs are another type of software tool. Most common are multimedia encyclopedias on CD-ROM, although almost any type of reference work available in print can be found in software format. One multipurpose reference tool is *Microsoft Bookshelf.* This CD-ROM contains 9 references in-

Inclusion Tips for the Teacher

Introducing Students to Database Management Programs

Lesson Title	Lesson 1: Introducing Database Management
Grade Level	4–12
Content Area	Language, Social Studies, Critical Thinking
Goal	Students will understand what a database is and how it works.
Time Required	1–3 hours
Preparation	Materials needed: File box, file folders, labels, computer, database program, blank disk, blackboard, paper and pencil for each student

Conducting the Lesson

1. Ask students if they've ever used a file box, file cabinet, etc., and if they know what it's used for.
2. Open the box and ask how you would find what you're looking for (label on box, folders, etc.).
3. Ask students if they would like to teach the computer to be an electronic file cabinet, and see who can find information best—an electronic file cabinet or a person with a file box.
4. Put a label on the file box: *Mrs. Smith's Class* (use *your* name).
5. Ask the class to brainstorm the kinds of information that might "fit" into the box. List these on the blackboard (for example, names of students, birthdays, hobbies, favorite subjects).
6. Have the class select three. Ask each student to write the three categories on his/her paper and fill in the information (for example, Name, Suzie Smith; Birthday, June 3, 1973; Favorite Color, Red).
7. Load the database program into the computer, insert the file disk, and design a form to collect the data while the students watch.
8. Ask for a volunteer to sit in the computer chair and enter his/her data. (You may need to point to the keys to speed up the process.) If time allows, let 2–3 others also enter data. Finish the class's data entry yourself.
9. Give each student a file folder and a label. Ask them to put their name on it and to put their papers in it. Put the folders in the file box.
10. Ask students if they think the computer remembers what was entered. Flash through the files to make sure.
11. Ask for a volunteer to race the computer to see how many students were born in 1973. Set up the program to sort by year of birth, and give the file box to the volunteer.
12. Read out the data as it is sorted by the computer.
13. Ask the students which was faster, more fun, easier, etc.

Follow-Up
Ask the students for other categories to sort. Ask the students if there is additional information that should go in the file box.

Note. From *Special Magic: Computers, Classroom Strategies, and Exceptional Students* (p. 69) by M. Male, 1988, Mountain View, CA: Mayfield. Copyright 1988 by Mayfield Publishing. Reprinted by permission.

cluding a dictionary, thesaurus, atlas, almanac, book of quotations, and encyclopedia.

Programs for Teacher Use

Although programs of this type are used by teachers rather than students, they are considered educational software because they support the delivery of instruction. Word processors and other tools such as database management programs could be placed in this category; however, usually they are not because they are designed for a general audience. A separate body of software has been created specifically for use by educators.

Spotlight on Technology

PLANalyst, a Lesson Planning Program

PLANalyst is a software tool that helps teachers develop and refine lessons. The teacher identifies the purpose of the lesson, the instructional events that will occur, the learners and context, any needed materials, and specific procedures for each instructional event. In addition, the teacher can seek expert advice from Dr. Anna Liszt about how to improve the lesson.

This is the first screen of a sample lesson on writing a business letter. The lesson name, authors, and objectives appear on the left; the events in the lesson are listed on the right.

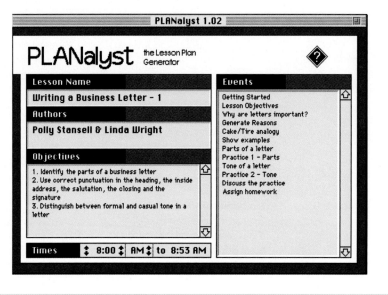

PLANalyst 1.02

PLANalyst the Lesson Plan Generator

Lesson Name
Writing a Business Letter – 1

Authors
Polly Stansell & Linda Wright

Objectives
1. Identify the parts of a business letter
2. Use correct punctuation in the heading, the inside address, the salutation, the closing and the signature
3. Distinguish between formal and casual tone in a letter

Times ↕ 8:00 ↕ AM ↕ to 8:53 AM

Events
Getting Started
Lesson Objectives
Why are letters important?
Generate Reasons
Cake/Tire analogy
Show examples
Parts of a letter
Practice 1 – Parts
Tone of a letter
Practice 2 – Tone
Discuss the practice
Assign homework

Authoring programs are one example. These programs assist in the creation of computer-based lessons and presentations. They are quite easy to use so that teachers can develop software for their students without learning the intricacies of computer programming. *HyperStudio* is one example. This multimedia authoring tool is widely used in schools not only by teachers but also by students.

There are a number of tools available to help teachers manage information about students. Examples are gradebook programs and software for managing and evaluating student portfolios. In addition, teachers can choose from a variety of programs that assist in the preparation of instructional materials. Examples are programs to generate crossword puzzles, word finds, and math fact worksheets. See "Spotlight on Technology" for information about another type of teacher tool, a lesson planning program.

SELECTING APPROPRIATE SOFTWARE

Good quality software is the key to effective computer use. Software is what brings the computer to life, what transforms the potential instructional value of this technology into a classroom reality. Thus, selection of appropriate software is one of the most important decisions educators face in the use of computers.

Try Before You Buy

There is no substitute for sitting down at the computer with a program and trying it out. Software cannot be adequately evaluated by reading an advertisement in a magazine or a description in a catalog, as many disappointed teachers have learned after purchasing a program sight unseen. Computers are an interactive medium, and it is necessary

```
┌─────────────────────────────────────────────────────────┐
│ ▓▓▓▓▓▓▓▓▓▓▓▓ PLANalyst 1.02 ▓▓▓▓▓▓▓▓▓▓▓▓▓▓               │▣│
│                                                           │
│       👤👤 👫  Learners & Context 🏛 🏢                   │
│                                                           │
│  In the field to the right, write a short description of the │
│  learners and the context of the lesson or presentation. E.g.: │
│  "Sophomores in week 6 of BIO 232. Class held in lab." Then │
│  use the pop-up buttons to describe the situation more fully. │
│                                                           │
│                         ┌─────────────────────────────┐   │
│  Age Level     │ Middle or junior high ▼│             │
│  Ability Level │ Medium              ▼│               │
│  Ability Range │ Wide                ▼│               │
│  Motivation    │ Medium              ▼│               │
│  Language      │ A few LEP learners  ▼│               │
│  Class Size    │ 11-30               ▼│               │
│                                                           │
│                        ( Cancel )   ((  OK  ))            │
└─────────────────────────────────────────────────────────┘
```

Middle school inner city language arts class. They've recently had practice in clustering as a pre-writing activity. First in a series of five lessons.

This lesson was designed for a class of middle school students with a wide ability range, including some students with limited proficiency in English.

continued

to see how programs respond to and interact with the user.

First, be sure that the software you are previewing is compatible with your computer. Although many programs today are designed for both Windows and Macintosh platforms, some are not. Pick programs designed for *your* computer and its capabilities. One common problem is a mismatch between the amount of memory a program requires and the amount installed in your machine.

In trying out a program, the teacher should begin by attempting to do everything right: start with the first activity, follow a logical navigation path through the program, and answer all questions correctly. If the program is poorly designed or its directions are unclear or ambiguous, this may not be possible—a sure sign that the program is not of the best quality. Next, the teacher should go through the program making mistakes that students might make. What happens when you skip from one activity to another without completing the first? How are incorrect answers handled? Does an error result in an unpleasant noise or message on the screen? How many times must you attempt to answer a question before the program moves on?

This experience provides the teacher with adequate information to judge a program's worth. There is no substitute for hands-on evaluation. Most software publishers now have websites that provide information about their programs and sometimes demonstration versions; see "Window on the Web" on page 216 for more information. Many publishers will supply teachers with demonstration disks or CD-ROMs. When previewing a program is simply not possible, software reviews can provide critical information about a program's value. Reviews are published in professional journals and by several different agencies; they are also available on the Web.

Evaluate with Particular Students in Mind

Software cannot be evaluated in a vacuum. A program may be appropriate for one group of learners

Spotlight on Technology

PLANalyst, a Lesson Planning Program (continued)

The teachers have described each instructional event in detail. The instructional purpose served by this event is information acquisition (shown in the blue box). Teachers choose from several purposes: prior knowledge activation, information preview, motivation, information acquisition, practice and feedback, closure, and other (e.g., administrative duties, breaks, etc.). Then teachers select specific procedures. For example, there are 17 choices for information acquisition including discussion, definitions and examples, fact presentation, procedure presentation, silent reading, and inquiry (individual or group).

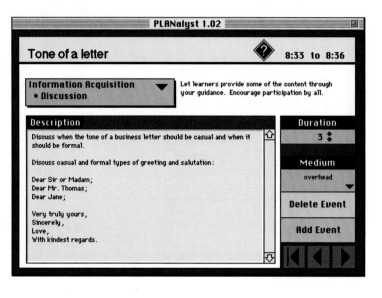

but not for another; for example, it may meet the needs of kindergarten students but be much too juvenile for third graders. Take into account not only students' current grade in school but also their skill levels (which may differ from school placement) and any special needs they may have. The instructional purpose must also be considered; an excellent drill-and-practice program will not suffice if a tutorial is needed.

Look Carefully at the Program's Content and Mode of Instruction

First, the teacher should consider what the software publisher says about the general purpose of the program and its educational objectives. This information usually appears in the program's documentation (i.e., the print materials that accompany the software). Then teachers should review the program to form their own opinions. The fact that a program is labeled as reading software does not necessarily mean that it teaches reading skills;

it could ask students to spell words, not read them. Or a program said to address the curriculum area of writing could cover only one small aspect of this skill, such as capitalization or forming possessives.

The mode of instruction is also a concern. Many programs advertised as tutorials are, in reality, drill programs. When the program's curricular content and type have been identified, the teacher can decide whether the program is worth further review. If its purpose and type are not what the teacher is looking for, the review process can be discontinued.

Determine Whether the Program Makes Use of the Computer's Capabilities

Today's computers are multimedia; visual information appears on the screen and speakers broadcast auditory information. Visual information can be in the form of text (i.e., letters, numbers, and symbols), still or animated graphics, and still photos or videos.

At any point in lesson development, teachers can ask for advice. The expert was generally positive about this lesson on writing a business letter but did suggest some improvements. *PLANalyst* was developed by Dr. Bernie Dodge at San Diego State University. It is available from Customer Service at Aztec Shops at that university (619-594-7535); its item number is 031304061B. You can find Dr. Dodge's home page at:

http://edweb.sdsu.edu/ people/bdodge/bdodge.html

Auditory information includes sound effects, music, and speech. All types of information should be clear and comprehensible to learners. Text should be legible and easy to read; the size of the text is an important consideration, particularly for younger students and those with visual impairments.

The hallmark of the computer as an instructional device is its ability to interact with the learner. Programs that appear to be electronic textbooks (or, as some call them, electronic page turners) do not capitalize on the computer's capabilities. A program does not need to take advantage of all features of the medium, but it should be more than a software translation of an instructional material that exists (or should exist) in print form.

Consider the Demands Placed on the Student

The demands that software places on students, over and above the requirements of the instructional content, can prevent students from being able to interact successfully with the program. There are 5 areas of concern:

1. *Computer use demands.* Before using any type of software, students must be trained to operate the computer. Usually it takes little time before students are running programs independently. However, some programs are difficult to operate and may pose problems for young or inexperienced computer users.

2. *Academic demands.* Reading and spelling skills are needed to profit from many educational programs. Programs may present textual information that must be read by the student, even when the purpose of the program is to teach math skills or introduce content subject information. In addition, spelling skills are required for programs in which students type words or sentences to respond to questions. The reading and spelling levels required for program use are a

Window on the Web

Websites of Software Publishers

PEP Registry of Educational Software Publishers

http://microweb.com/pepsite/software/publishers.html

This website for parents, educators, and publishers provides access to more than 1,000 publishers of educational software. Names of software companies, arranged in an alphabetical list, are linked to their websites.

A Sampling of Publishers' Websites

Broderbund Software (www.broderbund.com), publisher of the *Living Books* series, *The Print Shop, Kid Pix,* and the *Carmen Sandiego* series

Davidson & Associates (www.davd.com), best known for the *Math Blaster* and *Reading Blaster* series, its *Fisher-Price* programs, and *Typing Tutor*

Edmark Corporation (www.edmark.com), source of the *Imagination Express* and *Thinkin' Things* series and early learning programs such as *Bailey's Book House* and *Millie's Math House*

The Learning Company (www.learningco.com), publisher of *The Writing Center, The Oregon Trail,* and the *Reader Rabbit* series

Don Johnston, Inc. (www.donjohnston.com), a company that offers assistive technologies and software for students with special needs (e.g., *Co:Writer* and *Write:OutLoud*)

IntelliTools Inc. (www.intellitools.com), producer of the IntelliKeys adapted keyboard and software for students with special needs (e.g., *IntelliTalk*)

---

major consideration, particularly for students with academic learning problems.

3. *Physical demands.* In most educational programs, students respond by typing on the keyboard. The easiest type of keyboard response is pressing any key, a response mode used in discovery programs for preschoolers. More difficult is pressing one of a limited number of keys (e.g., *A, B, C,* or *D*), and most difficult is typing connected text (words, phrases, or sentences). Some programs get away from keyboard and typing demands by having the student respond with a mouse or joystick. However, some manual dexterity is required to operate such devices. Students with physical impairments may use special assistive devices so that they can

enter information without using the keyboard or mouse.

4. *Speed demands.* Another important concern is the pace of the program and whether it is under the control of the user. Some programs present information quickly and the student cannot regulate the speed with which information appears on the screen; other programs require students to respond within a time limit. When programs are under user control, the pace is controlled by the student so that he or she can spend as much time as needed on any one part of the program.

5. *Accuracy demands.* Programs differ in error handling capabilities. In some, the student can type the response, correct any typing errors, and then

signal that the response is complete (e.g., by pressing the Return or Enter key on the keyboard); in others, whatever the student first types is considered the final response. Error trapping is another concern. In some programs, if the student types *yse* instead of *yes,* the program accepts the response as correct or provides a prompt ("Not quite. Try again."). Programs without this capability simply count the response as incorrect.

Check the Adequacy of Instructional Procedures

The first step here is to evaluate the directions given to students. Are they clear and easy to follow or ambiguous and misleading? Then the content presented in the program is checked for accuracy and clarity of presentation.

Another aspect to consider is how the program provides feedback to students about the accuracy of their responses. At the minimum, students should receive knowledge of results after each response; the program should tell the student whether the answer was right or wrong.

When students make incorrect responses, how does the program react? Is the student informed and another trial provided? How many trials are given before the program shows the correct answer and moves on to the next question? Some programs do not advance until the student answers correctly; this procedure encourages guessing and then frustration if the student cannot come up with the answer. It is also important to determine whether the consequences of an incorrect response are more attractive than those of a correct response. For instance, in some arcade-type programs, the monster destroys the spaceship when errors occur, whereas the only consequence of correct responses is more questions to answer.

Programs use different techniques to reinforce students for correct responses. Some simply confirm the response; others confirm and add a text message of praise ("Right, Joey. Good job!"). Graphics or sound effects can also be used as reinforcers. Of course, the reward should be appropriate for the student's response. "GREAT!!!!" flashing in color on the screen with bells ringing for 15 seconds is not a suitable reward for success on the third try.

Evaluate the Program's Motivational Value

Perhaps the best way to determine a program's motivational value is to try it out with students to see how they like it. This is not a foolproof method, however, because students may like a program at first but quickly tire of it.

Many programs include game features as motivational devices. For example, the student may receive points for each question answered correctly; the student's score is displayed throughout the program so that he or she can watch it increase. Some programs are designed for two or more players to compete to earn the highest score.

Arcade-type programs put academic content into the format of arcade games. The student "shoots" the correct answer to an addition problem or travels through a maze to find the letters to spell a word. Other programs use games as rewards for successful performance; if the student answers a certain number of questions correctly in the drill section of the program, he or she can play a game.

The interest level of a program should also be examined. A program that features nursery rhyme characters will be insulting to middle school students, even if the content and skill level of the program are appropriate. Programs that will appeal to learners must suit their age and their interests. With older students who have academic skill problems, it may be necessary to seek out high interest–low skill level instructional programs.

Look for Program Flexibility

One indicator of a flexible program is that it allows users to make choices. For example, at the start of the program, students may be able to select from a range of different activities, determine the number of questions they will attempt, and then choose the difficulty level of those questions. Teachers may also be offered choices. They may be able to turn the program sound on or off, set the number of questions the program will present, and control important instructional variables, such as the amount of time allowed for responding.

Another aspect of flexibility is whether instructional software offers record-keeping and authoring features. Some educational programs record data on student performance so that the teacher

Inclusion Tips for the Teacher

Ten Reasons for Automatically Rejecting a Program

A few short years ago, we were generally pleased if a program would run. Today we demand much more from the courseware that we purchase. My "Terrible Ten" may differ from yours. Each of us applies our own criteria to the evaluation process. Yet I urge you to reject programs with any of the negative factors outlined here and to communicate to the publisher your reasons for the rejection. Our refusal to purchase courseware that is merely "adequate" can help to upgrade the overall quality of the instructional software market.

1. *Audible response to student errors.* Drill and practice programs are the worst offenders. They are most frequently used by the less able students, and NO student should be forced to advertise to the entire class that s/he has just made another mistake.
2. *Rewarding failure.* Hangman programs are classic examples of making it more fun to fail, by use of clever graphics, than to succeed.
3. *Any sound that cannot be controlled.* Sound can be effective as motivation or reward, but it is often distracting in the classroom or library media center. Constant repetition of the same sound also becomes annoying.
4. *Technical problems.* Programs marketed today MUST run smoothly without errors.

5. *Uncontrolled screen advance.* It is frustrating to have the screen advance while you are still reading it, and it is boring to wait for long seconds after finishing it. It is unnecessary to guess how long a screen should be displayed; let the user control the speed.
6. *Inadequate instructions.* We are no longer willing to guess how to operate a program.
7. *Errors of any kind.* Mistakes in factual content, spelling, grammar, etc., are totally unacceptable.
8. *Insults, sarcasm and derogatory remarks.* Students MUST NOT be attacked or belittled by the program.
9. *Poor documentation.* Instructional objectives, suggested student activities, instructions for teacher modification of the program and other classroom-related information should be standard with good courseware.
10. *Denial of a back-up copy.* If publishers insist on copy-locking their software, they should provide one free back-up copy. We are responsible for showing our good faith by refusing to make or to accept illegal copies of software for classroom use and by using our back-up copy for archival purposes only.

Note. From "The Terrible Ten in Educational Programming (My Top Ten Reasons for Automatically Rejecting a Program)" by A. Lathrop, 1982, *Educational Computer, 2*(5), p. 34. Copyright 1982 by *Educational Computer*. Reprinted by permission.

can review each student's progress at any time to see what skills have been mastered and what types of errors are occurring. Also, teachers may be able to customize a program to the needs of specific students by revising its content or adding new content. For example, the *Math Blaster* programs and others from Davidson & Associates have built-in authoring systems, and most spelling programs allow new lists of spelling words to be added.

See Whether the Documentation Is Clear and Complete

Print (or on-screen) documentation should provide a full, clear explanation of the purpose of the software and its method of operation. Field-test data should be reviewed, if these are included, to see whether they support the program's effectiveness. Sometimes documentation suggests ways to use the program in the classroom and recommends learn-

FIGURE 8-2   Success Stories

Almost every teacher who uses technology has at least one success story to share, one story that shows how powerful a force technology can be in helping students with special needs. The following stories were contributed by special educators in California.

- My favorite story concerns a student with very little self-confidence in the regular classroom. My program has had our computer much longer than his regular class. He now explains software to the other students, can run the printer, and even finds solutions when minor difficulties arise.
- An 11-year-old, nonoral student participated verbally for the first time in a class project. It was a "Monster Contest," and each student had to make up a monster, write about it, and then recite their description to the class. This student wrote her description on an Apple IIe using a single switch, then programmed it into her Epson Speech Pak. When it was her turn, she recited using her own "voice" for the first time—the Speech Pak.
- One student with mild retardation whose father lives in Hawaii is able to write to him successfully for the first time using a word processing program and the printer.
- For students with hearing impairment, color is like stereo to hearing students. Students' interest levels have increased dramatically with the color monitor on the computer screen.
- One of my students, a quadriplegic young woman with cerebral palsy, told me two years ago that she wanted more than anything else to be a writer. She had a difficult time managing conventional writing tools. Our Title IX Office sponsors a creative writing contest each year and thanks to computer-based word processing my student entered the contest and came in second place among all 11th and 12th grade entries. Incidentally, there were more than 1900 total essays submitted from throughout the district!
- I had a new sixth grade boy reading at first grade level who was my best Terrapin Logo student. He brought his mother and deaf uncle to Open House. First time since first grade.
- A "non-reader" was able to learn a math program without another student or adult sitting by him due to the speech synthesizer. He had completed something *on his own* for the first time!
- It's wonderful seeing students with attention spans of 15 seconds be able to concentrate for 10 minutes at a computer.

Note. From *Special Education Technology in Action: Teachers Speak Out* by R. B. Lewis, S. J. Dell, E. W. Lynch, P. J. Harrison, and F. Saba, 1987, and *Technology in Special Education: California's Exemplary Programs* by P. J. Harrison, E. W. Lynch, R. B. Lewis, F. Saba, and S. J. Dell, 1987, San Diego, CA: San Diego State University, Department of Special Education. Copyright 1987. The development of these books was supported by the State of California, Department of Education, Contract #4175. Adapted by permission.

ing activities to supplement or extend the program's content. If activity books or other print resources for students are part of the documentation, they should offer clear, complete, and easily understood directions for using the software.

Making a Decision

After all these factors have been considered, it is up to the teacher to decide whether the instructional program is worth adding to the classroom software collection. No piece of software will be perfect in every respect. Instead, it is necessary to weigh the advantages and disadvantages to determine whether a program will be a useful addition to the instructional resources already available within the classroom. However, there are certain characteristics that immediately signal an unsatisfactory program. In "Inclusion Tips for the Teacher" are Lathrop's (1982) 10 reasons for automatically rejecting a program.

ASSISTIVE TECHNOLOGIES FOR SPECIAL STUDENTS

Some students, like those with severe physical impairments or those who are blind, cannot interact with a standard computer system unless special

Spotlight on Technology

The IntelliKeys Keyboard

IntelliKeys is a versatile and easy-to-use alternative keyboard. It works with all major types of computers and installation is simple: IntelliKeys plugs into the computer's keyboard port. When IntelliKeys is installed, the standard keyboard and mouse remain operational.

IntelliKeys comes with several standard "smart" overlays that fit on its surface. To use an overlay, the teacher simply places it on the keyboard; a bar code on the back of the overlay tells IntelliKeys which standard overlay is in place. The photo shows students using one of the ABC overlays. Spaces separate the large yellow "keys," which are easy to see against

the darker background. At the left in the photo is the Numbers overlay often used with math software. Overlays are also available in standard keyboard format (i.e., the keys are arranged in QWERTY order) for Macintosh and PC-compatible computers. The Arrows overlay contains the arrow keys and command keys needed for interacting with many drill programs and software games.

The Setup overlay is used to configure IntelliKeys for students with special physical needs. Several adjustments are possible, including changing the response and repeat rate of keys. Also, keys such as Shift can be set so that the student presses them in sequence, not simultaneously (e.g., press Shift, then press the key of the letter to be capitalized). This helps students who have difficulty pressing two keys on the keyboard at the same time.

If the standard overlays do not meet the needs of a particular student, the teacher can easily create a new overlay and reprogram the IntelliKeys keyboard. The *Overlay Maker* program is used for this purpose. A talking word processor, *IntelliTalk,* is designed for use with IntelliKeys but works equally well with standard keyboards for students able to access them.

adaptations have been made. Assistive technologies are available today that allow such students and others with less serious disabilities to use computers for learning. The two major types of adaptations are alternative input devices (i.e., alternatives to or enhancements of the standard computer keyboard) and alternative output devices (i.e., alternatives to or enhancements of the standard computer monitor).

In addition, several other types of assistive devices are designed to meet the instructional needs of learners with physical, sensory, and communication impairments. Special educators report that computers and other technologies can cause dramatic changes in the skills, abilities, and attitudes of students with disabilities (Lewis & Harrison, 1988); see Figure 8-2 for a sampling of success stories.

Alternatives to the Computer Keyboard

Special input devices can be used to enhance or bypass the keyboard for students who are not able to enter information into the computer by typing. These devices are most often used with young children, particularly preschoolers, and persons with physical impairments that affect control of hand and finger movement.

Sometimes all that is necessary is a simple adaptation to the standard keyboard or an alternative way of typing on that keyboard. For example, a student who is partially paralyzed but has good control of head and neck muscles might be able to type using a headpointer, a device like a hat or headband with a stick attached. The student positions the pointer on the key to be typed and then depresses that key. A keyguard can be used with a student with tremor. Keyguards are covers that fit over the standard keyboard with holes cut out so that a student can reach down and press one key without touching the keys around it.

Alternate keyboards attach to the computer and bypass the standard keyboard. They may be larger or smaller than the regular keyboard; typically less pressure is required to activate their "keys." Most alternative keyboards are one flat, touch-sensitive surface. Instead of having separate keys, the surface is divided into "key" areas. These areas may be larger than the keys on a standard keyboard, and/or there may be space between them so that the "keys" are easier to locate.

The "key" areas on alternate keyboards are arranged in different ways. Keys may be in the traditional configuration used on typewriters, they may be in alphabetical order for young children, or the keyboard may feature pictures or words rather than individual letters and numbers. For example, on the Muppet Learning Keys, an alternate keyboard designed for young children, there is a chalkboard with the letters of the alphabet in order, a ruler with numbers, and a paint box with colors. IntelliKeys, a more versatile alternate keyboard, is described in "Spotlight on Technology" on page 220.

Other devices bypass the keyboard by allowing students to respond via the screen of the computer monitor. For example, with a touch screen, the student simply touches the area of the screen where the chosen response is shown. Light pens work in a similar fashion; the student places the pen on the screen to select a response. Devices such as these are usu-ally limited to software designed specifically to accept touch or light input.

Students with severe physical limitations can use switches to interact with computers. Switch input is possible if the student is able to make some type of consistent movement: a movement of the head from side to side, movement of a hand or elbow back and forth, movement of a foot up and down, or even a wrinkling of the eyebrow or a sucking motion. Switches come in many forms to accommodate students' movement repertoires. Examples are plate, leaf, brow wrinkle, and "suck-and-puff" switches. Switches work only with specially designed software unless a special device is added to the computer. These devices make switch input possible with any program by placing an array of letters and numbers somewhere on the screen display. The letters and numbers are scanned (e.g., first the letter *A* is highlighted, then the letter *B*, and so on), and the student selects one by pressing the switch.

Scanning through a series of letters or other possible responses is a laborious process. A more efficient (but more expensive) mode of interacting with the computer is speech recognition. With a speech recognition device, the student simply speaks into a microphone to enter information. First, however, the student must "train" the device to recognize his or her voice; the student's vocabulary is then stored for use with any software. See Figure 8-3 for photos of a speech recognition device and other methods of bypassing the standard computer keyboard.

Alternatives to the Computer Monitor

Alternative output devices bypass or enhance the visual display on the screen of the computer's monitor. One modification often used with students with visual problems is enlargement of the screen display. The regular monitor is replaced with a large-screen monitor, or a magnification device is used to increase the size of the screen display.

Speech can be added to the computer's output for young nonreaders, older students with reading difficulties, and students who are blind. One common way of adding speech is to install a hardware device called a speech synthesizer; many of the newer computers come equipped with synthesizers.

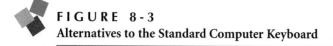

FIGURE 8-3
Alternatives to the Standard Computer Keyboard

Muppet Learning Keys™

TouchWindow

Discover:Switch for computer input

Speech recognition device

Speech synthesizers use voice chips that store phonemic rules; words are built or synthesized from phonemes as letters are typed in, and mispronunciations can occur when words do not follow phonemic rules. Synthesized speech typically sounds somewhat robotic, although it is usually clear enough to be intelligible to students. Synthesizers work with programs written to take advantage of their speech capabilities; they do not work with all software. Many of the newer multimedia programs use digitized (rather than synthesized) speech. This higher-quality, more natural-sounding speech is produced by recording actual speech and storing it as part of the program.

Software Designed for Students with Special Needs

Some software has been specially designed to accommodate the needs of students with disabilities. For example, there are talking word processing programs for students who are blind; when the student types in a letter, a speech synthesizer says the name of that letter as it appears on the screen. The student can also direct the synthesizer to read the program's menus and other on-screen directions and to review what has been written, either letter by letter or as words and sentences. Some beginning reading programs also talk, as do programs designed for students with delayed oral language. In addition, software has been developed to teach everyday living and vocational skills to students with mild cognitive disabilities.

However, most students with special needs can benefit from the software intended for average learners, if that software is well designed (Eiser, 1986; Shepard, 1986). In fact, special educators report that the software they use most often with students with mild disabilities is general education software (Lewis, 1997; Lewis & Harrison, 1988). Although teachers of general education classrooms may need to take extra care in the selection of instructional programs, the range of software available today offers many options appropriate for students with mild learning needs.

Electronic communication aid

Assistive Technologies for Students with Physical Impairments

Mobility is a major need of some students with physical impairments. Some students use standard wheelchairs, that is, chairs they propel with their hands and arms. Others, with limited strength or movement in their upper bodies, use power chairs (or scooters) equipped with motors and batteries. Power chairs are usually controlled by a joystick that the student operates by moving his or her hand, arm, foot, head, or chin.

Braces and prosthetic devices such as artificial limbs are aids that strengthen or replace portions of the body. In recent years, the design of these devices has improved, and lighter and stronger materials have been used in their construction. These changes have made braces and prosthetic devices more comfortable and better looking, which increases the likelihood that their owners will wear them. Now under development are prostheses that use microprocessors (such as those found in computers) to improve mobility and motor control.

In the classroom, students who have difficulty writing often use computers and calculators with print output. Audiotapes serve several purposes: recording class lectures, "reading" taped texts, and taping assignments or exams so they don't have to be written. Manual or electronic pageturners assist students by holding a book in an open position for reading; to turn the page, the student activates the device with a chin or mouth movement.

Communication Aids

Some students are unable to speak, or their speech is very difficult to understand. To bypass this problem, communication aids are used. Communication aids allow students to "talk" by simply pointing or pressing a button. For example, a simple communication board may be a piece of cardboard with pictures, letters, or words on it; a student could point to a picture of a glass to indicate thirst or use an alphabet to spell out greetings or requests. Electronic communication aids are more sophisticated because they "talk." One type of electronic communication device uses prerecorded speech. Spoken messages are recorded by a family member, teacher, or peer; to "speak," the student simply selects one of the available messages. Other communication devices contain speech synthesizers. The student may spell out words by typing on the device's keyboard or messages may be preprogrammed so that they can be activated by pressing a single key or a switch. When a word or phrase has been entered, the synthesizer pronounces it.

FIGURE 8-4
Print Enlarger

Note. Photo courtesy of TeleSensory Company.

Assistive Technologies for Students with Visual Impairments

Audio aids help students with visual impairments learn by listening. For example, students can gain access to printed information by listening to tapes of books, magazines, and textbooks. Sometimes tapes use compressed speech; in this mode, the spoken word is speeded up so that large amounts of information can be reviewed in less time. Tape recorders can also be used to tape lectures or class notes so that information is available for later access. A talking calculator resembles a regular pocket calculator, but it provides both a visual and an audible display. When a key is pressed or a calculation completed, the calculator speaks.

Magnification devices enlarge visual images for students able to use their residual vision. Devices called low vision aids resemble small telescopes or magnifying glasses; they are used to read print and look at drawings and maps. Closed-circuit television systems are used to enlarge reading materials; the book or paper is placed on a platform and a video camera projects its image to a monitor that looks like a television screen (see Figure 8–4). Print is greatly enlarged, and the student can control the size and brightness of the display and whether the image is black on a white background or white on a dark background.

Devices that translate print to some other communication mode are designed for students unable to use sight for reading. Most devices convert printed material to synthesized speech. The Optacon, in contrast, converts print to a tactile image. The student moves a small camera across the reading material and places the other hand on a tactile display; this display contains rods that vibrate to form the shape of the text (or other visual information) seen by the camera.

Electronic mobility aids have been developed to help persons with visual impairments travel safely and independently. These aids use ultrasonic sound or laser beams to detect environmental obstacles. The user carries or wears the aid, and when an obstacle is detected, the aid produces an auditory and/or tactile signal (Lewis, 1993).

Assistive Technologies for Students with Hearing Impairments

Several technologies assist students with hearing impairments to communicate with each other and persons in the hearing world. Hearing aids have become smaller and more versatile as a result of transistors and printed circuits. There are four basic types of hearing aids: (1) the body aid (approximately the size of a portable calculator, it is strapped to the body or carried in the pocket and connected by a wire to an earpiece), (2) the behind-the-ear aid that hangs over the ear, (3) the eyeglass aid, and (4) the all-in-the-ear aid. All aids use an ear mold, a plastic earpiece customized to fit the individual. The in-the-ear aid contains all electronic components within the earpiece; in other types of aids, the ear mold serves to direct the amplified sound into the ear.

Cochlear implants are being attempted with some individuals with serious hearing losses. The implants consist of a tiny external microphone, signal processor, and transmitter that are attached to a receiver implanted in the mastoid bone behind the ear, just under the skin. Electrical signals are transmitted from the receiver to the intact auditory nerve in the inner ear, bypassing the damaged cochlea or sensory organ. This system converts

For Your Information

Resources for Information About Special Education Technology

Closing the Gap

http://www.closingthegap.com

The Closing the Gap organization offers publications and a yearly conference on applications of technology for persons with disabilities. Its newspaper, *Closing the Gap,* is published 6 times yearly. The annual *Closing the Gap Resource Directory* is a comprehensive guide to hardware, software, publishers, and organizations related to special education technology. The website includes an Online Resources Library with recent articles and columns from the newspaper. (Address: P.O. Box 68, Henderson, MN 56044)

Trace Research and Development Center

http://trace.wisc.edu

The Trace Center is one of the oldest organizations concerned with technology for persons with disabilities. It publishes a comprehensive database of technology resources in both print *(Trace Resourcebook)* and CD form *(Co-Net CD-ROM).* The Trace Center website provides links to sites with access software (freeware and shareware) and a Cooperative Electronic Library. One of the features of the library is Hyper-ABLEDATA, a searchable database with descriptions of more 20,000 products. (Address: University of Wisconsin–Madison, S-151 Waisman Center, 1500 Highland Ave., Madison, WI 53705)

National Center to Improve Practice in Special Education (NCIP)

http://www.edc.org/FSC/NCIP

This website provides a wealth of information about technology applications for students with disabilities. Its resources include:

- NCIPnet, a moderated newsgroup with discussions about technology and students with disabilities
- Spotlights on specific technologies (e.g., speech recognition)
- Links to other sites related to technology and disabilities
- NCIP Library, with information on a range of technologies (e.g., word prediction, multimedia, technologies for students with visual impairments)
- Online workshops (ongoing) and resources from past workshops

University of Kentucky Assistive Technology Project

http://serc.gws.uky.edu/www/ukat/ukatmenu.html

This website offers links to assistive technology and special education websites, each of which is described in some detail. Background information on assistive technology and descriptions of research at the University of Kentucky are also available.

---

sounds to electrical signals that are transmitted to the brain for interpretation (Lowenbraun & Thompson, 1986). Although this option is not appropriate for all individuals, it does provide an option to many persons with profound hearing losses, particularly adults who have lost their hearing within the past two or three years. However, the use of cochlear implants has not been without controversy (D'Antonio, 1993). Representatives of the Deaf community have objected to the use of implants as a method to "fix" deafness, especially for children who are not yet old enough to decide for

themselves if they wish to belong to the Deaf culture or the hearing culture.

Telecommunication Devices for the Deaf (TDDs) allow persons who are deaf or others who are nonverbal to communicate on the telephone. These devices resemble a portable typewriter or computer; the individual types a message on the keyboard and looks at a visual display for the response. Some TDDs also have printers so that a record of the telephone conversation can be made. TDDs can communicate only with other TDDs. However, the Americans with Disabilities Act requires that all companies providing phone services also provide relay services. Relay services allow TDD users and hearing persons to communicate; in effect, the relay operator acts as a translator. When the hearing person speaks, the operator types the message for the TDD user; when the TDD user types a response, the operator reads it aloud. Devices for individuals who are hard of hearing amplify telephone conversations through the handset of the telephone.

Closed captioning allows students with hearing impairments to enjoy regularly scheduled television programs. Written captions transmitted along with the television signal are decoded by a special device and projected onto the screen. The Americans with Disabilities Act requires that all televisions sold in the United States contain built-in decoding devices. Open captioned films and television programs provide captions visible to all viewers and do not require a special decoder. Amplification devices using infrared transmission facilitate television use for viewers who are hard of hearing.

Other types of assistive devices include

- visual alerting systems for the telephone, doorbell, alarm clock, fire alarm, and smoke detector (these use bright strobe lights to attract attention);
- amplification systems in classrooms, cinemas, theaters, auditoriums, and other public facilities, for use with or without hearing aids; and
- tactile or vibrating devices for speech therapy, alarm clock systems, and paging systems.

Clearly, classroom computers represent only one of the technologies that can facilitate inclusion of students with disabilities in school and in the community. Assistive technologies such as the ones described in the preceding paragraphs also help students to bypass or compensate for disabilities that could interfere with their ability to succeed in the general education classroom. In addition, new technologies continue to emerge. For more information about special education technologies and for a list of resources, see "For Your Information" (on page 225).

Throughout this book, the "Spotlight on Technology" sections highlight applications of technology with special relevance for students with special needs and their teachers. Sometimes, as in chapter 7, the technologies are familiar instructional tools like tape recorders. In other cases, the technologies are less well known but equally useful. The focus is usually on technologies for students, but occasionally teachers (or both teachers and students) are the technology users. In all cases, these sections focus on practical suggestions for the use of technology to improve the inclusion experience.

STRATEGIES FOR CLASSROOM COMPUTER USE

Obtaining classroom computers and selecting appropriate software are only the first steps in computer use. What must also occur is an integration process, in which the computer is "fully included" into the instructional activities of the classroom. Computers are instructional tools like textbooks and chalkboards, and, if they are to be used effectively, the teacher must consider them as one of the many resources available to assist in the teaching-learning process. "Inclusion Tips for the Teacher" (on page 228) presents the basic principles to consider when integrating computers and other technologies into the general education classroom. The following paragraphs describe a few of the approaches that teachers can take to make computers a part of the classroom learning environment.

Design an Instructional Unit Around a Software Program

One of the adventure games, discovery programs, simulations, or problem-solving programs can be used as the basis for a series of class activities. For example, the teacher might begin by demonstrating the simulation *The Oregon Trail* to the entire class and then breaking the class into several teams, each of which will attempt to survive the trek westward to Oregon. As part of the unit, students can keep a log of their journey, write letters home, keep records of their expenses and the status of their stores of provisions, read about the adventures of actual pioneers, and chart their progress on the map.

Use Software and the World Wide Web to Enrich and Extend Classroom Instruction

Software and the Web can be used to expand the instructional content to which students are exposed.

For example, if students are learning about the political process in the United States, they can extend their knowledge with a computer program that simulates a presidential election or by visiting the websites of Congress and the major political parties. If the subject of instruction is addition and subtraction of decimals, a home budget program or a money management simulation can provide a set of practical problems for students to solve.

Use Computer Drills to Expand Practice Opportunities

Drill-and-practice programs are the most common type of instructional software; although they may be less creative than other types, they serve an important classroom function. All students, particularly those with learning problems, need to practice the skills they are learning, and drill programs provide an additional way for this to occur. Most drills give students immediate feedback, and thus the practice provided is guided practice. In addition, unlike teachers, computers never tire:

They can repeat the same questions or problems to 1 student or 30, provide consistent feedback when students make errors, and reinforce each and every instance of appropriate responding.

Make Free Time with the Computer a Classroom Reward

Because students like to work with computers, computer time can become a free time activity that students work to earn. Possible rewards are playing a computer game of the student's choice, using a graphics program to create a picture, spending time with a word processor to complete a homework assignment, and having free time to explore any program in the classroom.

Encourage Students to Use Software Tools for Assignments

Computers can assist students in preparing any assignment in which text must be written, charts or pictures drawn, or computations performed. If stu-

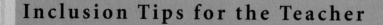

Inclusion Tips for the Teacher

Principles for Integrating Technology

1. Start with the curriculum, not the technology. The needs of individual students and the curriculum designed to meet those needs should drive the selection of technologies and the ways in which they are used.
2. Take advantage of the motivational value of technology, but don't limit its use to that of a reward or a leisure time activity. Technology has too much value as a teaching tool to ignore its use in instruction.
3. Use technology to reinforce skills taught by the teacher. Technology can present guided practice activities, monitor students' responses, and provide students with immediate feedback.
4. Select technology activities that match the goals of instruction and the skill levels of individual students. No matter how dazzling the technology or how superb the instructional strategy, teaching an irrelevant skill is a waste of time.
5. Take advantage of the customization options that some technologies offer. Features such as the ability to control content and instructional parameters make it easier to adapt learning activities to students' needs.
6. Monitor students' work at the computer or with other technologies with the same diligence used to monitor other types of classroom work. If performance data are collected by the technology, use that information in making instructional decisions.
7. Use technology to present new information to students. Although technology is certainly not the only instructional strategy available for this purpose, it does provide teachers with an additional resource for introducing new material.
8. Enrich and extend the curriculum through technology. Technology opens doors to experiences that students can't access in other ways, and these experiences can expand both the depth and breadth of the standard curriculum.
9. Teach students to use technologies as tools, then provide opportunities and encouragement for practice. Technology can help students bypass or compensate for disabilities, empowering them to achieve greater levels of independence.
10. Extend the benefits of technology to teachers. Technology is truly mainstreamed when it becomes an important tool not only for students but also for teachers.

Note. From *Special Education Technology: Classroom Applications* by R. B. Lewis. Copyright © 1993 by Brooks/Cole Publishing Company, Pacific Grove, CA. Reprinted by permission of Wadsworth Publishing Co..

dents learn how to use software tools to perform these tasks, they are gaining experience in valuable computer applications that can be used in a variety of situations. For example, when students learn to write with a word processor, they gain a tool that can facilitate all sorts of writing tasks: letters, essays, poems, book reports, lab notes, term papers, shopping lists, memoranda, and so on.

Promote Cooperative Learning by Forming Computer Work Groups

Computer use does not need to be a solitary activity. With many educational software programs, there is no reason that small groups of students cannot work together on one computer. Students can take turns reading the questions and typing in the answers; they can collaborate in solving a problem or arriving at the best response. By grouping students together and structuring the task in this way, the teacher promotes cooperative learning and provides an opportunity for socialization as well.

Experiment!

Computers can contribute to the richness of the learning environment in countless ways. Some of these have just been described; others can be found in magazines such as *Electronic Learning* and *Technology & Learning*. Still others are waiting to be dis-

Things to Remember

- Classroom computers are becoming more and more common, and educational software is increasing in both quality and quantity.
- Computers can teach, be taught, or serve as tools for accomplishing other tasks.
- Among the advantages of computers are their capacities for individualizing instruction, motivating students, and allowing new types of learning; with students with special needs, computers can help bypass or compensate for disabilities.
- All computer systems are made up of 5 parts: input, output, central processing unit, memory, and storage; the most common input and output devices are the keyboard and the computer monitor.
- The Internet and World Wide Web offer many learning opportunities to students including a wealth of information resources and the ability to communicate with others throughout the world.
- There are many types of educational programs, including tutorials, drill-and-practice programs, simulations, problem-solving programs, discovery programs, educational games, software tools

such as word processors, and programs for teacher use.
- In evaluating educational software, teachers should try a program before buying it and evaluate the program's instructional features with particular students in mind.
- Computer adaptations for students with special needs include modified keyboards, input alternatives such as single switches and speech recognition devices, speech synthesizers that add the spoken word to programs, and special software.
- Assistive devices help students with physical, sensory, and communication impairments.
- Computers can be integrated or "fully included" into the classroom in many ways. For example, educational software can enrich classroom instruction, expand students' opportunities for practice, and promote cooperative learning.
- Teachers are just beginning to explore how classroom computers can be used to assist in the education of students with special needs and their regular class peers.

covered. Experiment! The only limits are the boundaries of your imagination.

This chapter has focused on strategies for the effective use of computers and other technologies in the general education classroom. The next chapters describe specific techniques for teaching different types of students with special needs. Before turning to chapter 9 and considering students with learning disabilities, consult "Things to Remember" to review the primary concerns in classroom technology use.

ACTIVITIES

1. Visit a school and observe how teachers use computers in instruction. Find out where computers are located (in classrooms, a central computer lab, the library or media center, or a combination of these arrangements), what types of software are available, and what learning activities students accomplish with computers. For example, do students use computers for drill and practice? Word processing? Science or social studies simulations?

2. Observe a classroom or lab in which students are using computers. Are students actively involved in the learning task, or does their attention wander? Do they appear excited about learning? Watch the interactions among students. Is any cooperative learning taking place?

3. Use the information presented in this chapter as a guide in reviewing an educational software program. Be sure to consider your student population as you run the program and evaluate its strengths and weaknesses. Also, check to see whether the program would be appropriate for students with special learning needs.

4. Several professional organizations are concerned with computers in education, but one that focuses on technologies for individuals with disabilities is the Technology and Media (TAM) Division of The Council for Exceptional Children. Visit CEC's website (www.cec.sped.org) or write to TAM (1920 Association Drive, Reston, VA 22091) to find out about the services it provides.

5. Look through recent print or online issues of *Electronic Learning* (www.scholastic.com/EL), *Technology & Learning* (www.techlearning.com), or other educational computing magazines and journals. Select an article that provides suggestions for classroom computer activities. Write a short summary of the article, then add your ideas for adapting the activities for students with special needs.

chapter 9

Teaching Students with Learning Disabilities and Attention Deficit Hyperactivity Disorders

Cases

Jane is a seventh grader with a learning disability; she has great difficulty remembering what she has learned, particularly in the area of written language. It took Jane several years to acquire basic reading and spelling skills; now, she can read fourth grade material with adequate word recognition and good comprehension, and in spelling she performs at the third grade level. This year in seventh grade, Jane attends general education classes for all subjects except English; during that period, she visits the special education resource teacher for reading and spelling instruction. With the help of her seventh grade teacher, Mr. Henry, Jane is earning passing grades in math, science, and social studies. Classroom adaptations for Jane include taped textbooks and modified exams and assignments. Portions of Jane's special education assessment report and IEP appear later in this chapter.

Danny is a student with learning disabilities who is 8 years old and in second grade. Although Danny can read and spell quite well for his age, he has difficulty with handwriting and math. His printing is large and uncoordinated, and he has trouble staying within the lines. Several of his letters and numbers are written incorrectly; for example, he confuses b and d, n and u, and 6 and 9. In math, Danny has learned some of the basic addition facts but has not yet begun subtraction. His math papers are messy and difficult to read; the margins are irregular, and the columns of numbers poorly aligned. Danny visits the resource teacher for an hour each day for special help in math and handwriting. During the rest of the day, Danny participates in the activities of his second grade classroom. Mrs. Rose, Danny's second grade teacher, provides him with extra practice in math facts to help him progress more quickly. Handwriting assignments are also modified so that Danny can complete them successfully. Later we will see how Danny's second grade teacher assesses his specific educational needs.

A learning disability is a perplexing condition. Students with learning disabilities are of average intelligence and learn some things quickly and easily. However, because of deficits in attention, perception, and memory, they acquire other skills only with extreme difficulty. Students with learning disabilities may read well yet spell poorly. Or they may fail a written test but be able to answer every question correctly on an oral exam. These special students are often members of general education classes; they can participate successfully if instructional modifications are made.

Students with learning disabilities have special needs in academic, classroom behavioral, physical, and social performance. However, the most common area requiring adaptation of classroom procedures is academic instruction. Students like Danny need extra help in acquiring basic skills; reading, handwriting, spelling, written expression, or math can be trouble areas. Older students, such as Jane, benefit from assistance in content area subjects. Class requirements may need to be modified in science, social studies, and English courses to help students compensate for poor basic skills.

This chapter explores the characteristics of students with learning disabilities and provides methods for the general education teacher to use in gathering data, teaching basic skills, and modifying content area instruction. In addition, the last section of this chapter suggests strategies for instructional modifications for another group of learners who often experience academic difficulties: students with attention deficit hyperactivity disorder (ADHD).

INDICATORS OF LEARNING DISABILITIES

For students with learning disabilities, the general education teacher is a vital member of the inclusion team. Classroom teachers are usually the first to notice signs of learning disabilities and refer students for special education assessment. In addition, general educators assist in gathering assessment information and in coordinating special services.

The legal definitions of learning disabilities and other disabilities were discussed in chapter 3. However, a learning disability is one of the most difficult disabilities to define. Debate over definitional issues has continued since the passage of PL 94-142, and new definitions of learning disabilities have been proposed. One example is the definition of the National Joint Committee on Learning Disabilities (1994), a coalition of organizations concerned with this disability:

Learning disabilities is a general term that refers to a heterogeneous group of disorders manifested by significant difficulties in the acquisition and use of listening, speaking, reading, writing, reasoning, or mathematical abilities. These disorders are intrinsic to the individual and presumed to be due to central nervous system dysfunction. . . . Even though a learning disability may occur concomitantly with other handicapping conditions . . . or environmental influences . . . it is not the direct result of those conditions or influences.

Common to this and other definitions of learning disabilities is an extreme difficulty in the acquisition of basic school skills despite adequate intellectual ability.

Students may be identified as learning disabled at any age, but most are noticed during the early elementary grades. There are two major indicators of learning disabilities. First, students appear capable but experience extreme difficulty in some area(s) of learning. This is a discrepancy between expected and actual achievement. For example, a young child might be verbal and appear bright but be very slow to learn the alphabet, write his or her name, and

count to 20. The second indicator is variation in performance; that is, there is a discrepancy among different areas of achievement. A fourth grader might perform well in math but read and spell poorly. Or a tenth grader might be a good science student except when required to express ideas in writing. In addition to these two main indicators of learning disabilities, teachers should watch for several other signs, including the following:

- Speaks well but reads poorly
- Confuses similar letters and words, such as *b* and *d, was* and *saw*
- Guesses constantly when reading
- Has extreme difficulty with math
- Is clumsy; has difficulty with laces, buttons, ball-catching
- Has trouble understanding or following directions
- Has difficulty expressing thoughts
- Has trouble understanding time and distance
- Confuses up/down, left/right, and front/back
- Has a short attention span; is easily distracted
- Is overactive; or inactive, listless
- Is impulsive; cannot wait; cannot foresee consequences (California Association for Neurologically Handicapped Children [now the Learning Disabilities Association of California], 1980, p. 3)

Although it is a rare individual who displays all these characteristics, most students with learning disabilities exhibit at least one or two.

Poor **learning strategies** may also be a sign of learning disabilities (Lerner, 1997; Mercer, 1997; Reid, Hresko, & Swanson, 1996). Learning strategies are the methods students use to plan, begin, and complete learning tasks; students with learning disabilities tend to use less effective strategies than average achievers. For example, with memory tasks, average achievers rehearse the information they are trying to commit to memory, whereas students with learning disabilities do not. This difference in performance has led Torgesen (1977) to call students with learning disabilities inactive learners because they fail to become actively involved in the learning task. In contrast, Swanson (1989) suggests that these students are not passive but "*actively inefficient* learners" (p. 10).

Many school districts have developed checklists to help general education teachers identify students with learning disabilities, and several commercial measures such as the *Learning Disability Evaluation Scale* (McCarney, 1996) are also available. A teacher

Window on the Web

Websites About Learning Disabilities

http://www.ldonline.org

LD OnLine is a service of The Learning Disabilities Project at WETA in Washington, DC. LD On-Line provides information about learning disabilities and attention deficit hyperactivity disorders in

the interactive guide to learning disabilities for parents, teachers, and children

several ways: the ABCs of LD and ADD (for basic information), LD In Depth, Finding Help (including links to other sites), and Audio Clips (listen to experts speak on various topics). First Person features accounts from families and individuals with learning disabilities. The KidZone includes art and writing by young people as well as the Just for Kids bulletin board. Bulletin boards are also available for parents and teachers and these address topics such as social skills, postsecondary education, and parenting a child with learning disabilities. Visitors to LD OnLine can sign up to receive a free e-mail newsletter.

http://www.ldresources.com

The LD Resources site is hosted by Richard Wanderman, a nationally known expert on learning disabilities who calls himself a "suc-

LD Resources

cessful dyslexic adult." Features of this site are articles and essays on learning disabilities and on learning disabilities and writing; links to other resources; Macintosh software (freeware and shareware) that can be downloaded; and back issues of the *LD Reader,* an e-mail newsletter. Information about how to subscribe to this free newsletter is also provided.

http://www.ldanatl.org

This is the website of the national Learning Disabilities Association, the first parents' organization in the field of learning disabilities. It provides information about LDA, links to state LDA pages, and several resources. These include LDA's position papers on current topics of interest (e.g., inclusion, violence in schools), bulletins about legislation and lobbying efforts, Fact Sheets (e.g., early childhood, educational standards, spoken language problems), and information about publications and resources related to learning disabilities.

Note: Courtesy of LD Online, LD Resources, and LDA.

can use this rating scale to screen students for learning disabilities in academic areas (e.g., listening, thinking, speaking, reading, writing, spelling, math) and in areas such as attention, auditory discrimination, visual perception, fine-motor skills, and memory.

ASSESSMENT PROCEDURES

When learning disabilities are suspected, the general education teacher refers students for special education assessment. Parents are notified of the reasons for referral and are presented with an assessment plan prepared by the multidisciplinary team. If consent is given for special education evaluation, the team begins to collect information about the student.

Assessment is an information-gathering process that includes both formal testing and informal procedures such as observation, inventories, and work sample analyses. In the assessment of learning disabilities, information is collected about the student's current intellectual functioning, academic achievement, and performance in areas related to the disability: information processing and strategies for learning. Figure 9–1 presents a portion of the special education assessment report for Jane, one of the students introduced at the beginning of this chapter.

Intellectual functioning is assessed by intelligence tests, such as the *Wechsler Intelligence Scale for Children-Third Edition (WISC-III)* (Wechsler, 1991). This is an individual test, appropriate for students from age 6 to 17, that is administered by the school psychologist. Several intelligence quotient (or IQ) scores are obtained. The test average (or mean) is 100; scores between IQ 85 and 115 are considered to be within the average range of performance, and those between IQ 70 and 85 are considered low average (McLoughlin & Lewis, 1994). In this interpretation system, approximately 68% of the population falls within the average range of performance, 14% show low average performance, and 2% show below average performance. Most states require students to achieve an IQ score in the low average range or above to qualify for special education services for learning disabilities.

WISC-III results include a total test score called the Full Scale IQ, and two other global scores, Verbal IQ and Performance IQ. Verbal subtests require students to listen to questions and reply orally; performance subtests are made up of visual-motor tasks. Also available are Index scores that describe performance in the areas of Verbal Comprehension, Perceptual Organization, Freedom from Distractibility, and Processing Speed. IQ scores, Index scores, and scores on individual subtests are all of interest to professionals in the interpretation of *WISC-III* results. As the report in Figure 9–1 indicates, Jane scored within the average range in most areas. However, her performance fell in the low average range on the Digit Span subtest, a measure of short-term memory, and on the Freedom from Distractibility factor.

After the student's general ability level has been determined, academic achievement is assessed. One commonly used measure is the *Peabody Individual Achievement Test-Revised (PIAT-R)* (Markwardt, 1989). It is administered individually by the school psychologist or the special education resource teacher and is appropriate for students in kindergarten through grade 12. The *PIAT-R* assesses several areas of school achievement, and results include grade scores, age scores, percentile ranks, and standard scores. *PIAT-R* standard scores, like the IQ scores on the *WISC-III,* have a mean of 100; the range of average performance extends from standard score 85 to 115.

Jane's *PIAT-R* results also appear in Figure 9–1. There is a discrepancy between her performance on the *PIAT-R* (Total Test standard score of 84) and her overall intellectual performance (Full Scale IQ of 101). Also, there is variation among the different academic areas: Jane's achievement is average in math, reading comprehension, and general information but low average in reading recognition and spelling.

The third area of assessment is information processing. Several older measures are available; examples are the *Motor-Free Visual Perception Test* (Colarusso & Hammill, 1972), the *Auditory Discrimination Test* (Reynolds, 1987; Wepman, 1975), the *Goldman-Fristoe-Woodcock Auditory Skills Test Battery* (Goldman, Fristoe, & Woodcock, 1976), and the *Illinois Test of Psycholinguistic Abilities* (Kirk, McCarthy, & Kirk, 1968). However, the psychometric quality of many information processing measures has been heavily criticized (McLoughlin & Lewis, 1994; Salvia & Ysseldyke, 1991), and in many schools older tests such as these are no longer used.

Instead, newer measures such as the *Woodcock-Johnson Psycho-Educational Battery-Revised* (Woodcock & Johnson, 1989) and the *Detroit Tests of Learning Aptitude* (3rd ed.) (Hammill, 1991) provide information about students' functioning in areas such as memory, processing speed, auditory and visual processing, and attention. Tests are often supplemented with results of informal assessments such as observations of the student's strategies for learning. In Jane's case, a memory problem is indicated by test results and her teachers' observations.

FIGURE 9-1   **Special Education Assessment Results**

Student: Jane   **Age:** 13 years, 2 months   **Grade:** 7

Intellectual Performance

The *Wechsler Intelligence Scale-Third Edition* was administered to Jane by Ms. Ducharme, the school psychologist. Jane performed within the average range on all Verbal subtests except Digit Span, a measure of short-term memory, attention, and freedom from distractibility. She earned a scaled score of 6 on this subtest, which indicates low average performance. All Performance subtest results were within the average range. Jane's Intelligence Quotient (IQ) scores were as follows:

Verbal IQ	108
Performance IQ	92
Full Scale IQ	101

All IQ scores fell within the average range as did Index scores for Verbal Comprehension, Perceptual Organization, and Processing Speed. One Index score, Freedom from Distractibility, fell within the low average range because of Jane's poor performance on the Digit Span subtest. These results indicate that, overall, Jane shows average capabilities for academic learning. However, short-term memory may be a weak area for Jane.

Academic Performance

Mr. Ross, the resource teacher, administered the *Peabody Individual Achievement Test-Revised.* On this measure, Jane showed average performance in Mathematics, Reading Comprehension, and General Information (a measure of content area knowledge). However, her performance fell within the low average range in Reading Recognition and Spelling. She earned these standard scores:

General Information	98
Reading Recognition	82
Reading Comprehension	88
Mathematics	101
Spelling	72
TOTAL TEST	84

Jane scored at the fourth grade level in decoding, as measured by the Reading Recognition subtest. Spelling, at grade 3, was her weakest area. These results are consistent with the observations of Mr. Henry, Jane's seventh grade teacher. Despite average intellectual performance, Jane continues to experience difficulty in some academic tasks.

Learning Abilities and Strategies

To find out more about Jane's memory skills, Ms. Ducharme administered portions of the *Woodcock-Johnson Psycho-Educational Battery-Revised, Tests of Cognitive Ability.* Jane's performance was within the low average range on tests of Long-Term Retrieval and tests of Short-Term Memory. Mr. Henry notes that Jane appears to comprehend grade 7 material but has great difficulty committing facts to memory. Mr. Ross, Jane's resource teacher, reports that Jane is beginning to learn strategies for memorizing information but is not yet able to use these strategies consistently. These teacher observations and test results point to a learning disability in the area of memory and the need for continued instruction in strategies for learning and recalling academic information.

Once it has been established that a student is eligible for special education services for pupils with learning disabilities, the team begins to gather information about educational needs. The general education teacher can provide valuable assistance at this point in the assessment process. For example, for Danny (the second grader described at the beginning of this chapter), specific data about math and handwriting performance must be collected. Formal tests are available, but

more specific information is obtained from informal measures.

The general education teacher might decide to devise an informal procedure for a particular student. As shown in Figure 9–2 on page 240, Danny's teacher prepared a criterion-referenced test of addition facts to assess current math skills; results indicate that Danny has not yet mastered the basic facts of addition. The teacher might also wish to obtain a sample of Danny's handwriting and analyze it to locate typical error patterns.

Other assessment procedures available to the classroom teacher are informal inventories, curriculum-based measurement, direct observation, and classroom tests. Also useful are the results from recently administered group achievement measures and placement tests for educational materials and programs. One area of special need for many students with learning disabilities is reading. "Inclusion Tips for the Teacher" on page 241 suggests several ways to assess reading in the classroom. These include methods to determine students' reading levels and to measure the readability of textbooks and other instructional materials.

 **SPECIAL SERVICES**

When assessment is complete, the team meets to plan the student's IEP. Figure 9–3 on page 243 presents portions of the IEP for Jane. Like most students with learning disabilities, she is a general education student who leaves her classroom for only a short time each day for special education services.

Although the resource room is the most typical placement for students with learning disabilities, some districts provide self-contained special classes for those with comprehensive learning needs. In addition to part- or full-day special education, many students with learning disabilities receive assistance in oral language development from speech-language clinicians. Some receive counseling from the school psychologist, social worker, or counselor; those with motor problems may attend special physical education classes. For the general education teacher, consultant services are available to assist in including students with learning disabilities. To learn more about this group of students, consult "For Your Information" on page 244.

CLASSROOM ADAPTATIONS

Academic instruction is the primary area in which adaptations are made for students with learning disabilities in the general education classroom; the rest of this chapter focuses on methods for meeting academic needs. Some students with learning disabilities also require assistance in classroom behavior; methods for teaching study skills and controlling disruptive behavior can be found in chapter 11. For students who have difficulty relating to classmates, chapter 6 presents ways to increase social acceptance.

Two approaches are available for the instruction of students with learning disabilities. In the **remediation** approach, the teacher instructs the student in skills that are areas of need. For example, extra assistance in spelling might be provided to a fourth grader who spells at the second grade level. **Compensation,** on the other hand, attempts to bypass the student's weaknesses. For instance, to compensate for the reading and writing problems of a high school student, the teacher might administer class tests orally. Remediation techniques are used to teach basic skills and are most appropriate for elementary-aged students. Compensation techniques bypass deficiencies in basic skills in order to teach content area subjects; they are used most commonly in the late elementary grades, middle school, and high school.

The following sections of this chapter present several remediation techniques and compensatory strategies. Methods of teaching basic skills to

FIGURE 9-2   Informal Assessment

Student: Danny	**Age:** 8 years, 4 months	**Grade:** 2

Criterion-Referenced Test of Basic Addition Facts

Objective: When presented with any 20 one-digit plus one-digit basic addition facts problems (e.g., 1 + 1, 4 + 3, 8 + 5), the student will write the correct answer to at least 18 problems within 2 minutes.

Test and Student's Responses:

1 +4 **5**	5 +2 **7**	3 +3 **6**	9 +4 **(14)**	0 +7 **7**	2 +7 **(8)**	4 +5 **9**
8 +1 **(10)**	5 +6 **11**	3 +5 **8**	7 +0 **7**	3 +8 **(12)**	4 +2 **6**	9 +7 **16**
6 +3 **9**	8 +9 **(16)**	1 +1 **2**	6 +8 **(15)**	2 +8 **10**	7 +9 **(14)**	

Criterion for Acceptance Performance: 18 correct responses in 2 minutes

Student's Score: 13 correct responses in 2 minutes

younger students and methods for adapting content area instruction are included. In the latter section, secondary teachers can find ideas for modifying assignments and exams, using taped texts, and compensating in other ways for the academic difficulties of students with special needs.

TEACHING BASIC SKILLS

Reading, handwriting, spelling, written expression, and math are often called basic skills; these "tool" subjects, once acquired, are used in the acquisition of new information and concepts. Although most students learn the rudiments of basic skills in the early elementary grades, students with special needs may not. They may require additional instruction in order to progress. In general, basic skills instruction is provided to special students by the general education teacher if it is a part of the classroom curriculum. Some students may receive tutoring in some skills as part of their special education program, but most will take part in at least some of the basic skills instruction in the regular classroom. The general education teacher can enhance the learning of special students by modifying the techniques used to teach basic skills. Three

Inclusion Tips for the Teacher

Determining Reading Levels

To ensure effective instruction, the teacher must match reading materials to the skills of special students. There are several ways to accomplish this.

Oral Reading Sample

To check oral reading skills, the teacher can simply have the student read a portion of a textbook or other reading material aloud. If the student can read at least 95% of the words and successfully answer at least 75% of the comprehension questions the teacher asks, it is likely that the text is appropriate for the student (Kirk, Kliebhan, & Lerner, 1978). Oral reading samples should be collected in a private setting so that students are not embarrassed by the errors they make.

Cloze Procedure

With the cloze procedure, students can read silently or orally. This procedure is a valuable (and quick) way to determine whether class textbooks in subjects such as science, history, or shop are written at an appropriate level for students. The student reads a short passage in which every fifth (or seventh or *n*th word) has been replaced with a blank. The student must insert appropriate words in the blanks. If at least 44% to 57% of the missing words are correctly supplied, the passage is at the student's instructional level (Bormuth, 1968; Burron & Claybaugh, 1977).

Informal Reading Inventories

Another approach is to first determine the instructional reading level of the student and then select materials written at this level. Informal reading inventories (IRIs) are useful for this purpose. These measures contain several reading passages and comprehension questions for each passage. The student reads (usually aloud) and answers the questions; results are used to determine three reading level scores: Independent, Instructional, and Frustration.

According to McLoughlin and Lewis (1994), materials at the student's Independent Level can be read easily without assistance from the teacher, those at the Instructional Level are more difficult but appropriate for classroom reading instruction, and

those at the Frustration Level are too difficult for the student. Students are expected to show 90% to 100% accuracy in comprehension at the Independent Level, 75% to 90% accuracy at the Instructional Level, and less than 75% accuracy at the Frustration Level (Kirk, Kliebhan, & Lerner, 1978).

Three popular IRIs that are available commercially are the *Analytical Reading Inventory* (5th ed.) (Woods & Moe, 1995), *Classroom Reading Inventory* (6th ed.) (Silvaroli, 1990), and *Ekwall Reading Inventory* (2nd ed.) (Ekwall, 1986); all are appropriate for students reading between the primer and grade 8 or 9 reading levels. It is important to remember that published IRIs may focus on a different set of reading skills than those emphasized by the classroom reading series or other instructional materials.

If a student achieves an instructional reading level of grade 6 on an IRI, then books at that reading level will generally be appropriate for instruction. However, that student may not be able to read a sixth grade science text. Grade levels of content area texts refer to subject matter, not reading level, and such texts often require above-grade-level reading ability. For example, a fourth grade social studies book can have a reading level of fifth, sixth, or even seventh grade.

Readability Measures

To select instructional materials that are appropriate for students with special needs, the teacher must match the reading levels of students with those of texts and other materials. A readability formula or graph can be used to discover the reading level of the books in a classroom. There are many readability measures that teachers can use to determine the reading level of materials such as textbooks (e.g., Dale & Chall, 1948; Flesch, 1951; Spache, 1953).

One relatively quick and easy method is that suggested by Fry (1968). It is appropriate for use with materials that range from first grade to college levels; extended versions are available for preprimer and primer materials (Maginnis, 1969) and reading matter at college and graduate school levels (Fry, 1977). Use the Fry readability graph and the directions on pages 242 and 243 to discover the approximate reading levels of texts, supplementary read-

continued

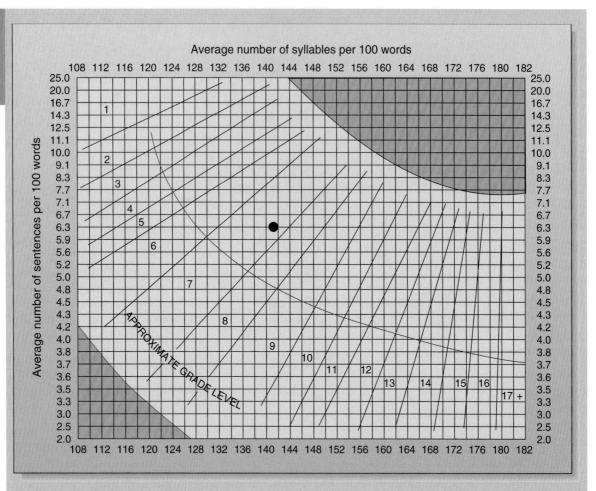

ing materials, newspapers and magazines, and any other type of reading matter you might use in your classroom. Once potentially appropriate materials have been identified by readability analyses, their suitability for particular students can be determined by oral reading samples or the cloze procedure.

DIRECTIONS: Randomly select 3 one hundred word passages from a book or an article. Plot average number of syllables and average number of sentences per 100 words on graph to determine the grade level of the material. Choose more passages per book if great variability is observed and conclude that the book has uneven readability. Few books will fall in [the] blue area but when they do grade level scores are invalid.

Count proper nouns, numerals and initializations as words. Count a syllable for each symbol. For example, "1945" is 1 word and 4 syllables and "IRA" is 1 word and 3 syllables.

EXAMPLE:

	Syllables	Sentences
1st Hundred Words	124	6.6
2nd Hundred Words	141	5.5
3rd Hundred Words	158	6.8
AVERAGE	141	6.3

READABILITY 7th GRADE (see dot plotted on graph)

EXPANDED DIRECTIONS FOR WORKING READABILITY GRAPH

1. Randomly select three (3) sample passages and count out exactly 100 words beginning with the beginning of a sentence. Do count proper nouns, initializations, and numerals.
2. Count the number of sentences in the hundred words estimating length of the fraction of the last sentence to the nearest 1/10th.
3. Count the total number of syllables in the 100-word passage. If you don't have a hand counter

available, an easy way is to simply put a mark above every syllable over one in each word, then when you get to the end of the passage, count the number of marks and add 100. Small calculators can also be used as counters by pushing numeral "1", then pushing the "+" sign for each word or syllable when counting.

4. Enter graph with average sentence length and average number of syllables; plot dot where the two lines intersect. Area where dot is plotted will give you the approximate grade level.

5. If a great deal of variability is found in syllable count or sentence count, putting more samples in the average is desirable.

6. A word is defined as a group of symbols with a space on either side; thus, "Joe," "IRA," "1945," and "&" are each one word.

7. A syllable is defined as a phonetic syllable. Generally, there are as many syllables as vowel sounds. For example, "stopped" is one syllable and "wanted" is two syllables. When counting syllables for numerals and initializations, count one syllable for each symbol. For example, "1945" is 4 syllables and "IRA" is 3 syllables, and "&" is 1 syllable.

Note. From "Fry's Readability Graph: Clarifications, Validity, and Extension to Level 17" by E. Fry, 1977, *Journal of Reading*, 21, 242–252. Reproduction permitted. No copyright.

FIGURE 9-3   **EP Goals and Services for Jane**

Annual Goals

1. By the end of the school year, Jane will read sixth grade material with adequate word recognition skills and comprehension.
   Person responsible: Resource teacher

2. By the end of the school year, Jane will correctly spell all words on a high-frequency word list such as the Dolch list.
   Person responsible: Resource teacher

3. By the end of the school year, Jane will correct her spelling errors by using the dictionary or a word processing program with a spelling checker.
   Person responsible: Resource teacher

4. Jane will successfully complete all requirements for seventh grade math, science, and social studies.
   Person responsible: Seventh grade teacher

Amount of Participation in General Education

Jane will attend all seventh grade classes in general education with the exception of English.

Special Education and Related Services

1. Jane will receive special education services from the resource teacher (annual goals 1, 2, and 3) for one period daily.

2. The resource teacher will provide consultation to Jane's seventh grade teacher as needed (annual goal 4).

---

adaptations are recommended: providing prompts, giving additional instruction, and allowing extra guided practice.

Prompts are features added to learning tasks; they are particularly helpful for students with learning disabilities and others who have difficulty focusing attention on relevant instructional cues. Prompts also structure the task and help the student know exactly what to do. Danny could use the prompts in Figure 9–4 on page 245 to help improve his printing.

Providing additional direct instruction and allowing extra guided practice are adaptations that aid students with poor recall. To ensure successful

For Your Information

Students with Learning Disabilities

- Students with learning disabilities make up about 5% of the school-aged population (U.S. Department of Education, 1997a).
- Learning disabilities are the most common disability; in 1995–1996, 51% of the students served in special education were identified as learning disabled (U.S. Department of Education, 1997a).
- Four times as many boys are identified as having learning disabilities as girls (Lerner, 1997).
- Reading is one of the academic skills in which students with learning disabilities experience difficulty most frequently. Other common problem areas are math, spelling, handwriting, and written expression.
- Among the most typical behavioral characteristics of students with learning disabilities are hyperactivity, impulsivity, and disorders of attention (Tarver & Hallahan, 1976).
- Terms such as *dyslexia* (a difficulty in reading) and *dyscalculia* (a computational difficulty) are sometimes used in reference to learning disabilities. Medical terms such as these do little to describe the learning problem and should be avoided. Instead of calling a student dyslexic, it is better to say he or she has a learning disability in the area of reading.
- Most students with learning disabilities are in general education classrooms for the majority of the school day and receive part-time special education services in areas of need. For example, in 1994–1995, approximately 81% of the students identified as learning disabled in the United States were served in regular classrooms (U.S. Department of Education, 1997a).
- Famous people with learning disabilities include Winston Churchill, Thomas Edison, Albert Einstein, Nelson Rockefeller, Leonardo da Vinci, and Woodrow Wilson.

learning, the teacher should break down the subject matter into small steps and present it as slowly as necessary. Several practice opportunities should be available; the teacher can monitor performance during practice, enlist the aid of a peer tutor or adult volunteer, or use self-correcting materials. The basic math self-instructional materials in Figure 9–5 on page 246 can help Danny learn addition facts.

Reading

Word recognition and comprehension are the two most important subskills of reading. Word recognition is the ability to decode printed symbols; decoding is accomplished by sight if the word is familiar or by analysis of the word's phonetic components or its structure (i.e., roots, prefixes, suffixes, etc.). Reading comprehension—the ability to understand what is read—involves knowing the meanings of individual words, following the sequence of events in a passage, detecting the main ideas, drawing conclusions, and making inferences.

There are two major approaches to teaching reading skills: the code-emphasis approach and the meaning-emphasis approach. According to Mercer and Mercer (1998), code-emphasis programs teach decoding first, then comprehension; instruction in decoding stresses the regular relationships between letters and sounds. In contrast, meaning-based programs emphasize comprehension from the start; students practice decoding by reading common words.

The whole language approach to reading instruction is an example of a meaning-emphasis program. In this approach, reading is not broken down into separate skill areas; thus, skills such as decoding are not taught separately. Instead, reading is integrated with the other language arts of listening, speaking, and writing (Lapp & Flood, 1992). McLoughlin and Lewis (1994) provide this description:

> In the whole language classroom, language learning takes place in a social context where students use language for real (i.e., authentic) purposes. Students read whole texts, not fragments, and those texts tend to be

FIGURE 9-4   **Prompts for Basic Skills Instruction**

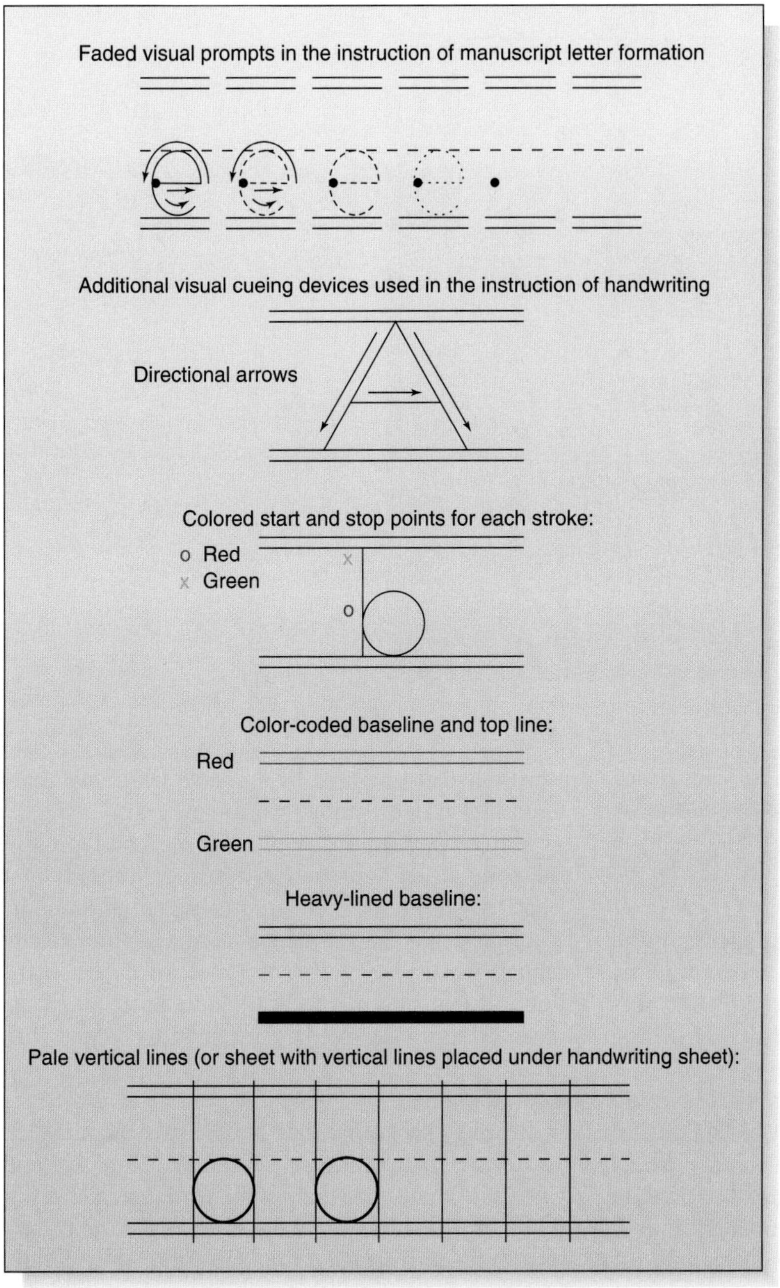

Faded visual prompts in the instruction of manuscript letter formation

Additional visual cueing devices used in the instruction of handwriting

Directional arrows

Colored start and stop points for each stroke:

o Red
x Green

Color-coded baseline and top line:

Red

Green

Heavy-lined baseline:

Pale vertical lines (or sheet with vertical lines placed under handwriting sheet):

Note. Reprinted with permission of Merrill, an imprint of Macmillan Publishing Company, from *Teaching the Mildly Handicapped in the Regular Classroom* (2nd ed., p. 108) by J. Affleck, S. Lowenbraun, and A. Archer. Copyright © 1980 Merrill Publishing Company, Columbus, Ohio.

FIGURE 9-5 Materials for Independent Practice

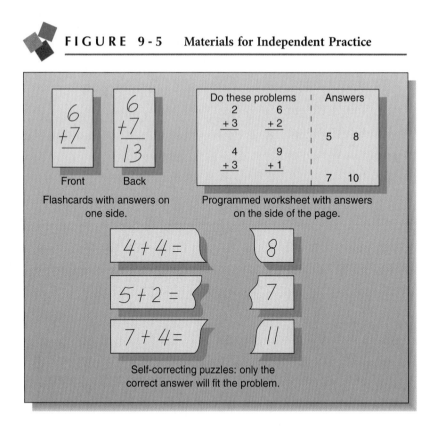

Flashcards with answers on one side.

Front   Back

Programmed worksheet with answers on the side of the page.

Do these problems | Answers

Self-correcting puzzles: only the correct answer will fit the problem.

children's literature rather than stories constructed solely for inclusion in textbooks. Throughout meaning and motivation are emphasized; the development of isolated skills is deemphasized. (p. 285)

Although the whole language approach is quite popular, research results suggest that code-emphasis programs are more effective, particularly for students with special needs and those at risk for learning problems (Chall, 1967, 1977, 1983, 1989; Stahl & Miller, 1989). In particular, students with learning disabilities will likely require explicit instruction in skills such as decoding if they are to succeed in whole language classrooms (Lerner, Cousin, & Richeck, 1992; Mather, 1992). Table 9–1 compares implicit (i.e., meaning-emphasis) approaches to reading instruction such as whole language to explicit (i.e., code emphasis) and interactive approaches.

Code-emphasis programs provide beginning readers with a systematic method of decoding unfamiliar words. Students learn decoding strategies and then practice with words that can be read using these strategies. Code-based reading materials feature a controlled vocabulary, that is, one limited to

words that can be read by students who have mastered the strategies taught in the program.

Materials based on the phonics method represent the code-based approach to reading. Students first learn the sound for each letter (phoneme-grapheme combinations) and practice reading phonetically regular words; later, other types of words are introduced. Linguistic methods are an adaptation of the phonics approach; reading instruction begins with phonetically regular word families such as *at, bat, cat, rat,* and *sat.*

Reading programs that begin with a controlled vocabulary help students acquire skills quickly and gain confidence in their ability to decode print; however, students eventually must make the transition to a more conventional vocabulary selection. One way to accomplish this is to teach students to read common words that appear with high frequency in the English language. Because many of these words are irregular and therefore not readily decodable with phonics strategies, they are often taught as sight vocabulary. The *Dolch Basic Sight Word List* (Dolch, 1953) is one example of a high-frequency word list; an updated version of the

TABLE 9-1   Approaches to Reading Instruction

Explicit	Interactive	Implicit
Reading Concepts		
Bottom-up reading (code emphasis)	Combination	Top-down reading (meaning emphasis)
Part-to-whole learning	Combination	Whole-to-part learning
Teacher-directed instruction	Combination	Student-directed instruction
Skill emphasis	Combination	Immersion emphasis
Reading viewed as a learned behavior that requires much teacher assistance		Reading acquired naturally through exposure to text
Reading Approaches and Programs		
Basals: *Palo Alto Reading Program; Merrill Linguistic Reading Program*	*Success for All*	Basals: *Ginn 720; New Open Highways*
Literature-Based Approach with systematic phonics	*Reading Recovery*	Literature-Based Approach with little or no phonics
Phonics Approach	*B.A.L.A.N.C.E.*	Whole Language Approach
Phonological Awareness Training	Reciprocal Teaching	Language Experience Approach
Reading Mastery and *Corrective Reading Program*	Learning Strategies	Individualized Reading Approach
Linguistic Approach		Neurological Impress Method
Multisensory Reading Method (Fernald; Gillingham; Word Imprinting)		High Interest–Low Vocabulary Method
Glass Analysis		

Note. Reprinted with the permission of Merrill from *Teaching Students with Learning Problems* (5th ed.) by C. D. Mercer and A. R. Mercer (p. 337). Copyright © by Prentice-Hall, Inc.

Dolch list (Johnson, 1971) is shown in Table 9–2. Simms and Falcon (1987) suggest dividing this word list into categories for instruction. Categories might include self words (e.g., *I, me*), moving words *(come, play)*, size words *(big, little)*, and question words *(who, when)*.

Reading is a problem area for many students with special needs, not only those with learning disabilities. Some have difficulty learning (or applying) word recognition skills; others fail to understand what they have read despite adequate decoding skills. Still others require assistance in both word recognition and comprehension. The following suggestions for modifying reading instruction for students with special needs include examples of prompts and ways to enhance the practice of reading skills:

• Add cues to help students decode troublesome words; for example, mark long vowels (se͞ed),

cross out silent letters (mak¢), and divide words into syllables (dis-crim-i-na̅t¢).

• Provide markers for students who lose their place while reading. They can move their finger along under the line of print or use an index card with an arrow for a guideline; cards with windows can be placed on the page to expose only a few words at a time.

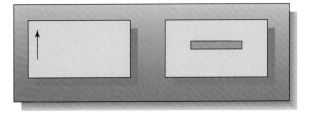

• To enhance reading comprehension, tell students the purposes for reading and what to look for in the passage. For example, they might read a story

TABLE 9-2   **High-Frequency Word List**

Preprimer	Primer	First	Second	Third
1. the	45. when	89. many	133. know	177. don't
2. of	46. who	90. before	134. while	178. does
3. and	47. will	91. must	135. last	179. got
4. to	48. more	92. through	136. might	180. united
5. a	49. no	93. back	137. us	181. left
6. in	50. if	94. years	138. great	182. number
7. that	51. out	95. where	139. old	183. course
8. is	52. so	96. much	140. year	184. war
9. was	53. said	97. your	141. off	185. until
10. he	54. what	98. may	142. come	186. always
11. for	55. up	99. well	143. since	187. away
12. it	56. its	100. down	144. against	188. something
13. with	57. about	101. should	145. go	189. fact
14. as	58. into	102. because	146. came	190. through
15. his	59. than	103. each	147. right	191. water
16. on	60. them	104. just	148. used	192. less
17. be	61. can	105. those	149. take	193. public
18. at	62. only	106. people	150. three	194. put
19. by	63. other	107. Mr.	151. states	195. thing
20. I	64. new	108. how	152. himself	196. almost
21. this	65. some	109. too	153. few	197. hand
22. had	66. could	110. little	154. house	198. enough
23. not	67. time	111. state	155. use	199. far
24. are	68. these	112. good	156. during	200. took
25. but	69. two	113. very	157. without	201. head
26. from	70. may	114. make	158. again	202. yet
27. or	71. then	115. would	159. place	203. government
28. have	72. do	116. still	160. American	204. system
29. an	73. first	117. own	161. around	205. better
30. they	74. any	118. see	162. however	206. set
31. which	75. my	119. men	163. home	207. told
32. one	76. now	120. work	164. small	208. nothing
33. you	77. such	121. long	165. found	209. night
34. were	78. like	122. get	166. Mrs.	210. end
35. her	79. our	123. here	167. thought	211. why
36. all	80. over	124. between	168. went	212. called
37. she	81. man	125. both	169. say	213. didn't
38. there	82. me	126. life	170. part	214. eyes
39. would	83. even	127. being	171. once	215. find
40. their	84. most	128. under	172. general	216. going
41. we	85. made	129. never	173. high	217. look
42. him	86. after	130. day	174. upon	218. asked
43. been	87. also	131. same	175. school	219. later
44. has	88. did	132. another	176. every	220. knew

Note. From "The Dolch List Reexamined" by D. D. Johnson, 1971, *The Reading Teacher, 24,* pp. 455–456. Copyright 1971 by the International Reading Association. Reprinted by permission of D. D. Johnson and the International Reading Association.

to discover the main characters and the sequence of events, or a textbook chapter to learn important facts and main ideas. **Advanced organizers** that provide an overview of the passage to prepare students for what they will be reading are an effective strategy for increasing comprehension (Graham & Johnson, 1989). Mercer and Mercer (1993) suggest giving students a list of questions to guide their reading and the page numbers of the text on which answers can be found.

- Use peer tutors and volunteers for sight word drill.
- Provide **high interest–low vocabulary** reading materials to aid in the practice of silent reading. They appeal to students who read at a lower grade level than expected for their age; examples appear in Table 9–3. Another good resource is *Easy Reading: Book Series and Periodicals for Less Able Readers* (2nd ed.) (Ryder, Graves, & Graves, 1989), which is available from the International Reading Association (800 Barksdale Rd., Newark, DE 19711).
- Tape texts or stories; students can read the passage while listening to correct word pronunciation and phrasing of sentences.
- Use computer software to help teach basic reading skills. For example, many multimedia programs talk, allowing students to develop sight vocabulary as they read and listen to stories, poems, and other texts. (See "Spotlight on Technology" in chapter 10 for more information about reading software.)
- Provide practice in reading comprehension with materials such as the *Specific Skill Series* (Boning, 1990). This program includes activities for skills such as using context clues, locating facts, following directions, and drawing conclusions. A source of ideas for other activities for comprehension practice is *Locating and Correcting Reading Difficulties* (6th ed.) (Ekwall & Shanker, 1993).
- To increase reading fluency, have students reread a passage several times. **Repeated readings** increase both speed and accuracy, which helps students master a selection before attempting more difficult selections. Sindelar (1987) says that "mastery is seldom achieved with a single reading, especially for students experiencing difficulty in learning to read" (p. 59).
- Teach students strategies for approaching comprehension tasks. In one study (Jenkins, Heliotis, Stein, & Haynes, 1987), students improved their comprehension of stories by learning to name the most important person *(Who?)* and the major event *(What's happening?)* in each paragraph.
- Another strategy, the SQ3R method (Robinson, 1961), can help students improve their comprehension of expository reading materials such as content area textbooks. (*SQ3R* stands for *Survey, Question, Read, Recite,* and *Review.*) Expository text is usually more difficult to understand than narrative text (i.e., stories). In the SQ3R method, students begin by surveying the passage to get a general idea of its contents. Students ask questions about the text, then read to find the answers. The answers are recited without reference to the text, and then the entire passage is reviewed.
- **Reciprocal teaching** is an instructional approach developed by Palinscar and Brown (1988) that involves four interrelated strategies. Teachers help students develop comprehension skills and the ability to monitor their own comprehension by involving students in dialogues about texts. Lerner (1997) describes the four strategies: "*summarizing* the content of a passage, *asking questions* about a central point, *clarifying* the difficult parts of the material, and *predicting* what would happen next" (p. 139).

Handwriting, Spelling, and Written Expression

Writing skills are built on reading skills, and many special students need extra assistance in this area. One important subskill is handwriting, the mechanical process of forming letters and words. The goal in handwriting instruction is for students to write legibly and with sufficient speed. Usually students learn manuscript writing (printing) first, then they are introduced to cursive writing in the middle elementary grades. For students with difficulty in letter formation and spacing, cursive writing may be less demanding. For example, in printing, the letters *b* and *d* require a similar motor pattern and are easily confused; in cursive, they are written quite differently.

Students who fail to make a complete transition from printing to cursive writing often continue forming capital letters in manuscript while writing the rest of the word in cursive. If legibility and speed

TABLE 9-3 High Interest–Low Vocabulary Reading Materials

Title	Publisher	Reading Grade Level	Interest Grade Level
American Adventure Series	Harper & Row	3–6	4–8
Basic Vocabulary Books	Garrard	2	1–6
Breakthrough Series	Allyn & Bacon	2–6	6–12
Checkered Flag Series	Field Educational Publications	2–4	7–12
Childhood of Famous Americans Series	Bobbs-Merrill	4–5	7–9
Cowboy Sam Series	Benefic Press	PP–3	1–6
Dan Frontier Series	Benefic Press	PP–4	1–7
Deep Sea Adventures	Field Educational Publications	2–5	3–11
Everyreader Series	McGraw-Hill	6–8	5–12
Fastback Books	Globe/Fearon	4–5	6–12
First Reading Books	Garrard	1	1–4
Focus on Reading	SRA	1–6	3–12
Folklore of the World Books	Garrard	2	2–8
Interesting Reading Series	Follett	2–3	7–12
Jim Forest Readers	Field Educational Publications	1–3	1–7
Junior Science Books	Garrard	4–5	6–9
Morgan Bay Mysteries	Field Educational Publications	2–4	4–11
Morrow's High Interest/Easy Reading Books	William Morrow	1–8	4–10
Mystery Adventure Series	Benefic Press	2–6	4–9
Pacemaker Classics	Globe/Fearon	2	7–12
Pacemaker True Adventure	Globe/Fearon	2	5–12
Pacemaker Story Books	Xerox Education Publications	2	7–12
Pal Paperback Kits	Xerox Education Publications	1–5	5–12
Perspectives Set	High Noon Books	3–4	6–12
Phoenix Everyreaders	Phoenix Learning Resources	4	4–12
Pleasure Reading Books	Garrard	4	3–7
Racing Wheels Series	Benefic Press	2–4	4–9
Reading For Concepts Series	McGraw-Hill	3–8	5–12
Reading Reinforcement Skilltext Series	SRA	1–5	1–8
Reading Skill Builders	Reader's Digest Services	1–4	2–5
Sailor Jack Series	Benefic Press	PP–3	1–6
Scoreboard Series	High Noon Books	2	3–10
Space Science Fiction Series	Benefic Press	2–6	4–9
Sports Mystery Stories	Benefic Press	2–4	4–9
Sprint Libraries	Scholastic	1–3	3–6
Super Kits	Warner Educational Services	2–5	4–12
Superstars Series	Steck-Vaughn	4–6	7–12
Teen-Age Tales	D. C. Heath	4–6	6–11
Tom & Ricky Mystery Series	High Noon Books	1	3–8
Top Picks	Reader's Digest Services	5–7	5–12
Turning Point	Phoenix Learning Resources	1–4	7–12
What Is It Series	Benefic Press	1–4	1–8

Note. Reprinted with the permission of Merrill from *Teaching Students with Learning Problems,* 5/e, by Cecil D. Mercer and Ann R. Mercer (p. 331). Copyright © 1998 by Prentice-Hall, Inc.

are not affected, this style is acceptable. In fact, many of the special cursive alphabets developed for students with handwriting problems contain print-style capitals; in addition, letters and words are written almost vertically with little slant. One example is found in *D'Nealian Handwriting* (Thurber & Jordan, 1981). In the modified alphabet proposed by Spalding and Spalding (1986), after students learn to form manuscript letters and five connecting strokes, the transition to cursive can be made with ease.

Spelling is the arrangement of letters to form words. Because English is not a completely phonetic language, many words cannot be spelled the way they sound. Although consonants have fairly reliable phoneme-grapheme correspondence, vowel letters take on several different sounds; for example, the letter *a* produces distinct sounds in *at, ate, all,* and *father.* For this reason, teaching spelling solely by phonics is probably not the best practice, particularly for students who learn words slowly. Although phonics skills should be a part of the spelling curriculum, words that appear frequently in written language should also be stressed; see, for example, the high-frequency word list in Table 9–2 on page 248. Combining basic instruction in phonics (with emphasis on consonant sounds) and instruction in spelling common words as well as words selected by the student is a practice that produces an excellent individualized spelling program.

When basal spelling programs are used, lessons can be modified for special students as necessary; for instance, the number of words to be learned each week can be reduced. Teachers should carefully monitor the words included in each lesson. For example, if lists include similar words, such as *receive* and *piece,* students may become confused and, as a result, acquire few new spelling words.

Written expression is the process of putting one's thoughts down on paper. Several skills are needed: the mechanics of writing, such as handwriting, spelling, punctuation, and capitalization; language skills such as knowledge of word meanings and syntax (grammar); and thinking skills such as organization, sequence, and logic. Although written expression used to be "the neglected basic skill" (Freedman, 1982, p. 34), the whole language movement has resulted in increased emphasis on writing as part of the language arts curriculum. As Lerner, Cousin, and Richeck (1992) comment, "Writing takes on a new role in whole language instruction and is just as important as reading" (page 227). As in reading, the whole language approach to writing stresses meaning rather than the development of specific skills. However, for many students with special needs, written language skills must be taught directly.

Several ideas for teaching spelling, handwriting, and composition in the general education classroom are listed here, along with examples of prompts and suggestions for practice activities. Also, see "Spotlight on Technology" later in this chapter on page 254 for information about using computers to teach writing skills.

- Help students who are poor spellers begin to use the dictionary as an aid; provide them with a minidictionary or "My Words" booklet that contains high-frequency words and words that they often misspell.
- Use the test-study-test method for spelling instruction (Graham & Miller, 1979). Begin with a pretest to identify words students have already mastered, then focus study activities on the words they need to learn. Students also should correct their own spelling tests under the teacher's direction. In a review of research on strategies for teaching spelling skills, Graham and Miller say that this approach is "the single most important factor in learning to spell" (p. 10).
- Provide handwriting prompts such as those shown in Figure 9–4. Fade the prompts as quickly as possible.
- Review rules for capitalization and punctuation before students begin writing; post rules on the bulletin board.
- Use instructional tapes for the practice of high-frequency and phonetically irregular spelling words. Students listen to the word, attempt to write it, and listen again to hear the correct spelling.
- For students who form letters slowly and laboriously, use newsprint and felt-tip pens for handwriting practice. When students write slowly on newsprint, the ink spreads, making individual letters indecipherable. Students must increase speed in order for their handwriting to be legible.
- Provide many different opportunities to practice written expression. Have students keep a daily journal, write three-sentence stories, compose a note to a friend each day, and/or describe an event or person. At first, keep writing activities brief; encourage clarity and accuracy.

FIGURE 9-6   **Organizational Map for an Essay on Scorpions**

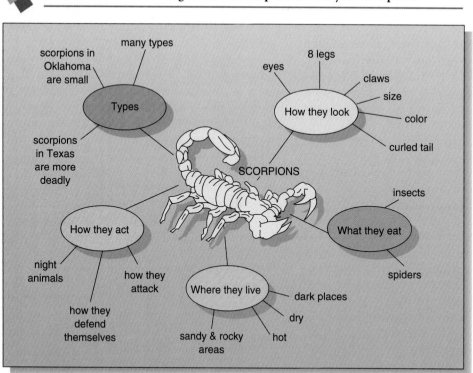

Note. From "On Your Mark, Get Set, Write!" by G. E. Tompkins and M. Friend, 1986, *Teaching Exceptional Children,* *18*(2), p. 86. Copyright 1985 by The Council for Exceptional Children. Reprinted by permission.

• Teach writing as a multistage process. Isaacson (1987) describes three stages: prewriting (or planning), writing, and rewriting (or revising). Mercer (1997) identifies five: prewriting, drafting, revising (making changes in content), editing (correction of errors), and publishing. Whatever process model is used, provide guided practice at each stage. At the prewriting stage, for instance, students can engage in a variety of activities to generate ideas and gather information for writing. Students can think about the topic, read, or research ideas; they can observe or interview others or listen to speakers, watch demonstrations, or take part in field trips (Tompkins & Friend, 1986; Whitt, Paul, & Reynolds, 1988).

• Give students a format for writing compositions or essays. For example, have them list the main ideas they wish to present and formulate a title. The main ideas are then converted to topic sentences for paragraphs, and supporting sentences are added.

• **Mapping** is another strategy to help students organize their ideas for writing. Students list the key words and ideas they have identified for the topic they will write about, then draw a map showing the relationship between the main topic and key words (Tompkins & Friend, 1986). Figure 9–6 shows a map developed by a group of students for a report on scorpions.

• Teach students specific strategies for planning the content of their writing. For narratives, Graham and Harris (1989) suggest the CSPACE strategy:

C character
S setting
P problem or purpose
A action
C conclusion
E emotion

The TREE strategy (Graham & Harris, 1989) is used when planning opinion essays:

T topic
R reasons
E examples
E ending

- Include structured activities for the revising stage of writing. One possibility is the formation of writing groups in the classroom. Each student reads his or her composition aloud to the group, and peers comment on specific strengths in the writing; the writer then asks for help (e.g., "Did the ending make sense?") (Tompkins & Friend, 1988). Students can also evaluate their own work using guides like the self-edit think sheet described by Englert and Raphael (1988). With this guide, students

    first look back at their papers, star the parts they like best, and anticipate readers' questions by putting question marks next to the unclear parts. Next, they rate the extent (e.g., "yes," "sort of," "no") to which they answered the text structure questions (e.g., Did I . . . "Tell what was being explained?" "Tell what materials you need?" "Make the steps clear?" etc.). (p. 518)

- Also teach strategies for locating and correcting writing errors. Schumaker, Nolan, and Deshler (1985) recommend the COPS strategy:

    C capitalization
    O overall appearance
    P punctuation
    S spelling

- Teach students to use word processors for writing. See "Spotlight on Technology" for word processing tools that assist students in the drafting, revising, and editing stages of writing.
- Teach students what to do when spelling checkers in word processing programs detect a misspelling but cannot suggest the correct alternative. Spelling checkers are able to supply the correct word for spelling errors only about 50% of the time for students with learning disabilities (MacArthur, Graham, Haynes, & DeLaPaz, 1996). One reason for this is that students' spellings are often far from accurate and the pro-

gram is unable to "guess" the word the student is attempting to write. Ashton (1997) suggests the CHECK strategy. This strategy helps students make systematic changes in their word (altering the beginning letter, consonants, and vowels), attend to the words suggested by the program, and remain persistent.

C Check the beginning sound
H Hunt for the correct consonants
E Examine the vowels
C Changes in word lists may give hints
K Keeping repeating steps 1 through 4

Math

Many students with special needs require extra assistance in math. Within the area of math are two important subskills: computation and reasoning. Computation is based on the prerequisite skills of number concepts, reading and writing numerals, and counting. It includes mastery of number facts in the basic operations (addition, subtraction, multiplication, and division) and knowledge of **algorithms,** the procedures for performing operations. For example, in the algorithm for adding 2 two-digit numbers such as 25 and 48, it is necessary to begin with the right-hand or ones column (5 + 8 = 13); if the sum of the ones column is more than 9 (in this case 13), then the ones portion (3) is written in the ones column, and the tens portion (1) is carried over to the tens column.

In math reasoning, computation skills are used to solve problems. A typical classroom example is the word or story problem in which students are presented with a situation and asked to find a solution. Some students find these difficult because poor reading skills interfere with their understanding of the problem; others have trouble separating essential from superfluous information, determining the appropriate algorithm, and computing the answer. Educational reform efforts have attempted to make problem solving a more important part of the math curriculum. For example, the National Council of Teachers of Mathematics (1989) recommends that students be actively engaged in authentic problem-solving tasks beginning in the early grades. Students who perform poorly in math reasoning tasks should receive extra instruction and practice in this area.

Spotlight on Technology

Write:OutLoud and *Co:Writer,* Word Processing Tools for Writers with Special Needs

Writing has been described as a schizophrenic activity because the writer must assume two roles, that of an author and that of a secretary (Smith, 1982). Students with learning disabilities have particular difficulties with the secretarial aspects of writing: handwriting, spelling, capitalization and punctuation, usage, and written grammar.

Word processing programs may help alleviate some of these problems (Lewis, 1993, 1998). One of the major advantages of word processors is that writers can easily manipulate the text to revise and improve it. Spelling checkers, present in most word processors, help in the correction of spelling errors. Another advantage is that the writer's final product is printed; it is neater and easier to read than a handwritten paper. This is very important for students with learning disabilities and others with poor handwriting. As one teacher commented about a student who had learned to word-process, "Now, even with hunt and peck, his written assignments are done willingly, on time, and *I can read them!!!*" (Lewis, Dell, Lynch, Harrison, & Saba, 1987, p. 61).

Write:OutLoud

Write:OutLoud is one of the many word processing programs designed for classroom use. It has three major advantages for students with special needs. It's easy to learn and easy to operate. It talks, that is, it has the ability to read aloud whatever the student has written. And, third, it contains a spelling checker that also talks.

In *Write:OutLoud,* students can easily change the size and color of the letters and the color of the background. The program can be set to speak text automatically as it is entered. Choices include hearing each letter name, each word, each sentence, and/or each paragraph. Students also have the option of hearing any portion of the

Note. Courtesy of Don Johnston, Inc.

Ways of modifying math instruction in the general education classroom are presented here. Prompts to aid students in computation and reasoning and suggestions for classroom practice activities are included.

- Add visual prompts to help students solve computation problems; see the examples presented in Figure 4–11.
- For students who have trouble spacing math problems and writing numbers, use paper that

has been marked off in squares, or add guidelines so that students write within boundaries.

- Include only a few problems per page if students appear confused by several problems or if they have difficulty finishing their work.
- Use self-instructional materials for drill in number facts; see Figure 9–5 for ideas for materials that can be made by teachers. Or select one of the many software programs for math drill and practice. (Example programs are described in "Spotlight on Technology" in chapter 11.)

text read aloud after they've finished writing. To do that, they simply select the text they want to hear and click on the button with the speaker.

The spelling checker in *Write:OutLoud* works like a typical spelling checker. When the student chooses Spell Check, the program scans the text to locate spelling errors. When a misspelling is identified, the students see the misspelled word in a sentence (which can be read aloud) and several possible alternatives. Each alternative can be read aloud, a useful feature for students who may have problems in reading.

Co:Writer

Co:Writer is a word prediction program. It works with other programs, such as word processors, to reduce the amount of typing students must do. Word prediction programs were originally developed for individuals with physical impairments to reduce the motor demands of the writing task. However, these programs have also been found useful with students with learning disabilities and others who have difficulty spelling (Lewis, Ashton, & Kieley, 1996).

When students are writing with a word processor, they activate *Co:Writer* by pressing the "=" key. A window pops up (right) and the student begins writing. When the first letter of a word is typed, *Co:Writer* attempts to predict the word the student wants to enter in the document. For example, when this writer typed *m,* the program predicted *most, main, mall, man,* and *men.* The student can hear any of these words read aloud and, if one is correct, select it by clicking on it or typing its number. If the list of suggested words does not contain the word the student wants, he or she types a second letter and another set of words is predicted.

Both *Write:OutLoud* and *Co:Writer* were developed by Don Johnston, Inc. Visit this company's website at www.donjohnston.com.

```
┌──────────────────────────────────────┐
│ ≡≡≡  Co:Writer Rena's Writer  ≡≡≡  ▣ │
│                    ▼                  │
│  I went to the m                      │
│               1: most                 │
│               2: main                 │
│               3: mall                 │
│               4: man                  │
│               5: men                  │
│                                       │
└──────────────────────────────────────┘
```

Note. Courtesy of Don Johnston, Inc.

- Work toward automatic recall of number facts. Facts are automatic when students no longer need to rely upon counting strategies; their responses are quick, accurate, and consistent. To develop **automaticity,** Hasselbring, Goin, and Bransford (1987) suggest introducing no more than two or three facts and their reciprocals at a time. Timed drills are used for practice, with the goal being a 1-second response time.
- Manipulative objects help some students learn basic number concepts and relationships; for example, use beans, blocks, or poker chips to teach counting, the relationship of multiplication to addition, and so on.
- Provide verbal prompts to assist in the application of algorithms; for instance, Affleck, Lowenbraun, and Archer (1980) recommend the following for two-digit multiplication: "Multiply by the one's column first. Remember to line up the numbers carefully. Remember to cross multiply" (p. 109).
- Use real situations for word problems. For example, the students' own performance data or the

number of points earned for appropriate behavior provide material for practice problems.

- Help students begin to analyze story problems by identifying the key words that often (but not always) signal the different operations. Mercer and Mercer (1989) call these "clue words" and give these examples:

> *Addition:* Altogether, sum, and, plus, finds
> *Subtraction:* Left, lost, spent, remains
> *Multiplication:* Rows, groups, altogether
> *Division:* Share, each, cost per month (p. 254)

- Set up a class store, bank, or stock exchange, and devise different activities for practice in math reasoning.

MODIFYING CONTENT AREA INSTRUCTION

In the late elementary grades, the curriculum shifts in emphasis from the acquisition of basic skills to the use of these tool subjects to gain other types of information. Content areas such as English, science, health, history, and social studies begin to dominate the curriculum. In high school, most courses are content subjects, and there is great variety—art, music, business education, shop and woodworking, home economics, physical education and sports, driver education, vocational subjects such as welding and auto mechanics, and so on.

Content area instruction assumes that students have mastered the basic skills of reading, writing, and math. For many special students, this is simply not the case. For these students to benefit from instruction, modifications must be made. Two types of changes are recommended: changing the criteria for task performance and altering the characteristics of content area tasks. Task criteria include speed and accuracy demands and the amount of work required. Task characteristics, in contrast, refer to the basic skills necessary for performance.

Compensatory strategies are used with older special students to enhance their chances of success. The most common strategy is the replacement of written language requirements with oral language requirements. Instead of reading and writing, students listen and speak; they use areas of strength to compensate for poor basic skills.

The following paragraphs describe several of the task demands that cause difficulty for special students in content area instruction; suggestions for modifications are also presented.

Reading Assignments

Students whose reading level is less than expected for their grades often find content subjects unmanageable. They may be unable to read textbook assignments, or they may be able to read only slowly and with great effort. To help such students acquire the information presented in assigned readings, teachers can try the following modifications:

- Reduce the amount of reading required. Permit students to read only part of the assignment or to concentrate on the most important elements, such as headings, italicized words, and chapter previews and summaries.
- Substitute materials written on a lower reading level. For example, use a sixth grade history text for tenth graders. Many remedial reading versions of content subject texts are available from commercial publishers.
- Present the information through another medium. Possible methods are lecture; class discussion; visual aids such as photos, maps, slides, and filmstrips; audiovisual aids such as movies, videotapes, and television; resource people who can be interviewed; peer tutors and volunteers who act as readers; and audiotapes of reading material. One of the most typical adaptations is the use of taped texts. For more information about preparing and using these aids, see "Inclusion Tips for the Teacher."

Written Assignments and Exams

Because they may be unable to read directions and questions, students with reading problems find written assignments and exams troublesome. For these students, the adaptations previously suggested can be used. For students who perform poorly in writing despite adequate reading skills, try the following modifications:

- For students who work slowly, reduce the length of the written task or extend the time limits.
- Allow students with poor handwriting to print, use a typewriter, or write with a word processor.
- Provide poor spellers with a dictionary or a list of commonly misspelled words.

Inclusion Tips for the Teacher

Taped Textbooks

Deshler and Graham (1980) present guidelines for the use of tape-recorded materials with secondary students with special needs:

1. Teachers should decide what material is to be taped; it is probably necessary to record only key sections of reading assignments, rather than entire texts or chapters.
2. Tapes can be used not only to present content area information but also to provide instruction in study skills. As Deshler and Graham note,

   While taping a reading assignment, a teacher has an excellent opportunity to demonstrate how to differentiate between main and supportive material within a chapter; how to use illustrations, graphs, charts, etc., to aid comprehension; how to use questions at the end of a section or chapter to determine major points; and how to use chapter titles, section headings, etc. to skim a reading section for main ideas. (p. 53)

3. To facilitate the acquisition of study skills, the teacher can mark the text to indicate important information, less crucial content that will be paraphrased, the point at which to stop the tape to complete activities, and so on.
4. Tapes should be of sufficient quality to ensure comprehension.
5. Principles of learning should guide tape preparation. Deshler and Graham list several important characteristics of an instructional tape:

   - Is well organized
   - Provides a variety of activities
   - Highlights or cues important points
   - Contains a variety of questions designed to facilitate recall and critical analyses
   - Repeats key concepts or ideas
   - Accommodates the assimilation and/or practice of new concepts or ideas
   - Provides immediate and delayed feedback. (p. 54)

6. Edwards (1980) adds that it is necessary to determine whether students learn best with or without the text in front of them while listening to the tape. She suggests conducting a quick, informal assessment of all students to see whether they should listen and read simultaneously or simply listen.

- Consider a dictionary designed for poor spellers, available in most bookstores. In this dictionary, students look up words by their phonetic spellings to find the correct version. The Franklin Spelling Master is an electronic version of a poor speller's dictionary. It is a small, portable device; the student types in a phonetic spelling (e.g., *reseve* for *receive*), and a list of possible options is generated: *resolve, receive, reserve,* and so on.
- Permit students to write using a word processor with a spelling checker program to help identify and correct spelling errors.
- Design assignments and exams so that writing requirements are minimized. For example, use multiple-choice and completion formats rather than essays.
- Have students who are unable to compose and write at the same time compose on a tape recorder and then transcribe what they have dictated.

- Have students respond through a medium other than writing. Two possible methods are telling answers to peer tutors or volunteers who write them for the student and giving oral responses to the teacher.

Math Skills

Content area subjects often require that students have rudimentary math skills. Basic facts and algorithms are necessary for success in algebra, geometry, trigonometry, home economics, woodshop, and auto mechanics. In some areas, such as higher math and vocational classes, computation skills are essential. Classes like English, history, and social studies can demand quantitative reasoning; for instance, graphs and charts are often used to convey important information.

The most common adaptation for students with poor math skills is the use of aids. Students can rely on facts tables for basic computation or use calculators for problems requiring more complex operations. This compensatory strategy is a useful one, and many adults also rely on electronic aids. However, simply providing students with calculators will probably not result in successful performance. Students need to learn how to operate calculators, estimate what the answer should be, and check their results.

By providing special students with compensatory strategies for reading assignments, written work and exams, and math skills, the general education teacher helps bypass basic skills deficits in order to facilitate content area instruction. Many students with special needs rely on compensatory procedures for their entire lives. Consider the words of Nelson Rockefeller, a former governor of New York and later vice president of the United States, who was learning disabled:

> If it helps a dyslexic child to know that I went through the same thing . . .
> But can conduct press conferences today in three languages . . .
> And can read a speech on television . . .
> (Though I may have to rehearse it six times . . .
> (With my script in large type . . .
> (And my sentences broken into segments like these . . .
> (And long words broken into syllables) . . .
> And learned to read and communicate well enough to be elected Governor of New York four times. . . .
> (Rockefeller, 1976, p. 14)

◆ ADAPTING INSTRUCTION FOR STUDENTS WITH ATTENTION DEFICIT HYPERACTIVITY DISORDERS

Students with attention deficit hyperactivity disorder have many of the same needs as students with learning disabilities and others with academic learning problems. However, unlike students with learning disabilities, students with ADHD may experience difficulty in most, if not all, school subjects. Problems with inattention, distractibility, impulsiveness, and hyperactivity affect all areas of learning. For some students with ADHD, these problems cause serious delays in academic achievement; for others, the effects are less severe.

Students with ADHD are identified by the behaviors they display. The definition currently accepted by most professionals is that of the American Psychiatric Association (1994). Figure 9–7 on page 261 presents the major elements of the definition included in the fourth edition of that organization's *Diagnostic and Statistical Manual of Mental Disorders* (often called the *DSM-IV*). See "Inclusion Tips for the Teacher" to learn more about attention deficit hyperactivity disorders.

ADHD is not recognized as a disability under the current version of IDEA. However, some students may be eligible for special education services because they meet criteria for another disability such as learning disabilities, behavioral disorders, or health impairments. Others may qualify for services under Section 504 of the Rehabilitation Act of 1973. Such services may include special education, related services, and adaptations in general education programs. The U.S. Department of Education (1991) gives these examples of possible classroom modifications:

> providing a structured learning environment; repeating and simplifying instructions about in-class and homework assignments; supplementing verbal instructions with visual instructions; using behavioral management techniques; adjusting class schedules; modifying test delivery; using tape recorders, computer-aided instruction, and other audiovisual equipment; selecting modified textbooks or workbooks; and tailoring homework assignments. (p. 7)

Inclusion Tips for the Teacher

Myths About ADHD

Read the myths below, then check the facts. Note that ADD, as used here, is synonymous with ADHD.

MYTH: Attention Deficit Disorder (ADD) does not really exist. It is simply the latest excuse for parents who do not discipline their children.

FACT: Scientific research tells us ADD is a biologically-based disorder that includes distractibility, impulsiveness, and sometimes hyperactivity. While the causes of ADD are not fully understood, recent research suggests that ADD can be inherited and may be due to an imbalance of neurotransmitters—chemicals used by the brain to control behavior—or abnormal glucose metabolism in the central nervous system. Before a student is labeled ADD, other possible causes of his or her behavior are ruled out.

MYTH: Children with ADD are no different from their peers; all children have a hard time sitting still and paying attention.

FACT: Before children are considered to have ADD, they must show symptoms that demonstrate behavior greatly different from what is expected for children of their age and background. They start to show the behaviors characteristic of ADD between ages three and seven. . . .These behaviors are persistent and occur in many different settings and situations. Furthermore, the behavior must be causing significant social, academic, or occupational impairment for the child to be diagnosed educationally as having ADD.

MYTH: Only a few people really have ADD.

FACT: Estimates of who has ADD range from 3 to 5 percent of the school-age population (between 1.46 and 2.44 million children). While boys outnumber girls by 4:1 to 9:1, experts believe that many girls with ADD are never diagnosed.

MYTH: Medication can cure students with ADD.

FACT: Medicine cannot cure ADD but can sometimes temporarily moderate its effects. Stimulant medication such as Ritalin, Cylert, and Dexedrine is effective in 70 percent of the children who take it. In these cases, medication causes children to exhibit a clear and immediate short-term increase in attention, control, concentration, and goal-directed effort. Medication also reduces disruptive behaviors, aggression, and hyperactivity.

However, there are side effects and no evidence for long-term effectiveness of medication. For example, recent studies show that medication has only limited short-term benefits on social adjustment and academic achievement. While medication can be incorporated into other treatment strategies, parents and teachers should not use medication as the sole method of helping the child.

MYTH: The longer you wait to deal with ADD in students, the better the chances are that they will outgrow it.

FACT: ADD symptoms continue into adolescence for 50–80 percent of the children with ADD. Many of them, between 30–50 percent, still will have ADD as adults. These adolescents and adults frequently show poor academic performance, poor self-image, and problems with peer relationships.

MYTH: There is little parents and teachers can do to control the behavior of children with ADD.

FACT: Teachers and parents have successfully used positive reinforcement procedures to increase desirable behaviors. A behavioral modification plan can give the child more privileges and independence as the child's behavior improves. Parents or teachers can given tokens or points to a child exhibiting desired behavior—such as remaining seated or being quiet—and can further reward children for good school performance and for finishing homework. Mild, short, immediate reprimands can counter and decrease negative and undesirable behaviors. Students with ADD can learn to follow classroom rules when there are pre-established consequences for misbehavior, rules are enforced consistently and immediately, and encouragement is given at home and in school.

MYTH: Students with ADD cannot learn in the regular classroom.

continued

FACT: More than half of the children with ADD succeed in the mainstream classroom when teachers make appropriate adjustments. Most others require just a part-time program that gives them additional help in a resource room. Teachers can help students learn by providing increased variety. Often, altering features of instructional activities or materials, such as paper color, presentation rate, and response activities, help teachers hold the attention of students with ADD. Active learning and motor activities also help. ADD students learn best when classroom organization is structured and predictable.

Note. From *Attention Deficit Disorder: Beyond the Myths* developed by the Chesapeake Institute, Washington, D.C., as part of a contract from the Office of Special Education Programs, U.S. Department of Education. No copyright.

Interventions for students with ADHD are often multimodal (Lerner & Lowenthal, 1993; Lerner, Lowenthal, & Lerner, 1995; Reeve, 1990). That is, they include not only instructional adaptations but also behavior management programs and medical treatment. Strategies for modifying instruction are discussed here; chapter 11 describes behavioral and medical interventions.

The major approach to adapting instruction for students with ADHD is to increase the structure of the classroom learning environment. In addition, the teacher attempts to decrease the sources of distraction within the classroom and, at the same time, make learning materials and activities more powerful so they will attract and sustain students' attention. Lerner and Lowenthal (1993) provide several specific suggestions drawn from the work of Abramowitz and O'Leary (1991) and Ysseldyke, Algozzine, and Thurlow (1992):

- Place the youngster in the least distracting location in the class. This may be in front of the class, away from doors, windows, air conditioners, heaters, and high-traffic areas. It may be necessary for the child to face a blank wall or be in a study carrel to enable the child to focus attention.
- Surround the student with good role models, preferably peers that the child views as *significant others*. Encourage peer tutoring and cooperative learning.
- Maintain a low pupil-teacher ratio whenever possible through the use of aides and volunteers.
- Avoid unnecessary changes in schedules and monitor transitions, because the child with ADD often has difficulty coping with changes. When unavoidable disruptions do occur, prepare the student as much as possible by explaining the situation and what behaviors are appropriate.
- Maintain eye contact with the student when giving verbal instructions. Make directions clear, concise, and simple. Repeat instructions as needed in a calm voice.

- Combine visual and tactile cues with verbal instructions since, generally, multiple modalities of instruction will be more effective in maintaining attention and in increasing learning.
- Make lists that will help the student organize tasks. Have the student check them off when they are finished. Students should complete study guides when listening to presentations.
- Adapt worksheets so that there is less material on each page.
- Break assignments into small chunks. Provide immediate feedback on each assignment. Allow extra time if needed for the student to finish the assignment.
- Insure that the student has recorded homework assignments each day before leaving school. If necessary, set up a home-school program in which the parents help the child organize and complete the homework.
- If the child has difficulty staying in one place at school, alternate sitting with standing and activities which require moving around during the day.
- Provide activities that require active participation such as talking through problems or acting out the steps.
- Use learning aides such as computers, calculators, tape recorders, and programmed learning materials. They help to structure learning and maintain interest and motivation.
- Provide the student opportunities to demonstrate strengths at school. Set up times in which the student can assist peers. (pp. 4–5)

Reeve (1990) adds these recommendations:

- Help the child get started with individual seat work. Have the child verbalize to you what the task is and how he or she is to approach it. Check back periodically to see if the child is still on track.
- Make frequent contact with the child by touching or speaking the child's name. Be sure that you have his or her attention before speaking. . . .

FIGURE 9-7 Definition of ADHD

The American Psychiatric Association (1994) identifies several characteristics that may indicate attention deficit hyperactivity disorder. These characteristics must appear before age seven, persist for at least six months, be present in more than one environment (e.g., home, school, work), and cause "clinically significant distress or impairment in social, academic, or occupational functioning" (p. 84).

The first set of characteristics relates to inattention and the second to hyperactivity-impulsivity. Three classifications are possible: predominantly inattentive, predominantly hyperactive, or combined. For example, a student who shows six or more of the inattention characteristics but fewer than six of the hyperactivity-impulsivity characteristics would be identified as having ADHD, Predominantly Inattentive Type. The two sets of characteristics follow.

Inattention
Six (or more) of the following symptoms of **inattention** have persisted for at least 6 months to a degree that is maladaptive and inconsistent with developmental level:

Inattention
(a) often fails to give close attention to details or makes careless mistakes in schoolwork, work, or other activities
(b) often has difficulty sustaining attention in tasks or play activities
(c) often does not seem to listen when spoken to directly
(d) often does not follow through on instructions and fails to finish schoolwork, chores, or duties in the workplace (not due to oppositional behavior or failure to understand instructions)
(e) often has difficulties organizing tasks and activities
(f) often avoids, dislikes or is reluctant to engage in tasks that require sustained mental effort (such as schoolwork or homework)
(g) often loses things necessary for tasks or activities (e.g., toys, school assignments, pencils, books, or tools)
(h) is often easily distracted by extraneous stimuli
(i) is often forgetful in daily activities

Hyperactivity-Impulsivity
Six (or more) of the following symptoms of **hyperactivity-impulsivity** have persisted for at least 6 months to a degree that is maladaptive and inconsistent with developmental level:

Hyperactivity
(a) often fidgets with hands or feet or squirms in seat
(b) often leaves seat in classroom or in other situations in which remaining seated is expected
(c) often runs about or climbs excessively in situations in which it is inappropriate (in adolescents or adults, may be limited to subjective feelings of restlessness)
(d) often has difficulty playing or engaging in leisure activities quietly
(e) is often "on the go" or often acts as if "driven by a motor"
(f) often talks excessively

Impulsivity
(g) often blurts out answers before questions have been completed
(h) often has difficulty waiting in turn
(i) often interrupts or intrudes on others (e.g., butts into conversations or games). (pp. 83–84)

Note. Reprinted with permission from the *Diagnostic and Statistical Manual of Mental Disorders,* Fourth Edition. Copyright © 1994 by the American Psychiatric Association.

- Give the child extra time to work on assignments or exams, without criticism or fanfare. . . .
- If note taking is a problem, arrange to have a more attentive classmate share notes by photocopying or using carbon paper; or give the child your notes.
- Use multiple choice or one-to-one oral tests to assess the child's mastery of content.
- Give regular feedback and praise successes. (p. 75)

CH.A.D.D.

http://www.chad.org

This website, sponsored by CH.A.D.D. (Children and Adults with Attention Deficit Disorders), provides a description of the organization, membership information, updates on new legislation and lobbying efforts related to ADHD, and information about the disability, including ADD Facts Sheets. Example topics are The Disability Named ADD, Attention Deficit Disorder in the Classroom, Parenting a Child with Attention Deficit Disorder, Adults with Attention Deficit Disorder, and 50 Tips on the Classroom Management of Attention Deficit Disorders. Articles from past issues of *Attention!* magazine are also online, and visitors can read descriptions of audiotapes and publications in the CH.A.D.D. Store.

Note: Courtesy of CH.A.D.D.

Finally, Bender and Mathes (1995) present these suggestions for organizing the classroom:

- Use a physically structured classroom rather than an "open" classroom. Having walls and a door will block out distractions in the hallway.
- Seat students away from noise. Be cognizant of auditory as well as visual distractions. Seat students away from the door and from auditory distractions.
- Place desks away from each other. Space desks one arm or leg length apart. . . .
- Provide two desks for each student with ADHD. Students with ADHD may stand up and leave their desk without realizing why. Provide a second desk for them to go to when this happens, and acknowledge to the class that the student has a right to change desks when he or she wishes.
- Alternate activities to eliminate desk fatigue. Provide activities that encourage active responding, such as working at the board, "Simon Says," or

standing or sitting to indicate a "yes" or "no" answer. (p. 229)

"Window on the Web" describes the website of CH.A.D.D., an organization for parents and families of individuals with ADHD. This site is a rich source of ideas for classroom adaptations.

In this chapter, you have learned about ways to adapt classroom instruction for students with learning disabilities and those with ADHD. In the next chapter, you will meet another group of students who are often members of general education classes, students with mental retardation. Methods for teaching functional academics and improving general work habits will be presented. But first, check "Things to Remember" to review ways to meet the needs of students with learning disabilities and others with academic learning problems.

Things to Remember

- The most common area in which adaptations must be made for general education students with learning disabilities is academic instruction; these students may require assistance in acquiring basic skills and/or learning content area information.
- Major indicators of learning disabilities are a discrepancy between expected and actual achievement and variation in performance.
- In assessment of learning disabilities, information is gathered about intellectual performance, academic achievement, information processing abilities, and strategies for learning; the general education teacher assists by collecting classroom performance data.
- Two approaches to the instruction of students with learning disabilities are remediation and compensation. The goal of remediation is the improvement of weaknesses; compensatory strategies, on the other hand, bypass or make up for weaknesses by using the strengths of the student.

- Remediation is used to teach younger students the basic skills of reading, handwriting, spelling, written expression, and math.
- In basic skills instruction, three adaptations are recommended: prompts, extra instruction, and additional guided practice.
- With older students, compensatory strategies are used to bypass basic skill deficiencies in order to teach content area subjects.
- In content area instruction, reading assignments, written work and exams, and math demands are modified by changing task criteria and characteristics.
- The most common compensatory strategy is the substitution of oral language tasks for reading and writing tasks.
- Inattention, distractibility, impulsiveness, and hyperactivity are indicators of ADHD.
- Instruction is modified for students with ADHD by increasing the structure of the learning environment and by eliminating distractions that compete with academic tasks for students' attention.

ACTIVITIES

1. Visit a special education resource room that serves students with learning disabilities. Observe the students and talk with the teacher. In what school subjects do students experience the most difficulty? What subjects are taught by the special education teacher? In what instructional activities do these students participate in the general education classroom?

2. Select one of the special education journals that focus on learning disabilities. Choose from the *Journal of Learning Disabilities, Learning Disabilities Quarterly, Learning Disabilities Research & Practice,* and *Learning Disabilities: A Multidisciplinary Journal.* Look through recent issues for articles that present inclusion suggestions. Collect ideas for making instructional adaptations in the general education classroom.

3. Two of the websites described in this chapter's "Window on the Web" sections are parent and family organizations: the Learning Disabilities Association (LDA) and CH.A.D.D. (Children and Adults with Attention Deficit Disorders). Visit these websites, then visit that of The Council for Exceptional Children to learn about its Division for Learning Disabilities (DLD). How does the site of a professional organization (DLD) differ from sites sponsored by parent groups? Which type of site is a better source of ideas for classroom teachers?

4. Pretend that you are a student with learning disabilities enrolled in a college course. You are doing quite well but anticipate that you will have trouble on the final exam. You fear that you won't be able to finish in the allotted 2 hours. How would you explain this to your instructor? What alternatives or instructional modifications could you suggest?

5. If possible, review one of the word processing programs described in "Spotlight on Technology." What are the program's major advantages for students with learning disabilities? Do you see any drawbacks? Would the program be equally effective for elementary and secondary students? If these programs are not available, try using your own word processor to check the spelling of the following sentences written by a sixth grader with learning disabilities.

The student wrote:

once a upon a time ther was some gis and women in the woods. thes man and women are like cavmen.

(The student read:

Once upon a time there was some girls and women in the woods. These men and women are like cavemen.)

Did your spelling checker find all of the errors? Was it able to suggest the correct spelling?

chapter 10

Teaching Students with Mild Retardation and Severe Disabilities

Cases

Judy is a fourth grade student with mild mental retardation. In most areas of academic and social development, 10-year-old Judy performs like a student who is 7 or 8. Her reading and math computation skills are at the second grade level, and her spelling skills are at the first grade level. At home, most of Judy's playmates are younger than she is; she enjoys interacting with first and second graders but doesn't appear interested in the more advanced games and activities of her age-mates. At school, Judy spends most of her day in a regular fourth grade classroom and she has made friends with several of her classmates. In the morning, the special education resource teacher comes to Judy's classroom to teach reading to Judy and four other students. In the afternoon, Judy visits the resource room for instruction in spelling, handwriting, and written expression. Judy receives instruction from Mrs. Thomas, her fourth grade teacher, in math, art, music, and physical education. To help Judy succeed in fourth grade math, Mrs. Thomas modifies assignments and exams and provides Judy with extra practice in computational skills. Also, Judy's math program includes practice in the application of basic skills to daily life problems. For instance, she is learning to add and subtract money and to make change. We will see portions of Judy's special education assessment results and her IEP later in this chapter.

Joe is a high school student with mild retardation who is 15 years old and in the ninth grade. Joe wants to learn a marketable skill in high school so that he can get a job when he graduates. Because his basic academic skills are at approximately the fifth grade level, Joe attends special education classes in Basic English and Basic Math. He is also enrolled in Career Exploration, a special education course that surveys several job options and provides instruction in general vocational skills, such as punctuality, job-related social skills, work completion, and filling out job applications. Joe attends two general education classes—Auto Mechanics I and Physical Education. With the assistance of his general and special education teachers, Joe is earning passing grades in auto mechanics. Ms. Frye, Joe's reading teacher, provides tapes of textbooks so that Joe can keep up with reading assignments. Mr. Nash, the auto mechanics teacher, adapts the written assignments for Joe and allows him to take quizzes and exams orally. In addition, Joe's Career Exploration teacher works closely with Mr. Nash to ensure that Joe acquires the basic work skills important in auto shops. If Joe continues to succeed in his vocational education class, next year he will advance to Auto Mechanics II.

Mental retardation is a comprehensive disability. It affects not only school learning but also the development of language, social, and vocational skills. Students with mental retardation are able to learn, but their learning proceeds more slowly than that of students with average ability. Consequently, students with retardation often perform at a level expected of younger students. At age 6, pupils with mild retardation may act like average 4-year-olds; at age 10, their school achievement may resemble that of second or third graders. Because it is difficult for these students to learn quickly, it is crucial that instruction focus on important areas that will help them become self-supporting adults. For most students with mild retardation, much of this instruction occurs in the general education classroom. With the aid and assistance of general and special educators, students with mild retardation can successfully participate in many classroom activities.

Students with mild retardation have special needs in academic, classroom behavioral, physical, and social performance and may require individualized assistance from special educators in several of these areas. In addition, when students with mild retardation are included in regular classes, the general education teacher must often modify classroom procedures for academic instruction. Younger students, like Judy, may need extra help in basic skills such as reading, math, and spelling; such students may also require help in learning to generalize skills from one situation to another. In middle school and high school, students like Joe often continue their study of basic skills and begin to acquire important career skills; when included in general ed-ucation, they may participate in regular vocational education classes. Throughout the school years, instruction for youngsters with mild retardation focuses on the development of basic academic skills and the application of these and other skills to career preparation.

Window on the Web

Websites About Mental Retardation

http://thearc.org

Founded in 1950, The Arc of the United States (formerly the Association for Retarded Citizens) is the largest national volunteer organization related to mental retardation. The Arc website contains many resources including fact sheets on topics in mental retardation and developmental disabilities, updates on legislation and other current events (see the Government Reports and Capitol Insider features), descriptions of The Arc programs and projects, and the organization's mission and position statements. Visitors can also search the website for specific topics, visit the active Discussion Board, or access links to other sites related to mental retardation.

Note. Courtesy of The Arc.

http://www.aamr.org

The American Association on Mental Retardation (AAMR), founded in 1876, is the nation's oldest organization for professionals and others interested in mental retardation. AAMR's website provides information for its members and others about the organization's policies and positions, journals, publications, and annual meeting. In the Disability Resources portion of the site are links to AAMR affiliates, national organizations, and more than 50 sites with disability-related information.

Note. Web page Courtesy of AAMR.

http://www.acf.dhhs.gov/programs/pcmr/

The President's Committee on Mental Retardation was created in 1961 by President John F. Kennedy. This committee advises the president on issues related to citizens with mental retardation and prepares an Annual Report to the President. At this website, visitors can learn about the mission of the committee, its history, its publications, and projects such as the National Collaboration Academy on Mental Retardation. Publications, such as the most recent Annual Report, can be ordered by e-mail. The site also provides links to national organizations, federal agencies, and state resources.

This chapter describes the characteristics of students with mild mental retardation. It also presents methods for the general education teacher to use in gathering data, teaching functional academic skills, and improving students' general work habits. Most students identified as mentally retarded have mild disabilities. Students are considered severely disabled when their retardation is moderate or severe, rather than mild. Students with severe disabilities are often members of special classes located within neighborhood schools; some are included in regular classrooms. The final section of this chapter addresses this group of learners; suggested are ways to promote the inclusion of students with severe disabilities as members of the school community and to adapt classroom instruction to meet severe learning needs. To become more familiar with the disability of mental retardation, consult one of the resources described in "Window on the Web."

INDICATORS OF MENTAL RETARDATION

The general educator is an important member of the inclusion team for students with mild retardation. These students usually begin their education in the general education classroom and are referred for special education assessment when they are slow to acquire basic academic skills. The classroom teacher plays a role in not only instruction but also identification and referral; in addition, general education services are coordinated with the services of special educators such as the resource teacher.

Students are generally identified as having mild retardation during the first few years of school. There are two main indicators of mild mental retardation. First, although such students are able to learn, their rate of learning is slow. Because of this, their level of development resembles that of younger children. For example, a second grade student may be just beginning to learn to say the alphabet, count, and write his or her name. The second indicator is that most areas of development are delayed. Unlike students with learning disabilities, individuals with mild retardation perform poorly on most tasks when compared to age peers. Their disability is comprehensive; it impinges on performance at school, at home, in the neighborhood, and in the community. These students fail to meet age expectations in intellectual and language development, academic achievement, social competence, and prevocational skills.

Students with mild retardation, although characterized by slower learning rates, are able to profit from many of the instructional activities in the general education classroom. These individuals make up the great majority of all persons with retardation, and, according to the Association for Retarded Citizens (n.d.), "Their retardation is not usually apparent until they enter school. And then, as adults, they often lose their identity as retarded when they enter the job market and daily community life" (p. 5).

Students with mild retardation learn in the same ways that average students do. However, some types of learning cause them particular difficulty. For example, reading comprehension skills appear more difficult for students with mild retardation than reading recognition. Similarly, such students are less successful with math problem solving than math computation (Thomas & Patton, 1990). Evidence also suggests that students with mild retardation have memory and attention problems and difficulty applying learned skills to new situations (Drew, Logan, & Hardman, 1992; Forness & Kavale, 1993).

These and other indicators of mild mental retardation can be noticed by the general education teacher. Students who learn slowly, perform at a level appropriate for younger individuals, and show consistent delays in several areas are prime candidates for referral for special education assessment. Consult "For Your Information" to learn more about students with mild retardation.

ASSESSMENT PROCEDURES

When mental retardation is suspected, the multidisciplinary team meets and prepares an assessment plan. According to McLoughlin and Lewis (1994), it is important to collect information about at least three areas of current performance: academic achievement, intellectual functioning, and adaptive behavior. However, there is some variation in the specific guidelines that states use to determine eligibility for public school services for students with retardation. States differ in the IQ scores used as cutoffs for determining retardation. Also, although impaired adaptive behavior is generally accepted as an important indicator of retardation, not all states include this area

For Your Information

Students with Mild Retardation

- Mental retardation is one of the most common disabilities; in 1995–1996, 12% of the students served in special education programs were identified as mentally retarded (U.S. Department of Education, 1997a).
- There is still concern today about the overrepresentation of students from minority groups in special education programs for individuals with mild retardation (Artiles & Trent, 1994; Chinn & Hughes, 1987; Janesick, 1995). According to the National Coalition of Advocates for Students (1985), "Black students are more than three times as likely to be in a class for the educable [i.e., mildly] mentally retarded as white students, but only half as likely to be in a class for the gifted and talented" (p. 10). In a more recent study, Harry (cited in U.S. Department of Education, 1996) found African American students made up 16% of the U.S. school population but 35% of students identified as mildly retarded.
- The President's Committee on Mental Retardation (1997) estimates that approximately 3% of the population is mentally retarded.
- Individuals with mild retardation account for 85% to 90% of the persons identified as retarded (Arc, 1993).

- For most persons with mild retardation, the cause of the disability is unknown (Hallahan & Kauffman, 1988; Morrison & Polloway, 1995).
- According to Kirk and Gallagher (1979), students with mild retardation are those who are able to profit from academic instruction; the IQ range associated with this group is 50 to 70 or 75, which is equivalent to that of adults with mental ages of 7.5 to 11 years (Becker, Engelmann, & Thomas, 1975).
- During their school years, students with mild retardation acquire basic academic skills up to approximately the sixth grade level; as adults they can achieve the necessary social and vocational skills to become at least minimally self-supporting (President's Committee on Mental Retardation, 1975).
- The most typical special education placement for students with mild retardation is part-time service in a resource room or special class. During the remainder of their school day, they are included with age peers in the general education classroom (Blake, 1981; Heward & Orlansky, 1992).

in their definition of mental retardation (Bruininks, Thurlow, & Gilman, 1987; Patrick & Reschly, 1982). Therefore, teachers must become aware of the specific guidelines in force in their states and school districts.

When individuals are referred for consideration for special education services for students with retardation, academic achievement is measured to determine whether there is an educational performance problem. The *Peabody Individual Achievement Test-Revised (PIAT-R)* (Markwardt, 1989), which was described in chapter 9, can be administered, or the team can select another individual measure, such as the achievement portion of the *Woodcock-Johnson Psycho-Educational Battery-Revised (WJ-R)* (Woodcock & Johnson, 1989).

The *WJ-R*, which is generally administered by the school psychologist or special educator, is appropri-

ate for students from age 2 through adulthood. Its standard battery assesses reading, mathematics, written language, and knowledge (science, social studies, and humanities). Grade and age scores, standard scores, and percentile rank scores are available for each subtest and each academic skill area. The mean (or average) standard score on the *WJ-R* is 100, and scores between 85 and 115 are considered to be within the average range of performance. The assessment results in Figure 10–1 show that Judy, introduced at the beginning of this chapter, is performing below grade-level expectations in all academic subjects assessed by the *WJ-R*.

Another major step in assessment is the determination of the student's general ability level. This is particularly important if mild retardation is suspected because below average intellectual performance is one of the criteria for this disability. The

FIGURE 10-1   **Special Education Assessment Results**

Student: Judy   **Age:** 10 years, 5 months   **Grade:** 4

Academic Performance

Judy was administered the standard achievement battery of the *Woodcock-Johnson Psycho-Educational Battery-Revised* by Mrs. Simeon, the resource teacher. These results were obtained:

Area	Grade Score	Standard Score	Percentile Rank
Broad Reading	1.8	68	2
Broad Mathematics	2.8	73	3
Broad Written Language	1.6	62	1

Judy's skills fall in the low average to below average range of performance in all areas, a result confirmed by her fourth grade teacher, Mrs. Thomas. Judy's grade scores indicate performance at the grade 1 to grade 2 level. In Broad Reading, she earned a percentile rank of 2, which indicates that her performance was equal to or better than that of only 2 percent of her age peers in the test's norm group. In Broad Written Language, she achieved a percentile rank of 1. Her performance was somewhat better in Math, where she earned a percentile rank of 3. These results indicate serious achievement problems in three basic skill areas, with the most severe problems occurring in reading and written language skills.

Intellectual Performance

The *Wechsler Intelligence Scale-Third Edition* was administered to Judy by Mr. Henry, the school psychologist. Judy's intelligence quotient (IQ) scores were as follows:

Verbal IQ	64
Performance IQ	61
Full Scale IQ	59

All IQ scores fall within the below average range. These results point to the possibility of mild mental retardation.

Adaptive Behavior

Mrs. Simeon interviewed Judy's parents to learn more about Judy's performance at home and in community situations. The *Scales of Independent Behavior-Revised* were used for this purpose, with the following results:

Area	Standard Score
Motor Skills	82
Social Interaction and Communication Skills	65
Personal Living Skills	68
Community Living Skills	72

Judy's adaptive behavior, as reported by her parents, fell in the below average range of performance in two areas, Social Interaction and Communication Skills and Personal Living Skills. This finding, along with the results of other measures and the information provided by Judy's classroom teacher, supports the conclusion of mild mental retardation. Intellectual performance is below average, adaptive behavior appears to be impaired, and academic achievement falls within the low average and below average ranges.

Wechsler Intelligence Scale for Children-Third Edition (WISC-III) (Wechsler, 1991), which was described in chapter 9, is usually used to assess global ability in school-aged children. Judy's assessment results in Figure 10–1 include *WISC-III* scores; her Verbal, Performance, and Full Scale IQs fall below 70, which indicates current functioning within the below average range.

Adaptive behavior is a third consideration in assessment when mental retardation is suspected. According to the American Association on Mental Retardation's definition of mental retardation, it is important to document not only below average intellectual performance but also impaired adaptive behavior. Measures such as the *AAMR Adaptive Behavior Scale-School* (2nd ed.) (Lambert, Nihira, & Leland, 1993) and the *Scales of Independent Behavior Revised (SIB-R)* (Bruininks, Woodcock, Weatherman, & Hill, 1996) can be used to gather information about the student's social competence.

On the *AAMR* scale, teachers and others rate the student's performance in areas such as independent functioning, physical development, economic activity, language development, and numbers and time; the scale is appropriate for use with students aged 3 to 21. The *SIB-R*, designed for preschool through adulthood, uses interviews with parents, teachers, or others to gather information about current functioning levels. This measure assesses several different aspects of adaptive behavior: Motor Skills, Social Interaction and Communication Skills, Personal Living Skills, and Community Living Skills. Several types of scores are available, including standard scores and percentile ranks. The case of Judy in Figure 10–1 illustrates a student with low performance in two areas of adaptive behavior.

If a student is found to perform below age expectations in academic achievement, general intellectual ability, and adaptive behavior, the team may decide that the student is eligible for special education services for students with retardation. The next step is to determine the precise educational needs of the student. All members of the team, including the student's parents, have valuable information to contribute; however, the general education teacher is probably the person most knowledgeable about the student's current academic skill levels. Before an educational program for a student with mild retardation can be planned, information is needed about current school performance and the student's ability

to use basic academic skills to solve daily life problems. Also, the prevocational and career skills of the student must be considered. Teachers can develop informal assessments for this purpose, or they can choose from commercially available measures, such as the criterion-referenced tests by Brigance.

BRIGANCE® inventories are available for preschool, elementary, and secondary students: the *Inventory of Early Development-Revised* (Brigance, 1991) for children from birth to developmental age 7, the *Comprehensive Inventory of Basic Skills* (Brigance, 1983) for grades kindergarten through 9, and the *Inventory of Essential Skills* (Brigance, 1981) for assessment of grade 4 through grade 11 achievement. A special feature of the secondary *BRIGANCE*® instrument is its coverage of basic skills not only in isolation but also as applied to daily life and vocational areas. Table 10–1 on page 274 presents a listing of functional skill subtests from which teachers can choose.

The *BRIGANCE*® inventories allow teachers to determine which skills have been mastered by the student and which must still be taught. Each criterion-referenced test includes simple directions for administration and scoring, plus a recommended instructional objective for the skill. For example, on the Warning/Safety Signs subtest the student is asked to read 40 signs, such as *Keep Out* and *High Voltage;* the objective recommended for this skill is

> By (date), when presented with a list of 40 words and phrases frequently seen on warning and safety signs, (student's name) will read (number) correctly.

These objectives, if appropriate for the student, can aid the team in preparation of the IEP.

◆ SPECIAL SERVICES

Individualized education programs for students with mild retardation usually contain several annual goals. Typical areas of instruction are reading, math, oral language, written language, and vocational preparation and other types of transition services. Special education services can be provided by the resource teacher or, for students with severe delays, the teacher of a special class. Others such as the speech-language clinician and the adapted physical education teacher often provide support services for children and adolescents with mild retardation.

TABLE 10-1   Functional Skills Assessed by the *BRIGANCE*® *Diagnostic Inventory of Essential Skills*

Area	Subtests
Functional Word Recognition	Basic Sight Vocabulary
	Direction Words
	Abbreviations
	Warning/Safety Signs
	Reads Number Words
Schedules and Graphs	Reads Class Schedule
	Reads Television Schedule
	Identifies and Interprets Graphs
Forms	School Information Form
	Computer Base Form
Measurement	Equivalent Values of Coins and the Dollar Bill
	Total Values of Collections of Coins and Bills
	Conversion of Coins
	Time
	Equivalent Units of Time
	Conversion of Units of Time
	Equivalent Calendar Units
	Conversion of Calendar Units
	Calendar
	Dates
	Ruler
	Equivalent Units of Measurement
	Conversion of Units of Measurement
	Meters and Gauges
	Concepts of Fahrenheit Temperature
Health and Safety	Medical Vocabulary
	Medical Labels
	Health Evaluation Form
	Health Practices and Attitude Rating Scale
	Self-Concept Rating Scale
	Warning Labels
Vocational	Attitude Rating Scale
	Personality Rating Scale
	Responsibility and Self-Discipline Rating Scale
	Job Interests and Aptitudes
	Health and Physical Problems/Handicaps
	Application for a Social Security Number
	Choosing a Career
	Employment Signs
	Employment Vocabulary
	Employment Abbreviations
	"Help Wanted" Advertisements
	Simple Application for Employment
	Complex Application for Employment
	Job Interview Questions
	Job Interview Preparation Rating Scale
	Job Interview Rating Scale

TABLE 10-1 Continued

Area	Subtests
	W-4 Form
	Future Time on Clock
	Past Time on Clock
	Time Duration on Clock
	Payroll Deductions
	Federal Income Tax Return—Form 1040A
	Unemployment Compensation Form
Money and Finance	Price Signs
	Computes Totals for Amounts of Money
	Making Change
	Comprehends and Computes Purchase Savings
	Computes Expenses Using Charts and Tables
	Banking and Credit Vocabulary
	Manages a Checking Account
	Computes Interest on Loans
	Reads and Comprehends a Credit Agreement
	Application for a Credit Card
	Reads and Comprehends Monthly Credit Statement
Travel and Transportation	Traffic Signs
	Traffic Symbols
	Car Parts Vocabulary
	Identifies Car Parts
	Application for Driver's Instruction Permit
	Auto Safety Rating Scale
	Gas Mileage and Cost
	Mileage Table
	Bus Schedule and Map of Route
	Road Map
Food and Clothing	Food Vocabulary
	Food Preparation Vocabulary
	Basic Recipe Directions
	Food Labels
	Conversion of Recipes to Different Servings
	Foods for a Daily Balanced Diet
	Computes Cost of Purchasing Different Quantities
	Food Quantity at Best Price
	Personal Sizes of Clothing
	Clothing Labels
Oral Communication and Telephone Skills	Speaking Skills
	Speaking Skills Rating Scale
	Listening Skills
	Listening Skills Rating Scale
	Telephone
	Telephone Book
	Telephone Yellow Pages

Note. From the *BRIGANCE® Diagnostic Inventory of Essential Skills.* Copyright 1981 by Curriculum Associates. Reproduced by permission of the publisher.

FIGURE 10-2   IEP Goals and Services for Judy

Annual Goals
1. By the end of the school year, Judy will read grade 2 material with adequate word recognition and comprehension.
   Person responsible: Resource teacher
2. By the end of the school year, Judy will correctly spell a minimum of 100 high-frequency words.
   Person responsible: Resource teacher
3. By the end of the school year, Judy will legibly print all lower- and uppercase manuscript letters.
   Person responsible: Resource teacher
4. By the end of the school year, Judy will write simple sentences and personal information, such as her name, address, and telephone number.
   Person responsible: Resource teacher
5. By the end of the school year, Judy will perform math computation problems at grade 3.5 level.
   Person responsible: Fourth grade teacher
6. By the end of the school year, Judy will achieve minimum competencies in math application skills such as time, money, and measurement.
   Person responsible: Fourth grade teacher
7. Judy will successfully complete minimum requirements for fourth grade art, music, and physical education.
   Person responsible: Fourth grade teacher

Amount of Participation in General Education
Judy will receive instruction in the regular fourth grade class for the entire day except for 1 hour in the afternoon.

Special Education and Related Services
1. The resource teacher will provide special education services to Judy for 1 hour each morning in the fourth grade classroom (goal 1) and for 1 hour each afternoon in the resource room (goals 2, 3, and 4).
2. The resource teacher will provide consultation for Judy's fourth grade teacher as needed.

These special students are included in general education programs to the maximum extent appropriate. Some may participate in only nonacademic classroom activities such as art, music, and physical education; others, like Judy and Joe, are included in academic programming. A portion of Judy's IEP in Figure 10–2 shows that, although Judy visits the resource room for an hour each afternoon, the majority of her instruction takes place in the fourth grade classroom.

CLASSROOM ADAPTATIONS

Classroom instruction is the primary area in which adaptations are made for students with mild retardation in general education programs; this section focuses on methods for meeting the special academic needs of these students. Some individuals with mild retardation also require assistance in the area of classroom conduct; chapter 11 presents

strategies for controlling disruptive behaviors. Chapter 6 contains suggestions for increasing the social acceptance of special students who have difficulty relating to classmates.

Habilitation is the major approach to the education of mainstreamed students with mild retardation. The goal is not to remediate or compensate for skill deficiencies; instead, instruction is directed toward the development of the crucial skills necessary for successful adulthood. Habilitation is the process of becoming capable or qualified; for students with mild retardation, this means the acquisition of skills that are important for daily life, citizenship, and a future career. Because these special students learn more slowly than their age peers, their educational program must concentrate on the most crucial and functional skills.

Transition and **career education** services are one way of conceptualizing the habilitation process for students with mild retardation. According to the

FIGURE 10-3   Important Competencies for Adulthood

Daily Living Skills
Managing family finances
Selecting, managing, and maintaining a home
Caring for personal needs
Raising children—family living
Buying and preparing food
Buying and caring for clothing
Engaging in civic activities
Utilizing recreation and leisure
Getting around the community (mobility)

Personal-Social Skills
Achieving self-awareness
Acquiring self-confidence
Achieving socially responsible behavior
Maintaining good interpersonal skills
Achieving independence
Achieving problem-solving skills
Communicating adequately with others

Occupational Skills
Knowing and exploring occupational possibilities
Selecting and planning occupational choices
Exhibiting appropriate work habits and behaviors
Exhibiting sufficient physical-manual skills
Obtaining a specific occupational skill
Seeking, securing, and maintaining employment

Note. Reprinted with permission of Merrill, an imprint of Macmillan Publishing Company, from *Career Education for Handicapped Individuals* (2nd ed., pp. 46–47) by C. J. Kokaska and D. E. Brolin, Copyright © 1985 Merrill Publishing Company, Columbus, Ohio.

Council for Exceptional Children (1993a), career education and transition are "the totality of experiences through which one learns to live a meaningful, satisfying work life." Brolin (1986) expands this definition:

Career education is not simply preparation for a job. It is also preparation for other productive work roles that comprise one's total career functioning. This includes the work of a homemaker and family member, the participation as a citizen and volunteer, and the engagement in productive leisure and recreational pursuits that are of benefit to oneself and others. (p. vii)

Kokaska and Brolin (1985) identify three major curriculum areas important in preparing for adulthood: daily living skills, personal-social skills, and occupational skills; specific competency areas are listed in Figure 10–3. In the system described by Cronin and Patton (1993), life skills are organized into six major domains: employment-education, home and family, leisure pursuits, personal responsibility and relationships, emotional-physical health, and community involvement.

One important factor to consider in a transition and career education program is the sequence in which competencies are presented. Kokaska (1980) recommends the following progression for special students:

- career awareness (Kindergarten onward)
- career exploration (Grade 6 onward)
- career preparation (Grade 6–7 onward)
- career placement, follow-up, and continuing education (Grade 10 onward). (p. 38)

In the last two stages, career preparation and career placement, students may have the opportunity to participate in supervised job placements on the school campus and in the community. Community-based training is an important component of career preparation for students with mild retardation because it promotes the generalization of work skills to actual work environments.

Transition and career education training can be infused into the general education classroom curriculum in several ways. First, by providing academic skill instruction, the general education teacher emphasizes one important component of career preparation: literacy, which is essential for most work and many life tasks. Second, the classroom teacher can help students by providing instruction and practice in the application of basic school and work skills to life problems. Such assistance is particularly important for students with mild retardation, who often have difficulty generalizing skills and information from one situation to another. Third, a portion of the general education curriculum can be devoted to career awareness and exploration. At the secondary level, much of the curriculum is already career oriented; students learn specific job skills in vocational classes, and in college preparatory courses students acquire skills and information necessary for further training.

The following sections present methods for teaching students with mild retardation in the general education classroom. Included are ways to teach functional academic skills and techniques for improving students' general work habits.

TEACHING FUNCTIONAL ACADEMICS

Students with mild retardation need special help to acquire the basic skills of reading, handwriting, spelling, written expression, and math. Typically, they receive instruction in these areas from the special education teacher; many students also participate in instructional activities in the general education classroom. In teaching basic skills to persons with mild retardation, the classroom teacher will find the techniques recommended for students with learning disabilities useful. As described in chapter 9, academic instruction is adapted to special needs by providing prompts, giving additional instruction, and allowing extra guided practice. Several strate-

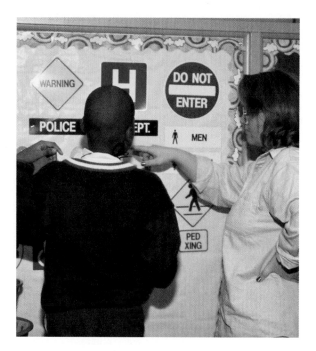

gies for adapting basic skills instruction were suggested in chapter 9. For students who learn slowly and require much repetition and practice, computers can be a useful tool for learning academic skills. See "Spotlight on Technology" for information about using talking software to teach reading skills.

The need to provide instruction and practice in skill generalization is a major consideration in teaching students with mild retardation. These students have difficulty applying skills and information learned in one situation to a new but similar problem or situation. For example, a student might add and subtract whole numbers easily when given a worksheet of computation problems but be unable to apply this skill to adding and subtracting coins. For this reason, educational programs for students with retardation focus on **functional skills,** that is, skills required for the satisfactory performance of everyday life tasks. Basic skills instruction must go beyond textbooks and workbook pages; it must extend into the real world if special students are to use tool subjects to solve the problems of everyday life.

There are two major strategies for teaching functional academic skills. In one, the **unit approach,** instruction in several basic skill areas is integrated around a central theme of interest and value to the students; this approach is probably best used with younger students. In the other approach, reading, writing, and math are taught as separate subjects,

Spotlight on Technology

Talking Reading Software

Computers can be used to teach basic reading skills to children just beginning to learn to read and to older students with difficulties in reading. For this to occur, however, it is necessary to use software that talks. The speech that talking programs produce can be either digitized or synthesized. Digitized speech is re-corded speech; it sounds like human speech because it is. Synthesized speech is not as natural sounding; in some programs, it sounds somewhat robotic. Synthesized speech is used for talking word processing programs because it has the ability to pronounce any combination of letters that the writer enters. Digitized speech is preferred for reading software. The programs described here all use digitized speech.

Note. Kid Phonics, courtesy of Davidson & Associates, Inc. © 1996 and 1997 Davidson & Associates, Inc. All rights reserved.

Talking Phonics Software

Talking reading programs teach many skills, including phonics. One popular example is *Kid Phonics* from Davidson & Associates (www.davd.com). At the menu, students can click on any of the Sound Buster characters to hear a song. Each song presents a basic concept such as rhyme, rhythm, or the relationship between letters and sounds. Clicking on "hot spots" in the picture produces actions. For example, clicking on the boat causes it to animate with sound effects and the word *boat* to be pronounced.

continued

but functional practice activities are designed to promote generalization of skills to life problems.

The Unit Approach

Instructional units allow the teacher to present functional academics in a meaningful context. First, an important life theme is selected; then, basic skills are presented, and practice opportunities related to the theme are provided. Meyen (1981) provides two examples. The first unit, "Time," is intended for intermediate grade students. Basic skills instruction and practice are included within subtopics such as recreation, seasons, measurement, money, and holidays. The second unit, "Home Safety and Maintenance," is also for intermediate grade students. It features subtopics such as basic first aid, emergencies, and drugs and poisonous substances.

Many unit themes would be appropriate for special students and other members of general education classrooms. For example, "Becoming a Consumer" is a topic that could be adapted to varying skill, age, and interest levels. For younger students, this unit could be used to teach basic money skills, such as identifying coins and bills, adding and subtracting amounts of money, and making change. For older (or more capable) students, appropriate consumer skills are reading advertisements, comparison shopping, and installment buying. Other flexible unit themes are transportation (e.g., riding the school bus, using public transportation, driving a car), getting a job (e.g., chores at home, the want ads, job applications and interviews), and money management (e.g., budgeting your allowance, using the bank, handling paychecks and taxes).

In the Sound Buster Game in *Kid Phonics,* students complete a series of activities: discriminating and matching sounds, blending sounds together to make a word, and putting words together to make a sentence. In the screen shown at left, students hear the *a* sound in *ate,* then must listen to the sound spoken by each character and find the one that matches. A correct response causes part of the hidden picture (beneath the umbrellas) to be revealed. The picture shows several things (e.g., jungle animals), and the student selects one to take to the Word Builder.

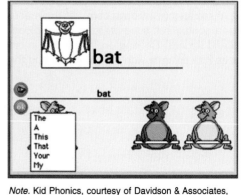

The Word Builder shows the picture the student has chosen (here a bat) and the first letter in the word *bat.* The student finds the correct ending for the word, then builds a sentence. In the screen shown here, the student can decide to start the sentence with *The, A, This, That, Your,* or *My.* The student can hear each of these words and the completed sentence read aloud. The student can color the picture and then print it, the word, and the sentence on a dictionary page.

Functional Practice Activities

The classroom teacher can design practice activities in any basic skill area so that they relate to daily life problems. One source of ideas for functional activities is a transition and career education curriculum, such as the one outlined in Figure 10–3. The key factor to be kept in mind when developing practice tasks is their relevance to life and work activities. Of course, the teacher must also consider the students' skill levels and the amount of supervision required during student practice.

Reading is an excellent skill to practice with everyday materials. Activities can focus on reading for information or reading as a leisure pastime. Some examples of reading materials appropriate for functional activities are listed here:

- Signs commonly found in buildings and in the community (e.g., *Women, Men, Stop, Do Not Enter*)
- Adult and student newspapers and magazines
- Menus for fast-food and regular restaurants
- Schedules for classes, television, movies, buses, and trains

Talking Storybook Programs

Talking storybook software may help to develop both word recognition and reading comprehension skills. These programs present a children's story on CD-ROM with rich, colorful illustrations and text that is read aloud. In most programs, students can interact with both text and graphics to make the story come alive.

One of the most popular sets of talking storybooks is Living Books (www.broderbund.com). The series contains several programs including stories by Mercer Mayer, Dr. Seuss, the Berenstains, and Marc Brown. *Arthur's Reading Race* by Marc Brown is shown here. As the story begins, the text on the page is read aloud and the teacher asks for a volunteer to read the big book. When Arthur is chosen, he reads the word and jumps up and down to show what the word means.

Note. Copyright 1996 Living Books and Marc Brown.

The student can hear the sentence (or individual words in the sentence) read aloud as many times as desired. Also, clicking on "hot spots" within the illustration causes actions. For example, when students click on the piano, the piano plays and the teacher sings a song about reading. When a letter of the alphabet is selected, its name is read aloud by several children. When the poster "Why are books delicious things?" is selected, the dinosaur on the poster reads the text aloud and another dinosaur sticks its head in the window and answers the question.

Arthur's Reading Race contains three literacy activities that supplement the story. For example, on some storybook pages, students can play "I Spy" and attempt to find specific objects within the illustration. There are three levels in this activity. In the easiest, the program reads the name of the object the student must find. In more difficult levels, the program reads only a clue or instructions. Reading Race (shown on page 282) is an on-screen board game for one or two players. The object is to read words and move around the board to reach the ice cream store first. In this screen, it's Arthur's turn. The players have chosen the easy level so Arthur must listen to the program read the word card aloud, then click on the picture of the sun.

continued

- The phone book
- Advertisements for consumer goods and jobs
- Directions for building models, assembling toys, or completing forms
- Labels on foods, medicines, and clothing

Figure 10–4 on page 283 lists important career and vocational words suggested by Schilit and Caldwell (1980); practice of words such as these is appropriate for secondary students.

Many daily life activities can be used to practice handwriting, spelling, and written expression. The tasks that follow emphasize writing as a means of communication:

- Making a shopping or a things-to-do list
- Leaving a note for a friend or family member
- Writing a postcard, invitation, or friendly letter
- Completing a job application
- Ordering something by mail by filling in an order blank
- Writing a business letter
- Applying for a social security number or a driver's permit

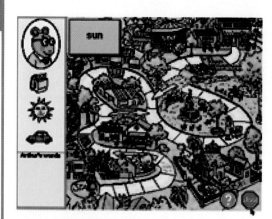

Note. Copyright 1996 Living Books and Marc Brown.

When he answers correctly, *sun* will appear in the list of Arthur's words.

There is much variation among the talking storybook programs available today. Some provide several opportunities to interact with the text in a story but few with the illustrations; examples are the stories in the *Reader Rabbit's Reading Development Library* series (www.learningco.com). Some programs are full of fun activities, although these activities do not relate directly to reading; examples are *101 Dalmatians, Toy Story,* and *Hercules* from the Disney's Animated Storybooks series (www.disneyinteractive.com). For more information about this type of software, visit the website of Project LITT (Literacy Instruction Through Technology). This site contains Software Profiles for more than 200 talking storybook programs.

Note. Courtesy of Project LITT, San Diego State University.

http://edweb.sdsu.edu/SPED/ProjectLitt/LITT

• Writing down a telephone message for someone

The skill area of math also offers numerous opportunities for functional practice. Computation ability is often required in everyday life, particularly in tasks involving time, money, and measurement. Examples are

• making a purchase
• budgeting an allowance or paycheck
• comparison shopping
• using a checking or savings account
• using a credit card
• applying for a loan
• selecting and preparing food
• using measurement, as in reading a thermometer, determining a person's weight and height, and measuring the length and width of a room

• using time, as in telling time, using a calendar, and computing time (e.g., "If it takes 20 minutes to walk to school, at what time must you leave home to arrive at school at 8:00 a.m.?")

Functional tasks often require more than one basic skill. For instance, in planning and cooking a meal, several skills are needed: reading (ads, labels, cooking and preparation directions), writing (shopping list), and math (buying foods, measuring ingredients, computing cooking times). When tasks such as these are used with special students, the teacher should be sure that the students are proficient in all necessary skills; that is, a math practice activity should be designed so that low reading skills are not an obstacle.

When students with mild retardation are included in general education for basic skills instruction, the

FIGURE 10-4 **Important Career and Vocational Words**

1. rules	26. supervisor	51. entrance	76. withholding
2. boss	27. vacation	52. responsibility	77. vote
3. emergency	28. apply	53. hospital	78. break
4. danger	29. fulltime	54. hourly rate	79. cooperation
5. job	30. income	55. schedule	80. dependable
6. social security	31. quit	56. instructions	81. money
7. first-aid	32. check	57. save	82. physical
8. help-wanted	33. careful	58. union	83. hazardous
9. safety	34. dangerous	59. credit	84. net income
10. warning	35. employee	60. elevator	85. strike
11. signature	36. layoff	61. punctuality	86. owner
12. time	37. take-home-pay	62. rights	87. repair
13. attendance	38. unemployed	63. hours	88. alarm
14. absent	39. cost	64. payroll	89. gross income
15. telephone	40. deduction	65. attitude	90. manager
16. bill	41. fired	66. reliable	91. reference
17. hired	42. closed	67. work	92. uniform
18. overtime	43. parttime	68. caution	93. hard-hat
19. punch in	44. correct	69. license	94. authority
20. directions	45. foreman	70. poison	95. training
21. paycheck	46. time-and-a-half	71. office	96. holiday
22. wages	47. worker	72. power	97. late
23. appointment	48. buy	73. qualifications	98. personal
24. income tax	49. raise	74. earn	99. tools
25. interview	50. on-the-job	75. transportation	100. areas

Note. From "A Word List of Essential Career/Vocational Words for Mentally Retarded Students" by J. Schilit and M. L. Caldwell, 1980, *Education and Training of the Mentally Retarded, 15*, p. 115. Copyright 1980 by The Council for Exceptional Children. Reprinted by permission.

assignment of grades is often difficult. Students can be working hard and making progress, but their performance may remain at a lower level than that expected for their grade placement. Alternatives for grading students with special needs are suggested in "Inclusion Tips for the Teacher" on page 284.

IMPROVING GENERAL WORK HABITS

Work habits can be viewed as the behaviors a person exhibits when presented with a task to perform. Many work behaviors apply to all types of tasks. For example, no matter what type of work is involved, it is necessary to begin work promptly, stay on task, and complete the task. Important not only on the job but also in school and daily life, work habits are a necessary part of the curriculum for children and youth with mild retardation. Kokaska and Brolin (1985) identify these important work behaviors:

- following directions
- working with others
- working at a satisfactory rate
- accepting supervision
- recognizing the importance of attendance and punctuality
- meeting demands for quality work
- demonstrating occupational safety skills (pp. 157–160)

Several of these skills are just as important for classroom success as they are for vocational endeavors.

General education teachers can help students develop and improve their general work habits in three ways. First, the acquisition of work habits must be accepted as a valuable educational goal. Second, students must receive instruction and practice in specific work behaviors. Third, good work performance must be reinforced. The following paragraphs suggest ways to promote three general work habits.

Inclusion Tips for the Teacher

Differential Grading

Report cards are a major way for teachers to inform parents of their children's progress in school. However, with students with special needs, grading performance in general education classes is often difficult. How should the teacher grade Judy, who is included in the fourth grade class but is successfully completing math assignments at the third grade level? Here are some alternatives:

1. State the student's current grade level in the academic subject, and grade the student's performance at that grade level.

    Judy, Grade 4
    Math grade level <u>3</u>
    Math performance at Grade 3 level <u>B</u>

2. State the student's current grade level in the academic subject, and grade the student's work behaviors rather than skill performance.

    Judy, Grade 4
    Math grade level <u>3</u>
    Works independently <u>B</u>
    Completes assignments <u>B+</u>
    Neatness <u>B</u>

3. State the student's IEP goals and objectives in the academic subject, and indicate which have been met and which still require work.

Judy, Grade 4
Goal: By the end of the school year, Judy will perform math computation problems at the 3.5 grade level. <u>in progress</u>
Objectives:

a. Judy will add and subtract two-digit numbers with regrouping with 90% accuracy. <u>achieved</u>
b. Judy will write multiplication facts with 90% accuracy. <u>achieved</u>
c. Judy will multiply two-digit numbers with regrouping with 90% accuracy. <u>in progress</u>
d. Judy will write division facts with 90% accuracy. <u>in progress</u>

Other options include replacing traditional letter grades with simplified grading systems such as pass/fail or satisfactory/needs improvement (McLoughlin & Lewis, 1994). Teachers also can assign multiple grades in a subject area; for example, the student might earn one grade for reading achievement and another for effort in reading activities (Banbury, 1987).

Attendance and Punctuality

These work habits are key ingredients in successful school and job performance. Students with poor attendance and those who are frequently tardy may fall behind their classmates in important school skills. Adults whose work records show frequent absences and late arrivals may find themselves unemployed. Attendance and punctuality are typically expected by teachers but are not addressed directly in instruction. For many special students, these work habits must become part of the curriculum so that students are taught the behaviors, provided with practice opportunities, and rewarded for successful performance. To teach these work habits, the teacher first communicates to students that attendance and punctuality are important. One way

to do this is to incorporate these behaviors into the class rules. For example, the rule for punctuality might be "When the bell rings, be in your seat." It is also necessary to explain why attendance and punctuality are important for students (and for employees). To do this, the teacher might lead the class in a discussion of the disadvantages of being tardy for school (or work).

When students are aware of the teacher's expectations, then appropriate work behaviors can be rewarded. There are several ways to reinforce students for attending class and arriving on time:

• Keep a record of attendance and punctuality. At the end of each week, allow students with good records to participate in a special free-time activity.

- Have students keep a log of their own attendance and punctuality. This can be done in the form of a journal or graph or even with a time clock.
- Present a certificate or award to students with good attendance. Begin gradually by rewarding students who come to school each day for 1 week.
- Encourage punctuality by scheduling a favorite activity at the beginning of the class period.
- Use individual contracts for students who are chronically absent or habitually late. Negotiate the terms of the contract so that acceptable performance is followed by a privilege, activity, or reward that the student values.

Work Completion

A second important work behavior critical for school and job success is task completion. Students and employees are expected to complete their work assignments. In school, the teacher must be sure that learning tasks are appropriate for the skill levels of the student. Kolstoe (1976) offers the following suggestions for teachers of students with retardation:

- The tasks should be uncomplicated. . . .
- The tasks should be brief. . . .
- The tasks should be sequentially presented. . . .
- Each learning task should be the kind in which success is possible. . . .
- Learning tasks should be applied to objects, problems, and situations in the learner's life environment. (p. 27)

When tasks are at an appropriate level for the learner, the teacher can concentrate on building work completion skills. Students should first be told that they are expected to finish their work. Then, task completion should be reinforced by the teacher. Ways to encourage and reward work completion are identified here:

- Make free-time activities contingent on work completion. For example, tell students, "If you finish your work, then you may listen to a tape or read a magazine."
- Have students record the number of tasks they complete each day. They can then graph the data and see how they progress from day to day.
- For students who are overwhelmed by lengthy assignments, break the work into several short

tasks. Reward these students after the completion of each short task.
- Begin gradually with students who rarely complete tasks. First, expect and reward one task per day, then two tasks, and so on.

Working with Others

In many situations at school and on the job, people must work closely with one another. This interaction necessitates communication, cooperation, and civility. Job-related social skills are particularly important for youngsters with mild retardation because, as Kokaska and Brolin (1985) note, one of the most common reasons for job failure is the inability to get along with coworkers and supervisors.

Practice in working with others can begin at any age. In most general education classrooms, students have many opportunities to work with peers. Besides the most typical examples of group instruction and class discussions, the teacher can design special projects to be completed by teams of students: for example, preparing group science reports, writing a class newspaper, putting up a bulletin board, or planning a class field trip.

When students work in groups, the teacher must often provide instruction and guidance in important interpersonal skills. Students need to learn to share work materials, work quietly with others, be polite to coworkers, and complete tasks by working cooperatively. These skills can be practiced in any classroom and, once acquired, are among the most valuable of all general work habits for student and adult workers alike.

By helping students with special needs learn functional academic skills and work habits, the teacher is providing them with important tools that they will use for the rest of their lives. Consider the story of Bill Yore, as told by Kokaska and Brolin (1985). Bill, a young man who was in special education programs all his life, graduated from high school at age 19 and was selected by his classmates as one of the commencement speakers. In his speech, Bill said:

> It isn't easy competing with other kids, even when you are normal much less handicapped. But, the love and the patience were there for 19 long years. And, tonight I am proud to stand here and say that I am that boy—almost condemned to an institution. True, I am not an A student. But neither am I a dropout. I may never go

to college but I won't be on the welfare rolls either. I may never be a great man in this world, but I will be a man in whatever way I am able to do it. (p. 386)

STRATEGIES FOR WORKING WITH STUDENTS WITH SEVERE DISABILITIES

The educational needs of students with severe disabilities are more complex than those of students with mild retardation. There is a greater degree of retardation, and poor intellectual performance may be accompanied by physical impairments, sensory impairments, or even emotional disturbance. According to Pumpian (1988), "individuals are typically identified as severely [disabled] . . . when the severity and/or multiplicity of their [disabilities] . . . pose major challenges to them, their families, and society in general in nearly all aspects of growth, development, and functioning" (p. 181).

Until quite recently, such students were educated almost exclusively in special schools and residential facilities; prior to the passage of PL 94-142, many were denied the opportunity to participate in public education in any form. However, within the past decade, advances in research and changes in educational philosophy have led to increased participation of students with severe disabilities in public school life. In the 1994–1995 school year, for example, approximately 93% of the students identified as mentally retarded in the United States attended regular schools in which special education services were delivered in a general education classroom, resource room, or special class (U.S. Department of Education, 1997a). Although many of these students were mildly retarded, a significant number were those identified as having severe disabilities.

Although many students with severe disabilities now attend regular schools, physical proximity is not sufficient to guarantee their successful integration into the school community. Falvey, Grenot-Scheyer, and Bishop (1989) identify several other factors that must be considered. In an optimal program, students with severe disabilities would attend neighborhood schools with same-age peers; however, no school would enroll a disproportionate number of students with severe (or other) disabilities. Special educators and support staff would be available to provide students with an appropriate instructional program. And the school would be both physically and socially accessible to students with severe disabilities.

Social accessibility refers to the availability of opportunities for interaction between students with and without disabilities. When students with severe disabilities are members of a special class within a regular school, they should have the same access to school functions and activities as others within the school community. For example, they should arrive at and depart from school at the same times and places as other students, they should attend school assemblies and social events, they should eat lunch at one of the regular lunchtimes, and their recess or physical education activities should be scheduled similarly to those of other classes.

Research supports the benefits of integration, not only for students with severe disabilities but also for their peers without disabilities. Positive interactions occur between these groups of students, and typical students begin to develop more positive attitudes toward individuals with disabilities (Brinker, 1985). Parents of students with severe disabilities also report satisfaction (McDonnell, 1987). Few reported that their children were mistreated or isolated; most said that their children had made or will make friends at school with peers without disabilities.

In addition to providing opportunities for interaction, it is also possible to set up structured programs that facilitate the building of relationships between students with and without disabilities. One approach is a peer tutoring program in which general education students are trained as tutors for students with severe disabilities (e.g., Kohl, Moses, & Stettner-Eaton, 1983). Special class students benefit from positive peer models and the additional instructional resources, while typical peers develop an understanding of and appreciation for individual differences. Tutors may also gain social status among their general education classmates (Sasso & Rude, 1988). A more innovative approach is the "Special Friends" program of Voeltz (1980, 1982). In this program, the relationship between peers with and without disabilities is social rather than pedagogical; the outcome is the building of new friendships and a positive change in the attitudes of general education students.

Full Inclusion

In the past several years, advocates for students with severe disabilities have taken the position that all students should be members of general education classrooms (Stainback & Stainback, 1988, 1990b, 1992; Stainback, Stainback, & Forest, 1989; Thousand & Villa, 1990). Called *full inclusion,* this movement encourages full-time general education placement for students with severe disabilities and others with identified special education needs. The general education teacher becomes responsible for the education of all students, although special educators and other staff are available to support students and teachers as needed. When a student with severe disabilities is fully included, general and special educators collaborate to ensure that the following occur:

(a) The student's natural participation as a regular member of the class
(b) The systematic instruction of the student's IEP objectives
(c) The adaptation of the core curriculum and/or materials to facilitate student participation and learning (Neary, Halvorsen, & Smithey, 1991, p. 1)

One of the major goals of full inclusion is the development of friendships between students with and without disabilities. Opportunities for social interactions increase when students with severe disabilities are full-time members of general education classrooms. Also, students without disabilities can be directly involved in the full inclusion effort. For example, Forest and Lusthaus (1989) recommend

two strategies, circles of friends and MAPS. A circle of friends is a network of students who volunteer to offer friendship to a student with disabilities; see "Inclusion Tips for the Teacher" on page 288 to see how a circle works.

MAPS stands for Making Action Plans (York, Doyle, & Kronberg, 1992); it was originally called the McGill Action Planning System (Lusthaus & Forest, 1987; Vandercook, York, & Forest, 1989). It is a team approach to planning the inclusion process. Members of the team include the student him- or herself, parents (and perhaps other family members), professionals, and the student's circle of friends. In the MAPS process, the team addresses seven major questions:

1. What is the individual's history?
2. What is your dream for the individual?
3. What is your nightmare?
4. Who is the individual?
5. What are the individual's strengths, gifts, and abilities?
6. What are the individual's needs?
7. What would the individual's ideal day at school look like and what must be done to make it happen? (Vandercook et al., 1989, pp. 207–208)

When students with severe disabilities are included in general education classrooms, it is often necessary to adapt instructional procedures. One concern is the curriculum, and Giangreco, Cloninger, and Iverson (1990) present four alternatives. First, the student with severe disabilities can participate in the same learning activities with the same goals as other students in the class. Second, in a multilevel curriculum, the student can work in the same curriculum area as classmates but at a different level. For example, while peers work on algebraic problems, a student with severe disabilities might practice addition and subtraction skills (York et al., 1992). Or, while classmates read a book and write a book report, a student with severe disabilities might listen to a story on tape, tape-record reactions to the story, and draw a picture illustrating the story (Wehman, 1997).

Third, in curriculum overlapping, all students participate in the same learning activities but pursue goals in different subject areas. Giangreco and colleagues (1990) provide this example:

Suppose students are in science lab learning about properties of electricity. A student with special needs may be involved in these activities for the primary

Inclusion Tips for the Teacher

Circles of Friends

Forest and Lusthaus (1989) provide this example to describe the establishment of a circle of friends for May, a student with disabilities who is going to join a seventh grade general education class.

In September, a few days before May Russell would be attending her new seventh grade classroom, an integration consultant visited the class to speak with the students. She asked them the following series of questions. The students' actual responses are included here, too.

Consultant (C)—"Hi, I've come to talk to you about May who is coming to your class next week. You met her last week when she visited with her mother. For years May has gone to a segregated school or been in a self-contained life skills class. What does that mean?"

Students (S)—"Places for retarded people"
"Schools for kids who are really bad"
"Like the one near my house where all the wheelchairs go"

C—"Well, May is coming here and I'll tell you a secret. Everyone is really scared. Her mother and father are scared. Mr. Gorman [teacher] is scared. Mr. Cullen [principal] is scared. I'm scared. Why do you think all of us are so scared?"

S—"You all think we'll be mean to her."
"You think we'll tease her and be mean to her."
"You think she'll be left out."

C—"There are some things we don't want you to do when she arrives. What do you think these are?"

S—"Don't treat her like a baby."
"Don't pity her."
"Don't ignore her."
"Don't feel sorry for her."

C—"Why are we doing this? Why is May coming to this class?"

S—"Why not? She's our age, she should be here."
"How would you feel if you were 12 and never were with kids your own age?"
"It's dumb for her not to be here."

"She needs friends."
"She needs a boy friend."

C—"What do you think we want you to do?"

S—"Treat her like one of us."
"Make her feel welcome."
"Help her make friends."
"Help her with her work."
"Call her and invite her to our parties."

C—"I want to switch gears for a few minutes and ask you to all do an exercise with me called 'circle of friends.' I do this very same thing with teachers and parents and I think you are all grown up enough to handle it."

(The consultant handed out a sheet with four concentric circles on it. After the first circle, each circle was a little larger and farther away from the center of the page where a stick person was drawn.)

C—"There are four circles. On each circle you are to list people you know. I want you to think about whom you would put in your first circle. These are the people closest to you, people you really love. You can do this privately or in pairs, and you can tell us or keep it private."

(The consultant filled in her own circles on the chalkboard while the students did theirs at their seats. When finished, the facilitator shared her circles and then asked for volunteers to share theirs.)

S—"OK. In my first circle I put in my mom, my dad, Matt who is my best friend, and Stacey—that's my Mom's best friend and she often helps me when I have a problem."

C—"Why did you put those people in your first circle?"

S—"They are people I feel close to. I love them."

C—"What do you do with the people in circle one?"

S—"I share my secrets, I can be myself, I go to them when I'm hurt, I trust them, I love them."

C—"Now let's do circle two—these are people you really like but not enough to put in circle one."

S—"I put in my dog and my two best friends Tim and Todd, and my teacher Mr. Gorman. I put them in because I can do everything with them and we have fun together and we visit a lot."

C—"The third circle is groups of people you like or people you do things with, like Scouts, swimming, hockey, etc."

S—"I have lots—I'm in Boy Scouts, my church, my Sunday school, this class, my street hockey group, and my family is like a group."

C—"The last circle is for people you pay to be in your lives, like your doctor, dentist, and so on."

S—"I put in my doctor and my eye glass doctor, that's all."

C—"Now I want you to think about a person's circle. Here's a fantasy person named Sebastian. He's your age (12) and his circle looks like this. He only has his Mom in circle one and the rest of his circles are empty except for circle four, which is filled with doctors, social workers, therapists, etc. Think hard for a few minutes because this is real serious. How would you feel if your life looked like Sebastian's?" (This is a list of responses from the seventh grade students in the brainstorming session.)

S—"Lonely, depressed, unwanted, terrible, disgusted, like what's the use of living, I'd want to commit suicide, like dying, awful, crazy, hurt, nobody cares, angry, furious, mad."

C—"How do you think you'd act?"

S—(Again, a list of responses from the brainstorming.) "I'd hide and keep my head down all day, I'd hit people, I'd cry all day, I'd hate everyone, I'd kill myself, I'd want to kill others, I'd steal, I'd curse and spit, I'd fight."

C—"OK, I want to wind this up for today and I'll be back in a few weeks to see what's happening. Remember, I came and we started talking about May who will be in your class soon. Well, right now her life looks a bit like Sebastian's imaginary circle. So why did I do all this?"

S—"To help us understand about all the new kids who are coming into our classes—about how they must feel."

C—"What I'd like is for a group of you to act as a welcome committee and another group to act as a telephone crew. I want a phone caller for each day of the week. Do you think that's a good idea?"

S—"Wow, yeah—what a neat idea!"

C—"Remember, friends don't develop overnight. This is just the start. Not all of you will be May's friends—though all of you can be 'friendly.' My dream and hope is that out of this great class May will have at least six friends who will do things with her in school and most of all after school and on weekends. This won't happen fast, but I bet it will happen. Who wants to help?"

Note. From "Promoting Educational Equity for All Students" by M. Forest and E. Lusthaus in *Educating All Students in the Mainstream of Regular Education* (pp. 47–49) by S. Stainback, W. Stainback, and M. Forest (Eds.), 1989. Copyright 1989 by Paul H. Brookes, P.O. Box 10624, Baltimore, MD 21285-0624. Reprinted with permission from Dr. Marsha Forest, Inclusion Press, 416-658-5363 or fax 416-658-5067, Web page http://inclusion.com.

purpose of pursuing objectives from other curriculum areas (e.g., communication, socialization) such as following directions, accepting assistance from others, or engaging in a school job with a nonhandicapped peer. (as cited in Thousand & Villa, 1990, p. 15)

The fourth option is an alternative curriculum. This is recommended for use only when it is impossible to address a student's educational goals within the general education classroom setting.

Vandercook and York (1990) have developed the Regular Classroom Integration Checklist to help teachers assess progress toward full inclusion of students with severe disabilities. As can be seen in Figure 10–5, that checklist is divided into four sections. The first, "Go with the Flow," is used to determine whether all students follow the same classroom routines. "Acting Cool" is concerned with participation in class activities, "Talking Straight" with communication, and "Looking Good" with

FIGURE 10-5 **Inclusion Checklist**

Directions: Record a "y" for yes and an "n" for no on the blank preceding each item. If the answer to any of the items is "no" your team may wish to consider whether any changes should be made and what those changes might be.

Go with the Flow:

_____ Does the student enter the classroom at the same time as classmates? _____
_____

_____ Is the student positioned so that she or he can see and participate in what is going on? _____
_____

_____ Is the student positioned so that classmates and teachers may easily interact with him or her (e.g., without teacher between the student and his or her classmates, not isolated from classmates)? _____
_____

_____ Does the student engage in classroom activities at the same time as classmates? _____
_____

_____ Does the student make transitions in the classroom at the same time as classmates? _____
_____

_____ Is the student involved in the same activities as his or her classmates? _____
_____

_____ Does the student exit the classroom at the same time as classmates? _____
_____

Acting Cool:

_____ Is the student actively involved in class activities (e.g., asks or responds to questions, plays a role in group activities)? _____
_____

_____ Is the student encouraged to follow the same classroom and social rules as classmates (e.g., hugs others only when appropriate, stays in seat during instruction)? _____
_____

_____ Is the student given assistance only as necessary (assistance should be faded as soon as possible)?
_____

_____ Is assistance provided for the student by classmates (e.g., transitions to other classrooms, within the classroom)? _____
_____

_____ Are classmates encouraged to provide assistance to the student? _____
_____

_____ Are classmates encouraged to ask for assistance from the student? _____
_____

_____ Is assistance provided for the student by classroom teachers? _____
_____

_____ Does the student use the same or similar materials during classroom activities as his or her classmates (e.g., Tom Cruise notebooks, school mascot folders)? _____
_____

Talking Straight:

_____ Does the student have a way to communicate with classmates? _____
_____

_____ Do classmates know how to communicate with the student? _____
_____

FIGURE 10-5   Continued

_____ Does the student greet others in a manner similar to that of his or her classmates? _____

_____ Does the student socialize with classmates? _____

_____ Is this facilitated? _____

_____ Does the student interact with teachers? _____

_____ Is this facilitated? _____

_____ Do teachers (e.g., classroom teachers, special education support staff) provide the same type of feedback (e.g., praise, discipline) for the student as for his or her classmates? _____

_____ If the student uses an alternative communication system do classmates know how to use it? _____

_____ If the student uses an alternative communication system do teachers know how to use it? _____

_____ Is the system always available to the student? _____

Looking Good:

_____ Is the student given the opportunity to attend to his or her appearance as classmates do (e.g., check appearance in mirror between classes)? _____

_____ Does the student have accessories which are similar to his or her classmates (e.g., oversize tote bags, friendship bracelets, hair jewelry)? _____

_____ Is the student dressed similarly to classmates? _____

_____ Is clothing that's needed for activities age appropriate (e.g., napkins instead of bibs, "cool" paint shirts)?_____

_____ Are personal supplies or belongings carried or transported discreetly? _____

_____ Is the student's equipment (e.g., wheelchair) kept clean?_____

Given the opportunity (and assistance as needed):

_____ Is the student's hair combed?

_____ Are the student's hands clean and dry?

_____ Does the student change clothing to maintain a neat appearance?

_____ Does the student use chewing gum, breath mints, breath spray?

Note. From "A Team Approach to Program Development and Support" by T. Vandercook and J. York in _Support Network for Inclusive Schooling_ (pp. 117–118) by W. Stainback and S. Stainback (Eds.), 1990. Copyright 1990 by Paul H. Brookes, P.O. Box 10624, Baltimore, MD 21285-0624. Reprinted with permission.

personal appearance. Items receiving a "no" response should be addressed by the team when it meets to discuss ways to improve the inclusion process.

Research is beginning to emerge about the effect of full inclusion on students with severe disabilities, their families, their peers, and their teachers. In a review of inclusion research, Hunt and Goetz (1997) summarized their conclusions in these six guidelines:

1. Parental involvement is an essential component of effective inclusive schooling. . . .
2. Students with severe disabilities can achieve positive academic and learning outcomes in academic settings. . . .
3. Students with severe disabilities realize acceptance, interactions, and friendships in inclusive settings. . . .
4. Students without disabilities experience positive outcomes when students with severe disabilities are their classmates. . . .
5. Collaborative efforts among school personnel are essential to achieving successful inclusive schools. . . .
6. Curricular adaptations are a vital component in effective inclusion efforts. . . . (pp. 25–26)

However, it is important to note that very little research has focused on the academic achievement of fully included students with severe disabilities or the ways in which the general education curriculum should be adapted for these students (Hunt & Goetz, 1997; Nietupski, Hamre-Nietupski, Curtin, & Shrikanth, 1997). Despite this, Werts, Wolery, Snyder, and Caldwell (1996) report that special and general educators are in full agreement about the types of supports general education teachers need to make full inclusion programs successful. Three supports were identified as most critical: sufficient training, support from a team of professionals, and additional personnel to provide assistance in the general education classroom.

In this chapter you have learned ways to adapt classroom instruction to help students with mild retardation learn functional academic skills and basic work habits. You have also learned more about students with severe disabilities and strategies for increasing their participation as members of the school community. In the next chapter, you will meet students with behavioral disorders. Methods for teaching study skills and handling disruptive behavior will be presented. First, however, consult "Things to Remember" to review ways to help students with retardation succeed in the general education classroom.

ACTIVITIES

1. Visit a special education classroom, either a resource room or a special class, that serves students with mild retardation. Observe the students and talk with the teacher. In what school subjects do students experience the most difficulty? What subjects are taught by the special education teacher? Are transition and career education services part of the curriculum? Find out how many of the students are included in general education for at least part of the school day. Do they participate in academic instruction in the regular classroom? In nonacademic subjects such as music and art? In social activities?

2. Select one of the special education journals that focus on mental retardation. Choose from the *American Journal on Mental Retardation, Education and Training in Mental Retardation and Developmental Disabilities,* and *Mental Retardation.* Look through recent issues for articles with suggestions that classroom teachers can use. Collect ideas for teaching functional academics and for incorporating transition and career education skills into the general education curriculum.

3. Make a list of the questions you have about mental retardation and the inclusion of students with retardation in general education classrooms. Visit at least five websites to find answers to your questions. Start with the sites described in "Window on the Web" and use the links they provide to locate other resources. In your opinion, which site is most valuable for teachers?

4. Imagine that you are a general education teacher with several students with mild retardation in your class. Design an instructional program to improve the general work habits of all your students. What work habits will you include in your program? How will you explain the program to the class? How will you implement the program? Outline a method to use to evaluate your program.

5. Contact local school districts to find out how students with severe disabilities are served. Do students attend special classes located in regular neighborhood schools? Are students fully included in general education classes? Visit an integrated site and observe how students with severe disabilities participate in school life. If the school has a full inclusion program, use the checklist in Figure 10–5 to guide your observation.

Things to Remember

- Academic instruction is the most common area in which adaptations must be made in the general education classroom for students with mild retardation. They require assistance in acquisition of basic skills and work habits and in the application of these skills to daily life and career situations.

- Major indicators of mild retardation are a slow rate of learning and consistent delays in most areas of development.

- In assessment of mild retardation, information is gathered about academic achievement, intellectual performance, and adaptive behavior. The general education teacher assists by collecting classroom performance data.

- The major approach to the education of students with mild retardation is habilitation; instruction is directed toward development of the critical skills necessary for successful adulthood.

- Transition and career education services are one way to view habilitation of students with mild retardation; in this approach, students are prepared for adult life by instruction in functional academic, daily living, personal-social, and vocational skills.

- When students with mild retardation participate in general education classes for basic skills instruction or vocational education, the teacher assists by teaching functional academic skills and improving the general work habits of the students.

- Two approaches to teaching functional academics are instructional units and functional practice activities; both help students generalize learned skills to daily life and vocational situations.

- General work habits important for school and later employment include attendance and punctuality, work completion, and working with others. The general education teacher promotes the development of these skills in students with mild retardation with instruction, guided practice, and reinforcement of appropriate performance.

- Students with severe disabilities may attend special classes within regular schools or be fully included in general education classrooms. Both options offer opportunities for interactions between peers with and without disabilities and participation in age-appropriate school activities.

chapter 11

Teaching Students with Behavioral Disorders

Cases

Jake is 15 years old, in the eighth grade, and identified as a student with behavioral disorders. He is often late for classes and, as soon as he has arrived, draws attention to himself by his restlessness and constant activity. He frequently argues with teachers, other students, and even the few friends he has in his neighborhood. At present, Jake attends general education classes for social studies, English, physical education, and shop; he also spends two periods a day in the resource room. The special education teacher works with Jake to improve his math and reading performance, study skills, and classroom behavior. Jake's academic progress is adequate when he completes his work; however, Jake often argues with the teacher over the assignment and begins to work only when the class period is almost over. These conduct problems are evident in all classes except shop. Jake is never late to his shop class; he enjoys working on small motors and reading books that will help him build the go-cart that is his project for the year. Observational data and portions of the IEP for Jake will be described later in this chapter.

Six-year-old Tina is a first grade student who is small for her age. At school, she seldom talks to other children and withdraws when others try to talk to her. She speaks with the teacher but only in a very soft voice. Tina plays alone during recess; her favorite classroom activity is art, and she enjoys painting. Tina's full-day placement is in the general education classroom; in addition, she visits the speech-language clinician twice a week, and once a week she spends a half hour with the school social worker. Tina's parents are concerned about her lack of social relationships. At home, she spends her time drawing and watching television rather than playing with the neighborhood children. Tina's teacher is also concerned. Although Tina's written classwork is of average quality, she does not participate in class discussions and refuses to respond orally in class.

*Mike is a nine-year-old fourth grader who continually displays serious behavioral problems with his teachers, other school personnel, and the students at his school. He always appears to be agitated and is described by adults at the school as aggressive and a bully. Mike gets into at least one fight on the playground each week, he has temper tantrums when he doesn't get his way, and in class he is extremely uncooperative; he repeatedly interrupts classroom in-*struction and refuses to complete assigned schoolwork. He has displayed similar behaviors since he came to the school in the first grade. While Mike is considered to be quite capable academically, he continues to fall farther and farther behind in academic areas because of his pattern of conflict with adults and other children.*

Even though the problem behaviors of Jake, Tina, and Mike are quite different, students such as these can be equally perplexing to a classroom teacher. Jake, Tina, and Mike are all capable of meeting the academic demands of the general education classroom, yet their behaviors interfere. Jake's difficulty is his conduct in the classroom; his tardiness, poor work habits, and argumentativeness prevent successful performance. Tina, on the other hand, is withdrawn; she attends to her work but refuses to engage in social interaction. Mike's conduct leads him to encounter problems throughout the school; his aggression and defiance interfere with his academic progress and his acceptance by adults and his peers. These students present three examples of the many types of behavioral disorders that can be found in the general education classroom.

As noted in chapter 3, many attempts have been made to define the term *behavioral disorders;* however, there is no common agreement on any one definition. One reason for this is that no single pattern of behaviors identifies a student as having behavioral disorders. Instead, many student behaviors can be indicative of a behavioral disorder, ranging from high levels of aggression to extreme withdrawal. In the schools, the prereferral team studies the needs of each student, explores all possible adjustments in the general education program, and then decides whether to assess the student to determine eligibility for special education services.

Students with behavioral disorders can have special needs in several areas, such as classroom behavior, social skills, and academic instruction. In classroom behavior, the student's problem can lie in school conduct or the application of appropriate study skills. For example, students with poor conduct may disregard class rules or disrupt instructional activities; those with poor study skills may not pay attention to classroom instruction, may fail to complete assignments, or may work hastily and carelessly. Students with social skill problems may

Window on the Web

Websites About Behavioral Disorders

http://www.gwu.edu/~ebdweb/index.html

The Resources in Emotional or Behavioral Disorders (EBD) website is sponsored by George Washington University. This site offers a Resources page with ideas for teachers and parents, a feature called "Ask Your Question" where visitors can read answers to questions asked by others and ask their own questions, and "The Writing Room," which contains brief papers on topics related to behavioral disorders. Resources in EBD also provides links to websites with information about behavioral disorders, ADHD, parent resources, teaching resources, and other topics.

http://earthvision.asu.edu/BD/

This is the website of *Behavioral Disorders,* the journal of the Council for Children with Behavioral Disorders (CCBD), a division of The Council for Exceptional Children. Included is information about the journal and CCBD as well as abstracts of selected articles from current issues of *Behavioral Disorders.*

Note. Courtesy of the editors of *Behavioral Disorders.*

http://www.psych.org

APA Online is the website of the American Psychiatric Association, an organization of physicians who specialize in mental and emotional illnesses. The Public Information section of this site contains resources that parents and teachers might find useful. For example, in the category "Families and Children" is information about childhood problems such as depression, ADHD, anxiety, and conduct disorders.

Note. Reprinted by permission of the American Psychiatric Association.

The following websites provide information on several disabilities, including behavioral disorders. All contain lists of links to sites that may be of interest to teachers and parents of children and youth with behavioral disorders.

- Special Education Resources on the Internet (SERI),

  http://www.hood.edu/seri/serihome.htm

- Mental Health Net,

  http://www.cmhc.com/mhn.htm

- Family Village,

  http://www.familyvillage.wisc.edu

have difficulty getting along with their peers or the teacher and other adults. In academic instruction, students with behavioral disorders, like students with learning disabilities and those with mild retardation, may require extra assistance to learn and apply basic school skills; chapters 9 and 10 offered suggestions for modifying academic instruction. Other students can have more serious problems, such as involvement in drug abuse or severe depression that could lead to suicide. Students with problems such as these, and others at risk for school failure, will be discussed further in chapter 17.

This chapter focuses on the needs of students with behavioral disorders. It includes ways to identify such students in the general education program, techniques for collecting useful assessment data, and methods for improving both classroom conduct and study skills.

INDICATORS OF BEHAVIORAL DISORDERS

Teachers in general education classrooms are typically the first professionals to bring students with behavioral disorders to the attention of the prereferral team. These students can be identified at any age, but they are most likely to be noticed at the middle or upper levels of elementary school. Male students are more often identified as having behavioral disorders than are female students. Although both males and females can exhibit acting-out or withdrawn behaviors, boys are typically referred for aggressive behaviors and girls for withdrawal.

There are three major indicators of a behavioral disorder. According to Nelson (1993), a student's behavior "may be judged disordered (1) if it deviates from the range of behaviors for the child's age and sex which significant adults perceive as normal; (2) if it occurs very frequently or too intensely; or (3) if it occurs over an extended period of time" (p. 549). These indicators can be used by the classroom teacher and the planning team to study a student's need for special education services.

Another important sign is academic underachievement. Many students with behavioral disorders experience difficulty in coping with the academic demands of the classroom. They may read poorly and have trouble in math and other basic school subjects. In many cases, there is overlap between this group of students and those with learning disabilities; inappropriate classroom behaviors

can be either the cause or result of poor academic performance.

Other frequently mentioned characteristics of students with behavioral disorders are hyperactivity, distractibility, and impulsivity. **Hyperactivity** refers to excessive activity; students are considered hyperactive when they are constantly in motion and when the amount of movement is inappropriate for their age and the task at hand. For example, 2-year-old children are very active, but their constant motion, directed toward exploration of the environment, is appropriate for their age. Equal activity from a 10-year-old during a classroom discussion would not be considered appropriate.

Distractibility concerns attention to task (or lack of it); when students are easily distracted from school tasks and unable to maintain attention, they can be considered distractible. Again, however, it is necessary to consider the circumstances. A student who has missed breakfast and is hungry may be justifiably distractible in the class period before lunch.

Impulsivity is characterized by actions that occur without careful thought and deliberation. When students act impulsively and do not pause to reflect, their actions are more likely to be inappropriate and their classroom responses inaccurate. Examples of impulsive students are those who shout out answers in class before hearing the entire question and students who rush through the assignment, putting down the first response that comes into their heads.

When hyperactivity, distractibility, and impulsivity occur together (or in some combination), the label **attention deficit hyperactivity disorder (ADHD)** is often used to describe the student's difficulty in maintaining attention to task. These characteristics are highly interrelated; the child who is hyperactive is likely also to be distractible and impulsive. These attributes are associated not only with students with behavioral disorders but also with other groups of special students, such as individuals with learning disabilities and those with mild retardation. The school problems of students with these characteristics are sometimes attributed to some sort of internal deviation, such as brain damage. However, this attribution can be misleading and hinder the evaluation of the student's abilities and the development of an appropriate intervention strategy. As Kauffman (1997) notes, there is empirical evidence that the behavior of students considered hyperactive, distractible, and impulsive can be improved by the use of systematic instructional/management techniques.

As with most educational problems, speculation about the medical etiology does not contribute useful information to educators for planning instructional programs. However, many students with ADHD can benefit when they receive an appropriate type and dosage of psychostimulant medication such as Ritalin (methylphenidate), Dexedrine (dextroamphetamine), or Cylert (pemoline). While these medications do not remediate academic problems or teach new behaviors, it has been demonstrated that they can help improve behavior and facilitate learning by making the student more teachable. As noted in chapter 5, when students are receiving medication, it is best if their physician seeks information from the teacher about how the medication is influencing behavior and whether any side effects are apparent in the school setting; an inappropriate dosage may actually impair learning. Because the medications used with students with ADHD or other behavioral disorders are constantly changing, it is important for the parents and teachers of these students to review information on potential effects. Articles such as that by Sweeney, Forness, Kavale, and Levitt (1997) can provide important information on the use of these medications and their potential effects on the behaviors of the students.

It is important to note that ADHD is not considered to be a disability under IDEA; students are eligible for special education services under IDEA only if they qualify for one of the existing disability categories. Some students with ADHD may meet criteria for learning disabilities or behavioral disorders; others may qualify as other health impaired if they are determined to have a "chronic or acute health problem resulting in limited alertness, which adversely affects educational performance" (U.S. Department of Education, 1991). In addition, if the ADHD limits a major life activity (e.g., learning) and interferes with school performance, students may be protected by the provisions of Section 504 of the Vocational Rehabilitation Act. If this is the case, the local education agency must make an individualized determination of the student's educational needs and provide appropriate adaptations and interventions in the general education classroom (Task Force on Children with Attention Deficit Disorder, 1992). Many of the adaptations and interventions discussed in this chapter are appropriate for meeting the unique educational needs of students considered to have ADHD.

The great many indicators of behavioral disorders do not provide one hard-and-fast rule that tells teachers when to refer a student for consideration for special services; teachers, therefore, are sometimes understandably confused. Several guidelines may be useful. First, all students exhibit inappropriate behavior at some time during their school careers. Such behavior should be considered a possible problem only when it interferes with a student's academic performance, relationships with teachers or peers, or the operation of the instructional program. Second, the behaviors of concern should occur consistently over an extended period of time. In most cases, one instance of an unacceptable behavior is not sufficient to warrant the attention of the teacher. However, if the behavior in question is extreme (e.g., one that could lead to the injury of another student), then just one occurrence may be justification for a referral.

Several other indicators of behavioral disorders appear regularly in the professional literature. These include descriptors such as *disobedient, defiant, attention seeking, irritable, anxious, timid, preoccupied,* and *passive.* Although these terms suggest student behaviors that may concern teachers, they have limited value because they are subjective and can be interpreted differently. Before clear communication can occur, there must be a careful definition of terms; what one teacher considers "hyper" or attention seeking may be perfectly acceptable to another. It is also important to look at the reasons for student behaviors that suggest such labels: a student who is passive may be tired, and one who is anxious and irritable may be concerned about the illness of a family member.

Another guideline suggests that the nature of the inappropriate behavior be considered. The actions of students with behavioral disorders will differ from what teachers expect of typical students. The difference can lie in the frequency of the inappropriate behavior; such students may talk out in class not once or twice a period but once or twice a minute. They may have more intense reactions; a student may become extremely upset over an incident that most students would treat lightly. Or behaviors may be of longer duration; instead of quickly calming down after a disagreement, a student may remain upset throughout the school day.

For Your Information

Students with Behavioral Disorders

- For many years the U.S. Office of Education estimated that 2% of school-aged students had behavioral disorders; it lowered its estimate to a range of 1.2% to 2.0% in the mid-1980s. Research literature in the field suggests that 3% to 6% is a more realistic estimate, although current programs for students with behavioral disorders serve slightly under 1% of the school-age population (Kauffman, 1997).
- Students with behavioral disorders are found in both elementary and secondary schools; at least 50% of the public school programs for students with behavioral disorders are at the secondary level (Grosenick & Huntze, 1980).
- Nelson (1993) states that "although studies do not consistently find more boys than girls with behavior problems, boys tend to be overrepresented in programs for behaviorally disordered children as much as ten to one" (p. 542).
- The majority of students with behavioral disorders spend most of their school day in the general education classroom.

- As many as 70% to 80% of the children in need of mental health services do not receive appropriate care (U.S. Office of Technology Assessment, 1986). Many of these children do not receive any services until their problems are so extreme that they require residential treatment (Knitzer, 1989).
- Most students with behavioral disorders encounter problems in the general education classroom because they lack appropriate social and study skills. Instruction in these areas will lead to skill improvement that will enhance their chances for success when they are included in the general education program (Sugai & Lewis, 1996).
- The intelligence level of students with behavioral disorders does not vary significantly from that of the general school population. However, these students fall behind their peers in academic achievement, and the gap seems to widen as the students progress through school, unless they receive high-quality academic instruction.

Different professionals hold different views on what constitutes typical and disordered behavior. Such behavioral expectations influence teachers' decisions about which students should be referred for consideration for special services. If a teacher prefers a quiet and orderly classroom in which students remain seated at their desks, an active student may be perceived as a problem. However, this student may fit quite well in a classroom in which student activity, movement, and interaction are encouraged by the teacher. Prior to initiating a referral, the teacher should attempt all possible interventions in the general education class. Often this is accomplished with the assistance of a special education consultant.

The problems of substance abuse and suicide are gaining increased attention from educators. **Substance abuse** is the voluntary intake of chemicals with adverse social and physical consequences. Alcohol and various other drugs (e.g., narcotics, depressants, marijuana, cocaine) can cause side effects

that have a detrimental impact on the student's ability to perform appropriately in the school environment. For example, teachers may observe changes in the student's ability to attend to instruction; temperament; work quality; attitudes toward school, parents, or peers; or self-concept (Coleman, 1986; Kerr & Nelson, 1998). In addition, many children who were born to mothers who were addicted to alcohol or drugs enter school with behavioral disorders "that include an inability to control anger and other impulses" (Guetzloe, 1996, p. 4). Suicide is one of the leading causes of death in adolescents; it occurs more frequently in males, although females have a much higher rate of suicide attempts (Kauffman, 1997). It is often associated with feelings of depression and hopelessness and is more likely to occur among active drug and alcohol abusers. Educators should not attempt to deal with such students without outside assistance. However, teachers should be alert to the problem and aware of resources within the school and community for suicide prevention and crisis intervention. Additional information on these and other related topics is provided in chapter 17.

Students with severe behavioral disorders are less likely to be found in general education classroom programs. Disorders such as **autism** (extreme withdrawal and poorly developed communication or language skills) and **psychosis** (lack of contact with reality) are typically identified in the preschool years or early grades. School districts generally provide special programs in which these students spend the majority of their time in special classes or special schools. If students with severe behavioral disorders are returned to the general education program, they and their teachers receive a great deal of support from special educators.

ASSESSMENT PROCEDURES

When behavioral disorders are suspected, and the behavior problems exhibited by a student do not respond to the interventions available in the general education classroom, the student is referred to the assessment team to determine eligibility and need for special education services. Parents are notified of the referral and the team's plans for special education assessment. When parents grant permission, the team can begin to collect formal assessment information.

As with students with learning disabilities and mild retardation, several major areas are addressed in the special education assessment of students with behavioral disorders. Academic performance is one; measures such as the *Peabody Individual Achievement Test-Revised* (Markwardt, 1989) and the *Woodcock-Johnson Psycho-Educational Battery-Revised* (Woodcock & Johnson, 1989) help determine whether reading, spelling, and math are areas of need. Intellectual ability is another area of concern; tests such as the *Wechsler Intelligence Scale for Children-Third Edition* (Wechsler, 1991) provide information about intellectual functioning. In many states, students must perform within an average IQ range to be considered for programs for individuals with behavioral disorders.

A third major concern is classroom behavior. Information about the student's typical patterns of behavior is gathered from teachers and parents. Interviews can be conducted, or the team can consider results from behavior checklists and rating scales.

The *Behavior Rating Profile* (2nd ed.) (Brown & Hammill, 1990) uses the input of teachers, parents, peers, and students themselves to determine whether students have significant difficulty in home behavior, school conduct, or relationships with peers. With the *Behavior Evaluation Scale-2* (McCarney & Leigh, 1990), teachers rate the frequency of five types of behaviors: Learning Problems, Interpersonal Difficulties, Inappropriate Behavior, Unhappiness/Depression, and Physical Symptoms/Fears. Other measures such as projective tests are sometimes used; however, the information they provide is of little use to the teacher and the prereferral or IEP teams in planning an appropriate intervention plan. On projective tests, students are asked to describe ambiguous stimuli such as inkblots, and the students' personality traits are inferred from their responses.

Direct observation, as described in chapters 5 and 6, is the best source of data for planning behavioral change programs. Observation gives the teacher specific information about the current behavior of the student and later serves as a basis for evaluation of student progress. Because a variety of measurement systems are available, the teacher can select or design one to generate the type of data needed to plan appropriate interventions for any particular student.

Assessment of student behavior is most effective when specific behaviors are pinpointed and accurate information is collected about the occurrence of these behaviors. In the case of Jake, the eighth grader described at the beginning of this chapter, Mr. Johnson, Jake's English teacher, was particularly concerned about two of Jake's problem behaviors: tardiness and failure to complete assignments on time. To gather more data on these behaviors, Mr. Johnson set up the observation system shown in Figure 11–1. Each day Mr. Johnson noted the number of minutes that Jake was late to class (duration recording), the number of assignments that were due, and the number of assignments that Jake completed on time (event recording). The results of this observation were then used as a basis for developing and evaluating the intervention plan for Jake. If Jake's behavior were more severe (e.g., aggressive behaviors), it would be important to also conduct a functional analysis to collect information on (a) the elements in the setting that influence the behavior (e.g., the presence of particular students; recess versus classroom; individual versus group interactions), and (b) specific events that occur before and

FIGURE 11-1   Observational Data

Student: Jake

Behaviors Observed: Number of minutes late to class
                         Number of assignments completed on time/number of assignments due

Setting: English 8, Period 3

Day	Number of Minutes Late	Assignments Completed/ Assignments Due	Percentage of Assignments Completed
1	10	0/5	0
2	5	1/4	25
3	2	1/2	50
4	7	0/3	0
5	11	0/4	0
6	4	2/6	33
7	4	1/4	25
8	6	0/2	0
9	3	0/2	0
10	8	0/3	0

after the behavior (i.e., antecedents and consequences). This information on factors that contribute to the occurrence of the behavior would be essential in designing an appropriate intervention.

In some cases, it is not necessary to collect new assessment information. For example, Tina's first grade teacher was also concerned about specific behaviors. The teacher considered gathering data on the frequency of Tina's interactions with other students and her participation in class discussions. However, an observation period was not really necessary because Tina never exhibited these behaviors. Instead, the teacher decided to begin the intervention program at once.

Mike's case was reviewed by the prereferral team and his interactions at home, in the classroom, and on the playground were carefully examined to determine the factors that were influencing his behavioral problems. Observations by the school psychologist and the special education teacher determined that interactions between Mike and adults, both in school and at home, tended to be quite negative. Moreover, as Mike's resistance to adult direction and the level of his acting-out behavior increased, the adults interacting with him tended to become even more coercive. The initial interventions with Mike involved improving the ways in which the adults in Mike's life interacted with him: increasing the preciseness of the directions given to Mike, avoiding angry interchanges with him, and increasing positive feedback to Mike for those appropriate behaviors that he did exhibit. In addition, the prereferral team worked with his teacher to implement social skills instruction that focused on improving Mike's skills in: (a) avoiding situations in which he typically became angry and (b) learning adaptive strategies for coping with these situations.

FIGURE 11-2   **IEP Goals and Services for Jake**

Annual Goals

1. By the end of the school year, Jake will complete and return to the teacher all assignments at the time they are due.
   Persons responsible: Resource teacher, eighth grade teachers
2. By the end of the school year, Jake will arrive on time to classes at least 4 out of 5 days per week.
   Persons responsible: Resource teacher, eighth grade teachers
3. By the end of the school year, Jake will remain in his seat during class time unless he is given permission to leave.
   Persons responsible: Resource teacher, eighth grade teachers
4. By the end of the school year, Jake will reduce the number of his arguments with teachers and other students to less than two per week.
   Persons responsible: Resource teacher, eighth grade teachers
5. Jake will continue to perform at the eighth grade level or above in reading and math.
   Person responsible: Resource teacher

Amount of Participation in General Education

Jake will attend the general education eighth grade social studies, English, physical education, and shop classes.

Special Education and Related Services

1. Jake will receive special education services from the resource teacher (annual goals 1, 2, 3, 4, and 5) for two periods daily.
2. The resource teacher will provide consultation to Jake's eighth grade teachers as needed to accomplish annual goals 1, 2, 3, and 4.

SPECIAL SERVICES

If assessment results indicate that an individual is eligible for services for students with behavioral disorders, the team meets to design the IEP. Most students identified as having behavioral disorders remain in the general education classroom for at least a portion of the school day. As shown in Figure 11–2, Jake will participate in four general education classes and receive special education services from the resource teacher for two periods each day. In addition, consultation services are available to Jake's general education teachers.

Other professionals can also provide support to students with behavioral disorders. In addition to the special instruction provided for the student by the resource teacher, the resource teacher or another consultant may be available to assist the student's general education classroom teacher. Students can also visit the school psychologist, school counselor, or school social worker for regular counseling ses-

sions. Some students and their families can be referred to community agencies that offer family counseling or other appropriate services.

Although most students with behavioral disorders are educated in the general education class, those with severe disabilities may attend special classes or special schools. In extreme cases, residential or hospital settings may be the most appropriate placement.

CLASSROOM ADAPTATIONS

When students with behavioral disorders are included in the general education program, the classroom teacher may find it necessary to make program adaptations in three areas: classroom behavior, social skills, and academic instruction. Suggestions for classroom modifications to meet academic needs were presented in the previous two chapters; the techniques and strategies described for students with learning disabilities and mild retardation are also applicable to students with behavioral disorders. See the "Spotlight on Technology" for additional ideas for teaching math skills, an area in which students with behavioral disorders often experience difficulty.

Techniques for social skills training were discussed in chapter 6. This chapter provides additional suggestions for improving social skills as well as methods for improving classroom conduct and teaching study skills. Although these strategies are suggested for students with behavioral disorders, they can be used with equal success with any student, special or typical, who disrupts classroom activities or has not yet acquired effective study skills.

Several approaches have been advocated for use with students with behavioral disorders. Some of these strategies assume that it is necessary to determine what is wrong with the student and study the student's past for possible causes; for example, the history of the student's family and his or her early childhood experiences might be investigated. This approach offers little aid to the classroom teacher in dealing with problem behaviors encountered daily in the classroom. As chapter 5 explained, the teacher is most effective in controlling behavior problems if the emphasis is on the current status of the student and if information is gathered about the status of the student's observable behaviors and the factors that influence these behaviors. This chapter adopts the same viewpoint.

In systematic management of behavior, the teacher first identifies the behavior(s) of interest, collects data on their current status, examines the factors that may contribute to the occurrence of the behaviors, designs and institutes an intervention program, and then collects additional data to evaluate the effectiveness of the intervention and determine whether it should be continued, modified, or abandoned. There are three possible instructional goals: to increase the occurrence of an appropriate behavior, decrease the occurrence of an inappropriate behavior, or teach a new behavior that is presently absent from a student's repertoire. Examples of these goals are increasing the number of times Johnny comes to class on time, decreasing the number of times Harvey leaves his seat during class, and teaching Esther a new study strategy, such as skimming a chapter for major ideas before reading it.

Teachers must assume that students with behavioral disorders can learn the appropriate behaviors

expected of all students in the general education classroom. The teachers who work directly with students with special needs hold the primary responsibility for planning and carrying out interventions to change problem behaviors. Although others, such as the psychologist or counselor, can provide some assistance, the general education teacher spends the majority of the school day with the student and is therefore responsible for bringing about improvement in classroom behavior.

Many students who exhibit behavioral disorders at school may also display some of these behaviors at home. It can be very helpful to involve parents by informing them of the interventions that are being implemented at school and to consider providing them with suggestions regarding activities they may use at home. Concerned parents are generally open to suggestions regarding dealing with difficult behaviors. These recommendations can be communicated at conferences, through written suggestions, at specific training meetings, or through suggested readings. Publications such as *Understanding ADHD: A Practical Guide for Teachers and Parents* (Bender, 1997) can help parents understand problem behaviors and also provide specific recommendations regarding strategies they can use at home.

The remainder of this chapter presents several ways to handle disruptive behavior in the classroom and help students acquire effective study skills. Before selecting one of these interventions (or designing an alternative), the teacher should carefully consider each of the following questions:

Spotlight on Technology

Math Software

There is a large collection of math software. In fact, more programs are available for math than any other academic subject (Lewis, 1993). Most common are programs for math computation, although software is available for math readiness, problem solving, and everyday math skills such as time, money, and measurement.

Millie's Math House is one of a set of readiness programs from Edmark Corporation (www.edmark.com). This program talks, so no reading is required. It introduces young children to shapes, patterns, counting skills, and math concepts such as size. For example, in the activity shown here, students must find shoes to fit the Big, Middle, and Little characters.

Note. Used by permission of Edmark © 1998.

Trudy's Time & Place House, another Edmark readiness program, includes beginning map, calendar, and time-telling activities. In Time Twins (shown at right), the learner can experiment in the exploratory mode by changing the time on one clock and seeing it change on the other. In the question mode of the program, either Analog Ann or Digital Dan shows a time and the learner must change the time of the other clock to match. When the time has been set, the learner clicks "Done" and the time is read aloud.

Note. Used by permission of Edmark © 1998.

continued

1. Can the intervention be carried out in the classroom? That is, is it feasible? Consider the type of problem (e.g., tardiness versus drug abuse), the age of the students involved, the resources within the classroom (e.g., availability of an aide, the experience and training of the teacher), the factors that contribute to the occurrence or maintenance of the behavior (e.g., attention of the teacher or peers, instructional situation versus recess), and the structure of the classroom.

2. Can the intervention be implemented consistently? If it cannot, another strategy should be selected.

3. How will data be collected to assess student progress? Can this be done consistently?

4. Do students have the prerequisite skills necessary to learn the appropriate behavior? If not, what skills must be taught?

5. Are there dangerous behaviors involved that require immediate elimination or remediation? If not, which intervention being considered is the most positive and the least intrusive?

6. How can students be involved in the intervention? Can they record their own performance data? Help to develop contingency contracts? Serve as models or recorders for other students?

Edmark also publishes the *Mighty Math* programs for more advanced students. This series includes:

- *Carnival Countdown* (ages 5 to 8)
- *Zoo Zillions* (ages 5 to 8)
- *Number Heroes* (ages 8 to 12)
- *Calculating Crew* (ages 8 to 12)
- *Cosmic Geometry* (ages 12 to 14)
- *Astro Algebra* (ages 12 to 14)

All programs feature problem solving, reasoning, and logic but each highlights a specific set of skills. For example, *Zoo Zillions* focuses on counting and number line concepts, early geometry, story problems, addition and subtraction facts, and money skills.

Fish Stories is the story problem activity in *Zoo Zillions*. In the example shown here, the student must add fish to the aquarium. Then the task is to determine the total number of fish in the tank.

Note. Used by permission of Edmark © 1998.

Note. Used by permission of Edmark © 1998.

7. What reinforcers are meaningful to the student(s) for whom the program is designed? Is it possible to use these reinforcers with the program?
8. What resources are needed? Does the intervention require teacher time? Aide time? Reinforcers? Are these available?
9. What other factors must be considered? For example, must the physical arrangement of the classroom be changed? Must peer tutors be recruited and trained?
10. What criteria and evidence will be used to determine the success or failure of the program?

What alternative interventions can be used if the original program fails?

It is important to remember that there are few specific strategies for effectively improving the behaviors of students with emotional and behavioral disorders. However, in order for programs to be effective with these students, the implementation of these strategies (e.g., data-based interventions, continuous assessment and monitoring of progress) requires a high level of precision, duration, and intensity in their implementation (Kauffman, Lloyd, Baker, & Riedel, 1995).

One of the features of the *Mighty Math* series is that all activities have multiple levels. For example, the story problems in Fish Stories can range from simple addition problems (with sums up to 6) to missing number and multiplication and division problems.

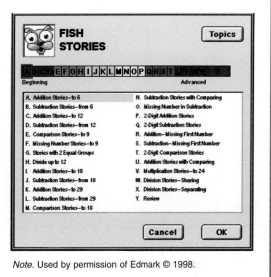

FISH STORIES

Topics

A B C D E F G H I J K L M N O P Q R S T U V W X Y

Beginning — Advanced

A. Addition Stories—to 6
B. Subtraction Stories—from 6
C. Addition Stories—to 12
D. Subtraction Stories—from 12
E. Comparison Stories—to 9
F. Missing Number Stories—to 9
G. Stories with 2 Equal Groups
H. Divide up to 12
I. Addition Stories—to 18
J. Subtraction Stories—from 18
K. Addition Stories—to 29
L. Subtraction Stories—from 29
M. Comparison Stories—to 18

N. Subtraction Stories with Comparing
O. Missing Number in Subtraction
P. 2-Digit Addition Stories
Q. 2-Digit Subtraction Stories
R. Addition—Missing First Number
S. Subtraction—Missing First Number
T. 2-Digit Comparison Stories
U. Addition Stories with Comparing
V. Multiplication Stories—to 24
W. Division Stories—Sharing
X. Division Stories—Separating
Y. Review

Cancel   OK

Note. Used by permission of Edmark © 1998.

continued

 ## CONTROLLING DISRUPTIVE BEHAVIORS

One of the most common concerns of classroom teachers is the student who disrupts the instructional process. Whether typical or special, students with conduct problems call attention to themselves by arriving late, talking out in class, moving about the classroom, and interacting poorly with others. These inappropriate behaviors indicate poor social skills or poor general work habits. Whereas chapters 6 and 10 have discussed methods for developing good social and work skills, the following sections concentrate on what to do with students who have acquired inappropriate work habits or social skills that interrupt classroom activities.

Tardiness

Students who arrive late begin the school day or class period at a disadvantage. Tardiness affects the performance of these students and interrupts and distracts the teacher and other students. Most stu-dents are late occasionally; however, frequent tardiness is an inappropriate behavior that must be resolved so that the student can become an active classroom participant. Suggestions for decreasing tardiness are presented next. Before implementing one of these plans, though, the teacher must be sure to collect data on current performance.

- Reward students for arriving on time. For example, students who arrive before the late bell rings can get tickets for a raffle or have the opportunity to copy answers from the board for a couple of quiz questions. More structured programs may provide points or tokens redeemable for reinforcers. Criteria can be set up to encourage improvement in arrival time. For example, students can earn 5 points if they arrive on time and 2 points if they arrive less than 5 minutes late. Gradually reduce the number of minutes students are allowed to arrive late until it is possible to earn points only by being on time.
- Help students analyze the skills or steps required to arrive on time. For example, determine the times they should leave home, arrive at school,

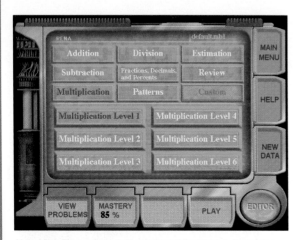

Math Blaster is a series of programs from Davidson & Associates (www.davd.com). It includes *Math Blaster* for ages 4 to 6, 6 to 9, and 9 to 12, *Math Blaster Pre-Algebra, Math Blaster Algebra,* and *Math Blaster Geometry.* All the programs use an arcade-game format to provide students with practice in a variety of math skills. For example, in *Math Blaster Ages 6 to 9,* students can choose different types of problems—basic operations (addition, subtraction, multiplication, division), fractions, decimals, percentages, number patterns, and estimation—and can vary the level of difficulty. In this example, the student has selected Level 1 of Multiplication. Parents and teachers can also add their own sets of problems to meet the needs of individual learners.

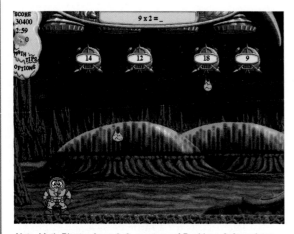

The mission in *Math Blaster Ages 6 to 9* is to rescue Spot, Blasternaut's best friend. Spot has been captured by the evil Gelator, the Brain Drainer. To succeed in the rescue mission, the student must complete five activities: Space Zapper, Math Blaster, Cave Runner, Equationator, and Space Zapper 2. In Math Blaster, shown here, the student helps Blasternaut by shooting the answer to the problem that appears at the top of the screen.

and be in the area of the classroom. Use this task analysis to establish a program to help students gradually master the skills needed for punctuality.

• Place a sign-in sheet at the door so students can record their name and time of arrival. Students who are late can leave tardy slips or excuses in an envelope attached to the sign-in sheet. The teacher can review these at a time that does not disrupt other classroom activities (Emmer, Evertson, Sanford, Clements, & Worsham, 1989).

• Schedule activities that students enjoy at the start of the class period. Allow only those students who are on time to class to participate.

• Set up contracts with students to specify the consequences of tardiness and punctuality. Be sure to identify clearly the criteria for success, who will keep the records, and the reinforcers that the students can earn. Students can record their own data if teachers periodically verify their accuracy.

- Discuss student tardiness with parents. Alert them to the extent of the problem, and encourage them to support the school's rules and to require, and reinforce, punctuality at home.
- Encourage parents to give their children watches so that students can keep track of time. If this is not possible, help students locate public clocks that they can consult.
- Arrange with parents to provide rewards at home. When students meet the prespecified punctuality criteria, they receive the rewards.
- Set up a system in which tardy students lose an equal number of minutes in a favorite activity.
- Group students into teams, and provide special reinforcers each week for the team with the best punctuality record.
- Assign peer tutors to help students get from class to class or from playground to classroom on time. As students develop appropriate skills, reduce the amount of assistance.
- Provide additional grade points for on-time arrival. For example, a student might earn 5 bonus points on an assignment if the assignment is started at the beginning of class.
- When students arrive on time, allow them to choose where they will sit. That is, use classroom seating preferences as reinforcers.

When any one of these interventions is implemented in the classroom, the teacher must continue to collect data on student performance to assure that the program is effective. An alternative should be selected only after the intervention has been consistently implemented over a period of time, modifications have been made, and collected data have proved that the intervention is not working.

Verbal Outbursts

When students talk out in class, they disrupt the orderly flow of classroom activities. The teacher is distracted, and the work of other students is interrupted. Examples of verbal outbursts considered inappropriate by most teachers are answering out of turn, making irrelevant comments, arguing with the teacher or peers, and chatting with classmates during instruction. The following strategies are used to decrease the occurrence of this problem behavior:

- Establish clearly stated classroom rules regarding student verbal interactions. State the specific circumstances under which students are permitted to talk (e.g., when asked a question by the teacher, when asking the teacher a question after being called on, during assigned group work), and model the acceptable and unacceptable voice levels for each occasion. Teach these rules and provide students with opportunities to practice with teacher supervision and to obtain feedback that provides recognition for appropriate interactions and correction of inappropriate behaviors.
- Reinforce students who are good behavioral models for others, that is, those who speak out in class only at appropriate times or when teacher permission has been granted. Make the reinforcers strong enough so that students with problem behaviors will consider changing their ways. Teachers might try reinforcers such as early departure for recess or lunch, first place in line, or a certain number of minutes in a special activity.
- Recognize and reinforce problem students when they exhibit an appropriate behavior that is incompatible with the inappropriate verbal behavior, such as raising their hands and gaining recognition before answering questions in class. Clearly identify why the reinforcer is provided. For example, the teacher might say, "I like the way you raised your hand before you talked. You may take this book to the office for me." A statement such as this identifies the appropriate behavior and provides both a social reward and an activity reinforcer. Often these students are used to gaining recognition only when they exhibit inappropriate behaviors.
- Set up a system in which a loss of points results if students talk out. List the cost of talking out on the reinforcement menu or the student contract.
- Have students record the number of times they talk out in class each day. They can graph the data each day for a week and then compute the weekly total. Their goal for the next week is to decrease the number of times they talk out. Provide reinforcers if they meet their targets.
- Set up time periods in which students receive reinforcers for not talking out. Start with short time segments and gradually increase these to longer periods. The teacher might begin with 5-minute periods, then 10-minute, and so on until students are able to refrain from making

verbal outbursts for an entire class period or activity.

- If classroom noise (caused by several loud students) becomes a problem, use an obvious signal such as "Stop talking!" or briefly turning off the classroom lights to alert students to be quiet.

Moving About the Classroom

A familiar conduct problem is the active student who moves about the classroom at inappropriate times. Such students leave their seats during instruction and interrupt the teacher's attempt to present information. They also move about when they have been assigned independent work tasks at their desks, interfering with their own academic progress and also disturbing the work of others. Some students remain at their desks but are constantly in motion; they wiggle and squirm in their seats, bounce up and down, tap their desks with their fingers, and kneel on their chairs.

Active behaviors such as these are described by some as hyperactivity. However, this label does not specify an observable behavior that can be counted or measured in any way. "Hyper" behaviors can be improved, but first they must be pinpointed and described in appropriate, observable terms. Consult the suggestions here for ways to decrease the occurrence of inappropriate activity in the classroom:

- Find out whether students fully understand the class rules about when they should remain in their seats and when they can move about the room. Demonstrate appropriate "in seat" and transition behaviors, and clarify any misinterpretations the students may have. Reteach and provide practice for any rules the students do not remember. Briefly remind students of the rules before a transition time. As needed, provide reinforcement and correction.
- Provide frequent reinforcers for appropriate behavior; for example, students might receive rewards for remaining in their seats during instruction. If students are permitted to share reinforcers with other students seated nearby, these peers will often encourage the target students to behave appropriately.
- Record the amount of time the student is out of his or her seat; reduce time in a favorite activity

by an equal amount or provide for a loss of points for each minute away from the desk.

- Allow opportunities for movement. Set up a system in which students can earn the chance to move about the room or travel to other parts of the school. For example, running errands to the office can serve as a reinforcer.
- Use extinction to reduce the occurrence of inappropriate movement. That is, provide no attention or reinforcement for inappropriate behaviors, but reward appropriate ones.
- Anticipate student movement and arrange to be near students when they are most likely to leave their seats. Often the proximity of the teacher, or a reminder provided by the teacher, will prevent inappropriate movement.
- Have students record their own in-seat behavior. They can begin with 5- or 10-minute intervals and note whether they remain seated during this time; if they leave their seats during the interval, they do not receive a check mark for that time period. At first, students can be reinforced for each successful interval. Then requirements are gradually increased so that students must perform successfully in 8 out of 10 intervals to earn reinforcers. The requirements are increased until expectations are consistent with those for all students in the class.
- Use a timing device to check student behavior. This can be a timer or a tape recording with preset random signals. When the signal is heard, reinforce students only if they are exhibiting appropriate behavior. Be sure to vary the number of minutes between signals so that students are not aware of when their behavior will be observed.

Social Relationships

Many students have difficulty getting along with others. This type of classroom conduct problem can be characterized by either aggressive behaviors or withdrawal; in either case, students do not establish and maintain satisfactory social relationships with teachers and peers. Examples of aggressive behaviors are fighting, swearing, arguing, refusing to follow directions, and antagonizing others. Withdrawn students, in contrast, may have limited interactions with teachers and peers and may avoid both physical proximity and verbal communication.

Many of the programs mentioned in chapter 6 provide specific problem-solving strategies and lessons for teaching the behaviors associated with appropriate social skills. The following suggestions can also help improve the social behaviors of students in the classroom:

- Provide students with examples of nonaggressive behaviors that can be used in situations that might lead to aggression. One way to do this is with good models; these can be adults, peers such as classmates or peer tutors, or films and videotapes.
- Use role playing to help students practice nonaggressive responses. Simulations provide students with an opportunity to learn appropriate behaviors before encountering difficult situations in daily life.
- Teach students acceptable responses to verbal or physical attacks. Options include calling for assistance, leaving the area, or saying something nonaggressive, such as "You played well in the softball game yesterday" or "I like the car I saw you driving after school." If students have not learned options such as these, they may react by fighting back or verbally attacking the aggressor. They need to learn a range of alternative responses and know which are appropriate for use in which situation.
- Reinforce students who substitute appropriate, nonaggressive responses for the aggressive behaviors they previously exhibited. For example, provide a special reinforcer when students spend the lunch period or recess playing a game rather than arguing, fighting, or name calling.
- Use extinction for inappropriate verbal behaviors such as swearing, arguing, and teasing. Supply reinforcers for other students in the classroom to encourage them to ignore this type of problem behavior.
- Provide a penalty or punisher when a student exhibits an inappropriate behavior. This action might be removing the student to a setting without reinforcement (time-out), taking away activity time or other reinforcers earned (response cost), or introducing an aversive such as scolding or notification of parents. This type of intervention should be used sparingly, but it is sometimes necessary to stop a problem behavior quickly. Punishment, when used, should be administered immediately each time the inappropriate behavior occurs. Punishment is most effective when used in conjunction with positive reinforcement of appropriate behaviors. In fact, Walker (1995)

indicates that the combination of teacher praise, token reinforcement, and response cost "represents the most powerful and potentially effective intervention for changing the behavior of acting-out children" (p. 197).

- Carefully review the social skills of withdrawn students, and determine their specific strengths and weaknesses. Provide instruction in important areas of need, such as how to greet others or what to do to start and participate in a conversation with others.
- Encourage the social interaction of withdrawn students with reinforcement techniques. Reinforcers can be used with the withdrawn student to encourage interaction, but, especially at first, it may be better to reinforce the student's peers. Focusing a great deal of attention on the withdrawn student at the start of the intervention may cause further withdrawal and avoidance of interactions.
- Include the withdrawn student in a classroom group assigned to complete a project or activity. Furnish specific activities that lead to interactions. For example, in completing worksheets, each student can be given a different portion of the materials needed to answer the questions. Provide reinforcers to the entire group when the target student is an active participant.
- Pair a withdrawn student with a peer tutor, cross-age tutor, or adult volunteer. The tutor or volunteer should model appropriate social interactions and reinforce the target student for like behaviors.

Spotlight on Technology

Technology as a Reward

A consideration in any intervention program designed to change the behavior of students is the selection of reinforcers. One option is technology. Most students enjoy media as consumers; they may also be enthusiastic about becoming producers. Listed here are several ways in which classroom technologies can be transformed into reinforcers.

Consuming Media

Students can earn the right to

- listen to instructional tapes
- listen to music tapes or CDs
- listen to the radio
- view a music videotape
- rent tapes, CDs, or videotapes to play at home
- play electronic learning games
- view instructional films or videotapes
- view films or videotapes for entertainment
- watch television either at school or at home
- use the computer to practice in an instructional area such as spelling or math
- use a word processor or desktop publishing program on the computer to write a story or complete an assignment.

Malouf (1987–1988) points out that computer activities are motivating to students with disabilities, particularly when academic tasks are presented in a game format. He reports the results of a study comparing two language arts programs, one incorporating arcade game features and the other an identical program without game features. Students showed equal gains under both conditions but the game resulted in higher levels of continuing motivation. Semmel and Lieber (1986) warn that the game features in software can distract students' attention from the academic task. However, that is not a concern if the program is used primarily as a reinforcer rather than an instructional tool.

Producing Media

Students can earn the right to

- make an audiotape of a story they have read or written
- tape-record a message to a friend
- produce a videotape of a class skit
- take photographs for a bulletin board or a class book or project
- use a video camera to create a film
- prepare an overhead transparency of a favorite poem or drawing
- use a computer graphics program to create a sketch or drawing
- create a poster, banner, or greeting card using a program such as *Print Shop*
- author a multimedia computer-based lesson or presentation with a program such as *HyperStudio.*

Many of the techniques suggested here for controlling disruptive behaviors involve the use of reinforcers. Rossett and Glassman (1979) maintain that one very effective reinforcer for improving classroom behavior is technology. Consult "Spotlight on Technology" for ideas on how to use technology to change behaviors.

It is important to note that students with more severe antisocial or acting-out behavioral problems (e.g., hostility or aggression toward others, a willingness to commit rule infractions or to violate social norms, defiance of adult authority) may require more intensive interventions to deal with their problem behaviors. Typically, special education programs have specialists or consultants available to assist general education teachers in designing and implementing these interventions. In addition, there are many books on the subject that provide detailed descriptions of strategies and interventions to deal with more severe challenging behaviors. Examples are listed here:

- *The Acting-Out Child: Coping with Classroom Disruption* (2nd ed.) by Walker (1995)
- *Antisocial Behavior in School: Strategies and Best Practices* by Walker, Colvin, and Ramsey (1995)
- *Strategies for Managing Behavior Problems in the Classroom* (3rd ed.) by Kerr and Nelson (1998)

The 1997 Individuals with Disabilities Education Act outlines specific requirements that educational agencies must follow when administering discipline to students with disabilities, especially those exhibiting more severe behavioral problems. These new regulations expedite the discipline process and make it possible for schools to make appropriate changes in the placement of a student with disabilities without going to court to make the same determination (Bootel, 1997). See "Inclusion Tips for the Teacher" on page 314 for more information.

TEACHING STUDY SKILLS

Students with poor study habits are at a distinct disadvantage in the general education classroom (Archer & Gleason, 1995; Heron & Harris, 1993). They may have difficulty maintaining attention in class, staying on task, organizing their work, or producing accurate responses. These problems have grave effects on academic performance and hinder a teacher's instructional effort. With students who fail to complete assignments, assessing current skill levels and progress is difficult because few work samples are available. As these students fall further and further behind their classmates, teachers become frustrated, and the probability increases that classroom conduct problems will occur.

Teachers have not typically taught study skills in a systematic fashion. However, programs such as *Skills for School Success* (Archer & Gleason, 1989b) provide teachers with a method, and the materials,

to teach students a wide range of school and study skills such as organizing a notebook, keeping a calendar, writing neat papers, and completing assignments. Skills such as these should be included as part of the school curriculum; they should be taught directly with opportunities for guided and independent practice. The sections that follow discuss strategies to promote several important study skills; included are ideas to help students increase their ability to maintain attention, organize their work, and respond accurately.

Maintaining Attention

Students with classroom behavior problems often spend a great deal of instructional time engaging in off-task behavior; their attention is not directed toward the appropriate classroom activity. They may stare into space, watch other students, doodle on their papers, or attend to stimuli that are irrelevant to the instructional task. These students are often referred to as distractible; they do not attend to the appropriate task for an adequate time period. The task in question can be any classroom activity: a worksheet, text chapter, class discussion, teacher lecture, or oral directions. Such students do not make effective use of independent study time. Instead of maintaining attention on the specific task, they attend to other features of the environment. Or their attention span is brief, and they shift attention from the instructional task to some other aspect of the classroom. Some engage in disruptive behaviors and interrupt the concentration of others. One of the following strategies might help students improve their on-task behavior:

- Before presenting important verbal information to students, use a cue to alert them, such as "Listen," "Ready?" or "It's time to begin the lesson!" Establish a standard way of beginning lessons, and use the signal word or phrase only at times when you wish to obtain everyone's attention.
- Make teacher attention or other reinforcers contingent on attending behavior. Students with severe attention problems will need strong reinforcers provided immediately. This approach is much more effective than scolding students for not attending.
- When presenting information to students, seat them in a semicircle or U-shaped formation to

Inclusion Tips for the Teacher

Discipline Provisions of the 1997 IDEA Amendments

Discipline of Children with Disabilities. The legislation adds substantial provisions that address the discipline of children with disabilities. Provisions allow school personnel to order a change in the placement of a child with a disability to an appropriate interim alternative education setting (IAES), another setting, or suspension, for not more than 10 school days (to the extent such alternative would be applied to children without disabilities).

- **Weapons and Drugs.** A child that carries a weapon to school or to a school function, or who possesses or uses illegal drugs or sells or solicits the sale of a controlled substance while at school or a school function can be placed in an IAES for the same amount of time that a child without a disability would be subject to discipline, but for not more than 45 days.
- **Behavior Intervention Plan.** The legislation requires that either before or not later than 10 days after taking the disciplinary action, the LEA [local education agency] convene an IEP meeting to develop an assessment plan to address the problem behavior (if the LEA did not conduct a functional behavior assessment and implement a behavior intervention plan for the child before the problem behavior), or if the child already has a behavior intervention plan, the IEP team will review the plan and modify it, as necessary, to address the behavior.
- **Injury to Self or Others.** A hearing officer may order a change in placement of a child with a disability to an IAES for not more than 45 days if the officer determines that the public agency has demonstrated by substantial evidence that maintaining the current placement of the child is substantially likely to result in injury to the child or to others, considers the appropriateness of the current placement, considers whether the agency has made reasonable efforts to minimize the risk of harm in the current placement (including the use of supplementary aids and services), and determines that the IAES meets the requirements.
- **Interim Alternative Educational Setting (IAES).** The legislation requires the IAES to be determined by the IEP team and to be selected

so as to enable the child to continue to participate in the general curriculum, continue to receive services and modifications that will enable the child to meet the goals in the IEP, and include services and modifications designed to address the problem behavior.
- **Manifestation Determination Review.** If a disciplinary action is contemplated as a result of drugs, alcohol, or injury to self or others, or if a disciplinary action involving a change of placement for more than 10 days is contemplated for a child with a disability who had engaged in other behavior that violated any rule or code of conduct: (1) not later than the date on which the decision to take action is made, parents must be notified of the decision and of all procedural safeguards; and (2) immediately, if possible, but in no case later than 10 school days after the date on which the decision to take that action is made, a review must be conducted of the relationship between the child's disability and the behavior subject to the disciplinary action. The review is to be conducted by the IEP team and other qualified personnel.
- **Requirements for Finding that Behavior is not a Manifestation of the Disability.** In order to find that the behavior was not a manifestation of the disability, the team must determine: (1) that the child's IEP and placement were appropriate and that special education services, supplementary aids and services, and behavior intervention strategies were provided consistent with the IEP and placement; (2) the child's disability did not impair the ability of the child to understand the impact and consequences of the behavior; and (3) the child's disability did not impair the ability of the child to control the behavior.
- **Implications of Manifestation Review.** If it is determined that the behavior of the child with a disability was not a manifestation of the child's disability, the relevant disciplinary procedure applicable to children without disabilities may be applied to the child in the same manner in which that would be applied to children without disabilities, except that they will continue to receive a free appropriate public education.

- **Parent Appeal and Child Placement During Appeal.** New provisions allow parents who disagree with a determination that the child's behavior was not a manifestation of the disability to request a hearing, and for the SEA [state education agency] or LEA to arrange for an expedited hearing. During the appeal, the child shall remain in the IAES pending the decision of the hearing officer or until the expiration of the time limit, whichever occurs first, unless the parent and the SEA or LEA agree otherwise. If a child is placed in an IAES and school personnel propose to change the child's placement after expiration of the IAES, the child shall remain in the current placement (prior to the IAES) during the pendency of any proceeding to challenge the proposed change in placement, unless school personnel maintain that it is dangerous for the child to be in the current placement, in which case the LEA may request an expedited hearing.
- **Children Not Yet Eligible for Special Education.** A child who has not been determined to be eligible for special education and related services and who has engaged in behavior that violated any rule or code of conduct of the LEA, may assert any of the protections if the LEA had knowledge that the child had a disability before the behavior occurred. If the LEA did not have knowledge that the child had a disability, the child may be subjected to the same disciplinary measures as applied to children without disabilities. The LEA will be considered to have knowledge of the disability if: (1) the parent has expressed concern in writing (unless the parent is illiterate or has a disability that prevents compliance) to personnel of the appropriate educational agency that the child is in need of special education and related services; (2) the behavior or performance of the child demonstrates the need for such services; (3) the parent has requested an evaluation of the child; or (4) the teacher, or other personnel of the LEA, has expressed concern about the behavior or performance of the child to the director of special education or to other personnel of the agency.

If a request is made for an evaluation of a child during the time in which the child is subjected to disciplinary measures, the evaluation shall be conducted in an expedited manner. If the child is determined to have a disability, the agency shall provide special education and related services.

Referral to and Action by Law Enforcement. The legislation clarifies that nothing prohibits an agency from reporting a crime committed by a child with a disability to appropriate authorities or prevents State law enforcement and judicial authorities from exercising their responsibilities with regard to crimes committed by a child with a disability. An agency that reports a crime committed by a child with a disability must ensure that copies of the special education and disciplinary records of the child are transmitted for consideration by the authorities. (Council for Exceptional Children, 1997)

---

assure that all students can maintain visual contact with the teacher.
- Provide clear directions. Students with attention problems may be unable to follow long sets of directions with several steps. Simplify the directions and provide reinforcement when students complete each step. Avoid directions such as "Everyone return to your seat, get out your science book, turn to page 28, and answer the first five questions." Instead, start with the first step ("Everyone return to your seat") and provide reinforcement when students comply.
- Present lessons at a brisk pace. Time spent on unimportant points or skills already mastered by the group can contribute to student inattention.
- Continually monitor whether students are attending to the lesson. Be prepared to modify your instructional approach if students seem confused or inattentive or if the material is too difficult.
- Use physical proximity to encourage attention. When students start to shift attention from the task, move closer to them.
- Reduce the predictability of your actions by varying the presentation of lessons. Ask different kinds of questions, vary the intonation of your voice, and let students know that they may be asked questions at any time.
- Provide students with individual work areas in which there are few distractions. These can be cubicles, carrels, or study booths. Be sure to consider both visual and auditory distractions when selecting an appropriate place for student offices.

- Hold students accountable for attending to the lesson and learning the material presented. Periodic teacher checks of students' understanding with techniques such as random questioning can increase student involvement.
- Simplify instructional materials so that only relevant information remains. For example, pictures or drawings can be distracting in reading materials.

Organizational Skills

Some students lack the ability to plan ahead. They are unorganized and use class time poorly. Such students can miss the important parts of task directions; fail to ask appropriate questions about assignments; and neglect to bring pens, pencils, and other necessary equipment to class. At test time, they are not prepared and have difficulty using the time allotted for the test effectively. The following suggestions may help students learn to plan ahead and become more organized:

- To help students budget their time, develop a schedule that divides the class period into short segments, each a few minutes in length. Make a list of activities to be finished during each time period, and reinforce students when these tasks are completed. Gradually allow students to help in devising the daily schedule until this is an independent activity. As students learn to complete their work, make the reinforcers more difficult to earn. For example, reinforcement might be delivered only after the satisfactory completion of work for two intervals rather than one.
- State directions for assignments and classroom work clearly and concisely; include only essential information. Alert students well ahead of time to work that is due and provide older pupils with a weekly schedule of assignments.
- Assist students in organizing their materials. This may involve teaching them how to organize their desk or how to set up a notebook. Student notebooks should contain a calendar, a place for recording assignments due, and sections for notes and assignments for each subject or class; they can also hold materials such as paper, pencils, pens, and rulers. The teacher should check notebooks periodically and reinforce or reinstruct students as necessary. Parents should be informed of the notebook requirements and en-

couraged to compliment students for organizing their work.
- Present directions for assignments and classwork both verbally and in writing. Students can practice by first listening to directions and taking notes and later checking their accuracy with written directions.
- Begin with work directions that have only a few steps. Reinforce students for following each step. Gradually increase the standards for success; the time period allowed for task completion can be shortened, or the accuracy criterion raised. When students are able to follow simple directions, then introduce ones that are more complex.
- Teach students to ask appropriate questions about directions and assignments by providing a model. The model can be a demonstration by the teacher or a written set of questions to ask when a task is unclear. Allow students to practice asking questions about hypothetical assignments.
- Group students together for completing individual assignments. Reinforce the group if all members finish their work and meet the criterion for accuracy.
- Make a list of materials needed to complete an assignment, and have students assemble these before beginning work. Later, require that students prepare such a list before they start an assignment. Grade both the list and the assignment itself.
- Encourage parents to set aside quiet time—with no television, radio, or telephone—each evening for their children to study and complete assignments.
- Work with parents in setting up a home program to reinforce studying. Parents can talk with the teacher each week or sign a checksheet to report whether the student has spent the appropriate time studying at home.

Other sources of information about teaching organizational skills to special students, particularly those in middle school and high school, are *Teaching Adolescents with Mild Disabilities* by Platt and Olson (1997), *Teaching Students with Learning and Behavior Problems* (3rd ed.) by Rivera and Smith (1997), and *Teaching Students with Mild Disabilities at the Secondary Level* by Sabornie and deBettencourt (1997). Woodward (1981) also presents many useful ideas; Figure 11–3 lists Woodward's suggestions for helping secondary students learn study techniques.

FIGURE 11-3 Study Techniques for Secondary Students

1. The student should first obtain an overview of the assignment. He should begin by writing exactly the assignment task the teacher has given—is he to read? to answer questions? to outline?
2. With a definitive purpose in mind, the student can more efficiently address the task. He should write what he hopes to gain as a result of his effort so that he has a clear and concrete goal to serve as a guide.
3. The student should use the aids provided through the structure of the text. Chapter titles, subheadings, summaries are valuable to the student taking notes of "important" information. Further they provide "cues" to the student of the information that is important.
4. The next step is actually outlining or noting information in an organized manner. The teacher can assist here by asking the student to write only the information he feels is the most important and using this as a basis for comparing with the teacher's notes. (A tendency of many students is to copy verbatim or to take excessive notes without really assimilating the information.)
5. The student should attempt to summarize the material in the assignment (with the goal he has established for the reading in mind). He should ask himself the following questions: have I the necessary information to meet the goal? am I able to discuss the main points in my own words? what does this material really mean?

Note. From *Mainstreaming the Learning Disabled Adolescent* (p. 33) by D. M. Woodward, 1981, Austin, TX: PRO-ED. Copyright 1981 by PRO-ED, Inc.

Increasing Accuracy

Inaccurate responses occur for many reasons. For students with behavioral disorders, a rapid response rate is one common cause. In this instance, students work quickly, without taking time to think about their answers or check them for accuracy. In class discussions, these students may blurt out a response before carefully considering the question. Such students are characterized by the speed with which they work and the resulting high number of incorrect responses; a term used to describe this behavior is *impulsivity*. To help hasty students increase the accuracy of their work, teachers can try one of the strategies described here:

• When giving assignments, remind students that part of the task is checking for accuracy, and reinforce students for completing this step. Teachers can observe students to see whether they are checking their work, or reinforcement can be contingent upon a continual decrease in the number of errors.
• Provide reinforcement for accurate responses. For example, students might earn tokens for each correct response.
• Model appropriate proofreading procedures. Show the class examples of work containing errors, and review how to make corrections. Students may be taught to use a proofreading strategy such as COPS, in which students check Capitalization, Overall appearance, Punctuation, and Spelling (Schumaker, Nolan, & Deshler, 1985).
• Carefully design instructional materials to achieve high rates of student success, which is associated with higher levels of student learning. Poorly designed instruction leads to student frustration and poor levels of performance.
• Teach students strategies for taking tests and examinations. An example of a program to improve test-taking skills appears in Figure 11–4; teachers might also be interested in the article "Improving Test-Taking Skills of LD Adolescents" by Markel (1981).
• Encourage students to think before they speak. For example, after asking a question, require students to observe a short 5- to 10-second "thinking time" before making a response. As students learn to deliberate before answering, gradually reduce the structure of this requirement.
• Use a cognitive training technique to help students learn to direct their own problem solving. Consult "Inclusion Tips for the Teacher" on page 319 for information about the self-instructional training program described by Finch and Spirito (1980).
• Kauffman (1997) suggests that careless student errors can be reduced through the use of response cost procedures. That is, when errors are

FIGURE 11-4   How to Be a Better Test-Taker

To the Student:

If you have ever studied for a test only to find your efforts didn't pay off in a good grade because you didn't study efficiently, this packet can help. Follow the suggestions in the order presented. Read each item carefully. Review wherever you feel necessary. Begin!

1. When taking a test, don't panic! Be prepared with a pencil (with eraser), pen, and paper.
2. Carefully examine the entire test before starting to answer any questions. It is very important that you understand what you are to do in response to the test. Knowing whether the teacher wants one word answers or discussion responses, for example, makes a difference in the correctness of your response.
3. After you have looked at the number of questions and the type of response required, estimate how much time you are going to devote to each question or area. Pay particular attention to the weight each question carries. An essay question worth 25 points out of a 100 possible points must be given more time than two multiple-choice questions of 2 points each.
4. Answer first those questions you feel most confident of the answers.
5. When you are responding to an essay question, it is a good idea to write down the key ideas or main points in brief form. This will help you include everything you feel is of importance in your answer.
6. It is a good idea to try to answer all the questions in a test (unless you're told that you could be penalized for wrong answers). If you are really stumped on a question, go on to another. Sometimes another question will help you to remember the answer to the question you have been struggling with.
7. Write clearly. You are likely to lose points if the teacher has great difficulty reading your writing.
8. Leave time to reread your paper before you hand it in. Pay attention to punctuation and spelling. Most importantly, ask yourself if you wrote what you intended.
9. In objective tests, don't waste time on questions that are confusing to you.
10. Once you have made a guess to a question you are unsure of, you should not change it; first guesses are usually best.

Note. From *Mainstreaming the Learning Disabled Adolescent* (p. 35) by D. M. Woodward, 1981, Austin, TX: PRO-ED. Copyright 1981 by PRO-ED, Inc.

made, students lose something, such as part of their recess time. The procedure can be made more effective by adding a provision that students must complete an additional question or problem correctly for each error made.

• Use peer tutors to help students correct work or practice correct responses. For instance, the teacher might provide tutors with questions likely to be asked in class, and the tutor and student could then practice those questions. Tutors should be reminded to encourage students to think before they respond.

In this chapter, you have learned ways to handle disruptive behavior in the general education classroom and improve the study skills of students with behavioral disorders and others with similar needs. Techniques for teaching students with communication disorders in the general education classroom will be described next. Before proceeding, check "Things to Remember" to review strategies used to meet the needs of students identified as having behavioral disorders.

ACTIVITIES

1. Observe a student who has been identified as having behavioral disorders in a general education classroom. Describe how this student's behavior differs from that of typical class peers. How does the teacher treat this student? How do classmates react? For this student and one or two "normal" students, try to get a count of the number of positive and negative interactions with the teacher and with other students; compare your data. Look back through this chapter for intervention ideas that might be appropriate for the student. Select one and defend your choice.

2. Interview a special educator who works with students with behavioral disorders. Ask that teacher for recommendations of appropriate

Inclusion Tips for the Teacher

Self-Instructional Training

According to Finch and Spirito (1980), self-instructional training is a procedure in which students learn a step-by-step system for attacking a problem by means of specific verbalizations. That is, students learn specific strategies to talk themselves through problem situations; they themselves give the instructions.

Finch and Spirito (1980) describe the four general types of verbal messages used in the program:

1. Problem definition ("What is it I should do in this situation?")
2. Focusing of attention ("I have to concentrate and do what I'm supposed to do.")
3. Coping statements ("Even though I made a mistake, I can continue more slowly.")
4. Self-reinforcement ("Great! I did it! That was good.")

Students learn this strategy by observing the teacher, who models completion of a task using the verbalization procedures. Then the students perform the task and begin by instructing themselves out loud. Next, they perform the task using only whispered instructions. Eventually, the instructions are internalized, and students are able to direct their own problem-solving behavior.

---

techniques to use in the general education classroom. In the teacher's view, what are the important differences between students with behavioral disorders who succeed in the general education program and those who require a special class? Write a summary of your interview, and discuss any of the teacher's points with which you disagree.

3. Read two articles that discuss techniques for working with students with behavioral disorders. *Behavioral Disorders, Journal of Applied Behavior Analysis, Teaching Exceptional Children, Education and Treatment of Children, The Pointer,* and *Behavior Therapy* are journals in which such articles often appear. Carefully consider the articles you have read, and describe how these techniques could be used in a general education class.

4. Survey your local community for agencies that provide services to students with behavioral disorders. These agencies may deal with acting-out or withdrawn students, drug abuse, or suicide prevention. Local school districts or mental health organizations may be able to provide the names of some appropriate agencies. Contact two agencies and find out what types of services they offer. How do these programs differ from school programs? Are services offered to parents? In your view, how useful are these programs?

5. Presume that you have been selected to explain behavioral disorders to another teacher. Prepare an outline of your presentation, including the benefits of these students being included in the general education program. Formulate four questions that you anticipate the teacher is likely to ask, and prepare answers for these questions.

6. Watch a movie that includes information about individuals who have unusual or disordered behavior (such as *To Sir With Love, Rain Man,* or *Blackboard Jungle*). Describe their behaviors in terms that would be meaningful in planning for their educational needs. Explain how a general education teacher could accommodate a school-aged individual with similar needs in his or her classroom. What type(s) of special support or services might be needed by the student? By the teacher? Discuss any questions you would have about the feasibility and appropriateness of the placement.

Things To Remember

- The most common areas in which adaptations must be made for students with behavioral disorders are social skills and classroom behavior. Although these students usually require assistance in academic instruction, the most urgent needs are generally control of disruptive behaviors and acquisition of appropriate social and study skills.
- The major indicators of behavioral disorders are actions that deviate significantly in frequency, intensity, and duration from those expected of the student's typical peers of the same age and gender.
- Many students with behavioral disorders have academic needs that closely resemble those of students with learning disabilities and require the use of similar instructional interventions.

- Assessment of behavioral disorders is most useful when data are gathered about the current status of students' problem behaviors.
- Typical disruptive behaviors of students include tardiness, verbal outbursts and other acting-out behaviors, inappropriate physical activity, and poor social relationships.
- In the area of study skills, students with behavioral disorders experience difficulty maintaining attention, organizing work, and responding with accuracy.
- Students with behavioral disorders are capable of learning to act appropriately; their school conduct and work habits can be improved with proper instructional and behavioral management techniques.

chapter 12

Teaching Students with Communication Disorders and Autism

Cases

There are three children with communication problems in Ms. Ranson's first grade class. Despite their speech and language difficulties, these students participate in all regular class activities. Each also receives individual help twice each week from the speech-language pathologist. We will look more closely at the special education needs of two of these children—Elaine and Rocky—later in the chapter.

Elaine speaks clearly and distinctly but has difficulty producing the r sound. Because of this articulation problem, she calls her teacher Ms. Wanson.

Jeff's speech is like that of a much younger child. He mispronounces sounds, omits some, and speaks hurriedly and indistinctly. Jeff's teacher and classmates often find it difficult to understand what he is saying.

Rocky speaks intelligibly but makes many grammatical errors. He uses incomplete sentences and may mix plural nouns with singular verbs ("boys runs"). In addition, his speaking vocabulary is limited, and his knowledge of word meanings is poor for his age.

Willy stutters. He is in 10th grade and is a good student. On written reports, assignments, and exams, Willy excels. However, because of his dysfluency in speech, he is reluctant to answer questions in class, participate in discussions, or give oral reports. Willy has several close friends around whom he is comfortable speaking, but he is hesitant to talk with persons he does not know well. Although attending general education classes for all his academic work, Willy receives special education services from the speech-language pathologist. This special teacher is working with Willy to reduce his dysfluency and to overcome his embarrassment in speaking. She also consults with Willy's general education teachers to help them provide a nonthreatening classroom environment in which Willy will feel comfortable and will practice speaking in front of others.

When children enter school, they are expected to be able to communicate. This expectation may not be realized in students with speech and language impairments. Communication disorders, one of the most common of all disabilities, affect a student's ability to interact with teachers and classmates. Students with

speech problems may mispronounce words or sounds, speak with **dysfluency,** or have an unusual voice quality; as a result, their speech is difficult for the listener to understand. Students with language problems may fail to understand the speech of others and may have trouble expressing their own thoughts in words. Although communication disorders can accompany other disabilities such as learning disabilities, mental retardation, and hearing impairment, most students with speech and language impairments remain in the general education classroom. Special services are provided to them on a part-time basis by professionals such as speech-language pathologists.

The special needs of students with communication problems fall in the areas of academic and social performance. In instruction, the general education teacher may need to make minor adaptations in order to stress language, listening, and speaking skills for such students. Creating an accepting classroom environment is also important. Students with communication impairments are more likely to practice verbal interactions with others if their classmates and teacher are tolerant, accepting, and supportive.

This chapter describes the characteristics of students with communication disorders and suggests methods for the general education teacher to use in gathering data, teaching listening and speaking skills, and creating an accepting classroom environment. The last section of this chapter presents suggestions for working with students with another disability that affects communication skills: autism. To become more familiar with speech and language impairments and their impact on communication, try one of the simulations described in Table 12–1.

INDICATORS OF COMMUNICATION DISORDERS

Because students with communication disorders typically remain members of general education classrooms for their entire educational careers, the general education teacher is an important professional on the inclusion team. It is the general education teacher who notes signs of communication difficulties, refers individual students for special education assessment, helps gather assessment information, and later coordinates students' classroom instruction with special speech and language services.

Window on the Web

American Speech-Language-Hearing Association (ASHA)

http://www.asha.org

ASHA is the major professional organization in the field of communication disorders. Its website is divided into sections for three categories of visitors: Professionals, Students (and prospective students), and Consumers. The Consumer section describes ASHA's mission and the professional roles of speech-language pathologists and audiologists. It also provides online brochures on topics such as "Recognizing Communication Disorders," "Child Language," "Articulation Problems," "Stuttering," and "Voice Problems." The Student segment of this site focuses on information about careers, graduate programs, and certification. The Professional portion of the site offers choices such as Library, Professional Issues and Information, Governmental Affairs and Advocacy, Publications, and Treatment Outcomes. Also available is Technology 2000, a set of resources on the use of technology in speech-language pathology.

Note. Reprinted with permission of the American Speech-Language-Hearing Association (ASHA).

TABLE 12-1   Simulations of Speech and Language Impairments

Communication Situation	Type of Disorder	Suggested Simulation
You are speaking to a group of teachers and parents. Describe the instructional program in your classroom.	Delayed speech	Deliver your speech without talking. You may gesture.
You have just met your new principal. Introduce yourself and welcome him or her to your school.	Articulation	Introduce yourself after you have placed one or two saltine crackers in your mouth. Don't chew.
You are reporting to the school board about the new parent involvement program at your school.	Poor voice quality	Tape record your speech and then play it back at the wrong speed.
You are chatting with the parents of several of your students about the upcoming school play.	Dysfluency or stuttering	S-say th-the f-first s-sound o-of e-each w-word, th-then th-the w-word i-itself.

Inclusion Tips for the Teacher

Recognizing Speech Impairments

Perhaps the best way to determine whether a person has a speech problem is to ask yourself the following questions:

1. *Can I understand this person?* This is the simplest judgment you will have to make. If you cannot understand or can understand only with difficulty what a person is saying, she has a communication disorder.

2. *Does this person sound strange?* If you can understand someone, but he doesn't sound like you expect him to, he has a problem. An adult who sounds like Elmer Fudd, a 200-pound adult male who sounds like a nine-year-old girl, and a person who has a flat, expressionless manner of speaking all have communication problems.

3. *Does this person have any peculiar physical characteristics when speaking?* A person who has distracting mannerisms that interfere with his message has a problem. These mannerisms might include unnecessary or unexpected movements of the lips, tongue, nostrils, arms, legs, or posture.

4. *Is the communication in a style inappropriate to the situation?* We do not expect the president of the United States to greet Congress before his annual State of the Union address by saying, "Hey, baby, what's happenin'? It's cool at my pad, what's goin' down here?". . . . Our point is that we normally shift our style of communication to fit a given situation. A speaker unable to do this may have a problem.

5. *Do I enjoy listening to this speaker?* This is a judgment we all feel comfortable making. If the reason we don't enjoy a speaker is that we don't like her message, the speaker doesn't have a problem. If, on the other hand, we don't enjoy a speaker for one of the reasons mentioned here, she probably does have a problem. . . . Speakers who can alienate people merely by introducing themselves need help.

6. *Is the speaker damaging his communication mechanisms?* Like most other parts of the body, the organs used in communication can be misused. Although diagnoses of physiological abuse can only be made by specialists, listeners can often detect signs of strain in a speaker. Teachers should always refer to professionals children they think may be injuring their voices. An unnecessary referral hurts no one, but overlooking a symptom can have disastrous consequences.

7. *Does the speaker suffer when attempting to communicate?* This is difficult to judge, because a listener cannot usually determine how a person feels about her efforts to communicate. Many people considered normal communicators by their peers suffer emotionally as a result of shortcomings they imagine. Communication problems such as these that do not have obvious symptoms are among the most difficult to treat.

Note. From *An Introduction to Special Education* (2nd ed.) by William H. Berdine and Edward Blackhurst. Copyright © 1985 by William H. Berdine and A. Edward Blackhurst. Reprinted by permission of Addison Wesley Educational Publishers, Inc.

Communication disorders are of two types: those that affect language and those that affect speech. **Language** is the ability to communicate using symbols; it includes both oral and written communication and requires both expression and reception of ideas. **Speech** is one aspect of oral language; it is the vehicle by which thoughts are expressed in oral communication.

According to the American Speech-Language-Hearing Association (ASHA) (n.d.), language and speech disorders can be differentiated as follows:

A *language disorder* is characterized by an inability to use the symbols of language through (a) proper use of words and their meanings, (b) appropriate grammatical patterns, and (c) proper use of speech sounds.

A *speech disorder* is characterized by difficulty in (a) producing speech sounds (articulation), (b) maintaining speech rhythm (fluent speech), and (c) controlling vocal production (voice). (p. 1, italics added)

The National Information Center for Children and Youth with Disabilities (1997b) includes as characteristics of language disorders "improper use of words and their meanings, inability to express ideas, inappropriate grammatical patterns, reduced vocabulary, and inability to follow directions" (p. 1). Thus, students with language disorders experience difficulty understanding or expressing ideas appropriate to their age. Those with speech impairments show poor speech sound production, fluency, or voice quality for their age.

Most speech problems are detected at an early age; articulation disorders are most commonly found among children in the first few grades of school. Language disorders are also identified in young children but can persist throughout the elementary and secondary years. Speech disorders are usually obvious to the listener. In fact, Van Riper (1978) maintains that one criterion for identifying a communication disorder is speech unusual enough to bring attention to itself. *Unusual,* however, is not a very precise description of a possible problem. The questions in "Inclusion Tips for the Teacher" can assist in obtaining more specific information.

ASSESSMENT PROCEDURES

When communication disorders are suspected, the assessment team meets to prepare an assessment plan. One important consideration is the student's hearing; the school nurse is consulted to determine whether a hearing loss is contributing to poor speech or language performance. If the problem appears to be a minor speech disorder, the speech-language pathologist takes primary responsibility for assessment. If more serious difficulties are suspected, several specialists participate in gathering assessment information. Formal assessment begins when the parents of the referred student have given written consent.

In evaluating a student's speech, the speech-language pathologist can administer a standardized measure such as the *Goldman-Fristoe Test of Articulation* (Goldman & Fristoe, 1986). The specialist also talks with the student in an informal setting in order to evaluate speech fluency and voice quality. The classroom teacher may be asked to contribute observations concerning the usual speech patterns of the student.

Figure 12–1 presents a checklist that the teacher may use to evaluate the speech of young elementary children. Voice quality, speech fluency, and sound production are included. The checklist also provides

the ages at which students are expected to produce the various speech sounds; these are general guidelines and should be used with caution when evaluating the performance of an individual child.

Most children have mastered the sounds of the English language by the age of 8. Some, however, progress more slowly. Consider Elaine, the first grader introduced at the beginning of this chapter who has yet to master the *r* sound. Her articulation error is one of substitution; she replaces the *r* sound with the *w* sound. Other types of articulation errors are omissions, distortions, and additions of sounds.

The assessment of language disorders requires the expertise of several disciplines. In addition to the general education teacher and the speech-language pathologist, the assessment team may include the school nurse, an audiologist or other specialist in the detection of hearing losses, the school psychologist, and the special education teacher. The student is evaluated in many areas: hearing, intellectual performance, academic achievement, and language skills.

Language assessment typically focuses on both reception and expression. The student's ability to receive and understand information from language is evaluated; likewise, the student's skill in using the symbols of language to express thoughts is assessed. One standardized measure that looks at both of these dimensions is the *Test of Language Development-Primary* (3rd ed.) (Newcomer & Hammill, 1997), an individual test appropriate for students aged 4 to 9. This test assesses three important features of language: **semantics,** the meaningful aspects of language; **syntax,** the grammatical aspects of language; and **phonology,** the sound system of language.

Figure 12–2 on page 329 presents a portion of the assessment report for Rocky, the first grader with grammar and vocabulary problems who was described at the beginning of this chapter. The results of the *Test of Language Development-Primary* show that Rocky understands language well but has difficulty in expression, particularly in semantics and syntax.

Many other measures are available to the speech-language pathologist or special education teacher responsible for language assessment. Examples include the *Test of Language Development-Intermediate* (3rd ed.) (Hammill & Newcomer, 1997) for students aged 8 to 13, the *Clinical Evaluation of Language Fundamentals-3* (Semel, Wiig, & Secord,

FIGURE 12-1   Speech Checklist

Student _____ Age _____ Grade _____
Teacher _____ Date of Evaluation _____

1. **Voice Quality** (check all that are appropriate)
   The student's *usual* voice quality is
   ____ pleasant to listen to   ____ monotone
   ____ unpleasant to listen to   ____ very high-pitched
   ____ hoarse or husky   ____ very low-pitched
   ____ like a whisper   ____ very loud
   ____ nasal   ____ very soft

2. **Speech Fluency** (check one)
   The student's *usual* speech is
   ____ very fluent
   ____ generally fluent with occasional hesitations, repetitions, and/or prolongations of sounds and syllables
   ____ frequently dysfluent and characterized by hesitations, repetitions, and/or prolongations of sounds and syllables

3. **Sound Production** (check each sound that the student *usually* produces clearly and correctly)*
   Sounds expected by age 5[†]
   ____ /p/ as in *pal*   ____ /g/ as in *goat*   ____ /n/ as in *not*   ____ /t/ as in *tap*
   ____ /m/ as in *map*   ____ /d/ as in *dog*   ____ /b/ as in *ball*   ____ /ng/ as in *ring*
   ____ /f/ as in *fat*   ____ /h/ as in *hit*   ____ /k/ as in *kill*   ____ /y/ as in *year*
   Sounds expected by age 6[†]
   ____ /r/ as in *rag*   ____ /l/ as in *lad*
   Sounds expected by age 7[†]
   ____ /ch/ as in *church*   ____ /sh/ as in *ship*   ____ /j/ as in *junk*
   ____ /th/ (voiceless) as in *thank*
   Sounds expected by age 8[†]
   ____ /s/ as in *son*   ____ /z/ as in *zoo*   ____ /v/ as in *very*
   ____ /th/ (voiced) as in *this*
   Sounds expected after age 8[†]
   ____ /zh/ as in *azure* or *pleasure*

* Only consonant sounds are listed because most children are able to produce vowel and diphthong sounds upon entry to school.
[†] Age norms derived from Sander (1972).

1995) for students aged 6 to 21, and the *Test of Adolescent and Adult Language-3* (Hammill, Brown, Larsen, & Wiederholt, 1994) for individuals aged 12 to 25. These measures concentrate on semantics, syntax, and phonology.

To assess the fourth dimension of language, pragmatics, professionals often rely on informal procedures. **Pragmatics** is the use of language, that is, how language functions in the various situations in which communication occurs. Clearly, language use varies according to the purpose of communication, audience, and setting. For example, when the message to be communicated is that today's homework has not been completed, the language a student uses to communicate that message to the teacher is likely to differ from that used with a classmate.

In addition, a student's parents and general education teacher are valuable sources of information about language performance. These team members have observed the student over long time periods and can comment on the student's usual facility with language tasks. By observing typical classroom activities, the teacher can gather data about the student's performance of language skills such as

- understanding oral directions,
- speaking in complete sentences,

FIGURE 12-2   **Special Education Assessment Results**

Student: Rocky   **Age:** 6 years, 2 months   **Grade:** 1

Classroom Performance
Ms. Ranson, Rocky's first grade teacher, reported that Rocky is experiencing difficulty in classroom language tasks. According to Ms. Ranson's observations, Rocky appears to be a bright child but one who has not yet learned the grammatical rules and vocabulary expected of a first grade student. Rocky's progress in math is adequate, but he makes mistakes in oral reading that reflect his problems with grammar. Also, he has difficulty expressing his thoughts when speaking in class and in play situations with the other children.

Hearing
Results of a routine hearing screening at the beginning of the school year indicated that Rocky's hearing is adequate.

Intellectual Performance
Mr. Scott, the school psychologist, administered the *Wechsler Intelligence Scale for Children-Third Edition* to Rocky. All subtest and IQ scores were within the average range, which indicates adequate intellectual performance.

Oral Language Skills
To learn more about Rocky's oral language skills, Mrs. Putnam, the speech-language pathologist, administered the *Test of Language Development-Primary* to Rocky. This test includes measures of both receptive and expressive language. On the receptive language tests, Rocky scored within the average range; he shows adequate skills in understanding the semantic, syntactical, and phonological aspects of language.

Expressive language tasks were more difficult for Rocky, as the following results indicate. (Average performance is indicated by standard scores of 85 to 115.)

Language Area	Subtest	Standard Score
Expressive Semantics	Oral Vocabulary	78
Expressive Syntax	Sentence Imitation	80
Expressive Syntax	Grammatic Completion	76
Expressive Phonology	Word Articulation	95

Expressive phonology, assessed by the Word Articulation subtest, was within the average range. However, other expressive skills fell within the low average range of performance. Rocky's major areas of need are expressive semantics and syntax. Rocky's oral vocabulary is more typical of a 4- or 5-year-old child than a first grader, and his command of grammatical structures is limited for his age.

- using age-appropriate vocabulary in oral communication, and
- using correct grammar in speech.

SPECIAL SERVICES

As with all individuals with disabilities, the special services provided to students with communication disorders depend on the severity and extent of the students' educational needs. For many students with speech problems, only minor educational adaptations are necessary. Such students are members of general education classrooms and fully capable of participation in instructional activities. They leave the classroom only for short periods of time to receive special services from the speech-language pathologist on a daily or weekly basis. Elaine, the first grader introduced earlier, is an example of a student with a speech disorder who is successfully included in general education. Elaine's problem was identified early in her school career, and she is receiving the special help she needs to overcome her problem.

For Your Information

Students with Communication Disorders

- It is estimated that students with communication disorders make up about 2% of the school-aged population. Communication disorders are the second most prevalent disability, accounting for approximately one-fifth of the students served by special education (U.S. Department of Education, 1997a).
- The most typical types of communication disorders in school-aged children are articulation problems and language impairments (Heward, 1996; Smith, 1998).
- Speech and language problems are most often found in young children. The prime time for identification of communication disorders is the first and second grades.
- Expectations for communication skills are related to the age of the child. For example, young preschool children are expected to pass through a developmental stage in which dysfluencies are

common (American Speech-Language-Hearing Association, 1997; Swift, 1988).
- The great majority of school-aged children with communication disorders remain in general education, and only a very few receive special services in a special class or school; in 1994–1995, 95% of students with speech or language impairments were educated in the general education classroom for the majority of the school day (U.S. Department of Education, 1997a).
- Every child and adult who speaks makes articulation errors, and everyone's speech at one time or another is marked by dysfluencies. Deviations in speech are considered communication disorders only when they become frequent and severe enough to interfere with the ability to communicate.
- Speech characterized by an accent or dialect is different but is *not* considered disordered.

FIGURE 12-3   IEP Goals and Services for Rocky

Annual Goals
1. By the end of the school year, Rocky will speak in grammatically correct sentences with agreement in number between subjects and verbs.
   Person responsible: Speech-language pathologist
2. By the end of the school year, Rocky will increase his speaking vocabulary by at least 100 words.
   Person responsible: Speech-language pathologist
3. Rocky will successfully complete all requirements for first grade reading, language arts, math, and other academic subjects.
   Person responsible: First grade teacher

Amount of Participation in General Education
Rocky will attend the general education first grade class for all academic instruction.

Special Education and Related Services
1. Rocky will receive special education services from the speech-language pathologist (annual goals 1 and 2) for 30 minutes daily.
2. The speech-language pathologist will provide consultation to Rocky's first grade teacher as necessary.

Other types of communication disorders may require more extensive special programming. Rocky, the first grader with difficulty in expressive language, requires special help to learn better language skills. Figure 12–3 shows that his IEP goals focus on improvement of expressive vocabulary and grammar. However, Rocky remains with his first grade class for instruction in all academic subjects.

Some students with communication disorders also have social needs. Because of their speech or language problems, they have difficulty interacting with others and may feel isolated or disliked. Willy, the 10th grade student described at the beginning of this chapter, is keenly aware of his dysfluent speech and, as a result, remains silent throughout most of the school day. The IEP for Willy stresses not only more fluent speech but also an increased number of interactions with teachers and classmates.

The general education classroom is the most typical placement for students with speech and language impairments. If communication problems are related to other disabilities such as learning disabilities, resource services may be provided. If more severe disabilities such as mental retardation or hearing impairment are present, the intensive services available in a special class setting may be needed. Most students, however, remain in the general education classroom and receive special services only on a part-time basis. The general education teacher provides all academic instruction and receives consultant help from the speech-language pathologist as necessary. To learn more about individuals with communication disorders, consult "For Your Information."

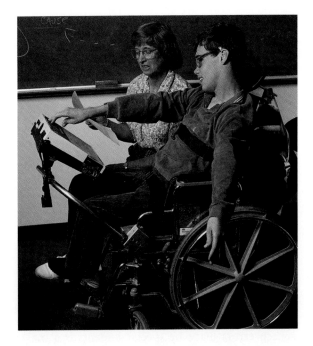

CLASSROOM ADAPTATIONS

The general education teacher usually does not have to make major classroom adaptations in order to meet the special needs of students with communication disorders. Even though characterized by speech or language problems, these students are generally able to participate in all aspects of the general education curriculum. Special attention is needed in only two areas: speech and language skills and social acceptance.

Students with speech impairments may need to improve articulation, voice quality, or fluency. To meet these needs, an individualized special education program is provided by the speech-language pathologist. The major goal in the general education classroom becomes practice of oral communication. Students require a nonthreatening environment in which to try out the new speech skills they are learning in their special education program. By collaborating with the speech-language pathologist, the general education teacher can target these skills for reinforcement in the general education classroom. The classroom teacher assists by encouraging the students' participation and ensuring that their attempts at oral communication are accepted with tolerance and support by classmates.

Students with language impairments experience difficulty in the reception and expression of oral communication. Again, although the speech-language pathologist takes primary responsibility for instruction in the areas of educational need, students should have opportunities within the general education classroom to practice the new language skills they are learning. The general education teacher also assists by modeling appropriate grammar, stressing vocabulary development in all curriculum areas, and modifying the language aspects of classroom activities and assignments.

The following sections include methods for teaching students with communication disorders, ways to encourage practice of oral communication by students with speech disorders, and suggestions for teaching language skills to students with grammar and vocabulary needs.

ENCOURAGING ORAL COMMUNICATION

For students with speech impairments, the general education classroom should be a place where they can hear correct speech and feel comfortable enough to practice their newly learned communication skills. In order to accomplish this, the general education teacher must provide good speech models, an accepting environment, and opportunities for practicing oral communication skills.

Students with special needs require good models of oral communication. The teacher is the primary model and should be careful to speak clearly, fluently, and with appropriate articulation. Classmates are also able to help. By demonstrating appropriate speech, they, too, serve as important models for special students.

How the teacher and classroom peers react to speech errors made by special students is a major factor in encouraging oral communication. It is crucial that the communication attempts of students with speech disorders be treated with respect and tolerance. If the teacher and peers are accepting listeners, then special students will feel comfortable enough to practice oral communication. Guidelines for establishing a tolerant classroom climate are identified here:

- When students with speech problems speak, the teacher should listen with full attention and ensure that other students listen.
- Speech errors should not be criticized by teacher or classmates. However, the teacher may wish to demonstrate correct speech for the student by repeating what was said. For example, if the student says, "The story was about a wittle wabbit," the teacher might say, "Right! The story was about a little rabbit."
- The teacher should not call attention to speech errors. If the teacher accepts misarticulations and dysfluencies and attends to the content of what the student is saying, peers are more likely to do the same. This approach is particularly important with dysfluency problems that may become much more serious if attention is called to them.
- Peers should not be allowed to ridicule or make fun of speech errors. The teacher should make it clear that this is not appropriate behavior. One

way to help peers understand the problems of special students is by using simulations. Table 12–1 on page 325 presented ways to experience simulated oral communication problems.
- The teacher should take care when placing students with speech problems in situations in which their communication difficulties might interfere. For example, if class members are reading tongue twisters aloud, "six silly snakes" should be reserved for the student who can articulate the *s* sound. In other words, the teacher should carefully consider which oral classroom activities are appropriate to assign to students unsure of their communication abilities or embarrassed by speaking.
- Changing the nature of the communication situation can sometimes improve stuttering problems. Shames and Ramig (1994) report that dysfluencies often decrease (or, in some cases, disappear) when students sing, read aloud in unison with another person, whisper, speak in a monotone, speak in a higher or lower pitch than usual, or speak in time to a metronome.
- For some students with communication problems, speech is slow and labored. A stutterer may take a long time to produce a single sentence, a student with cerebral palsy may make facial grimaces as he or she struggles to articulate each word, and a person who communicates by means of a communication board or an electronic communication aid may require several seconds to select the message he or she wants to convey to the listener. Such students require patient listeners. Attempts to hurry them will likely result in slower, not faster, communication; finishing their sentences for them will discourage and frustrate them further.

The teacher should model appropriate listening skills for the class as well as attempt to sensitize students to the need to wait quietly and listen while others speak. In some situations, the teacher may want to speed communication by phrasing questions to students with speech problems so that only short responses are required. In other situations, these students should be encouraged to express their thoughts and opinions more fully. See "Spotlight on Technology" for more information on alternative methods of communication such as communication boards and electronic communication devices.

Spotlight on Technology

Augmentative Communication

When students do not talk or their speech is not intelligible, an **augmentative communication** system may be used to increase their ability to communicate. There are many types of augmentative communication systems. For example, if you have a cold and find it difficult to talk, you might augment your usual means of communication by using more gestures or even writing notes rather than speaking. In classrooms, two types of systems are used most often with students with communication disorders: communication boards and electronic communication devices.

Communication Boards

Communication boards are considered a "low" technology. According to Lewis (1993),

> A communication board can be as simple as a piece of paper or cardboard with two photographs pasted on it, or as elaborate as a notebook filled with pages of messages for a variety of different communication situations. The essential elements are the "board" itself, which may be composed of paper or a sturdier material, and the choices depicted on the board by photos, drawings, or some kind of symbol system. (p. 383)

Note. The Picture Communication Symbols © 1981–1998 used with permission from the Mayer-Johnson Company, P.O. Box 1579, Solana Beach, CA 92075, 619-550-0084 (phone), 619-550-0449 (fax), and Mayerj@aol.com (e-mail).

To use a communication board, the student simply points to one of the choices. For some students, all choices are depicted by photos or drawings. Other students are able to use communication boards with letters, words, and phrases.

Computers can be used to make communication boards with programs such as *Boardmaker* from Mayer-Johnson Company (www.mayer-johnson.com). This program contains more than 3,000 picture symbols from the Mayer-Johnson Picture Communication Symbol collection (Johnson, 1981, 1985, 1992). *Boardmaker* is easy to use. As the sample communication board shown here illustrates, it is possible to select symbols from several categories: social, verbs, feelings, food, and so on. The teacher has full control over the choice of symbols included on the board and the number and size of the symbols. Boards can be printed in black and white or color, and the print labels accompanying each symbol are available in 11 languages.

continued

Electronic Communication Devices

Electronic communication devices "talk." Because of this capability, they are sometimes called *voice output communication aids,* or VOCAs. Some electronic devices use prerecorded speech, others contain speech synthesizers, and still others use both technologies.

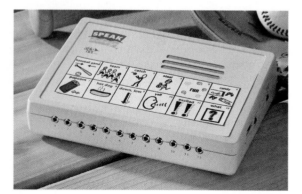

The SpeakEasy from AbleNet, shown here, is an example of an inexpensive VOCA. On its surface are 12 touch-sensitive "keys"; the student presses a key to play back a prerecorded message. Each key is covered by a photo, drawing, word, or phrase that illustrates its message. The SpeakEasy can store up to 4 minutes and 20 seconds of prerecorded speech, and it is very easy to record new mes-

Note. Photo courtesy of AbleNet Inc.

sages. Thus, as students move from one activity to another during the school day, the teacher (or a peer) could replace the messages needed for math class with those needed for science.

Devices such as the SpeakEasy, although inexpensive, may not be appropriate for a more advanced student because they can store only a limited number of messages. More sophisticated (and more expensive)

In addition to providing good speech models and an accepting environment, the classroom teacher should ensure that students with speech impairments have frequent opportunities to practice their communication skills. McCormick (1986) recommends that practice take place in a variety of contexts throughout the school day. Oral communication can be incorporated into most areas of the curriculum. Whether the subject is reading, math, or social studies, students can practice speaking with the teacher, in small work groups, and during class discussions. Lunchtime, work breaks, and recess create natural opportunities for socialization and talking with others, as do many free-time activities in the classroom. Culatta and Culatta (1993) provide these suggestions for creating communication opportunities:

- Do not anticipate needs. A child who is given paper without crayons or who is provided with only a small amount of juice at a time is encountering the need to communicate.
- Arrange for unusual or novel events to occur. A child who sees a box of cereal taped to the wall is

likely to want to share that event and seek information about it. Language can also be evoked by engaging in such actions as "inadvertently" throwing away toys, wearing clothes that are too big, and trying to eat soup with a fork.
- Arrange for the child to convey information to others. In the cafeteria the child may be asked to direct others to their seats, describe the menu, convey the location of utensils, and report the acceptability of the food to the cook. Many opportunities to convey experiences to others can be created throughout the day.
- Provide the child with choices. During a snack activity, the child can decide what to drink, where to sit, whether to use a napkin or a paper plate, and who should be responsible for cleaning up. Each decision requires communication. (pp. 251–252)

An important goal of any inclusion program is the participation of special students in as many classroom activities as possible. For students with speech problems, both social and academic activities should be considered. One way to promote acceptance while maximizing communication opportunities is to seat the student with special needs in the midst of several typical peers. In traditional devices may be required. These are available from companies such as Prentke Romich Company (www.prentrom.com), Sentient Systems Technology, Inc. (www.sentient-sys.com), Words+, Inc. (www.words-plus.com), and Zygo Industries, Inc.

Examples are the DynaVox 2 and Dynavox 2c from Sentient Systems. These augmentative communication devices offer synthesized speech. The screen display on the Dynavox 2 is in black and white; that of the 2c is in color. Users can touch the screen to make selections, and the choices shown can be customized to fit individual needs. The display is dynamic; once one choice is made, the screen changes and other choices appear.

Note. Photo courtesy of Sentient Systems Technology, Inc.

To learn more about augmentative communication, visit the Assistive Technology On-Line website (www.asel.udel.edu/at-online). This site is sponsored by the Applied Science and Engineering Laboratories of duPont Hospital for Children and the University of Delaware.

classrooms, students with special needs are usually seated near the teacher in an arrangement that does not encourage student interaction (see Figure 12–4). Instead, the classroom environment should be modified so that the student is surrounded by good speech models and has natural opportunities for communication.

TEACHING LANGUAGE SKILLS

Students with language impairments receive individualized help from the speech-language pathologist. They may require assistance in the development of receptive language skills and/or expressive language skills; instruction focuses on the area of need, whether it be grammatical constructions (syntax) or vocabulary development (semantics). The general education teacher can help students with language problems by modeling appropriate grammar, by helping expand their listening and speaking vocabularies, and by modifying classroom activities and assignments that require language skills.

For students with difficulty in the area of syntax, the classroom teacher must provide a consistent model of grammatically correct speech. The teacher should correct students' grammatical errors by demonstrating the proper construction. If, for instance, a student comments, "It's funner to swim than to water ski," the teacher can respond, "It's more fun to swim? Why?" With this approach, the student hears the grammatically correct version of the statement without being criticized for poor language.

Some students with language disorders need help in vocabulary development. They may not be familiar with the words their classmates and teachers use; they may fail to express themselves in the vocabulary expected of their age level. The classroom teacher can help these special students increase their receptive and expressive vocabularies by following these suggestions:

• Encourage students to ask about the meanings of words they do not understand.
• Use demonstration to teach the meanings of some words. Because prepositions and action verbs are often hard to explain in words, *show* students their meanings.

FIGURE 12-4   Traditional and Modified Classroom Environments

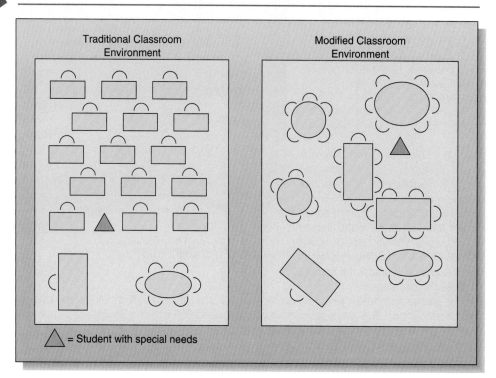

Note. Adapted with permission of Merrill, an imprint of Macmillan Publishing Company, from *Language Arts for the Mildly Handicapped* (pp. 201, 203) by S. B. Cohen and S. P. Plaskon. Copyright © 1980 Merrill Publishing Company, Columbus, Ohio.

- Use definitions, explanations, and examples to teach other words. For example, define *container* as something that holds something else; then give examples of objects that are containers and objects that are not.
- Provide multiple examples of word meanings. For example, if students are learning the word *break,* they might "break cookies and crackers, encounter objects that keep falling apart, break spaghetti in order to glue the pieces on a picture, and break carrot sticks for lunch" (Culatta & Culatta, 1993, p. 252).
- Include vocabulary instruction in all curriculum areas. Teach the meanings of new reading words, new math terms, and new vocabulary in science, social studies, and art.
- Teach students to use regular or picture dictionaries to discover the meanings of unfamiliar words.
- Give students opportunities throughout the school day to practice the new vocabulary they are learning.

In addition to helping students with language impairments acquire correct grammar and new word meanings, the general education teacher may need to make adaptations in classroom activities and assignments. With students who have difficulty listening with understanding, directions for school tasks should be brief, to the point, and in simple language. With students who find it hard to express themselves, questions that require a yes or no response are easier to answer than open-ended questions. For example, "Is the platypus a mammal?" may be an easier question for a student with language disorders than "What type of animal is the platypus?"

Some students may require direct instruction in listening skills. Bauwens and Hourcade (1989) suggest teaching the LISTEN strategy to improve students' ability to attend and listen to oral directions. *LISTEN* is an acronym for a six-step procedure: "Look, Idle your motor, Sit up straight, Turn to me, Engage your brain, Now . . ." (p. 61). The teacher

Inclusion Tips for the Teacher

When Students Leave the Classroom for Special Services

Many students with special needs leave the general education classroom for a short time each day to visit a special education teacher. While they are gone, the activities of the classroom continue. When they return, they may feel lost, confused, and unsure of what they should be doing. To help students reenter the classroom and regain their bearings quickly and easily, try these suggestions:

1. Work with the special education teacher to arrange the best time for each student to leave the classroom. Usually, it is better for students to receive special education services when their class is working on
   * independent practice rather than direct instruction
   * the student's best rather than worst subject
   * the student's least liked rather than favorite activity
2. Maintain a regular daily schedule so that you and the student know what will be missed each day.

3. Help the student take responsibility for leaving the classroom for special education services at the appropriate time. One method is to provide the student with a drawing of a clock showing the time to leave.
4. Arrange a communication system so that when the student returns, he or she knows how to find out what to do. The student might
   * go directly to the teacher for instructions
   * look for a note on the board
   * check in the work folder on his or her desk
   * consult a classmate who has been assigned as a buddy
5. Do not penalize the student for leaving the class for special education help. Avoid scheduling treats and special activities during the time the student is out of the room. Do not double the workload by requiring the student to keep up with the current class activity as well as make up what was missed during his or her absence.

models this strategy, and students practice it to mastery. The goal is for students to internalize the strategy so that they follow each step automatically whenever the teacher says, "Listen."

Older students may benefit from instruction in the skills needed for listening to lectures in content area classes. One activity for developing these skills uses tape recordings of news broadcasts (Forster & Doyle, 1989). The teacher prepares an outline of the news items, including major points but leaving space for students to add supporting details; the outline also lists background concepts and vocabulary with which students may be unfamiliar. Students begin the activity by reviewing the outline, and the teacher explains any terms or concepts that students do not recognize or understand. As students listen to the tape, they underline key points on the outline and add details. Students have the opportunity to ask questions before taking a quiz on the information presented in the news broadcast.

The general education teacher plays an important role in the education of students with communication disorders. When these students are provided with a classroom environment that encourages the learning and practice of speech and language skills, their chances for successful performance in school (and in life) increase. Many speech and language problems are developmental in nature; they appear in young children and, with maturation and appropriate treatment, may disappear. The special education program is only part of the appropriate treatment for students with communication disorders. Another important component is the instruction and support received from the teacher in the general education classroom.

Students who leave the classroom to visit the speech-language pathologist or resource teacher may return to discover that the class has moved on to a different activity. To help these students feel more a part of their classroom, see "Inclusion Tips for the Teacher."

Window on the Web

Autism Society of America

http://www.autism-society.org

Founded in 1965, the Autism Society is an organization of parents and others interested in autism. The mission of the society is to increase public awareness about this condition and to provide support to individuals with autism, their families, and professionals who work with them. The Autism Society website is a rich collection of resources with basic information about the condition ("What is Autism?"), information for families with newly diagnosed children ("Getting Started"), articles and resources for education ("Educating Children with Autism"), and an "Autism Checklist." The site provides online Information Packages on topics such as Educational Rights, Early Intervention, Challenging Behaviors, and Employment and Adults with Autism. Also available are a glossary of terms and abbreviations and news about current legislation, lobbying, and advocacy efforts.

SPECIAL CONSIDERATIONS FOR STUDENTS WITH AUTISM

Autism is usually considered a severe disability, and many students with autism have special needs in a number of areas, including communication. Some children with autism are nonverbal. Others have echolalic speech; that is, they repeat the words of other speakers. When students with autism are included in general education classrooms, special educators and other professionals should be available to assist the classroom teacher in adapting instruction and, when necessary, developing alternative learning activities.

Autism was recognized as a separate disability category in the 1990 Individuals with Disabilities Education Act. That law defined autism as "a developmental disability significantly affecting verbal and nonverbal communication and social interaction, generally evident before age 3 . . ." The Autism Society of America (1996) describes several areas that may be affected by autism:

- *Communication:* language develops slowly or not at all; use of words without attaching meaning to them; communicates with gestures instead of words; short attention spans
- *Social interaction:* spends time alone rather than with others; shows little interest in making friends; less responsive to social cues such as eye contact or smiles
- *Sensory impairment:* unusual reactions to physical sensations such as being overly sensitive to touch or underresponsive to pain; sight, hearing, touch, pain, smell, taste may be affected to a lesser or greater degree
- *Play:* lack of spontaneous or imaginative play; does not imitate others' actions; doesn't initiate pretend games
- *Behaviors:* may be overactive or very passive; throws frequent tantrums for no apparent reason; may perseverate on a single item, idea, or person; apparent lack of common sense; may show aggressive or violent behavior or injure self.

Autism is a low-incidence disability. In 1995–1996, special education served 22,827 students with autism, only .05% of the total school-age population (U.S. Department of Education, 1997a).

Inclusion Tips for the Teacher

A Teacher's Advice for Working with Students with Autism

- *Don't let the behavior overwhelm you.* Develop a behavior-management plan and implement small steps. Decide what you will put up with and what behaviors must stop, and target those.
- *Systematically expect more and more of the student.* At first the student might only be required to sit with the class with whatever it takes (a favorite object), then the student may be required to hold the reading book.
- *Develop a picture and word schedule for daily activities.* Use this to prepare the student for transitions to new activities. Introduce changes in routine slowly, and let the student know in advance that these changes are going to occur.
- *Talk to the student's parents and other teachers,* and find out what works and what does not work with this student.
- *Use peers to help redirect the student's behavior* and to interest him or her in the task.
- *Take "ownership" of the student* so that he or she feels like a real member of the class.

Note. From *Teaching Mainstreamed, Diverse, and At-Risk Students in the General Education Classroom* by S. Vaughn, C. S. Bos, and J. S. Schumm (p. 220). Copyright © 1997 by Allyn & Bacon. Reprinted with permission.

Vaughn, Bos, and Schumm (1997) describe the experiences of Robert Hernandez, a fourth grade teacher who worked with a student with autism in his classroom. "Inclusion Tips for the Teacher" presents Mr. Hernandez's words of advice to other general educators.

Wood, Lazzari, and Reeves (1993) offer these suggestions for working with students with autism in general education settings:

- Structure the learning environment so that it is predictable and consistent. This includes the physical structure of the classroom as well as routines, schedules, and teacher behavior.
- Design instructional programs to provide ways to help children learn to communicate. Remember that verbal communication is but one way to communicate; provide students with alternatives such as signing, writing, using the computer or facilitated communication. . . .
- Since students with autism have difficulty managing their own behavior without structure, develop individual and group behavior plans that stress positive behavior management and set forth clear instructions, rules, and consequences. . . .
- Work closely with the family to ensure consistency between school and home and other settings in approaches, methods of interaction, and response to students. (p. 115)

The second suggestion of Wood et al. mentions several alternative modes of communication. One of these, **facilitated communication,** is a controversial technique developed in Australia by Rosemary Crossley and popularized in the United States by Douglas Biklen (1990). In facilitated communication, the nonverbal person points to letters or types while another individual, the facilitator, provides some type of physical support. For example, the facilitator may help the nonverbal person isolate his or her index finger for pointing; hold the hand, wrist, forearm, or elbow of the nonverbal person; and then help the nonverbal person move his or her arm away from the letterboard or keyboard after a selection has been made (Lehr, 1992).

Biklen and his associates provide numerous examples of the successful use of facilitated communication with students identified as autistic and others without verbal communication skills. For example, Biklen and Schubert (1991) report the results of one study in which 18 of 21 students were able to produce sentences via facilitated communication. In their writings, students "revealed unexpected literacy, typing, for example, 'IM NOT RETARDED' . . ." (Biklen, Morton, Gold, Berrigan, & Swaminathan, 1992, p. 5).

However, facilitated communication is a controversial technique that has received much criticism (e.g., Prior & Cummins, 1992). As Calculator (1992) comments, "This communication technique remains one that is characterized by its ambiguity (e.g., lack

Things to Remember

- The primary areas of need for students with communication disorders are speech and language; because of their communication difficulties these students may also require assistance in social interactions.
- Major indicators of speech impairments are misarticulations of speech sounds, dysfluent speech, and unusual voice quality.
- Major indicators of language impairments are problems in reception or expression of grammatical constructions and vocabulary.
- In assessment of communication disorders, information is gathered about a possible hearing loss, current performance in speech and language, and, for serious problems, general intellectual performance.
- Students with communication disorders receive individualized special education from the speech-language pathologist. These students remain in the general education class and take part in special services for only short periods each day or several times each week.

- Major instructional adaptations are usually not necessary to accommodate the needs of students with communication disorders in the general education classroom.
- For students with speech impairments, the general education teacher provides an accepting classroom environment in which students can feel comfortable practicing newly acquired communication skills.
- For students with language impairments, the classroom teacher assists their acquisition of language skills by modeling appropriate grammar and helping them expand their listening and speaking vocabularies. Classroom activities and assignments that require language skills may need to be modified.
- Students with autism have challenging communication needs; when these students are members of general education classrooms, teachers should receive support from special educators and other professionals.

of specific teaching principles), mystique, recurring anecdotes and spiritual underpinnings" (p. 18). One major concern is the lack of experimental research supporting the effectiveness of facilitated communication (the studies of Biklen and his colleagues have been case studies, not experiments). In one experimental study (Wheeler, Jacobson, Paglieri, & Schwartz, 1993), students using facilitated communication were able to type the names of familiar objects correctly only when both they and their facilitators saw identical objects. When facilitators were shown one object and students another, students were unable to answer correctly.

One possible conclusion from these results is that the facilitator, perhaps unconsciously, is conveying his or her own message in facilitated communication by providing physical support to the nonverbal student. Another concern is the large number of sexual abuse allegations that have been made by students being facilitated; the evidence indicates that the majority of these charges are untrue (Chideya, 1993). Given these concerns, it appears best to choose techniques other than facilitated communi-

cation when working with students with autism. As Myles, Simpson, and Smith (1996) advise in discussing the results of their research on facilitated communication:

> We are of the opinion that facilitated communication has failed to demonstrate its worth as an educational tool. Hence, we contend that it is now time to acknowledge facilitated communication as an interesting phenomenon that has claimed its 15 minutes of fame, and to move on to more functional and potentially useful tools for improving the lives of individuals with autism. (pp. 43–44)

In this chapter, you have learned ways to teach language skills to students with communication disorders. You have also learned methods for creating a classroom climate that encourages the practice of speaking skills. In chapter 13, you will meet students with physical and health impairments. Before going on, check "Things to Remember" to review ways to help students with speech and language disorders succeed in general education.

ACTIVITIES

1. Interview a speech-language pathologist to find out more about students with communication disorders. Ask this professional to describe his or her caseload. How many students does he or she serve? What are their ages and typical problems? Do most students participate in general education classes for the majority of the day? If so, what effects do their speech and language disorders have on their performance in the general education classroom?

2. Locate one of the journals that deals primarily with communication disorders. You might select the *Journal of Speech and Hearing Disorders, Journal of Speech and Hearing Research,* or *Language, Speech, and Hearing Services in the Schools.* Look through recent issues for articles that present suggestions for encouraging oral communication and teaching language skills. Do you find any ideas that could be used by general education teachers?

3. The major professional organization in the field of communication disorders is the American Speech-Language-Hearing Association (ASHA). Its national headquarters are located at 10801 Rockville Pike, Rockville, MD 20852. Write to ASHA or visit its website (www.asha.org) to find out more about this organization. Or talk with a speech-language pathologist or audiologist who is an ASHA member.

4. Communication disorders can be found in persons of any age. Survey your community to locate agencies that provide services to adults with speech and language problems. What services are available? How do these differ from the services offered by the public schools to children and adolescents?

5. In a group, try one or more of the communication disorders simulations described in Table 12–1. Afterward, discuss your reactions to the following questions: What were the feelings of the person with the simulated speech or language disorder? Did he or she feel frustrated? Anxious? Angry? How did the listeners feel? Were they sympathetic? Impatient? Embarrassed? What recommendations can the group make to teachers of students with communication disorders?

6. Visit the website of the Autism Society (www.autism-society.org) to learn more about the controversy over facilitated communication. What does current research say about this approach? What is the position of the Autism Society on the use of facilitated communication?

chapter 13

Teaching Students with Physical and Health Impairments

Cases

Tim is a 16-year-old high school sophomore with spastic cerebral palsy. He is quite mobile with the aid of his braces and crutches; he is able to get from class to class, use the rest room, and eat in the lunchroom without assistance. Tim attends all general education classes during the day (except for adapted physical education) and is maintaining a B average this semester. He does not receive resource services, but the special education teacher is available to assist Tim's teachers when necessary. In class, Tim uses a portable computer and word processing program because his handwriting is poor; however, he is expected to complete assignments and exams within the usual time limits. Tim has been in general education classes since the first grade and has several friends at his high school. This semester he is taking the driver's education course, and he's very excited about getting his driver's license.

Maxine is 10 years old and in the fourth grade. She enjoys school and has many friends both at school and in her neighborhood. Every day Maxine must take the medication that has helped to control her epileptic seizures for the past 3 years. Despite this medication, she has generalized tonic-clonic seizures (formerly called grand mal seizures) at school about once a month. Mrs. Emerick, Maxine's teacher, knows what to do when a seizure occurs, and she and the school nurse have explained the nature of Maxine's problem to the other students in the class. Although her classmates are quite understanding, Maxine worries about what they think when seizures occur. In the past year she has become more concerned about this problem, and she visits the school counselor once a week to talk about her feelings. In all other respects, Maxine is typical. She is a good student. She performs well in all school subjects and is particularly interested in science and math.

Hank is 13 years old and attends Madison Middle School. When he was in the first grade, he suffered a spinal injury in a bike accident and now travels by wheelchair. He is able to get to all of his classes because some of the school's architectural barriers have been removed; for instance, a ramp has been built so that he can bypass the three steps up to the door of his English classroom. Hank missed much school during his elementary years and had difficulty acquiring reading skills. At present, he attends general education classes for the majority of the school day but continues to visit the special education teacher for assistance in reading. Hank is a sports enthusiast who keeps up with all the high school and professional teams. He attends an adapted physical education class but is often frustrated because he is not able to participate in many of the athletic activities in which he is interested. Hank has a small circle of close friends, and he is well liked by his teachers. He's an active participant in class discussions and usually maintains at least a C average. This semester he has had several medical appointments that have caused him to miss school at least one day each week; his grades have not yet suffered, but he is beginning to fall behind in some of his classes. We will take a look at a portion of Hank's IEP later in this chapter.

Students with physical and health impairments are an extremely heterogeneous group with a wide variety of conditions and diseases; **cerebral palsy,** paralysis, **epilepsy,** clubfoot, asthma, polio, **diabetes,** and allergies are just a few. Some physical and health impairments are **congenital,** that is, present at birth; others are acquired after birth through disease or injury. Physical and health problems can have grave, little, or no effect on school performance. Some students with physical and health impairments require no special adaptations; others need only modification of the physical environment. For others, it is necessary to adapt instructional activities in the general education classroom or to provide special instruction in areas of need, such as mobility, communication, and basic skills. A few of these students may have multiple disabilities with various medically related needs that require extensive services from the school nurse or other trained individuals. Students with similar impairments may have very different special needs; one student with lower-limb paralysis may be active and outgoing, whereas another may be withdrawn and unwilling to interact with others.

Teachers often believe that it is necessary to create a protective environment for students with physical and health impairments. However, such an environment discourages the development of skills

For Your Information

Students with Physical and Health Impairments

- The U.S. Department of Education (1997a) reports that 63,200 students (aged 6 to 21) with orthopedic impairments and 133,419 with other health impairments received special education services in the 1995–1996 school year. The number of students with other health impairments represented a 25% increase from the previous year and a 190% increase from 1987–1988.
- According to Reynolds and Birch (1982), "for every 20 children with medically significant conditions, perhaps 4 or 5 of them will be in need of special educational programming" (p. 301).
- Over 50,000 children between the ages of 1 and 14 are permanently crippled and disabled by accidents each year (Telford & Sawrey, 1981).
- In the school-aged population, 1 in 500 students is hospitalized each year because of a head injury (Mira & Tyler, 1991); head injuries are most common in males between the ages of 15 and 24 (Brain Injury Association, n.d.). Approximately 16% of hospital admissions in pediatrics are due to head trauma (Tucker & Colson, 1992) and traumatic brain injury is the leading cause of death and disability in U.S. children and adolescents (National Information Center for Children and Youth with Disabilities, 1997).
- It is estimated that students with physical and health impairments make up approximately 0.4% of the school-aged population; they account for only about 3.9% of the students with disabilities who receive special education services (U.S. Department of Education, 1997a).
- Cerebral palsy is one of the most complex of all physical impairments; because it results from damage to the brain, other areas of functioning including speech, vision, hearing, and intelligence can also be affected. However, there is no relationship between the extent of physical impairment and intellectual performance; individuals with severe motor involvement may be intellectually gifted.
- At the end of 1996, over 7,472 children under the age of 13 had been diagnosed as having AIDS in the United States (Centers for Disease Control, 1996). About 80% of these children were infected by their mothers during pregnancy and about 19% received contaminated blood products during transfusions (Byrom & Katz, 1991). While their educational needs are very similar to those of other students of similar age and ability, some interesting challenges are presented to educators serving this population of students because their right to participate alongside their peers in an educational program has often been questioned. The rights of these students to an appropriate education have been protected by the provisions of IDEA and the courts (Zirkel, 1989) as well as the provisions of Section 504 of the Rehabilitation Act (Heward, 1996).
- Different, and relatively new, diseases such as Lyme disease, Tourette's syndrome, or Reyes syndrome appear periodically (Sklaire, 1989). Lyme disease, which results from the bite of a deer tick, was first noticed in the 1970s. It starts with a rash and can lead to swollen joints and stiffness; complications can affect the heart and nervous system. Tourette's syndrome is a rare motor disorder that typically affects children between the ages of 2 and 15. While its cause is not known, it appears to be related to a chemical imbalance; youngsters with Tourette's syndrome are characterized by involuntary movements and behavior similar to students with ADHD. Reyes syndrome can result from administering aspirin to children and youth with flu or chicken pox, and it can be fatal. Education regarding the use of alternates to aspirin has led to a reduction in the number of cases of Reyes syndrome.
- Most students with physical and health impairments spend the majority of the school day in the general education classroom; many of these students also receive special education services from a resource teacher or other specialist(s), such as a physical therapist, occupational therapist, or adapted physical education teacher.
- Many famous people have had physical and health impairments, including several presidents of the United States: Theodore Roosevelt was asthmatic, Franklin Delano Roosevelt suffered from polio, and John F. Kennedy was plagued by back problems.

necessary for independence. Dependency is one of the greatest problems of these students, and teachers must take care not to add to this difficulty. Expectations for students with physical and health impairments should be realistic and geared toward the actual capabilities of individual students. The goal is the same as that for any other students: the development of skills that lead to independence.

This chapter describes the characteristics of students with physical and health impairments who are included in the general education program and presents methods for the general education teacher to use in gathering assessment data and modifying classroom procedures and activities to meet special needs. Consult "For Your Information" on page 345 to learn more about physical and health impairments.

INDICATORS OF PHYSICAL AND HEALTH IMPAIRMENTS

General education teachers are important members of the teams that assist in planning for students with physical and health impairments. Depending on the nature of the student's problem, the general education teacher may be involved in a variety of activities. He or she can help identify a physical or health impairment, provide the prereferral or assessment team with information about the student's current classroom performance, or take primary responsibility for the education and management of the student. In the general education classroom, a range of possible adaptations may be necessary; these include additional instruction for students with frequent absences, modification of the physical environment to allow mobility, and adaptations of instructional materials and activities.

Some students with physical and health impairments begin their school careers with an identified disability. With others, the problem is first noted after they enter school, or it may result from an accident or disease that occurs during the school years. Because students in this group may have many different physical disabilities and health problems that can serve as impairments, it is not possible to make a single list of signs or symptoms that identify this group. The glossary of terms in "For Your Information" describes several of the most common physical and health impairments.

Knowledge about a student's physical or health problem does not provide educators with much information about instructional programming. As Reynolds and Birch (1988) point out:

a. The names of the medical conditions give few clues to individual special education needs;
b. only a minority of children with these conditions have any special education needs at all; and
c. there is no educational justification for grouping these children in school by their medical diagnoses. (p. 269)

As with other students with special needs, it is necessary to go beyond the label and consider the individual needs of the student.

The special needs of students with physical and health impairments are almost as diverse as their physical disabilities. Some require no special assistance in school, others need minor modifications, and a few benefit from extensive special education services. One frequent area of need for students with physical impairments is mobility; for many, the major school adaptation necessary is proper arrangement of the physical environment. Other students may experience difficulty in learning academic skills, because of excessive absences, fatigue attributable to a medical condition or medication, or learning problems similar to those of pupils with learning disabilities, behavioral disorders, and mild retardation. Social skill development is often impeded by restricted opportunities to interact with others. Another possible area of need is social acceptance; teachers and peers may be hesitant to interact with a student whose disability is immediately obvious or with one whose condition seems strange and somewhat frightening. For example, the student with convulsive disorders who experiences epileptic **seizures** may be alarming to the observer unless this condition is understood. Figure 13–1 on page 348 presents information on the different types of seizures and the characteristics of each.

The general education teacher may be the first professional to identify the possible physical and health problems of students included in the general education program. Teachers should be aware of the general health status of their students and take note of any changes, whether sudden or gradual. With many physical and medical problems, it is possible to look for specific signs and symptoms. As Figure 13–2 on page 348 illustrates, several student behaviors can be indicative of the conditions of diabetes and epilepsy. If a physical or health impairment is suspected, the teacher should contact the school nurse or physician for further information.

For Your Information

Glossary of Medical Terms

Reynolds and Birch (1988) discuss several of the physical impairments and health problems that can be found in general education classrooms. Following is a list of the medical terms for these disabilities and a brief description of each.

Allergies: Adverse sensitivities or low tolerances to specific substances that are not problems to people in general. Reactions may take many forms; the most common are watering eyes, sneezing, nasal discharge, itching, or rash.

Arthritis: Inflammation of a joint, making motion difficult, painful, and limited.

Asthma: Repeated occurrence of wheezing coughs, difficult breathing, and feeling of constriction because of bronchial contractions.

Cerebral palsy: Several forms of paralysis due to damage to the brain. The most common forms are *ataxia,* shown by marked inability to coordinate bodily movements; *athetosis,* appearing as slow, repeated movements of the limbs; and *spasticity,* characterized by abrupt contractions of muscles or muscle groups, producing interference with and distortion of movement. All forms involve involuntary movements, and they appear in various combinations in different body locations depending on the nature and sites of the brain damage.

Congenital anomaly: Any body organ or part existing in an abnormal form from the time of birth. It can include, for example, the whole body, as in dwarfism (unusually small size) or albinism (absence of pigmentation); can be limited to one part (absence of an arm or a leg); can be clefts (cleft lip or palate); or can affect internal parts like the spine or spinal cord (spina bifida) or the heart.

Diabetes: Disorder of metabolism of carbohydrates that is indicated by excessive amounts of glucose in the blood or urine.

Epilepsy: Disorder of the brain sometimes resulting in convulsive movements and periods of unconsciousness lasting several minutes and sometimes in brief lapses of consciousness (up to 10 seconds) or feelings of unreality, dizziness, or semiconsciousness.

Hemophilia: A condition in which the normal blood clotting procedure is defective, with consequent difficulty in stopping bleeding when it occurs for any reason on the surface or within the body.

Leukemia: A form of cancer affecting the balance of cells in the blood and, therefore, the normal functioning of the blood.

Muscular dystrophy: A group of chronic inherited disorders characterized by progressive weakening and wasting of voluntary skeletal muscles.

Poliomyelitis: A viral infection that can result in the paralysis of body parts or systems, depending on the parts of the nervous system attacked.

Rheumatic fever: A disease that is characterized by fever, inflammation, and pain around the joints and inflammation of the muscle and valves of the heart.

Spina bifida: An anomaly characterized by a defect in the bone that encases the spinal cord.

Traumatic injuries: Impairments that result from accidents. They include a great variety of conditions ranging through amputations, paralyses, and limitations of body functions.

Note. Excerpted from *Adaptive Mainstreaming: A Primer for Teachers and Principals,* 3/e, by Maynard C. Reynolds and Jack W. Birch. Copyright © 1988 by Longman Publishers USA. Reprinted by permission of Addison Wesley Educational Publishers, Inc.

An increasing number of children with extensive health management or medical needs are entering the educational system because medical technology has allowed them to survive early medical crises and to be capable of attending school. Many of these students are considered to be **medically fragile** and their participation in a school setting requires the use of technology (e.g., heart monitors, oxygen tanks, or suctioning units), medical support (e.g.,

consultation or special emergency strategies), and other related services to survive and/or to participate in the educational program (Pendergast, 1995; Rapport, 1996). With the movement toward including a greater number of students with more severe special needs or multiple disabilities in general education, an increasing number of students who are medically fragile are likely to be placed in the general education classroom. Teachers in these general

FIGURE 13-1 Epileptic Seizures

The word *epilepsy* comes from the Greek word for "seizures." Seizures of one kind or another are the main symptoms of all forms of epilepsy. Seizures occur when there are excessive electrical discharges in some nerve cells of the brain. When this happens, the brain loses conscious control over certain body functions and consciousness may be lost or altered. Loss of control is temporary and the brain functions normally between seizures.

Generalized tonic clonic (grand mal) seizures are the most potentially disruptive in the classroom. The child becomes stiff and slumps to the floor unconscious. Rigid muscles give way to jerking, breathing is suspended and saliva may escape from the lips. The seizure may last for several minutes, and the child will regain consciousness in a confused or drowsy state, but otherwise unaffected.

Generalized absence (petit mal) seizures, most common in children, usually last only for 5 to 20 seconds. They may be accompanied by staring or twitching of the eyelids and are frequently mistaken for "daydreaming." The child is seldom aware he has had a seizure, although he may be aware that his "mind had gone blank" for a few seconds.

Complex partial (psychomotor or temporal lobe) seizures have the most complex behavior pattern. They may include constant chewing or lip smacking, purposeless walking or repetitive hand and arm movements, confusion and dizziness. The seizure may last from a minute to several hours.

Note. From *Epilepsy School Alert* by the Epilepsy Foundation of America, 1974, Washington, DC: Author. Copyright 1974 by the Epilepsy Foundation of America. Reprinted by permission.

FIGURE 13-2 Classroom Signs of Diabetes and Epilepsy

The Undiagnosed Diabetic

A listless, thin child who frequently needs to visit the restroom should put you on the alert. The diabetic child is typically lean, often undernourished, with an unhealthy skin color. These signs may point to an undiagnosed diabetic:

- breath with a sweet, fruity odor (ketone breath)
- frequent need to urinate
- frequent thirst
- recurring nausea and vomiting
- dry skin and mucous membranes
- air hunger (panting without exercise)
- muscular weakness
- localized short recurring pain, or general abdominal pain
- poor circulation, evidenced by cold feet and hands

If you observe these symptoms, mention your suspicion to the school nurse. If you've spotted a diabetic, good treatment and control will reward your teaching effort with a more alert and attentive child. (Byrne, 1981, p. 5)

Significant Signs of Epilepsy

Of course, there is little trouble recognizing a generalized tonic-clonic (grand mal) seizure. But keep your eyes open for repeated occurrences of two or more of the symptoms listed below happening together and without variation. They may indicate a petit mal or psychomotor epilepsy.

- staring spells
- tic-like movements
- rhythmic movements of the head
- purposeless sounds and body movements
- head dropping
- lack of response
- eyes rolling upward
- chewing and swallowing movements

If you suspect that one of your students has epilepsy, consult health personnel in your school. Only a physician, after thorough examination, can state that a person does or does not have the disorder. (Epilepsy Foundation of America, n.d.)

Note. From "Diabetes in the Classroom" by C. E. Byrne, September 1981, *ECO* (Washington, DC: National Education Association), p. 5; and from *Teacher Tips About the Epilepsies* by the Epilepsy Foundation of America, n.d., Washington, DC: Author. Reprinted by permission.

education classrooms should participate in the IEP meetings for the student and have a clear understanding of their specific responsibilities when the student is placed in their classroom. In addition, they should be provided information on the full range of related services required to meet the student's educational and medical needs and be aware of the other professionals and support personnel that are assigned the responsibility for implementing this part of the IEP.

ASSESSMENT PROCEDURES

Because of the diverse nature of the problems exhibited by students with physical and health impairments, the teams considering these students must take care to select appropriate assessment devices to gather information about educational needs. The procedures used can differ from student to student, and in many cases health professionals and other specialists must be included as part of the assessment team. For example, physical therapists, occupational therapists, adapted physical education teachers, and school nurses and physicians may provide important information about the effects of a disability on school performance. Other team members who play critical roles in assessment are the general education teacher, special educators, speech therapist, and school psychologist.

Students with physical and health impairments often require classroom adaptations to help them function successfully in general education settings. To obtain the information needed to design and implement these adaptations, the assessment team collects assessment data about current levels of performance in important skills. Sirvis (1988) suggests that assessment should focus on the following areas:

- *Activities of Daily Living.* Assessment of current and potential skills in self-help and daily living (e.g., eating, toileting, personal hygiene, cooking, travel on public transportation).
- *Mobility.* Current ability and potential to move from place to place and to become independent. Special equipment or assistive devices such as special wheelchairs or support devices may be required to facilitate mobility.
- *Physical Abilities and Limitations.* Identification of the effect of physical factors on the student's present and future plans for schooling, employment, recreation, and independent functioning.

- *Psychosocial Development.* Study of factors that interfere with social and emotional development and with the student's ability and opportunities to interact with others.
- *Communication.* Evaluation of the student's ability to understand and express language. May lead to the use of various communication devices such as electric typewriters, computers, communication boards, electronic communication aids, or other devices.
- *Academic Potential.* While the academic assessment may be similar to that used with other students, it is essential that the students are not penalized because of their physical limitations. This may require adaptations such as modifications in the physical setup, elimination of timed tasks, or alternative response modes such as verbal rather than written responses.
- *Adaptations for Learning.* Enhancement of the potential for independence by identifying needed classroom academic and physical adaptations for the student.
- *Transition Skills.* Identification of the factors necessary for a successful transition from school to living and working in the community. This is not limited to assessing job skills but should include other factors that will affect post-school performance.

Sirvis (1988) warns that standardized tests should be used cautiously with students with physical impairments. Communication problems or poor motor coordination can affect a student's ability to respond within the test's time limits or to provide adequate verbal responses. Sirvis also contends that students with physical impairments can be at a disadvantage in responding to norm-referenced tests because their physical problems may restrict their ability to explore the world around them. Their plight in this regard is similar to the test bias experienced by students who are economically disadvantaged or those from culturally and linguistically diverse backgrounds.

Criterion-referenced tests that compare a student's performance to the goals of the curriculum rather than to the performance of others are especially useful with this group of students with special needs. Criterion-referenced measures provide a way to evaluate a student's current level of performance and progress without the limitation of standardized tests. They also supply the teacher with information

Window on the Web

Websites About Physical and Health Impairments

A number of websites provide information about physical and health impairments. Several of these sites focus on one condition (e.g., epilepsy), while others are more general in nature.

Websites Focusing on Specific Conditions

- American Cancer Society (www.cancer.org)
- American Diabetes Association (www.diabetes.org)
- Brain Injury Association, Inc. (www.biausa.org)
- Epilepsy Foundation of America (www.efa.org)
- Leukemia Society of America (www.leukemia.org)
- Muscular Dystrophy Association (www.mdausa.org)
- Spina Bifida Association of America (www.sfaa.org)
- United Cerebral Palsy Association (www.ucpa.org/html)

More General Websites

- American Academy of Pediatrics (www.aap.org)
- Centers for Disease Control and Prevention (www.cdc.gov)
- Internet Resources for Special Children (www.irsc.org)
- National Easter Seal Society (www.seals.com)
- National Rehabilitation Information Center (www.naric.com/naric)

---

that is helpful in the design of instructional/management programs.

Direct observation is another useful technique. The teacher can collect data on a variety of student behaviors, such as academic performance, the frequency of seizures, the time taken to complete assignments, the types of interactions with others, and the frequency of inappropriate classroom behaviors. Classroom observation data provide the teams serving students with special needs with important information about the current performance of a student and can also be useful to the medical personnel responsible for management of the student's physical or health problems.

The general education teacher should review the assessment results of other professionals who aid in the evaluation of a student with physical or health impairments. The information gathered in assessment can be extremely useful for the teacher working with the student in the general education classroom. If portions of the assessment reports are unclear, the teacher should seek assistance from the school nurse, special educator, physician, other appropriate professionals, or the student's parents. For a classroom program that develops the independence as well as the academic and behavioral skills of students, a clear picture of their capabilities and limitations is imperative.

SPECIAL SERVICES

When assessment is complete, an IEP is developed by the IEP team for each student found eligible for special education services. For students with physical or health impairments, IEP goals may address several areas and involve services from a wide variety of professionals—for example, general education teachers, special education teachers, physical or occupational therapists, school nurses, social workers, counselors, speech and language specialists, adapted physical education teachers, and vocational counselors. Figure 13–3 shows portions of the IEP for Hank, the middle school student introduced at the beginning of this chapter. Although Hank is in-

---

◆ **FIGURE 13-3**   **IEP Goals and Services for Hank**

Annual Goals
1. By the end of the school year, Hank will demonstrate the basic skills necessary to participate in two group-oriented recreational activities.
   Person responsible: Adapted physical education teacher
2. By the end of the school year, Hank will participate in 4 hours of self-directed recreational activity each week.
   Person responsible: Adapted physical education teacher
3. By the end of the school year, Hank will read materials at the sixth grade level with adequate word recognition and comprehension.
   Person responsible: Resource teacher
4. Hank will successfully complete eighth grade math, English, social studies, and science.
   Persons responsible: Eighth grade teachers

Amount of Participation in General Education
Hank will attend eighth grade general education classes in math, English, social studies, and science.

Special Education and Related Services
1. Hank will receive special education services from the adapted physical education teacher (annual goals 1 and 2) for one period per day.
2. Hank will receive special education services from the resource teacher (annual goal 3) for one period per day.
3. The resource teacher, adapted physical education teacher, and school nurse will provide consultation to Hank's eighth grade teachers as needed.

---

cluded in the general education program for the majority of the school day, he receives help in reading from the resource teacher, and he is learning leisure time skills in adapted physical education.

Most students with physical and health impairments spend the majority of their day in the general education classroom and only attend a resource room for academic assistance or visit a specialist for some other type of necessary service. Special classes and schools are available for students with severe or multiple disabilities; these placements are usually reserved for individuals with complex physical needs accompanied by severe learning problems. As noted earlier in this chapter, there has been increased attention to including students who are medically fragile and those with more severe disabilities in the general education program whenever it is appropriate to meet their special educational needs. When students cannot attend school because of prolonged illness or the need for extensive medical services, homebound and hospital services can be provided. Consultant services are also available to the general education teacher from a variety of specialists who attempt to assist the teacher in mak-

ing classroom adaptations to facilitate the successful inclusion of students with health and physical impairments.

◆ **CLASSROOM ADAPTATIONS**

When students with physical and health impairments enter the general education classroom, one of the teacher's first tasks is to learn about their disabilities. Other students must also become aware of the problems of these students with special needs and learn about possible ways of helping them function as independently as possible. In addition, it may be necessary to adapt portions of the general education program to allow full participation of students with physical and health impairments. The areas in which modifications are usually required are the arrangement of the physical environment and the format and structure of instructional activities and assignments.

The following sections of this chapter describe methods for meeting physical and health needs in the general education classroom, modifying the physical environment, and adapting instructional

MEETING PHYSICAL AND HEALTH NEEDS

Students' physical and health needs are an important area of concern to any teacher. Students with identified physical and health impairments often require special diets, have restrictions placed on their physical activities, take medication during the school day, or require other health-related services (e.g., seizure, nutrition, or glucose monitoring; transfer and lifting) that are provided by the school nurse or other qualified person. The teacher's first step in meeting special physical and health needs is to learn as much as possible about each student's limitations and capabilities. One source of information is the assessment data collected by the assessment team. Recent evaluations will describe the current functioning levels of the student in important areas such as mobility, communication, academic achievement, classroom behavior, and social skills. Cross (1993) suggests that teachers contact the student's parents and the professionals who have worked with that student in the past to determine the best ways to meet physical and health needs. Figure 13–4 lists questions that teachers can ask to find out more about a student's specific requirements.

Medical personnel such as the school nurse and the student's physician are another excellent source of information. Typically the school nurse helps the assessment and IEP teams interpret medical reports and translate medical findings into educationally relevant information. The nurse might explain why certain students have activity restrictions, how different medications affect students' classroom behavior, and what the reasons are for medical treatments and procedures. The nurse can also help teachers learn to deal with unusual medical situations, such as epileptic seizures in the classroom. If teachers are aware of the proper procedures to follow should a seizure occur, they will face the situation more calmly and be of more assistance to the student and the student's peers. To learn about what to do in case of a seizure, see "Inclusion Tips for the Teacher."

When teachers are fully aware of the needs of students with physical and health impairments, the next step is consideration of what information to provide to other students in the class. This issue should be discussed with the prereferral and IEP

activities. For students with specific needs in academic instruction, the teacher should refer to the methods suggested for students with learning disabilities and mild retardation. If classroom behavior is a concern, the suggestions provided for students with behavioral disorders might prove helpful.

Reynolds and Birch (1988) point out that students with physical and health impairments "seldom need to be taught material that is outside the curriculum for all other pupils" (p. 281). That is, the general education curriculum with its emphasis on academic skills is appropriate. However, several additional curriculum areas may benefit students with physical and health impairments. Mobility training (instruction in planning travel within the school building) may help some students conserve their limited energy. For secondary students, continued instruction in writing skills (handwriting, typing, or using computers and word processors) may be necessary. Other possible areas of benefit are driver's training, recreation and use of leisure time, and sex education. In many cases, these additions to the general education curriculum are offered as part of the student's special education program.

Inclusion Tips for the Teacher

What to Do for Seizures

When tonic-clonic (also known as grand mal) seizures occur in the classroom, the teacher should remain calm, assist the child with the seizure, and assure the other students that their classmate is not in pain and that the seizure will last only a few minutes.

The Epilepsy Foundation of America (1987) suggests that the teacher take the following steps to safeguard the student having a tonic-clonic seizure:

- Keep calm. Reassure the other students that the child will be fine in a minute.
- Ease the child to the floor and clear the area around him of anything that could hurt him.
- Put something flat and soft (like a folded coat) under his head so it will not bang on the floor as his body jerks.
- You cannot stop the seizure. Let it run its course. Do not try to revive the child and do not interfere with his movements.
- Turn him gently on his side. This keeps his airway clear and allows saliva to drain away.

DON'T try to force his mouth open.
DON'T try to hold his tongue.
DON'T put anything in his mouth.
- When the jerking movements stop, let the child rest until he regains consciousness.
- Breathing may be shallow during the seizure, and may even stop briefly. In the unlikely event that breathing does not begin again, check the child's airway for obstruction and give artificial respiration.

Some students recover quickly after this type of seizure; others need more time. A short period of rest is usually advised. If the student is able to remain in the classroom afterwards, however, he or she should be encouraged to do so. Staying in the classroom (or returning to it as soon as possible) allows for continued participation in classroom activity and is psychologically less difficult for the student. If a student has frequent seizures, handling them can become routine once the teacher and classmates learn what to expect.

FIGURE 13-4 **Questions to Ask About Physical and Health Needs**

Medical Concerns
- In addition to the child's primary disorder, does the child have additional problems such as seizures or diabetes? Does the child have any sensory disorders?
- Does the child take medication? How frequently, and in what amounts?
- If medication is taken, is the school authorized to administer the medication during school hours?
- What are the expected side effects of the medication? What are the other possible side effects?
- What procedures should be followed in the event of a seizure, insulin shock, diabetic coma, or other problem, with regard to contacting the child's parents or medical personnel?
- Should the child's activities be restricted in any way?

Travel
- How will the child be transported to school?
- Will the child arrive at the usual time?
- Will someone need to meet the child at the entrance to the school to provide assistance in getting the child on and off the vehicle?
- Will the child need special accommodations to travel within the school building or the classroom?

continued

◆ **FIGURE 13-4   Continued**

Transfer and Lifting
- What methods are used to get the child on and off the school bus?
- What is the preferred way to lift and transfer the child out of a wheelchair and onto a chair or to the floor?
- What cautions or limitations are there regarding transfer and lifting?
- How much help does the child really need with movement and transfer?

Communication
- If the child does not communicate verbally, what particular or unique means of communication does the child use?
- Does the child have a speech or language problem?
- Does the child use gestures? If so, what are they? Is a pointer used? Does the child use the same signal consistently for *yes, no,* or other common words?
- Can the child write? Type? How?
- Is an electronic communication aid used? If so, are there any special instructions necessary for the child to use it or for the teacher to understand and maintain it? Are fresh batteries or a charger needed?
- Can the child make his or her needs known to the teacher? How?

Self-Care
- What types of help does the child need with self-care activities such as feeding, dressing, toileting, and so forth?
- What equipment, such as a special feeding tray, does the child need?

Positioning
- What positioning aids or devices (braces, pillows, wedges, etc.) does the child use?
- What particular positions are the most useful for specific academic activities? What positions for resting?
- What positions are best for toileting, feeding, dressing, and other activities?
- Are there any other special aids or devices that I should know about?

Educational Needs
- What is the child's current level of achievement and of developmental and vocational functioning?
- What are the child's strengths and weaknesses?
- To what extent is achievement in school affected by physical disabilities?
- What medical considerations must be taken into account (that is, to what extent is the child able to participate in classroom activities)?
- What physical modifications to the classroom need to be made?
- What special equipment must be acquired?
- What related services will be needed?

Note. From *An Introduction to Special Education*, 3rd ed., by William H. Berdine and Edward Blackhurst. Copyright © 1993 by Harper-Collins College Publishers. Reprinted by permission of Addison Wesley Educational Publishers, Inc.

teams, including the student's parents and, if appropriate, the student. In some cases, parents and students may be reluctant to have teachers inform students in the general education class about the specific nature of the problem. However, with disabilities and conditions that are obvious to a student's peers, the general education teacher or the school nurse should prepare the class by explaining the impairment and the ways in which it will affect the student's participation in class activities. Older students with special needs may want to give this explanation themselves. This approach should be encouraged because these students, as adults, will often have occasion to explain their disabilities to friends, acquaintances, and potential employers.

Information about physical and health needs of students should be presented factually, with emphasis not only on the student's problems but also the student's abilities. Any questions peers might have should be answered openly and accurately. This sharing of information is particularly important with young students, who may wonder whether needing to ride in a wheelchair is contagious or whether being naughty causes seizures. The teacher should anticipate such concerns and attempt to quell apprehensions with a matter-of-fact explanation.

One subject that many teachers find difficult to discuss with their students is death. If there is a child or adolescent in the class with a terminal illness, this discussion may become necessary. Some thoughts on death education are presented in Figure 13–5. Other resources that may be of interest are "Death in My Classroom?" by Postel (1986) or *Death Education: A Concern for the Living* by Gibson, Roberts, and Buttery (1982).

To accommodate the physical and health needs of students with special needs who are included in the general education classroom, alterations in some classroom routines and procedures may be necessary. These students should not be automatically excused from classroom activities simply because they have a disability. However, if there are medical restrictions that prevent participation or if their disabilities truly impose limits, then classroom standards should be changed. Examples of appropriate modifications appear here:

- If students in wheelchairs or those with mobility problems travel slowly, they can be dismissed a few minutes early from class so that they can arrive at their next class or activity on time.
- Students should be allowed to take breaks during the day if these are necessary for rest, a visit to the bathroom, medication, or a special diet.
- There should be classroom procedures for emergency situations. For example, in the case of a fire drill, someone should be assigned the responsibility of making certain that students with mobility problems are assisted in leaving the classroom quickly.
- For some students, it is hard to follow dietary or activity restrictions. The student who is on a low-carbohydrate diet may want to eat candy; one who is restricted to short exercise periods may want to join the others playing football at recess. These students should be provided with attractive alternatives to help them adhere to their medical regimens. For instance, instead of snacks for classroom rewards, activities can be used as reinforcers; or if students are unable to play sports, they can be appointed coaching assistants to the teacher.

Students with physical and health impairments may require some assistance, but it is equally important that these students be offered opportunities to learn to function independently. Often it is quicker and easier for the teacher or peers to do things for these students rather than allow them to do things for themselves. For example, a student may take 5 minutes to put on a jacket, whereas, with assistance, only a few seconds are required. However, such skills are acquired only with practice, and another's help may actually hinder learning.

MODIFYING THE PHYSICAL ENVIRONMENT

One major consideration in the education of students with physical and health impairments is the physical environment of the classroom and school. For some students with mobility problems, this may be the prime area in which modifications must be made. The following guidelines should help ensure that the physical environment is suitably arranged to accommodate students with disabilities:

- Evaluate the school and classroom for accessibility. Architectural barriers that restrict the travel of students in wheelchairs or students with physical limitations may prevent their full participation in the educational program. The most brilliant student cannot benefit from the best of programs if stairs are the only route to the classroom and the student uses a wheelchair. Use the checklist in "Inclusion Tips for the Teacher" on page 357 to evaluate the accessibility of your school building. If problems are evident, bring these to the attention of the

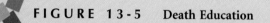

FIGURE 13-5   **Death Education**

A child once wrote a letter to God:

> Dear God,
> What is it like to die?
> Nobody ever told me.
> I just want to know.
> I don't want to do it.
> Your friend, Harry

This letter points out two important needs of children: (1) "nobody ever told me," people are reluctant to talk about death, and (2) "I don't want to do it," children feel anxiety about death.

- A challenge to teachers and parents is to put the thought and experience of death into the context of living. In this way, much of the child's fears and anxiety may be alleviated.
- Proper death education enhances the child's joy of life. Death education can reduce the child's fear of death thereby increasing the joy of living.
- Death education works to improve the quality of the child's total life span, birth, living, process of dying and death. . . .

What Can Teachers Do?

- The role of the teacher in death education is to disseminate the results of scientific studies and to facilitate the child's acceptance of death.
- What a teacher should do in any specific situation cannot be known for there are too many variables. The best thing one can bring to a terminally ill student is one's self. Every teacher, therefore, needs to clarify an individual philosophy for working with terminally ill students. . . .

What Teachers Need to Know

The dying child goes through a number of stages before accepting death. These stages may be experienced simultaneously; not every child experiences all of them. It is important that the child experience some of them if death is to be accepted. The stages and conjectured positive contributions are as follows:

1. *Shock and disbelief*—This serves as a temporary anesthesia holding the child's sense of self-esteem together for a brief time.
2. *Crying (sometimes hysterical)*—This usually provides the needed emotional release.
3. *Feelings of isolation and loneliness*—This may help the child feel the need for others and to experience the discomfort which alienation brings. A degree of personal untidiness may be observed at this stage.
4. *Psychosomatic symptoms*—This may momentarily deviate the child's attention from the fatal prognosis to lesser conditions.
5. *Panic*—This pushes the child to explore all possibilities and to eventually accept the fact that the dying process is occurring.
6. *Guilt feelings*—This eventually enables the child to accept the fact that nobody is to blame and that the process of dying is unlikely to be reversed.
7. *Hostility-resentment*—The child attempts to defend and protect his ego by projecting these negative feelings onto teachers, parents and friends.
8. *Resists usual routine*—The child questions the worth and complains of the difficulty in doing everyday activities in an effort to come to terms with the requirements for continued living.
9. *Reconciliation*—This very positive stage enables the child to avoid feelings of hopelessness and to begin the process of accepting the inevitability of death.
10. *Acceptance*—The child struggles to adjust to the reality that death is happening and that there is living and work yet to be accomplished. The child becomes a deeper more profound person—young in years but old in experience.

Note. From "What Parents and Teachers Should Know about Death Education" by R. Berner, 1977, *DOPHHH Journal, 3,* pp. 17–21. Copyright 1977 by DOPHHH, The Council for Exceptional Children. Reprinted with permission.

Inclusion Tips for the Teacher

Checking Your School for Accessibility

Sidewalks
Are there curb cuts which provide access?
Is there a width of at least 48"?
Are they level, without irregular surfaces?
Is there a level area 5' by 5' if the door swings in?

Ramps
Are handrails present (32" high)?
Is the grade of the ramp [less] than a 1" rise in every 12" length?
Does it have a non-slip surface in all types of weather?

Doors (including elevator)
Is there an opening of at least 32" when door is open?
Are floors level for 5' in both directions of the door?
Are the thresholds navigable (1/2")?

Floor
Do hallways, stairs, and class areas have carpeting or some other non-slip surface?

Toilets
Is one stall 3' wide by 4'8" deep with handrails 33" high?
Is the toilet seat 20" high and urinals 19" from floor?
Are sinks, towel dispensers, mirrors, etc. 36–40" from floor?

Water fountains
Are the controls hand operated?
Is the spout in the front of the unit?
Are they mounted 26–30" from the floor?

Note. From "Environmental Alternatives for the Physically Handicapped" by B. B. Greer, J. Allsop, and J. G. Greer in *Implementing Learning in the Least Restrictive Environment* (pp. 128–129) by J. W. Schifani, R. M. Anderson, and S. J. Odle (Eds.), 1980, Austin, TX: PRO-ED. Copyright 1980 by PRO-ED. Reprinted by permission.

school principal and the teams working with students with special needs.

• Arrange the classroom to facilitate mobility. Be sure sufficient room is allowed for students in wheelchairs or those who use crutches to travel from one work area to another.

• Make all areas and activities within the general education classroom accessible to students with mobility problems. This includes chalkboards, bookcases, storage cupboards, coatracks, art supplies, bulletin boards, display cases, computers, audiovisual equipment, activity centers, and so on.

• Consider the seating arrangements for students with special needs. Those in wheelchairs may need a special table or lapboard to write on. Others may require special chairs that provide extra support; for instance, arm- or footrests can help students maintain an upright position for reading and writing activities. Check with the school nurse, special education teacher, or physical therapist for specific information about the positioning needs of each student.

• Provide storage space for students' aids and equipment. For example, crutches should be within their owner's easy reach without presenting a hazard to others moving about the classroom. One method is to use crutch holders on the back or sides of a student's chair.

• Be sure that special equipment is kept in good working order. Check wheelchairs periodically for proper fit, comfort, and good repair. Figure 13–6 presents a checklist from *Wheelchair Prescriptions* (1968, 1976) that can be used for regular inspections. If there is need for modification or repair, notify the student's parents or the special educator who works with the student.

• For students with crutches, Glazzard (1982) suggests chairs with wheels to facilitate movement about the classroom; an office chair on rollers is appropriate. In rooms without carpets, crutches can slip when students use them to help themselves up from a sitting position. If assistance is needed, show their peers in the general education class how to use their foot as a brace to prevent the crutch from slipping.

• Students with limited strength or poor coordination may need easy access to work equipment. Desks with open storage space are preferable to those with a lid that must be raised. Pencil

FIGURE 13-6   **Wheelchair Checklist**

	No	Yes	Comments

I. With the student out of the wheelchair
   A. Arms
      1. Are the armrests and side panels secure and free of sharp edges and cracks?
      2. Do the armlocks function properly?
   B. Backs
      1. Is the upholstery free of rips and tears?
      2. Is the back taut from top to bottom?
      3. Is safety belt attached tightly and not frayed?
   C. Seat and frame
      1. Is the upholstery free of rips and tears?
      2. Does the chair fold easily without sticking?
      3. When the chair is folded fully are the front post slides straight and round?
   D. Wheel locks
      1. Do the wheel locks securely engage the tire surfaces and prevent the wheel from turning?
   E. Large wheels
      1. Are the wheels free from wobble or sideplay when spun?
      2. Are the spokes equally tight and without any missing spokes?
      3. Are the tires free from excessive wear and gaps at the joined section?
   F. Casters
      1. Is the stem firmly attached to the fork?
      2. Are the forks straight on sides and stem so that the caster swivels easily?
      3. Is the caster assembly free from excessive play both up and down as well as backward and forward?
      4. Are the wheels free of excessive play and wobble?
      5. Are the tires in good condition?
   G. Footrest/Legrest
      1. Does the lock mechanism fit securely?
      2. Are the heel loops secure and correctly installed?
      3. Do the footplates fold easily and hold in any position?
      4. Are the legrest panels free of cracks and sharp edges?
II. With the student sitting in the chair
   A. Seat width
      1. When your palms are placed between the patient's hip and the side of the chair (skirtguard), do the hands contact the hip and the skirtguard at the same time without pressure?
      2. Or, is the clearance between the patient's widest point of either hips or thigh and the skirtguard approximately 1 inch on either side?
   B. Seat depth
      1. Can you place your hand, with fingers extended, between the front edge of the seat upholstery and to the rear of the knee with a clearance for three or four fingers?
      2. Or, is the seat upholstery approximately 2 to 3 inches less than the student's thigh measurement?

FIGURE 13-6   Continued

		No	Yes	Comments
C. Seat height and footrest				
	1. Is the lowest part of the stepplates no closer than 2 inches from the floor?			
	2. Or, is the student's thigh elevated slightly above the front edge of the seat upholstery?			
D. Arm height				
	1. Does the arm height not force the shoulders up or allow them to drop significantly when in a normal sitting position?			
	2. Is the elbow positioned slightly forward of the trunk midline when the student is in a normal sitting position?			
E. Back height				
	1. Can you insert four or five fingers between the patient's armpit area and the top of the back upholstery touching both at the same time?			
	2. Is the top of the back upholstery approximately 4 inches below the armpit for the student who needs only minimum trunk support?			
III. With the student pushing or riding in the wheelchair				
	A. Is the wheelchair free from squeaks or rattles?			
	B. Does the chair roll easily without pulling to either side?			
	C. Are the large wheels and casters free of play and wobble?			

Note. From *Wheelchair Prescriptions: Measuring the Patient* and *Wheelchair Prescriptions: Care and Service* by Everest and Jennings, Los Angeles: Author. Copyright 1968 and 1976 by Everest and Jennings. Adapted by permission.

grooves on the desk top or a small box to hold pencils, pens, and erasers can help keep work materials close at hand.

ADAPTING INSTRUCTIONAL ACTIVITIES

In addition to meeting physical and health needs and modifying the classroom environment, it may also be necessary to adapt instructional activities and procedures. Glazzard (1982) suggests several ideas for assisting students with poor coordination or inadequate muscle control:

- Tape the student's paper to the desk with a piece of masking tape applied to the top and bottom of the paper.
- Attach one end of a string to a pencil and the other end to the desk with a thumbtack or masking tape so that a student can easily retrieve a dropped pencil.
- Appoint a student to bring teacher handouts to the student's desk.
- Allow students to answer questions orally, or have them record answers for later evaluation. It is often laborious for some . . . students [with disabilities] to write their answers. If they have poor muscle control in their hands they must exert much more energy than the . . . [typical] students to write their answers.
- Make a copy of your lecture notes for the child with disabilities who writes slowly or with difficulty. It would also be simple for a classmate to insert a sheet of carbon paper under his or her paper so that a duplicate set of notes can be supplied to the . . . student [with disabilities].
- Provide . . . students [with disabilities] with plastic or wooden rulers to use as bookmarks. They are easier to manipulate than paper markers.
- A . . . child [with disabilities] may use a shoulder bag to carry books and supplies from class to class. The book bag leaves arms free to handle crutches. (pp. 7–8)

Be creative, but remember that simple modifications are sometimes all that's necessary. Don't use clamps and tape if a paperweight will work just as well.

Many of the technological aids available to assist students with physical and health impairments in the general education program have been described in chapter 8. These devices help students compensate for the effects of their disabilities on mobility, communication, and academic learning. See "Spot-

light on Technology" for more information about switches and how these simple devices can provide access to a wide variety of activities in the classroom, at home, and in the community.

Some students with physical and health impairments may require further adaptations in instruction in order to keep pace in the general education classroom. When students miss school because of illness or medical treatment, extra instruction should be provided so that they do not fall far behind. For those who work slowly, the teacher can alter requirements for assignments and exams; more time can be allowed, or the amount of work can be reduced. If students have difficulty speaking or writing, other response modes can be substituted. For example, instead of writing, a student might type, tape-record, or dictate a response to a peer. By adapting instruction in these ways, the general education teacher creates a learning environment in which students with special needs have every chance for success. For more information about adaptations for one group of students with physical and health impairments, those with traumatic brain injuries, see "Inclusion Tips for the Teacher" on page 364.

When a child or adolescent receives a head injury, the first interventions will be medical. It is likely that the student will be hospitalized for some

Spotlight on Technology

Switch Access

Because of physical impairments, some students cannot grip a pencil or pen, hold a book or turn its pages, or play with toys designed for typical children. However, students can access these activities if they have voluntary control over at least one type of motor movement. That movement can involve any part of the body: lifting a finger, raising an eyebrow, moving a hand outward from the body, pressing downward with a foot, or blowing through a tube. Movements such as these allow students to operate a switch, and switches can control a number of different devices.

Note. Photo courtesy of AbleNet Inc.

There are many types of switches, but each requires only a single action. With some switches, the student pushes or pulls; with others, he or she pinches or squeezes, sucks or blows, changes the position of a body part, or makes a small muscle movement such as flexing the muscles in a hand. Switches requiring a pushing motion are most common; see photo for examples of push switches.

Students who are switch users can control toys, appliances, and even the lights in their home or classroom (Lewis, 1993). Here are some examples:

- *Battery-operated toys* can be converted for switch use by adding a device called a battery adapter. One source of battery adapters and similar assistive devices is AbleNet Inc. (1081 Tenth Ave. S. E., Minneapolis, MN 55414). Toys already adapted for switch users are available from companies such as Toys for Special Children and Enabling Devices (www.enablingdevices.com).
- *Electrical appliances* can be accessed by switch with a device such as the AbleNet PowerLink 2 Control Device. The appliance and the switch are plugged into the control device and it in turn is plugged into a wall socket. With this configuration, a student could press the switch to turn on a radio or television, blender, hair dryer, or fan.
- *Slide projectors* can be operated by switch with a special adapter. By pressing the switch, the student moves to the next slide.
- *Automatic pageturners* hold a book or magazine, then turn its pages when the reader presses a switch.
- Some *environmental control devices* can be operated by switch. Options these devices offer include turning on lights and appliances, automatically dialing the telephone, and automatically releasing a door lock.
- Some *electronic communication devices* accept switch input. To select a message, the student presses the switch rather than a key on the device's keyboard.
- *Computers* can also be adapted for switch users.

Computer Adaptations

Students who respond by switch can interact with computers in one of two ways. The first method requires a switch, a switch interface device (used to connect the switch to the computer), and special software. This software must be specifically designed to accept switch input. For example, Don Johnston Incorporated (www.donjohnston.com) offers a number of switch-operated programs for young students and those with severe disabilities. However, switch programs are not available in all subject areas for all ages; in fact, the collection is quite small compared to the number of programs on the market for typical learners.

continued

The second method allows switch users to access any software, including that designed for typical learners. This method requires a switch, any software program, and a special control device. This device allows the switch to control the computer in the same way that the keyboard and mouse do.

Discover:Switch is an access device from Don Johnston Incorporated that allows students to operate any computer program using a switch. It is a large switch with special control technology built in. The teacher plugs the Discover:Switch into the computer and an on-screen "keyboard" appears on the computer's monitor.

Discover:Switch allows students to "type" letters by pressing a switch.

Note. Photo courtesy of Don Johnston Incorporated.

The on-screen keyboard contains an array of choices. For example, the array might include the letters of the alphabet, mouse commands, special keys, punctuation marks, and numbers. Letters could be arranged in alphabetical order as shown in the photo.

The student makes choices through a process called scanning. The first row of the array is highlighted, then the second, and so on. The student presses the switch when the desired row is highlighted. For example, in the array shown on the computer screen, to type the word *dog,* the student would press the switch when the first row was highlighted. Then, blocks of letters are highlighted in turn: *abcd,* then *efghi,* then *jklm.* When a block of letters has been selected, each of the letters within that block is highlighted (e.g., first *a,* then *b,* etc.). To type *dog,* the student would press the switch to select the first group of letters *(abcd),* then press again to select the letter *d.* The process would be repeated to type the last two letters in *dog.*

Although scanning is a slow process, it is a powerful one because it allows students with severe physical disabilities to access any software program. With Discover:Switch, the on-screen keyboard that the student sees can be changed. The device comes with several preprogrammed arrays, and teachers can create new ones to meet the needs of individual students. On-screen keyboards can include graphics for younger students and those who are beginning readers, and any array can "talk" using synthesized speech.

period of time, then continue rehabilitation on an outpatient basis with professionals such as occupational and physical therapists. Depending on the length of hospitalization, the student may attend hospital school; once back at home, he or she may receive educational services from a teacher who visits several times a week. Planning the student's return to school requires a team approach; Mira and Tyler (1991) recommend collaboration between hospital staff, school personnel, and the student and his or her family. Consider, for example, the reentry plan developed for Barbara, a 16-year-old who sustained a severe head injury in an auto accident:

1. *Reduce course load:* Barbara enrolled in a limited number of academic courses with the understanding that others could be added.
2. *Special scheduling:* Barbara took her most taxing courses early in the day, when she was most alert.
3. *Resource room:* Barbara would begin and end the day in the resource room with an aide present to provide assistance.
4. *Rest breaks:* Barbara was allowed to rest in the nurse's office when she became fatigued.
5. *Adaptive physical education:* Barbara would receive adaptive PE with an aide present to assist her at all times, because of the danger of her falling.
6. *Student aide:* One of her friends would assist her in moving from one class to the next.
7. *Extra set of books:* Barbara was given an extra set of books to keep at home, to avoid having to carry them back and forth.
8. *Lunch room provisions:* Because Barbara was still physically unsteady, someone would carry her lunch tray and have her seated before the lunchroom crowds arrived.
9. *Counseling:* Meetings were scheduled with the school counselor, and she was given the option for other meetings as needed.
10. *Other modifications:* Barbara would be allowed to have someone take notes for her in her class and tape her lectures, and she would be able to take her exams in a setting other than the regular classroom, with extra time allowed. She also would have use of a computer to complete assignments. (p. 7)

In this chapter, you have learned about the special needs of students with physical and health impairments. Methods for accommodating their disabilities within the general education classroom, modifying the physical environment, and adapting instructional activities have been suggested. The next chapter describes ways to make accommodations for the educational needs of stu-dents with sensory disabilities—those with visual and hearing impairments.

ACTIVITIES

1. Use the checklist provided in "Inclusion Tips for the Teacher" on page 357 to check the accessibility of one of your local public schools. Also consider whether instructional activities within the classroom are accessible. Can a student in a wheelchair write on the chalkboard? Remove a book from the bookcase? Hang up a coat? Use the classroom computer? If possible, borrow a wheelchair and travel through the school and several classrooms to gain a better understanding of what environmental features can impose barriers.
2. Visit a school with a special education program for students with physical and health impairments. Talk with the teacher and find out what types of disorders the students have. Are most of the students included in the general education program? How are these students accepted by their peers? What adaptations are necessary in the general education classroom?
3. Interview a young person or adult with a physical or health impairment. What impact does this condition have on daily life? That is, how does it affect routine tasks such as eating, dressing, shopping, traveling, and working? How do others react to the disability, and how does the person with disabilities deal with these reactions?
4. Identify a school setting that has a medically fragile student included in the general education program. Visit the school and observe the student's educational program, talk with the teachers involved, and review any concerns that may arise in implementing the program. Prepare a short report on your findings related to the appropriateness of the program and its success.
5. Learn more about agencies that provide services to those with physical and health impairments by visiting the websites of the United Cerebral Palsy Association, Epilepsy Foundation of America, Brain Injury Association, American Diabetes Association, or others mentioned in "Window on the Web." Several of these organizations provide information on branches in your community and can help you locate their local office.

Inclusion Tips for the Teacher

Working with Students with Traumatic Brain Injury

Students with traumatic brain injury (TBI) may have special needs in a variety of areas including physical, academic, social-emotional, and behavioral performance. Although teachers expect students who have received serious head injuries to experience difficulty with learning tasks (and, depending on the injury, with tasks requiring physical skills), they often do not anticipate the social-emotional consequences that can accompany this disability. Tucker and Colson (1992) describe the types of behaviors that some students with TBI may show:

- *Overestimates abilities*—Student brags to friends that he or she is still the fastest runner or will win the spelling bee.
- *Lowered social inhibition and judgment*—Student tries to touch and hug everyone.
- *Lowered impulse control*—Student interrupts teachers and peers at inappropriate times.
- *Faulty reasoning*—Student confronts peers and teachers with unfair accusations.
- *Lowered initiative*—Student will not begin a task without a reminder or assistance.
- *Depression*—Student appears uninterested and passive, even in activities once considered highly enjoyable. The emotional stress of the injury may be prolonged and can be overwhelming.
- *Fatigue*—This can be a result of both the injury and medication. Sleep disorders are common.
- *Acting-out behavior*—Student may yell or curse about being asked to do a task he or she doesn't want to do. He or she may walk out of class or knock over a desk.
- *Impulsivity*—Student may be unable to wait his or her turn at a drinking fountain or in the cafeteria. He or she may talk out during a test or speak before being called on.
- *Rigidity*—Student may be unable to adapt to changes in schedule or routine. Student may be unwilling to go to an assembly if it is scheduled during the regular math period.
- *Flat affect*—Student seems to have no voice inflections. Face seems expressionless, eyes seem vacant, he or she doesn't laugh or smile appropriately.

- *Low motivation*—What appears as low motivation may be confusion and inability to conceptualize and plan how to do the task.
- *Agitation and irritability*—Varying degrees of agitation and irritability may manifest themselves, such as becoming annoyed over picky things to becoming aggressive toward self or teachers.

The following recommendations should be considered when dealing with the student with traumatic brain injury in the school setting (National Information Center for Children and Youth with Disabilities, 1997c):

It will be important to determine whether the child needs to relearn material previously known. Supervision may be needed (i.e., between the classroom and restroom) as the child may have difficulty with orientation. Teachers should also be aware that, because the child's short-term memory may be impaired, what appears to have been learned may be forgotten later in the day. To work constructively with students with TBI, educators may need to:

- Provide repetition and consistency;
- Demonstrate new tasks, state instructions, and provide examples to illustrate ideas and concepts;
- Avoid figurative language;
- Reinforce lengthening periods of attention to appropriate tasks;
- Probe skill acquisition frequently and provide repeated practice;
- Teach compensatory strategies for increasing memory;
- Be prepared for students' reduced stamina and increased fatigue and provide rest breaks as needed; and
- Keep the environment as distraction-free as possible.

Initially, it may be important for teachers to gauge whether the child can follow one-step instructions well before challenging the child with a sequence of two or more directions. Often attention is focused on the child's disabilities after the injury, which reduces self-esteem; therefore, it is important to build opportunities for success and to maximize the child's strengths (p. 3).

Note. From "Traumatic Brain Injury: An Overview of School Re-Entry" by B. F. Tucker and S. E. Colson, 1992, *Intervention in School and Clinic, 27,* p. 201. Copyright 1992 by PRO-ED, Inc. Adapted with permission. Also from *Traumatic Brain Injury,* p. 2, NICHCY (National Information Center for Children and Youth with Disabilities), 1997, Washington, DC. Not copyrighted.

Things to Remember

- The special needs of students with physical and health impairments are diverse and vary with each individual. Some students require no educational adaptations, some require modification of the physical environment because they have limited energy or mobility, and others require modification of instructional activities. Medically fragile students may have special health-management needs. However, the major goal for all of these students is circumvention of the restrictions imposed by their physical or health impairments.
- There are a great many conditions that can produce special physical and health needs. Among the most common are traumatic brain injuries, epilepsy, cerebral palsy, diabetes, and asthma.
- Some physical and health impairments are congenital, whereas others occur after birth and are due to injury, accident, or disease.

- The primary purpose of assessing physical and health impairments is to gather information about the impact of the disabilities on educational performance and participation in instructional activities. It is also important to consider the effect of the disabilities on the development of social, vocational, and leisure skills. Medical information is useful only when it is interpreted in relation to classroom functioning and special health needs.
- One primary need of students with physical and health impairments is the opportunity to develop independence. Students should be encouraged to learn the skills necessary to assume responsibility for their own needs.
- In the general education classroom, the teacher provides for physical and health needs, ensures an accessible environment, and accommodates learning difficulties by adapting instruction.

Determine what services these agencies provide and the information they provide for parents, teachers, and individuals with physical or health impairments. How does one go about obtaining additional information or services?

6. Locate journal articles that present suggestions for including students with physical and health impairments in the general education program. Good places to look include special education journals (e.g., *Teaching Exceptional Children* or *Intervention in School and Clinic*) and writings in the field of rehabilitation; try, for example, the *Journal of Rehabilitation* or *Rehabilitation Literature*.

chapter 14

Teaching Students with Visual and Hearing Impairments

Cases

Beverly is a 17-year-old junior in high school who has been blind since birth. She has attended general education classes since the first grade. She also has been active in choir, plays the guitar, and is in the drama club. This year, she attends general education classes for all of her academic subjects. In the regular physical education class, she excels in swimming and gymnastics. Beverly uses an electronic device to take class notes in Braille, transfers those notes to her computer, and completes her assignments with a talking word processor. In math, she uses a talking calculator and, when materials for her classes are not available in tape-recorded or Braille formats, two of her fellow students act as readers so that she can keep up with her reading assignments. Beverly receives special services from a mobility instructor who is helping her develop the skills needed to use public transportation to travel around town. An itinerant teacher of students with visual impairments provides assistance and special instructional materials to Beverly and also to her teachers when needed.

Morris is a third grader who is partially sighted; he spends the majority of his school day in a general education class. He is able to read large-print material if it is further enlarged through magnification. During the school day, Morris visits the resource room for an hour to use special magnification equipment and to obtain help in math. He has some social problems with other students, especially when they call attention to his thick glasses or call him "four eyes." The resource teacher provides special materials to the general education teacher, enlarges classroom worksheets and other papers, and is on call to assist with special needs as they arise. Goals and services from Morris's IEP will be presented later in this chapter.

Beatrice is a 10-year-old student who is hard of hearing and in the fourth grade. She acquired her moderate hearing loss 2 years ago as the result of an accident. Beatrice spends one period a day in the resource room getting help in speech, speechreading, and language. In the general education class, she is assisted by a careful seating arrangement, the teacher's awareness of her need to see him speaking, and her hearing aid. Beatrice had developed excellent speech before the ac-

cident and currently has little trouble communicating information to others. The students in her class accept Beatrice's hearing loss and have learned to talk directly and clearly to her.

Max is a high school sophomore who has a congenital hearing impairment that has resulted in a severe bilateral hearing loss. Max wears hearing aids that provide some assistance to him in understanding the speech of others. Although Max's reading and math skills are quite good, his speech, oral language, and written work are poor; his writing is characterized by incomplete sentences, errors in punctuation and word usage, and word omissions. Max attends general education classes; during two periods each day he works with the resource teacher of students with hearing impairments to improve his speechreading, oral and written language, and sign language skills. He is also learning to use a word processing program on a computer for written assignments. Max has an interpreter who attends general education classes with him; the interpreter helps Max understand lectures and class discussions and communicate with teachers and peers. Several of Max's friends have learned enough sign language to carry on simple conversations. Max hopes to graduate in 2 more years and then attend college. We will look at portions of Max's IEP later.

Each of the students just introduced has a specific and different hearing or visual impairment. They all, however, share a sensory loss. Such students can exhibit a wide range of abilities and can experience a variety of problems in school. Their visual and hearing impairments can be mild, moderate, or severe. Although their performance in most areas falls within a range similar to that of typical students, their school achievement is generally poorer than that expected for their age and grade. Students with visual impairments have difficulty with mobility and with reading print or other visual materials (Hazekamp & Huebner, 1989); those with hearing impairments experience problems in language development and oral communication (Luetke-Stahlman & Luckner, 1991). Both the degree of the disability and the specific characteristics of the student influence the nature and extent of the impairment.

For Your Information

Students with Sensory Impairments

- About 1 student in 1,000 has a highly significant, noncorrectable visual impairment, but only about 3 out of 10 of these students are considered blind for educational purposes (Reynolds & Birch, 1988).
- The loss of vision can slow the pace of intellectual and concept development because it limits access to the normal range and variety of experiences (Caton, 1993).
- Students with visual impairments may be somewhat below grade level in school because of factors such as school absences for medical reasons and the difficulty of acquiring adequate instructional materials in Braille or large print (Caton, 1993).
- Fewer than 1 out of 100 students has a hearing impairment severe enough to warrant special education services (Reynolds & Birch, 1988).
- Hearing losses are measured in decibels (dB) and can be categorized by severity; individuals with losses in the speech range may have a mild (20–40 dB), moderate (40–60 dB), severe (60–80 dB), or profound (80 dB or greater) hearing impairment.
- Amplification of unintelligible sounds may do nothing for the person with a hearing impairment except make the unintelligible sound louder.
- American Sign Language (called Ameslan or ASL) is the fourth most used language in the United States (after English, Spanish, and Italian). It employs both fingerspelling and signs, with its own system and rules for formation of signs; it is not merely a manual form of English (Cartwright, Cartwright, & Ward, 1995).
- Speechreading (or lipreading) is a system of interpreting a speaker's words and message without hearing the speaker's voice. The speechreader watches the lips, mouth, tongue, gestures, and facial movements of the speaker in order to decode the message. This approach is difficult because many words are identical in appearance. For example, the words *pie* and *buy* appear the same on the lips. According to Green and Fischgrund (1993), "only 30 to 40 percent of the sounds in our language are produced with visible lip movements, so the speechreader has many gaps to fill in" (p. 293).
- The majority of students with visual and hearing impairments spend most of their school day in the general education classroom.

Special education for students with sensory impairments may be provided in a special class or resource room; in many cases, students remain in the general education class and receive special instruction, materials, or equipment to supplement or enrich their educational program. The goal of special education for students with visual and hearing impairments is the same as it is for other students with disabilities—facilitation of learning. This may require teaching students to make use of remaining sensory abilities and/or helping them learn to use other abilities to compensate for their disabilities.

Students with visual impairments are taught to rely on unaffected senses, such as hearing and touch. For example, they may learn to read **Braille,** to develop their listening skills, and to travel using **orientation** and **mobility** skills. For students with visual impairments with some usable vision, the educational program may include instruction in the use of **low-vision aids,** such as magnification devices, large-print reading materials, and new technological devices. Students with hearing impairments may require instruction in speech and language, training in other communication systems such as **speechreading** and **sign language,** or assistance in learning to use and care for **amplification devices** such as hearing aids. It is generally necessary to provide **auditory training** to students with hearing impairments in order for them to develop listening skills by learning to use their residual hearing. In addition to the specific sensory needs of these students, adaptations in the general education classroom may be needed to give them the opportunity to participate in instructional activities and social interactions.

The characteristics of students with visual and hearing impairments, methods for gathering data and adapting the classroom environment, and instructional procedures for the general education teacher are described in this chapter. The "For Your Information" on page 369 feature provides readers with background information on individuals with sensory impairments and helps to familiarize teachers with the problems these students may encounter.

INDICATORS OF VISUAL AND HEARING IMPAIRMENTS

The general education teacher plays an important role on the various teams assigned to assist students with visual and hearing impairments. Many of these students are initially identified and referred for consideration for special education services by the general education classroom teacher. In addition, general education teachers assist in collecting information about their students' classroom performance and in coordinating the services provided by various specialists.

Visual and hearing impairments can be congenital or **adventitious.** An adventitious impairment is one that is acquired as a result of illness or accident. Students with severe impairments are generally identified by parents or a physician prior to entrance into school; those with impairments that are milder or that result from illness or accident may be identified during the school years. Students who acquire impairments after they have experienced normal vision or hearing (with normal development of speech and language) are usually affected less adversely than those whose impairments are present at birth.

The extent of a vision or hearing loss is determined only after all possible corrections have been made. If a sensory impairment can be corrected so that the student has adequate vision or hearing, then the student is not considered disabled and in need of special education. If impairments remain after corrections have been made (e.g., eyeglasses, hearing aids, and all possible medical treatments, including surgery), then the student is considered to have a disability.

Students with visual impairments may be **blind** or **partially sighted.** These designations are based on measures of visual acuity and may have little educational relevance, just as an IQ score is not always an accurate predictor of academic achievement.

Students who are blind are defined legally as (1) those whose visual acuity is 20/200 or less in the better eye with the best possible correction or (2) those whose field of vision is restricted to an angle subtending an arc of 20 degrees or less (National Information Center for Children and Youth with Disabilities, 1997a). A larger group is made up of students who are partially sighted, whose vision in the best eye is between 20/70 and 20/200 after correction. The designation of 20/200 roughly indicates that the individual can see at 20 feet what a person with normal vision can see at 200 feet. Grayson (n.d.) indicates that "the American Foundation for the Blind prefers that the term blindness be reserved for a complete loss which can accurately be determined by ophthalmic measurements" (p. 1).

Legal terminology to describe visual impairments often lacks meaning for the educator. Instead, teachers are primarily concerned with assessing and developing a child's functional use of residual vision. Teachers need to know whether the student's remaining vision will allow learning with visually presented material, whether learning must be through other senses, or what combination of these approaches will be most beneficial. Many students who are legally blind are not considered **educationally blind.** Some are able to read regular print; oth-

FIGURE 14-1   Signs of Possible Vision Problems

The National Society to Prevent Blindness (1977) urges teachers and parents to watch for these signs that a child might be experiencing vision problems.

Behavior
- Rubs eyes excessively
- Shuts or covers one eye, tilts head or thrusts it forward
- Has difficulty reading or doing other work requiring close use of the eyes
- Blinks more than usual or is irritable when doing close work
- Is unable to see distant things clearly
- Squints eyelids together or frowns

Appearance
- Crossed eyes
- Red-rimmed, encrusted, or swollen eyelids
- Inflamed or watery eyes
- Recurring sties

Complaints
- Itching, burning, or scratchy feeling in eyes
- Inability to see well
- Dizziness, headaches, or nausea following close work
- Blurred or double vision

If students exhibit any of these problems for a period of time, they should be referred to the school nurse or appropriate special education personnel.

ers can read print that is enlarged typographically or viewed through a magnifying device. Because of the limited educational relevance of the legal terms and acuity scores, teachers should be aware that it is important to acquire information on the visual functioning of students included in the general education program; assumptions regarding their ability to use their vision should not be based on a label or acuity score.

Students with visual impairments who have not been identified before entering school are often located in the periodic vision screening conducted for all students in a school. The general education teacher can play an important role by carefully observing students in the classroom. The signs and symptoms of vision problems listed in Figure 14–1 can alert the teacher to students in need of further investigation.

Students with hearing impairments may be **deaf** or **hard of hearing.** Students who are deaf are not able to use their hearing to understand speech, even with a hearing aid. Students who are hard of hearing have a significant hearing loss that requires some special adaptations; they are able to use hearing to understand speech, often through the use of a hearing aid (Heward, 1996).

Conductive hearing losses are caused by interference with the transmission of sound from the outer ear to the inner ear; this interference can occur in either the outer or the middle ear. Individuals with this type of loss are usually treated by medication or surgery, but occasionally hearing aids are prescribed. An impairment to the auditory nerve or inner ear results in a **sensorineural hearing loss.** Surgery and medication are generally less effective in treating this type of loss; most individuals with a sensorineural loss will benefit from the use of hearing aids. A mixed hearing loss involves both conductive and sensorineural impairments. Functional hearing losses have no known organic origin, can be due to emotional factors, and are generally not improved by sound amplification (National Information Center for Children and Youth with Disabilities, 1996).

FIGURE 14-2　Signs of Hearing Problems

Ear Problems
- Draining ears.
- Infected outer ear.
- Unpleasant odor in ears.
- Cotton in ears.
- Continuous mouth breathing.
- Consistent pulling or tugging of ears.

Hearing Defects
- Persistent inattentiveness.
- More awareness of movement or action than of sound.
- Extremely watchful of the teacher (lip reading).
- Turns head to one side in an effort to hear.
- Consistently asks that questions be repeated.
- Seems to confuse words that have similar sounds.
- Constantly interrupts conversations without awareness of interruption.
- Finds it difficult to follow verbal directions.
- Fails to locate source of sound in class.
- Has difficulty with articulation.
- Has a monotonous voice pitch.
- Mumbles without being aware of it.
- Speaks very quietly.

Note. From *School Health Problems* (p. 34) by J. Smolensky, L. R. Bonvechio, R. E. Whitlock, and M. A. Girard, 1968, Palo Alto, CA: Fearon. Copyright 1968 by Fearon. Reprinted by permission.

Frequency and intensity are two of the physical characteristics of sound used in measuring hearing loss. Frequency, or pitch, is expressed in a unit called hertz (Hz). An example of pitch is the musical scale; as the voice ascends the scale, pitch or frequency increases. Intensity, or loudness, is measured in decibels (dB). These symbols often appear on reports of students' hearing losses, with a loss indicated in dB at each Hz level. It is important for the educator to consider a hearing loss in relation to speech sounds. Most speech is between 500 and 2,000 Hz in frequency and between 40 and 65 dB in intensity (Green & Fischgrund, 1993). A student with a 75 to 80 dB loss in the 1,000 to 4,000 Hz range would have a severe loss that would affect his or her ability to understand speech.

Hearing losses not identified during the preschool years by parents or physicians are often detected during annual school hearing screenings. By also carefully observing the behaviors of students, the classroom teacher can be alert to signs and symptoms that indicate possible hearing impairments. Warning signals to watch for are listed in Figure 14–2; these and other indicators of visual or hearing impairments may be noticed by the teacher. Students who do not respond normally to visual or auditory stimuli are potential candidates for special education assessment.

ASSESSMENT PROCEDURES

When students are suspected of having visual or hearing impairments, they are referred to the prereferral team to determine if appropriate interventions can be implemented in the general education classroom. If this team determines there is a need for more extensive review, a referral is made to the special education assessment team. An assessment plan is then developed and presented to the parents, who must grant permission before it is implemented. This assessment should determine the student's intellectual functioning, academic achievement, and communicative status. It must be conducted in an appropriate mode of communication (e.g., Braille or sign language when appropriate) and must assess all areas that relate to the suspected sensory impairment. The assessment should determine the student's capabilities and identify factors that are interfering with school performance.

Assessments of students with visual and hearing impairments can be conducted by a variety of professionals. Several—such as special education teachers of students with visual or hearing impairments, ophthalmologists, and audiologists—may assess only this type of special student. Many instruments commonly used to evaluate the ability or achievement of other students with disabilities may be inappropriate for students with sensory impairments. To obtain accurate and reliable information about these individuals, measures must be selected carefully and, if necessary, adapted to allow students to circumvent their disabilities.

The intellectual functioning of pupils with visual and hearing impairments can be assessed with adapted, modified, or specially designed measures. The verbal section of the *Wechsler Intelligence Scale for Children-Third Edition (WISC-III)* has been used to assess students with visual impairments. The *Perkins-Binet Intelligence Scale* (Davis, 1980) is designed for students with visual impairments who are ages 2 to 22. This adaptation of the *Stanford-Binet Intelligence Scale* has two forms, one for those with nonusable vision and another for those with usable vision. Approximately 25% to 30% of the items are performance based, and the test yields both mental age and intelligence quotients. The *Nebraska Test of Learning Aptitude (NTLA)* (Hiskey, 1966) is a measure of the learning aptitude of individuals between the ages of 3 and 16 who are deaf. Each of the measures identified here is specifically designed to provide an indication of the capability of students with visual or hearing impairments.

Many academic assessment instruments for sighted or hearing students can be administered with little or no modification to individuals who are partially sighted or hard of hearing. Students with more severe impairments may require adaptations, such as communicating in sign language or transcribing portions of the test into Braille. In addition, students can be allowed extra time to finish portions of a test if this is necessary to reflect their skill levels adequately. However, if modifications have been made in the administration procedures of standardized tests, they must be noted in the assessment report.

Vision and hearing assessments are normally conducted by specially trained individuals. These assessments can be useful in indicating the extent of an impairment and determining possible remedies (e.g., glasses, low-vision aids, hearing aids) that can reduce the impact of the impairment on the student's educational performance. Students who are partially sighted should be encouraged to have their vision rechecked frequently because their visual efficiency may improve and adjustments may be needed in their optical aids or the type size used for their materials (Harley & Lawrence, 1984). Ophthalmologists are medical doctors who specialize in the diagnosis and treatment of defects and diseases of the eye. An optometrist is a nonmedical practitioner licensed to measure refractive errors and eye muscle disturbances. Both of these professionals measure vision and prescribe corrective lenses, but only the ophthalmologist may perform surgery, prescribe medication, and administer other medical treatments. Medical doctors concerned with hearing impairments are the otolaryngologist (who diagnoses and treats ear, nose, and throat disorders) and the otologist (who specializes in the treatment of ear diseases and disorders).

The **Snellen Chart** is commonly used for vision screening of students; its purpose is to identify students with possible visual acuity problems who are in need of a more thorough evaluation by a vision specialist. The chart is composed of rows of letters of various sizes, which students must identify from a preset distance. For young children, the Snellen Chart contains only the letter *E* in various sizes and orientations; this allows the child to point in the direction the *E* is facing rather than name various letters. Hearing is assessed with a device called an **audiometer.** The student listens to tones or speech delivered via air or bone conduction at a variety of frequencies and intensities.

A mobility specialist may meet with students with visual impairments to assess their orientation and mobility skills and to determine their need for training in these areas. Other specialists may evaluate students' ability to use low-vision aids or read printed material. For students with hearing impairments, the speech-language pathologist is the professional who determines current functioning in oral communication and language development. The educational audiologist is responsible for ensuring that hearing aids and other amplification systems are functioning properly.

Direct observation and informal assessment by the teacher can provide a great deal of information for the prereferral and assessment teams. Much of the data needed to determine a student's requirements for special services and to prepare the goals and objectives for the IEP can most effectively be gathered by the teacher or specialists while the student is performing under typical conditions in the general education classroom.

 SPECIAL SERVICES

Information gathered through the assessment process is used by the IEP team to develop a student's IEP. The IEPs of students with visual and hearing impairments usually contain several goals. Students with visual impairments often have goals in the use of vision aids, improvement of listening skills, development of Braille reading and writing ability, notetaking, mobility, and academic skill areas. Figure 14–3 shows portions of an IEP for Morris, one of the students introduced at the beginning of this chapter. Morris is a third grader who is partially sighted.

Students with hearing impairments may have goals in speechreading, speech and language, auditory training, sign language, and the use of amplification devices. Max, the high school student described at the start of this chapter, has a severe

---

 **FIGURE 14-3**   **IEP Goals and Services for Morris**

Annual Goals
1. By the end of the school year, Morris will increase his reading rate for print material enlarged through magnification.
   Person responsible: Resource teacher
2. By the end of the school year, Morris will decrease his math errors by correcting his work with a talking calculator.
   Person responsible: Resource teacher
3. By the end of the school year, Morris will decrease the number of inappropriate reactions to comments of other students about his glasses.
   Persons responsible: Resource teacher and grade 3 teacher
4. Morris will successfully complete third grade requirements.
   Person responsible: Grade 3 teacher

Amount of Participation in General Education
Morris will spend the entire day in the third grade classroom with the exception of 1 hour per day in the special education program.

Special Education and Related Services
1. Morris will receive special education services from the resource teacher (annual goals 1, 2, and 3) for 1 hour daily.
2. The resource teacher will provide consultation to Morris's third grade teacher and special materials such as large-print books as needed.

FIGURE 14-4   **IEP Goals and Services for Max**

Annual Goals
1. By the end of the school year, Max will use a word processor to write a 300-word composition with complete sentences, correct punctuation, and appropriate paragraph structure.
   Persons responsible: Resource teacher and English teacher
2. By the end of the school year, Max will use speechreading accurately for short lectures.
   Person responsible: Resource teacher
3. By the end of the school year, Max will be able to conduct an oral conversation with an adult.
   Person responsible: Resource teacher
4. By the end of the school year, Max will complete all requirements in English, math, chemistry, and driver's education.
   Persons responsible: General education teachers
5. By the end of the school year, Max will be able to carry on a complete conversation with a person competent in sign language.
   Person responsible: Resource teacher

Amount of Participation in General Education
Max will attend all general education classes with the exception of two class periods.

Special Education and Related Services
1. Max will receive special education services from the resource teacher (annual goals 1, 2, 3, and 5) for two periods each day.
2. The resource teacher will provide consultation services to Max's classroom teachers as needed.

bilateral hearing loss that resulted from a congenital hearing impairment. A portion of Max's IEP appears in Figure 14–4.

The majority of students with sensory impairments spend some portion of their school day included in the general education program. Many receive services from an itinerant special education teacher to supplement the activities provided in the general education class. For those spending the entire day in the general education classroom, teacher consultants may work with the general education teacher to help design needed classroom adaptations and provide special materials or equipment. Other students may attend a resource room. Very young students or those with multiple or more severe disabilities may spend the majority of their school day in a special class and participate in general education classroom activities when there is some assurance that they can have successful involvement and progress in the general curriculum. Students with sensory impairments receive services from a variety of specialists, such as speech-language pathologists, adapted physical education teachers, and vocational rehabilitation counselors. The school system or out-side agencies may offer these students special programs, such as instruction in daily living skills or recreational activities. The special services required for different students with similar impairments may vary considerably.

In making decisions about including students with disabilities in the general education program, it is necessary to consider the views of parents and those of students themselves. In the past few years, for example, many members of the Deaf community have become advocates for special schools for students who are deaf. This position reflects a growing awareness of Deaf culture and the Deaf community's pride in that culture. For example, in 1988, students at Gallaudet University, a university for students who are deaf, staged a protest until trustees named a person who was deaf as president. Another example is the testimony given by Jesse Thomas, a 15-year-old who is deaf, before the National Council on Disabilities:

> I think I have to explain that I am not disabled, I'm just deaf. Deaf persons are a minority group. They use American Sign Language (ASL) and are part of the

Window on the Web

Websites About Sensory Impairments

Websites About Visual Impairments

- American Council of the Blind (www.acb.org)
- American Foundation for the Blind (www.afb.org)
- American Printing House for the Blind, Inc. (www.aph.org)
- Blindness Resource Center (www.nyise.org/blind.htm)
- National Association for Visually Handicapped (www.navh.org)
- National Federation of the Blind (www.nfb.org)

Websites About Hearing Impairments

- Alexander Graham Bell Association for the Deaf (www.agbell.org)
- American Society for Deaf Children (www.educ.kent.edu/deafed/asdchome.htm)
- Educational Audiology Association (www.ehhs.cmich.edu/eaa)
- National Association of the Deaf (www.nad.org)
- National Council on the Education of the Deaf, Kent State University (www.educ.kent.edu/deafed)
- National Information Center on Deafness (www.gallaudet.edu:80/~nicd)
- National Institute on Deafness and Other Communication Disorders (www.nih.gov/nidcd)

Deaf Culture. One of the main reasons that mainstreaming is not good is because mainstreaming lacks Deaf Culture and ASL. I can't really explain Deaf Culture. I do know that Deaf Culture makes me proud of who I am—DEAF. (as cited in Heward, 1996, p. 376)

CLASSROOM ADAPTATIONS

Students with visual or hearing impairments who are in the general education program frequently require adaptations in the arrangement of the learning environment and in the structure of instructional procedures. Extensive curricular adaptations are typically not needed. Although additional hands-on experiences may be beneficial for students with sensory impairments, other adjustments correspond to those generally provided for typical students.

The idea of adapting instruction for students with visual and hearing impairments is not new. In 1900, for example, Helen Keller wrote specifications for her own classroom adaptations. Much has been written about the obviously gifted Helen Keller, who had severe impairments in both hearing and vision. Her familiar story and struggle to adapt to a world she could neither see nor hear is

captured in the letter she wrote to the chairman of the academic board at Radcliffe College. In this letter, she asks for adaptations to the regular, not special, college classroom.

Dear Sir:

As an aid to me in determining my plans for study the coming year, I apply to you for information as to the possibility of my taking the regular courses in Radcliffe College.

Since receiving my certificate of admission to Radcliffe last July, I have been studying with a private tutor, Horace, Aeschylus, French, German, Rhetoric, English History, English Literature and Criticism, and English Composition.

In college I should wish to continue most, if not all, of these subjects. The conditions under which I work require the presence of Miss Sullivan, who has been my teacher and companion for thirteen years, as an interpreter of oral speech and as a reader of examination papers. In college, she, or possibly in some subjects someone else, would of necessity be with me in the lecture room and at recitations. I should do all my written work on a typewriter, and if a Professor could not understand my speech, I could write out my answers to his questions and hand them to him after the recitation.

Is it possible for the College to accommodate itself to these unprecedented conditions, so as to enable me to pursue my studies at Radcliffe? I realize that the obstacles in the way of my receiving a college education are very great—to others they may seem insurmountable; but, dear Sir, a true soldier does not acknowledge defeat before the battle. (Keller, 1965, p. 151)

The classroom adaptations described in chapter 13 are similar to those required for students with visual and hearing impairments. The teacher should be sure to explain the special student's impairment(s) to the other students in the general education class. A careful explanation facilitates the acceptance of students with disabilities by their peers. However, teachers and students should be careful not to become overprotective of students with disabilities; they must be encouraged to develop independence.

◈ ARRANGING THE LEARNING ENVIRONMENT

Students with sensory impairments may require adaptations in the arrangement of the classroom, seating patterns, and other factors related to lighting, sound transmission, and proximity to activities. The following are suggestions for general education classroom teachers working with students with visual impairments:

- Be sure students' tables or desktops are large enough for braillewriters and other equipment (Maron & Martinez, 1980).
- Copyholders, easels, and adjustable tops on desks help students to maintain good posture for close-eye activities (Harley & Lawrence, 1984).
- Provide an accessible storage area with adequate space for large pieces of equipment such as optical devices or reading stands and Braille or large-print books (Torres & Corn, 1990).
- Do not place students who are partially sighted where they must face the glare of a primary source of light, such as a window (Pasanella & Volkmor, 1981). However, lighting should be adequate; some students may need additional light from a source such as a desk lamp or a window.
- Seat students so that they are able to participate in activities with other class members. A flexible seating arrangement will allow students to be close to different classroom activities or to adjust the amount of light available as needed. For example, a student might relocate to obtain a better view of the teacher, the chalkboard, or the projection screen, or to obtain a greater amount of light for a particular activity.
- Use copy machines to enlarge print materials for students with visual impairments (Torres & Corn, 1990).
- Allow students to become oriented to the classroom; permit them to explore (Maron & Martinez, 1980). Other suggestions for developing the mobility skills of students with visual impairments are listed in "Inclusion Tips for the Teacher" on page 378.

Students with hearing impairments require other types of adaptations to facilitate their successful inclusion in the general education program:

- The student's seat should be away from noise and close to the area where instruction takes place.
- Seating arrangements should permit the student to face the teacher and other students. Teachers should take care not to turn their back to students with hearing impairments while speaking. During a class discussion, it may be necessary to allow the student to move around the room to be able to see those who are speaking (Reynolds & Birch, 1988).

Inclusion Tips for the Teacher

Orientation and Mobility

For students who are blind, or those with limited vision, the orientation and mobility specialist provides instruction in how to travel from one place to another. According to Mandell and Fiscus (1981), "*Orientation* refers to the ability to understand the relationship between self and environment through intact sensory input. *Mobility* refers to one's ability to travel safely and independently through the physical environment" [emphasis added] (p. 209). Independent travel is an important skill for individuals who are blind, and several types of travel aids are available: a long cane, a guide dog (for older students and adults), and electronic devices that signal the presence of obstacles in the path of travel. The general education teacher can support and supplement the training provided by the mobility specialist, as Craig and Howard (1981) suggest:

- Eliminate unnecessary obstacles; inform students of changes in room arrangement or of any temporary obstacles, such as a portable movie screen.
- Keep doors completely closed or completely open to eliminate the possibility of the student running into a partially open door.
- Initially, allow the student to travel with a companion to frequently used rooms, such as the library, restroom, and auditorium. Discuss the route, pointing out right and left turns and any distinguishing landmarks.
- Allow the student to move about freely until he has familiarized himself with the room or route.

- Discourage reliance upon sighted guides once the student has demonstrated the ability to travel independently.
- If necessary, make provisions for a sighted guide for fire drills, field trips, assemblies, and seating in rooms that ordinarily have unassigned seating. (p. 191)

Recommendations for persons who will act as sighted guides are provided by the Arkansas Enterprises for the Blind (n.d.):

- When offering assistance to a . . . person [who is blind], be direct. Speak in a normal tone. Simply ask: "May I be of help?" Address him directly; this helps him locate you.
- Never "grab" . . . [the] arm [of a person who is blind]; he can't anticipate your movements if you do. Permit him to take your arm and say: "Here's my left arm" or the right, as the case may be. He knows, then, how to take your arm and he will respond to your motion much as a dancer follows a partner.
- In walking with a . . . person [who is blind] proceed at a normal pace; hesitate slightly before stepping up or down; don't drag him over the curb. After crossing a street, see that he is started in the direction he wants to take, and caution him of any unusual obstructions ahead.
- In showing a . . . person [who is blind] to a chair, place his hand upon the back of it; don't try to push him into it. His touch will tell him the type, width and height of the chair. (p. 2)

- If an interpreter is provided, that individual should be seated near the student. The student and the interpreter should have some flexibility in where they choose to sit.
- Speakers should avoid standing with a direct light behind them; if the teacher stands in front of a window, it may not be possible to see what he or she is saying (English, 1995).
- Keep classroom and background noise to a minimum; when students wear hearing aids, *all* sounds are amplified (Reynolds & Birch, 1988).
- Label items in the classroom to help in the development of vocabulary for the young student. This practice can also help other students in learning to read (Glazzard, 1980).

For many students with sensory impairments, special assistive aids and equipment (such as those described in chapter 8) are helpful, and students should be encouraged to use the special devices that have been provided. Become acquainted with one type of device designed to help students with visual impairments communicate with others by consulting "Spotlight on Technology."

Other adaptations are often required to meet the individual needs of students. Special educators, the students' parents, and often the students themselves can give suggestions for such adaptations. Careful observation of students in a classroom setting provides information on how the educational environment can best be modified.

Spotlight on Technology

Braille Personal Notetakers

Braille personal notetakers are portable electronic devices that allow students who are blind to take notes in class, complete written assignments, and write answers to exam questions. One example is the Braille Lite from Blazie Engineering (www.blazie.com). It is lightweight (approximately 2 pounds), quite small (8.25″ by 5″ by 1.75″), and is powered by a battery or household current. Its eight-key keyboard is designed for typing Braille, not standard text. Two keys are used solely for word processing. The other six correspond to the six dots found in Braille; the student presses one, two, three, or more keys depending on the Braille character he or she wants to type.

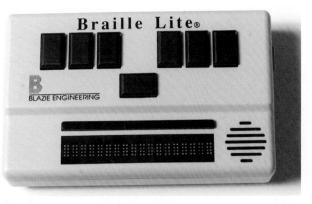

Note. Photo courtesy of Blazie Engineering.

Braille Lite contains a built-in speech synthesizer so that it can read the student's text aloud. It also converts Braille to standard text that can be edited with the full range of standard word processing features (including spellcheck) provided by the Braille Lite. In addition, the student can use the built-in talking clock, calendar, scientific calculator, stopwatch, and telephone directory.

Another feature of the Braille Lite is its dynamic Braille display. This is a tactile display; small reeds corresponding to the dots in the Braille cell are raised electronically to form Braille characters. Eighteen Braille cells are displayed at a time on the Braille Lite. This type of Braille is called paperless or refreshable Braille. It does not need to be printed on paper, and it can be reused (or refreshed) by lowering the reeds and then arranging them to form a different set of Braille characters. Another model, the Braille Lite 40, provides a 40-cell Braille display. This larger display allows the student to review more material at one time and improves the review of computer screen layouts.

Braille 'N Speak, another device from Blazie Engineering, is used by many students. Although it is smaller and less expensive than the Braille Lite, Braille 'N Speak contains many of the same word processing and notetaking features but provides only speech output; no refreshable Braille display is available. All of the notetakers (including Braille 'N Speak) can be interfaced with external refreshable Braille displays that display 40, 65, or 80 Braille cells in order to permit the student to review a greater number of characters at the same time.

When the students are ready to print their work, they can connect the personal notetaker to a Braille printer, a standard printer, or a printer that produces pages with text in both Braille and print formats. Printers with both Braille and print output are very useful in general education settings because a student who is blind and a teacher who is sighted can both read from the same copy. It is also possible to connect personal notetakers to computers. This allows the student to use the notetaker as a Braille keyboard to edit and spellcheck the text he or she has produced using a talking word processor designed for writers with visual impairments. These word processors "speak" everything on the screen (including instructions and menu choices), not just the text the student has written.

With assistive devices such as personal notetakers, students who are blind can participate in general education classroom activities without having to rely on others for notetaking or the production of written assignments. For example, when writing a paper, a student might draft the outline on the personal notetaker, print it in Braille to review it, use the notetaker's talking word processing program to expand the outline into a draft of the paper, then transfer the draft to a computer for a spelling check before printing the final version in print for his or her classmates and/or teacher.

FIGURE 14-5 Sources of Materials for Students with Sensory Impairments

Large-Print Materials
- American Printing House for the Blind, Inc., P.O. Box 6085, Louisville, KY 40206; (800) 223-1839; (502) 895-2405; Fax: (502) 895-1509
  e-mail: info@aph.org
  Web address: http://www.aph.org/
- National Association for Visually Handicapped, 22 West 21st Street, NY, NY 10010; (212) 889-3141; San Francisco: (415) 221-3201
  e-mail: staff@navh.org (western states: staffca@navh.org)
  Web address: http://www.navh.org

Braille Materials
- American Printing House for the Blind, Inc. (address above)
- Library of Congress National Library Service for the Blind and Physically Handicapped, 1291 Taylor Street, NW, Washington, DC 20542; (202) 707-5100; (800) 424-8567
  e-mail: nls@loc.gov
  Web address: http://www.loc.gov/nls

Tape-Recorded Materials
- American Printing House for the Blind, Inc. (address above)
- Library of Congress National Library Service for the Blind and Physically Handicapped (address above)
- Recording for the Blind, 20 Roszel Road, Princeton, NJ 08540; (800) 221-4792

Captioned Films and Videos
- Captioned Films/Videos for the Deaf, Modern Talking Picture Service, Inc., 5000 Park Street North, St. Petersburg, FL 33709; (800) 237-6213

MODIFYING INSTRUCTIONAL PROCEDURES

When students with visual or hearing impairments are present in the general education classroom, it may be necessary for the teacher to modify instructional procedures. These adaptations depend on the individual needs and capabilities of the included students and vary from minimal to extensive. Specialists are generally available to assist the teacher in developing and implementing modified instructional strategies.

Students with visual impairments who are included in the general education program may require instruction from a specialist to acquire the skills needed to use low-vision aids or to read and write Braille. In addition, some students need special materials or equipment; others use only those materials available in the classroom. Suggestions for teachers working with students with visual impairments in a general education setting are listed here:

- Change instructional procedures only when absolutely necessary. Curricular goals should remain the same for typical and special students (Blankenship & Lilly, 1981).
- Many of the print materials used in the general education classroom may be available in other formats. Work with the student's special education teacher to locate large-print, Braille, or tape-recorded texts. Start looking well ahead of the time materials are needed, to ensure their availability. For information about sources of materials for students with visual (and hearing) impairments, see Figure 14–5.
- When descriptive language is used to interpret events that involve facial expressions or gestures, students are less likely to be off-task (Spenciner, 1992).
- Allow adequate time for students with visual impairments to complete reading assignments; some students may need some extra time to locate their materials and to find the starting place (Spenciner, 1992).

- Encourage students to use a word processor or to type communications that must be read by sighted individuals; examples include written reports, homework assignments, and personal correspondence. The special education teacher may provide word processing and typing instruction; the general education teacher can help by allowing students access to a computer or a typewriter in the classroom.
- Say aloud material that is being written on the chalkboard or on the overhead projector (Spenciner, 1992).
- Provide students with instruction and experiences that develop critical listening skills; individuals with visual impairments do not automatically have better listening skills (Blankenship & Lilly, 1981).
- Occasionally provide tape-recorded materials to students who read Braille or large print in order to vary the presentation of reading material (Spenciner, 1992).
- Vigorous physical exercise is recommended for students with visual impairments. Encourage them to compete with sighted peers whenever possible (Reynolds & Birch, 1988).
- Become familiar with the various types of special equipment used by the students with visual impairments in your class. Let the special teacher know immediately of any necessary replacement or repairs. Perkins **braillewriters** are small machines that are often used to write (type) material in Braille; the **slate and stylus** is a small handheld device also used to write Braille. Devices such as an abacus, Braille ruler, or raised relief map are also useful for students. To learn more about the Braille system, consult Figure 14–6 on page 382.

In addition to the special equipment available for students with visual impairments, the teacher can use general education classroom materials more effectively by adapting them. Glazzard (1980) suggests several ideas for modification of materials:

- Use a heavy black marking pen on dittoed worksheets. It makes them easier to see.
- Use a marking pen to delineate lines on writing paper or purchase heavy-lined paper.
- Write chalkboard directions on a separate piece of paper for the child with poor vision. Keep copying work for the . . . student to a minimum.

- Ask parents or other students to read reference material or lengthy reading assignments to the . . . student [with visual impairments].
- Record reading material or other assignments for the . . . child [with visual impairments]. Aides, parents, volunteers, or other students are possible sources of help for recording assignments.
- A magnifying glass may be helpful for enlarging the print of regular class materials. It is less tiring for some . . . students [with visual impairments] to use such an aid. (pp. 27–28)

Pasanella and Volkmor (1981) provide additional suggestions that general education teachers might find helpful in communicating with students with visual impairments:

- Use a vocabulary that is related to sight, such as the words *see* and *look*. . . . [P]ersons [with visual impairments] use those words, too.
- Call the student by name when you are speaking to him.
- Talk directly to the student. Look him in the face and remind classmates to do the same.
- Some . . . students [with visual impairments] develop unusual mannerisms. Gently remind them about more appropriate behaviors.
- Tell the student who you are when you approach him or her and tell him when you leave.
- Encourage the student to use any adaptive aids s/he needs and to explain their use to other classmates. (pp. 186–187)

Students with hearing impairments may also require adaptations in the general education classroom. Specialists provide many of these students with instruction in speechreading, fingerspelling, and sign language. Educators of students with hearing impairments do not agree on the most appropriate communication method for this group, but many professionals advocate **total communication.** This approach combines the oral/aural method of communication (speech, speechreading, and audition) with the manual method (fingerspelling and sign language). The manual alphabet, shown in Figure 14–7 on page 383, allows students to fingerspell names and technical terms that are not available in sign language. The following suggestions can help the teacher work with students with hearing impairments who are included in the general education program:

- Teachers and students should speak naturally, use natural gestures, and maintain face-to-face

FIGURE 14-6 Braille: Tactile Communication for Individuals Who Are Blind

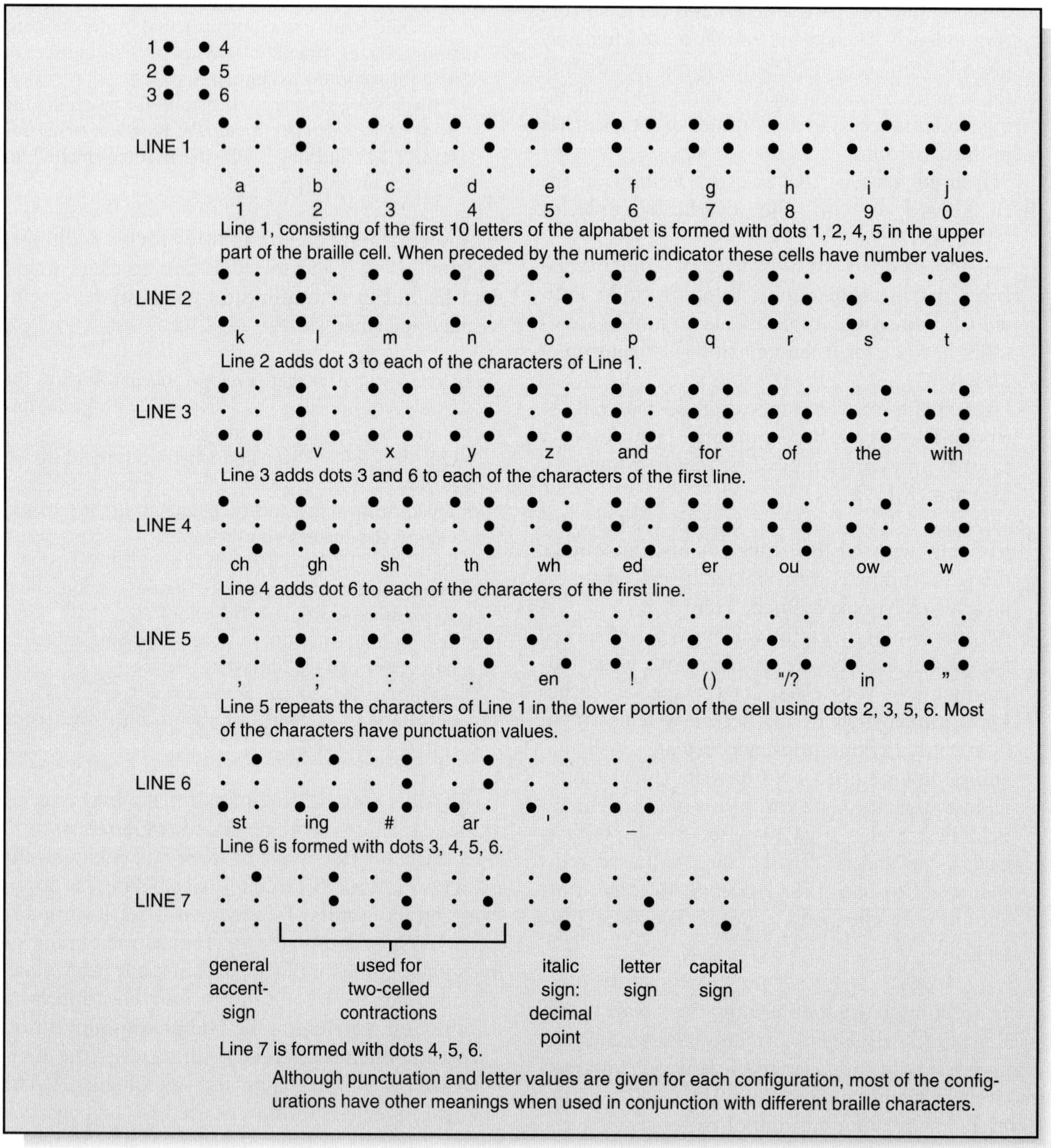

1 4
2 5
3 6
LINE 1
a b c d e f g h i j
1 2 3 4 5 6 7 8 9 0
Line 1, consisting of the first 10 letters of the alphabet is formed with dots 1, 2, 4, 5 in the upper part of the braille cell. When preceded by the numeric indicator these cells have number values.
LINE 2
k l m n o p q r s t
Line 2 adds dot 3 to each of the characters of Line 1.
LINE 3
u v x y z and for of the with
Line 3 adds dots 3 and 6 to each of the characters of the first line.
LINE 4
ch gh sh th wh ed er ou ow w
Line 4 adds dot 6 to each of the characters of the first line.
LINE 5
, ; : . en ! () "/? in "
Line 5 repeats the characters of Line 1 in the lower portion of the cell using dots 2, 3, 5, 6. Most of the characters have punctuation values.
LINE 6
st ing # ar ' _
Line 6 is formed with dots 3, 4, 5, 6.
LINE 7
general accent-sign
used for two-celled contractions
italic sign: decimal point
letter sign
capital sign
Line 7 is formed with dots 4, 5, 6.
Although punctuation and letter values are given for each configuration, most of the configurations have other meanings when used in conjunction with different braille characters.

Note. From *Understanding Braille* by the American Foundation for the Blind, n.d., New York: Author. Reprinted by permission.

contact when speaking with a student with a hearing impairment (Reynolds & Birch, 1988).

- Encourage students with hearing impairments to use their hearing aids at all times.
- Find out the best seating position for the student to speechread the teacher's verbal presentations to the class by discussing this with the student (Rees, 1992).

FIGURE 14-7   The Manual Alphabet

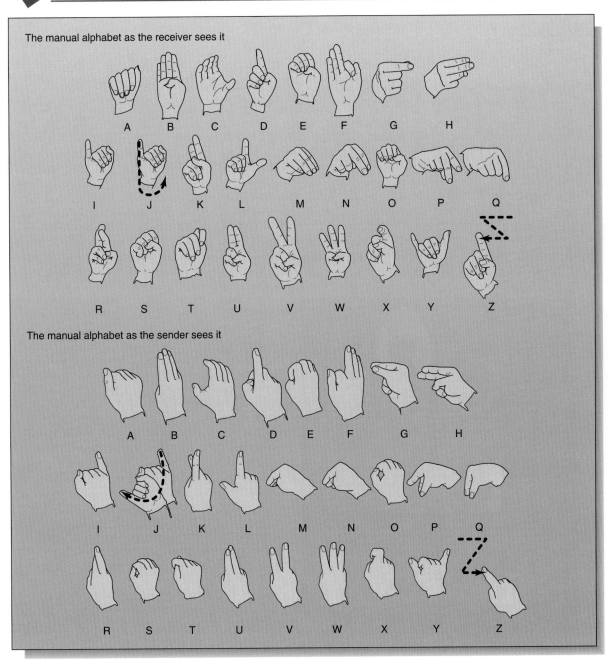

Note. From the National Association of the Deaf, n.d. Copyright by the National Association of the Deaf. Reprinted by permission.

- Use an overhead projector; it permits a teacher to write material that can be seen by all students while the teacher continues to face the class (English, 1995). It is best to use a projector with a quiet fan.

- Provide copies of the teacher's notes or those of two other students when material is presented in lecture format; it is not possible to speechread and take notes simultaneously. Write assignments

Spotlight on Technology

Classroom Amplification Devices

Students with hearing impairments benefit from technological devices that amplify sounds in order to optimize residual hearing. Some amplification systems also overcome the problem of listening in noisy situations.

Hearing aids differ in shape and style (see chapter 8), but all operate on the same principles. Sound is picked up by a microphone, amplified, and delivered to a receiver in the canal of the ear. Unfortunately, *all* sounds are amplified, making it difficult for the user to discriminate between conversation and all other noises in the background. In the classroom, a student with a hearing impairment will likely find it difficult to follow a teacher's instructions in the presence of competing noise (rustling paper, shuffling feet, pencil sharpeners, aquarium motors, heating systems, etc.).

The hearing aid user is also affected by two other factors: distance and direction. As distance between the speaker and the hearing aid user increases, the intensity of the speaker's voice decreases. To a person with a hearing impairment, this decrease has a significantly negative impact on speech perception. As a speaker turns away from a hearing aid user, the speech signal again becomes weaker and sometimes distorted. In order to overcome these limitations of a hearing aid, a teacher would need to directly face the student with a hearing impairment at all times, and speak at a distance of approximately 12 inches from the hearing aid microphone. Obviously, this strategy is not a practical recommendation.

Phonic Ear Personal FM System

Note. Photo courtesy of Phonic Ear, Inc.

Fortunately, technology is available to address these hearing aid limitations. FM technology is an instrument specially designed to address the problems of noise, distance, and direction (Flexer, Wray, & Ireland, 1989; Maxon, Brackett, & van den Berg, 1991). To use an FM system (previously called an auditory trainer), the classroom teacher wears a wireless microphone, and the student wears a wireless receiver. Some receivers look and operate like personal stereos. Recently, receivers have also been designed to be worn as behind-the-ear hearing aids. This new type of receiver is a preferred choice among students if cosmetic concerns become an issue.

The FM system has three advantages: (1) the teacher's voice is amplified 12 to 15 decibels above the classroom noise; (2) the teacher's voice is transmitted at an even intensity across a distance of up to 100 feet; and (3) the teacher's voice is not affected by direction. This three-fold "FM advantage" has helped make the FM system standard equipment in special classrooms for students with hearing impairments for many years. Because

and outlines of lectures on the board (Reynolds & Birch, 1988).

- Use **captioned films** whenever possible. Many films and videotapes used in the classroom are available in a captioned version. (See Figure 14–5 for information about the source for captioned films and videos.)

- Hearing aids should be checked daily. Consult with a speech-language pathologist or educational audiologist to determine who will assume the FM system is easy to use, it has been introduced into mainstreamed and inclusion settings with much success. However, because there is a real risk of overamplification, FM systems must be fitted and monitored by an audiologist.

Another amplification system used in classrooms is called sound field amplification. FM technology is used to transmit the teacher's voice by a microphone to one or more speakers placed around the classroom. The teacher's voice is slightly amplified and conveyed to the whole room (that is, the sound field); students in the back of class hear the teacher's voice as loudly as the students in front. If there is a student in the classroom with a hearing impairment, he or she may wear either an FM receiver or his or her personal hearing aids, depending on the audiologist's recommendation. Research indicates that all members in the class can benefit from sound field amplification: for example, students have demonstrated significant academic gains and an increase in on-task behavior. Teachers also report a noticeable reduction in vocal fatigue (Berg, 1987; Sarff, 1981; Zabel & Tabor, 1993).

Sound Field System from Phonic Ear

Note. Photo courtesy of Phonic Ear, Inc.

Developed by Kris English, Ph.D., CCC-A, educational audiologist and assistant professor at Duquesne University.

this responsibility. "Spotlight on Technology" describes the use of hearing aids and classroom amplification devices with students with hearing impairments.

• Question students with hearing impairments to determine whether they understand information presented in class. Do not assume that students understand the material.

Inclusion Tips for the Teacher

Students Who Are Hard of Hearing

Hearing Aid Basics

• Do not expect a hearing aid to "correct" hearing impairments like glasses correct visual impairments. The instrument will make sounds louder but not necessarily clearer. In addition, a conventional hearing aid amplifies all sounds; it cannot sort out the teacher's instruction from the general background noise. Recent advances in electronics allow some hearing aids to be "programmed" to reduce speech-in-noise problems; however, these are relatively expensive and not often recommended for children's use.

• If the aid "whistles" or produces feedback while in the child's ear, check the earpiece (or earmold) to see whether it has been inserted properly. Feedback will naturally occur if the aid is covered with a hand or a hat, or if the student leans close to a wall or turns the volume too high. However, if the earmold is fully in the ear, if the aid is not covered, and if the volume is at the appropriate setting, and feedback still occurs, the earmold may be too small and need to be replaced. Inform the parent of the situation. Reducing the volume is only a temporary solution.

• Obtain a battery tester and a hearing aid stethoscope from the school audiologist and request training in conducting a hearing aid check. Hearing aids must be checked every day.

• Ask parents to provide spare batteries to keep at school, and let them know when dead batteries are replaced.

• Encourage the student to develop self-management skills for hearing aid care. Students should be able to check their own hearing aid batteries by third grade. If a battery dies during the school day, students should advise their teachers immediately; reinforce these self-advocacy skills.

Classroom Acoustic Considerations

Noise has a detrimental effect on the listening abilities of all students, but particularly students with hearing impairments (American Speech-Language-Hearing Association, 1995). A classroom's acoustical environment can be immediately improved by reducing or eliminating noise sources. A careful "listening inspection" of the classroom will help the teacher identify noise sources that most adults have learned to ignore but most children find distracting; examples are fish tank filters, computers, printers, and fans from overhead projectors. If noise sources cannot be eliminated or reduced, the student with a hearing impairment should work away from noise as much as possible.

In addition to conducting a "listening inspection," teachers can request the following environmental modifications to significantly reduce noise and reverberation problems:

• Carpeting, acoustic ceiling tile, and walls covered with bulletin board or similar materials, which absorb rather than reflect noise.

• Acoustic treatments for noise sources such as rumbling plumbing, rattling window blinds, and buzzing fluorescent lights. Noise from heating, ventilation, and air conditioning (HVAC) systems can be reduced with inexpensive bafflers.

Acoustic modifications to a classroom can generally be accomplished by the site custodial staff at little cost and will result in an environment conducive for learning for students with normal hearing as well as those with hearing impairments.

Strategies to Optimize Visual Information

Students with hearing impairments need as much visual cueing as possible. Comprehension increases significantly when a student can watch the teacher's face in order to lipread, or more accurately, speechread. Here are some suggestions to improve speechreading conditions:

• Speak in a normal fashion, without exaggeration or an increase in volume. Speak in phrases, at a normal pace. If there is a misunderstanding, rephrase rather than repeat.

• As often as possible, the teacher should directly face a student with a hearing impairment, at eye level. Proximity is also very important: it is too difficult to speechread beyond 10 feet.

• When the room is darkened for films or slides, the student will not be able to speechread the teacher. Ask another student to take notes.

- Be aware that some people are naturally better speechreaders than others and that, even for the best speechreaders, only one-third of English speech sounds are visible. Speechreading becomes more difficult when the speaker has a foreign accent or a mustache that covers the mouth.

Other Teaching Strategies

- Students with hearing impairments often have some language deficits as a result of inconsistent auditory input. Pretutoring helps a student develop familiarity with new vocabulary and concepts before they are presented in class. Have the student read ahead on a subject to allow for extra time to consider new material. This can be accomplished as a homework assignment or with a resource teacher.

- As often as possible, write page numbers, homework assignments, public address announcements, key vocabulary, and so forth, on the chalkboard.
- Routinely check comprehension with questions that require more than yes or no answers. When simply asked, "Do you understand?" a student with a hearing impairment may prefer to nod his or her head rather than volunteer that he or she does not fully understand.
- For older students, it is helpful to have another student act as a notetaker. If the notes are made on NCR (no carbon required) paper, a copy can also be provided for a notebook available to any class member who may have missed information during class lectures. A student with a hearing impairment will then have a copy without conspicuously requiring special assistance.

Note. Developed by Kris English, Ph.D., CCC-A, educational audiologist and assistant professor at Duquesne University.

- Clearly explain concepts being taught. Use visual examples whenever possible, and keep terminology consistent.
- Do not talk when distributing handouts as the student with a hearing impairment cannot look for papers and watch the teacher at the same time (Rees, 1992).
- Talk in full sentences. Avoid the use of single words, and rephrase the entire sentence if it was not understood; content and meaning are easier to grasp in context (Reynolds & Birch, 1988).
- Provide assignments both orally and in writing to avoid confusion (Rees, 1992).
- Speechreading and attending to auditory stimuli with deficient hearing can be tiring tasks; watch for student fatigue.
- Start lectures with an outline of material to be presented and end the lecture with a summary of the key points (Rees, 1992).
- During class discussions, allow only one person to speak at a time and signal who is talking so the student with hearing impairment knows where to look (Rees, 1992).
- The academic problems of many students are related to their language impairments, not to a lack of intelligence. Closely monitor their achievement (Blankenship & Lilly, 1981).
- Classmates of a student with a hearing impairment may wish to learn sign language. Arrange

for instruction in this area if it is appropriate (Blankenship & Lilly, 1981).
- Encourage independence in students with hearing impairments and help them develop skills to act as their own advocates. English (1997) and Marttila and Mills (1995) have designed self-advocacy curriculums for students with hearing losses.
- Work closely with specialists to assure that students with hearing impairments are provided with appropriate experiences in the general education classroom.

Specific suggestions for working with students who are hard of hearing are presented in "Inclusion Tips for the Teacher." In addition, Harrington (1976) makes the following recommendations about communicating with a student with a hearing impairment:

(a) If you have difficulty understanding the child ask him to repeat; (b) Do not call attention to the child's speech errors in the classroom. Record and share them with the speech clinician; (c) Realize that the child may have limited vocabulary and syntax, both receptively and expressively. His/her failure to understand may be related to this language deficit as well as the inability to hear normally. (p. 25)

General education teachers ordinarily are not required to become proficient in specialized techniques,

Things to Remember

- Students with visual or hearing impairments commonly require modification of the learning environment and adaptation of instructional procedures to facilitate their performance in the general education classroom.
- Students with severe visual and hearing impairments are typically identified before they enter school. Milder impairments may be identified as a result of school screening programs or teacher observation and referral.
- Sensory impairments may be congenital, or they may occur as a result of illness or accident.
- Legal definitions of visual impairment have little educational relevance. Educators need to know whether students can use their remaining vision to learn or whether they must rely on other senses.
- An educator needs to know the effects of a hearing loss on a student's ability to use and understand speech. Speech and language are the most significant areas in which hearing impairments affect students educationally.
- Students with visual or hearing impairments can learn to use other senses to compensate for their disabilities. Individuals who are blind can develop tactile reading skills and improve their listening skills; persons with hearing impairments can learn to speechread and to communicate manually. Students with visual impairments may also need orientation and mobility training to facilitate independent travel in the school and community.
- Many technological developments have improved the opportunities for students with sensory impairments to communicate with others; examples include FM classroom amplification systems for students with hearing impairments and Braille notetakers and computer programs that provide speech or tactile output for students who are blind.
- Special educators are generally available to assist general education teachers in making classroom adaptations and obtaining appropriate materials for students with sensory impairments who are included in the general education classroom.

such as Braille or sign language. However, they must be aware of students' needs and be familiar with the specialists who provide assistance in adapting instructional procedures for students with sensory impairments. Many such students are fully capable of spending the majority of the school day in the general education classroom when appropriate adaptations are introduced.

This chapter has presented information on adapting the classroom environment and instructional procedures for students with visual and hearing impairments. In the next chapter, you will meet students who are gifted and talented and will learn methods for promoting the achievement of these individuals.

ACTIVITIES

1. Observe the classroom behavior of a student with a visual or hearing impairment. Keep a record of the adaptations made by the student and by others. What problems, if any, are encountered? Can the student adjust as unexpected events occur? What reactions do you observe from other students? From teachers? Write a brief summary of your observations.

2. Interview the parents of a student with a sensory impairment. When were they first aware of the disability? How did they react? Does the student encounter any difficulties at home or in the neighborhood? Has inclusion in the general education program been a positive experience for the student? Are the parents apprehensive about the student's eventual adulthood? How do they encourage their child to become independent? Describe your impressions of the interview.

3. Read two articles about students with sensory impairments, one about visual impairments and one about hearing losses. The *Journal of Visual Impairment and Blindness* and *The Sight-Saving Review* provide articles related to visual impairments; *American Annals of the Deaf*, *Volta Review*, and *Language, Speech, and Hearing Services*

in Schools discuss hearing impairments. Summarize each article's relevance for the general education teacher.

4. Contact a large and a small school district to determine what services they offer for students with visual and hearing impairments. Are all the services needed by these students provided within the district, or must services be contracted from another district? What personnel are employed to provide instruction for these students? Is the percentage of students with sensory impairments about the same in both districts? What services are provided for general education teachers?

5. Write a short report describing one of the new electronic devices being used by persons who are blind or deaf. You can find information about some of these devices by going to the website for the American Foundation for the Blind and examining the page on Braille Technology:

http://www.afb.org/afb/tc_bra.html

It provides information on equipment and how to obtain additional information from the vendors of the devices. Explain the way in which the device works, its advantages and disadvantages, cost, and special benefits to the user. If possible, interview an individual who actually uses the device. Find out how this person evaluates the device and include this information in your report. Determine whether the device is available for students in a local school district.

PART IV

Methods for Teaching Students with Other Special Needs in General Education

Teaching Students Who Are Gifted and Talented

Cases

Kay is a high school junior who was identified in the second grade as gifted. Since that time, special adaptations have been provided in much of her education, especially in the area of mathematics. Her current program allows her to complete a 3-year high school curriculum in 2 years, and she plans to enroll as a full-time college student at age 16. At present, she is taking courses in calculus and computer programming at the local junior college, in addition to her regular high school program. In her after-school hours, she plays on the school golf team, serves as president of the math club, and has helped with set designs for several of the drama club's plays.

Luis is a 6-year-old first grader who has recently been identified as gifted. He was able to read when he entered kindergarten and now is in an advanced reading group in the school's resource program for students who are gifted. The resource teacher assists the general education teacher by providing Luis with individualized assignments in most academic areas; much of the material appropriate for Luis's classmates he has already mastered. Math is an exception; Luis's performance in this area is only average. Although assessment results indicate that Luis is quite capable, his interest in math is low. As a result, his teacher is providing an individualized program in which Luis can earn extra reading time for each math development step. Luis is very interested in music and has learned to play both the piano and the guitar; he takes music lessons twice a week at the local recreation center. Later in this chapter we will take a look at the goals and services from Luis's IEP.

Johnny is a sixth grader with special talent in writing. Although he did not learn to read until he entered school, he began to write short stories and poems in first grade. Several of his pieces have been published in children's magazines. Although his spelling is not always the best, his vocabulary and ability to use words are far beyond those expected of a 12-year-old student. Johnny's school has no special programs for students who are talented, and he does not qualify for the gifted program because his achievement is average in all areas except writing. Despite the lack of special services, Johnny's teacher is interested in helping him progress and maintain his interest in writing. She allows him to select his own topics for classroom writing assignments, reads and critiques any poems or stories he brings to her, and is investigating ways to help Johnny enroll in the creative writing course offered at the high school in the summer.

Students who are gifted and talented are found at all ages and grade levels within the school system. They are "a minority distinguished not by race, socioeconomic background, ethnic origin, or impaired powers, but by its exceptional ability . . . members come from all levels of society, from all races and nationalities, and from both sexes in about equal numbers" (Lyon, 1981, pp. 15–16). Many believe that gifted and talented individuals are one of the most neglected and underserved of all groups of special students (Gallagher, 1988) because their special learning needs are neither universally recognized nor provided for.

Many teachers and parents do not clearly understand the needs of students who are gifted and talented. Some educators continue to believe that these students, because of their exceptional abilities, are capable of realizing their maximum potential without the benefit of specially designed educational adaptations or programs. Some teachers are somewhat in awe of gifted and talented pupils; others resent their probing minds and seemingly endless questions (Kennedy, 1995). There is also the question of resource allocation. In a supposedly egalitarian society, should monies be spent to promote the achievement of those who are already in some way superior (Culross, 1997; Mann & McIntyre, 1992)?

Many educators do not realize that students who are gifted and talented often have special learning needs that are not fully met by the general education program. Such students should be identified in order to adapt the general education program or provide special educational services. In this way, it is possible to help them achieve at a level commensurate with their potential (Culross, 1997; Parker, 1989).

This chapter examines the characteristics of students with special gifts and talents who are included in the general education program and also describes methods for the general education teacher to use in gathering data and designing and implementing program adaptations.

INDICATORS OF TALENT AND GIFTEDNESS

Some students who are gifted and talented have highly unusual abilities that are identified early in life by their parents. For most students, however, it is the classroom teacher who first notices their special abilities. Students who are gifted and talented can be identified at any time during their school careers, but they are most likely to come to their teachers' attention during the elementary school years.

Giftedness and talent have several indicators that teachers might look for. However, Heward (1996) cautions that general descriptions of group characteristics are not always effective in the identification of individuals; students may be gifted or talented and display several or none of the specific characteristics included on a list. As with all special individuals, the student's unique needs must be considered.

Although there is not universal agreement concerning a definition of this group of students, the description included in the Gifted and Talented Children's Act of 1978 (PL 95-561, Section 902) is often cited:

> The term *gifted and talented children* means children and, whenever applicable, youth who are identified at the preschool, elementary, or secondary level as possessing demonstrated or potential abilities that give evidence of high performance capabilities in areas such as intellectual, creative, specific academic, or leadership ability, or in the performing and visual arts, and who by reason thereof, require services or activities not ordinarily provided by the school.

In contrast to earlier definitions, this statement includes not only those who are intellectually gifted but also those with specific gifts or talents in the arts or in leadership. In general, **giftedness** is characterized by above-average intellectual ability, which may be accompanied by superior academic achievement and creative capability. **Talented** individuals, in contrast, excel in one or more specific areas of endeavor: drama, art, music, leadership, and so on. This distinction between giftedness and talent is expanded by Gardner (1987), who identifies seven different types of intelligence: linguistic, logical-mathematical, spatial, musical, bodily-kinesthetic, interpersonal, and intrapersonal.

Giftedness and talent may occur in combination or separately; that is, students may be either gifted or talented or both. It is also possible for an individual to be intellectually gifted and yet experience difficulty in school learning; the special problems of underachieving students who are gifted pose a real challenge to a classroom teacher.

"Inclusion Tips for the Teacher" on page 396 summarizes some of the major indicators of giftedness and talent that can be observed in the general education classroom. Although these special students do not generally display all these signs, the presence of one or two of them is cause for a teacher to consider further assessment.

Heward (1996) points out that even though descriptions of students who are gifted usually emphasize only positive characteristics, these students can also display less attractive behaviors. Figure 15–1 on page 397 presents both sides of the giftedness coin.

Several techniques are used to identify students who are gifted and talented. These include referrals from teachers, parents, peers, or students themselves; group measures of achievement or intellectual performance; and observation of special academic or creative achievements. Although teachers are the most common source of referrals, their accuracy as identifiers is questionable, especially with younger children and classes with many students from diverse ethnic, cultural, or linguistic groups (Baldwin, 1991; Kitano, 1989). Even with training, teachers tend to look for the stereotypical student

Inclusion Tips for the Teacher

Signs of Giftedness and Talent

There are numerous lists of characteristics or distinguishing features and attributes of gifted and talented children. Teachers and parents should interpret any single list, including this one, as only an example of possible traits.

Few gifted children will display all of the characteristics in a given list; however, when clusters of these characteristics are present, they do serve as fairly reliable indicators. Giftedness may exist in only one area of academic learning, such as mathematics, or may be quite general across the school curriculum. . . . These characteristics are signals to indicate that a particular child might warrant closer observation and could require specialized educational attention, pending a more comprehensive assessment.

General Behavioral Characteristics

* Many typically learn to read earlier with a better comprehension of the nuances of the language. As many as half of the gifted and talented population have learned to read before entering school. They often read widely, quickly, and intensely and have large vocabularies.
* They commonly learn basic skills better, more quickly, and with less practice.
* They are frequently able to pick up and interpret nonverbal cues and can draw inferences which other children have to have spelled out for them.
* They take less for granted, seeking the "hows" and "whys."
* They display a better ability to work independently at an earlier age and for longer periods of time than other children.
* They can sustain longer periods of concentration and attention.
* Their interests are often both widely eclectic and intensely focused.
* They frequently have seemingly boundless energy, which sometimes leads to a misdiagnosis of "hyperactive."
* They are usually able to respond and relate well to parents, teachers, and other adults. They may prefer the company of older children and adults to that of their peers.
* They are willing to examine the unusual and are highly inquisitive.

* Their behavior is often well organized, goal directed, and efficient with respect to tasks and problems.
* They exhibit an intrinsic motivation to learn, find out, or explore and are often very persistent. "I'd rather do it myself" is a common attitude.
* They enjoy learning new things and new ways of doing things.
* They have a longer attention and concentration span than their peers.

Learning Characteristics

* They may show keen powers of observation, exhibit a sense of the significant, and have an eye for important details.
* They may read a great deal on their own, preferring books and magazines written for youngsters older than themselves.
* They often take great pleasure in intellectual activity.
* They have well developed powers of abstraction, conceptualization, and synthesizing abilities.
* They generally have rapid insight into cause-effect relationships.
* They often display a questioning attitude and seek information for the sake of having it as much as for its instrumental value.
* They are often skeptical, critical, and evaluative. They are quick to spot inconsistencies.
* They often have a large storehouse of information regarding a variety of topics which they can recall quickly.
* They show a ready grasp of underlying principles and can often make valid generalizations about events, people, and objects.
* They readily perceive similarities, differences, and anomalies.
* They often attack complicated material by separating it into its components and analyzing it systematically.

Creative Characteristics

* They are *fluent* thinkers, able to produce a large quantity of possibilities, consequences, or related ideas.

- They are *flexible* thinkers able to use many different alternatives and approaches to problem solving.
- They are *original* thinkers, seeking new, unusual, or unconventional associations and combinations among items of information. They also have an ability to see relationships among seemingly unrelated objects, ideas, or facts.
- They are *elaborative* thinkers, producing new steps, ideas, responses, or other embellishments to a basic idea, situation, or problem.
- They show a willingness to entertain complexity and seem to thrive in problem situations.
- They are good guessers and can construct hypotheses or "what if" questions readily.

- They often are aware of their own impulsiveness and the irrationality within themselves and show emotional sensitivity.
- They have a high level of curiosity about objects, ideas, situations, or events.
- They often display intellectual playfulness, fantasize, and imagine readily.
- They can be less intellectually inhibited than their peers in expressing opinions and ideas and often exhibit spirited disagreement.
- They have a sensitivity to beauty and are attracted to aesthetic dimensions.

Note. From "Characteristics of Intellectually Gifted Children" (Digest 344) by J. R. Whitmore, 1985, *Digests on the Gifted* (Reston, VA: The Council for Exceptional Children), pp. 1–2. Material is in the public domain.

FIGURE 15-1   Two Sides of Gifted Behavior

List A: Positive Aspects
1. Expresses ideas and feelings well
2. Can move at a rapid pace
3. Works conscientiously
4. Wants to learn, explore, and seek more information
5. Develops broad knowledge and an extensive store of vicarious experiences
6. Is sensitive to the feelings and rights of others
7. Makes steady progress
8. Makes original and stimulating contributions to discussions
9. Sees relationships easily
10. Learns material quickly
11. Is able to use reading skills to obtain new information
12. Contributes to enjoyment of life for self and others
13. Completes assigned tasks
14. Requires little drill for learning

List B: Not-So-Positive Aspects
1. May be glib, making fluent statements based on little or no knowledge or understanding
2. May dominate discussions
3. May be impatient to proceed to the next level or task
4. May be considered nosey
5. May choose reading at the expense of active participation in social, creative, or physical activities
6. May struggle against rules, regulations, and standardized procedures
7. May lead discussions "off the track"
8. May be frustrated by the apparent absence of logic in activities and daily events
9. May become bored by repetitions
10. May use humor to manipulate
11. May resist a schedule based on time rather than task
12. May lose interest quickly

Note. Reprinted with the permission of Prentice-Hall, Inc., from *Exceptional Children*, 5th ed., by William L. Heward. Copyright © 1996 by Prentice-Hall, Inc.

---

who is gifted—who is highly motivated and adjusted to school—and often overlook the unique student with a set of unusual skills and abilities.

Behavior checklists or rating scales can prove helpful to the teacher. For example, the *Scales for Rating the Behavior Characteristics of Superior Stu-* dents (Renzulli, Smith, White, Callahan, & Hartman, 1976) is used by a teacher to rate a student's performance in the areas of learning, motivation, and creativity. This type of scale provides information on a student's strengths and is useful for both identification and educational planning.

For Your Information

Students Who Are Gifted and Talented

- It is estimated that, under the current U.S. Office of Education definition of giftedness and talent, 3% to 5% of the school-aged population is eligible for special services. "This percentage includes talented children who might be excluded under a definition that is based only on general intellectual ability" (Pendarvis, 1993, p. 566).

- The Council of State Directors of Programs for the Gifted found that there was an increase in the number of public school students served in gifted programs from 2.7% in 1984 to 4.5% in 1987. Program growth was also illustrated by the fact that $289 million was allocated to local districts by 41 states, Puerto Rico, and Guam (Reis, 1989). In 1990, 37 states and trust territories reported spending $395 million on these programs; this represented about 2 cents out of every $100 spent on elementary and secondary education (Programs for Improvement of Practice, 1993).

- A nationwide poll (Rose, Gallup, & Elam, 1997) indicates that "a small majority (52%) of the public supports the placement of gifted and talented students in separate classes. This response takes added significance from the fact that 66% of poll respondents also said they believe that grouping students according to ability will improve student achievement a great deal or quite a lot" (p. 53).

- Many students who are gifted may have high levels of activity in the classroom because of boredom or intense interest in an activity and may be considered to be hyperactive (e.g., have ADHD) and in need of special education services. This possibility should be carefully evaluated before decisions are made regarding changes in their programs (Webb & Latimer, 1993).

- Teachers of children and adolescents who are gifted do not necessarily have to be gifted themselves, but they "must be flexible, curious, tolerant, competent, and self-confident" (Heward & Orlansky, 1988, p. 437).

- Males and females do not differ in intellectual ability, but there have traditionally been significant differences in their achievement. Girls tend to achieve better than boys until puberty, when boys begin to excel, especially in math and science. In the adult years, the expectations of society continue to have a negative effect on the achievement of many women (Kerr, 1991; Pendarvis, 1993). Females are frequently found to disguise their abilities and limit their achievement to "socially acceptable" levels (Parke, 1989).

- Professionals and parents interested in gifted education are concerned that the school reform movement designed to increase the inclusion of students with disabilities in general education programs will also lead to a reduction in the opportunities to provide specialized programs for students who are gifted and talented (Culross, 1997).

Stephens and Wolf (1978) suggest that identification of students with giftedness and talent should be tied directly to the goals of the program in which they will be placed. To assure a better match between student and program, these authors recommend the following steps:

1. Establish Program Goals
2. Develop Objectives
3. Specify Requisite Student Characteristics
4. Locate Students
5. Assign Students (p. 390)

Kitano (1989) provides several suggestions to teachers to assist them in improving their accuracy in identifying gifted children:

- Consider all children as potential candidates for giftedness. For example, a hyperactive, disruptive, or unkempt child may also be gifted.
- Recognize that "negative" traits [e.g., List B in Figure 15–1] . . . do not disqualify a child from consideration as gifted. Although gifted and average children may display negative behaviors, gifted children will also demonstrate their strengths when provided with opportunities to do so.
- Look for and analyze the strengths exhibited by all children, including those who do not display stereotypical achieving, cooperating, and conforming behaviors. For example, the child who touches expensive equipment after being admonished not to touch may be exhibiting extreme curiosity rather than defiance.

- Provide opportunities for and encourage children to express their abilities. For example, the teacher can informally assess reading and writing skills by inviting children individually to read to them at the book center and encouraging volunteer efforts to write their names and other words.
- Use parents as informants. Parents serve as effective identifiers of gifted children. . . . Moreover, they can provide accurate observations about what their children can and cannot do. (p. 60)

Special attention should be paid to the inclusion of qualified students from diverse ethnic, cultural, or linguistic groups and those with disabilities in programs for students who are gifted and talented (Karnes & Johnson, 1991; Klein, 1989). Total reliance on standardized tests should be avoided; norm-referenced measures can lead to the exclusion of many such students who are excellent candidates for programs for students who are gifted and talented. Educators should use several different measures, rather than only one or two, and stress procedures that reduce cultural bias to identify students from these populations (Kitano & Kirby, 1986). To learn more about students with special gifts and talents, consult "For Your Information."

ASSESSMENT PROCEDURES

When a student is identified as a potential candidate for special education services for students who are gifted and talented, the next step is a comprehensive assessment. The purpose is to gather information about the learning needs and abilities of the student in order to assist in planning appropriate educational modifications. Both formal and informal measures are used; examples of possible informal procedures are direct observation, inventories, checklists, and analysis of various types of work samples. In some states, there are specific guidelines for determining eligibility for special education programs for gifted and talented pupils; in others, this decision is left to the discretion of the local school district (Dettmer, 1994). Care should be taken to gather only information that will be used in the actual identification process. It is inappropriate to collect a variety of data and then determine eligibility solely on the basis of an intelligence test score (Reis & Renzulli, 1985; Sternberg, 1991).

In the past, many programs for students who are gifted relied almost exclusively on norm-referenced tests of intelligence for assessment. Measures such as the *Wechsler Intelligence Scale for Children-Third Edition* (Wechsler, 1991) and the *Stanford-Binet Intelligence Scale* (4th ed.) (Thorndike, Hagen, & Sattler, 1986) remain in use today, particularly for identification of students who are academically talented. Practices vary widely regarding minimum scores for eligibility for services for students who are gifted; a *WISC-III* score of IQ 115 may qualify a student in one state or school district, whereas a score of 130 or 135 may be necessary in another.

Although individual IQ tests such as the *WISC-III* and the *Stanford-Binet* are considered the single most reliable indicator of intellectual giftedness, they have many drawbacks. They are expensive to use and can be administered only by special personnel. They are biased in favor of middle- and upper-class students and discriminate against those students who have disabilities or come from diverse ethnic, cultural, or linguistic groups. In addition, they fail to assess such important abilities as creativity, leadership, and specific talents.

Measures such as the *Torrance Tests of Creative Thinking* (Torrance, 1966) can be used to assess creativity. Such tests help identify divergent

Window on the Web

Websites About Giftedness and Talent

Organizations Related to Gifted and Talented Education

- National Association for Gifted Children (NAGC) (www.nagc.org/)
- TAG Family Network (www.teleport.com/~rkaltwas/tag/)
- GT World (www.gtworld.org)

Web Resources

- Gifted Education Connection (www.netc.org/web_mod/gifted_ed/)
- Gifted and Talented (TAG) Resources Home Page (www.eskimo.com/~user/kids.html)
- Gifted and Talented (205.121.65.141/Millville/Teachers/TAG/gifted2.htm)

Special Programs and Research Centers

- Center for Academic Precocity, Arizona State University (www-cap.ed.asu.edu)
- Connie Belin and Jacqueline N. Blank International Center for Talented & Gifted Education, University of Iowa (www.uiowa.edu/~belinctr/)
- CTDNet (The Center for Talent Development), Northwestern University (ctdnet.acns.nwu.edu)
- Duke Talent Identification Program (TIP) (www.jayi.com/tip)
- NRC/GT (The National Research Center on the Gifted and Talented), University of Connecticut (www.gifted.uconn.edu/nrcgt.html)
- The Johns Hopkins University Institute for the Academic Advancement of Youth (IAAY) (www.jhu.edu/~gifted/)

thinkers who may be overlooked on intelligence tests. In describing these instruments, Gay (1981) notes that

> one such test asks the individual to list as many uses as he or she can think of for an ordinary brick. Think about it and list a few. If you listed uses such as build a school, build a house, build a library, etc., then you are not very creative; all of those uses are really the same, namely, you can use a brick to build something. Now, if you are creative, you listed different uses such as break a window, drown a rat, and hit a robber on the head. (p. 128)

Creativity test results should be supplemented with information from other sources, such as analysis of students' creative products and performances and direct observation of student behavior.

Observation techniques help to objectively assess and describe a student's academic and social performance in the classroom. For example, it is possible to observe the amount and reading levels of material the student reads each week, the number of social interactions per class period, or the time taken to complete an assignment. Information such as this not only helps to determine the student's current performance levels but also assists in the development of program modifications.

Analysis of work samples is conducted somewhat differently with students who are gifted and talented. Instead of searching for error patterns, the purpose is to discover a student's strengths and potential for further achievement. In the area of academics, a teacher looks for advanced school skills or competence in a subject matter not normally taught in the general education curriculum. Examples include the precocious kindergartner who reads and understands fourth grade material and the second grader who has special knowledge in botany and zoology. For information about specific talents, the teacher should consider a wide variety of student products, such as writings, artwork, musical compositions, and inventions; other possibilities are dramatic or musical performances. A teacher can analyze these work samples or ask for assistance from others. Subject matter experts and practicing artists, musicians, or writers may be better able to judge whether students' work is exceptional and whether students have potential to benefit from advanced study in the area.

In addition to the strengths of students who are gifted and talented, areas of relative weakness must also be considered. This is particularly important for students with major discrepancies between ability and achievement and those who excel in one or two areas but not in others. The assessment procedures suggested for students with learning disabilities and behavioral disorders are appropriate for gathering information about academic achievement and school conduct. The procedures suggested in chapter 6 can be helpful if social acceptance problems are suspected.

SPECIAL SERVICES

When the assessment data have been collected, the educational planning team meets to plan an appropriate educational program for the student. If special education services for students who are gifted and talented are not available, the team may be composed of only the general education teacher and the student's parents. In districts where appropriate services are offered, the team may include a full complement of specialists; possible team members are teacher-consultants, special class teachers, psychologists, administrators, and subject matter experts or professionals practicing in a student's area of talent. Even if IEPs are not required for students who are gifted and talented, it is good practice to develop a written educational plan. Figure 15–2 presents portions of the individualized plan for Luis, the first grader introduced at the beginning of this chapter.

Special services for students who are gifted and talented can be provided in many ways. As shown in Figure 15–3, these approaches span a continuum from fully mainstreamed or included programs to complete segregation (Reynolds & Birch, 1988). The most appropriate placement is selected for each student on the basis of individual learning needs. As with students with disabilities, the restrictiveness of the environment is an important consideration; the appropriate placement closest to the general education program may be judged the least restrictive but it may not be the most appropriate for exceptionally gifted or talented students.

FIGURE 15-2 **IEP Goals and Services for Luis**

Annual Goals
1. By the end of the school year, Luis will read fifth grade material with adequate comprehension.
   Person responsible: Resource teacher
2. By the end of the school year, Luis will successfully complete all requirements for first grade math.
   Person responsible: First grade teacher
3. By the end of the school year, Luis will write short reports (with correct spelling and sentence structure) on topics of his choice.
   Persons responsible: First grade teacher and resource teacher
4. By the end of the school year, Luis will successfully play a series of songs on both the guitar and the piano.
   Person responsible: Parent

Amount of Participation in General Education
Luis will attend the regular first grade class for all subjects except reading.

Special Education and Related Services
1. Luis will receive special education services from the resource teacher for students who are gifted (annual goals 1 and 3) for 1 hour daily.
2. The resource teacher will provide consultation to Luis's first grade teacher as needed.

FIGURE 15-3   **Placement Alternatives for Students Who Are Gifted**

Full Mainstreaming   Complete Segregation

- Special summer programs
- Special schools
- Clustered special classes in regular schools
- Limited enrollment seminars and courses
- Resource rooms and clinical centers
- Limited participation field trips and events on school time

- Cluster groups within the regular class
- Limited participation in before-and after-school groups
- Tutoring carried on in regular class
- Independent and individualized study in the context of the regular class

Note. From *Adaptive Mainstreaming: A Primer for Teachers and Principals,* 3/e, by Maynard C. Reynolds and Jack W. Birch. Copyright © 1988 by Longman Publishers USA. Reprinted by permission of Addison Wesley Educational Publishers.

CLASSROOM ADAPTATIONS

Educational adaptations are made for students who are gifted and talented who fail to attain their full potential in the general education program. According to Stephens and Wolf (1978):

> Bright students should receive systematically differentiated instruction throughout their school lives because they learn differently. While the objectives for the gifted are similar to those for other students, the ways to meet them differ. Emphasis should be on creativity, intellectual initiative, critical thinking, social adjustment, responsibility, and leadership. (pp. 398–399)

Instruction is the most typical area in which classroom adaptations must be made for students who are gifted and talented. For those who excel, advanced instruction is appropriate; for those with achievement problems, additional help with basic school subjects may be needed. The following sections of this chapter address ways in which the general education teacher can select appropriate educational options, promote the development of creativity and problem solving, and assist underachieving students in better realizing their capabilities.

EDUCATIONAL OPTIONS FOR STUDENTS WHO ARE GIFTED AND TALENTED

Individualized programs can be delivered in several ways to students who are gifted and talented. In many of these options, the student remains in the general education classroom with age peers. Special instruction can be provided within this class by the general education teacher, on a part-time basis by a special teacher in a special class or resource room, or in a setting outside the school when school is not in session.

The selection of an appropriate method for providing service depends on many factors. One important consideration is the relationship between student needs and program goals. According to Pendarvis (1993), educational modifications for students who are gifted and talented can be designed to accomplish the following things:

- Quicken the pace of learning by moving the student through activities faster than would be appropriate for children of average ability.
- Broaden the range of experiences and knowledge of gifted children by teaching subjects not offered in the general education curriculum at the children's grade level.

- Develop skills of analysis and expression in academic or artistic disciplines.
- Provide opportunity for concentrated, in-depth study of areas in which the students are especially interested or able. (p. 587)

Feldhusen, Van Winkle, and Ehle (1996) stress the importance of determining what knowledge and skills have already been mastered by students in order to determine the level at which instruction will begin. They indicate that the Diagnostic Testing followed by Prescriptive Instruction (DT-PI) model accomplishes this. In this model, the student's current level of knowledge is assessed, the results are used to identify areas of weakness, instruction is provided in these areas, and the student is then reassessed to evaluate mastery. When mastery is demonstrated, the teacher moves on to the next higher level and repeats the process.

Curriculum compacting is one method of adapting general education programs for students who are gifted and talented. The goal is to expand the amount of time academically capable students have to work on more challenging material by "either eliminating work that has been mastered previously or streamlining work that may be mastered at a pace commensurate with the student's ability" (Feldhusen et al., 1996, p. 50). This permits the student to replace unnecessary repetition of the basics with enriched and accelerated learning activities (Kennedy, 1995). The curriculum compacting technique also ensures that the gifted students cover the essential elements of the general education curriculum and it "is one of the major techniques for adapting and developing curriculum for talented students in the regular classroom" (Heward, 1996, p. 565). According to Heward, to effectively implement curriculum compacting, teachers need specific training to be able to (a) assess the curriculum content areas, (b) identify content to be eliminated, and (c) replace it with more appropriate content.

Enrichment and **acceleration** are two other typical ways in which the general education program is altered to meet the needs of students who are gifted and talented (Heward, 1996). In enrichment, something is added to the general education program. Students may study the same subjects as their peers but in greater depth. Or the curriculum may be broadened to include areas of study not generally

covered; examples include after-school instruction in chess for first and second graders or the investigation by middle school students of finance policies in state government.

In acceleration, students progress through the general education curriculum at a faster rate than that in the regular classroom. They may be admitted to school at a younger-than-usual age or be allowed to skip one or more grades. Another way to accelerate is the telescoping of grades; for instance, the course of study for two grades might be compressed into one school year. Research conducted on acceleration programs establishes that students enrolled in these programs achieved at a much higher rate than their talented same-age peers who were not accelerated and as well as talented older peers in the same classes, while experiencing no negative effects on social-emotional development (VanTassel-Baska, 1994).

One of the primary advantages of enrichment is that students remain with age peers in the general education classroom. Acceleration, in contrast, requires either removal from the general education class to a special setting or placement in a regular class with students of older chronological ages. To learn more about the available educational options for providing enrichment and acceleration, consult the list of programs described in Figure 15–4.

Not only the needs of the student but also the resources of the school and community must be considered in determining the most appropriate instructional adaptation for individual students. Kirk and Gallagher (1979) present specific guidelines for selecting a suitable option:

1. When a child's pattern of growth in physical, social, mental, and educational areas . . . [is] accelerated beyond the chronological age . . . acceleration in grade placement should be considered.
2. When the physical, social and emotional areas are equal to chronological age, but the educational achievement is advanced, a special class or resource room can be considered.
3. When the school system is too small (not providing sufficient numbers of gifted children of a particular kind for a special class), enrichment, tutoring, or itinerant teachers for the gifted children in the regular classroom may be necessary.
4. When the class in which a gifted child is placed contains a preponderance of children of superior intelligence, even though it is not designated as a class

FIGURE 15-4   Options for Providing Enrichment and Acceleration

Acceleration
- Subject matter acceleration—remaining at grade level while advancing in specific subject areas (e.g., advanced placement classes).
- Telescoping—covering more than a full year's work in a given year (e.g., multiage grouping).
- Grade skipping—bypassing at least one year of instruction (e.g., early graduation).
- Early entrance—entering school at least one year younger than the norm (e.g., early admission to kindergarten or college).

Enrichment in the Regular Classroom
- Individualized programming
- Independent study
- Ability grouping
- Cluster grouping—all students who are gifted at a grade level are placed with one teacher to facilitate differentiated instruction.
- Flexible scheduling—students attend class less often than peers, perhaps for only 4 days each week.
- Use of faster-paced, higher-level materials
- Field trips
- Use of community resource persons at school

Special Classes
- Honors classes and seminars
- Extra course work
- Special course offerings (e.g., Junior Great Books)
- Use of a resource room or itinerant teacher on a weekly basis
- Segregated "pull-out" program for part of the day or week
- Full-time placement in a special class
- Special study centers
- Magnet schools—one may specialize in science, another in language arts. Students choose to enroll in a school that will serve them best.
- School within a school—a portion of the school is reserved for specialized classes for students who are gifted.
- Specialized school for students who are gifted (e.g., Bronx High School of Science)

Flexible Scheduling [i.e., Offerings Outside the School Day]
- Extracurricular clubs
- Early-bird classes—special classes held before school
- Extended day
- Extended school year
- Saturday or after-school workshops, classes, excursions
- Summer courses
- Evening courses

Off-Campus Options
- Mentorships
- Individual study with a community member
- Internships—working in the field with a specialist
- Outreach activities—programs developed for students who are gifted at local museums, colleges, businesses, etc.
- Residential summer institutes
- Community-based career education
- Student exchange programs
- Credit for educational experiences outside school (e.g., travel)

Note. From "Gifted and Talented" by L. K. Silverman in *Exceptional Children and Youth* (3rd ed., pp. 281–283) by E. L. Meyen and T. M. Skritic (Eds.), 1988, Denver: Love. Copyright 1988 by Love. Adapted by permission.

Inclusion Tips for the Teacher

Promoting Appropriate Instruction for Gifted Students

Kennedy (1995) provides several suggestions for general education teachers to consider when reviewing their classroom practices with gifted students:

1. **Resist policies requiring *more* work of those who finish assignments quickly and easily.** Instead, explore ways to assign *different* work, which may be more complex, more abstract, and both deeper and wider. Find curriculum compacting strategies that work, and use them regularly.

2. **Seek out supplemental materials and ideas which extend, not merely reinforce, the curriculum.** Develop interdisciplinary units and learning centers that call for higher level thinking. Don't dwell on comprehension-level questions and tasks for those who have no problems with comprehension. Encourage activities that call for analysis, synthesis, and critical thinking, and push beyond superficial responses.

3. **De-emphasize grades and other extrinsic rewards.** Encourage learning for its own sake, and help perfectionists establish realistic goals and priorities. Try to assure that the self-esteem of talented learners does not rest solely on their products and achievements.

4. **Encourage intellectual and academic risk-taking.** The flawless completion of a simple worksheet by an academically talented student calls for little or no reward, but struggling with a complex, open-ended issue should earn praise. Provide frequent opportunities to stretch mental muscles.

5. **Help all children develop social skills to relate well to one another.** For gifted children this may require special efforts to see things from other viewpoints. Training in how to "read" others and how to send accurate verbal and nonverbal messages may also be helpful. Tolerate neither elitist attitudes nor anti-gifted discrimination.

6. **Take time to listen to responses that may at first appear to be off-target.** Gifted children often are divergent thinkers who get more out of a story or remark and have creative approaches to problems. Hear them out, and help them elaborate on their ideas.

7. **Provide opportunities for independent investigations in areas of interest.** Gifted children are often intensely, even passionately, curious about certain topics. Facilitate their indepth explorations by teaching research skills as needed, redirecting them to good resources, and providing support as they plan and complete appropriate products.

8. **Be aware of the special needs of gifted girls.** Encourage them to establish realistically high-level educational and career goals, and give them additional encouragement to succeed in math and science. (pp. 233–234)

---

for the gifted, enrichment of the program is probably more desirable than special classes or acceleration, neither of which may be necessary.

5. When the child is gifted but underachieving, special attention to social and emotional problems or to possible areas of weakness is called for. Intensive counseling and parent education or even remedial instruction may be more important for the child than classroom placements.

6. When inner discrepancies in growth are quite marked, as we often find in children with extremely high IQs, a tutorial or individualized method of instruction may be necessary, especially when the child is found to be unable to adjust to existing educational situations.

7. When school systems feel that enrichment in the regular grades is the most feasible plan, a special teacher or coordinator for gifted children is advisable. (pp. 95–96)

General education teachers should take the instructional needs of gifted and talented students in account when planning the classroom program. "Inclusion Tips for the Teacher" presents strategies for improving the ways in which instruction is provided to these students.

PROMOTING CREATIVITY AND PROBLEM SOLVING

When students who are gifted and talented are included in the general education classroom, their teacher is responsible for making program adaptations that facilitate maximum growth and development. Reynolds and Birch (1982) present six principles to help teachers provide appropriate educational experiences for this group of special students:

1. Teach pupils to be efficient and effective at independent study, instilling and polishing the skills called for in self-directed learning and in analyzing and solving problems on one's own.
2. Help pupils to invoke and apply complex cognitive processes such as creative thinking, critiques, and pro and con analyses.
3. Encourage pupils to press discussions of questions or issues all the way to the culminating activity of decision making and to clear communication to others of plans, status reports, or solutions based on the decisions.
4. Establish the human interaction skills necessary to work smoothly with groups of all ages and of all levels of cognitive development.
5. Aid pupils in acquiring respect for all other humans whatever their gifts or talents and in understanding themselves in relation to all others.
6. Build pupils' positive expectations about careers and about lives as adults that optimize their talents and gifts. (p. 185)

Creativity and problem solving are two important areas in which students who are gifted and talented may require special attention and instruction. **Creativity,** according to Kirk and Gallagher (1979), is the production of "a unique product (from the child's point of view) from the available data or information" (p. 81). Creativity can also be conceptualized as the ability to generate novel solutions to specific problems.

One component of creativity is **divergent thinking.** In divergent thinking, several solutions to one problem are suggested. Four factors are important:

- *Fluency*—the ability to generate many responses.
- *Flexibility*—the ability to change the form, modify information, or shift perspectives.

- *Originality*—the ability to generate novel responses.
- *Elaboration*—the ability to embellish an idea with details. (Silverman, 1988, p. 276)

For ideas about ways to encourage creative thinking in gifted and talented students, consult the following suggestions:

- Provide regular opportunities for creative thinking. Creativity can be incorporated into most school subjects as soon as basic skills are acquired. Do not, however, accept novelty when accuracy is the goal. For example, spelling is one of the areas in which creativity should not be encouraged.
- Develop fluency with brainstorming sessions. Present a problem and see how many possible solutions can be suggested within a certain period of time. Do not evaluate the proposed solutions; instead, encourage a high rate of response. Younger students can practice with problems such as how to finance a trip to the toy store; older students may wish to suggest solutions for societal problems, such as how to provide proper health care for senior citizens or funding for public education.

Spotlight on Technology

HyperStudio®, a Multimedia Authoring Tool for Students and Teachers

HyperStudio® is an easy-to-use multimedia authoring program. The student (or teacher) designs a series of "cards" that are linked together in a "stack" or program. Cards can contain text and graphics. In addition, program creators can add animation, photographs, sound effects, recorded voice, video, QuickTime movies, and Internet links. "Buttons" are placed on cards to allow users to access features (e.g., to watch a QuickTime movie or listen to a tape recording) and to move from card to card. For example, a button shaped like an arrow might move the user to the next screen.

The *HyperStudio®* program "Bobcats" begins with the author reading the title of her story. To hear the title and author's name again, the user clicks on the tape in the upper left-hand corner. When the drawing of the little girl is selected, Kristin explains why she wrote this stack. Clicking on the arrow moves the program to the next card.

The second card (shown on the right) presents four choices. Clicking on "Behavior" (or one of the other choices) brings the user to a different card.

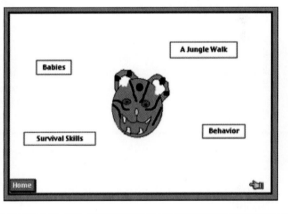

continued

- Encourage flexibility. For students who tend to generate one solution and remain with it loyally, require two suggestions. Keep increasing the number of solutions required until the student is able to generate several spontaneously.
- Flexibility also involves the ability to change one's perspective. Have students list solutions to a school problem from their own point of view. Then, have them adopt the viewpoint of the teacher, the principal, the school board, or their parents.
- Originality is the creation of new solutions. As Kirk and Gallagher (1979) suggest, this means that the solution must be new to its creator, not

necessarily new to society. For instance, the student who discovers an old idea or invents an existing device should be given credit for originality. Develop original thinking by providing opportunities for its occurrence. Suggest problems or needs, and direct students to come up with novel solutions. For example, ask students to suggest new ways of solving everyday problems, such as how to keep the toothpaste container and its cap together or how to prevent injuries caused by falls in the bathtub. Better yet, have students think of important problems and then generate novel solutions. One possibility is to challenge students to invent assistive devices to

The card on the left describes the behavior of the bobcat. In the "Bobcats" program, the author created all of her own graphics. It is also possible to import photographs. For example, the card on the right is the title page for a program on Rwanda.

HyperStudio® is produced by Roger Wagner Publishing, Inc. Visit their website at www.hyperstudio.com to download a trial version of the program; this version allows you to experiment with the features in the program and create small stacks, but you cannot save what you've created. The site also provides links to schools that use *HyperStudio*® and a library of stacks to download.

Note. HyperStudio® is a registered trademark of Roger Wagner Publishing, Inc. There is no relationship between Roger Wagner Publishing, Inc. and Prentice Hall. The views expressed herein are solely those of the authors, and Prentice Hall takes full responsibility for the content of this publication.

help bypass some of the limitations imposed by disabilities such as physical impairments, blindness, and deafness.

- In elaboration, ideas are expanded and made more detailed. Give students practice in elaborative thinking by presenting simple statements that they must expand. Use quotations or sayings, such as "All's well that ends well" and "All people are created equal." Or consider one of the novel responses produced in an original thinking exercise; have students expand the idea to include directions for implementation, ways of evaluating effectiveness, potential advantages, and possible disadvantages.

"Spotlight on Technology" describes a software program students can use to express their creativity. *HyperStudio*® is a multimedia authoring program that allows students (and their teachers) to design computer-based presentations that incorpo-

rate text, graphics, animation, music, sound effects, and video.

Problem solving is an extension of divergent thinking. It is important for students to become sensitive to the fact that problems exist and that they possess the skills required to develop appropriate solutions for these problems (Feldhusen, 1989). In his structure of intellect model, Guilford (1967) describes five types of mental operations: cognition, memory, divergent production, convergent production, and evaluation. Cognition and memory relate to the gathering of information about a specific problem. In divergent thinking, several solutions are proposed; in convergent thinking, one "best" solution is selected. The final step is evaluation, in which the success of the selected solution is assessed; if the result is unsatisfactory, another solution can be chosen.

These different types of mental operations relate closely to the problem-solving model suggested by

Gordon (1974). In this approach, conflicts are resolved by means of a six-step process:

1. Defining the problem
2. Generating possible solutions
3. Evaluating the solutions
4. Deciding which solution is best
5. Deciding how to implement the solution
6. Assessing how well the solution solved the problem (p. 228)

In the second step, all possible solutions are specified (divergent production). Then the solutions are considered, and one is selected (convergent production). The process ends with implementation and evaluation of the chosen alternative.

The Gordon model is one that can be taught to students included in the general education program and then used for the solution of classroom problems. It is also useful as a general strategy for attacking any problem situation. To students who are gifted and talented, it represents a powerful tool to guide analysis, synthesis, and evaluation activities.

ASSISTING STUDENTS WHO ARE UNDERACHIEVING

Underachieving students who are gifted and talented are one of the great tragedies of education. Because their potential for achievement is so great, their failure to thrive in school is doubly disappointing. The reasons for underachievement are many and complex. Some, particularly students from diverse ethnic, cultural, or linguistic groups and those with disabilities, may simply be overlooked. Hallahan and Kauffman (1988) address this issue and others in their recommendations to general education teachers:

1. The teacher should periodically review the characteristics of all the pupils in the class in order not to overlook any child who may be gifted. Which students in the class show particular ability, creativity, and task commitment? Are there pupils in the class, especially pupils who are economically disadvantaged or . . . [from a diverse ethnic, cultural, or linguistic] group, whose abilities may be less obvious according to white middle-class standards or who may be masking their abilities because of peer pressure for conformity?
2. The teacher must analyze and adjust his or her educational requirements for gifted pupils. Is the gifted child turned off to education because the work is not challenging or is not suitable for his superior intellectual powers? Is the gifted child underachieving simply because he is not being given appropriate work? Especially with the disadvantaged or culturally different gifted, it is important to present specific educational tasks in a structured environment with the firm and consistent expectation that they will be completed. . . .
3. The teacher must seek out and employ the resources of the school and community that can be used to the advantage of gifted children. Are there other teachers or older students with knowledge of the problems and methods of inquiry in a field of special interest who can help the child in independent study or small-group activities? Are there residents of other communities with special expertise who are willing to tutor the child or use him as an assistant?
4. The teacher should support whatever movement there may be in the school system toward establishing special programs for the gifted. Are there parents of gifted children whose pleas for special programs should be encouraged? Are there workshops for teachers? Does the school system employ resource teachers or specialists who will help . . . [general education] teachers find methods, materials, community resources? (pp. 453–454)

Another factor in underachievement is motivation. When students are uninterested in academic pursuits or bored with school activities, poor performance can result. Several suggestions for whetting students' appetites for learning appear in "Inclusion Tips for the Teacher." Hallahan and Kauffman (1988) also recommend the *Handbook of Instructional Resources and References for Teaching the Gifted* by Karnes and Collins (1980).

Pendarvis (1993) adds several ideas gleaned from various sources for removing the barriers to achievement:

- Don't give the students lectures or "pep talks" to get them to try harder. This has been shown to have detrimental effects on achievement.
- Show support and respect for the student's efforts.
- Establish appropriate standards and provide the instruction, guidance, and support to help students meet them.
- Encourage cooperation, rather than competition, in the classroom.
- Reward small gains in achievement, and don't expect quick success. (p. 583)

Levy (1981) also discusses ways to meet the needs of students who are gifted and talented. Three of these suggestions are particularly appropriate for the teacher of underachievers:

Inclusion Tips for the Teacher

Motivating Underachievers

Many bright students need little encouragement. Some, however, have not yet developed the motivation to learn. With these individuals, Stephens and Wolf (1978) suggest the following tactics:

- Provide recognition for their efforts
- Provide extra credit for novel ideas or products
- Stress positive comments in all teacher-pupil exchanges
- Offer special privileges for specified performances
- Permit high-achieving students to be "teacher"
- Encourage student-initiated projects and activities for those who have completed assignments
- Make special arrangements for high-achieving students to take selected subjects in higher grades
- Introduce elementary age students to research methods

- Teach debating skills and encourage students to sponsor and participate in debates on topics of their choice
- Have high-achieving math students create mathematical puzzles
- Encourage students to write scripts for TV and radio programs and "participate in" the programs
- Have students present a synopsis of a magazine or newspaper article to the class in a way that is interesting and understandable
- Have a "crazy idea" session where only unusual notions can be discussed
- Conduct a traditional brain-storming session
- Let them express themselves in art forms such as drawings, creative writing, and role playing
- Have them dramatize their readings
- Have a great books seminar to introduce students to the classics

Note. Reprinted with permission of Merrill, an imprint of Macmillan Publishing Company, from "The Gifted Child" by T. M. Stephens and J. S. Wolf in *Behavior of Exceptional Children* (2nd ed., pp. 403–404) by N. G. Haring (Ed.). Copyright © 1978 Merrill Publishing Company, Columbus, Ohio.

Things to Remember

- For achievement to be commensurate with potential, students who are gifted and talented require special educational adaptations in the general education class or in separate programs.

- Students who are gifted and talented are characterized by their above-average ability. Their gift or talent can be in intellectual performance, creativity, academic achievement, leadership potential, or special areas of endeavor such as art or music.

- This group of special students is composed of both males and females and individuals representing all socioeconomic strata and cultures. As a group, students who are gifted and talented are more verbal, learn more rapidly, and are better adjusted than their typical class peers.

- The major educational adaptations for students who are gifted and talented are curriculum compacting, enrichment, and acceleration. In the general education class, curriculum compacting reduces the coverage of material already mastered, whereas enrichment expands both the depth and breadth of study.

- One important goal in the education of this group of special students is the development of creativity and problem-solving skills. Divergent thinking is encouraged, and appropriate solutions to problems are sought through convergence and evaluation.

- Students who are gifted and talented do not all excel in school; some, considered underachievers, remain unidentified and/or lack sufficient motivation to perform near their potential.

- Most students who are gifted and talented remain in the general education program for the majority of their school careers. To meet their special learning needs, educators must adapt the instructional procedures in the general education classroom.

- It is not necessary to be gifted or talented to be an effective teacher of such students. It is more important to be an adept facilitator of learning than an expert in all subject matter areas.

- Let them teach you what they need. By listening to them and observing them, you can make guesses about what is needed . . . these students are articulate. They also appreciate a good listener. I constantly experience delight in my encounters with them.
- Let them teach each other. Often my students teach each other content and processes that are way beyond my comprehension. As the teacher, I am not responsible to be the sole source of knowledge. I see myself as a facilitator of student learning . . . [two students] taught each other more in 5 months of computer instruction than I could have in a year, considering my other teacher responsibilities. They also provided each other with more minutes of instruction than I could have done in several years of being their classroom teacher.
- Enjoy them. They are interesting people who are fun to have in class. (p. 142)

In this chapter, you have learned about some of the characteristics of students who are unusually bright and those with special gifts and talents. Methods for identifying appropriate educational options, promoting creativity and problem solving, and assisting underachievers have been suggested. In the next chapter, you will meet another group of students with special needs—those from culturally and linguistically diverse backgrounds.

ACTIVITIES

1. Observe a general education classroom in which there are one or more students identified as gifted or talented. Are these pupils involved in any special programs outside the classroom or school? What special provisions are made in the general education classroom? Are techniques such as curriculum compacting used to eliminate the need for students to work on material they have already mastered or to streamline the pace at which they master other materials? Do the behaviors of these students differ in any way

from those of their peers? Are they well accepted by their classmates and teacher?

2. Interview children or young adults who have been identified as gifted or talented. What are their current interests? What do they like and dislike about school? Ask them to suggest ways in which the school experience could be made more valuable to them.

3. Locate articles that discuss education of pupils who are gifted and talented. *G/T/C* (Gifted/Talented/Creative), *Roeper Review, Journal of Creative Behavior, Journal for the Education of the Gifted,* and *The Gifted Child Quarterly* are possible sources. Do you find suggestions for general education class adaptations? For assisting underachievers? For students from diverse ethnic, cultural, or linguistic groups?

4. Contact local schools to find out what services are available for youngsters who are gifted and talented. Are there special classes? Early admission? Resource services? Enrichment programs to augment the general education classroom? What assistance is available to the general education teacher?

5. Ask several members of your community to define the terms *gifted* and *talented*. You might select teachers, students, school administrators, parents of school-aged children, and others with no current connection with the public school system. Compare their definitions to see whether there is any consensus. Use the information you have collected to prepare a set of local definitions meaningful to the persons in your community. Be clear and concise, and use language understandable to both educators and the general public.

chapter 16

Teaching Culturally and Linguistically Diverse Students

Let's begin with the case of Juanito, or Pablo, or Pedro, who is attending school for the first time. He comes to school with a language that has served him quite well for his first five years and with possibly some knowledge of English. He has grown up in a Mexican American family with traditional values unique to his culture and has been socialized in this culture. He goes to a school which reflects the values of the dominant society. This child comes in having a different language and a different culture from that of the school. He finds himself in a strange and threatening situation, not only with the need to master a new language, but to make immediate use of it in order to function as a student. Moreover, many of the social relationships and cultural attitudes on which the total school program is based are completely outside his experience. (Sierra, 1973, p. 43)

Chau became an honor student this year. Seventeen years old and a tenth grader, she is enrolled in a college prep curriculum with plans for becoming a counseling psychologist. . . . Born to a privileged Vietnamese family, Chau was six years old when the North Vietnamese entered Saigon as victors. She remembers hiding for hours with relatives in a cellar until the shooting stopped and then walking home over, and on, the bodies of those massacred. She remembers the government troops replacing a picture of her grandparents with one of Ho Chi Minh and then removing all furniture, clothes, and other belongings from her home. . . . And she remembers her first attempt to flee Vietnam with two brothers. Discovered by roving government troops, one brother escaped, one was killed, and Chau was shot and left for dead. (Cegelka, 1988, p. 547)

The United States is a culturally diverse nation, and the composition of many general education classrooms reflects this diversity. Students may differ from one another and from their teachers in culture and in language. These differences, when encouraged and fostered by society, are known as **cultural pluralism** (Rueda & Prieto, 1979).

Although each person is an individual with distinct characteristics, each is influenced by the cul-ture in which he or she is reared and in which he or she lives. Aragon (1973) describes five major components that define a culture:

> First is a common pattern of communication, sound system or language which is unique to that group. Second is a common basic diet and method of preparing food. If the group adorns and protects their bodies with the same kinds of dress, or if the group has common costuming, they meet the third criterion of culture. And if the relationships within the group—woman-man, mother-child, uncle-niece—are predictable, or if there are common socialization patterns within the group, they have met the fourth. And finally, the group must subscribe to a common set of values and beliefs or have a common set of ethics. (p. 26)

Students in schools in the United States represent many different cultures. The dominant culture, or *macroculture,* has its roots in western European traditions. According to Gollnick and Chinn (1990), "the major cultural influence on the United States, particularly on its institutions, has been white, Anglo-Saxon, and Protestant" (p. 12). Persons living in the United States are influenced by the macroculture whether or not they choose to adopt all of its values and belief systems.

Each individual is also influenced by his or her membership in several microcultures. A *microculture* is a group of individuals who share some, but not all, of the cultural patterns of the macroculture *and* a common set of cultural patterns distinct from those of the macroculture (Gollnick & Chinn, 1998). Microcultures may be based on factors such as ethnicity or national origin, socioeconomic class, religion, gender, age, disability, or the area of the country in which a person lives (Gollnick & Chinn, 1998). Consider, for example, the differences between the customs and mores of New England and those of the Deep South or the differences in cultural patterns among Irish Americans, Mexican Americans, and Chinese Americans.

The term *minority* is used to describe groups with fewer members than the "majority" group. In the United States, census data and other sources of demographic information often define these populations as minorities: (a) Black, (b) Hispanic, (c) Asian and Pacific Islander, and (d) American Indian, Eskimo, and Aleut. It is important to recognize that each of these groups is itself heterogeneous. For example, among people with Asian roots are those who identify themselves as Chinese, Vietnamese, Laotian, Hmong, Cambodian, Filipino, Korean, and Japanese (Cheng, 1991). Also, the Native American population is made up of more than 500 tribes with over 200 different languages (McDonald, 1989).

Minority is considered to be a pejorative term. In addition, in many parts of the country, it is inaccurate. Consider these statistics about the changing nature of the U.S. population:

- America's racial profile is rapidly changing. Between 1980 and 1990, the rate of increase in the population for white Americans was 6 percent, while the rate of increase for racial and ethnic minorities was much higher: 53 percent for Hispanics, 13.2 percent for African-Americans, and 107.8 percent for Asians.
- By the year 2000, this Nation will have 275,000,000 people, one of every three of whom will be either African-American, Hispanic, Asian-American, or American Indian.
- Taken together as a group, it is a more frequent phenomenon for minorities to comprise the majority of public school students. Large city school populations are overwhelming minority, for example: for fall 1993, the figure for Miami was 84 percent; Chicago, 89 percent; Philadelphia, 78 percent; Baltimore, 84 percent; Houston, 88 percent; and Los Angeles, 88 percent. [PL 105-17, Individuals with Disabilities Education Act Amendments of 1997, Sec. 601(c)(7)]
- The limited English proficient population is the fastest growing in our Nation, and the growth is occurring in many parts of our Nation. In the Nation's 2 largest school districts, limited-English students make up almost half of all students initially entering school at the kindergarten level. [PL 101-476, Individuals with Disabilities Education Act, 1990, Sec. 610 (j)(1)]

There have been many approaches to the education of students from culturally and linguistically diverse groups. Kitano (1991) describes the two major philosophical positions underlying these approaches: assimilation and pluralism. In assimilation, the goal is to move students away from their original culture and teach them the skills needed to compete in the macroculture. In pluralism, students are encouraged to retain their original culture, and, to promote educational success, schools make accommodations based upon students' experiential backgrounds.

Multicultural education is an instructional approach based on the pluralistic perspective. According to the policy statement, "No One Model American," of the American Association of Colleges for Teacher Education (1973):

Multicultural education is education which values cultural pluralism. Multicultural education rejects the view that schools should seek to melt away cultural differences or the view that schools should merely tolerate cultural pluralism. To endorse cultural pluralism is to endorse the principle that there is no one model American. To endorse cultural pluralism is to understand and appreciate the differences that exist among the nation's citizens. It is to see these differences as a positive force in the continuing development of a society which professes a wholesome respect for the intrinsic worth of every individual. (p. 264)

When this viewpoint is adopted, the general education classroom begins to meet the needs of students from diverse cultural and linguistic backgrounds.

Gollnick and Chinn (1998) identify six fundamental beliefs and assumptions underlying the concept of multicultural education:

- Cultural differences have strength and value.
- Schools should be models for the expression of human rights and respect for cultural differences.
- Social justice and equality for all people should be of paramount importance in the design and delivery of curricula.
- Attitudes and values necessary for the continuation of a democratic society can be promoted in schools.
- Schooling can provide the knowledge, dispositions, and skills for the redistribution of power and income among cultural groups.
- Educators working with families and communities can create an environment that is supportive of multiculturalism. (p. 28)

Figure 16–1 presents a checklist developed by Ortiz (1988) for evaluating a school or district's educational environment and its effectiveness for culturally diverse learners. Among the factors to consider are the relevance of the curriculum, parental participation, student involvement, and opportunities for teachers to continue to refine their skills.

FIGURE 16-1   Evaluating the Educational Context

For each of the items below, circle "Yes" if the statement is characteristic of your school (or your district, if you prefer). Circle "No" if the statement is not characteristic of your school or district.

Yes   No   1. My school/district supports cultural pluralism.

Yes   No   2. The curriculum incorporates students' contemporary culture, not only history, customs and holidays.

Yes   No   3. The curriculum helps students strike a balance between cultural pride and identity on one hand and appreciation of cultures different from their own on the other.

Yes   No   4. The curriculum teaches certain humanistic values such as the negative effects of prejudice and discrimination.

Yes   No   5. My school/district is integrated (or facilitates opportunities for cross-cultural interaction).

Yes   No   6. Inservices routinely incorporate considerations in teaching linguistically/culturally diverse students.

Yes   No   7. Children are encouraged to use their native language.

Yes   No   8. The administration supports bilingual education.

Yes   No   9. Minority parents are actively encouraged to participate in school activities.

Yes   No   10. Training is provided to facilitate involvement of minority parents in their children's education.

Yes   No   11. The regular classroom curriculum is appropriate for the diverse student populations served.

Yes   No   12. Regular classroom (not only bilingual education or ESL) teachers understand how limited English proficient students acquire English competence and incorporate language development activities in subject matter instruction.

Yes   No   13. Minority students do as well on achievement tests as do Anglo students.

Yes   No   14. Poor students do as well as middle- and upper-income students on tests of academic achievement.

Yes   No   15. As much emphasis is given to developing higher cognitive skills as is given to basic skill attainment.

Yes   No   16. Teachers are facilitators of learning as opposed to transmitters of information and facts.

Yes   No   17. Teachers adjust instructional approaches and activities to accommodate culturally-conditioned learning styles.

Yes   No   18. Informal assessment is given as much emphasis as is formal assessment in psychoeducational evaluations of linguistically/culturally different students.

Yes   No   19. Teachers are trained in informal assessment procedures.

Yes   No   20. Reading and writing instruction is characterized by student control and an emphasis on meaningful communication and creativity.

Yes   No   21. There is a well-articulated prereferral process in place to assure that students receive appropriate educational opportunities before they are referred to special education.

Yes   No   22. The emphasis of assessment is on gleaning information to guide intervention.

Yes   No   23. Students participate in school governance.

Yes   No   24. Teachers are involved in planning and selecting inservice training topics and activities.

Yes   No   25. My school/district would be described as a "happy" place by minority students and parents.

Note. This questionnaire was developed by Alba A. Ortiz, Department of Special Education, The University of Texas at Austin; it appeared in the *Bilingual Special Education Newsletter* (Vol. 7, Spring 1988) published by The University of Texas at Austin. The questionnaire may be reproduced without special permission when appropriate credit is given to the author.

For Your Information

Cultural and Linguistic Diversity in the United States

- Gollnick and Chinn (1998) report that "the United States is comprised of at least 276 ethnic groups, including 170 Native American groups" (p. 78).
- Asian Americans include (but are not limited to) Japanese, Chinese, Filipino, Korean, Vietnamese, Cambodian, Laotian, Guamanian, Indian, Pakistani, Burmese, Thai, Marshallese, Saipanese, Ponapean, and Yapese individuals (Cheng, 1991; Decano, 1979; Garcia, 1978). Asian Americans are the fastest-growing "minority" group, now numbering more than 7 million (Chan, 1992).
- Native Americans number more than 2 million and show great diversity in culture and language, as evidenced by the more than 200 different Native American languages in use today (Garcia, 1978; Joe & Malach, 1992; McDonald, 1989; Pepper, 1976).

- African Americans are the largest "minority"; the more than 33 million African Americans make up 13% of the U.S. population (U.S. Census Bureau, 1997; Willis, 1992).
- The second largest group (and the largest bilingual group) is Hispanics (sometimes called Latinos). Numbering more than 19 million persons, they are largely concentrated in New York and Florida and the southwestern states of Arizona, California, New Mexico, Colorado, and Texas (Baca & de Valenzuela, 1998; Garcia, 1978; Smith, 1979; U.S. Department of Commerce, 1989; Zuniga, 1992).
- More than 31 million people in the United States speak languages other than English at home (Schmidt, 1992).

DIVERSITY IN THE GENERAL EDUCATION CLASSROOM

Students are considered culturally diverse when their home culture is at variance with that of the school. According to Hodgkinson (1993):

> . . . the population of American schools today truly represents the world. Children come to school today with different diets, different religions (there were more Moslems than Episcopalians in the U.S. in 1991), different individual and group loyalties, different music, different languages. (p. 620)

Some culturally diverse students were born in the United States and have lived there all their lives; others are recent immigrants still experiencing the shock of adapting to an entirely new culture. Immigrants come from all parts of the world, but in recent years the majority have been Latin Americans and Asians (Hodgkinson, 1993; Kellogg, 1988). Some are refugees who were forced to flee their homelands. The article "Educating Refugees: Understanding the Basics" (1989) reports that "in many cases, refugees

have had to abruptly leave their home culture, language, family and friends, and may never be able to return to their countries" (p. 1).

Some students differ from their peers in not only cultural background but also language. They may speak with an accent or in a dialect; some may know little English and may feel more comfortable speaking the language of their home. Correa and Heward (1996) estimate that there are now more than 8 million U.S. students with limited proficiency in English. The population of a single district or school may reflect several of the more than 3,000 languages spoken in the world (Cheng, 1991). Smith (1998) reports that more than 100 languages are spoken in four urban districts in the United States: New York, Chicago, Los Angeles, and Fairfax County, Virginia. Cegelka (1988) provides examples of individual schools in California that serve 25 to 38 different language groups.

Some culturally diverse students have special learning needs, and others do not. Some have disabilities, some are gifted, and others are average achievers. Like their peers, most are best served in the general education classroom. However, the general

education teacher must recognize the impact of cultural and linguistic diversity on the performance of these students. Knowledge of and respect for differences among cultural groups will help the teacher provide a more successful educational experience for all students.

◆ CULTURAL DIVERSITY

Culture influences behavior. Within each culture is a set of values and beliefs that guide the members of that culture in social interactions. However, what is accepted as desirable conduct in one culture may be considered inappropriate in another. The classroom teacher must be aware of such differences in order to understand the behavior of students from diverse groups.

Before proceeding, it is important to point out that descriptions of cultures are necessarily generalizations. As such, they provide some guidance in understanding the customs and beliefs of a *group* of persons but little information about specific individuals within that group. As Lynch (1992) warns:

> Culture is only one of the characteristics that determine individuals' and families' attitudes, values, beliefs, and ways of behaving. . . . Assuming that

culture-specific information . . . applies to all individuals from the cultural group is not only inaccurate but also dangerous—it can lead to stereotyping that diminishes rather than enhances cross-cultural competence. When applying culture-specific information to an individual or family, it is wise to proceed with caution. (p. 44)

Pepper (1976) observes that there are many differences between the values of the dominant culture in the United States and those of the Native American culture; several of these differences appear in Table 16–1. For example, whereas the macroculture emphasizes competition and individual achievement, Native American culture stresses cooperation and group achievement. Also, in contrast to the dominant culture, in which words are the primary mode of communication, Native American students are more likely to express themselves through actions. These cultural differences can affect a student's ability to conform to the expectations of the school. In discussing points of divergence between the two cultures, Walker (1988) notes:

- Family or cultural expectations for child behavior may differ from the expectations of the educational setting. For example, levels of independence in decision making might be greater for American Indian children.
- Identification of a child with his or her peer group may be more important than selection or recognition as an individual, thus inhibiting performance [by] noncompetitiveness.
- Cultural and family expectations for verbal interactions with adults may be contradictory to teacher expectations. (pp. 50-51)

Other cultures also have value systems that may be in conflict with the expectations of the dominant-culture school. Kitano (1973) describes several characteristics of Asian culture that may affect student behavior:

- The Asian doesn't do anything that would make him stand out from the group. . . .
- The Asian culture utilizes a much more indirect or subtle means of communication than we usually find here in this country. . . .
- The Asian family structure is based on the traditional agrarian family model; males are considered more desirable than females. . . .
- Very few Asians engage in free participation in group discussions. Generally, they feel that if they say something, it must be profound and important. (p. 14)

TABLE 16-1 Native American and Dominant-Culture Values

Native American	Dominant Culture
Excellence is related to a contribution to the group—not personal glory.	Competition and striving to win or to gain status is emphasized.
Cooperation is necessary for group survival.	Competition is necessary for individual status and prestige.
Good relationships and mutual respect are emphasized.	Success, progress, possession of property and rugged individualism are valued above mutual respect and maintaining good relationships.
People express their ideas and feelings through their actions.	People express themselves and attempt to impress others through speech.
People are usually judged by what they do.	People are usually judged by their credentials.
Time is present oriented—this year, this week—NOW—a resistance to planning for the future.	Time is planning and saving for the future.
Clocktime is whenever people are ready—when everyone arrives.	Clocktime is exactly that.
Work is when necessary for the common good. Whatever Indian people have, they share. What is mine is ours.	Work is from 9–5 (specified time) and to obtain material possessions and to save for the future. What is mine, stays mine.
Going to school is necessary to gain knowledge. Excelling for fame is looked down upon by the Indian.	Going to school is necessary to gain knowledge and to compete for grades.

Note. Adapted from "Teaching the American Indian Child in Mainstream Settings" by F. C. Pepper in *Mainstreaming and the Minority Child* (pp. 135–136) by R. L. Jones (Ed.), 1976, Reston, VA: The Council for Exceptional Children. Reprinted by permission.

TABLE 16-2 Incongruities Between American Teachers' Expectations and Asian Parents' Expectations

American Teachers' Expectations	Asian Parents' Expectations
Students need to participate in classroom activities and discussion.	Students are to be quiet and obedient.
Students need to be creative.	Students should be told what to do.
Students learn through inquiries and debate.	Students learn through memorization and observation.
Asian students generally do well on their own.	Teachers need to teach; students need to "study."
Critical thinking is important. Analytical thinking is important.	It is important to deal with the real world.
Creativity and fantasy are to be encouraged.	Factual information is important; fantasy is not.
Problem solving is important.	Students should be taught the steps to solve problems.
Students need to ask questions.	Teachers are not to be challenged.
Reading is a way of discovering.	Reading is the decoding of new information and facts.

Note. From *Assessing Asian Language Performance* (p. 14) by L. L. Cheng, 1991, Oceanside, CA: Academic Communication Associates. Reprinted by permission.

Teachers' expectations for student performance often come into conflict with the expectations of Asian parents, as Table 16–2 illustrates.

Several authors have addressed the effects of Latino culture on student behavior (Aragon & Marquez, 1973; Condon, Peters, & Sueiro-Ross, 1979; Rodriguez, Cole, Stile, & Gallegos, 1979; Sierra, 1973; Zuniga, 1992). Cultural characteristics frequently mentioned are the existence of close family ties and strong family loyalties, preference

Window on the Web

Websites Related to Diversity and Multicultural Education

General Websites

We Hold These Truths to be Self-Evident
http://edweb.sdsu.edu/people/CMathison/truths/truths.html
This site is an online learning activity on democratic schooling designed for educators. Included are resources and information on students with disabilities, gender issues in education, and a number of cultures: Latino, Gay and Lesbian, African American, American Indian, and Asian American.

Online Culture and Language Learning
http://edweb.sdsu.edu/CSP/ocll.html
Among the resources offered by this site are links to online resources on Latino/Hispanic, Native American, Asian–Pacific Islander, and African American cultures.

American Studies Web: Race and Ethnicity
htty://www.georgetown.edu/crossroads/asw/race.html
Part of the American Studies Crossroads Project at Georgetown University, the American Studies Web contains dozens of links categorized by group: African American, Asian American, Native American, Latino and Chicano, and other racial and ethnic resources.

NCBE Web Site
http://www.ncbe.gwu.edu/
The website of the National Clearinghouse for Bilingual Education is operated by George Washington University and funded by the Office of Bilingual Education and Minority Languages Affairs of the U.S. Department of Education. It features an online library and links to sites on bilingual education and ESL, multiculturalism, and specific languages and cultures.

NABE
http://www.nabe.org
NABE, the National Association for Bilingual Education, sponsors this site for its members and others interested in bilingual education.

Websites About Specific Cultures

African American Culture

- The African American Mosaic, A Library of Congress Resource Guide
  (lcweb.loc.gov/exhibits/african/intro.html)
- African American Web Connection (www.aawc.com/aawc.html)
- Black/African Related Resources (www.sas.upenn.edu/African_Studies/Home_Page/mcgee.html)
- National Civil Rights Movement (www.mecca.org/~crights/nc2.html)

Asian American Culture

- Hmong Homepage (www.hmongnet.org)
- Philippine History (pubweb.acns.nwu.edu/~flip/history.html)

- Southeast Asia Web (www.gunung.com/seasiaweb)
- VietGATE, Gateway to the Online Vietnamese Community (www.vietgate.net)

Native American Culture

- Alaska Native Knowledge Network (zorba.uafadm.alaska.edu/ankn/index.html)
- Native American Home Pages (www.pitt.edu/~lmitten/indians.html)
- Native American Resources on the Internet (hanksville.phast.umass.edu/misc/NAresources.html)
- NativeWeb (www.nativeweb.org)

Latino/Hispanic Culture

- CLNet (Chicano/Latino Net) (latino.sscnet.ucla.edu)
- Hispanic Heritage: Hispanic Pages in the USA (coloquio.com/index.html)
- HISPANIC Online (www.hisp.com)
- LatinoWeb (www.latinoweb.com)

for cooperative rather than competitive activities, emphasis on interpersonal relationships rather than tasks, and a relaxed sense of time (in relation to that of the macroculture).

Likewise, values of the African American culture can influence students' classroom behavior. Teachers expect students to speak one at a time and to listen quietly while others are speaking. However, African American culture emphasizes general audience participation and spontaneity, not taking turns (Ratleff, 1989). Schools value verbal expression over other modes of communication. In contrast, African American culture encourages not only speech but other forms of expression as well, including body language, nonverbal communication, and visual and dramatic expression (Ratleff, 1989; Rivera & Rogers-Adkinson, 1997). Franklin (1992) adds that African American students prefer student-centered classrooms with multiple opportunities for interpersonal interactions.

Although all persons are influenced by their cultures, they remain individuals; no group of people is homogeneous. However, it is worthwhile for teachers to attempt to gain insight into the cultural backgrounds of their students—and to identify their own values and belief systems. Lynch (1992) identifies three components of cross-cultural competence for teachers and other professionals: awareness of one's own culture, awareness and understanding of students' cultures, and development of cross-cultural communication skills.

LINGUISTIC DIVERSITY

Language is another important consideration in the education of students from diverse backgrounds. Although some students are quite competent in English, others enter school speaking little or no English. The language of a student's family also concerns the teacher. Even if a child is fluent in English, the parents may not feel comfortable conversing in that language. For many (but certainly not all) culturally diverse students, the language spoken in the home is not English. Their parents and siblings may speak Spanish, one of many Asian languages, or one of many Native American tongues. Students who enter school with few English language skills are at a distinct disadvantage; as noted by Sierra (1973), the school expects these students not only to speak English but also to use that language to acquire other school skills.

At present, Spanish speakers make up the largest group of bilingual individuals in the United States. Much has been written regarding the overlap between language and culture and the difficulties this overlap presents in the education of students whose dominant language is Spanish. Condon, Peters, and Sueiro-Ross (1979) cite the examples of Lado (1968), which identify communication problems that can occur among speakers of Spanish and speakers of English:

- The Spanish compliment "Qué grueso estás," which is translated literally as "how fat you are," becomes an insult in English.
- The use of the name "Jesús" for a boy is quite common in Hispanic society, but not in the Anglo-Saxon community, where it is regarded as inappropriate, if not sacrilegious.
- To be "informal" in Spanish is "to be neglectful," but to be so in English simply conveys the notion of "casual" behavior.
- "Compromiso" as it applies to negotiations carries a negative connotation in Hispanic culture which is not found in its English counterpart "compromise." (p. 82)

Evans and Guevara (1974) discuss other problems of communication that result from the interdependence of language and culture. Several of their examples are presented in Figure 16–2.

When children acquire English as a second language, their speech may sound somewhat different from that of students who are native speakers of English. A teacher may note that they speak with an accent. One reason for this is the nonequivalence of speech sounds between languages. Taylor (1986) points out that Spanish speech sounds can interfere with English pronunciation. For instance, a Spanish speaker may substitute *chair* for *share* and *watch* for *wash* in English. These and other examples appear in Table 16–3.

It should be noted that not all culturally diverse students are bilingual; for many, English is the language of their home, and it is the only language that they know. However, they may speak a dialect of English rather than the standard English of the public school. One example is Black English, considered by many experts to be a dialect of standard English. Black English is also called Vernacular Black English or Ebonics (Gollnick & Chinn, 1998). As shown in Table 16–4, on page 426 Black English is characterized by its own formal rules and structures.

ASSESSMENT AND SPECIAL SERVICES

Although most culturally diverse students receive their education in the general education classroom, some may be referred for assessment if they appear to have special learning needs. If students are identified as disabled, gifted, or talented, they may be

FIGURE 16-2 **Relationships Between Language and Culture**

- **It is sometimes not possible to translate a word from one language to another.**

  Example: In studying a unit on animals, young English speakers understand *pet*. However, translation into Spanish results in *animal doméstico* (a domesticated animal) or perhaps *animalito* (a little animal), neither of which . . . [carries] the same meaning. The word *pet* is an English culture concept and the difficulty lies in the impossibility of translating the culture.

- **Translation may result in misinformation.**

  Example: For many English speakers, the word *tools* is a general category label indicating objects which are used in different occupations or tasks. At the end of a study unit on community helpers, the child may be asked to subcategorize tools on the basis of occupation (those used by a carpenter, janitor, gardener, etc.). In Spanish, there is no single general term for *tools* and translation may result in *fierros* (objects made of iron or steel), *herramientas* (implements), *instrumentos* (instruments), *equipo* (equipment), or *útiles* (utensils). Tools used by a carpenter are *fierros* while those used by a janitor may be referred to as *equipo.* It is impossible to teach a child to subdivide a category label that does not exist.

- **A word specifying one concept in one language may specify several concepts in another.**

  Example: The positional terms *in, on,* and *over* carry distinct concepts in English. However, in Spanish *en* is the equivalent of both *in* and *on; sobre* may mean *on* or *over;* and *encima* and *arriba de* can also mean *on* or *on top of.* To translate an activity written in English in which in, on and over are taught as contrasting concepts is not only confusing but may result in teaching erroneous concepts.

  Example: In English *hot* or the phrase "it is hot" may be used in multiple ways such as describing the weather, a heated object, or degree of food seasoning. For example:

  1. "It (stove) is hot."
  2. "It (weather temperature) is hot."
  3. "It (highly seasoned chili) is hot."

  However, in Spanish, these ideas must be expressed in a completely different manner. For example:

  1. "Está caliente."
  2. "Hace calor."
  3. "(El chile) pica."

Note. From "Classroom Instruction for Young Spanish Speakers" by J. Evans and A. E. Guevara, 1974, *Exceptional Children, 41,* p. 17. Copyright 1974 by The Council for Exceptional Children. Adapted by permission.

TABLE 16-3 **Examples of Spanish Interference with English Speech Sounds**

English Sound	Sound Substituted	Examples
initial sound of *ship*	initial sound of *chip*	*chair* for *share*
		watch for *wash*
initial sound of *zoo*	initial sound of *see*	*sip* for *zip*
		racer for *razor*
final sound of *ring*	final sound of *in*	*sin* for *sing*
initial sound of *voice*	initial sound of *boy*	*bat* for *vat*
initial sound of *thing*	initial sound of *see* or initial sound of *top*	*tin* or *sin* for *thin*
initial sound of *that*	initial sound of *do*	*den* for *then*
		ladder for *lather*
initial sound of *in*	initial sound of *eat*	*cheap* for *chip*

Note. Reprinted with permission of Merrill, an imprint of Macmillan Publishing Company, from "Language Differences" by O. L. Taylor in *Human Communication Disorders* (2nd ed., p. 400) by G. H. Shames and E. H. Wiig (Eds.). Copyright © 1986 Merrill Publishing Company, Columbus, Ohio.

TABLE 16-4　Characteristics of Black English

Linguistic Categories	Characteristics	Examples	
		Standard English	**Black English**
Phonological Differences			
Initial position	Merging of /f/ with /th/	thigh	fie
	Merging of /v/ with /th/	Thou	vow
Medial position	Deletion of /r/	Carol	cal
	Merging of /i/ and /e/	pen	pin
	Merging of /v/ with /th/	mother	movver
	Merging of /f/ with /th/	birthday	birfday
Final position	Deletion of /r/	sore	saw
	Deletion of /l/	Saul	saw
	Simplification of consonant clusters:		
	/st/	past	pass
	/ft/	left	leff
	/nt/	went	wen
	/nd/	wind	wine
	/zd/	raised	raise*
	/md/	aimed	aim*
	/ks/	six	sick
	/ts/	it's	it*
	/lt/	salt	saught
Morphological differences			
Future	Loss of final /l/	you'll	you
Past tense	Simplification of final consonants such as:		
	/st/	passed	pass
	/nd/	loaned	loan
Plural	Deletion of final /s/ and /z/	50 cents	50 cent
		3 birds	3 bird
Syntactical differences			
Auxiliary verb	Deletion of auxiliary	He is gone.	He goin.
Subject expression	Repetition of subject	John lives in NY.	John, he live in NY.
Verb form	Substitution of past participle for simple past form	I drank the milk.	I drunk the milk.
Verb agreement	Deletion of /s/ for third person singular present tense	He runs home.	He run home.
Future form	Substitution of a variation of present progressive tense	I will go home.	I'ma go home.
Negation	Use of double negative	I don't have any.	I don't got none.
Indefinite article	Deletion of /n/	I want an apple.	I want a apple.
Pronoun form	Substitution of objective for nominative case	We have to do it.	Us got to do it.
Preposition	Difference in preposition	He is over at his friend's house.	He is over to his friend's house.
Copula ("be")	Use of durative be for is	He is here all the time.	He be here.

*These items also are morphological differences.

Note. From "Special Education and the Linguistically Different Child" by D. N. Bryen, 1974, *Exceptional Children, 40,* p. 593. Copyright 1974 by The Council for Exceptional Children. Reprinted by permission.

provided with appropriate special education services. Others may qualify for bilingual education services, if these are available within the district. According to Gonzalez (1978), students are in need of bilingual instruction if (1) their primary or home language is other than English and (2) their school performance indicates academic underachievement.

Bilingual education is concerned with both language and culture, and programs take many forms depending on their goals. According to Baca (1998), *transitional* or "early-exit" bilingual education programs utilize the student's native language and culture to facilitate the acquisition of English. The goal is to integrate the student into the general education curriculum as quickly as possible. *Maintenance* or "late-exit" programs, in contrast, are designed to develop the student's native language skills and cultural competence as well as to teach English; the goal is to maintain the first language and augment (not replace) it with English. Gersten and Woodward (1994) prefer the term *native language emphasis* to describe programs with strong native language components. According to Gersten and Jiménez

(1998), this model of bilingual education is the most common in use today.

Cummins (1989) maintains that educators should encourage students to develop proficiency in their first language (L1), even if bilingual education programs are not available. To do this, teachers should follow these suggestions:

- Encourage students to use their L1 around the school.
- Provide opportunities for students from the same ethnic group to communicate with one another in their L1 where possible (e.g., in cooperative learning groups on at least some occasions).
- Recruit people who can tutor students in their L1.
- Provide books written in the various languages in both classrooms and the school library.
- Incorporate greetings and information in the various languages in newsletters and other official school communications. (Cummins, 1989, p. 113)

Another approach to the education of students with limited proficiency in English is *sheltered English,* sometimes called structured immersion. Like earlier approaches such as ESL (English as a second language) and ESOL (English for speakers of other languages), in sheltered English instruction takes place only in English, and no effort is made to maintain or develop proficiency in the student's first language. Schools often use this approach when there are insufficient numbers of non-English-speaking students to form a bilingual education class, when students represent a number of different language groups, and/or when there is a shortage of teachers fluent in the language spoken by students. See "Spotlight on Technology" on page 428 for information about a desktop publishing program designed for Spanish-speaking students who are learning English language skills.

When students from culturally diverse backgrounds are evaluated either for special education or bilingual education services, it is necessary to ensure that assessment procedures are nonbiased. That is, measurement devices must not discriminate on the basis of race, culture, or language (McLoughlin & Lewis, 1994). The language of the student is an obvious consideration. If the student has limited proficiency in English, it is futile to use an English-language test to assess aptitude or school achievement. In fact, if the student's primary language is Spanish, Navajo, or Tagalog, the only justification for testing in English is to determine the student's facility in this second language.

Spotlight on Technology

The Bilingual Writing Center

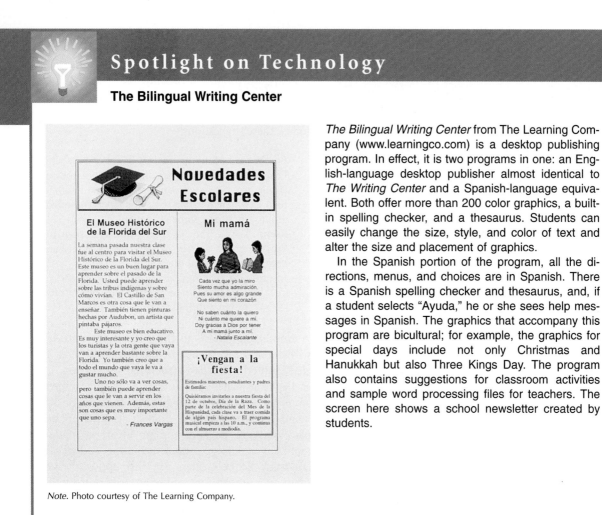

The Bilingual Writing Center from The Learning Company (www.learningco.com) is a desktop publishing program. In effect, it is two programs in one: an English-language desktop publisher almost identical to *The Writing Center* and a Spanish-language equivalent. Both offer more than 200 color graphics, a built-in spelling checker, and a thesaurus. Students can easily change the size, style, and color of text and alter the size and placement of graphics.

In the Spanish portion of the program, all the directions, menus, and choices are in Spanish. There is a Spanish spelling checker and thesaurus, and, if a student selects "Ayuda," he or she sees help messages in Spanish. The graphics that accompany this program are bicultural; for example, the graphics for special days include not only Christmas and Hanukkah but also Three Kings Day. The program also contains suggestions for classroom activities and sample word processing files for teachers. The screen here shows a school newsletter created by students.

Note. Photo courtesy of The Learning Company.

The cultural background of the student is another important concern. If a measure has been designed for use with dominant-culture students, those who differ in experiential background are unjustly penalized. Consider the example of Williams (1974) that is cited by Alley and Foster (1978):

> "When is Washington's birthday?" If you are of the majority culture, you probably would answer "February 22." This response would be scored correct according to the Wechsler Adult Intelligence Scale scoring criteria. . . . If, however, you were to respond "April 5," your response would be scored as incorrect, using that scoring criteria. The implication is that you must associate George rather than Booker T. with Washington. This item could be classified as culture-biased. (p. 1)

In the general education classroom, the teacher should also take care in assessing students from various cultural backgrounds. Many typical classroom measures are in opposition to the values held by some cultures. For instance, students who are not influenced by clock time will fare poorly on tests of speed or timed assignments. Those who prefer cooperation to competition may feel threatened by class contests. Individuals who are reluctant to stand out from the group may not respond to awards, prizes, and recognition as incentives.

CLASSROOM ADAPTATIONS

Most culturally and linguistically diverse students are full-time members of general education classes. Although some students with special needs may receive services from a special education resource teacher or from an expert in bilingual education, most of their school career is typically spent in general education settings. Therefore, the general education teacher must be aware of cultural and linguistic differences and their effects on performance in academics, classroom conduct, and social interactions.

Multicultural education is the major approach to instruction of students from diverse backgrounds. According to Gonzales (1979), multicultural education includes five major components:

1. Staffing composition patterns throughout the organization hierarchy that reflect the pluralistic nature of American society;
2. Curricula that are appropriate, flexible, and unbiased, and that incorporate the contributions of all cultural groups;
3. Affirmation of the languages of cultural groups as different rather than deficient;
4. Instructional materials that are free of bias, omissions, and stereotypes; that are inclusive rather than supplementary; and that show individuals from different cultural groups portraying different occupational and social roles;

5. Educational evaluation procedures, which assess not only the content of the curricula and instructional materials, but also how well the experience and materials help encourage better understanding and respect for humankind. (p. 15)

These principles help guide the development of instructional programs that promote not only the acceptance of students who differ from their peers in culture and language but also their academic success.

In addition, teachers can use several strategies to adapt instruction to better meet the needs of students from diverse groups. One approach recommended by experts is **cooperative learning** (e.g., Baca & Almanza, 1991; Franklin, 1992; Ruiz, 1989). Many cultures value cooperation over competition and prefer interpersonal interactions to interactions with tasks. Cooperative learning, in which students work together to accomplish a common goal, is therefore more congruent with the values of these cultures than individualistic or competitive learning situations. See chapter 6 for descriptions of several types of cooperative learning strategies and the research supporting this approach.

Inclusion Tips for the Teacher

Teaching a Sheltered English Lesson

Echevarria (1995) suggests that teachers follow six steps in presenting sheltered English instruction to students with limited proficiency in English:

1. *Target Vocabulary.* Select several terms or words critical to the lesson. Define those words at the outset of the lesson and keep them posted for visual reference for the students. The vocabulary then becomes part of a word bank to which words are continually added. As previous lessons are built upon, the word banks serve to orient students and create a context for greater understanding.

2. *Select a Main Concept.* Most chapters or lessons can be summarized by one or two key concepts. Focus on the main concept, with the lesson's goal being attainment of that concept. Chapter readings can be outlined or reduced to manageable parts, making the content more comprehensible. A unit of study is more valuable when students fully understand the main ideas and have developed the related academic vocabulary rather than covering every detail with only a cursory understanding.

3. *Create a Context.* This is where the teacher's creativity is put to work. Anything and everything should be used to provide a context for the information to make it more understandable: visuals, sketches on an overhead, gestures, real objects (realia), facial expressions, props, manipulatives, bulletin boards, and the like. Demonstrate what the book is talking about; provide the students with the requisite experiences to add meaning to the topic. If they have difficulty understanding the story's reference to a phrase like "Her attitude was as sour as a lemon," give them the experience of tasting a lemon; if the lesson involves learning the name and function of the teeth, give each child a slice of apple to test out the function of each tooth (e.g., incisor cuts and bicuspid crushes).

4. *Make Connections.* Provide the students with opportunities to relate their background experiences to the topic at hand. The teacher may need to facilitate this process by asking probing questions and then relating the students' comments to the topic. Being able to identify with the topic makes instruction more meaningful to students.

5. *Check for Understanding.* Second-language learners require repetition, clarification, and elaboration. Check frequently for understanding by reviewing target vocabulary and concepts. Use different types of questions to elicit responses and assess understanding in a variety of ways. Above all, maintain a supportive atmosphere in which students are comfortable asking for clarification and participating in the lesson.

6. *Encourage Student-to-Student Interaction.* Because sheltered instruction is highly interactive in nature, it provides students with an optimum opportunity to practice the language they are acquiring. Planning needs to include cooperative activities and projects that group native speakers of English with non-native speakers. For example, partners might work together with a globe to locate specific areas. Cooperative groups might complete a worksheet together, or small groups might plan and execute role playing of the topic.

Note. From "Sheltered Instruction for Students with Learning Disabilities who have Limited English Proficiency" by J. Echevarria, 1995, *Intervention in School and Clinic, 30*, p. 303. Copyright 1995 by PRO-ED, Inc. Reprinted by permission.

Franklin (1992) discusses the major characteristics of culturally sensitive instruction for African American students, which include:

• Presenting instruction at a faster pace, with greater verve and rhythm
• Increasing the amount of stimulation in the classroom by combining media (e.g., speech, singing, music, print, movement, visuals) and by providing a variety of different types of activities
• Using several types of verbal activities such as rap, choral reading, chants, and responsive reading
• Encouraging divergent thinking
• Considering students' individual experiential backgrounds when choosing instructional materials and activities

- Incorporating real-life tasks into the curriculum
- Increasing the "people focus" of instruction so there are many opportunities for person-to-person interactions
- Frequently using small groups for cooperative learning and peer tutoring

Ruiz's (1989) work focuses on another group of students: those who enter school less proficient in English than in Spanish. Ruiz presents the following guidelines for planning instruction for students learning English. Although these guidelines address the language arts curriculum in the elementary grades, many are also applicable to other subjects and other age groups.

- Take into account students' sociocultural backgrounds and their effects on oral language, reading and writing, and second-language learning. . . .
- Follow developmental processes in literacy acquisition.
- Locate curriculum in a meaningful context where the communicative purpose is clear and authentic.
- Connect curriculum with the students' personal experiences.
- Incorporate children's literature into reading, writing, and English-as-a-second language (ESL) lessons.
- Involve parents as active partners in the instruction of their children.
- Give students experience with whole texts in reading, writing, and ESL lessons.
- Incorporate collaborative learning whenever possible. (p. 134)

Sheltered English is another strategy often used with students who are learning English. In this approach, the goal is to teach English language skills at the same time that students are learning specific content area knowledge (California Teachers of English to Speakers of Other Languages, 1992; Northcutt & Watson, 1986). To do this, the teacher analyzes the content of the lesson to identify key concepts and vocabulary. Then, he or she systematically teaches those concepts and vocabulary by using instructional techniques designed to maximize students' ability to comprehend English language input (Krashen, 1987). These techniques include linking new information to students' background knowledge; use of clear, consistent language with many repetitions; and incorporation of extralingual cues such as visual aids, media, props,

realia (i.e., real objects), demonstrations, dramatizations, and so forth (Freeman & Freeman, 1988; Gersten & Jiménez, 1998; Ratleff, 1989; Towell & Wink, 1993). If the teacher or aide speaks the language of the student, key concepts can be pretaught in that language prior to the start of the lesson. See "Inclusion Tips for the Teacher" for Echevarria's (1995) recommendations for sheltered English instruction.

PROMOTING ACCEPTANCE OF DIVERSITY

Peer acceptance is a special need for many culturally and linguistically diverse students. Students who appear different by virtue of language, dress, or customs may find interactions with classmates difficult. One way to overcome this problem is through instruction. When students learn about the language and culture of groups other than their own, differences become less frightening and easier to understand. When students learn about cultural pluralism, diversity is more likely to be treated not only with tolerance but also with respect. McCormick (1990) lists 10 suggestions to assist the teacher of the general education classroom; these appear in "Inclusion Tips for the Teacher" on page 432.

It is also important that the school curriculum and instructional materials such as textbooks reflect the contributions of all cultural groups. That is not always the case, as these examples provided by the National Coalition of Advocates for Students (1985) show:

Witnesses told us of Native American children sitting through lessons about "taming the frontier" and of Columbus "discovering America"; of world history texts which devote no more than a few paragraphs to Africa; of Asian history courses that treat "all Japanese, Chinese, and Filipino people, whose histories are all different and all need to be told" as if they were one; of schools in the Southwest which teach the history of their region with little more than a cursory look at its rich pre-Anglo culture. (p. 17)

Vaughn, Bos, and Schumm (1997) make several recommendations to help teachers include multicultural content in the classroom program:

- To teach cultural content you need knowledge of cultural groups. Read at least several books that survey the histories of cultural groups in the United States. . . .

Inclusion Tips for the Teacher

Teaching Students from Diverse Groups

1. As you identify the different ethnic groups in your classroom, become informed about their characteristics and learning styles.
2. Encourage and assist students in sharing their culture in the classroom; you can start the process by sharing your own cultural values and traditions.
3. Avoid textbooks and materials that present cultural stereotypes.
4. Know as much as possible about . . . [diverse] students' home and community, interests, talents, skills, and potentials and develop an instructional program accordingly.
5. Find out how the . . . [diverse] students in your class wish you to refer to their ethnic group; for example, some Mexican Americans prefer to be called Chicanos while others may take offense at the term.
6. Include ethnic studies in the curriculum to help . . . [diverse] students gain a more positive self-image.
7. Make parents your partners in educating . . . [diverse] students.
8. Treat all students equally; do not fall into the trap of reverse racism.
9. Be sure assessment techniques used are appropriate and take into account cultural differences.
10. Avoid imitating speech patterns of . . . [diverse] students; rather than an aid in education, this may be viewed as mockery.

Note. Reprinted with permission of Merrill, an imprint of Macmillan Publishing Company, from "Cultural Diversity and Exceptionality" by L. McCormick in *Exceptional Children and Youth* (5th ed., p. 75) by N. G. Haring and L. McCormick (Eds.). Copyright © 1990 by Merrill Publishing Company, Columbus, Ohio.

• Make sure that your room conveys positive im-ages of various cultural groups (through bulletin boards, posters, literature, software, and so on).
• Plan time in which you and your students can learn about each other's cultural backgrounds. . . .
• Be culturally conscious in selecting teaching materials. If the materials you use include stereotypes or present only one perspective, point out the limitation to the students.
• Use trade books, films, videotapes, and recordings to supplement the textbook and to present more varied perspectives.
• Use literature to enrich students' understanding of cultural pluralism. . . .
• Make sure that not only classroom but also school-wide activities (such as plays, sports, and clubs) are culturally integrated. (p. 287)

Garcia (1978) has compiled a set of techniques for promoting acceptance of diversity. Some of Garcia's suggestions are appropriate for students of all ages, whereas others are particularly useful in the secondary grades.

• Students can study and discuss their ethnic heritages.
• Ethnic minority group parents can be invited to school to visit and talk with students.
• Students can study the contributions that all ethnic groups have made to the community.
• Students can conduct surveys of their own ethnic group's geographic distribution and develop charts to record the information.
• Students can make a multi-ethnic map of U.S. society using pictures from old magazines.
• Any special ability of ethnic minority students, such as bilingualism, may be used to build their sense of belonging to the class. Sharing folktales, ethnic games, or songs are examples.
• Playground activities can be monitored so that students practice cooperation and fair play.
• Field trips to other schools with diverse student populations can be planned so that students of different ethnic backgrounds can have one-to-one cultural exchanges.
• A multi-ethnic reading table or reading shelf can be maintained by the teacher and student. It might contain ethnic magazines, newspapers, and books. . . .

- Students and teachers may work with P.T.A. groups to conduct activities, such as a multi-ethnic song fest, that are cultural exchanges designed to improve community group relations.
- A multi-ethnic student welcoming committee can be organized to greet all new students, teachers, and school personnel.
- Role playing can be used to help students learn to take the role of out-groups as well as in-groups.
- A multi-ethnic bulletin board can be maintained by the students to display reports, pictures, and other items about persons from various ethnic groups.
- Students can work out a code covering sports, games, elections, and classroom behavior in which all students are treated as equals.
- Students and teachers can discuss frankly instances in which namecalling, prejudice, or discrimination are practiced by students or teachers.
- A teacher can use an intergroup incident that occurs in the school or community for helping students acquire a sound perspective.
- A science teacher might demonstrate the similarities of racial groups by studying the blood samples of blacks, Asians, etc.
- Teachers in all subject areas can make an effort to incorporate a study of ethnic groups as they relate to the curriculum, e.g., Chinese math discoveries, black scientists, and American inventions.
- Schoolwide activities, Chicano dramas, blues festivals, and dances should be planned and conducted to offer students positive multi-ethnic experiences.
- Students should not be encouraged to develop fraternities, sororities, clubs, or cliques that would divide students along racial, ethnic, or socioeconomic lines. Instead, multi-ethnic clubs should be encouraged. (pp. 35–36)

The suggestions that follow are designed to help refugee students adjust to their new culture and school environment ("Educating Refugees: Understanding the Basics," 1989). However, several of these strategies apply equally well to all culturally diverse students:

Adjusting to a New Culture

- Enhance students' self-esteem by focusing on their positive qualities and the progress they have already made.
- Help students develop realistic expectations for adjustment to the United States.
- Help students develop coping skills such as not overreacting to stressful situations and making the best of difficult situations.

Culture and Family

- Learn about cultural differences and be sensitive to these differences when working with students.
- Provide opportunities for students to share information about their culture during social studies, geography, and other classes.
- Familiarize yourself with different cultural, medical, and religious practices, such as fasting or holiday celebrations, that might affect students' school attendance and participation.
- Learn to correctly pronounce students' names in the proper order and how to address students' parents. For example, the order of Vietnamese names is family name, middle name, and first name. Vietnamese people are usually addressed using their first name.

Educational Concerns

- When new students arrive, have students from the same linguistic and cultural background who have been at the school longer become "buddies" to help the new students become oriented.
- During class, pose questions related to the content of instruction to check if students have understood; do not assume they understand simply because they appear to have understood.
- Use nonverbal gestures to supplement your instruction.
- Make sure newly arrived students meet and interact with American students, especially in classes that do not require much English proficiency, such as art, physical education, and music.
- Write out class assignments and important instructions to reinforce your oral statements. (p. 1)

Another important consideration for the general education teacher is communication with parents of culturally diverse students. Lynch (1981), in a study of parents' views of special education services, identified several barriers to parents' participation in the public school programs of their children. Two major roadblocks were language and cultural barriers. Suggestions for overcoming these barriers are presented in "Inclusion Tips for the Teacher."

In summary, multicultural education is an attempt to affirm the value and worth of cultural diversity. In many ways, the mainstreaming movement of the past and the inclusion movement of today echo this ideal: Mainstreaming and inclusion are attempts to integrate but not obliterate differences. This point is well made by McLaughlin-Williams (1977):

Inclusion Tips for the Teacher

Overcoming Language and Cultural Barriers

Overcoming Language Barriers

- If you are not bilingual, have someone available who is when you talk to parents. Better yet, encourage them to bring a bilingual friend or relative. Make an attempt to learn words, phrases, and to say something positive about the child in the family's preferred language.
- Be sure that printed materials for parents are available in their preferred language.
- Provide a sign language interpreter for parents who are deaf or hard of hearing.

Overcoming Cultural Barriers

- Learn as much as you can about the cultures that your students represent through talking with the parents and other staff, reading books, attending in-service sessions, and viewing films. Family structures, values, and child-rearing practices vary greatly. You can then use the cultural differences as strengths rather than working at cross-purposes.
- Instead of lumping all groups together, recognize the many differences that exist within groups of Hispanics, Anglos, blacks, Pan-Asians. Each country, each region, and most important, each individual has unique ways of interpreting their cultural experience.
- Weed out the stereotypes and prejudices that have been acquired through your own cultural roots. Try to approach people individually and openly.
- Use cultural differences to bring schools and families together. Utilize celebrations and the special traditions that go with them as ways of learning and working together.
- Never feel that you have to apologize for your own culture or ethnicity. We all have something special to contribute.

Note. From *But I've Tried Everything! A Special Educator's Guide to Working with Parents* (pp. 37–39) by E. W. Lynch, 1981, San Diego, CA: San Diego State University. The development of this book was supported by the State of California, Department of Education, Project Number 37-3062-80-3293-7100. Reprinted by permission.

Mainstreaming can become a force for the valuing of individual differences, a process to foster acceptance of varying physical, psychological, educational, and racial characteristics, and a futuristic model to celebrate variance as a desirable state. (as cited in Fuchigami, 1980, p. 640)

ACTIVITIES

1. Write a short paper that describes your cultural background. Include your family's traditions for holidays, foods, ceremonies such as weddings, child-rearing practices, and so on. Exchange papers with one of your classmates. What similarities do you find? What differences?

2. Interview someone who learned English as a second language. Ask that person to describe some of the problems that occur in translating from one language to another. Are there some concepts that cannot be expressed in the English language?

3. Look through several of the textbooks used in elementary or secondary classrooms. Do these texts include information about the contributions of several cultures? Do the illustrations depict a multicultural society?

4. Observe in a classroom that serves culturally and linguistically diverse students. Can you identify any special needs? In what ways does the teacher adapt instruction to meet the needs of diverse students? How are social interactions among students encouraged?

5. It was noted that inclusion is an attempt to integrate but not obliterate differences. Discuss this statement in relation to the "No One Model American" policy statement of the American Association of Colleges for Teacher Education.

Things to Remember

- General education classrooms often reflect the cultural and linguistic diversity of the United States.
- Cultural pluralism is the belief that cultural and linguistic diversity is a strength, not a weakness.
- African Americans make up the largest "minority" group, whereas Hispanics represent the largest bilingual culture.
- A student's language and culture can affect school behavior and academic success; if the student's background is discrepant from the culture of the school, the student may fail to meet scholastic expectations.
- Students who enter school with few English-language skills are at a distinct disadvantage; however, not all culturally diverse students have limited English proficiency.
- Most culturally and linguistically diverse students are educated in general education classes. Those with special learning needs may receive special education services or bilingual education services.
- Assessment of students from diverse groups must be nonbiased; measures must not discriminate on the basis of race, culture, or language.
- The major approach to instruction of diverse students is multicultural education; students who learn about the language and culture of others are more likely to accept diversity.
- Inclusion and multicultural education share the same goal: to teach students to appreciate the value of individual differences.

chapter 17

Teaching Students at Risk for School Failure

The kindergartner who comes to school hungry, the 15-year-old who is 2 months pregnant, the young boy who seeks solace from drugs when his stepfather beats him, the lonely adolescent who sees little reason for living: These are students at risk. The factors that place them at risk—substance abuse, delinquency, abusive caregivers, and so on—interfere with their ability to benefit from the school experience.

A Phi Delta Kappa study considered children at risk "if they are likely to fail—either in school or in life" (Frymier & Gansneder, 1989, p. 142). The inclusion of failure "in life" in the definition considers the individual's involvement in areas such as drug abuse, suicide, physical or sexual abuse, delinquency, or other factors that may contribute to future problems. Although these students usually have not been identified as individuals with disabilities (and may never be considered eligible for special education services), it is important that educators provide them with educational experiences appropriate to their special needs.

Ogden and Germinario (1988) describe the problem as follows:

> All children are at times students-at-risk and there is a portion of every school population that consistently shows a lack of the necessary intellectual, emotional and/or social skills to take full advantage of the educational opportunities available to them. Often these students become disenchanted, and ultimately openly or passively reject school—they are then students-at-high-risk.
>
> The purpose of school is to maximize learning for all students. The most obvious way in which schools attempt to carry out their mission is through direct instruction in the curriculum areas. However, another way of maximizing learning is by controlling or eliminating the effects of those factors which limit the learning and potential of children. (p. xvii)

McWhirter, McWhirter, McWhirter, and McWhirter (1998) indicate that the various at-risk groups are a concern to professionals in the fields of education, psychology, medicine, social work, and economics. They provide this definition:

> We use *at risk* to denote a set of presumed cause-and-effect dynamics that place the child or adolescent in danger of negative *future events*. Youngsters who use tobacco, for example, are at risk for alcohol use. Children and adolescents who use illicit drugs are at risk for drug abuse. Thus, a specific behavior, attitude, or

deficiency provides an initial marker of later problem behavior. Conduct disorders, aggression, and low achievement in elementary school become markers that predict later delinquent and antisocial behavior in adolescence. To us, then, *at risk* designates a situation that is not necessarily current (although we sometimes use the term in that sense too) but that can be anticipated in the absence of intervention.

> Perhaps even more important, at-riskness must be viewed not as a discrete, unitary diagnostic category but as a series of steps along a continuum. (p. 7)

Although educators generally agree that many students are at risk, they do not necessarily agree on who these students are or how to deal with their problems. All 50 states have made some attempt to consider the question; only 25 states have formally defined the at-risk population. These definitions vary widely, from limiting the group to only dropouts to associating students at risk with a long list of adverse social and economic conditions (e.g., truancy, absenteeism, drug abuse, delinquency, teenage pregnancy, poverty). The states have had a similar piecemeal approach to providing programs that attempt to remedy the problems of students at risk. At this point, only pilot programs that provide limited interventions have been introduced (Manning & Baruth, 1995; Mirga, 1988a, 1988b).

According to various sources, from 25% to 35% (Frymier & Gansneder, 1989; Hodgkinson, 1993) to as many as 35% to 40% (Siegel & Senna, 1994; "Technology," 1988) of the K–12 school population can be considered at risk. High numbers of students at risk can be found in schools in urban (Cuban, 1989), suburban, and rural (Helge, 1991) communities. The potential for being identified as at risk is higher for students raised in disadvantaged or impoverished home settings (Biddle, 1997). These students are often not able to meet the academic demands of the school because of their delayed physical and psychological development (Butler, 1989). The longer students live under poverty conditions, the more likely they are to be underachievers in school (Manning & Baruth, 1995; Reeves, 1988) and to experience emotional or behavioral problems (Recer, 1989). Many other factors such as drug or alcohol abuse, child abuse or neglect, eating disorders, suicide, delinquency, single-parent homes, and teenage pregnancy are thought to be related to a student's potential inclusion in the at-risk population.

For Your Information

Students at Risk for School Failure

- Close to one-third of the children born in 1992 will become students who are at the greatest risk for school failure and should be the focus of the energies and talents in education in the United States (Hodgkinson, 1993).
- Of the children entering school in the fall of 1987, 14% were the children of teenage mothers, as many as 15% were non-English-speaking immigrants, and in many states almost 25% lived below the poverty line (Olson, 1988).
- "Each year, nearly 1 million students drop out of the nation's public schools" (Butler, 1989, p. 50).
- Less than 75% of the students enrolled in the ninth grade graduate from high school in four years (McMillen, Kaufman, & Whitener, 1996).
- "In 1993 more than 23% of America's children were living below the poverty line and thus were at risk of failing to fulfill their physical and mental promise" (Hodgkinson, 1993, p. 620).
- More than one out of five teachers working with students at risk in urban schools do not believe that all students are capable of learning; these low expectations can become a self-fulfilling prophecy. Many teachers now believe that the responsibility for working with these students belongs to someone else, such as a specialist (Reeves, 1988).
- Although the practice of retention is often considered appropriate, its effectiveness is open to question (Frymier & Gansneder, 1989). According to Gastright (1989), "80% of the dropouts had been retained at least once; 16% of these had been retained two or more times. A study of ninth-grade students showed that almost 90% of the students who had never been retained later received a diploma. The probability of graduating decreased to 41% for students who were retained once and less than 19% for students who were retained twice" (p. 2).
- Poor basic skills are characteristic of disadvantaged youth; in a survey of 19- to 23-year-old disadvantaged persons, results indicated that 85% were dropouts, 72% were unemployed, 79% were welfare dependents, 68% had been arrested, and 85% of the women were unwed mothers (Berlin & Sum, 1988).

- Businesses and corporations spend from $25 billion to $40 billion a year on remedial education to supplement that currently provided by the educational system (Reeves, 1988; "Technology," 1988).
- Students at risk will continue to be served primarily by general education programs; only 5% of state education funds are being used specifically for programs for these students, and such programs serve only between 4% and 10% of those in need (Mirga, 1988a).
- It is estimated that approximately 1,000 teens attempt suicide every day (Patros & Shamoo, 1989).
- Although the dropout rate has been declining for several years, the 28th Gallup Poll on Education reports that 64% of the population believes that it is higher than it was 25 years ago (Elam, Rose, & Gallup, 1996).
- A majority of the public (59%) expresses a willingness to spend more tax money to expand child care centers for all preschool children as part of the public school system. A majority (61%) also indicated they would be willing to pay more taxes to fund these programs for children whose parents were unable to pay (Elam, Rose, & Gallup, 1993).
- "High-quality preschool education for three- and four-year-olds helped reduce by about half later dropout behavior, criminal involvement, teen pregnancy, welfare dependency, and the need for remedial education" (Butler, 1989, p. 51).
- Poverty and the child-raising methods associated with it contribute to the number of youth identified as emotionally and behaviorally troubled (over 20% of some inner-city populations) (Recer, 1989).
- The reduction in later delinquency that results from preschool programs, prenatal care, and nutrition programs for women and infants provides taxpayers with a saving of $3 to $6 for every $1 spent (Butler, 1989).
- Cohen (1992) reports that $4.75 would be saved for every $1 spent on preschool programs by reducing special education, crime, and welfare costs; yet, in 1990, half the states spent less

continued

- than $25 per child on early childhood care and education.
- Some states have begun to deny driver's licenses to dropouts. Advocates of such an approach believe that it will encourage students to complete school. Opponents feel that this program does not consider the many other factors that strongly influence the student's lack of achievement and eventual dropping out of school (Russell & Fessenden, 1989).
- Dropping out of high school is not an irrevocable action. Many dropouts later complete high school, often within a short period after dropping out. Nearly half (46%) of the dropouts from the sophomore class of 1980 had completed high school by 1986, that is, within four years of the expected date of their graduation (Frase, 1989).
- "A substantial number of today's young people from low-income ethnic and racial minorities are unequipped to find jobs when they leave school" (Cuban, 1989, p. 782).

School personnel encounter a number of unique challenges in providing appropriate educational programs for students at risk. First, this group does not generally benefit from the equal access provisions of laws and policies designed to ensure that appropriate educational programs or special services are provided for other students, such as those with disabilities. Second, students at risk require an adequate education to ensure that they will be contributors to society rather than future recipients of welfare or institutional services. Third, schools are being given the responsibility to teach life and social skills needed by many of these students, which was once the domain of the family. Finally, if the educational needs of these students are not met, their negative attitudes are likely to deleteriously affect the behavior, achievement, and attitudes of other students currently in school and those of their own children in the future (McWhirter et al., 1998; Ogden & Germinario, 1988; Reeves, 1988; Stevens & Price, 1992).

In recent years the needs of gay or lesbian students have not received the increased attention that has been directed toward homosexuality in the adult population of our culture, although many of these students are considered to be disproportionately at risk in the areas considered in this chapter (McWhirter et al., 1998). McWhirter et al. provide this explanation of the needs of this group:

> Most gay and lesbian youth experience stress in their lives because of their sexual orientation. On one hand, adverse responses of disapproval and rejection to an adolescent's homosexual orientation from family members, friends, and peers [are] common. On the other hand, inability or unwillingness to accept or acknowledge same-sex attraction leads to early feelings of confusion and alienation. These young people are vulnerable because of their fear of reaction from family and friends regarding their sexual orientation. However, not disclosing to family and friends may also be stressful, as it frequently entails living a lie, becoming emotionally isolated, and feeling terribly lonely.
>
> Although lesbian and gay young people receive services from multiple systems, including education, mental health, child welfare, juvenile justice, and health, these service providers rarely identify or address the special needs of this population. Lesbian and gay young people are particularly vulnerable to alcohol and other drug abuse as they cope with the isolation, rejection, and stressors they experience. Homosexuals are probably the most frequent victims of hate violence, and because educators do little to support gay and lesbian adolescents, they frequently leave school before graduation. Finally, the suicide rate of homosexual youths is considerably higher than that of heterosexual youths. (p. 15)

Members of every community should carefully review the potential consequences of not responding to the special needs of students at risk. Failing to respond to these needs can increase both dropout rates and the likelihood that students at risk will fail. Additional information about students at risk can be found in "For Your Information."

Many of the techniques and classroom strategies mentioned earlier in this text are highly appropriate for use with students at risk because they are similar to other students with special needs in many of their characteristics and educational requirements. Technologies such as the AlphaSmart 2000 keyboard (which is described in "Spotlight on Technology" can also prove useful with this population of students. Students at risk require appropriate educa-

Spotlight on Technology

The AlphaSmart 2000 Keyboard

The AlphaSmart 2000 from Intelligent Peripheral Devices, Inc., is a small, lightweight, portable keyboard designed for students to use for word processing. This durable keyboard runs on 3 AA batteries, and batteries typically last 120 to 300 hours. Text is stored in 8 different files, and it is possible to store up to 64 pages of single-spaced text at one time. The AlphaSmart 2000 also contains a spell checker.

The major advantage of this device for students and teachers is its ease of use. All the student has to do is press the "on" key and start typing. Text is saved automatically, and the keyboard turns itself off automatically if not used for 3 minutes. Text can be printed directed from the AlphaSmart by connecting it to a printer. Or students can send their text to a computer for further editing. The AlphaSmart is compatible with PC, Macintosh, and Apple IIGS computers.

The major advantage of the AlphaSmart for schools is its low cost. Each AlphaSmart costs approximately $250 (January 1998 prices), and the price is reduced when several keyboards are purchased. Thus, for the price of one $2,000 computer, a school could buy eight AlphaSmarts. This greatly increases the number of students with access to word processing technology. For more information and ideas for classroom applications, visit the AlphaSmart website at www.alphasmart.com.

tional interventions as well as optimum behavior management and instruction in academics and social skills. If these components are provided as part of their educational program, it is likely that students will experience gains in achievement and develop an overall sense of confidence and personal worth. However, teachers and other school personnel are not expected to become therapists. Their primary role is to work on the learning problems of the student as part of their daily instructional responsibilities, and, when appropriate, to help identify other more serious problems (e.g., addiction, suicide, child abuse) and refer these cases to experts (Manning & Baruth, 1995; McWhirter et al., 1998; Ogden & Germinario, 1988).

Educators working with students at risk must be aware of specific information about and techniques used with people in the at-risk categories. The importance of this need is cited in a study (Frymier & Gansneder, 1989) indicating that professionals "lacked skill with or confidence about particular approaches to working with at risk students" (p. 145).

The remainder of the chapter will present information about the at-risk categories of dropouts, suicide, drug and alcohol abuse, teenage pregnancy and sexually transmitted diseases, child abuse and neglect, eating disorders, and delinquency. The extent of each problem, contributing factors, potential prevention and intervention techniques, and alternative services available outside the school setting will be discussed.

DROPOUTS

Case

By his sophomore year, Bill had become so disenchanted with his monotonous school program that he began cutting class regularly. He recalls that the year he dropped out he went to school no more than 60 days. Bill explains that since both his parents worked, "It was easy; I'd cut out and go home to watch TV, get

high with friends, or sleep all day. Nobody did any-thing about it." Bill's family had moved six times since kindergarten, and he reported that he had not yet found a school he considered worth going to. The times he was in school were, in his opinion, "a waste of time." He often asked, "Why are we learning this?" He thought about going to see his counselor but decided, "why bother?" In his two years of high school, Bill saw his counselor for one 10-minute interview, despite failing several classes each semester. "At the end they called twice to tell me to come in and sign out, but I didn't." No one tried to talk Bill out of dropping out. In fact, it was easy; he just never came back. (Gross-nickle, 1986, p. 11)

Although educators and researchers agree that the number of students dropping out of school is a major problem, they currently do not agree on who should be considered dropouts. The U.S. Census Bureau provides the most concise definition; it considers a **dropout** to be anyone over the age of 18 who is no longer enrolled in and has not graduated from high school. The current national dropout rate, using this definition, is reported to be 14% (Woodring, 1989). Other figures from the National

Center for Education Statistics (Frase, 1989) indicate that 13% of 16- to 20-year-olds had not completed high school and that, between 1985 and 1988, a total of 4.4% of the students in grades 10 to 12 dropped out of school each year. Dropout rates in inner-city schools are often cited as being over 50% ("Technology," 1988) and sometimes as high as 80% (Bowen, 1988); rates may be as high as 40% to 50% in small or rural schools (Phelps & Prock, 1991).

Reeves (1988) reported that an examination of the 17-year-olds in school determined that 13% of the students are functionally illiterate and 44% are marginally literate; also, 60% of the dropouts at this age are functionally illiterate. In addition, the "rate of delinquency is significantly higher for those who drop out of school than among those who do not" (Siegel & Senna, 1994, p. 356). It is estimated that the cost to the nation of welfare, crime prevention, unemployment, and lost tax revenues resulting from dropouts alone is at least $60 billion annually—possibly as high as $228 billion; this is at least $60,000 per dropout (McNergney & Haberman, 1988). These figures make the importance of providing for the educational needs of this group of students at risk readily apparent.

Assumptions based solely on the data on current dropout rates may be somewhat misleading because over the past 100 years or so there has actually been a reduction in the dropout rate and an increase in the number of students completing high school. In 1890, only 6.7% of 14- to 17-year-olds attended high school; 3.5% of 17-year-olds graduated. By the 1970s, this figure had increased to 76% and, by the mid 1990s, to 89%. The major problem is that during this period there has been an overall increase in the expected skill levels needed to function effectively in society and thus a decrease in the probability that the dropout will be a contributing member of society (Berliner & Biddle, 1995).

In discussing the results of a 1986 longitudinal study of high school students, Kunisawa (1988) described the general characteristics of the contemporary dropout in this way:

> Dropouts are usually from low-income or poverty settings, often from a minority group background (although not often Asian-American), and have very low basic academic skills (especially in reading and math). Their parents are not high school graduates, are generally uninterested in their child's progress in school, and do not provide a support system for academic progress. English is often not spoken in the home, and

many dropouts are children of single parents. Dropout rates are higher among males than females. Males are more likely to leave school to get a job (which usually turns out to be a failure), while females tend to drop out in order to have a child. Dropouts are generally bored in school; they perceive themselves accurately as failures in the school culture and are usually very alienated from school. (p. 62)

Reducing the dropout rate is a major challenge for educators. The call to raise the standards for student performance as part of the movement to reform educational programs has created additional problems for students at risk. The increase in standards has not been accompanied by an increase in assistance for the students who had difficulty meeting the old standards (Hill, 1989; Woodring, 1989). Although the dropout rate has decreased over the past 100 years, the ability of the dropout to assimilate into society has also decreased. The number of jobs available for workers lacking basic skills is much smaller (Slavin, 1989), and the dropouts can no longer "go West" or return to the farm as they did earlier in the century (Woodring, 1989).

The school can play an important role in helping reduce the number of dropouts. Information gathered from other studies can do little more than provide a general framework for a prevention program; educators must examine their own local setting to identify their specific needs as part of the development of the components of this program (Gastright, 1989). A variety of recommendations are provided here for preventing students from dropping out of school:

- Early prevention programs are needed that provide services such as prenatal and postnatal care for young mothers, day care and preschool programs, and health care programs for students at risk. Such programs are the most promising and cost-effective interventions (Butler, 1989; Hill, 1989; Kunisawa, 1988).
- Teachers can play an important role by developing an interest in the progress of all students and establishing a level of personal interaction that communicates this interest to the students (Barone, 1989).
- "Prevention and early intervention are much more promising than waiting for learning deficits to accumulate and only then providing remedial and special education services" (Slavin, Madden, & Karweit, 1989, p. 355).

- Although teachers and administrators seem to have a good basic knowledge of the characteristics and attributes of potential high school dropouts, they appear to have a negative outlook regarding their own ability to encourage a dropout to return to school (Soderberg, 1988).
- Teachers must communicate a feeling that the student is capable of achieving and be accountable for providing the type of instruction designed to ensure that achievement will occur (Gajar, Goodman, & McAfee, 1993; McWhirter et al., 1998).
- Effective programs for students at risk accommodate instruction to individual needs while maximizing direct instruction and following models such as mastery learning and cooperative learning. Quality instruction that improves students' skills increases the likelihood that they will achieve and benefit from their school experiences (Cuban, 1989; Slavin et al., 1989).
- Consistent attendance is critical if students are to benefit from the educational program, and students missing a great deal of school are more likely to drop out. Strong attendance policies should be established and enforced. Teachers and staff should be involved in following up on student absences and should reinforce students for attendance (Gajar et al., 1993; Kerr & Nelson, 1998).
- Job training programs that provide for the development of specific job skills and work behaviors (e.g., reporting on time, following directions) are needed to initiate and support the employment of students at risk because they are likely to be a group with a high rate of unemployment ("Project," 1988; Snider, 1988).

The importance of involving parents in their children's education is stressed by many experts. Parents need to be informed of their child's progress and encouraged to be supportive of their child's education and attendance at school. It may be necessary to provide parents with assistance in order for them to gain the skills and attitudes necessary for supporting the educational opportunities provided by the school. School personnel may also need to assist parents in obtaining services from social or health agencies in the community. It is critical that every available resource be directed at reducing the risk factors that potentially lead students to drop out of school. The school's efforts should focus on making the student a success in school and in life.

Window on the Web

Websites Related to Risk Factors

Dropouts

- National Dropout Prevention Center/Network (www.dropoutprevention.org)
- U.S. Department of Education (www.ed.gov)

Suicide

- American Academy of Child and Adolescent Psychiatry (www.aacap.org)
- American Foundation for Suicide Prevention (www.afsp.org)

Substance Abuse

- National Institute on Drug Abuse, National Institutes of Health (www.nida.nih.gov)
- National Institutes of Health, Consumer Health Information (www.nih.gov/health/consumer/conicd.htm)
- PREVLINE (Prevention Online), National Clearinghouse for Alcohol and Drug Information (www.health.org)
- YouthInfo, sponsored by U.S. Department of Health and Human Services (youth.os.dhhs.gov)

Teenage Pregnancy and Sexually Transmitted Diseases

- American Foundation for AIDS Research (www.amfar.org)
- National Institutes of Health, Consumer Health Information (www.nih.gov/health/consumer/conicd.htm)
- YouthInfo, sponsored by the U.S. Department of Health and Human Services (youth.os.dhhs.gov)

Child Abuse and Neglect

- American Academy of Child and Adolescent Psychiatry (www.aacap.org)
- National Clearinghouse on Child Abuse and Neglect Information, sponsored by the U.S. Department of Health and Human Services (www.calib.com/nccanch)
- National Committee to Prevent Child Abuse (www.childabuse.org)

Eating Disorders

- American Academy of Child and Adolescent Psychiatry (www.aacap.org)
- American Anorexia/Bulimia Assocation, Inc. (members.aol.com/amanbu/index.html)
- National Institute of Mental Health, National Institutes of Health (www.nimh.nih.gov)

Delinquency

- Children's Defense Fund (www.childrensdefense.org)
- Justice Information Center, sponsored by the National Criminal Justice Reference Service (www.ncjrs.org)
- Juvenile Justice Clearinghouse, Florida State University (www.fsu.edu/~crimdo/jjclearinghouse/jjclearinghouse.html)
- Office of Juvenile Justice and Delinquency Prevention, U.S. Department of Justice (www.ncjrs.org/ojjhome.htm)

SUICIDE

Cases

To the casual observer, Jimmy was a fairly typical teenager—reticent, especially around adults, and a moderate achiever in school. He had few close friends, all of them quiet and unassuming around the tougher kids at school. According to his homeroom teacher, Jimmy kept mostly to himself. These traits are typical of adolescents and aren't necessarily reason for special concern or attention. That's why Jimmy's death was initially thought to be an accident. One dark weekday morning, while delivering papers on his bike, Jimmy suddenly swerved into the path of an oncoming truck and was killed instantly. At first police thought that the unsafe conditions—darkness and light drizzle that made the road slippery—caused Jimmy to lose control of his bike. That was until a note describing his feelings of hopelessness and rejection was found in his school locker. Part of his note read, "Why me, why always me? They make fun of everything I do, everything that I am. It's such a cruel punishment."

Jeanine was an ebullient 16-year-old. Her grades were good, and she was popular enough to be elected to homecoming court. She was regarded by the faculty as a model student and a fine representative of her school. Then, gradually, she became apathetic. Parents and teachers thought the change was only a temporary emotional "phase" that many young women go through. Her death by drug overdose shocked everyone. How could this lovely, popular young lady with a promising future do such a terrible thing? She left no note to explain the confusion. However, subsequent investigations uncovered the apparent cause: Jeanine had been rejected by three of her friends who became jealous of her success and popularity. They apparently started a rumor that Jeanine was promiscuous and had contracted a venereal disease. Feeling overwhelmed and isolated, Jeanine took what she thought was the only way out. (Kirk, 1993, p. 5)

Suicide is the third leading cause of death among adolescents (after unintentional injury and homicide) (Centers for Disease Control & Prevention, 1993). The rate of suicide for this group has in-

creased dramatically over the past 35 years, climbing 300% among males and 230% among females (Edwards, 1988; Garfinkel et al., 1988; Pfeifer, 1986). Suicides account for over 5,000 deaths of young people each year (Guetzloe, 1993). While the rate of suicides is much lower for children under 14, the suicide rate for this age group increased notably in the 1980s (Kirk, 1993). Some experts would argue that it is the leading cause of death in this age range, but they contend that it is difficult to get an accurate count because the stigma placed on suicide often leads suicides to be labeled accidents (Kauffman, 1997).

A recent study of high-school-age students in the United States (Centers for Disease Control, 1995) estimated that 24% of this group seriously considered suicide in 1995 and 9% attempted to take their own lives. Among high school students, as many as 350 suicides are attempted for every 1 completed; in the 14 and under group, each year "suicide attempts lead to the hospitalization of an estimated 12,000 youngsters" (Guetzloe, 1993, p. 34).

Males are four to five times as likely to complete the act of suicide, yet females are three to nine times more likely to attempt suicide (Kirk, 1993; Vannatta, 1997). It should be noted that special education students, especially those with severe behavioral disorders, often have a disproportionately high representation in the group attempting suicide (Guetzloe, 1988, 1989).

Teachers can play an important role in identifying students who may be suicide candidates, although suicide attempts often occur without warning. As part of a prevention program, school staff should be trained to identify warning signs and follow appropriate procedures after these signs have been noted. Warning signs are provided in Figure 17–1 on page 446.

Adolescent suicide is usually precipitated by a combination of factors. Depression, impulsivity, stress, physical or sexual abuse, or drug and alcohol abuse are frequently associated with suicide attempts.

Another factor that often contributes to suicide among students is the death of another adolescent from suicide or an accident (Dismuke, 1988; Garfinkel et al., 1988). Such an event often causes a contagion effect that leads to cluster suicides (i.e., a series of suicide attempts by friends or acquaintances). Specific suggestions for dealing with suicide

FIGURE 17-1 **Suicide Warning Signs**

At-Risk Adolescent Checklist

Listed below are several factors associated with at-risk adolescents. None of these factors alone is an indication of suicidal tendencies; but educators should be alert to clusters of these factors, which could indicate potential problems.

1. Inability to compete in school, failing grades.
2. Family instability (divorce, blended family, neglect, and abuse).
3. Death or chronic illness of a loved one or pet, or the anniversary of such an event.
4. Failure to communicate feelings of unhappiness.
5. Health problems.
6. Major disappointment or humiliation (real or imagined).
7. Economic insecurity.
8. Parental role failure.
9. Desire for revenge against a girl friend, boy friend, or significant other.
10. Sense of not belonging to anyone (family, community, school).
11. Family history of suicide or suicide attempts.

Symptoms of Suicidal Youth Checklist

1. Extreme mood swings (violent or rebellious behavior, sudden cheerfulness).
2. Difficulty concentrating.
3. Sudden lifestyle changes.
4. Withdrawal or isolation from peers, family, or school activities.
5. Neglect of personal appearance.
6. Previous suicide attempts.
7. Loss of friends (boy friend, girl friend, best friend).
8. Giving away possessions, pulling affairs together, voluntarily cleaning room, or throwing things out.
9. Decline in school work, failing grades, cheating.
10. Noticeable change in sleeping habits and energy level.
11. Frequent suicidal talk (revealed through writing, drawings, or indirect verbal expression).
12. Drug use (half of suicidal youngsters are involved in substance abuse).
13. Many unexplained absences.

Note. From *Responding to Adolescent Suicide* (pp. 25–26) by B. D. Garfinkel, E. Crosby, M. R. Herbert, A. L. Matus, J. K. Pfeifer, and P. L. Sheras (The Phi Delta Kappa Task Force on Adolescent Suicide), 1988, Bloomington, IN: The Phi Delta Kappa Educational Foundation. Copyright 1988 by The Phi Delta Kappa Educational Foundation. Reprinted by permission.

threats and with potential cluster suicides are found in "Inclusion Tips for the Teacher."

Teachers and other school personnel can be involved in a variety of activities that can potentially reduce the number of suicides. Social skills training programs (such as those mentioned in chapter 6) can contribute to the development of skills that will permit students to establish a network of social relationships and reduce their vulnerability to social isolation and possible depression (Patros & Shamoo, 1989). Providing experiences that lead to the development and reinforcement of personal self-worth is important in programs designed to prevent suicide (Guetzloe, 1989).

Schools serving adolescents should consider their legal responsibilities regarding the physical and psychological safety of students (such as those noted in Figure 17–2 on page 448), develop a plan for dealing with suicide, and communicate this to all staff members. In addition, it is essential that mental health clinics, crisis centers, counseling agencies, suicide hotlines, and other community resources in the area of suicide prevention be identified and information provided to the entire staff describing how these services supplement those provided by the school. It is also important that the staff be aware of the referral process that must be used for each of these agencies; often there is not a great deal

Inclusion Tips for the Teacher

Dealing with Potential Suicides

Suicide Threat Checklist

Do these things:

1. Remain calm. Stay with the student. Remember, the student is overwhelmed, confused, as well as ambivalent.
2. Get vital information if possible (name, address, home phone number, parent's work number). Send another teacher or student to get help.
3. Clear other students from the scene. Direct them to return to class.
4. Assure the student that he or she has done the right thing by talking to you. Try to win the student's trust. Assure the student that emergency help is coming. Tell the student that there are options available.
5. Get the student to talk. Listen! Listen! Listen! Repeat back what you hear the student saying (help the student define the problem). Acknowledge the student's feelings ("You are really angry." "You must feel humiliated.").
6. Establish direct eye contact with the student. Speak in a calm, low voice. If student is about to commit suicide, buy time. Say, "Don't jump. Stand there. Talk with me. I'll listen." Show that you are not shocked by discussing suicide.
7. Try to get the student to agree to a verbal "no suicide" contract ("No matter what happens, I will not kill myself.").
8. Monitor the student's behavior constantly.
9. Make a mental note at the time of the incident of what the student says.
10. Ask the principal or another administrator to contact the parents with the message that their child is hurt and they will be called back immediately with the name of the hospital where they can join their child. Tell them to keep the telephone line clear.

Do not do these things:

1. Do not ignore your intuitions if suicide is suspected.
2. Do not minimize the student's threat. Take it seriously.
3. Do not be concerned about long periods of silence. Give the student time to think.
4. Do not leave the student. Do not let him or her go to the restroom.
5. Do not lose patience with the student.
6. Do not argue with the student about whether suicide is right or wrong.
7. Do not promise confidentiality. Instead promise help and promise privacy.
8. Do not discuss the incident in the teacher's lounge or with another student. (Garfinkel et al., 1988, p. 26)

Reducing the Effects of a Suicide

The following are recommendations to help communities prevent young people from killing themselves and, when a young person does commit suicide, to help communities handle the situation as well as possible.

1. Plan community action to deal with any event or situation that might cause a suicide cluster before trouble starts.
2. Appoint a committee of community representatives and a community agency to coordinate a response to suicide among the young.
3. Identify people and groups in the community who can help prevent suicide clusters or respond when one occurs.
4. Put the response plan into action when a suicide cluster occurs—or when one is suspected.
5. When such a situation arises, immediately prepare the groups that are key to the community response to take up their assigned responsibilities.
6. Avoid any action that could be interpreted as glorifying suicide, and minimize any sensational aspects of suicides or suicide attempts.
7. Identify people who may be especially likely to kill themselves and put them in touch with a counselor.
8. Arrange for a timely flow of accurate, appropriate information to the news media after a suicide.
9. Identify elements in the environment—school, home and community—that might increase the likelihood of suicide. Change those elements—or get rid of them.
10. If a group of youngsters do kill themselves, find out whether their deaths are connected to any long-term issue—and, if so, deal with it. (Dismuke, 1988, p. 21)

Note. From *Responding to Adolescent Suicide* (p. 26) by B. D. Garfinkel, E. Crosby, M. R. Herbert, A. L. Matus, J. K. Pfeifer, and P. L. Sheras (The Phi Delta Kappa Task Force on Adolescent Suicide), 1988, Bloomington, IN: The Phi Delta Kappa Educational Foundation; and from "Reducing Suicides" by D. Dismuke, November 1988, *NEA Today* (Washington, DC: National Education Association), p. 21. Reprinted by permission.

FIGURE 17-2   **Liability Issues in Dealing with Suicide**

Guidelines for determining what to do with a student when psychological impairment is suspected are not always clear. What is clear is that when a life is in jeopardy, the school system must provide every available resource to save that life. How that responsibility translates into legal risk is the focus of . . . [this section].

The basic concern must be the life of the student. As a society, we seem reasonably aware of the need to protect children and adolescents, but obviously suicidology is not an exact science. Administrators and educators need to know, as do all professionals, what their legal obligations are in the case of a suicidal student. The following points are generally accepted legal guidelines, but each state, and even certain school districts within states, may have different statutes or guidelines. [It is important that each educator determine the specific policies and procedures that apply to his or her own school assignment.]

- School personnel are not responsible for the suicide death of a student unless they aided and abetted the student in death or during a period of obvious suicidality. This is interpreted as specifically assisting the student in attempting or completing the act of suicide by providing the means or by intentionally doing nothing, knowing that the suicide was going to occur.
- When a student is assessed as or suspected of being suicidal, the parents or guardians must be informed about the assessment and the actions being taken to alleviate or treat the vulnerability. This should be done as quickly as possible without jeopardizing the life of the student.
- When an employee or consultant to the school system becomes aware of the possibility of suicidal ideation in a student, he or she should consider immediate assessment and intervention. If this is not possible, immediate referral to an appropriate professional within or outside the school system should be made while the safety of the student is simultaneously ensured. The specific school administrator responsible for the student, such as the building principal, should always be apprised of suicide vulnerability and what staff and faculty are doing to counter the process with any student.
- The rules of confidentiality can be broken when information that suggests that a student is suicidal is obtained. The suspicion need only be slight, but it must be concrete. The statement or behavior that leads the educator to suspect a suicidal process needs to be documented. It is always prudent to err on the side of safety. Thus, breaking confidentiality to consult with a professional when suicidal ideation is suspected will result in a more effective assessment process.
- All communications, conversations, and actions taken with regard to the assessment, intervention, and referral of a suicidal (or suspected suicidal) student should be documented and recorded. These records should be kept in the student's confidential file. Some teachers and school clinicians keep what is known as "working files," which are not necessarily subject to legal seizure. However, if information regarding suicidal vulnerability remains only in a working file, the information does little to facilitate suicide prevention or intervention.
- When the suicide process is accurately assessed, regardless of risk level, the student should be referred to a therapist or clinic specializing in the evaluation and treatment of depression and suicide. Referral to professionals saves lives and provides educators with a measure of legal protection.

If all faculty, pupil personnel specialists, and administrators are trained in suicide assessment and referral, they might not be as hesitant to intervene with students for fear of legal troubles. Stated simply, educators are responsible for taking all signals and threats seriously and for acting professionally, effectively, and quickly on the information available. Following these guidelines should keep intervention in the school setting on firm legal footing. When all educators have access to the information and training they need in order to handle these types of situations, we will surely see a reduction in the loss of life.

Note. From *Adolescent Suicide: A School-Based Approach to Assessment and Treatment* (pp. 105–107) by W. G. Kirk, 1993, Champaign, IL: Research Press. Copyright 1993 by W. G. Kirk. Reprinted by permission.

of time available to search for this information. School personnel should not assume responsibilities for follow-up or long-term counseling if they do not have the expertise or time available. The responsibility for this care should be delegated to the appropriate agency in the community (Capuzzi, 1988).

DRUG AND ALCOHOL ABUSE

Case

They started young, usually with pot, and moved on to coke—sometimes snorted, sometimes injected, sometimes freebased. Now they're patients at Phoenix House, a residential treatment center in Orange County, Calif. "When I first smoked rock I fell in love," says Samantha. "I wanted to do more right away. I would lie, steal—anything for a hit off the pipe. It gets hold of you real fast." To Amy, "coke was the wonder drug, and freebasing was better than sex. I had no morals: I'd do anything with my body for coke." Dan, a bleached-blond 15-year-old from Orange County stole from his parents, from his employer and from neighbors. "I used all the cash for drugs," he says. "I didn't care about food, I didn't care about a bed. It was scary on the street, but the cocaine made it all right." Dan says about half the kids at his old high school now use coke. (Morganthau, 1986, p. 63)

From 1986 to 1992, a series of national Gallup polls found that the general public considered the use of drugs to be the major problem faced by the public schools (Elam, Rose, & Gallup, 1993). In 1996 the Gallup Poll again listed drug abuse as the number one problem in schools, and it was ranked the number three problem in 1997, only a narrow one-point margin below lack of discipline and financial support for schools (Rose, Gallup, & Elam, 1997). Other figures (National Institute on Drug Abuse [NIDA], 1997) indicate that the most prevalent drug use activities among high school seniors are drinking alcohol (79%) and smoking (64%), although nearly 51% had tried at least one illicit controlled substance or drug (marijuana was tried most frequently—by 45%).

Alcohol and tobacco appear to be the most abused drugs because they are the most readily available and the most highly visible due to the amount of advertising they receive (Horton, 1985). Data reported by NIDA (1997) indicate that, in the 12-month period prior to being polled, 40% of the students in the 12th grade group had used an illicit drug; 31% had been drunk in the past month; 30% admitted to binge drinking (five or more drinks in a row) during the past 2 weeks. Marijuana had been used at some time by 45% of this group, and 22%

currently used it. In this NIDA study it was also determined that 7% of high school seniors had used cocaine at least once; 13% of the students had used LSD; 21% of the eighth graders included in the study had used inhalants (i.e., glues, aerosols, and solvents). An earlier report indicated that the average age at which students first used alcohol was 12.8 years (Needham, 1989).

The data on **drug and alcohol abuse** for students are not completely surprising when considered next to statistics on the adult population. For example, alcohol consumption is at its lowest level in 30 years, and still 56% of Americans drink alcoholic beverages ("Alcohol Use," 1989). Individuals who abuse drugs or alcohol are very much at risk for failure in school and in other aspects of their lives (Elmquist, 1991).

Factors such as having friends who provide drugs and encourage their use, low socioeconomic status, disturbed families, adult family members using drugs, poor school performance, stressful life events, deviant behaviors, depression, or anxiety can all contribute to the possibility that an individual will be at risk for use or abuse of alcohol and drugs. The greater the number of these factors influencing a specific student, the more likely that student is to abuse alcohol and other drugs (Newcomb & Bentler, 1989). Figure 17–3 lists a series of symptoms that can help educators to identify students involved in drug and alcohol abuse.

A variety of programs directed at preventing and/or treating drug and alcohol abuse have been developed, and many have had limited success. These programs have often attempted to reduce the use of milder drugs such as cigarettes, alcohol, and marijuana on the theory that their use will lead to the use of harder drugs. Prevention programs whose sole purpose is to provide information on drug and alcohol abuse have not been highly successful. Programs that involve improving peer interactions and enhancing social skills and assertiveness or refusal skills have been the most effective in reducing the use of drugs, but they have had less impact on individuals currently abusing drugs. Interventions that involve individuals in alternative activities, build their confidence, broaden their experiences, and improve social competence were the most successful in reducing the abuse of drugs (Newcomb & Bentler, 1989).

Studies on the effectiveness of various types of treatment programs are needed so that programs

FIGURE 17-3   Signs of Alcohol and Other Drug Use

Signs of alcohol and other drug use [AOD] vary, but there are some common indicators of AOD problems. Look for changes in performance, appearance, and behavior. These signs may indicate AOD use, but they may also reflect normal teenage growing pains. Therefore, look for a series of changes, not isolated single behaviors. Several changes together indicate a pattern associated with use.

Changes in Performance:
- Distinct downward turn in grades—not just from Cs to Fs, but from As to Bs and Cs
- Assignments not completed
- A loss of interest in school; in extracurricular activities
- Poor classroom behavior such as inattentiveness, sleeping in class, hostility
- Missing school for unknown reasons
- In trouble with school, at work, or with the police
- Increased discipline problems
- Memory loss

Changes in Behavior:
- Decrease in energy and endurance
- Changes in friends (secrecy about new friends, new friends with different lifestyles)
- Secrecy about activities (lies and avoids talking about activities)
- Borrows lots of money, or has too much cash
- Mood swings; excessive anger, irritability
- Preferred style of music changes (pop rock to heavy metal)
- Starts pulling away from the family, old friends, and school
- Hostile or argumentative attitude; extremely negative, unmotivated, defensive
- Refusal or hostility when asked to talk about possible alcohol or other drug use

Changes in Appearance and Physical Changes:
- Weight loss or gain
- Uncoordinated
- Poor physical appearance or unusually neat. A striking change in personal habits
- New interest in the drug culture (drug-related posters, clothes, magazines)
- Smells of alcohol, tobacco, marijuana
- Frequent use of eye drops and breath mints
- Bloodshot eyes
- Persistent cough or cold symptoms (e.g., runny nose)
- Always thirsty, increased or decreased appetite, rapid speech
- AOD paraphernalia (empty alcohol containers, cigarettes, pipes, rolling papers, baggies, paper packets, roach clips, razor blades, straws, glass or plastic vials, pill bottles, tablets and capsules, colored stoppers, syringes, spoons, matches or lighters, needles, medicine droppers, toy balloons, tin foil, cleaning rags, spray cans, glue containers, household products)

Note. From "School-Based Alcohol and Other Drug Prevention Programs: Guidelines for the Special Educator" by D. L. Elmquist, 1991, *Intervention in School and Clinic, 27*(1), p. 14. Copyright 1991 by PRO-ED, Inc. Reprinted by permission.

can become more accountable to the students they serve and their families. Problems have occurred when programs have placed individuals into the wrong type of program (sometimes because of an error and other times because of a need to fill that program's beds). For example, if parents agree to have a mildly involved adolescent (i.e., one who has used a drug infrequently as a result of normal experimentation or social pressure) "thrown in" with youth who are truly drug abusers, the adolescent may be alienated from his or her family and exposed to an environment that may actually encourage fur-

Inclusion Tips for the Teacher

Elements of a Successful Drug Abuse Prevention Program

Listed here are a series of elements that are considered essential in developing a school drug abuse prevention program:

1. Establish a clear, well-defined policy for teachers and students spelling out how teachers and administrators will deal with apparent or substantiated drug use or possession.
2. Encourage teachers to establish a basic drug education curriculum for their grade levels—keeping it simple, brief, and nonjudgmental and emphasizing the teachers' concern for the students' physical and psychological welfare.
3. Help teachers increase their awareness of local drug problems and use community service agencies.
4. Provide an atmosphere in which the teacher can develop the skills and sensitivity for resolving classroom and individual problems and for leading group discussions about topics such as adolescent development and drug use.
5. Develop an intervention program that involves families as well as students by offering both one-to-one and group counseling centers and drop-in centers within the school. (A drop-in center could be staffed by an education counselor with some training in drug abuse counseling.)
6. Try to get all teachers to review their role perceptions. If they feel their jobs are basically unfulfilling and that they are unable to empathize with students and deal with affective as well as cognitive training, this may lead to constructive career reorientation.
7. Develop peer-group approaches with positive role models for group or individual support. Different types of peer programs are discussed in the National Institute on Drug Abuse publication, "Adolescent Peer Pressure" (NIDA Publication No. ADM 83-1152).
8. Promote understanding of the emotional structure and perceptions that often accompany drug use. Many drug-using students feel they are incompetent and unreasonably rejected by adults and peers. They need an understanding approach rather than a disciplinary and judgmental attitude that confirms their belief that teachers and administrators are only concerned about keeping order, not about helping students.

Note. This list is reprinted with permission of Merrill, an imprint of Macmillan Publishing Company, from "Drug Abuse Management in Adolescent Special Education" by S. Miksic in *Helping Adolescents with Learning and Behavior Problems* (p. 245) by M. M. Kerr, C. M. Nelson, and D. L. Lambert, Copyright © 1987 Merrill Publishing Company, Columbus, Ohio.

ther drug abuse (Newcomb & Bentler, 1989). Any recommended treatment must be matched to the individual needs of the student. Also, treatments should include attempts to provide for family involvement because programs tend to be more effective if they involve other members of the family. Miksic (1987) has outlined the essential elements of a prevention program for drug abuse; see "Inclusion Tips for the Teacher."

Many aspects of the treatment program for students who are drug or alcohol abusers will incorporate the services of public or private community agencies. Teachers should not expect to be counselors or investigators; their responsibility is to make appropriate referrals when there are signs of drug use or abuse. In addition, teachers may be called on to assist in managing suspected drug abuse episodes involving intoxication or withdrawal crises. At these times, they should remain calm and nonconfrontational because demonstrating control is not as important as ensuring safety (Kauffman, 1997).

The long-term effects of the use and abuse of drugs are not yet known. It is well documented that drug and alcohol abuse impairs the ability of students to function effectively in school and in their interactions with others. Educators can play an important role in decreasing the number of students who use and abuse alcohol and other drugs by including accurate information on drug and alcohol use in the school curriculum, being aware of the signs of potential problems, and helping to refer students to the appropriate professional resources.

TEENAGE PREGNANCY AND SEXUALLY TRANSMITTED DISEASES

Cases

At age 15, Barbara quit school in the fourth month of her pregnancy. She was afraid that the baby might be "damaged" due to heavy drug use at the time of conception, but she has decided to keep the baby rather than have an abortion. Her boyfriend had denied that the baby is his. Barbara suspects it was her boyfriend who smashed the windshield of her mother's car as a threat to leave him out of this "mess." Barbara's mother is unemployed and on welfare. Their plan is to have the mother babysit and Barbara will get a job to support the three of them. Barbara does not see returning to school as an option for her. She feels that her problems with school were mostly her fault and does not blame her teachers or the school. (Grossnickle, 1986, pp. 13–14)

Joshua is a 17-year-old teenager from a typical American family. He has been diagnosed with AIDS. He contracted the virus through sexual experimentation. He has been prevented from attending school. His mother and father cry and feel helpless in the battle to keep him alive. He now weighs 86 pounds. He is often too sick to go out of the house. He will die soon. He is very frightened. (Gray & House, 1989, p. 231)

Each year, 12 million to 13 million teen and preteen girls are sexually active (Cartwright, Cartwright, & Ward, 1989). Adolescents in the United States have pregnancy rates that are "dramatically higher than those of other developed countries (21% compared to 14–15% elsewhere)" (Muccigrosso, Scavarda, Simpson-Brown, & Thalacker, 1991, p. 1). Every day, 2,740 teenagers become pregnant, and 1,293 have babies ("Data Bank," 1989). Of the nearly 1 million teenage girls who become pregnant each year, (a) 50% never complete high school (Woodring, 1989), (b) 40% of the pregnancies end in abortion (Furstenberg, Brooks-Gunn, & Chase-Lansdale, 1989), and (c) 90% of the babies that are born are kept and raised by the teenage mothers (Mathes & Irby, 1993). Re-

cent figures indicate that 23.9% of all women become pregnant before the age of 18 and 43.5% before the age of 20 (Furstenberg et al., 1989); about 13% of all babies are born to teenagers (Mathes & Irby, 1993). Sixty percent of white males are sexually active by age 18, and 60% of African American males are sexually active by age 16.

While the teenage birthrate declined from 1990 to 1994, the current rates are still much higher than they were in the mid-1970s. Although the birthrates have steadily declined for both white and African American mothers, the rates for Hispanic mothers continue to be quite stable. Birth and infant mortality rates are somewhat lower for white teenagers than for both African American and Hispanic teenage mothers, yet all groups are likely to have low-birth-weight infants and to lack timely prenatal care (Jacobson, 1996; National Center for Health Statistics, 1996).

The high level of sexual activity reported in teenagers also increases the possibility of contracting **sexually transmitted diseases** (STDs) such as acquired immune deficiency syndrome (AIDS), genital warts, herpes, syphilis, or gonorrhea (Brooks-Gunn & Furstenberg, 1989). It is estimated that more than 3 million teenagers acquire an STD every year (Donovan, 1993). The most frequently diagnosed STD among adolescents is chlamydia, an infection of the vagina or urinary tract (McWhirter et al., 1998). Males (1993) estimates that the rate of STDs among teenage girls is 2.5 times higher than that of boys in the same age group. More than 50% of the teenagers who are known to have AIDS are from ethnic minority groups (Steel, 1995).

When a teenage mother plans to raise her baby, a number of potential problems arise. She is generally unprepared for this role and is very likely to terminate her education by failing or dropping out of school. Many of the babies born to teenage mothers are likely to be premature and/or have medical problems and a higher than average risk of poor cognitive development. These difficulties may occur because many of the mothers do not have appropriate nutrition or health care during pregnancy, and it is not likely that they will be able to provide these essentials for their child. The teenager's child is apt to be at high risk for failure because of potential health, nutritional, and emotional problems, and it is probable that he or she will need special attention at school (Bonjean & Rittenmeyer, 1987; Cartwright et al., 1995; Mathes & Irby, 1993).

Many factors contribute to the level of teenage sexual activity and pregnancy. Social attitudes and the attitudes of peers often encourage sexual activity. Many teenagers have not been exposed to sex education or the use of contraceptives, and they lack knowledge about pregnancy prevention and the consequences of their sexual behavior. Lack of close relationships with parents or friends may contribute to a need to participate in sexual activities in order to be "accepted" by others (Brooks-Gunn & Furstenberg, 1989; Cartwright et al., 1989).

The school must play several roles in dealing with this issue. First, educational programs must provide information on sex education and STDs to assure that students are aware of the possible ramifications of sexual activity. Second, because Title IX of the Education Amendments of 1972 protects the teenage mother from discrimination, schools are obligated to continue to provide educational programs for these students (Bettinger, 1989). Finally, because children of teenage mothers are more likely to be at risk for potential failure, the school can improve the probability of their success by supporting the development of infant and preschool programs and attending to their risk status and their needs when they enter the general education program (Furstenberg et al., 1989).

While many educators believe that the school can play an important role in the areas of teenage pregnancy and AIDS education, only about 35% to 40% of the public indicate that they have confidence in the school's ability to deal with these topics (Gallup & Elam, 1988). Prevention programs introduced in schools typically provide general information on sexuality and contraception, attempt to modify attitudes in order to discourage early sexual activity, or provide specific information on family planning or contraception. These primary prevention programs have had limited success and "may promote healthier—but probably not less—childbearing by teenagers" (Males, 1993, p. 568). At present, many experts believe that actually providing family planning and contraception is most likely to reduce the early childbearing rate. A sex education curriculum should be carefully developed to provide information on the "social, health and economic risks related to sex and teen pregnancies" (Ogden & Germinario, 1988, p. 150).

In addition to informing students about all STDs, Yarber (1987) recommends that students be specifically taught about how AIDS is transmitted (i.e., via sexual intercourse or exchange of blood) and the ways in which the transmission of this deadly disease can be prevented. After carefully reviewing many AIDS education programs, Popham (1993) indicates that in order for programs to teach students to "avoid behavior that places them at risk of HIV infection, students need to be *knowledgeable* about HIV and AIDS, *skilled* in avoiding behaviors that place them at risk of infection, and *motivated* to use their HIV–relevant skills and knowledge" (p. 561).

Students must be provided with the information they will need to make their own decisions regarding their sexual activity. In some communities, the school must approach this topic with a great deal of care. Teachers must take into account the values of parents, students, and the community, and they must carefully examine their own values when they provide instruction and guidance in this area. Cartwright and others (1989) provide teachers with an important reminder:

> A teacher may be the one person a girl who thinks or knows she is pregnant approaches for advice or for help. It is essential that teachers be aware of their own reactions to this situation and be able to control their own feelings in order to provide the assistance requested or to arrange for referrals to appropriate health-care agencies. (pp. 430–431)

CHILD ABUSE AND NEGLECT

Kara, age 5, always presented a neat, well-ordered picture. Although not expensive, her clothes were well-chosen, clean, and pressed. Her long-sleeved blouses and colorful tights seemed a bit strange in warmer weather, but the teacher made no comments about them. The child was very affectionate, almost to the point of smothering; her endearing ways made her an easy candidate for teacher's pet. It was not until Kara unexplainably wet her pants and the teacher helped her remove her tights to clean up, that anything seemed amiss. Kara's small legs revealed numerous bruises in various stages of healing. An examination by the school nurse attested to the abuse Kara had suffered over her entire body. (Tower, 1987, p. 24)

Child abuse and neglect can occur in many forms. The National Clearinghouse on Child Abuse and Neglect (1997) provides information on the federal law related to these problems, The Child Abuse Prevention and Treatment Act (CAPTA). As amended and reauthorized in October 1996 (PL 104-235, Section 111; 42 U.S.C. 5106g), CAPTA defines child abuse and neglect as, at a minimum, any recent act or failure to act:

- Resulting in imminent risk of serious harm, death, serious physical or emotional harm, sexual abuse, or exploitation
- Of a child (a person under the age of 18, unless the child protection law of the State in which the child resides specifies a younger age for cases not involving sexual abuse)
- By a parent or caretaker (including any employee of a residential facility or any staff person providing out-of-home care) who is responsible for the child's welfare.

CAPTA defines sexual abuse as:

- Employment, use, persuasion, inducement, enticement, or coercion of any child to engage in, or assist any other person to engage in, any sexually explicit conduct or any simulation of such conduct for the purpose of producing any visual depiction of such conduct; or
- rape, and in cases of caretaker or inter-familial relationships, statutory rape, molestation, prostitu-

tion, or other form of sexual exploitation of children, or incest with children. . . .

Each State is responsible for providing definitions of child abuse and neglect within the civil and criminal context. Civil laws, or statutes, describe the circumstances and conditions that obligate mandated reporters to report known or suspected cases of abuse, and they provide definitions necessary for juvenile/family courts to take custody of a child alleged to have been maltreated. Criminal statutes specify the forms of maltreatment that are criminally punishable. (National Clearinghouse on Child Abuse and Neglect, 1997, p. 1)

Reports indicate that in 1996 there were over 3 million reported cases of child abuse and neglect (National Committee to Prevent Child Abuse, 1997); in 1994, over 115,000 cases of child sexual abuse were reported (McCurdy & Daro, 1995). Bauer and Shea (1989) indicate that abused and neglected children may not relate well with peers or adults and are likely to have "deficits in measured intelligence, academic performance, and readiness to learn" (p. 303).

Inclusion Tips for the Teacher

Identifying Suspected Child Abuse

School personnel need assistance in determining if a situation they have observed is a case of child abuse that should be reported. The following list of descriptions of abuse, and the indicators for each, will be useful in helping educators recognize child abuse.

Physical Abuse

Physical abuse is characterized by inflicting physical injury by punching, beating, kicking, biting, burning, or otherwise harming a child. Although the injury is not an accident, the parent or caretaker may not have intended to hurt the child.

Physical Abuse—Physical Indicators
Child shows evidence of unexplained or repeated injury or injuries in the form of:
a. lacerations, punctures, or missing teeth
b. fractures, sprains, or dislocations
c. rope burns, immersion burns, or cigarette or cigar burns (especially on soles of feet, palms, back, or buttocks—these are seldom self-inflicted)
d. bruises or welts reflecting shape of object used to inflict the injury or injuries on several different surface areas
e. new injuries before old injuries have healed

Physical Abuse—Behavioral Indicators
The child is or may be:
a. wary of adult contacts
b. consistently on the alert for danger
c. subject to frequent and severe mood changes
d. frightened of parents and avoids home (consistently arrives at school early or leaves late)
e. apprehensive when other children cry
f. demonstrating behavioral extremes (aggressive, disruptive, or destructive; or unusually shy, withdrawn, passive, or overly compliant)

Child Neglect

Child neglect is characterized by failure to provide for the child's basic needs. Neglect can be physical, educational, or emotional. Physical neglect includes refusal of or delay in seeking health care, abandonment, expulsion from home or not allowing a runaway to return home, and inadequate supervision. Educational neglect includes permission of chronic truancy, failure to enroll a child of mandatory school age, and inattention to a special educational need. Emotional neglect includes such actions as chronic or extreme spouse abuse in the child's presence, permission of drug or alcohol use by the child, and refusal of or failure to provide needed psychological care.

Neglect—Physical Indicators
Child shows evidence of:
a. constant fatigue or listlessness
b. unattended physical problems or medical needs
c. consistent hunger (begs for food, undernourished)
d. poor hygiene, unbathed, filthy clothing, or inappropriate dress for the weather
e. abandonment

Neglect—Behavioral Indicators
Child is or may be:
a. constantly hungry, begs for food
b. rejected by other children because of offensive body odor
c. constantly falling asleep in class
d. constantly arriving at school early and leaving late
e. left alone for substantial periods of time

Sexual Abuse

Sexual abuse includes fondling a child's genitals, intercourse, incest, rape, sodomy, exhibitionism, and sexual exploitation. To be considered child abuse, these acts have to be committed by a parent [or other caregiver] responsible for the care of a child.

Sexual Abuse—Physical Indicators
Child shows evidence of:
a. difficulty in walking or sitting
b. torn, stained, or bloody underclothes
c. pain or itching in genital area
d. semen around the genitals or on clothing
e. lacerations, bruises, or bleeding in external genitalia, vaginal, or anal area
f. venereal disease (especially in young children)
g. pregnancy

continued

Sexual Abuse—Behavioral Indicators
Child shows evidence of:
a. bizarre, sophisticated, or unusual sexual behavior or knowledge
b. regression (Some sexually abused children, especially younger ones, will retreat into a fantasy world, or exhibit infantile behaviors, which may be interpreted as retardation.)
c. delinquency or aggression (The anger and hostility these children, particularly teenagers, feel toward the perpetrator may cause them to adopt aggressive behavior toward others.)
d. poor peer relationships (Because of guilt feelings the child cannot form relationships with peers.)
e. running away to escape from the home situation (Running away may be an indirect manner of asking for help in a situation in which they feel powerless.)
f. unwillingness to participate in physical activities (Young children who have been highly stimulated sexually or have had forced sexual intercourse may find it painful to sit during school or to play at active games.)
g. drug use/abuse (The use of alcohol and other drugs may be the child's method of handling his/her guilt and anxieties.)
h. indirect allusion (Sometimes sexually abused children confide in someone they feel may be helpful by using vague or indirect allusions to the home situation; e.g., "I'm afraid to go home tonight," "I'd like to come and live with you," or "I want to live in a foster home.")
i. seductive behavior (If a child views sexual contact as a positive source of attention, he/she may adopt seductive behaviors with peers or adults.)

Emotional Maltreatment
This form of child abuse and neglect includes acts or omissions by the parents that have caused, or could cause, serious behavioral, cognitive, emotional, or mental disorders. Examples include: refusal to acknowledge the child's worth and needs, depriving them of normal social experiences, verbally terrorizing them and creating a climate of fear, ignoring them, or corrupting them through encouragement to engage in destructive behavior and reinforcing the deviance.

Emotional Maltreatment—Physical Indicators
Child shows evidence of:
a. habit disorders (sucking, biting, rocking)
b. conduct disorders (hyper- or hypo-activity, antisocial, destructive)
c. neurotic traits (sleep disorders, speech [disorders], enuresis, inhibition of play)
d. psychoneurotic reactions (hysteria, obsessions, depression, compulsion, phobias, hyprochondria)
e. physical manifestations of nervous disorders (overweight, skin rashes)

Emotional Maltreatment—Behavioral Indicators
Child shows evidence of:
a. low self-esteem
b. behavior extremes (compliant and passive or aggressive, demanding, disruptive)
c. overly compliant behavior
d. developmental lags (physical, mental, and emotional)
e. seeking affection
f. attempting suicide
g. excessive temper tantrums

Note. From *The School's Role in the Prevention of Child Abuse* (pp. 19–22) by S. B. London and S. W. Stile, 1982, Bloomington, IN: The Phi Delta Kappa Educational Foundation. Copyright 1982 by The Phi Delta Kappa Educational Foundation. Also from *Abuse and Neglect of Exceptional Children* (pp. 3–4) by C. L. Warger, S. Tewey, and M. Megivern, 1991, Reston, VA: The Council for Exceptional Children. Adapted by permission.

No single set of characteristics can be associated with those who abuse children. The abusive behavior commonly can occur as the result of various types of stress (e.g., marital stress), lack of basic knowledge of appropriate child-rearing practices, a low tolerance for child behaviors such as crying or whining, or an inaccurate assessment of the motivation for the child's misbehavior (Emery, 1989). London and Stile (1982) indicate that the following characteristics are often found in child abusers:

• A history of being abused and/or neglected as a child.
• Uses physical punishment as the primary method of disciplining a child.
• Has unrealistic expectations that are inconsistent with the developmental age of the child.
• Has had no models of successful family relationships and, therefore, has little notion of parenting skills.
• Does not have friends or family to help with the heavy demands of caring for small children.
• Reports that there was not much love or emotional support from adults during his/her childhood.

- Has poor impulse control.
- Has an undue fear of "spoiling" the child by "giving in" to the child or allowing the child to "get away with" anything. (p. 11)

It is possible that abuse is more likely to occur with students with special needs than with their "typical" peers (Warger, Tewey, & Megivern, 1991). Some students with special needs are more difficult to control in the home, or they may exhibit high levels of inappropriate and/or irritating behaviors. Others may lack the skills required to respond as appropriately as the parent would like them to in social situations, or they are "easy marks" because they are incapable of defending themselves. "Inclusion Tips for the Teacher" on pages 455–456 provides information on identifying suspected child abuse.

The actual number of cases of child abuse and neglect is hard to determine because experts estimate that only 20% of the cases are reported. It is difficult to obtain accurate statistics in this area because (a) definitions and reporting requirements vary across states and agencies, (b) people are not trained to recognize abuse, (c) individuals are unwilling to report cases because they do not want to get involved, and (d) agencies assigned to protect children have a difficult time obtaining evidence that maltreatment has occurred.

Educators have legal, ethical, and professional responsibilities to report cases of abuse and neglect and assist these children at school. It is their obligation to obtain the information necessary to report these cases accurately and provide for the needs of these students in the school setting (London & Stile, 1982). Educators are legally responsible for reporting child abuse, and "every state provides immunity by law from civil suit and criminal prosecution that might arise from the reporting of suspected child abuse or neglect" (Fischer & Sorenson, 1985, p. 188). Guidelines for a school's reporting policy and a set of suggested procedures for teachers to follow in preparing reports on child abuse and neglect are presented in Figure 17–4. It is important, however, that each teacher know the required guidelines and timelines for reporting abuse in his or her own school assignment.

In the area of child abuse and neglect, the responsibilities of educators do not end with identifying and reporting suspected cases of abuse or neglect. Educators should also (a) model appropriate adult-pupil interactions; (b) support positive pupil-pupil interactions; (c) include opportunities for students to develop parenting skills as part of the school's curriculum; (d) support and participate in the development of prevention activities that involve parents; (e) encourage the development of programs that respond to the specific needs of students at risk; and (f) assure that cases are monitored, reported, investigated, and that the school is informed of the disposition of the case (London & Stile, 1982).

Students need to be informed (a) that all individuals have basic human needs (i.e., for food, shelter, safety, and affection); (b) of acceptable ways that adults interact with children so that they would be able to tell whether they were being abused or exploited; (c) that an adult should be contacted if they are confused or concerned about something that is occurring in their life; (d) how they should deal with others to protect themselves from possible abuse; (e) of resources available to them in the community; and (f) who should be notified in the case of an emergency situation, such as someone approaching them on the street or attempting to enter their home when their parents are away (Tower, 1987). These topics should be covered at each appropriate grade level and may be included as part of the programs for sex education or the teaching of parenting skills.

EATING DISORDERS

Case

Julie is a pretty, intelligent 15-year-old who has been hospitalized twice for anorexia nervosa. She is the youngest of three children in an intact family. Her father is a professor at a prominent university and her mother is an artist with her studio in the home. The two older children are also bright and successful. The oldest, a son, has graduated from one of the Ivy League schools and is now in medical school. The older sister is currently attending a small, private, liberal arts school and earning almost straight As. She, too, expects to do graduate work. Julie has always been a good student and, according to her parents, after numerous food allergies as a baby, was the easiest to raise. Julie, however, thinks she is ugly, fat, not well-

FIGURE 17-4   Reporting Child Abuse and Neglect

School Reporting Policy

Although educators are responsible for reporting child abuse and neglect, it is important that the school system has an established reporting procedure. Such a policy should include specific information such as:

1. At what point should the teacher report child abuse? Suspicion? Reasonable cause to believe? (This may be based not only on school policy but also on state law.)
2. Whom does the teacher notify? Nurse? Principal? School social worker?
3. What specific information does the teacher need to know to report?
4. What actions should the teacher have taken before reporting to validate suspicions?
5. What other school personnel should be involved?
6. Who makes the report to the appropriate authorities? How?
7. What information should be included in the report? (This may be dictated by state law or protective agency policy.)
8. What follow-up is expected on reported cases?
9. What role will the school play in possible community/child protection teams?
10. What commitment does the school have to inservice training or community programs?

Teacher's Checklist for Preparing to Report

Certainly reporting child abuse is neither easy or clear-cut. But the potential benefit for the abused child is worth every effort you are able to expend. Consider the following points when preparing to report:

1. Have you documented your data and written down the information to organize it in your own mind?
2. Have you analyzed your data? What causes you to suspect abuse/neglect? List the symptoms—physical or behavioral.
3. Have you been able to observe the parent/child interaction? Does the parent see the child as worthwhile or different and/or hard to handle?
4. Have you spoken with other professionals within the school? Do they have reason to suspect abuse/ neglect? Why?
5. Do you know the reporting policy of your school? Do you know the answers to the questions listed above (i.e., in **School Reporting Policy**)? To whom do you report?
6. Do you have the necessary information required for a report? State law usually requires the following information:
   • names of the child and parents
   • address
   • age and sex of the child
   • type and extent of the child's injuries or complaints
   • evidence of prior injuries
   • explanation of the injuries given by the child
   • name and telephone number of the reporter
   • actions taken by the reporter (such as detaining the child, photographs)
   • other pertinent information
7. Do you (or does the school) have the exact telephone number and address of the agency to which you should report?
8. Have you talked with your administrator about the support you will receive once the report is made? What if the parents try to remove the child from your class? Will you have the support of the administration?
9. Does the school have on hand the necessary report forms?
10. Have you set up a support system for yourself with other teachers or administrators? (After the report is made, you may feel vulnerable and need to talk.)

Now you should be ready to report, knowing that you are providing a chance for both the child and the family to receive much-needed help.

Note. From *How Schools Can Help Combat Child Abuse and Neglect* (2nd ed., pp. 50–51, 53, 67–68) by C. C. Tower, 1987, Washington, DC: National Education Association. Copyright 1987 by National Education Association of the United States. Adapted by permission.

liked by her peers, and not as competent as her siblings. She also thinks her parents think the two older siblings are brighter and more productive. When she was 13, Julie started overeating and then gagging herself afterwards. This quickly led to strict dieting and strenuous exercise. Julie had a boyfriend, Nick, but shortly before the second hospitalization, they quit dating. There had been much conflict between them: Nick wanted more sexual intimacy than Julie. She finally acquiesced, but felt much ambivalence and guilt afterward. She feels Nick broke up with her because he thought she was promiscuous. (Epanchin, 1987, p. 175)

About 25% of all adolescents exhibit symptoms of anorexia nervosa, bulimia, or obesity (Maloney & Klykylo, 1985). Problems related to their condition can contribute to their risk for failure in school and in their interactions with others. Although these students may require services provided by professionals outside the school setting, it is important that educators be aware of the symptoms of these disorders and be able to identify and refer these students for the appropriate treatment.

Individuals with **anorexia nervosa** choose to restrict their intake of food to such an extent that they lose 20%–25% of their appropriate body weight. Approximately 90% of the cases occur in young women who are overly concerned about being overweight and have a distorted idea of their body appearance (often thinking they are fat when they are actually underweight). Anorexia is most likely to occur in 14- or 15-year-old girls and usually begins with dieting that turns into an obsession with weight loss. At one time, approximately 10%–20% of anorexic individuals died from starvation or from complications arising from the disorder; this number has dropped sharply as awareness of the disorder has increased (Coleman, 1986).

Bulimia nervosa involves primarily young women who have recurrent episodes of binge eating that are followed by induced vomiting and the use of laxatives, fasting, or drugs to reduce weight. Bulimics tend to go on a food binge when they are under stress, angry, depressed, or lonely and then try to remove the food from their body before it can be digested. They are preoccupied with both eating and losing weight. Frequently these individuals hide their disorder from others (Levine, 1987).

Obesity occurs when body weight exceeds ideal weight by 20% or more. It may occur because of in-appropriate eating habits, family eating behaviors and attitudes, or genetic factors (Maloney & Klykylo, 1985).

The school's health curriculum should include information on eating disorders and provide a forum for developing knowledge and skills in (a) how to deal with stress, depression, and anxiety; (b) the role of society in setting specific expectations for physical appearance; (c) normal growth and development; and (d) appropriate nutrition. Educators who identify students who are at risk because of a potential eating disorder should consider contacting the school nurse or a counselor or referring the student to local mental health support services. Individuals with anorexia have responded well to behavioral interventions that provide positive reinforcement for weight gain, and bulimics often respond positively to treatment for depression or to participation in support groups with other bulimics (Coleman, 1986). Obesity can often be treated through behavioral approaches (e.g., self-monitoring and reinforcement) and the teaching of appropriate eating habits (Doleys & Bruno, 1982).

DELINQUENCY

Case

The child, nicknamed "Scarface" because of the cuts and scars on his face, was ten years old, only five feet tall, and weighed just 90 pounds. His spindly legs barely touched the floor as he sat in detention, waiting for his court-appointed lawyer. He was accused of molesting a ten-year-old girl on the school grounds while one of his friends held her down. The judge released him into the custody of his parents. Over the next ten weeks, he was arrested five more times—more times than any other juvenile in Washington, D.C. in that year, 1985. His other arrests were for holding up and robbing two men, threatening a woman with an iron pipe, participating in a brawl, illegally entering a car, and roughing up a woman and snatching her purse. (Kauffman, 1997, p. 396)

Of the 2.3 million juveniles arrested in 1986, 1.4 million were arrested for crimes such as vandalism, drug abuse, or running away; 900,000 were arrested for more serious crimes such as larceny-theft, robbery, or forcible rape. These figures may represent a very small percentage of the actual delinquent acts

Things to Remember

- The factors that place students at risk—substance abuse, delinquency, abusive caregivers, and so on—interfere with their ability to benefit from the school experience.
- Definitions of students at risk vary greatly from state to state and sometimes from district to district within the same state.
- Students at risk do not belong exclusively to any one group, community, or population.
- The potential for being identified as at risk is higher for students raised in disadvantaged or impoverished home settings.
- Students at risk do not generally benefit from the equal access provisions of laws and policies designed to ensure that appropriate educational programs or special services are provided for other students, such as those with disabilities.
- Educators can increase the probability that many students at risk will be contributors to society.
- The attitudes that students at risk take with them as they leave school will affect the attitudes of their younger siblings and, later, of their own children.
- Students at risk require appropriate educational interventions as well as optimum behavior management and instruction in academics and social skills.
- Teachers and other school personnel are not expected to become therapists for students at risk, but they can assist in referring them to appropriate services.
- A dropout is anyone over the age of 18 who is no longer enrolled in and has not graduated from high school.

- Suicide is the third leading cause of death among 15- to 24-year-olds.
- Teachers and other school personnel can be involved in a variety of activities that can potentially reduce the number of suicides among students.
- Drug abuse is viewed by the general population as one of the top problems in our schools and the nation at large.
- Both the teenage mother and her children are at high risk for failure.
- The high level of sexual activity reported among teenagers increases the possibility that they will contract sexually transmitted diseases.
- No single set of characteristics is associated with those who abuse children.
- The actual number of cases of child abuse and neglect is difficult to determine because experts estimate that only 20% of the cases are reported.
- About one-fourth of adolescents show symptoms of eating disorders such as anorexia nervosa, bulimia, and obesity.
- The most promising interventions for delinquents combine specific training in child management practices for the parents with training in social skills and academic remediation for the students.
- It is important that educators be aware of the symptoms and characteristics of students at risk and be able to identify and refer these students for the appropriate treatment.

(Siegel & Senna, 1994), perhaps as few as 2% of the violations that are actually committed by delinquents (Patterson, DeBaryshe, & Ramsey, 1989).

Delinquents are much more likely to be boys. Those who show early signs of delinquent behavior and are initially arrested before they are 12 are more likely to continue their antisocial behavior as adults (Kauffman, 1997). Those initially arrested later in their teens are more likely to be one-time offenders. About 50% of the children who are antisocial become adolescent delinquents, and approximately 50% to 75% of the adolescent delinquents become

adult offenders (Patterson et al., 1989). Each year, about 450,000 delinquents are placed in juvenile detention centers and state training schools, while 300,000 are sent to adult jails (Leone, Rutherford, & Nelson, 1991).

Many factors have been noted as contributing to **delinquency.** Low intelligence, constitutional differences, location of the community (urban versus rural), cultural forces, community attitudes, failure in school, drug or alcohol abuse, poor self-concept, poor impulse control, and emotional problems have all been identified as contributing to the occurrence of delinquency (Cartwright et al., 1989). Patterson and others (1989) suggest that ineffective parenting (lack of appropriate discipline and monitoring) is a major contributor to the antisocial behavior of children. Antisocial behaviors eventually contribute to failure in academic areas and rejection by peers, and these failures can in turn lead to seeking acceptance in a deviant peer group and eventually to delinquency. The peer group is thought to provide the adolescent with antisocial attitudes and an opportunity to commit delinquent acts. Usually peers shape behavior by positively reinforcing deviant acts and punishing socially conforming behavior. Families with a history of antisocial behavior, low socioeconomic status, divorce, marital conflict, low educational level of the parent(s), unemployment, and the use of physical discipline have also been found to be related to the likelihood of delinquent behavior.

When interventions such as academic remediation, parent training, or social skills training have been attempted independently, they have at best had limited success that generally did not endure over time. The most receptive candidates for effective interventions are likely to be elementary students identified as lacking social and academic skills and exhibiting antisocial behaviors. Potential interventions that show the most promise combine specific training for the parents to improve their child management practices (e.g., effective, positive, and consistent discipline; appropriate supervision and monitoring) with training in social skills and academic remediation for the students (Kauffman, 1997; Patterson et al., 1989). Educators should be actively involved in developing programs that identify these students early in their school years, and they should work to coordinate the efforts and resources of the school and those of appropriate community agencies that can assist in working with the parents.

*The material presented in this chapter should help you identify students at risk and understand the difficulties they experience that are likely to interfere with their success in school, at home, and in the community. Many of the specific educational techniques described in earlier chapters will prove to be helpful in working with students at risk because their skills and educational needs in some areas are often similar to those of other students with special needs. When edu-*cators work to provide educational experiences that are appropriate for these students, their opportunities for success increase and the likelihood that they will experience failure in school and life decreases.*

ACTIVITIES

1. Write a short paper that establishes your position on providing mandatory educational programs tailored to meet the needs of students at risk. Tell how students would be identified, how eligibility for these services would be determined, and who would be responsible for providing the services.

2. Contact a local school district, and determine the types of programs they offer for students at risk. Establish who supervises these programs (e.g., special education, remedial services), the specific programs offered, the type of training required for the personnel who deliver the services, and any agencies they work with in the community. From what you know about both the community and students at risk, does the program seem to be adequate? Be prepared to describe your findings and state what changes you would recommend.

3. Identify a student with whom you are familiar who would fit into one of the at-risk groups described in the chapter. Write a brief description of the student's background as well as his or her current progress (or lack of it) in school. Explain how you would use specific methods or techniques discussed in this chapter, or earlier in the book, to reduce the likelihood that the student would experience failure.

4. Locate community agencies that serve individuals who are at risk. Consider agencies such as telephone hotlines for suicide prevention, child abuse, or drug abuse. Determine the types of services they provide and whether their services are readily available to school-age students.

5. Obtain information that will help you to determine the policy and procedures for identifying and reporting child abuse and neglect in a local school or school district. If possible, also include specific information on the state laws and the penalties for not reporting cases of abuse or neglect in a timely fashion. Prepare a written description of these, with information on the agencies that work with the school to investigate

the reports and enforce the laws related to abuse and neglect.

6. Write a letter to a legislator in which you describe what you consider to be the types of societal changes that would reduce the number of students at risk for failure in school, and tell how legislation could produce or influence those changes. Explain the types of losses that we currently experience (in both human and financial terms) as a result of the high number of students at risk.

Epilogue

Inclusion Today . . . and Tomorrow

Past Mistakes

Is Inclusion Working?

Critical Issues for the Future

Disability is a natural part of the human experience and in no way diminishes the right of individuals to participate in or contribute to society. Improving educational results for children with disabilities is an essential element of our national policy of ensuring equality of opportunity, full participation, independent living, and economic self-sufficiency for individuals with disabilities. (PL 105-17, Individuals with Disabilities Education Act Amendments of 1997, italics added)

Today, inclusion is part of the reality of public schooling in the United States. Although it is not possible to fix an exact date for the birth of this movement, the passage of the Education for All Handicapped Children Act in 1975 stands out as one of the critical starting points. With this law, students with disabilities were guaranteed the right to a free, appropriate public education. That education was to take place in the Least Restrictive Environment (LRE); to the maximum extent appropriate, youngsters with disabilities were to be educated alongside their peers without disabilities. To many educators, this exhortation for placement in the LRE became a mandate for mainstreaming in the 1970s and 1980s and for inclusion in the 1990s.

What has happened as a result of the implementation of PL 94-142 and its amendments? As countless teachers and administrators have asked, is inclusion working? What have we learned, what mistakes have we made, and, most important, how can we make it better? What can be done to improve the effectiveness of inclusion?

PAST MISTAKES

As mainstreaming became a common practice in public schools in the years following the passage of PL 94-142, mistakes were made, and the educational community learned from them. Perhaps the most critical error was the overenthusiastic endorsement of the general education classroom as the optimal placement for all children and youth with disabilities. The evils of special classes as segregated settings that perpetuate labeling and misclassification of culturally and linguistically diverse students were well publicized (e.g., Dunn, 1968). The alternative—placement in the mainstream with special education services as support—appeared a better approach.

In a conscientious attempt to right past wrongs, educators in the late 1970s rushed to place a massive mainstreaming program into operation. However, along the way, several important mistakes were made.

- *Inadequate preparation of mainstreaming participants.* Many programs began without attempts to inform and prepare general education teachers, other school personnel, students without disabilities, and concerned parents of the changes that would occur in the regular classroom. Such preparation is vital not only to counteract negative attitudes toward individuals with disabilities (Alexander & Strain, 1978) but also to provide skills and information to the professionals responsible for the education of students with disabilities.
- *Misunderstanding of the principle of Least Restrictive Environment.* In many cases, the mandate for placement in the LRE was equated with full-time placement in general education classes. The term "Least Restrictive Environment," however, presupposes a continuum of service alternatives for students with disabilities; general education is only one option, albeit the one deemed least restrictive. In the selection of placements, although the restrictiveness of the educational environment should be considered, the primary goal is an appropriate match between the services provided and the student's needs.
- *Inappropriate selection of students for full-time mainstreaming.* Full-time placement in the general education classroom simply is not appropriate for all students with disabilities. Some students require more intensive services, at least for part of the school day or for a portion of their school career. In the early days of mainstreaming, this reality was often overlooked in an overzealous attempt to serve students in a more normalized (and less expensive) educational setting.
- *Insufficient support for mainstreamed students.* Students with disabilities usually require support and assistance from special education professionals to perform adequately and independently in the general education environment. Early mainstreaming programs devoted little effort to this crucial component of the inclusion process.
- *Insufficient support for general education teachers.* General education teachers often require aid and assistance from special educators, particularly when mainstreaming is a new venture. This support has not always been available. Special educators, committed to a variety of other duties, have often lacked the time (and, in some cases, the expertise) to provide appropriate and ongoing consultation services.

• *Inadequate communication among team members.* One component of mainstreaming is the complex network of communication among team members: general education teachers talking with special education teachers, educators building communication links with the home, and older students with disabilities being allowed a voice in their own education. This team approach has not always proved successful. At worst, it has resulted in acrimony as professionals haggle over territorial rights and parents are relegated to the role of passive observers. At best, it has required enormous amounts of time and energy as professionals and parents have learned to work together.

The mistakes of early mainstreaming efforts should not be used as an indictment of the entire movement. Many of the errors made were developmental in nature, a result of hasty implementation in the light of unforeseen contingencies. Inclusion in general education remains one of the appropriate options for educating students with disabilities. Our past experiences serve best as a guide for the improvement of present programs and the launching of better efforts in the future.

IS INCLUSION WORKING?

Determining the effectiveness of inclusion is a complex task. Inclusion affects several constituent groups, and expected benefits vary from group to group. Some of the questions that arise in the evaluation of inclusion are identified here:

1. What effects does placement in the general classroom have on *students with disabilities?* Are such students accepted by peers and teachers? If not, what are the consequences in terms of lowered self-esteem? Is general education classroom instruction (even when augmented by part-time special services) sufficient to bring about the satisfactory progress of learners with disabilities in crucial academic, social, and vocational skill areas? What are the lifelong effects of inclusion? That is, does inclusion in the classroom result in inclusion in the community?
2. How does the inclusion of special students influence the educational experience of *students without disabilities?* What are the social and personal benefits that accrue from interactions with individuals with disabilities in the general education setting? How does instruction change when inclusion occurs? Does instructional quality decline when teachers are forced to divide attention between able and less able students? Or does the overall quality of instruction improve as teachers learn new techniques for the solution of educational problems?
3. Is inclusion a positive experience for *general education teachers* or only another claim placed on the time and energy of overworked professionals? Do teachers become more tolerant of individual differences with the inclusion of students with disabilities? Are sufficient support services available, and do teachers know when and how to use these services? How does inclusion affect the teacher's ability to present instruction, provide practice, ensure mastery, and manage classroom behavior?
4. How has inclusion affected *special education teachers?* How have the roles of special educators changed as the duties of consultation and collaboration were added to the central function of instruction? Have special education resource programs become tutorial services, acting only as an adjunct to the general education program? Is the consultant function one that most special educators perform effectively?

Is inclusion working? Although this is much too simplistic a question, it can be answered. The answer is yes; inclusion is working very well for some students and some teachers in some schools. The answer is also no; it is not working perfectly everywhere for everyone. The literature on inclusion (and its predecessor, mainstreaming) provides more specific answers to questions about effectiveness.

Early Research on Mainstreaming

Much of the research on the effectiveness of mainstreaming predates the federal mandate for service in the LRE. In large part this literature is composed of comparisons of regular class versus special class placement for students with mild retardation (for reviews of this research, see MacMillan, 1982; Strain & Kerr, 1981; Zigler & Muenchow, 1979). Studies of effects on the academic achievement of students with disabilities and their acceptance by peers do not consistently favor either placement. According to Zigler and Muenchow (1979), "The data on the merits of educating retarded children with their nonretarded peers are simply inconclusive" (p. 994).

More recent analyses shed some light on this issue. Using a technique called meta-analysis, Carlberg and Kavale (1980) synthesized the results of 50 studies of special versus general education class placement. These authors reported negative effects of special class placement on pupils with low IQs but more positive effects on students with learning disabilities and those with behavioral disorders. Forness, Kavale, Blum, and Lloyd (1997) contend that the overall results of the 1980 meta-analysis support the conclusion that special class placement is an intervention that doesn't work.

Leinhardt and Pallay (1982) reviewed the results of research on a range of educational environments, including special classes, resource programs, general education classes with support services, and general education classes with no support services. They concluded:

> There were several examples of successful programs for mildly handicapped students that used isolated environments. Among the two isolated environments, resource rooms and self-contained classes, there is weak evidence that the less restrictive of the two, the resource room, may be superior. There are also examples of successful programs which help nonachieving students in the mainstream without removing them from the regular class. (p. 564)

Madden and Slavin (1983) present a somewhat different perspective. Their conclusions from a review of the literature are that "research favors placement in regular classes using individualized instruction or supplemented by well-designed resource programs for the achievement, behavior, and social emotional adjustment of academically handicapped students" (p. 519).

Differences in the interpretation of research results can be attributed to two major factors. First, there is no one optimal placement for all students with disabilities; the search for such a panacea in efficacy research is an impossible quest. For some students with disabilities, the general education class with resource support is most appropriate; for others, the more intensive intervention of a special class is necessary, at least at some point in their educational career. Second, studies of the relative effectiveness of a range of educational placements are asking the wrong question. As Forness and Kavale (1984) point out, "*Where we teach may not be as im-portant as what and how we teach*" (p. 242). That is, it is not the location of the teaching act that is critical but the quality of the curriculum taught and the instructional procedures used to teach it.

Leinhardt and Pallay (1982) share this view, identifying several curricular and instructional factors that promote the achievement of students with disabilities:

- Small class size
- Consistency between curricular goals and instructional activities
- Mastery learning and a formal management system
- Increased time for cognitive activities
- Increased instructional time

These factors are the same as those identified by teacher effectiveness research as important for the achievement of students without disabilities (Brophy & Good, 1986). Good teaching is good teaching, whatever the setting and whoever the audience.

Advocacy Efforts

Two advocacy efforts that marked the late 1980s and early 1990s influenced the direction of school programming for students with disabilities: the Regular Education Initiative (REI) and full inclusion. The REI movement advocated collaboration between special and general education, provision of special services within the regular classroom, and a commitment to serve all students with learning problems, not just those with identified disabilities. In the article considered the position statement for the REI, "Educating Children with Learning Problems: A Shared Responsibility," Will (1986b) called the current service delivery system a "flawed vision of education for our children" (p. 412). She pointed to the large number of students not eligible for special education who experience difficulty in school and exhorted special educators to "establish a partnership with regular education to cooperatively assess the educational needs of students with learning problems and to cooperatively develop effective educational strategies for meeting those needs" (p. 415).

While the REI focused primarily on students with mild disabilities, full inclusion was concerned with a broader population including those with the most severe disabilities. The full inclusion movement began in the field of severe disabilities, and its proponents advocate full-time general education class placement for all students, regardless of the severity of their disability (Biklen, 1985; Lipsky & Gartner, 1989; Thousand & Villa, 1990; York & Vandercook, 1991). Full inclusion is based on the premise that all students have the right to be members of the school community and that no student should be excluded. According to Stainback and Stainback (1990a), "An inclusive school is one that educates all students in the mainstream. . . . An inclusive school is a place where everybody belongs. . . ." (p. 3).

In support of this position, Taylor (1988) points out that the concept of Least Restrictive Environment may be a faulty one for students with severe disabilities. LRE legitimizes restrictive environments and confuses the intensity of service needed with the amount of segregation. Taylor contends that it is not necessary to segregate students with severe disabilities in order to meet their many educational needs. Brown and others (1991) offer a more moderate view. Although the "homeroom" of all students should be a general education classroom, students with severe disabilities should have the opportunity to spend time in other educational environments, depending on their individual needs.

The REI and full inclusion movements have caused much controversy within the field of special education. The major issue appears to be the need for a continuum of special education services, as required by federal laws. Proponents of REI and full inclusion endorsed full-time placement in general education; critics of these movements pointed to the need for a range of service options. As Braaten, Kauffman, Braaten, Polsgrove, and Nelson (1988) comment, "Research clearly does not support the assertion that all students can be managed and taught effectively in regular classrooms" (p. 23). Similar views have been expressed by several of the professional organizations concerned with the education of students with mild disabilities, including the Council for Learning Disabilities (1993), the National Joint Committee on Learning Disabilities (1993), and the Learning Disabilities Association of America (1993). These organizations argue that no one placement option is appropriate for all students.

One of the major fears of special educators who opposed the REI and full inclusion is that students with disabilities will be placed in general education classrooms on a full-time basis without adequate support. Although provision of special services within the general education class is a viable model for some students, others require more intensive intervention. Kauffman, Lloyd, Baker, and Riedel (1995) contend that general education is not the best placement for all students with emotional or behavioral disorders, students who according to these authors have problems that are "severe, pervasive, and chronic—not minor, situational, or transitory" (p. 542). In addition, Schumaker and Deshler (1988) point out that full-time inclusion faces many barriers at the secondary level. In middle school and high school, there are large gaps between the skills of students with mild disabilities and the demands of the instructional setting, and instruction tends to be teacher-centered rather than student-centered. Bringing about the systems changes needed to implement either the REI or full inclusion in secondary schools would be a difficult and lengthy process.

Another consideration is the already difficult task facing the general education teacher as he or she attempts to meet the needs of the diverse group of learners who make up a regular class. The general education classroom includes an increasing number of students at risk for school failure, as chapter 17 has described. It is the view of Kauffman, Gerber, and Semmel (1988) that "more variability than now exists in most regular classrooms is not a reasonable option without additional protected resources for the teacher" (p. 10). In a challenge to advocates of full inclusion, Fuchs and Fuchs (1994) ask:

> Why do full inclusionists believe general education can respond appropriately to all students heretofore receiving special education (as well as Chapter 1 and English as a second language instruction)? How can the mainstream improve so dramatically to incorporate an increase in diversity when it has such obvious difficulty accommodating the student diversity it already has . . . ? (p. 302).

Compounding the increased variability in the general education classroom are trends in educational reform such as higher academic standards, increased graduation requirements, more rigorous evaluation of student achievement, and improved discipline (Braaten & Braaten, 1988; Timar & Kirp, 1989). Such reforms have direct implications for learners with disabilities and students at risk. Braaten and Braaten (1988) suggest that "the increased demand for greater skill development in mathematics, science, foreign language, and technology may benefit the general population but further burden students with special needs who are having difficulty coping with current requirements" (p. 46).

As in most debates, both advocates and critics of REI and full inclusion have made several valid points. More collaboration is needed between general and special education, and the general education classroom is an appropriate full-time placement for many students with disabilities as long as adequate support is provided to those students and their teachers. However, the general education classroom should remain one of a set of placement options for students with disabilities. As Will (1986a) describes it, the basic principle underlying the concept of least restrictive environment "is that placement decisions must be made on an individual basis and that various alternative placements must be available in order to ensure that each handicapped child receives an education which is appropriate to his or her individual needs" (p. 1).

Research on Full Inclusion

The research base for full inclusion is beginning to develop, although it is not yet substantial. In 1997, the *Journal of Special Education* published a special issue on research in severe disabilities. One highlight of this issue was a review by Hunt and Goetz (1997) of the research to date on inclusive programs for students with severe disabilities. Hunt and Goetz identified 19 studies which addressed five areas related to full inclusion: parents' perceptions of full inclusion, school and classroom practices, costs, achievement outcomes for students with severe disabilities, and social outcomes.

Researchers in severe disabilities were most concerned with the social effects of inclusion (Hunt & Goetz, 1997). Six studies on social relationships and friendships were conducted, and results suggest positive outcomes for students with severe disabilities. Only two studies addressed student achievement (Hunt, Staub, Alwell, & Goetz, 1994; Sharpe, York, & Knight, 1994, both as cited in Hunt & Goetz, 1997). Both examined the effects of inclusion on the academic achievement of general education students without disabilities. One also investigated whether students with severe disabilities were able to acquire basic communication skills as part of their participation in cooperative learning experiences in math in general education classrooms (Hunt et al., 1994). Results indicate that the achievement of typical peers is not affected by inclusion and that students with severe disabilities can acquire communication skills in the general education setting. A more recent study (Logan & Keefe, 1997) found that students with severe disabilities included in general education classrooms received more academic instruction, more one-to-one instruction, and more teacher attention than similar students in self-contained special education classrooms.

In contrast, the research on full inclusion of students with mild disabilities tends to focus on academic, rather than social, outcomes. Zigmond and colleagues (1995) report on the results of three large-scale research projects at the University of Pittsburgh, University of Washington, and Vanderbilt University. Each developed a model inclusion program using research-based practices for students with learning disabilities and implemented that program in general education classrooms over a three- or four-year period. All projects "required large investments of time and resources for preparation, planning, training, technical assistance, and support. All three were able to win the cooperation of general education school personnel in a genuine restructuring effort" (p. 539).

Despite these efforts, the academic outcomes for students with learning disabilities were disappointing. Zigmond et al. (1995) report:

> . . . a majority of students with learning disabilities (63%) did not register average or better achievement gains. Even more disconcerting, we found that, for 40% of our LD sample, gains were less than half the size of the grade-level averages. In other words, 40% of students with learning disabilities who were being educated full-time or primarily in general education settings not only were failing to make average gains, but also were slipping behind at what many would consider a disturbing rate." (p. 539)

The authors concluded that "general education settings produce achievement outcomes for students with learning disabilities that are neither desirable nor acceptable" (p. 539).

This body of research places in stark relief the differences between professionals who advocate full inclusion for students with severe disabilities and those who are more skeptical about full-time general education placement for students with milder disabilities. Professionals concerned with severe disabilities focus on social outcomes and the ways in which inclusion can enhance the social acceptance and participation of students with disabilities. Those concerned with milder disabilities, particularly learning disabilities, are more interested in academic outcomes and whether general education programs can foster the development of reading, math, and written language skills for students with problems in these areas. Roberts and Mather (1995) summarize the position of professionals in learning disabilities in these words: "To be anti–full inclusion is not to be pro-exclusion (Lieberman, 1992), but instead to support appropriate, individualized educational programs" (p. 54). That is the position espoused in this book and our rationale for choosing the term *inclusion* (rather than *full inclusion*) to describe the participation of students with disabilities in general education.

CRITICAL ISSUES FOR THE FUTURE

Inclusion is basically an equity issue; it is an expression of the belief that all students, including those with disabilities, have an equal right to participate in the educational experience. Inclusion is also an integration issue, promoting the concept that students should not be excluded from the normal educational program solely on the basis of a physical, cognitive, or emotional disability. The inclusion movement has forced U.S. education to reconsider one of its basic issues: Is education designed to serve only those who learn quickly and easily when placed in the standard instructional environment, or is the goal to educate all students, even those who learn with difficulty?

One important result of inclusion has been to focus attention on students who, although not identified as disabled, encounter failure in the educational system. As students with disabilities joined the ranks of the regular classroom, it soon became apparent that some of their peers without disabilities had similar needs and benefited from similar instructional modifications. As we move into the future, let us attempt to improve the quality of education for all students who are members of general education classrooms—students with disabilities and those without, students who represent the U.S. macroculture and those from diverse cultural and linguistic backgrounds, gifted students and students at risk for school failure. To this end, the following recommendations are offered:

- **Continue to evaluate the practice of inclusion and to identify effective approaches to educating students with disabilities in the general education classroom.** Research should continue to examine the effects of inclusion on all participants. In addition, it is necessary to document effective inclusion strategies and seek out or develop promising new approaches. Determining what has gone wrong can prevent the recurrence of past mistakes; identifying effective practices can increase the probability of future successes.
- **Increase the use of technology and nonprofessional personnel in the general education classroom.** The teacher need not be the only instructional resource in the general education classroom. With proper training, instructional aides, adult volunteers, and peers can substantially increase a given classroom's capability to provide students with opportunities to learn. For this to occur, educators must recognize that direct delivery of instruction is not the only valid role of the teacher. Management of instruction delivered by others is also appropriate and may be the more efficient method to guarantee appropriate educational experiences for all students included in the general education classroom setting. Also often overlooked as aids to the classroom teacher are computers and other technologies. When educators overcome their reluctance to deal with hardware, they discover the potential of such devices not only in the delivery of instruction but also in the management of classroom information.
- **Search out ways to predict the success of inclusion in the general education classroom.** One pressing need in inclusion is the development and refinement of a set of criteria or indicators to determine when inclusion in a particular classroom is likely to be successful for a particular student. However, such judgments cannot be based solely on the student's characteristics; the nature of the classroom environment in which the student is to function must also be considered (Dardig, 1981; Wood & Miederhoff, 1989). To determine the probability of successful inclusion, it is necessary to take into account the characteristics of the classroom, the instructional techniques in use, the capabilities of the general education teacher and his or her skills in adapting instruction to meet individual needs, and the kinds of special education services and personnel

required to support the student's and teacher's efforts.

- **Develop strategies to assist students with disabilities in the generalization and maintenance of important functional skills.** Students with disabilities are often plagued by difficulty in transferring information learned in one setting to another situation or environment. This problem becomes critical when students acquire skills under the tutelage of the special education teacher in the resource room and then are expected to generalize and maintain those skills in the general education classroom setting. Steps toward a solution to this problem will benefit students with disabilities, particularly when emphasis is placed on functional skills that are both currently relevant and important to successful adulthood.

- **Increase efforts to ensure nonbiased assessment.** In an attempt to safeguard against the misidentification of students from diverse groups as disabled, PL 94-142 and IDEA mandate procedures for nondiscriminatory assessment. Evaluation measures are to be administered by trained personnel; validated for the purpose for which they are used; in the student's native language; and nondiscriminatory in terms of race, culture, and disability. Although the requirements of the law are clear, they have been difficult to implement because of the lack of appropriate assessment tools (McLoughlin & Lewis, 1994). Many measures in widespread use lack adequate validation, appropriate instruments have not been developed for all purposes in all languages, and the problem of measuring skills and abilities without cultural bias has not been solved (de Valenzuela & Baca, 1998). Work must continue to assure the fair and unbiased assessment of culturally and linguistically diverse students.

- **Examine current practices in the labeling and classification of students with disabilities.** One unfortunate result of the current system of labeling and classifying special students on the basis of disability has been the erroneous conclusion that students with different labels require totally different treatments (Lovitt, 1982). Although there may be different curriculum concerns for various groups of students, instructional techniques remain the same across different areas of exceptionality. That is, the skills appropriate for students with mild retardation may be different from those appropriate for students with learning disabilities, but the ways in which teachers go about skill instruction do not vary across groups (Hallahan & Kauffman, 1976). To put it simply, good teaching has the same characteristics whether it occurs in science instruction in the general education class, vocational training in the special class, or individualized reading instruction in the resource room. The ideal classification system for students with disabilities would reflect both the salient differences in curriculum and the universality of instructional techniques.

- **Increase the use of direct instruction and other educational approaches with empirical support.** Research on instructional factors affecting student achievement has produced important results, and the teacher's role is quite clear. Students learn when they spend time engaged in the learning process, when learning activities are related to the goals of instruction, and when they have ample opportunity to respond and receive feedback on their responses. Because it promotes these conditions, direct instruction has emerged as an effective strategy for teaching basic academic skills. Although research must continue, educators should begin to discard unsubstantiated teaching methodologies and employ in their stead those approaches with empirical support.

- **Increase the meaningful involvement of parents and students in the inclusion process.** The right to make educational decisions does not belong exclusively to educators. Parents and students are also concerned; and their interest is more immediate, more personal, and more enduring than that of professionals. Education will command higher regard from its constituents when it begins to welcome and not merely permit the continuous participation of these involved individuals.

- **Transform inclusion from a school-based practice to a lifelong condition for individuals with disabilities.** The ultimate test of the inclusion movement is its effect on the adulthood of today's children and adolescents. If students with disabilities mature into competent adults who are included within the workplace and the social fabric of the community, then inclusion has been a success. Although the general education classroom is only the first step, it is a crucial one. If we are successful today, the next generation of teachers and students will regard inclusion of individuals with disabilities in general education as an expected, ordinary, and unexceptional occurrence.

GLOSSARY

Academic problems. Difficulties encountered in the acquisition, maintenance, and generalization of basic school skills and content area subjects.

Acceleration. Progress through the curriculum at an increased rate.

Access. Ease of entry to and travel from place to place within a building or location.

Acquisition. The initial learning of information or skills.

Adapted physical education teacher. A specialist who modifies physical education instruction to meet the needs of students with special needs.

Adaptive behavior. The individual's ability to change in order to cope with the demands of the environment; also called *social competence.*

Advanced organizers. Information presented to students prior to an instructional task as a preview or overview.

Adventitious. Acquired after birth; for example, as a result of illness or accident.

Algorithm. A procedure used to perform an operation in mathematics.

Amplification device. Anything that increases the volume of sound.

Anorexia nervosa. The disorder in which individuals (usually young women) choose to restrict their intake of food to such an extent that they lose 20%–25% of their appropriate body weight.

Antecedent. Anything that precedes or comes before a behavior; it can be manipulated to control the behavior.

Architectural barriers. Obstructions in the physical environment that prevent access.

Assessment. The process by which information about students is gathered in order to make educational decisions.

Assistive technology. Any technology designed specifically for individuals with disabilities; includes add-ons to computer systems and stand-alone devices.

Assistive technology specialist. Individual responsible for advising the team serving students with special needs regarding the selection, acquisition, or use of assistive technology devices that can increase, maintain, or improve the functional capabilities of students with a disability.

At risk. See *Students at risk for school failure.*

Attention deficit hyperactivity disorder (ADHD). A term used in psychiatric classification systems to describe individuals who show poor attention, impulsivity, and sometimes hyperactivity.

Audiologist. A specialist trained in the evaluation of hearing and detection of hearing losses.

Audiometer. A device to assess hearing ability.

Auditory training. Instruction to improve listening skills by teaching individuals with hearing impairments to use as much of their residual hearing as possible.

Augmentative communication. Any system or device designed to enhance the communication abilities of individuals who are nonverbal or whose speech is difficult to understand.

Authoring program. A type of computer program designed to facilitate the teacher's authoring (i.e., writing) of computer-based lessons.

Autism. A disability characterized by extreme withdrawal and poorly developed communication/language skills.

Automaticity. In skill learning, the ability to perform a skill both accurately and quickly without thought.

Baseline data. Information collected about a behavior before an intervention is implemented.

Basic skills. The "tool" subjects of listening, speaking, reading, writing, spelling, and mathematics.

Behavioral disorder. A disability in which students are characterized by inappropriate school behavior.

Blind. A legal designation, often with little educational relevance, that indicates (a) visual acuity of 20/200 or less in the better eye with the best possible correction or (b) a field of vision restricted to an angle subtending an arc of 20 degrees or less.

Blindness. The condition in which so little information is received through the eye that other senses must be used for learning.

Braille. A system of raised dots that can be decoded by touch.

Braillewriter. A machine used to type material in Braille.

Bulimia nervosa. The disorder in which individuals (primarily young women) have recurrent episodes of binge eating that are followed by induced vomiting, using laxatives, fasting, or taking drugs to reduce weight.

Captioned film. A film adapted for viewers who are deaf; dialogue appears in print superimposed on the screen.

Career education. Instruction in the application of basic skills and content area information to problems of daily life, independent living, and vocational independence.

Cerebral palsy. A motor impairment due to damage to the brain, usually occurring before, during, or shortly following birth.

Child abuse and neglect. The physical or mental injury, sexual abuse or exploitation, negligent treatment, or maltreatment of a child under the age of 18 or the age specified by the child protection law of the state in question, by a person who is responsible for the child's welfare, under circumstances which indicate that the child's health or welfare is harmed or threatened.

Choral responding. An instructional technique in which groups of students answer the teacher's question in unison.

Classroom conduct problems. Inappropriate school behaviors that interfere with classroom instruction, impede social interaction with teachers and peers, or endanger others.

Clinical teaching. An instructional technique in which data are gathered both before and during the implementation of an intervention in order to evaluate the effectiveness of that intervention.

Cloze procedure. A method used to determine whether reading material is appropriate for a particular student.

Cognitive training. The behavior change method that attempts to teach students new thinking strategies for controlling their own behavior.

Compensation. The instructional technique in which a student's weaknesses are bypassed.

Computer-assisted instruction. The delivery of instruction to learners via computers.

Conductive hearing loss. A hearing loss caused by interference with the transmission of sound by air or by bone conduction.

Congenital. Present at birth.

Consequence. Anything that follows a behavior; it can be manipulated to control the behavior.

Content area subjects. Bodies of knowledge in the academic curriculum; for example, English and other languages, the sciences, mathematics, and the social sciences.

Contingency contract. A written agreement between a student and a teacher that states what the student must do to earn a specific reward.

Contingent observation. A type of time-out procedure in which a student is removed from a reinforcing event and can watch but not participate.

Cooperative learning. The instructional model in which students work together as a team to complete activities or assignments (in contrast to *competitive learning*, in which each student works alone).

Creativity. The ability to generate novel solutions to specific problems.

Criterion-referenced test. An informal assessment device that measures whether students have mastered the educational goals stated in instructional objectives.

Cultural pluralism. The belief that cultural and linguistic diversity is a strength.

Culturally and linguistically diverse students. Students whose home cultures (and perhaps languages) differ from that of the school. Such students may require special assistance to succeed in general education.

Curriculum-based assessment. The use of current classroom performance as the basis for determining students' educational needs.

Curriculum-based measurement. A type of curriculum-based assessment in which the teacher takes frequent, brief samples of student performance in important skill areas to evaluate progress toward curricular goals. See also *Curriculum-based assessment.*

Curriculum compacting. Eliminating repetition, minimizing drill, and accelerating instruction in basic skills or lower level classes so that gifted students can move to more challenging material.

Database management program. A type of computer program that facilitates the storage of information and its retrieval.

Deaf. See *Deafness.*

Deafness. The condition in which so little information is received through the sense of hearing that other senses must be used for learning.

Delinquency. Offenses against the legal and social standards of society. The term refers to unacceptable behavior on the part of young people, classified by law as underage, that causes them to be charged as law breakers.

Demonstration. The instructional procedure in which a new skill is modeled.

Desktop publishing program. A computer program that allows the user to manipulate both text and graphics.

Diabetes. A disorder of metabolism.

Direct teaching. The teacher's demonstration of appropriate strategies for the performance of a learning task, encouragement of maximal student response opportunities, and provision of frequent systematic feedback on task performance; also called *direct instruction* or *active teaching.*

Discovery learning. An instructional technique in which the teacher presents students with opportunities for learning; skills are not taught directly.

Distractibility. Difficulty in maintaining attention.

Divergent thinking. The production of several solutions to one problem.

Dropout. Any individual over the age of 18 who is no longer enrolled in and has not graduated from high school.

Drug and alcohol abuse. Use of alcohol or other drugs that cause negative reactions or other adverse consequences to the individual user, others, or property.

Duration recording. The system of recording observation data in which the length of time a behavior occurs is noted.

Dysfluency. Difficulty in the production of fluent, rhythmic speech; for example, stuttering.

Early interventionist. A specialist who provides educational services to infants, toddlers, and preschoolers with special needs and to the families of these children. These services may be provided in the home, school, or other settings.

Educationally blind. Having vision impaired to the extent that tactile or auditory materials must be used for reading.

E-mail. Electronic mail; the type of mail sent over the Internet.

Engaged time. The actual time during which students are actively involved and participating in instruction.

Enrichment. The instructional technique in which something is added to the regular school program in order to enrich it.

Epilepsy. A convulsive disorder of the central nervous system.

Error analysis. The technique in which student work samples are studied for patterns of errors.

Etiology. Cause.

Event recording. The system of recording observation data in which the number of times a behavior occurs is noted.

Extinction. A procedure used to decrease the occurrence of a behavior by removing reinforcers that have previously followed the behavior.

Facilitated communication. A controversial augmentative communication strategy in which a facilitator provides physical support to a nonverbal person as he or she types or points to letters. See also *Augmentative communication.*

Flexible grouping. A method of instructional grouping in which arrangements of students change frequently and placement decisions are made on a variety of criteria (e.g., skills, interests, proximity).

Full inclusion. Full-time integration in general education classrooms of all students with special needs, regardless of the severity of their disabilities. See also *Inclusion.*

Functional analysis. A systematic process designed to collect data to help educators (a) understand a problem behavior and (b) develop effective methods for modifying the behavior.

Functional skills. Important skills selected for instruction because of their usefulness in everyday life.

Generalization. The application or transfer of learned material to similar situations and problems.

Gifted and talented students. Exceptional students with intellectual gifts or special abilities in areas such as the arts and leadership.

Giftedness. Superior intellect; it can be accompanied by creative ability.

Group contingencies. Reinforcement provided to members of a group dependent on whether the entire group has reached a criterion level established by the teacher.

Guided practice. The performance of a task under supervision; feedback, correction, and confirmation are immediate.

Habilitation. The instructional approach directed toward the development of the critical skills necessary for successful adulthood.

Hard of hearing. Characterized by a condition in which hearing, although impaired, can be used as one of the senses for learning.

Hearing impairment. A disability characterized by a decrease in the ability to hear; see also *Deafness* and *Hard of hearing.*

Heterogeneous grouping. A method of instructional grouping that places together students whose instructional needs are somehow dissimilar.

High interest–low vocabulary. Reading materials that appeal to students who read at a lower grade level than that expected for their age.

Hyperactivity. Excessive activity.

Hypermedia. A computer program in which the user, not the program, determines the sequence of events; the user decides which media (text, voice, video, etc.) to access and when to access them.

Impulsivity. Lack of reflectivity; activity without careful thought and reflection.

Inclusion. Meaningful participation of students with special needs in general education classrooms and programs.

Independent practice. The performance of a skill without supervision; feedback is delayed.

Individualized Education Program (IEP). A written educational plan that specifies a special student's current levels of educational performance, annual goals, and short-term instructional objectives; prepared by a team that includes the student's parent(s), teacher(s), and, if appropriate, the student.

Individualized instruction. Instruction designed to meet the needs of each student; it can be group instruction or tutorial as long as a high proportion of correct responses is maintained.

Informal assessment. The process of gathering information about students with measures and techniques such as inventories, criterion-referenced tests, and observation; teachers often design their own informal assessment strategies.

Informal reading inventory. An informal assessment device that aids in determining a student's instructional reading level.

Information processing. The method by which persons receive, store, and express information; also called *psychological processing.*

Instruction. The teaching process. See also *Direct teaching* and *Individualized instruction.*

Instructional environment. In the context of the classroom, the procedures, materials, and equipment used by the teacher to increase student performance.

Instructional technology. Any technology that can support the teaching-learning process; see also *Assistive technology.*

Internet. A worldwide computer network that includes e-mail, the World Wide Web, and other resources.

Interval recording. The system of recording observation data in which the occurrence or nonoccurrence of a behavior within a specific time interval is noted.

Inventory. An informal assessment device that samples a variety of skills within a subject matter area; for example, an informal reading inventory.

Itinerant teacher. A professional who travels from school to school rather than providing instruction at one school site.

Knowledge of results. Information provided to students about the accuracy of their responses.

Language. The ability to communicate using symbols.

Learning center. An area of the classroom designed for use of self-instructional materials for independent practice.

Learning disability. A disorder in the ability to process information that can result in attention, perception, or memory deficits. Students with learning disabilities experience difficulty in school learning despite adequate hearing, vision, and intelligence.

Learning strategies. Methods students use to acquire, rehearse, organize, and recall information.

Least Restrictive Environment (LRE). The most appropriate educational placement that is closest to general education.

Listserv. An electronic mailing list to which a user subscribes to receive e-mail messages related to a specific topic.

Local education agency. Typically a local school district that is governed by a public board of education to provide public elementary and/or secondary schools in a city, township, or county.

Low vision. The condition in which vision, although impaired, can be used as one of the senses for learning.

Low-vision aid. Any device that aids vision by magnification.

Mainstreaming. The inclusion of students with special needs in the general educational program for any part of the school day. See also *Inclusion.*

Maintenance. The recall of information previously learned.

Mapping. An instructional strategy to help students organize ideas for writing; students draw a map showing the relationship between the main topic and key words.

Mediated instruction. Any instructional procedure that includes the use of media.

Medically fragile. Students with a chronic medical condition that requires ongoing medical management and accommodation during the school day.

Mental retardation. A disability in which subaverage general intellectual functioning is associated with deficits in adaptive behavior.

Mobility. The ability to move from place to place.

Modeling. The reinforcement of another individual, the model, for exhibiting the desired behavior in the presence of the target student. When the target student imitates the desired behavior, he or she is then reinforced.

Modem. A device that links one computer to another over telephone lines; in most cases, modems link home or school computers to the Internet or a commercial Internet service provider.

Multicultural education. The instructional approach that emphasizes the value of diverse cultures.

Multimedia. Computers and computer software that present information to the user through a variety of media such as photos, video, voice, and music.

Narrative recording. A system of observation in which the observer describes all behaviors that occur.

Negative attention. Use of a negative verbal or nonverbal response (e.g., "Stop" or a frown) that indicates disapproval of a student's behavior. The procedure attempts to reduce the behavior quickly without interfering with ongoing classroom activities.

Negative reinforcement. A procedure used to increase the occurrence of a behavior by following it with the removal of an aversive event or condition.

Newsgroup. An online discussion group where users can read and post messages related to a specific topic.

Norm-referenced test. A test designed to compare the performance of one student with that of students in the norm group of the same age or grade; used to determine whether students have significant problems in relation to peers.

Obesity. The condition in which the body weight of an individual exceeds the ideal weight by 20% or more.

Occupational therapist. A specialist who provides therapy and instruction to students with motor disabilities.

Operant behavior. A behavior that is learned and therefore under the voluntary control of the individual.

Orientation. The determination of one's position in space, especially in relation to objects or reference points in the environment.

Partially sighted. Having vision that is impaired but can be used as one of the senses for learning.

Peer tutor. A student who provides instruction to another student.

Permanent product recording. The system of recording observation data in which permanent products (such as written assignments, videotapes, and audiotapes) are evaluated.

Phonology. The sound system of language.

Physical and health impairments. Physical disabilities and medical conditions that result in chronic health problems.

Physical environment. In the context of the school, the classroom and its furnishings.

Physical therapist. A specialist who provides treatment under the supervision of a physician to students with motor disabilities.

Portfolio assessment. The process of gathering information about students by assembling samples of their work over time.

Positive reinforcement. A procedure used to increase the occurrence of a behavior by following it with a pleasant or positive event.

Practice. The performance of a learned skill. See also *Guided practice* and *Independent practice.*

Pragmatics. The use of language; language within the context of communication.

Premack principle. The practice of providing a reinforcement after the completion of a less desired task; for example, if Joan takes out the garbage, then she may watch television.

Prereferral interventions. Modifications of the general education program designed to promote a student's success in the regular classroom and prevent referral for services such as special education.

Problem solving. The process of gathering information about a problem, proposing solutions, selecting a solution, and evaluating the result.

Programmed instruction. A method of instruction in which learners progress at their own pace through small, incremental steps that provide immediate feedback about response accuracy.

Prompt. Any feature added to learning tasks that assists students in task performance. Prompts can be verbal, visual, or physical.

Psychosis. A type of emotional disturbance characterized by lack of contact with reality.

Punishment. A procedure used to decrease the occurrence of a behavior by following it with the presentation of an aversive event.

Readability measure. A method of determining the reading level of a given material.

Reciprocal teaching. An approach to teaching reading comprehension skills in which teachers engage students in dialogues about texts.

Referral. The process by which a student is identified for study; it can result in consideration for special education services.

Reinforcement. Anything that increases the probability of occurrence of a behavior. See also *Positive reinforcement* and *Negative reinforcement.*

Reinforcement menu. A listing of reinforcers and the number of points or tokens needed to purchase each; it is used in a token economy system.

Related services. Auxiliary services such as psychological services for assessment, transportation, or physical therapy that are available to help students with disabilities derive maximum benefit from special education.

Remediation. The instructional approach that focuses on correcting the weaknesses of the student.

Repeated readings. An instructional technique in which students read a passage several times to increase comprehension.

Resource room. A service arrangement in which special education is provided to students for a portion of the school day. Typically the student is placed in a general education classroom and visits the resource room only for short periods.

Response cost. A mild form of punishment in which an inappropriate behavior is followed by the loss or withdrawal of earned reinforcers or privileges.

Seizure. The loss or alteration of consciousness due to a convulsive disorder.

Self-correcting materials. Instructional materials that provide the student with the correct response so that answers can be checked for accuracy.

Self-instruction. A procedure in which students learn specific strategies to talk themselves through problem situations.

Self-instructional learning materials. Instructional materials that provide feedback to students and thus allow independent practice.

Self-monitoring. Observing, recording, and evaluating one's own behavior; for example, students might observe/record the number of times they leave their chairs, graph the data, and review the graph daily to determine whether they are improving.

Semantics. The aspects of language related to meaning.

Sensorineural hearing loss. A hearing loss caused by impairment of the auditory nerve.

Sequence analysis. A system of observation in which the observer describes each behavior and attempts to identify its antecedent and consequence.

Sexually transmitted diseases (STDs). Diseases such as chlamydia, genital warts, gonorrhea, syphilis, herpes, and acquired immune deficiency syndrome (AIDS) that are transmitted most frequently through sexual contact with an individual who has the disease, although newborns may be infected *in utero* or during passage through the birth canal.

Shaping. The reinforcement of successive approximations or small, progressive steps toward a desired behavior.

Sheltered English. A teaching technique for students learning English in which content area lessons include systematic instruction in English language skills.

Sign language. The system of manual communication in which gestures express thoughts.

Simulation. A type of computer program that allows students to participate in an experience resembling a real-life or historic event.

Skill-specific group. A homogeneous instructional group made up of students who require instruction in the same area.

Slate and stylus. A small hand-held device used to write Braille.

Snellen Chart. A measure used in screening for visual acuity problems.

Sociometric measure. An assessment device used to determine how students perceive their peers.

Special class. A service arrangement in which students with special needs are grouped together in a self-contained class; students may leave the special class for short periods to participate in general education activities.

Special education. Instruction that is specially designed to meet the unique educational needs of students with disabilities.

Special educator. A professional educator trained to meet the instructional needs of students with special needs; usually, an educator who serves students with disabilities or gifted and talented students.

Special students. Those students with special learning needs who require instructional adaptations in order to learn successfully; includes students with disabilities, gifted and talented students, culturally and linguistically diverse students, and students at risk for school failure.

Speech. The vehicle by which thoughts are expressed in oral communication.

Speech and language impairments. Disabilities characterized by deficits in speech, receptive language, and/or expressive language.

Speech-language pathologist. A specialist who serves students with speech and language impairments.

Speechreading. The process of decoding speech by watching the speaker's face.

Students at risk for school failure. General education students who show poor achievement and/or are likely to drop out of school.

Students with disabilities. Students with special learning needs due to physical, sensory, cognitive, or emotional impairments. Included are students with learning disabilities, mental retardation, behavioral disorders, speech and language impairments, physical and health impairments, visual impairments, hearing impairments, autism, traumatic brain injury, and multiple disabilities.

Study skill problems. Inappropriate classroom behaviors that interfere with the student's own academic performance or with the teacher's ability to assess academic progress.

Substance abuse. The voluntary intake of chemicals (e.g., alcohol, narcotics) that can produce adverse social and physical consequences.

Supplementary aids and services. Supports provided to students with disabilities to enable them to participate in general education programs.

Syntax. The grammatical aspects of language.

Talented. Having a special ability in an area such as music or leadership.

Task analysis. The process of breaking down a task into smaller subtasks.

Team-based contingencies. Reinforcement provided to team members based on the performance of their team; teams can compete against each other or against a preset criterion level.

Technology. See *Assistive technology* and *Instructional technology.*

Time management. The organization and scheduling of time for its most effective use.

Time-out. A mild form of punishment in which either the individual is removed from an event that is reinforcing or reinforcement is withdrawn for a specified period of time.

Token economy. A behavior change system in which students are presented with tokens rather than reinforcers after the occurrence of a desired behavior; the tokens can be cashed in for reinforcers at a later time.

Total communication. A method of communication combining oral techniques (speech and speechreading) and manual techniques (fingerspelling and sign language).

Transition. Process of preparing students to meet the challenges of adulthood including those involved in postsecondary education, vocational pursuits, and home and community life.

Traumatic brain injury. A disability caused by injury or accident involving damage to the brain.

Unit approach. A method of organizing the curriculum by important life themes.

Visual impairment. A limitation in the ability to see.

Vocational rehabilitation counselor. A specialist who assists individuals with disabilities in obtaining employment.

Volunteer. A classroom assistant from the community.

Word processing program. A type of computer program that facilitates written composition by making it easy to manipulate text.

World Wide Web (WWW). That portion of the Internet in which information is presented not only in text but also in graphics; audio, video, and other multimedia features are sometimes available.

REFERENCES

Abramowitz, A. J., & O'Leary, S. G. (1991). Behavior interventions for the classroom: Implications for students with ADHD. *School Psychology Review, 20,* 221–235.

Affleck, J. Q., Lowenbraun, S., & Archer, A. L. (1980). *Teaching the mildly handicapped in the regular classroom* (2nd ed.). Columbus, OH: Merrill Publishing Company.

Aiello, B. (1979). Hey, what's it like to be handicapped? *Education Unlimited, 1*(2), 28–31.

Alcohol use. (1989, September 27). *Los Angeles Times,* p. A1.

Alexander, C., & Strain, P. S. (1978). A review of educators' attitudes toward handicapped children and the concept of mainstreaming. *Psychology in the Schools, 15,* 390–396.

Algozzine, B., Christenson, S. L., & Ysseldyke, J. E. (1982). Probabilities associated with the referral to placement process. *Teacher Education and Special Education, 5*(3), 19–23.

Alley, G., & Foster, C. (1978). Nondiscriminatory testing of minority and exceptional children. *Focus on Exceptional Children, 9*(8), 1–14.

Allinder, R. M., & Peterson, R. L. (1992). Readability, interest, and content of current mainstreaming textbooks. *Teacher Education and Special Education, 15,* 202–210.

Alves, A. J., & Gottlieb, J. (1986). Teacher interactions with mainstreamed handicapped students and their nonhandicapped peers. *Learning Disability Quarterly, 9,* 77–83.

American Association of Colleges for Teacher Education, Commission on Multicultural Education. (1973). No one model American. *Journal of Teacher Education, 24,* 264–265.

American Association on Mental Retardation. (1992). *Mental retardation: Definition, classification, and systems of supports* (9th ed.). Washington, DC: Author.

American Federation of Teachers. (1996). *Making standards matter 1996* [Online]. Available: http://www.aft.org//research/reports/standard/index.htm#Table

American Psychiatric Association. (1994). *Diagnostic and statistical manual of mental disorders* (4th ed.). Washington, DC: Author.

American Speech-Language-Hearing Association. (1995, March). Position statement and guidelines for acoustics in educational settings. *Asha, 37* (Suppl. 14), 15–19.

American Speech-Language-Hearing Association. (1997). *American Speech-Language-Hearing Association answers questions about stuttering* [Online]. Available: http://www.asha.org/consumers/brochures/stuttering.htm [1997, December 13].

American Speech-Language-Hearing Association. (n.d.). *Speech and language disorders and the speech-language pathologist.* Rockville, MD: Author.

America 2000. (1990). Washington, DC: U.S. Department of Education.

Andersen, M., Nelson, L. R., Fox, R. G., & Gruber, S. E. (1988). Integrating cooperative learning and structured learning: Effective approaches to teaching social skills. *Focus on Exceptional Children, 20*(9), 1–8.

Aragon, J. (1973). Cultural conflict and cultural diversity in education. In L. A. Bransford, L. M. Baca, & K. Lane (Eds.), *Cultural diversity and the exceptional child* (pp. 24–31). Reston, VA: The Council for Exceptional Children.

Aragon, J., & Marquez, L. (1973). Highlights of Institute on Language and Culture: Spanish-speaking component. In L. A. Bransford, L. M. Baca, & K. Lane (Eds.), *Cultural diversity and the exceptional child* (pp. 20–21). Reston, VA: The Council for Exceptional Children.

Arc. (1993). *Introduction to mental retardation* [Online]. Available: http://thearc.org/faqs/mrqa.html [1997, November 30].

Archer, A. L., & Gleason, M. M. (1989a). *Design and delivery of lessons.* Paper presented at the annual meeting of The Council for Exceptional Children, San Francisco.

Archer, A. L., & Gleason, M. M. (1989b). *Skills for school success.* North Billerica, MA: Curriculum Associates.

Archer, A. L., & Gleason, M. M. (1995). Skills for school success. In P. T. Cegelka & W. H. Berdine (Eds.), *Effective instruction for students with learning difficulties* (pp. 227–263). Boston: Allyn & Bacon.

Archer, A., Gleason, M. M., Englert, C. S., & Isaacson, S. (1995). Meeting individual instructional needs. In P. T. Cegelka & W. H. Berdine (Eds.), *Effective instruction for students with learning difficulties* (pp. 195–225). Boston: Allyn & Bacon.

Archer, A., Gleason, M. M., & Isaacson, S. (1995). Effective instructional delivery. In P. T. Cegelka & W. H. Berdine (Eds.), *Effective instruction for students with learning difficulties* (pp. 161–194). Boston: Allyn & Bacon.

Arkansas Enterprises for the Blind. (n.d.). *10 rules of courtesy to the blind.* Little Rock: Author.

Artiles, A. J., & Trent, S. C. (1994). Overrepresentation of minority students in special education: A continuing debate. *Journal of Special Education, 27,* 410–437.

Asher, S. R., & Taylor, A. R. (1981). Social outcomes of mainstreaming: Sociometric assessment and beyond. *Exceptional Education Quarterly, 1*(4), 13–30.

Ashton, T. M. (1997). *Making technology work in the inclusive classroom.* Unpublished manuscript, San Diego State University.

Ashton-Coombs, T. M., & James, H. F. (1995). Including all of us: A K–8 bibliography. *California English, 31*(2), 12–13, 26–27.

Association for Retarded Citizens. (n.d.). *The truth about mental retardation.* Arlington, TX: Author.

Autism Society of America. (1996). *What is autism?* [Online]. Available: http://www.autism-society.org/autism.html#symptoms [1997, December 14].

Axelrod, S., & Bailey, S. A. (1979). Drug treatment for hyperactivity: Controversies, alternatives, and guidelines. *Exceptional Children, 45,* 544–550.

Axelrod, S., Hall, R. V., & Tams, A. (1972). *A comparison of common seating arrangements in the classroom.* Paper presented at the meeting of the Kansas Symposium on Behavior Analysis in Education, Lawrence.

Baca, L. (1998). Bilingualism and bilingual education. In L. M. Baca & H. T. Cervantes (Eds.), *The bilingual special education interface* (3rd ed.) (pp. 26–45). Upper Saddle River, NJ: Merrill/Prentice Hall.

Baca, L. M., & Almanza, E. (1991). *Language minority students with disabilities.* Reston, VA: The Council for Exceptional Children.

Baca, L., & de Valenzuela, J. S. (1998). Background and rationale for bilingual special education. In L. M. Baca & H. T. Cervantes (Eds.), *The bilingual special education interface* (3rd ed.) (pp. 2–25). Upper Saddle River, NJ: Merrill/Prentice Hall.

Bacon, E. H., & Schulz, J. B. (1991). A survey of mainstreaming practices. *Teacher Education and Special Education, 14,* 144–149.

Baldwin, A. Y. (1991). Ethnic and cultural issues. In N. Colangelo & G. A. Davis (Eds.), *Handbook of gifted education* (pp. 416–427). Boston: Allyn & Bacon.

Banbury, M. (1987). Testing and grading mainstreamed students in regular education subjects. In A. Rotatori, M. Banbury, & R. A. Fox (Eds.), *Issues in special education* (pp. 177–186). Mountain View, CA: Mayfield.

Barone, T. (1989). Ways of being at risk: The case of Billy Charles Barnett. *Phi Delta Kappan, 71,* 147–151.

Bauer, A. M., & Shea, T. M. (1989). *Teaching exceptional students in your classroom.* Boston: Allyn & Bacon.

Bauwens, J., & Hourcade, J. J. (1989). Hey, would you just LISTEN. *Teaching Exceptional Children, 21*(4), 61.

Becker, W. C., Englemann, S., & Thomas, D. R. (1975). *Teaching 2: Cognitive learning and instruction.* Chicago: Science Research Associates.

Bender, W. N. (1997). *Understanding ADHD: A practical guide for teachers and parents.* Upper Saddle River, NJ: Merrill/Prentice Hall.

Bender, W. N., & Mathes, M. Y. (1995). Students with ADHD in the inclusive classroom: A hierarchical approach to strategy selection. *Intervention in School and Clinic, 30,* 226–234.

Berdine, W. H., & Blackhurst, A. E. (Eds.). (1985). *An introduction to special education* (2nd ed.). Boston: Little, Brown.

Berdine, W. H., & Cegelka, P. T. (1980). *Teaching the trainable retarded.* Columbus, OH: Merrill Publishing Company.

Berg, F. (1987). *Facilitating classroom listening: A handbook for teachers of normal and hard of hearing students.* Austin, TX: PRO-ED.

Berlin, G., & Sum, A. (1988). *Toward a more perfect union: Basic skills, poor families, and our economic future.* New York: Ford Foundation.

Berliner, D. C., & Biddle, B. J. (1995). *The manufactured crisis: Myths, fraud, and the attack on America's public schools.* Reading, MA: Addison-Wesley.

Bettinger, M. M. (1989). Educating the pregnant teen. *CTA Action, 28*(2), 9.

Biddle, B. J. (1997). Foolishness, dangerous nonsense, and real correlates of state differences in achievement. *Phi Delta Kappan, 79,* 9–13.

Biklen, D. (1985). *Achieving the complete school.* New York: Teachers College Press.

Biklen, D. (1990). Communication unbound: Autism and praxis. *Harvard Educational Review, 60,* 291–314.

Biklen, D., Morton, M. W., Gold, D., Berrigan, C., & Swaminathan, S. (1992). Facilitated communication: Implications for individuals with autism. *Topics in Language Disorders, 12*(4), 1–28.

Biklen, D., & Schubert, A. (1991). New words: The communication of students with autism. *Remedial and Special Education, 12*(6), 46–57.

Binkard, B. (1985). A successful handicap awareness program—run by special parents. *Teaching Exceptional Children, 18*(1), 12–16.

Blake, K. A. (1981). *Educating exceptional pupils.* Reading, MA: Addison-Wesley.

Blankenship, C., & Lilly, M. S. (1981). *Mainstreaming students with learning and behavior problems.* New York: Holt, Rinehart & Winston.

Boning, R. A. (1990). *Specific skill series* (4th ed.). Baldwin, NY: Barnell Loft.

Bonjean, L. M., & Rittenmeyer, D. C. (1987). *Teenage parenthood: The school's response.* Bloomington, IN: Phi Delta Kappa Educational Foundation.

Bootel, J. (JACKIB@cec.sped.org). (1997, November 12). *CEC model letter re: discipline.* E-mail to Alliance 2000 (alliance@unm.edu).

Bormuth, J. R. (1968). The cloze readability procedure. *Elementary English, 45,* 429–436.

Bossert, S. T., & Barnett, B. G. (1981). *Grouping for instruction: A catalog of arrangements.* San Francisco: Far West Laboratory for Educational Research and Development. (ERIC Document Reproduction Service No. ED 201 052)

Bowen, E. (1988, February 1). Getting tough. *Time,* pp. 52–58.

Bower, E. M. (1969). *Early identification of emotionally handicapped children in school* (2nd ed.). Springfield, IL: Thomas.

Braaten, B., & Braaten, S. (1988). Reform: For everyone? *Teaching Exceptional Children, 21*(1), 46–47.

Braaten, S., Kauffman, J. M., Braaten, B., Polsgrove, L., & Nelson, C. M. (1988). The regular education initiative: Patent medicine for behavioral disorders. *Exceptional Children, 55,* 21–27.

Brady, M. P., & McEvoy, M. A. (1989). Social skills training as an integration strategy. In R. Gaylord-Ross (Ed.), *Integration strategies for students with handicaps* (pp. 213–231). Baltimore: Brookes.

Brain Injury Association (n.d.). *The costs and causes of traumatic brain injury* [Online]. Available: http://www. biausa.org/ [1997, November 21].

Brigance, A. H. (1981). *BRIGANCE® diagnostic inventory of essential skills.* North Billerica, MA: Curriculum Associates.

Brigance, A. H. (1983). *BRIGANCE® diagnostic comprehensive inventory of basic skills.* North Billerica, MA: Curriculum Associates.

Brigance, A. H. (1991). *BRIGANCE® diagnostic inventory of early development-Revised.* North Billerica, MA: Curriculum Associates.

Brinker, R. P. (1985). Interactions between severely mentally retarded students and other students in integrated and segregated public school settings. *American Journal of Mental Deficiency, 89,* 587–594.

Brolin, D. E. (1986). *Life centered career education: A competency based approach* (Rev. ed.). Reston, VA: The Council for Exceptional Children.

Brooks-Gunn, J., & Furstenberg, F. F., Jr. (1989). Adolescent sexual behavior. *American Psychologist, 44,* 249–257.

Brophy, J. E., & Good, T. L. (1986). Teacher behavior and student achievement. In M. C. Wittrock (Ed.), *Handbook of research on teaching* (3rd ed., pp. 328–375). New York: Macmillan.

Brown, L., & Hammill, D. D. (1990). *Behavior rating profile* (2nd ed.). Austin, TX: PRO-ED.

Brown, L., Schwarz, P., Udvari-Solner, A., Kampschroer, E. F., Johnson, F., Jorgensen, J., & Gruenewald, L. (1991). How much time should students with severe intellectual disabilities spend in regular education classrooms and elsewhere? *Journal of The Association for Persons with Severe Handicaps, 16*(1), 39–47.

Bruininks, R. H. (1977). *Manual for the Bruininks-Oseretsky test of motor proficiency.* Circle Pines, MN: American Guidance Service.

Bruininks, R. H., Thurlow, M. L., & Gilman, C. J. (1987). Adaptive behavior and mental retardation. *Journal of Special Education, 21*(1), 69–88.

Bruininks, R. H., Woodcock, R. W., Weatherman, R. F., & Hill, B. K. (1996). *Scales of independent behavior-Revised.* Chicago: Riverside Publishing.

Bryan, T. (1997). Assessing the personal and social status of students with learning disabilities. *Learning Disabilities Research & Practice, 12,* 63–76.

Bryan, T. H., & Bryan, J. H. (1977). The social-emotional side of learning disabilities. *Behavioral Disorders, 2,* 141–145.

Bryan, T. H., Pearl, R., Donahue, M., Bryan, J. H., & Pflaum, S. (1983). The Chicago Institute for the Study of Learning Disabilities. *Exceptional Education Quarterly, 4*(1), 1–22.

Bryan, T. H., & Pflaum, S. (1978). Social interactions of learning disabled children: A linguistic, social, and cognitive analysis. *Learning Disability Quarterly, 1*(3), 70–79.

Bulgren, J. A., & Carta, J. J. (1992). Examining the instructional contexts of students with learning disabilities. *Exceptional Children, 59,* 182–191.

Burron, A., & Claybaugh, A. L. (1977). *Basic concepts in reading instruction* (2nd ed.). Columbus, OH: Merrill Publishing Company.

Butler, O. B. (1989). Early help for kids at risk: Our nation's best investment. *NEA Today, 7*(6), 50–53.

Byrne, C. E. (1981, September). Diabetes in the classroom. *ECO,* pp. 5, 19. (Available from the National Education Association)

Byrom, E., & Katz, G. (Eds.). (1991). *HIV prevention and AIDS education: Resources for special educators.* Reston, VA: The Council for Exceptional Children.

Calculator, S. N. (1992). Perhaps the emperor has clothes afterall: A response to Biklen. *American Journal of Speech Language Pathology, 1*(2), 18–20.

California Association for Neurologically Handicapped Children. (1980). *If they aren't learning, don't write them off.* Sacramento: Author.

California Governor's Committee for Employment of Disabled Persons. (1990). *Language guide on disability.* Sacramento: State of California, Employment Development Department.

California Teachers of English to Speakers of Other Languages. (1992). *Catesol position paper on specially-designed academic instruction in English (sheltered instruction)* [Online]. Available: http://www.catesol. org/shelter.html [1997, December 16].

Campbell, N. J., Dodson, J. E., & Bost, J. M. (1985). Educator perceptions of behavior problems of mainstreamed students. *Exceptional Children, 51,* 298–303.

Campbell, P. H. (1989). Students with physical disabilities. In R. Gaylord-Ross (Ed.), *Integration strategies for students with handicaps* (pp. 53–76). Baltimore: Brookes.

Capuzzi, D. (1988). Adolescent suicide: Prevention and intervention. In J. Carlson & J. Lewis (Eds.), *Counseling the adolescent: Individual, family, and school interventions* (pp. 41–56). Denver: Love.

Carlberg, C., & Kavale, K. A. (1980). The efficacy of special versus regular class placement for exceptional children: A meta-analysis. *Journal of Special Education, 14,* 295–309.

Cartledge, G., Frew, T., & Zaharias, J. (1985). Social skill needs of mainstreamed students: Peer and teacher perceptions. *Learning Disability Quarterly, 8,* 132–140.

Cartledge, G., & Milburn, J. F. (Eds.). (1986). *Teaching social skills to children: Innovative approaches* (2nd ed.). New York: Pergamon.

Cartledge, G., & Milburn, J. F. (1995). *Teaching social skills to children: Innovative approaches* (3rd ed.). Boston: Allyn & Bacon.

Cartwright, G. P., Cartwright, C. A., & Ward, M. E. (1989). *Educating special learners* (3rd ed.). Belmont, CA: Wadsworth.

Cartwright, G. P., Cartwright, C. A. & Ward, M. E. (1995). Educating special learners (4th ed.). Belmont, CA: Wadsworth.

Casto, G., & Mastropieri, M. A. (1986). The efficacy of early intervention programs: A meta-analysis. *Exceptional Children, 52,* 417–424.

Caton, H. R. (1993). Students with visual impairments. In A. E. Blackhurst & W. H. Berdine (Eds.), *An introduction to special education* (3rd ed., pp. 313–349). New York: HarperCollins.

Cegelka, P. T. (1988). Multicultural considerations. In E. W. Lynch & R. B. Lewis (Eds.), *Exceptional children and adults* (pp. 545–587). Glenview, IL: Scott, Foresman.

Cegelka, P. T. (1995a). An overview of effective education for students with learning problems. In P. T. Cegelka & W. H. Berdine (Eds.), *Effective instruction for students with learning difficulties* (pp. 1–17). Boston: Allyn & Bacon.

Cegelka, P. T. (1995b). Structuring the classroom for effective instruction. In P. T. Cegelka & W. H. Berdine (Eds.), *Effective instruction for students with learning difficulties* (pp. 135–160). Boston: Allyn & Bacon.

Centers for Disease Control. (1996). AIDS among children: U.S. *MMWR Weekly Report, 45*(46), 7–8.

Centers for Disease Control & Prevention. (1993). *Mortality trends, causes of death, and related risk behaviors among U.S. adolescents.* Atlanta, GA: U.S. Department of Health and Human Services.

Centers for Disease Control & Prevention. (1995). *Youth risk behavior surveillance report, 1995.* Atlanta, GA: U.S. Department of Health and Human Services.

Chalfant, J. C., & Pysh, M. (1989). Teacher assistance teams: Five descriptive studies on 96 teams. *Remedial and Special Education, 10*(6), 49–58.

Chall, J. S. (1967). *Learning to read: The great debate.* New York: McGraw-Hill.

Chall, J. S. (1977). *Reading 1967–1977: A decade of change and promise.* Bloomington, IN: Phi Delta Kappa Educational Foundation.

Chall, J. S. (1983). *Learning to read: The great debate* (Updated ed.). New York: McGraw-Hill.

Chall, J. S. (1989). *Learning to Read: The Great Debate* 20 years later—A response to "Debunking the great phonics myth." *Phi Delta Kappan, 70,* 521–538.

Chan, S. (1992). Families with Asian roots. In E. W. Lynch & M. J. Hanson (Eds.), *Developing cross-cultural competence* (pp. 181–257). Baltimore: Brookes.

Cheng, L. L. (1991). *Assessing Asian language performance.* Oceanside, CA: Academic Communication Associates.

Chideya, F. (1993, February 28). The language of suspicion. *Los Angeles Times Magazine,* pp. 34–36, 52, 54.

Chinn, P. C., & Hughes, S. (1987). Representation of minority students in special education classes. *Remedial and Special Education, 8*(4), 41–46.

Christenson, S. L., & Ysseldyke, J. E. (1986). *Academic responding time as a function of instructional arrangements.* Paper presented at the annual meeting of the American Educational Research Association, San Francisco. (ERIC Document Reproduction Service No. ED 271 917)

Close, D. W., Irvin, L. K., Taylor, V. E., & Agosta, J. (1981). Community living skills instruction for mildly retarded persons. *Exceptional Education Quarterly, 2*(1), 75–85.

Cochran, C., Feng, H., Cartledge, G., & Hamilton, S. (1993). The effects of cross-age tutoring on the academic achievement, social behaviors, and self-perceptions of low-achieving African-American males with behavioral disorders. *Behavioral Disorders, 18,* 292–302.

Cohen, D. L. (1992, March 11). Inadequate state funding seen impeding school readiness. *Education Week,* p. 13.

Cohen, S. B., & Hart-Hester, S. (1987). Time management strategies. *Teaching Exceptional Children, 20*(1), 56–57.

Colarusso, R. P., & Hammill, D. D. (1972). *Motor-free visual perception test.* San Rafael, CA: Academic Therapy Publications.

Coleman, M. C. (1986). *Behavior disorders.* Englewood Cliffs, NJ: Prentice Hall.

Condon, E. C., Peters, J. Y., & Sueiro-Ross, C. (1979). *Special education and the Hispanic child: Cultural perspectives.* Philadelphia: Temple University, Teacher Corps Mid-Atlantic Network.

Correa, W. I., & Heward, W. L. (1996). Special education in a culturally and linguistically diverse society. In W. L. Heward, *Exceptional children* (5th ed.) (pp. 91–129). Englewood Cliffs, NJ: Merrill.

Council for Exceptional Children (1993a). *Career education and transition* [Online]. Available: http://www.cec.sped.org/pp/cec_pol.htm#14 [1997, November 29].

Council for Exceptional Children. (1993b). CEC policy on inclusive schools and community settings. *Teaching Exceptional Children, 25*(4), supplement.

Council for Exceptional Children. (1997). *Summary of the IDEA amendments of 1997: Discipline of children with disabilities* [Online]. Available: http://www.cec.sped.org/pp/idea-b.htm#46 [1997, November 7].

Council for Exceptional Children (1998). *CEC's comments on the proposed IDEA regulations* [Online]. Available: http://www.cec.sped.org/pp/regscom.htm [1998, February 20].

Council for Learning Disabilities. (1993). Concerns about the full inclusion of students with learning disabilities in regular education classrooms. *Journal of Learning Disabilities, 26,* 595.

Craig, R., & Howard, C. (1981). Visual impairment. In M. L. Hardman, M. W. Egan, & D. Landau (Eds.), *What will we do in the morning?* (pp. 180–209). Dubuque, IA: Brown.

Cronin, M. E., & Patton, J. R. (1993). *Life skills for students with special needs.* Austin, TX: PRO-ED.

Cross, D. P. (1993). Students with physical and health-related disabilities. In A. E. Blackhurst & W. H. Berdine (Eds.), *An introduction to special education* (3rd ed., pp. 350–397). New York: HarperCollins.

Cuban, L. (1989). The "at-risk" label and the problem of urban school reform. *Phi Delta Kappan, 70,* 780–784, 799–801.

Cuenin, L. H., & Harris, K. R. (1986). Planning, implementing, and evaluating timeout interventions with exceptional students. *Teaching Exceptional Children, 18,* 272–276.

Culatta, B. K., & Culatta, R. (1993). Students with communication problems. In A. E. Blackhurst & W. H. Berdine (Eds.), *An introduction to special education* (3rd ed., pp. 238–269). New York: HarperCollins.

Culross, R. R. (1997). Concepts of inclusion in gifted education. *Teaching Exceptional Children, 29*(3), 24–26.

Cummins, J. (1989). A theoretical framework for bilingual special education. *Exceptional Children, 56,* 111–119.

Dale, E., & Chall, J. S. (1948). A formula for predicting readability. *Educational Research Bulletin, 27,* 11–20.

D'Alonzo, B. J., D'Alonzo, R. L., & Mauser, A. J. (1979). Developing resource rooms for the handicapped. *Teaching Exceptional Children, 11,* 91–96.

D'Antonio, M. (1993, November 21). Sound & fury. *Los Angeles Times Magazine,* pp. 44–48, 60–63.

Dardig, J. C. (1981). Helping teachers integrate handicapped students into the regular classroom. *Educational Horizons, 59,* 124–130.

Data bank: Every day. . . . (1989). *NEA Today, 8*(3), 12.

Davis, C. (1980). *Perkins-Binet intelligence scale.* Watertown, MA: Perkins School for the Blind.

Decano, P. (1979). Asian and Pacific-American exceptional children: A conversation. *Teacher Education and Special Education, 2*(4), 33–36.

de Grandpre, B. B., & Messier, J. M. (1979). Helping mainstreamed students stay in the mainstream. *The Directive Teacher, 2*(2), 12.

Deno, S. L. (1985). Curriculum-based measurement: The emerging alternative. *Exceptional Children, 52,* 219–232.

Deno, S. L. (1987). Curriculum-based measurement. *Teaching Exceptional Children, 20*(1), 41–42.

Deno, S. L., & Fuchs, L. S. (1987). Developing curriculum-based measurement systems for data-based special education problem solving. *Focus on Exceptional Children, 19*(8), 1–16.

Deshler, D. D., & Graham, S. (1980). Tape recording educational materials for secondary handicapped students. *Teaching Exceptional Children, 12,* 52–54.

Dettmer, P. (1994). IEPs for gifted secondary students. *Journal of Secondary Gifted Education, 5*(4), 52–59.

de Valenzuela, J. S., & Baca, L. (1998). Issues and theoretical considerations in the assessment of bilingual children. In L. M. Baca & H. T. Cervantes (Eds.), *The bilingual special education interface* (3rd ed.) (pp. 144–166). Upper Saddle River, NJ: Merrill/Prentice Hall.

Diana v. State Board of Education. Civ. No. C-70 37 RFP (N. D. Cal. 1970, 1973).

Dinkmeyer, D., & Dinkmeyer, D., Jr. (1982). *DUSO-Revised: Developing understanding of self and others.* Circle Pines, MN: American Guidance Service.

Dismuke, D. (1988). Reducing suicides. *NEA Today, 7*(3), 21.

Division for Learning Disabilities. (1993). *Inclusion: What does it mean for students with learning disabilities?* Reston, VA: Author.

Dolch, E. W. (1953). *The Dolch basic sight word list.* Champaign, IL: Garrard.

Doleys, D. M., & Bruno, J. (1982). Treatment of childhood medical disorders. In A. S. Bellack, M. Hersen, & A. E. Kazdin (Eds.), *International handbook of behavior modification and therapy* (pp. 997–1016). New York: Plenum.

Donaldson, J. (1980). Changing attitudes toward handicapped persons: A review and analysis of research. *Exceptional Children, 46,* 504–514.

Donaldson, J., & Martinson, M. C. (1977). Modifying attitudes toward physically disabled persons. *Exceptional Children, 43,* 337–341.

Donovan, P. (1993). *Testing positive: Sexually transmitted disease and the public health response.* New York: The Alan Guttmacher Institute.

Doorlag, D. H. (1989a). Students with learning handicaps. In R. Gaylord-Ross (Ed.), *Integration strategies for students with handicaps* (pp. 33–52). Baltimore: Brookes.

Doorlag, D. H. (1989b, May). *Getting along better with others: How parents and professionals can improve the social skills of special students.* Paper presented at the Fifth Annual California Parent-Professional Collaboration Conference, San Diego, CA.

Doyle, W. (1986). Classroom organization and management. In M. C. Wittrock (Ed.), *Handbook of research on teaching* (3rd ed., pp. 392–431). New York: Macmillan.

Drabman, R. S., & Patterson, J. N. (1981). Disruptive behavior and the social standing of exceptional children. *Exceptional Education Quarterly, 1*(4), 45–56.

Drew, C. J., Logan, D. R., & Hardman, M. L. (1992). *Mental retardation* (5th ed.). New York: Merrill/Macmillan.

Dunn, L. M. (1968). Special education for the mildly retarded—Is much of it justifiable? *Exceptional Children, 35,* 5–22.

Dunn, R., & Dunn, K. (1978). *Teaching students through their individual learning styles: A practical approach.* Reston, VA: Reston.

Eaton, M. D., & Hansen, C. L. (1978). Classroom organization and management. In N. G. Haring, T. C. Lovitt, M. D. Eaton, & C. L. Hansen (Eds.), *The fourth R: Research in the classroom* (pp. 191–217). Columbus, OH: Merrill Publishing Company.

Echevarria, J. (1995). Sheltered instruction for students with learning disabilities who have limited English proficiency. *Intervention in School and Clinic, 30,* 302–305.

Edgar, E., & Davidson, C. (1979). Parent perceptions of mainstreaming. *Education Unlimited, 1*(4), 32–33.

Educating refugees: Understanding the basics. (1989). *NCBE Forum, 12*(3), 1, 3.

Edwards, L. L. (1980). Curriculum modification as a strategy for helping regular classroom behavior-disordered students. *Focus on Exceptional Children, 12*(8), 1–11.

Edwards, T. K. (1988). Providing reasons for wanting to live. *Phi Delta Kappan, 70,* 296–298.

Ehly, S. W., & Larsen, S. C. (1980). *Peer tutoring for individualized instruction.* Boston: Allyn & Bacon.

Eiser, L. (1986). "Regular" software for special ed. kids? Yes! *Classroom Computer Learning, 7*(2), 26–30, 35.

Ekwall, E. E. (1986). *Ekwall reading inventory* (2nd ed.). Boston: Allyn & Bacon.

Ekwall, E. E., & Shanker, J. L. (1993). *Locating and correcting reading difficulties* (6th ed.). Upper Saddle River, NJ: Merrill/Prentice Hall.

Elam, S. M., Rose, L. C., & Gallup, A. M. (1993). The 25th annual Phi Delta Kappa/Gallup poll of the public's attitudes toward the public schools. *Phi Delta Kappan, 75,* 137–152.

Elam, S. M., Rose, L. C., & Gallup, A. M. (1996). The 28th annual Phi Delta Kappa/Gallup poll of the public's attitudes toward the public schools. *Phi Delta Kappan, 78,* 41–59.

Ellett, L. (1993). Instructional practices in mainstreamed secondary classrooms. *Journal of Learning Disabilities, 26,* 57–64.

Elliot, S. N., & Gresham, F. M. (1993). Social skills interventions for children. *Behavior Modification, 17,* 287–313.

Elmquist, D. L. (1991). School-based alcohol and other drug prevention programs: Guidelines for the special educator. *Intervention in School and Clinic, 27*(1), 10–19.

Emery, R. E. (1989). Family violence. *American Psychologist, 44,* 321–328.

Emmer, E. T. (1981). *Effective management in junior high math classes* (Report No. 6111). Austin: University of Texas, Research and Development Center for Teacher Education.

Emmer, E. T., Evertson, C. M., Sanford, J. P., Clements, B. S., & Worsham, M. E. (1989). *Classroom management for secondary teachers* (2nd ed.). Englewood Cliffs, NJ: Prentice Hall.

Englert, C. S. (1984). Measuring teacher effectiveness from the teacher's point of view. *Focus on Exceptional Children, 17*(2), 1–14.

Englert, C. S., & Raphael, T. E. (1988). Constructing well-formed prose: Process, structure, and metacognitive knowledge. *Exceptional Children, 54,* 513–520.

English, K. M. (1995). *Educational audiology across the lifespan: Serving all learners with hearing impairment.* Baltimore: Paul H. Brookes.

English, K. M. (1997). *Self-advocacy for students who are deaf and hard of hearing.* Austin, TX: PRO-ED.

Epanchin, B. C. (1987). Anxiety and stress-related disorders. In B. C. Epanchin & J. L. Paul (Eds.), *Emotional problems of childhood and adolescence: A multidisciplinary perspective* (pp. 165–190). New York: Merrill/Macmillan.

Epilepsy Foundation of America. (1987). *Epilepsy school alert.* Washington, DC: Author.

Epilepsy Foundation of America. (n.d.). *Teacher tips about the epilepsies.* Washington, DC: Author.

Evans, J., & Guevara, A. E. (1974). Classroom instruction for young Spanish speakers. *Exceptional Children, 41,* 16–19.

Evertson, C. M., Sanford, J. P., & Emmer, E. T. (1981). Effects of class heterogeneity in junior high school. *American Educational Research Journal, 18,* 219–232.

Fad, K. S., Ross, M., & Boston, J. (1995). Using cooperative learning to teach social skills to young children. *Teaching Exceptional Children, 27*(4), 29–34.

Falvey, M. A., Grenot-Scheyer, M., & Bishop, K. (1989). Integrating students with severe handicaps. *California State Federation/CEC Journal, 35*(3), 8–10.

Feldhusen, J. F. (1989). Thinking skills for the gifted. In J. F. Feldhusen, J. Van Tassel-Baska, & K. Seeley (Eds.), *Excellence in educating the gifted* (pp. 239–259). Denver: Love.

Feldhusen, J. F., Van Winkle, L., & Ehle, D. A. (1996). Is it acceleration or simply appropriate instruction for precocious youth? *Teaching Exceptional Children, 28*(3), 48–51.

Fiedler, C. R., & Simpson, R. L. (1987). Modifying the attitudes of nonhandicapped students toward handicapped peers. *Exceptional Children, 53,* 342–349.

Finch, A. J., & Spirito, A. (1980). Use of cognitive training to change cognitive processes. *Exceptional Education Quarterly, 1*(1), 31–39.

Fischer, L., & Sorenson, G. P. (1985). *School law for counselors, psychologists, and social workers.* New York: Longman.

Flesch, R. (1951). *How to test readability.* New York: Harper & Row.

Flexer, C., Wray, D., & Ireland, J. C. (1989). Preferential seating is not enough: Issues in classroom management of hearing-impaired students. *Language, Speech, and Hearing in Schools, 20,* 11–21.

Fonner, K., & Zabala, J. (1997, October). *It really is a small world after all: Sharing knowledge and skill on the Internet.* Paper presented at the Closing the Gap Conference, Minneapolis, MN.

Forest, M., & Lusthaus, E. (1989). Promoting educational equality for all students. In S. Stainback, W. Stainback, & M. Forest (Eds.), *Educating all students in the mainstream of regular education* (pp. 43–57). Baltimore: Brookes.

Forness, S. R., & Kavale, K. A. (1984). Education of the mentally retarded: A note on policy. *Education and Training of the Mentally Retarded, 19,* 239–245.

Forness, S. R., & Kavale, K. A. (1993). Strategies to improve basic learning and memory deficits in mental retardation: A meta-analysis of experimental studies. *Education and Training in Mental Retardation, 28,* 99–110.

Forness, S. R., Kavale, K. A., Blum, I. M., & Lloyd, J. W. (1997). Mega-analysis of meta-analyses. *Teaching Exceptional Children, 29*(6), 4–9.

Forster, P., & Doyle, B. A. (1989). Teaching listening skills to students with attention deficit disorders. *Teaching Exceptional Children, 21*(2), 20–22.

Foster, S. L., Inderbitzen, H. M., & Nangle, D. W. (1993). Assessing acceptance and social skills with peers in childhood. *Behavior Modification, 17,* 255–286.

Fox, C. L. (1989). Peer acceptance of learning disabled children in the regular classroom. *Exceptional Children, 56,* 50–59.

Foyle, H. C., & Lyman, L. (1990). *Cooperative learning: What you need to know.* Washington, DC: National Education Association.

Franklin, M. E. (1992). Culturally sensitive instructional practices for African-American learners with disabilities. *Exceptional Children, 59,* 115–122.

Frase, M. J. (1989). *Dropout rates in the United States: 1988.* Washington, DC: U.S. Department of Education, Office of Educational Research and Improvement, National Center for Education Statistics.

Freedman, S. W. (1982). Language assessment and writing disorders. *Topics in Language Disorders, 2*(4), 34–44.

Freeman, D., & Freeman, Y. (1988). *Sheltered English instruction. ERIC Digest.* Washington, DC: ERIC Clearinghouse on Languages and Linguistics. (ERIC Document Reproduction Service No. ED 301 070)

Fry, E. (1968). A readability formula that saves time. *Journal of Reading, 11,* 513–516, 575–577.

Fry, E. (1977). Fry's readability graph: Clarifications, validity, and extension to level 17. *Journal of Reading, 21,* 242–252.

Frymier, J., & Gansneder, B. (1989). The Phi Delta Kappa study of students at risk. *Phi Delta Kappan, 71,* 142–146.

Fuchigami, R. Y. (1980). Teacher education for culturally diverse exceptional children. *Exceptional Children, 46,* 634–641.

Fuchs, D. S., & Fuchs, L. S. (1994). Inclusive schools movement and the radicalization of special education reform. *Exceptional Children, 60,* 294–309.

Fuchs, L. S. (1986). Monitoring progress among mildly handicapped pupils: Review of current practice and research. *Remedial and Special Education, 7*(5), 5–12.

Fuchs, L. S. (1987). Program development. *Teaching Exceptional Children, 20*(1), 42–44.

Furstenberg, F. F., Jr., Brooks-Gunn, J., & Chase-Lansdale, L. (1989). Teenaged pregnancy and childbearing. *American Psychologist, 44,* 313–320.

Gable, R. A., Laycock, V. K., Maroney, S. A., & Smith, C. R. (1991). *Preparing to integrate students with behavioral disorders.* Reston, VA: The Council for Exceptional Children.

Gable, R. A., Strain, P. S., & Hendrickson, J. M. (1979). Strategies for improving the status and social behavior of learning disabled children. *Learning Disability Quarterly, 2*(3), 33–39.

Gajar, A., Goodman, L., & McAfee, J. (1993). *Secondary schools and beyond: Transition of individuals with mild disabilities.* New York: Merrill/Macmillan.

Gallagher, J. J. (1988). National agenda for educating gifted students: Statement of priorities. *Exceptional Children, 55,* 107–114.

Gallup, A. M., & Elam, S. M. (1988). The 20th annual Gallup Poll of the public's attitudes toward the public schools. *Phi Delta Kappan, 70,* 33–45.

Gans, K. D. (1985). Regular and special educators: Handicap integration attitudes and implications for consultants. *Teacher Education and Special Education, 8,* 188–197.

Garcia, R. L. (1978). *Fostering a pluralistic society through multi-ethnic education.* Bloomington, IN: Phi Delta Kappa Educational Foundation.

Gardner, H. (1987). Beyond the IQ: Education and human development. *Harvard Educational Review, 57,* 187–193.

Garfinkel, B. D., Crosby, E., Herbert, M. R., Matus, A. L., Pfeifer, J. K., & Sheras, P. L. (1988). *Responding to adolescent suicide. A report of the Phi Delta Kappa Task Force on Adolescent Suicide.* Bloomington, IN: Phi Delta Kappa Educational Foundation.

Garrett, M. K., & Crump, W. D. (1980). Peer acceptance, teacher preference, and self-appraisal of social status of learning disabled students. *Learning Disability Quarterly, 3*(3), 42–48.

Gartner, A., & Riessman, F. (1977). *How to individualize learning.* Bloomington, IN: Phi Delta Kappa Educational Foundation.

Gastright, J. F. (1989, April). Don't base your dropout program on somebody else's problem. *Phi Delta Kappa Research Bulletin,* pp. 1–4.

Gay, L. R. (1981). *Educational research* (2nd ed.). Columbus, OH: Merrill.

Gersten, R., & Dimino, J. (1993). Visions and revisions: A special education perspective on the whole language controversy. *Special Education and Remedial Education, 14*(4), 5–13.

Gersten, R., & Jiménez, R. (1998). Modulating instruction for language minority students. In E. J. Kameenui & D. W. Carnine (Eds.), *Effective teaching strategies that accommodate diverse learners* (pp. 161–178). Upper Saddle River, NJ: Merrill/Prentice Hall.

Gersten, R., & Woodward, J. (1994). The language-minority student and special education: Issues, trends, and paradoxes. *Exceptional Children, 60,* 310–322.

Giangreco, M., Cloninger, C., & Iverson, V. (1990). *C.O.A.C.H.-Cayuga-Onondaga assessment for children with handicaps* (6th ed.). Stillwater: Oklahoma State University.

Gibson, A. B., Roberts, P. C., & Buttery, T. J. (1982). *Death education: A concern for the living.* Bloomington, IN: Phi Delta Kappa Educational Foundation.

Gickling, E. E., & Thompson, V. P. (1985). A personal view of curriculum-based assessment. *Exceptional Children, 52,* 205–218.

Gillung, T. B., & Rucker, C. N. (1977). Labels and teacher expectations. *Exceptional Children, 43,* 464–465.

Glass, G. V., & Smith, M. L. (1978). *Meta-analysis of research on class size and achievement.* Boulder: University of Colorado, Laboratory of Educational Research.

Glazzard, P. (1980). Adaptations for mainstreaming. *Teaching Exceptional Children, 13,* 26–29.

Glazzard, P. (1982). *Learning activities and teaching ideas for the special child in the regular classroom.* Englewood Cliffs, NJ: Prentice Hall.

Goldman, R. M., & Fristoe, M. (1986). *Goldman-Fristoe test of articulation.* Circle Pines, MN: American Guidance Service.

Goldman, R. M., Fristoe, M., & Woodcock, R. W. (1976). *Goldman-Fristoe-Woodcock auditory skills test battery.* Circle Pines, MN: American Guidance Service.

Goldstein, A. P., Sprafkin, R. P., Gershaw, N. J., & Klein, P. (1980). *Skillstreaming the adolescent: A structured learning approach to teaching prosocial skills.* Champaign, IL: Research Press.

Gollnick, D. M., & Chinn, P. C. (1990). *Multicultural education in a pluralistic society* (3rd ed.). New York: Merrill/Macmillan.

Gollnick, D. M., & Chinn, P. C. (1998). *Multicultural education in a pluralistic society* (5th ed). Upper Saddle River, NJ: Merrill/Prentice Hall.

Gonzales, E. (1979). Preparation for teaching the multicultural exceptional child: Trends and concerns. *Teacher Education and Special Education, 2*(4), 12–18.

Gonzalez, J. (1978). The status of bilingual education today: Un vistazo y un repaso. *National Association for Bilingual Education, 2*(1), 13–20.

Goodman, L. (1978). Meeting children's needs through materials modification. *Teaching Exceptional Children, 10,* 92–94.

Gordon, T. (1974). *Teacher effectiveness training.* New York: Wyden.

Gottlieb, J., & Leyser, Y. (1981). Facilitating the social mainstreaming of retarded children. *Exceptional Education Quarterly, 1*(4), 57–70.

Graden, J. L., Casey, A., & Christenson, S. L. (1985). Implementing a prereferral intervention system: Part I. The model. *Exceptional Children, 51,* 377–384.

Grady, E. (1992). *The portfolio approach to assessment.* Bloomington, IN: Phi Delta Kappa Educational Foundation.

Graham, S., & Harris, K.R. (1989). Improving learning disabled students' skills at composing essays: Self-instructional strategy training. *Exceptional Children, 56,* 201–214.

Graham, S., Harris, K. R., & Reid, R. (1998). Developing self-regulated learners. In R. J. Whelan (Ed.), *Emotional and behavioral disorders: A 25 year focus* (pp. 205–228). Denver: Love.

Graham, S., & Johnson, L. A. (1989). Teaching reading to learning disabled students: A review of research-supported procedures. *Focus on Exceptional Children, 21*(6), 1–12.

Graham, S., & Miller, L. (1979). Spelling research and practice: A unified approach. *Focus on Exceptional Children, 12*(2), 1–16.

Gray, L. A., & House, R. M. (1989). No guarantee of immunity: AIDS and adolescents. In D. Capuzzi & D. R. Gross (Eds.), *Youth at risk: A resource for counselors, teachers and parents* (pp. 231–263). Alexandria, VA: American Association for Counseling and Development.

Grayson, D. (n.d.). *Facts about blindness and visual impairment.* New York: American Foundation for the Blind.

Green, W. W., & Fischgrund, J. E. (1993). Students with hearing loss. In A. E. Blackhurst & W. H. Berdine (Eds.), *An introduction to special education* (3rd ed., pp. 271–311). New York: HarperCollins College Publishers.

Gregor, A. (1997). Filtering software can help make surfing safer for kids. *HOMEPC, 4*(11), 243–246.

Gresham, F. M. (1984). Social skills and self-efficacy for exceptional children. *Exceptional Children, 51,* 253–261.

Grosenick, J. K., & Huntze, S. L. (1980). *National needs analysis in behavior disorders: Adolescent behavior disorders.* Columbia: University of Missouri at Columbia, Department of Special Education.

Grossman, H. J. (Ed.). (1983). *Classification in mental retardation* (1983 revision). Washington, DC: American Association on Mental Retardation.

Grossnickle, D. R. (1986). *High school dropouts: Causes, consequences, and cure.* Bloomington, IN: Phi Delta Kappa Educational Foundation.

Guetzloe, E. (1996). Facts pertaining to children and youth with emotional/behavioral disorders. *Council for Children with Behavioral Disorders Newsletter, 10*(2), 4.

Guetzloe, E. C. (1988). Suicide and depression: Special education's responsibility. *Teaching Exceptional Children, 20*(4), 25–28.

Guetzloe, E. C. (1989). *Youth suicide: What the educator should know.* Reston, VA: The Council for Exceptional Children.

Guetzloe, E. C. (1993). Answering the cries for help—Suicidal thoughts and actions. *Journal of Emotional and Behavioral Problems, 2*(2), 34–38.

Guilford, J. P. (1967). *The nature of human intelligence.* New York: McGraw-Hill.

Guralnick, M. J. (1981). Programmatic factors affecting child-child social interactions in mainstreamed preschool programs. *Exceptional Education Quarterly, 1*(4), 71–92.

Hallahan, D. P., & Kauffman, J. M. (1976). *Introduction to learning disabilities.* Englewood Cliffs, NJ: Prentice Hall.

Hallahan, D. P., & Kauffman, J. M. (1988). *Exceptional children* (4th ed.). Englewood Cliffs, NJ: Prentice Hall.

Hammill, D. D. (1991). *Detroit tests of learning aptitude* (3rd ed.). Austin, TX: PRO-ED.

Hammill, D. D., & Bartel, N. R. (1986). *Teaching students with learning and behavior problems* (4th ed.). Austin, TX: PRO-ED.

Hammill, D. D., Brown, V. L., Larson, S. C., & Wiederholt, J. L. (1994). *Test of adolescent and adult language* (3rd ed.). Austin, TX: PRO-ED.

Hammill, D. D., & Newcomer, P. L. (1997). *Test of language development-Intermediate* (3rd ed.). Austin, TX: PRO-ED.

Hamre-Nietupski, S., McDonald, J., & Nietupski, J. (1992). Integrating elementary students with multiple disabilities into supported regular classes: Challenges and solutions. *Teaching Exceptional Children, 24*(3), 6–9.

Handlers, A., & Austin, K. (1980). Improving attitudes of high school students toward their handicapped peers. *Exceptional Children, 47,* 228–229.

Harley, R. K., & Lawrence, G. A. (1984). *Visual impairment in the schools.* Springfield, IL: Thomas.

Harrington, J. D. (1976). Hard-of-hearing pupils in the mainstream: Educational needs and services. In *Serving hard-of-hearing pupils: Alternative strategies for personnel preparation* (pp. 16–31). Minneapolis: University of Minnesota, Leadership Training Institute/Special Education.

Hasazi, S. B., Furney, K. S., & Hull, M. (1995). Additional preparation for adulthood: Transition planning. In P. T. Cegelka & W. H. Berdine (Eds.), *Effective instruction for students with learning difficulties* (pp. 419–443). Boston: Allyn & Bacon.

Hasselbring, T. S., Goin, L. I., & Bransford, J. D. (1987). Developing automaticity. *Teaching Exceptional Children, 19*(3), 30–33.

Hazekamp, J., & Huebner, K. M. (Eds.). (1989). *Program planning and evaluation for blind and visually impaired students: National guidelines for educational excellence.* New York: American Foundation for the Blind.

Helge, D. (1991). *Rural, exceptional, at risk.* Reston, VA: The Council for Exceptional Children.

Hemphill, B. (1997). *Taming the paper tiger.* Washington, DC: Kiplinger Washington Editors.

Hendrie, C. (1996). Enrollment crunch stretches the bounds of the possible. *Education Week, 16*(2), 1, 12–15.

Henker, B., Whalen, C. K., & Hinshaw, S. P. (1980). The attributional contexts of cognitive intervention strategies. *Exceptional Education Quarterly, 1*(1), 17–30.

Heron, T. E., & Harris, K. C. (1993). *The educational consultant* (3rd ed.). Austin, TX: PRO-ED.

Heron, T. E., Heward, W. L., & Cooke, N. L. (1980). *A classwide peer tutoring system.* Paper presented at the Sixth Annual Meeting of the Association of Behavior Analysis, Dearborn, MI.

Heward, W. L. (1996). *Exceptional children: An introduction to special education* (5th ed.). Englewood Cliffs; NJ: Merrill/Prentice Hall.

Heward, W. L., Courson, F. H., & Narayan, J. S. (1989). Using choral responding to increase active student response. *Teaching Exceptional Children, 21*(3), 72–75.

Heward, W. L., Gardner, R., Cavanaugh, R. A., Courson, F. H., Grossi, T. A., & Barbetta, P. M. (1996). Everyone participates in this class. *Teaching Exceptional Children, 28*(2), 4–10.

Heward, W. L., & Orlansky, M. D. (1988). *Exceptional children* (3rd ed.). New York: Merrill/Macmillan.

Heward, W. L., & Orlansky, M. D. (1992). *Exceptional children* (4th ed.). New York: Merrill/Macmillan.

Hill, D. (1989, September/October). Fixing the system from the top down. *Teacher Magazine,* pp. 50–55.

Hiskey, M. (1966). *Hiskey-Nebraska test of learning aptitude.* Lincoln, NE: Union College Press.

Hobbs, N. (1975). *The futures of children.* San Francisco: Jossey-Bass.

Hobbs, N. (1976). *Issues in the classification of children.* San Francisco: Jossey-Bass.

Hocutt, A. M. (1996). Effectiveness of special education: Is placement the critical factor? *The Future of Children, 6*(1), 77–102.

Hodgkinson, H. (1993). American education: The good, the bad, and the task. *Phi Delta Kappan, 74,* 619–623.

Hollinger, J. D. (1987). Social skills for behaviorally disordered children as preparation for mainstreaming: Theory, practice, and new directions. *Remedial and Special Education, 8*(4), 17–27.

Holzberg, C. S. (1991). Sound and image: The world on a disc. *inCider/A+, 9*(11), 30–34.

Horton, L. (1985). *Adolescent alcohol abuse.* Bloomington, IN: Phi Delta Kappa Educational Foundation.

Howell, K. W., Fox, S. L., & Morehead, M. K. (1993). *Curriculum-based evaluation* (2nd ed.). Pacific Grove, CA: Brooks/Cole.

Hunt, P., & Goetz, L. (1997). Research on inclusive educational programs, practices, and outcomes for students with severe disabilities. *Journal of Special Education, 31,* 3–29.

Idol, L. (1993). *Special educator's consultation handbook* (2nd ed.). Austin, TX: PRO-ED.

Idol, L., & West, J. F. (1991). Educational collaboration: A catalyst for effective schooling. *Intervention in School and Clinic, 27*(2), 70–78, 125.

Isaacson, S. L. (1987). Effective instruction in written language. *Focus on Exceptional Children, 19*(6), 1–12.

Israelson, J. (1980). I'm special too—A classroom program promotes understanding and acceptance of handicaps. *Teaching Exceptional Children, 13,* 35–37.

Jackson, N. F., Jackson, D. A., & Monroe, C. (1983). *Getting along with others: Teaching social effectiveness to children.* Champaign, IL: Research Press.

Jacobson, L. (1996, October 11). Falling birthrate leaves experts asking why. *Education Week,* p. 5

Janesick, V. J. (1995). Our multicultural society. In E. L. Meyen & T. M. Skrtic (Eds.), *Special education and student disability* (4th ed.) (pp. 713–727). Denver: Love.

Jenkins, J. R., Heliotis, J. D., Stein, M. L., & Haynes, M. C. (1987). Improving reading comprehension by using paragraph restatements. *Exceptional Children, 54,* 54–59.

Jenkins, J. R., & Jenkins, L. (1985). Peer tutoring in elementary and secondary programs. *Focus on Exceptional Children, 17*(6), 1–12.

Joe, J. R., & Malach, R. S. (1992). Families with Native American roots. In E. W. Lynch & M. J. Hanson (Eds.), *Developing cross-cultural competence* (pp. 89–119). Baltimore: Brookes.

Johnson, D. D. (1971). The Dolch list reexamined. *The Reading Teacher, 24,* 455–456.

Johnson, D. W., & Johnson, R. T. (1980). Integrating handicapped students into the mainstream. *Exceptional Children, 47,* 90–98.

Johnson, D. W., & Johnson, R. T. (1984). Classroom learning structure and attitudes toward handicapped students in mainstream settings. In R. L. Jones (Ed.), *Attitudes and attitude change in special education* (pp. 118–142). Reston, VA: The Council for Exceptional Children.

Johnson, D. W., & Johnson, R. T. (1989). Cooperative learning and mainstreaming. In R. Gaylord-Ross (Ed.), *Integration strategies for students with handicaps* (pp. 233–248). Baltimore: Brookes.

Johnson, L. J., & Pugach, M. C. (1990). Classroom teachers' views of intervention strategies for learning and behavior problems: Which are reasonable and how frequently are they used? *Journal of Special Education, 24,* 69–84.

Johnson, R. (1981). *The Picture Communication Symbols: Book I.* Solana Beach, CA: Mayer-Johnson.

Johnson, R. (1985). *The Picture Communication Symbols: Book II.* Solana Beach, CA: Mayer-Johnson.

Johnson, R. (1992). *The Picture Communication Symbols: Book III.* Solana Beach, CA: Mayer-Johnson.

Jones, F. H., & Eimers, R. C. (1975). Role playing to train elementary teachers to use a classroom management "skill package." *Journal of Applied Behavior Analysis, 8,* 421–433.

Jones, F. H., & Miller, W. H. (1974). The effective use of negative attention for reducing group disruption in special elementary school classrooms. *Psychological Record, 24,* 435–448.

Kameenui, E. J., & Simmons, D. C. (1990). *Designing instructional strategies.* New York: Merrill/Macmillan.

Karnes, F. A., & Collins, E. C. (1980). *Handbook of instructional resources and references for teaching the gifted.* Boston: Allyn & Bacon.

Karnes, M. B., & Johnson, L. J. (1991). Gifted handicapped. In N. Colangelo & G. A. Davis (Eds.), *Handbook of gifted education* (pp. 428–437). Boston: Allyn & Bacon.

Karweit, N. L., & Slavin, R. E. (1981). Measurement and modeling choices in studies of time and learning. *Educational Research Journal, 18*(2), 157–171.

Kauffman, J. M. (1977). *Characteristics of children's behavior disorders.* Columbus, OH: Merrill Publishing Company.

Kauffman, J. M. (1997). *Characteristics of emotional and behavioral disorders of children and youth* (6th ed.). Upper Saddle River, NJ: Merrill.

Kauffman, J. M., Gerber, M. M., & Semmel, M. I. (1988). Arguable assumptions underlying the regular education initiative. *Journal of Learning Disabilities, 21,* 6–11.

Kauffman, J. M., Lloyd, J. W., Baker, J., & Riedel, T. M. (1995). Inclusion of all students with emotional and behavioral disorders? Let's think again. *Phi Delta Kappan, 76,* 542–546.

Kaufman, M. J., Gottlieb, J., Agard, J. A., & Kukic, M. D. (1975). Mainstreaming: Toward an explication of the construct. In E. L. Meyen, G. A. Vergason, & R. J. Whelan (Eds.), *Alternatives for teaching exceptional children* (pp. 35–54). Denver: Love.

Keefe, C. H., & Keefe, D. R. (1993). Instruction for students with LD: A whole language model. *Intervention in School and Clinic, 28,* 172–177.

Keller, H. (1965). *The story of my life.* New York: Airmont.

Kellogg, J. B. (1988). Forces of change. *Phi Delta Kappan, 70,* 199–204.

Kennedy, D. M. (1995). Plain talk about creating a gifted-friendly classroom. *Roeper Review, 17,* 232–234.

Kerr, B. (1991). Educating gifted girls. In N. Colangelo & G. A. Davis (Eds.), *Handbook of gifted education* (pp. 402–415). Boston: Allyn & Bacon.

Kerr, M. M., & Nelson, C. M. (1998). *Strategies for managing behavior problems in the classroom* (3rd ed.). Upper Saddle River, NJ: Merrill/Prentice Hall.

King-Sears, M.E. (1997). Best academic practices for inclusive classrooms. *Focus on Exceptional Children, 29*(7), 1–22.

Kinnaman, D. E. (1992). 2.5 million strong—and growing. *Technology & Learning, 13*(1), 67.

Kirk, S. A., & Gallagher, J. J. (1979). *Educating exceptional children* (3rd ed.). Boston: Houghton Mifflin.

Kirk, S. A., Kliebhan, J. M., & Lerner, J. W. (1978). *Teaching reading to slow and disabled readers.* Boston: Houghton Mifflin.

Kirk, S. A., McCarthy, J. J., & Kirk, W. D. (1968). *Illinois test of psycholinguistic abilities* (Rev. ed.). Urbana: University of Illinois Press.

Kirk, W. G. (1993). *Adolescent suicide: A school-based approach to assessment and treatment.* Champaign, IL: Research Press.

Kitano, H. (1973). Highlights of Institute on Language and Culture: Asian component. In L. A. Bransford, L. M. Baca, & K. Lane (Eds.), *Cultural diversity and the exceptional child* (pp. 14–15). Reston, VA: The Council for Exceptional Children.

Kitano, M. K. (1989). The K–3 teacher's role in recognizing and supporting young gifted children. *Young Children, 44*(3), 57–63.

Kitano, M. K. (1991). A multicultural educational perspective on serving the culturally diverse gifted. *Journal for the Education of the Gifted, 15*(1), 4–19.

Kitano, M. K., & Kirby, D. E. (1986). *Gifted education: A comprehensive view.* Boston: Little, Brown.

Klein, E. (1989). Gifted and talented. In G. P. Cartwright, C. A. Cartwright, & M. E. Ward, *Educating special learners* (3rd ed., pp. 315–341). Belmont, CA: Wadsworth.

Knitzer, J. (1989). *Invisible Children Project: Final report and recommendations of the Invisible Children Project.* Alexandria, VA: National Mental Health Association.

Kohl, F. L., Moses, L. G., & Stettner-Eaton, B. A. (1983). The results of teaching fifth and sixth graders to be instructional trainers with students who are severely handicapped. *Journal of the Association for the Severely Handicapped, 8*(4), 32–40.

Kokaska, C. J. (1980). A curriculum model for career education. In G. M. Clark & W. J. White (Eds.), *Career education for the handicapped: Current perspectives for teachers* (pp. 35–41). Boothwyn, PA: Educational Resources Center.

Kokaska, C. J., & Brolin, D. E. (1985). *Career education for handicapped individuals* (2nd ed.). New York: Merrill/Macmillan.

Kolstoe, O. P. (1976). *Teaching educable mentally retarded children* (2nd ed.). New York: Holt, Rinehart & Winston.

Krashen, S. D. (1987). *Principles and practice in second language acquisition.* New York: Prentice Hall.

Kroth, R. (1981). Involvement with parents of behaviorally disordered adolescents. In G. Brown, R. L. McDowell, & J. Smith (Eds.), *Educating adolescents with behavior disorders* (pp. 123–139). Columbus, OH: Merrill Publishing Company.

Krouse, J., Gerber, M. M., & Kauffman, J. M. (1981). Peer tutoring: Procedures, promises, and unresolved issues. *Exceptional Education Quarterly, 1*(4), 107–115.

Kunisawa, B. (1988). A nation in crisis; The dropout dilemma. *NEA Today, 6*(6), 61–65.

Lambert, N., Nihira, K., & Leland, H. (1993). *AAMR adaptive behavior scale-School* (2nd ed.). Austin, TX: PRO-ED.

Lance, W. D. (1977). Technology and media for exceptional learners: Looking ahead. *Exceptional Children, 44,* 92–97.

Lapp, D., & Flood, J. (1992). *Teaching reading to every child* (3rd ed.). New York: Macmillan.

Larry P. v. Riles. C-71-2270-RFP (N. D. Cal. 1972), 495 F. Supp. 96 (N. D. Cal. 1979) Aff'r (9th Cir. 1984), 1983–84 EHLR DEC. 555:304.

Lathrop, A. (1982). The terrible ten in educational programming (My top ten reasons for automatically rejecting a program). *Educational Computer, 2*(5), 34.

Learning Disabilities Association of America. (1993). Position paper on full inclusion of all students with learning disabilities in the regular education classroom. *Journal of Learning Disabilities, 26,* 594.

Lehr, S. (1992). *If you look in their eyes, you know: Parents' perspectives on facilitated communication.* Syracuse: Institute on Facilitated Communication, Syracuse University.

Leinhardt, G., & Pallay, A. (1982). Restrictive educational settings: Exile or haven? *Review of Educational Research, 52,* 557–578.

Leone, P. E., et al. (1991). *Juvenile corrections and the exceptional student.* ERIC Digest #E509. Reston, VA: ERIC Clearinghouse on Handicapped and Gifted Children.

Leone, P. E., Rutherford, R. B., & Nelson, C. M. (1991). *Special education in juvenile corrections.* Reston, VA: The Council for Exceptional Children.

Lerner, J. W. (1997). *Learning disabilities* (7th ed.). Boston: Houghton-Mifflin.

Lerner, J. W., Cousin, P. T., & Richeck, M. (1992). Critical issues in learning disabilities: Whole language learning. *Learning Disabilities Research & Practice, 7,* 226–230.

Lerner, J. W., & Lowenthal, B. (1993). Attention deficit disorders: New responsibilities for special educators. *Learning Disabilities: A Multidisciplinary Journal, 4*(1), 1–8.

Lerner, J. W., Lowenthal, B., & Lerner, S. R. (1995). *Attention deficit disorders.* Pacific Grove, CA: Brooks/Cole.

Levine, M. P. (1987). *How schools can help combat student eating disorders: Anorexia nervosa and bulimia.* Washington, DC: National Education Association.

Levy, P. S. (1981). The story of Marie, David, Richard, Jane, and John: Teaching gifted children in the regular classroom. *Teaching Exceptional Children, 13,* 39–43.

Lewis, R. B. (1980). Performance technologists and the needs of special learners. *NSPI Journal, 19*(4), 20–21.

Lewis, R. B. (1983). Learning disabilities and reading: Instructional recommendations from current research. *Exceptional Children, 50,* 230–240.

Lewis, R. B. (1993). *Special education technology: Classroom applications.* Pacific Grove, CA: Brooks/Cole.

Lewis, R. B. (1997). Changes in technology use in California's special education programs. *Remedial and Special Education, 18,* 233–242.

Lewis, R. B. (1998). Assistive technology and learning disabilities: Today's realities and tomorrow's promises. *Journal of Learning Disabilities, 31,* 16–25, 54.

Lewis, R. B., Ashton, T., & Kieley, C. (1996). Word processing and individuals with learning disabilities: Overcoming the keyboard barrier. In *Eleventh Annual Conference of Technology for People with Disabilities, California State University, Northridge, submitted papers, 1996* [computer software]. Newport Beach, CA: Rapidtext.

Lewis, R. B., Dell, S. J., Lynch, E. W., Harrison, P. J., & Saba, F. (1987). *Special education technology in action: Teachers speak out.* San Diego, CA: San Diego State University, Department of Special Education.

Lewis, R. B., & Harrison, P. J. (1988, April). *Effective applications of technology in special education: Results of a statewide study.* Paper presented at The Council for Exceptional Children's 66th Annual Convention, Washington, DC.

Lipsky, D. K., & Gartner, A. (1989). *Beyond separate education: Quality education for all.* Baltimore: Brookes.

Lloyd, J. W., & Carnine, D. W. (Eds.). (1981). Foreword to structured instruction: Effective teaching of essential skills. *Exceptional Education Quarterly, 2*(1), viii–ix.

Lloyd, J. W., & Keller, C. E. (1989). Effective mathematics instruction: Development, instruction, and programs. *Focus on Exceptional Children, 21*(7), 1–10.

Lloyd, J. W., Crowley, E. P., Kohler, F. W., & Strain, P. S. (1988). Redefining the applied research agenda: Cooperative learning, prereferral, teacher consultation, and peer-mediated interventions. *Journal of Learning Disabilities, 21*, 43–52.

Lloyd, J. W., Kauffman, J. M., Landrum, T. J., & Roe, D. L. (1991). Why do teachers refer pupils for special education? An analysis of referral records. *Exceptionality, 2*, 115–126.

Logan, K. R., & Keefe, E. B. (1997). A comparison of instructional context, teacher behavior, and engaged behavior for students with severe disabilities in general education and self-contained elementary classrooms. *JASH, 22*, 16–27.

London, S. B., & Stile, S. W. (1982). *The school's role in the prevention of child abuse.* Bloomington, IN: Phi Delta Kappa Educational Foundation.

Lovaas, O. I., & Newsom, C. D. (1976). Behavior modification with psychotic children. In H. Leitenberg (Ed.), *Handbook of behavior modification and behavior therapy* (pp. 303–360). Englewood Cliffs, NJ: Prentice Hall.

Lovitt, T. C. (1982). What does the direct in directive teacher mean? [Interview with T. C. Lovitt]. *The Directive Teacher, 4*(1), 24–25, 27.

Lowenbraun, S., & Thompson, M. D. (1986). Hearing impairments. In N. G. Haring & L. McCormick (Eds.), *Exceptional children and youth* (4th ed., pp. 357–395). New York: Merrill/Macmillan.

Luetke-Stahlman, B., & Luckner, J. (1991). *Effectively educating students with hearing impairments.* White Plains, NY: Longman.

Luftig, R. L. (1989). *Assessment of learners with special needs.* Boston: Allyn & Bacon.

Lusthaus, E., & Forest, M. (1987). The kaleidoscope: A challenge to the cascade. In M. Forest (Ed.), *More education integration* (pp. 1–17). Downsview, Ontario: G. Allan Roeher Institute.

Lynch, E. W. (1981). *But I've tried everything! A special educator's guide to working with parents.* San Diego, CA: San Diego State University.

Lynch, E. W. (1992). Developing cross-cultural competence. In E. W. Lynch & M. J. Hanson (Eds.), *Developing cross-cultural competence* (pp. 35–59). Baltimore: Brookes.

Lyon, H. C. (1981). Our most neglected natural resource. *Today's Education, 70*(1), 14–20.

Maag, J. W., & Webber, J. (1995). Promoting children's social development in general education classrooms. *Preventing School Failure, 39*(3), 13–19.

MacArthur, C. A., Graham, S., Haynes, J. B., & DeLaPaz, S. (1996). Spelling checkers and students with learning disabilities: Performance comparisons and impact on spelling. *Journal of Special Education, 30*, 35–57.

Machado, R. E., Belew, A. D., Jans, M., & Cunha, A. (1996). Full inclusion. *SKOLE: The Journal of the National Coalition of Alternative Community Schools, 3*(1), 110–124.

MacMillan, D. L. (1982). *Mental retardation in school and society* (2nd ed.). Boston: Little, Brown.

Madden, N. A., & Slavin, R. E. (1983). Mainstreaming students with mild handicaps: Academic and social outcomes. *Review of Educational Research, 53*, 519–569.

Madsen, C. H., Becker, W. C., & Thomas, D. R. (1968). Rules, praise, and ignoring: Elements of elementary classroom control. *Journal of Applied Behavior Analysis, 1*, 139–151.

Mager, R. F. (1984). *Preparing instructional objectives* (Rev. ed.). Belmont, CA: Pitman Learning.

Maginnis, G. (1969). The readability graph and informal reading inventories. *The Reading Teacher, 22*, 534–538.

Maheady, L., Sacca, M. K., & Harper, G. F. (1988). Classwide peer tutoring with mildly handicapped high school students. *Exceptional Children, 55*, 52–59.

Males, M. (1993). Schools, society, and 'teen' pregnancy. *Phi Delta Kappan, 74*, 566–568.

Maloney, M. J., & Klykylo, W. M. (1985). An overview of anorexia nervosa, bulimia, and obesity in children and adolescents. In S. Chess & A. Thomas (Eds.), *Annual progress in child psychology and child development-1985* (pp. 436–453). New York: Bruner Mazel.

Malouf, D. B. (1987–1988). The effect of instructional computer games on continuing student motivation. *Journal of Special Education, 21*(4), 27–38.

Mandell, C. J., & Fiscus, E. (1981). *Understanding exceptional people.* St. Paul, MN: West.

Mann, A., & McIntyre, M. (1992, October). Debate: Should schools eliminate gifted and talented programs? *NEA Today,* p. 39.

Manning, M. L., & Baruth, L. G. (1995). *Students at risk.* Boston: Allyn & Bacon.

Manzo, K. K. (1996). Slow progress in reaching goals for 2000 reported. *Education Week, 16*(13), 6.

Marfilius, S., & Roznaksi, D. (1997, March). *List servers related to children with special needs.* Paper presented at the 4th Annual Wisconsin Assistive Technology Conference.

Markel, G. (1981). Improving test-taking skills of LD adolescents. *Academic Therapy, 16*, 333–342.

Markwardt, F. C. (1989). *Peabody individual achievement test-Revised.* Circle Pines, MN: American Guidance Service.

Maron, S. S., & Martinez, D. H. (1980). Environmental alternatives for the visually handicapped. In J. W. Schifani, R. M. Anderson, & S. J. Odle (Eds.), *Implementing learning in the least restrictive environment* (pp. 149–198). Baltimore: University Park Press.

Martin, E. W. (1974). Some thoughts on mainstreaming. *Exceptional Children, 41*, 150–153.

Marttila, J., & Mills, M. (1995). *Knowledge is power.* Bettendorf, IA: Mississippi Bend Area Education Agency.

Mather, N. (1992). Whole language reading instruction for students with learning disabilities: Caught in the cross fire. *Learning Disabilities Research & Practice, 7,* 87–95.

Mathes, P. G., & Irby, B. J. (1993). *Discussion guide: Teen pregnancy and parenting handbook.* Champaign, IL: Research Press.

Maxon, A., Brackett, D., & van den Berg, S. (1991). Classroom amplification use: A national long-term study. *Language, Speech, and Hearing Services in Schools, 22,* 242–253.

McCarney, S. B. (1996). *The learning disability evaluation scale.* Columbia, MO: Hawthorne.

McCarney, S. B., & Leigh, J. E. (1990). *Behavior evaluation scale-2.* Columbia, MO: Hawthorne Educational Services.

McCormick, L. (1986). Keeping up with language intervention trends. *Teaching Exceptional Children, 18*(2), 123–129.

McCormick, L. (1990). Cultural diversity and exceptionality. In N. G. Haring & L. McCormick (Eds.), *Exceptional children and youth* (5th ed., pp. 46–75). New York: Merrill/Macmillan.

McCurdy, K., & Daro, D. (1995). *Current trends in child abuse reporting fatalities: The results of the 1994 Annual Fifty State Survey.* Chicago, IL: National Committee to Prevent Child Abuse.

McDonald, D. (1989). A special report on the education of Native Americans: "Stuck in the horizon" [Special Report insert]. *Education Week, 7*(4), 1–16.

McDonnell, J. (1987). The integration of students with severe handicaps into regular public schools: An analysis of parents' perceptions of potential outcomes. *Education and Training in Mental Retardation, 22,* 98–111.

McGinnis, E., & Goldstein, A. P. (1984). *Skillstreaming the elementary school child.* Champaign, IL: Research Press.

McIntosh, R., Vaughn, S., & Zaragoza, N. (1991). A review of social interventions for students with learning disabilities. *Journal of Learning Disabilities, 24,* 451–458.

McLoughlin, J. A., & Lewis, R. B. (1994). *Assessing special students* (4th ed.). New York: Merrill/Macmillan.

McMillen, M. M., Kaufman, P., & Whitener, S. D. (1996). *Dropout rates in the United States: 1995.* Washington, DC: National Center for Education Statistics.

McNergney, R., & Haberman, M. (1988). Dropouts: Time for solutions. *NEA Today, 6*(10), 27.

McWhirter, J. J., McWhirter, B. T., McWhirter, A. M., & McWhirter, E. H. (1998). *At-risk youth: A comprehensive response.* Pacific Grove, CA: Brooks/Cole.

Medley, D. M. (1982). Teacher effectiveness. In H. E. Mitzel (Ed.), *Encyclopedia of educational research* (5th ed., pp. 1894–1903). New York: Free Press.

Meisgeier, C. (1981). A social/behavioral program for the adolescent student with serious learning problems. *Focus on Exceptional Children, 13*(9), 1–13.

Mercer, C. D. (1997). *Students with learning disabilities* (5th ed.). Upper Saddle River, NJ: Merrill/Prentice Hall.

Mercer, C. D., & Mercer, A. R. (1989). *Teaching students with learning problems* (3rd ed.). New York: Merrill/Macmillan.

Mercer, C. D., & Mercer, A. R. (1993). *Teaching students with learning problems* (4th ed.). New York: Merrill/Macmillan.

Mercer, C. D., & Mercer, A. R. (1998). *Teaching students with learning problems* (5th ed.). Upper Saddle River, NJ: Merrill.

Mercer, C. D., Mercer, A. R., & Bott, D. A. (1984). *Self-correcting learning materials for the classroom.* New York: Merrill/Macmillan.

Mercer, J. R. (1973). *Labeling the mentally retarded.* Berkeley: University of California Press.

Meyen, E. L. (1981). *Developing instructional units* (3rd ed.). Dubuque, IA: Brown.

Miksic, S. (1987). Drug abuse management in adolescent special education. In M. M. Kerr, C. M. Nelson, & D. L. Lambert, *Helping adolescents with learning and behavior problems* (pp. 225–253). New York: Merrill/Macmillan.

Mills, P. J. (1979). Education within the mainstream: Suggestions for classroom teachers. *The Directive Teacher, 2*(2), 16.

Mira, M. P., & Tyler, J. S. (1991). Students with traumatic brain injury: Making the transition from hospital to school. *Focus on Exceptional Children, 23*(5), 1–12.

Mirga, T. (1988a, September 21). States and the "at risk" issues: Said aware but still "failing." *Education Week,* pp. 1, 14, 15.

Mirga, T. (1988b, September 21). The first step: Some states' working definitions of students "at risk." *Education Week,* p. 14.

Montgomery, M. D. (1978). The special educator as consultant: Some strategies. *Teaching Exceptional Children, 10,* 110–112.

Morganthau, T. (1986, March 17). Kids and cocaine. *Newsweek,* pp. 57, 59–62, 63, 65.

Morrison, G. M., & Polloway, E. A. (1995). Mental retardation. In E. L. Meyen & T. M. Skrtic (Eds.), *Special education and student disability* (4th ed.) (pp. 212–269). Denver: Love.

Morsink, C. V., & Lenk, L. L. (1992). The delivery of special education programs and services. *Remedial and Special Education, 13*(6), 33–43.

Muccigrosso, L., Scavarda, M., Simpson-Brown, R., & Thalacker, B. E. (1991). *Double jeopardy: Pregnant and parenting youth in special education.* Reston, VA: The Council for Exceptional Children.

Munson, S. M. (1986). Regular education teacher modifications for mainstreamed mildly handicapped students. *Journal of Special Education, 20,* 489–502.

Murdick, N. L., & Petch-Hogan, B. (1996). Inclusive classroom management: Using preintervention strategies. *Intervention in School and Clinic, 31,* 172–176.

Myklebust, H. R. (1981). *The pupil rating scale revised.* New York: Grune & Stratton.

Myles, B. S., Simpson, R. L., & Smith, S. M. (1996). Impact of facilitated communication combined with direct instruction on academic performance of individuals with autism. *Focus on Autism and Other Developmental Disabilities, 11,* 37–44.

National Advisory Committee on Handicapped Children. (1968). *Special education for handicapped children* [First annual report]. Washington, DC: U.S. Department of Health, Education, and Welfare.

National Center for Health Statistics. (1996, December 19). *Teenage birth rates down in a majority of states.* [Online]. Available: http://www.cdc.gov/nchswww/releases/96facts/96sheets/teenbrth.htm [1997, November 11].

National Clearinghouse on Child Abuse and Neglect. (1997). *What is child maltreatment?* [Online]. Available: http://www.calib.com/nccanch/pubs/whatis.htm [1998, January 10].

National Coalition of Advocates for Students. (1985). *Barriers to excellence: Our children at risk.* Boston: Author.

National Commission on Excellence in Education. (1983). *A nation at risk: The imperative for educational reform.* Washington, DC: U.S. Government Printing Office.

National Committee to Prevent Child Abuse. (1997, April). *Child abuse and neglect statistics.* [Online] Available: http://www.childabuse.org/facts96.html [1998, January 10].

National Council of Teachers of Mathematics. (1989). *Curriculum and evaluation standards for school mathematics.* Reston, VA: Author.

National Education Goals Panel. (1997). *Commonly asked questions* [Online]. Available: http://www.negp.gov/caq.html

National Information Center for Children and Youth with Disabilities. (1996). *General information about deafness and hearing loss: Fact sheet number 3.* Washington, DC: Author.

National Information Center for Children and Youth with Disabilities. (1997a). *General information about visual impairments: Fact sheet number 13.* Washington, DC: Author.

National Information Center for Children and Youth with Disabilities. (1997b). *Speech and language disorders.* Washington, DC: Author.

National Information Center for Children and Youth with Disabilities. (1997c). *Traumatic brain injury.* Washington, DC: Author.

National Institute on Drug Abuse. (1997, November 24). Facts about teenagers and drug abuse. *NIDA Capsules* [Online]. Available: http://www.nida.nih.gov/NIDACapsules/NCTeenagers.html [1998, January 10].

National Joint Committee on Learning Disabilities. (1993). A reaction to full inclusion: A reaffirmation of the right of students with learning disabilities to a continuum of services. *Journal of Learning Disabilities, 26,* 596.

National Joint Committee on Learning Disabilities. (1994). *Collective perspectives on issues affecting learning disabilities.* Austin, TX: PRO-ED.

National Research Council. (1997). *Executive summary. Educating one & all: Students with disabilities and stan-*

dards-based reform. Washington, DC: National Academy Press.

National Society to Prevent Blindness. (1977). *Signs of possible eye trouble in children* (Pub. G-112). New York: Author.

NEA survey investigates teacher attitudes, practices. (1980). *Phi Delta Kappan, 62,* 49–50.

Neary, T., Halvorsen, A., & Smithey, L. (1991). *Inclusive education guidelines.* Sacramento, CA: California Department of Education, PEERS Project.

Needham, N. (1989). Meet C. Everett Koop: Gruff, tough, and no bluff. *NEA Today, 7*(7), 10–11.

Nelson, C. M. (1988). Social skill training for handicapped students. *Teaching Exceptional Children, 20*(4), 19–23.

Nelson, C. M. (1993). Students with behavioral disorders. In A. E. Blackhurst & W. H. Berdine (Eds.), *An introduction to special education* (3rd ed., pp. 528–561). New York: HarperCollins.

Newcomb, M. D., & Bentler, P. M. (1989). Substance use and abuse among children and teenagers. *American Psychologist, 44,* 242–248.

Newcomer, P. L., & Hammill, D. D. (1997). *Test of language development-Primary* (3rd ed.). Austin, TX: PRO-ED.

Nietupski, J., Hamre-Nietupski, S., Curtin, S., & Shrikanth, K. (1997). A review of curricular research in severe disabilities from 1976 to 1995 in six selected journals. *Journal of Special Education, 31,* 36–55.

Nirje, B. (1969). The normalization principle and its human management implications. In R. B. Kugel & W. Wolfensberger (Eds.), *Changing patterns in residential services for the mentally retarded* (pp. 231–240). Washington, DC: U.S. Government Printing Office.

Norris, W. C. (1977). Via technology to a new era in education. *Phi Delta Kappan, 58,* 451–453.

Northcutt, L., & Watson, D. (1986). *Sheltered English teaching handbook.* San Marcos, CA: AM Graphics & Printing.

Odom, S. L., McConnell, S. R., & Chandler, L. K. (1994). Acceptability and feasibility of classroom based social interaction interventions for young children with disabilities. *Exceptional Children, 60,* 226–236.

Oehring, S. (1992). Adventures with grandparents. *Instructor, 102*(2), 90, 102.

Office of Technology Assessment. (1988). *Power on! New tools for teaching and learning.* Washington, DC: U.S. Government Printing Office.

Ogden, E. H., & Germinario, V. (1988). *The at-risk student: Answers for educators.* Lancaster, PA: Technomic.

Olson, J. L., & Platt, J. M. (1996). *Teaching children and adolescents with special needs* (2nd ed.). New York: Merrill/Prentice Hall.

Olson, L. (1988, September 21). Despite years of rhetoric, most still see little understanding, inadequate efforts. *Education Week,* pp. 1–16.

Orr, L. E., Craig, G. P., Best, J., Borland, A., Holland, D., Knodel, H., Lehman, A., Mathewson, C., Miller, M., & Pequignot, M. (1997). Exploring developmental disabilities through literature: An annotated bibliography. *Teaching Exceptional Children, 29*(6), 14–17.

Ortiz, A. A. (1988, Spring). Evaluating educational contexts in which language minority students are served. *Bilingual Special Education Newsletter, 7,* 1, 3–4, 7.

Osguthorpe, R. T, & Scruggs, T. E. (1986). Special education students as tutors: A review and analysis. *Remedial and Special Education, 7*(4), 15–26.

Palinscar, A. S., & Brown, A. L. (1988). Teaching and practicing thinking skills to promote comprehension in the context of group problem solving. *Remedial and Special Education, 9*(1), 53–59.

Papert, S. (1980). *Mindstorms.* New York: Basic Books.

Parke, B. N. (1989). *Gifted students in regular classrooms.* Boston: Allyn & Bacon.

Parker, J. P. (1989). *Instructional strategies for teaching the gifted.* Boston: Allyn & Bacon.

Parson, L. R., & Heward, W. L. (1979). Training peers to tutor: Evaluation of a training package for primary learning disabled students. *Journal of Applied Behavior Analysis, 12,* 309–310.

Pasanella, A. L., & Volkmor, C. B. (1981). *Teaching handicapped students in the mainstream* (2nd ed.). Columbus, OH: Merrill.

Patrick, J. L., & Reschly, D. J. (1982). Relationship of state educational criteria and demographic variables to school-system prevalence of mental retardation. *American Journal of Mental Deficiency, 86,* 351–360.

Patros, P. G., & Shamoo, T. K. (1989). *Depression and suicide in children and adolescents: Prevention, intervention, and postvention.* Boston: Allyn & Bacon.

Patterson, G. R., DeBaryshe, B. D., & Ramsey, E. (1989). A developmental perspective on antisocial behavior. *American Psychologist, 44,* 329–335.

Pendarvis, E. D. (1993). Students with unique gifts and talents. In A. E. Blackhurst & W. H. Berdine (Eds.), *An introduction to special education* (3rd ed., pp. 563–599). New York: HarperCollins.

Pendergast, D. E. (1995). Preparing for children who are medically fragile in educational programs. *Teaching Exceptional Children, 27*(2), 37–41.

Pepper, F. C. (1976). Teaching the American Indian child in mainstream settings. In R. L. Jones (Ed.), *Mainstreaming and the minority child* (pp. 133–158). Reston, VA: The Council for Exceptional Children.

Perske, R., & Perske, M. (1988). *Circles of friends: People with disabilities and their friends enrich the lives of one another.* Nashville, TN: Abington.

Pfeifer, J. K. (1986). *Teenage suicide: What can the schools do?* Bloomington, IN: Phi Delta Kappa Educational Foundation.

Phelps, M. S., & Prock, G. A. (1991). Equality of educational opportunity in rural America. In A. DeYoung (Ed.), *Rural education issues and practice* (pp. 269–312). New York: Garland.

Platt, J. M., & Olson, J. L. (1997). *Teaching adolescents with mild disabilities.* Pacific Grove, CA: Brooks-Cole.

Platt, J. M., & Platt, J. S. (1980). Volunteers for special education: A mainstreaming support system. *Teaching Exceptional Children, 13,* 31–34.

Polloway, E. A., & Patton, J. R. (1993). *Strategies for teaching learners with special needs* (5th ed.). New York: Merrill/Macmillan.

Popham, J. P. (1993). Wanted: AIDS education that works. *Phi Delta Kappan, 74,* 559–562.

Postel, C. A. (1986). Death in my classroom? *Teaching Exceptional Children, 18,* 139–143.

Posth, M. A. (1997, March). Why the Web? *Mac Home Journal,* 36–37.

Prasad, S. (1994). Assessing social interactions of children with disabilities. *Teaching Exceptional Children, 26*(2), 23–25.

Prater, M. A. (1994). Improving academic and behavior skills through self-management procedures. *Preventing School Failure, 38*(4), 5–9.

President's Committee on Mental Retardation. (1969). *The six hour retarded child.* Washington, DC: U.S. Department of Health, Education, and Welfare.

President's Committee on Mental Retardation. (1975). *The problem of mental retardation.* Washington, DC: U.S. Department of Health, Education, and Welfare.

President's Committee on Mental Retardation. (1997). *Mission* [Online]. Available: http://acf.dhhs.gov/programs/pcmr/mission.htm [1997, November 30].

Prior, M., & Cummins, R. (1992). Questions about facilitated communication and autism. *Journal of Autism and Developmental Disorders, 22,* 331–337.

Programs for Improvement of Practice (1993). *National excellence: A case for developing America's talent.* Washington, DC: U.S. Department of Education.

Project seen helping "disconnected" young. (1988, September 21). *Education Week,* p. 17.

Pumpian, I. (1988). Severe multiple handicaps. In E. W. Lynch & R. B. Lewis (Eds.), *Exceptional children and adults* (pp. 180–226). Glenview, IL: Scott, Foresman.

Putnam, J. M. (1992). Teaching students with severe disabilities in the regular classroom. In L. G. Cohen (Ed.), *Children with exceptional needs in regular classrooms* (pp. 118–142). Washington, DC: National Education Association.

Quality Education Data, Inc. (1985). *Microcomputer usage in schools, 1984–1985.* Denver: Author.

Quay, H. C. (1979). Classification. In H. C. Quay & J. S. Werry (Eds.), *Psychopathological disorders of childhood* (2nd ed.). New York: Wiley.

Raison, S. B. (1979). Curriculum modification for special needs at the secondary level. *Education Unlimited, 1*(3), 19–21.

Rapport, J. K. (1996). Legal guidelines for the delivery of special health care services in schools. *Exceptional Children, 62,* 537–549.

Ratleff, J. E. (1989). *Instructional strategies for crosscultural students with special education needs.* Sacramento, CA: Resources in Special Education.

Ray, B. M. (1985). Measuring the social position of the mainstreamed handicapped child. *Exceptional Children, 52,* 57–62.

Recer, P. (1989, June 8). 12% of kids mentally troubled, study says. *Associated Press,* pp. 1–2.

Rees, T. (1992). Students with hearing impairments. In L. G. Cohen (Ed.), *Children with exceptional needs in regular classrooms* (pp. 98–117). Washington, DC: National Education Association.

Reeve, R. E. (1990). ADHD: Facts and fallacies. *Intervention in School and Clinic, 26,* 70–78.

Reeves, M. S. (1988, April 27). "Self-interest and the commonweal": Focusing on the bottom half. *Education Week,* pp. 14–21.

Reid, D. K., Hresko, W. P., & Swanson, H. L. (Eds.). (1996). *Cognitive approaches to learning disabilities* (3rd ed.). Austin, TX: PRO-ED.

Reid, R. (1996). Research in self-monitoring with students with learning disabilities: The present, the prospects, the pitfalls. *Journal of Learning Disabilities, 29,* 317–331.

Reis, S. M. (1989). Reflections on policy affecting the education of gifted and talented students: Past and future perspectives. *American Psychologist, 44,* 399–408.

Reis, S. M., & Renzulli, J. S. (1985). *Identification of the gifted and talented* (ERIC Digest, Clearinghouse on Handicapped and Gifted Children, No. 360). Reston, VA: The Council for Exceptional Children.

Renzulli, J. S., & Smith, L. H. (1978). *Learning styles inventory: A measure of student preference for instructional techniques.* Mansfield Center, CT: Creative Learning Press.

Renzulli, J. S., Smith, L. H., White, A. J., Callahan, C. M., & Hartman, R. K. (1976). *Scales for rating the behavior characteristics of superior students.* Mansfield Center, CT: Creative Learning Press.

Reschly, D. J., & Lamprecht, M. J. (1979). Expectancy effects of labels: Fact or artifact? *Exceptional Children, 46,* 55–58.

Research and Training Center on Independent Living. (1990). *Guidelines for reporting and writing about people with disabilities* (3rd ed.). Lawrence, KS: Author.

Reynolds, M. C., & Birch, J. W. (1982). *Teaching exceptional children in all America's schools* (Rev. ed.). Reston, VA: The Council for Exceptional Children.

Reynolds, M. C., & Birch, J. W. (1988). *Adaptive mainstreaming* (3rd ed.). New York: Longman.

Reynolds, M. C., Zetlin, A. G., & Wang, M. C. (1993). 20/20 analysis: Taking a close look at the margins. *Exceptional Children, 59,* 294–300.

Reynolds, W. M. (1987). *Wepman's auditory discrimination test manual* (2nd ed.). Los Angeles: Western Psychological Services.

Rich, H. L., & Ross, S. M. (1989). Students' time on learning tasks in special education. *Exceptional Children, 55,* 508–515.

Rieth, H., & Evertson, C. M. (1988). Variables related to the effective instruction of difficult-to-teach children. *Focus on Exceptional Children, 20*(5), 1–8.

Rivera, B. D., & Rogers-Adkinson, D. (1997). Culturally sensitive interventions: Social skills training with children and parents from culturally and linguistically diverse backgrounds. *Intervention in School and Clinic, 33,* 75–80.

Rivera, D. P., & Smith, D. D. (1997). *Teaching students with learning and behavior problems* (3rd ed.). Boston: Allyn & Bacon.

Roberts, R., & Mather, N. (1995). The return of students with learning disabilities to regular classrooms: A sellout? *Learning Disabilities Research & Practice, 10,* 46–58.

Robinson, F. P. (1961). *Effective study.* New York: Harper & Row.

Robinson, S., & Deshler D. D. (1995). Learning disabled. In E. L. Meyen & T. M. Skrtic (Eds.), *Special education and student disability* (4th ed.) (pp. 170–211). Denver: Love.

Rockefeller, N. A. (1976, October 16). Don't accept anyone's verdict that you are lazy, stupid, or retarded. *TV Guide,* pp. 12–14.

Rodriguez, R. C., Cole, J. T., Stile, S. W., & Gallegos, R. L. (1979). Bilingualism and biculturalism for the special education classroom. *Teacher Education and Special Education, 2*(4), 69–74.

Roland, P. (1989, August). A parent speaks to special educators. *Exceptional Times,* p. 3.

Rose, L. C., Gallup, A. M., & Elam, S. M. (1997). The 29th annual Phi Delta Kappa/Gallup poll of the public's attitudes toward the public schools. *Phi Delta Kappan, 79,* 41–58.

Rosenkoetter, S. E., & Fowler, S. A. (1986). Teaching mainstreamed children to manage daily transitions. *Teaching Exceptional Children, 19*(1), 20–23.

Rosenshine, B., & Stevens, R. (1986). Teaching functions. In M. C. Wittrock (Ed.), *Handbook of research on teaching* (3rd ed., pp. 376–391). New York: Macmillan.

Rossett, A., & Glassman, B. O. (1979). Technology and desirable school behavior. *Journal of Technological Horizons in Education, 6*(2), 37–39.

Rubin, R. A., & Balow, B. (1978). Prevalence of teacher identified behavior problems: A longitudinal study. *Exceptional Children, 45,* 102–111.

Rueda, R., & Prieto, A. G. (1979). Cultural pluralism: Implications for teacher education. *Teacher Education and Special Education, 2*(4), 4–11.

Ruiz, N. T. (1989). An optimal learning environment for Rosemary. *Exceptional Children, 56,* 130–144.

Russell, B., & Fessenden, B. (1989). Debate: Should dropouts be denied driver's licenses? *NEA Today, 8*(3), 39.

Ryder, R. J., Graves, B. B., & Graves, M. F. (1989). *Easy reading: Book series and periodicals for less able readers* (2nd ed.). Newark, DE: International Reading Association.

Sabornie, E. J., & deBettencourt, L. U. (1997). *Teaching students with mild disabilities at the secondary level.* Upper Saddle River, NJ: Merrill/Prentice Hall.

Sabornie, E. J., & Kauffman, J. M. (1985). Regular classroom sociometric status of behaviorally disordered adolescents. *Behavioral Disorders, 10,* 268–274.

Safran, S. P., & Safran, J. S. (1996). Intervention assistance programs and prereferral teams: Directions for the twenty-first century. *Remedial and Special Education, 17,* 363–369.

Sailor, W., Gee, K., & Karasoff, P. (1993). Full inclusion and school restructuring. In M. E. Snell (Ed.), *Instruction of students with severe disabilities* (4th ed., pp. 1–30). New York: Merrill/Macmillan.

Sale, P., & Carey, D. M. (1995). The sociometric status of students with disabilities in a full-inclusion school. *Exceptional Children, 62,* 6–19.

Salend, S. J. (1987). Group-oriented behavior management strategies. *Teaching Exceptional Children, 19*(1), 53–55.

Salpeter, J. (1988). Answers to your questions about CD-ROM. *Classroom Computer Learning, 8*(6), 18.

Salpeter, J. (1997). Industry snapshot: Where are we headed? *Technology & Learning, 17*(6), 22–24, 28–32.

Salvia, J., & Ysseldyke, J. E. (1991). *Assessment* (5th ed.). Boston: Houghton Mifflin.

Sander, E. K. (1972). When are speech sounds learned? *Journal of Speech and Hearing Disorders, 23*(1), 55–63.

Sarff, L. (1981). An innovative use of free field amplification in regular classrooms. In R. Roesser & M. Downs (Eds.), *Auditory disorders in school children* (pp. 263–272). New York: Thieme Stratton.

Sasso, G., & Rude, H. A. (1988). The social effects of integration on nonhandicapped children. *Education and Training in Mental Retardation, 23,* 18–23.

Schilit, J., & Caldwell, M. L. (1980). A word list of essential career/vocational words for mentally retarded students. *Education and Training of the Mentally Retarded, 15,* 113–117.

Schinke, S. P., & Gilchrist, L. D. (1984). *Life skills counseling for adolescents.* Baltimore: University Park Press.

Schlosser, L. Y., & Algozzine, B. (1980). Sex, behavior, and teacher expectancies. *Journal of Experimental Education, 48,* 231–236.

Schmidt, P. (1992). Census data find more are falling behind in school. *Education Week, 11*(38), 1, 9.

Schubert, M., Glick, H., & Bauer, D. (1979). *The least restrictive environment and the handicapped student.* Dayton, OH: Wright State University.

Schulte, A. C., Osborne, S. S., & McKinney, J. D. (1990). Academic outcomes for students with learning disabilities in consultation and resource programs. *Exceptional Children, 57,* 162–172.

Schultz, J. B., & Torrie, M. (1984). Effectiveness of parent-hood education materials for mainstreamed vocational Home Economics classes. *Journal of Vocational Education Research, 9*(1), 46–56.

Schulz, J. B., & Turnbull, A. P. (1983). *Mainstreaming handicapped students* (2nd ed.). Boston: Allyn & Bacon.

Schumaker, J. B., & Deshler, D. D. (1988). Implementing the regular education initiative in secondary schools: A different ball game. *Journal of Learning Disabilities, 21,* 36–42.

Schumaker, J. B., & Hazel, J. S. (1984). Social skills assessment and training for the learning disabled: Who's on first and what's on second? Part I. *Journal of Learning Disabilities, 17,* 422–431.

Schumaker, J. B., Nolan, S. M., & Deshler, D. D. (1985). *Learning strategies curriculum: The error monitoring strategy.* Lawrence: University of Kansas.

Scrogan, L. (Ed.). (1988). The OTA report: New technologies *are* making a difference. *Classroom Computer Learning, 9*(2), 33–42.

Searcy, S. (1996). Friendship interventions for the integration of children and youth with learning and behavior problems. *Preventing School Failure, 40*(3), 131–134.

Semel, E., Wiig, E. H., & Secord, W. A. (1995). *Clinical evaluation of language fundamentals-Third edition.* San Antonio, TX: Psychological Corporation.

Semmel, M. I., & Lieber, J. A. (1986). Computer applications in instruction. *Focus on Exceptional Children, 18*(9), 1–12.

Shames, G. H., & Ramig, P. R. (1994). Stuttering and other disorders of fluency. In G. H. Shames, E. H. Wiig, & W. A Secord (Eds.), *Human communication disorders* (4th ed., pp. 336–386). New York: Merrill/Macmillan.

Shatz-Akin, T. (1997). DVD comes to the Mac. *MacUser, 13*(7), 74–77.

Shepard, D. H. (1986, November). Special students and regular software. *The Computing Teacher,* pp. 18–19.

Shinn, M. R., & Hubbard, D. D. (1993). Curriculum-based measurement and problem-solving assessment: Basic procedures and outcomes. In E. L. Meyen, G. A. Vergason, & R. J. Whelan (Eds.), *Educating students with mild disabilities* (pp. 221–253). Denver: Love.

Siegel, L. J., & Senna, J. J. (1994). *Juvenile delinquency: Theory, practice and law.* St. Paul: West.

Sierra, V. (1973). Learning style of the Mexican American. In L. A. Bransford, L. M. Baca, & K. Lane (Eds.), *Cultural diversity and the exceptional child* (pp. 42–49). Reston, VA: The Council for Exceptional Children.

Silvaroli, N. J. (1990). *Classroom reading inventory* (6th ed.). Dubuque, IA: Brown.

Silver, L. B. (1987). The "magic cure": A review of the current controversial approaches for treating learning disabilities. *Journal of Learning Disabilities, 20,* 498–504, 512.

Silverman, L. K. (1988). Gifted and talented. In E. L. Meyen & T. M. Skrtic (Eds.), *Exceptional children and youth: An introduction* (3rd ed., pp. 263–291). Denver: Love.

Simms, R. S., & Falcon, S. C. (1987). Teaching sight words. *Teaching Exceptional Children, 20*(1), 30–33.

Simpson, R. L. (1980). Modifying the attitudes of regular class students toward the handicapped. *Focus on Exceptional Children, 13*(3), 1–11.

Sindelar, P. T. (1987). Increasing reading fluency. *Teaching Exceptional Children, 19*(2), 59–60.

Sirvis, B. (1982). The physically disabled. In E. L. Meyen (Ed.), *Exceptional children and youth* (2nd ed., pp. 382–405). Denver: Love.

Sirvis, B. (1988). Physical disabilities. In E. L. Meyen & T. M. Skrtic (Eds.), *Exceptional children and youth: An introduction* (3rd ed., pp. 387–411). Denver: Love.

Sivin-Kachala, J., & Bialo, E. R. (1996). *Report on the effectiveness of technology in schools, '95–'96.* Washington, DC: Software Publishers Association.

Sklaire, M. (1989). Today's kids face different diseases. *NEA Today, 7*(8), 9.

Slate, J. R., & Saudargas, R. A. (1986). Differences in learning disabled and average students' classroom behaviors. *Learning Disability Quarterly, 9*(1), 61–67.

Slavin, R. E. (1987). *Cooperative learning: Student teams.* Washington, DC: National Education Association.

Slavin, R. E. (1989). Students at risk of school failure: The problem and its dimensions. In R. E. Slavin, N. L. Karweit, & N. A. Madden (Eds.), *Effective programs for students at risk* (pp. 3–19). Boston: Allyn & Bacon.

Slavin, R. E. (1990). *Cooperative learning: Theory, research, and practice.* Englewood Cliffs, NJ: Prentice Hall.

Slavin, R. E., Madden, N. A., & Karweit, N. L. (1989). Effective programs for students at risk: Conclusions for practice and policy. In R. E. Slavin, N. L. Karweit, & N. A. Madden (Eds.), *Effective programs for students at risk* (pp. 355–372). Boston: Allyn & Bacon.

Slavin, R. E., Madden, N. A., & Leavey, M. (1984). Effects of cooperative learning and individualized instruction on mainstreamed students. *Exceptional Children, 50,* 434–443.

Smith, D. D. (1998). *Introduction to special education* (3rd ed.). Boston: Allyn and Bacon.

Smith, F. (1982). *Writing and the writer.* New York: Holt, Rinehart & Winston.

Smith, J. (1979). The education of Mexican-Americans: Bilingual, bicognitive, or biased? *Teacher Education and Special Education, 2*(4), 37–48.

Smith, R. M., Neisworth, J. T., & Greer, J. G. (1978). *Evaluating educational environments.* Columbus, OH: Merrill Publishing Company.

Smith, T. E. C., Finn, D. M., & Dowdy, C. A. (1993). *Teaching students with mild disabilities.* Fort Worth, TX: Harcourt Brace Jovanovich.

Smith, T. E. C., Polloway, E. A., Patton, J. R., & Dowdy, C. A. (1998). *Teaching students with special needs in inclusive settings* (2nd ed.). Boston: Allyn and Bacon.

Snell, M., & Brown, F. (1993). Instructional planning and implementation. In M. Snell (Ed.), *Instruction of students with severe disabilities* (4th ed., pp. 99–151). New York: Merrill/Macmillan.

Snider, W. (1988, September 21). Hispanic students require income to remain in school, study finds. *Education Week,* p. 17.

Soderberg, L. J. (1988). Educators' knowledge of the characteristics of high school dropouts. *The High School Journal, 71,* 108–115.

Spache, G. (1953). A new readability formula for primary-grade reading materials. *The Elementary School Journal, 53,* 410–413.

Spalding, R. B., & Spalding, W. T. (1986). *The writing road to reading* (3rd rev. ed.). New York: Morrow.

Spenciner, L. J. (1992). Mainstreaming the child with a visual impairment. In L. G. Cohen (Ed.), *Children with exceptional needs in regular classrooms* (pp. 82–97). Washington, DC: National Education Association.

Stahl, S. A., & Miller, P. D. (1989). Whole language and language experience approaches for beginning reading: A quantitative research synthesis. *Review of Educational Research, 59,* 87–116.

Stainback, S., & Stainback, W. (Eds.). (1985). *Integrating students with severe handicaps into regular schools.* Reston, VA: The Council for Exceptional Children.

Stainback, S., & Stainback, W. (1988). Educating students with severe disabilities. *Teaching Exceptional Children, 21*(1), 16–19.

Stainback, S., & Stainback, W. (1990a). Inclusive schooling. In W. Stainback & S. Stainback (Eds.), *Support networks for inclusive schooling* (pp. 3–23). Baltimore: Brookes.

Stainback, W., & Stainback, S. (Eds.). (1990b). *Support networks for inclusive schooling.* Baltimore: Brookes.

Stainback, S., & Stainback, W. (1992). *Curriculum considerations in inclusive classrooms.* Baltimore: Brookes.

Stainback, S., Stainback, W., & Forest, M. (1989). *Educating all students in the mainstream of regular education.* Baltimore: Brookes.

Stainback, S., Stainback, W., & Slavin, R. (1989). Classroom organization for diversity among students. In S. Stainback, W. Stainback, & M. Forest (Eds.), *Educating all students in the mainstream of regular education* (pp. 131–142). Baltimore: Brookes.

Stainback, W., Stainback, S., & Froyen, L. (1987). Structuring the classroom to prevent disruptive behaviors. *Teaching Exceptional Children, 19*(4), 12–16.

Stainback, W., Stainback, S., & Wilkinson, A. (1992). Encouraging peer supports and friendships. *Teaching Exceptional Children, 24*(2), 6–11.

Steel, E. (1995). AIDS, drugs, and the adolescent. *National Institute on Drug Abuse Research Monograph, 156,* 130–145.

Stephens, T. M. (1978). *Social skills in the classroom.* Columbus, OH: Cedars.

Stephens, T. M. (1980). Teachers as managers. *The Directive Teacher, 2*(5), 4.

Stephens, T. M., & Wolf, J. S. (1978). The gifted child. In N. G. Haring (Ed.), *Behavior of exceptional children* (2nd ed., pp. 387–405). Columbus, OH: Merrill.

Sternberg, R. J. (1991). Giftedness according to the triarchic theory of human intelligence. In N. Colangelo & G. A. Davis (Eds.), *Handbook of gifted education* (pp. 45–54). Boston: Allyn & Bacon.

Stevens, L. J., & Price, M. (1992). Meeting the challenge of educating children at risk. *Phi Delta Kappan, 74,* 18–20, 22–23.

Stevens, R., & Rosenshine, B. (1981). Advances in research on teaching. *Exceptional Education Quarterly, 2*(1), 1–9.

Stitt, B. A., Erekson, T. L., Hofstrand, R. K., Loepp, F. L., Minor, C. W., Perreault, H. R., & Savage, J. G. (1988). *Building gender fairness in schools.* Carbondale: Board of Trustees, Southern Illinois University.

Stone, B., Cundick, B. P., & Swanson, D. (1988). Special education screening system: Group achievement test. *Exceptional Children, 55,* 71–75.

Stowitschek, J. J., Gable, R. A., & Hendrickson, J. M. (1980). *Instructional materials for exceptional children.* Germantown, MD: Aspen Systems.

Strain, P. S. (1981a). Peer-mediated treatment of exceptional children's social withdrawal. *Exceptional Education Quarterly, 1*(4), 93–105.

Strain, P. S. (Ed.). (1981b). *The utilization of peers as behavior change agents.* New York: Plenum.

Strain, P. S., & Kerr, M. M. (1981). *Mainstreaming of children in schools.* New York: Academic Press.

Strickland, B. B., & Turnbull, A. P. (1993). *Developing and implementing individualized education programs* (3rd ed.). New York: Merrill/Macmillan.

Sugai, G., & Lewis, T. J. (1996). Preferred and promising practices for social skills instruction. *Focus on Exceptional Children, 29*(4), 1–16.

Sugai, G. M., & Tindal, G. A. (1993). *Effective school consultation: An interactive approach.* Pacific Grove, CA: Brooks/Cole.

Sulzer-Azaroff, B., & Mayer, G. R. (1977). *Applying behavior-analysis procedures with children and youth.* New York: Holt, Rinehart & Winston.

Swanson, H. L. (1989). Strategy instruction: Overview of principles and procedures for effective use. *Learning Disabilities Quarterly, 12,* 3–14.

Swanson, H. L., & Cooney, J. B. (1996). Learning disabilities and memory. In D. K. Reid, W. P. Hresko, & H. L. Swanson, *Cognitive approaches to learning disabilities* (3rd ed.) (pp. 287–314). Austin, TX: PRO-ED.

Sweeney, D. P., Forness, S. R., Kavale, K. A., & Levitt, J. G. (1997). An update on psychopharmacologic medication: What teachers, clinicians, and parents need to know. *Intervention in Clinic and School, 33,* 4–21, 25.

Swift, C. A. (1988). Communication disorders. In E. W. Lynch & R. B. Lewis (Eds.), *Exceptional children and adults* (pp. 318–351). Glenview, IL: Scott, Foresman.

Tarver, S., & Hallahan, D. P. (1976). Children with learning disabilities: An overview. In J. M. Kauffman & D. P. Hallahan (Eds.), *Teaching children with learning disabili-*

ties: Personal perspectives (pp. 2–57). Columbus, OH: Merrill Publishing Company.

Task Force on Children with Attention Deficit Disorder. (1992). *Children with ADD: A shared responsibility.* Reston, VA: The Council for Exceptional Children.

Taylor, O. (1986). Language differences. In G. H. Shames & E. H. Wiig (Eds.), *Human communication disorders* (2nd ed., pp. 385–413). New York: Merrill/Macmillan.

Taylor, R. P. (Ed.). (1981). *The computer in the school: Tutor, tool, tutee.* New York: Teachers College Press.

Taylor, S. J. (1988). Caught in the continuum: A critical analysis of the principle of the least restrictive environment. *Journal of the Association for Persons with Severe Handicaps, 13*(1), 41–53.

Technology and the at-risk student. (1988, November/December). *Electronic Learning,* pp. 35–49.

Telford, C. W., & Sawrey, J. M. (1981). *The exceptional individual* (4th ed.). Englewood Cliffs, NJ: Prentice Hall.

Thomas, C. H., & Patton, J. R. (1990). Mild and moderate retardation. In J. R. Patton, M. Beirne-Smith, & J. S. Payne (Eds.), *Mental retardation* (3rd ed., pp. 197–226). New York: Merrill/Macmillan.

Thorndike, R. L., Hagen, E., & Sattler, J. (1986). *Stanford-Binet intelligence scale: Fourth edition.* Chicago: Riverside.

Thousand, J. S., & Villa, R. A. (1990). Strategies for educating learners with severe disabilities within their local home schools and communities. *Focus on Exceptional Children, 23*(3), 1–24.

Thurber, D. N., & Jordan, D. R. (1981). *D'Nealian handwriting.* Glenview, IL: Scott, Foresman.

Timar, T. B., & Kirp, D. L. (1989). Education reform in the 1980s: Lessons from the states. *Phi Delta Kappan, 70,* 505–511.

Tompkins, G. E., & Friend, M. (1986). On your mark, get set, write! *Teaching Exceptional Children, 18*(2), 82–89.

Tompkins, G. E., & Friend, M. (1988). After your students write: What's next? *Teaching Exceptional Children, 20*(3), 4–9.

Torgesen, J. K. (1977). The role of nonspecific factors in the task performance of learning disabled children: A theoretical assessment. *Journal of Learning Disabilities, 10,* 27–34.

Torrance, E. P. (1966). *Torrance tests of creative thinking.* Princeton, NJ: Personnel.

Torres, I., & Corn, A. L. (1990). *When you have a visually handicapped child in your classroom: Suggestions for teachers.* New York: American Foundation for the Blind.

Towell, J., & Wink, J. (1993). *Strategies for monolingual teachers in multilingual classrooms.* Turlock, CA: California State University, Stanislaus. (ERIC Document Reproduction Service No. ED 359 797)

Tower, C. C. (1987). *How schools can help combat child abuse and neglect* (2nd ed.). Washington, DC: National Education Association.

Tucker, B. F., & Colson, S. E. (1992). Traumatic brain injury: An overview of school re-entry. *Intervention in School and Clinic, 27,* 198–206.

Turnbull, A. P., & Schulz, J. B. (1979). *Mainstreaming handicapped students.* Boston: Allyn & Bacon.

U.S. Census Bureau. (1996). *Poverty: 1995 highlights* [Online]. Available: http://www.census.gov/hhes/poverty/pov95/pov95hi.html

U.S. Census Bureau. (1997). *Population profile of the United States: 1995, Highlights* [Online]. Available: http://www.census.gov/population/www/pop-profile/highlgt.html

U.S. Department of Commerce. (1989). *Statistical abstract of the United States 1989.* Washington, DC: U.S. Government Printing Office.

U.S. Department of Education. (1991, September 16). *Memorandum: Clarification of policy to address the needs of children with attention deficit disorders within general and/or special education.* Office of Special Education and Rehabilitative Services.

U.S. Department of Education. (1996). *Eighteenth annual report to Congress on the implementation of The Individuals with Disabilities Education Act.* Washington, DC: Author.

U.S. Department of Education. (1997a). *Nineteenth annual report to Congress on the implementation of The Individuals with Disabilities Education Act.* Washington, DC: Author.

U.S. Department of Education. (1997b). *Voluntary national tests* [Online]. Available: http://www.ed.gov/nationaltests/

U.S. Office of Technology Assessment. (1986). *Children's mental health problems: A background paper.* (Report No. OTA-BP-H-33). Washington, DC: Author.

Utley, C. A., Mortweet, S. L., & Greenwood, C. R. (1997). Peer-mediated instruction and interventions. *Focus on Exceptional Children, 29*(5), 1–23.

Vandercook, T., & York, J. (1990). A team approach to program development and support. In W. Stainback & S. Stainback (Eds.), *Support networks for inclusive schooling* (pp. 95–122). Baltimore: Brookes.

Vandercook, T., York, J., & Forest, M. (1989). The McGill Action Planning System (MAPS): A strategy for building the vision. *Journal of The Association for Persons with Severe Handicaps, 14,* 205–215.

Vannatta, R. A. (1997). Adolescent gender differences in suicide-related behaviors. *Journal of Youth and Adolescence, 26,* 559–568.

Van Riper, C. (1978). *Speech correction.* Englewood Cliffs, NJ: Prentice Hall.

VanTassel-Baska, J. (1994). *Comprehensive curriculum for gifted learners* (2nd ed.). Boston: Allyn & Bacon.

Vaughn, S., Bos, C. S., & Schumm, J. S. (1997). *Teaching mainstreamed, diverse, and at-risk students in the general education classroom.* Boston: Allyn & Bacon.

Vaughn, S. R. (1995, July). *Responsible inclusion for students with learning disabilities.* Paper presented at the conference of the International Academy for Research in Learning Disabilities, Phoenix, AZ.

Vergason, G. A., & Anderegg, M. L. (1991). Beyond the Regular Education Initiative and the resource room controversy. *Focus on Exceptional Children, 23*(7), 1–7.

Voeltz, L. M. (1980). Children's attitudes toward handicapped peers. *American Journal of Mental Deficiency, 84,* 455–464.

Voeltz, L. M. (1982). Effects of structured interactions with severely handicapped peers on children's attitudes. *American Journal of Mental Deficiency, 86,* 380–390.

Walker, H. M. (1995). *The acting out child: Coping with classroom disruption* (2nd ed.). Longmont, CO: Sopris West.

Walker, H. M., Colvin, G., & Ramsey, E. (1995). *Antisocial behavior in school: Strategies and best practices.* Pacific Grove, CA: Brooks/Cole.

Walker, H. M., McConnell, S., Holmes, D., Todis, B., Walker, J., & Golden, N. (1983). *The Walker social skills curriculum: The ACCEPTS program.* Austin, TX: PRO-ED.

Walker, H. M., Todis, B., Holmes, D., & Horton, G. (1988). *The Walker social skills curriculum: The ACCESS Program.* Austin, TX: PRO-ED.

Walker, J. L. (1988). Young American Indian children. *Teaching Exceptional Children, 20*(4), 50–51.

Warger, C. L., Tewey, S., & Megivern, M. (1991). *Abuse and neglect of exceptional children.* Reston, VA: The Council for Exceptional Children.

Webb, J. T., & Latimer, D. (1993). ADHD and children who are gifted. *Exceptional Children, 60,* 183–184.

Wechsler, D. (1991). *Wechsler intelligence scale for children-Third edition.* San Antonio, TX: Psychological Corporation.

Wehman, P. (1997). *Exceptional individuals in school, community, and work.* Austin, TX: PRO-ED.

Weil, M. L., & Murphy, J. (1982). Instruction processes. In H. E. Mitzel (Ed.), *Encyclopedia of educational research* (5th ed., pp. 890–917). New York: Free Press.

Weiner, J., & Harris, P. J. (1997). Evaluation of an individualized, context-based social skills training program for children with learning disabilities. *Learning Disabilities Research & Practice, 12,* 40–53.

Weinstein, C. S. (1979). The physical environment of the school: A review of research. *Review of Educational Research, 49,* 577–610.

Wepman, J. M. (1975). *Auditory discrimination test* (Rev. 1973). Palm Springs, CA: Research Associates.

Werts, M. G., Wolery, M., Snyder, E. D., & Caldwell, N. K. (1996). Teachers' perceptions of the supports critical to the success of inclusion programs. *JASH, 21,* 9–21.

Westby, C. E. (1992). Whole language and learners with mild handicaps. *Focus on Exceptional Children, 24*(8), 1–16.

Wheelchair prescriptions: Care and service. (1976). Los Angeles: Everest & Jennings.

Wheelchair prescriptions: Measuring the patient. (1968). Los Angeles: Everest & Jennings.

Wheeler, D. L., Jacobson, J. W., Paglieri, R. A., & Schwartz, A. A. (1993). An experimental assessment of facilitated communication. *Mental Retardation, 31,* 49–60.

Whelan, R. J. (1995). Emotional disturbance. In E. L. Meyen & T. M. Skrtic (Eds.), *Special education and student disability* (4th ed.) (pp. 270–336). Denver: Love.

White, K. R., Bush, D., & Casto, G. (1986). Let the past be prologue: Learning from previous reviews of early intervention efficacy research. *Journal of Special Education, 19,* 417–428.

Whitmore, J. R. (1985). *Characteristics of intellectually gifted children* (ERIC Digest, Clearinghouse on Handicapped and Gifted Children, No. 344). Reston, VA: The Council for Exceptional Children.

Whitt, J., Paul, P. V., & Reynolds, C. J. (1988). Motivate reluctant learning disabled writers. *Teaching Exceptional Children, 20*(3), 37–39.

Wiedmeyer, D., & Lehman, J. (1991). "The House Plan" approach to collaborative teaching and consultation. *Teaching Exceptional Children, 23*(10), 7–10.

Will, M. C. (1986a). Clarifying the standards: Placement in a least restrictive environment. *OSERS News in Print, 1*(2), 1.

Will, M. C. (1986b). Educating children with learning problems: A shared responsibility. *Exceptional Children, 52,* 411–415.

Willis, W. (1992). Families with African American roots. In E. W. Lynch & M. J. Hanson (Eds.), *Developing cross-cultural competence* (pp. 121–150). Baltimore: Brookes.

Winget, P., & Kirk, J. (1991). *California programs and services for students with serious emotional disturbances.* Sacramento, CA: Resources in Special Education.

Winston, S. (1991). *Getting organized* (Rev. ed.). New York: Warner Books.

Witherspoon, J. (1996). The evolving university: No longer virtual. *The Distance Educator, 2*(3), 1, 10–11, 18.

Wolfensberger, W. (1972). *The principle of normalization in human services.* Toronto: National Institute on Mental Retardation.

Wood, J. W., Lazzari, A., & Reeves, C. K. (1993). Educational characteristics and implications. In J. W. Wood (Ed.), *Mainstreaming* (2nd ed., pp. 78–120). New York: Merrill/Macmillan.

Wood, J. W., & Miederhoff, J. W. (1989). Bridging the gap. *Teaching Exceptional Children, 21*(2), 66–68.

Woodcock, R. W., & Johnson, M. B. (1989). *Woodcock-Johnson psycho-educational battery-Revised.* Chicago: Riverside.

Woodring, P. (1989). A new approach to the dropout problem. *Phi Delta Kappan, 70,* 468–469.

Woods, M. L., & Moe, A. J. (1995). *Analytical reading inventory* (5th ed.). Upper Saddle River, NJ: Merrill/Prentice Hall.

Woodward, D. M. (1981). *Mainstreaming the learning disabled adolescent.* Rockville, MD: Aspen Systems.

Worthen, B. R. (1993). Critical issues that will determine the future of alternative assessment. *Phi Delta Kappan, 74,* 444–454.

Yarber, W. L. (1987). *AIDS education: Curriculum and health policy.* Bloomington, IN: Phi Delta Kappa Educational Foundation.

York, J., Doyle, M. B., & Kronberg, R. (1992). A curriculum development process for inclusive classrooms. *Focus on Exceptional Children, 25*(4), 1–16.

York, J., & Vandercook, T. (1991). Designing an integrated program for learners with severe disabilities. *Teaching Exceptional Children, 23*(2), 22–28.

York, J., Vandercook, T., MacDonald, C., Heise-Neff, C., & Caughey, E. (1992). Feedback about integrating middle-school students with severe disabilities in general education classes. *Exceptional Children, 58,* 244–258.

Ysseldyke, J. E., Algozzine, B., & Thurlow, M. L. (1992). *Critical issues in special education* (2nd ed.). Boston, MA: Houghton Mifflin.

Ysseldyke, J. E., Thurlow, M. L., Wotruba, J. W., & Nania, P. A. (1990). Instructional arrangements: Perceptions from general education. *Teaching Exceptional Children, 22*(4), 4–8.

Zabel, H., & Tabor, M. (1993). Effects of soundfield amplification on spelling performance of elementary school children. *Educational Audiology Monograph, 3,* 5–9.

Zaragoza, N., Vaughn, S., & McIntosh, R. (1991). Social skills interventions and children with behavior problems: A review. *Behavioral Disorders, 16,* 260–275.

Zentall, S. S. (1983). Learning environments: A review of physical and temporal factors. *Exceptional Education Quarterly, 4*(2), 90–115.

Zigler, E., & Muenchow, S. (1979). Mainstreaming: The proof is in the implementation. *American Psychologist, 34,* 993–996.

Zigmond, N., Jenkins, J., Fuchs, D., Deno, S., & Fuchs, L. S. (1995). When students fail to achieve satisfactorily: A reply to McLeskey and Waldron. *Phi Delta Kappan, 77,* 303–306.

Zigmond, N., Jenkins, J., Fuchs, L. S., Deno, S., Fuchs, D., Baker, J. N., Jenkins, L., & Couthino, M. (1995). Special education in restructured schools: Findings from three multi-year studies. *Phi Delta Kappan, 76,* 531–540.

Zirkel, P. A. (1989). AIDS: Students in glass houses? *Phi Delta Kappan, 70,* 646–648.

Zirpoli, T. J., & Melloy, K. J. (1997). *Behavior management: Applications for teachers and parents* (2nd ed.). New York: Merrill/Prentice Hall.

Zuniga, M. E. (1992). Families with Latino roots. In E. W. Lynch & M. J. Hanson (Eds.), *Developing cross-cultural competence* (pp. 151–179). Baltimore: Brookes.

AUTHOR INDEX

Abramowitz, A. J., 260
Affleck, J. Q., 111, 183, 186, 193, 245, 256
Agard, J. A., 4
Agosta, J., 95
Aiello, B., 157
Akers, E., 120, 121
Alcohol use, 450
Alexander, C., 466
Algozzine, B., 38, 149, 260
Alley, G., 428
Allinder, R. M., 165
Allsop, J., 357
Almanza, E., 429
Alves, A. J., 103, 149, 179
Amadeo, D. M., 160
America 2000, 20
American Association of Colleges for Teacher Education, 417
American Association on Mental Retardation, 69
American Federation of Teachers, 21
American Foundation for the Blind, 382
American Psychiatric Association, 73, 260, 261
American Speech-Language-Hearing Association, 325, 326, 330, 341, 386
Ancona, G., 160
Anderegg, M. L., 92
Andersen, M., 158
Anderson, R. M., 357
Aragon, J., 416, 421
Arc, 271
Archer, A., 91, 111
Archer, A. L., 96, 183, 186, 193, 245, 313
Arkansas Enterprises for the Blind, 378
Artiles, A., 271
Aseltine, L., 160
Asher, S. R., 148, 154
Ashton, T. M., 17, 51, 253, 255
Ashton-Coombs, T. M., 159
Association for Retarded Citizens (ARC), 271
Austin, K., 151, 156, 157
Autism Society of America, 338
Axelrod, S., 125, 179

Baca, L. M., 419, 427, 429, 472
Bacon, E. H., 43

Bailey, S. A., 125
Baker, J., 306, 469
Baldwin, A. Y., 395
Balow, B., 68, 119
Banbury, M., 284
Barnett, B. G., 183
Barone, T., 443
Bartel, N. R., 195
Baruth, L. G., 438, 441
Bauer, A. M., 454
Bauer, D., 174, 183
Bauwens, J., 336
Becker, W. C., 186, 271
Bender, W. N., 262, 304
Bentler, P. M., 449, 451
Berdine, W. H., 10, 177, 185, 326, 354
Berg, F., 385
Berkus, C. W., 159
Berlin, G., 439
Berliner, D. C., 442
Berner, R., 356
Bernstein, J. E., 160
Berrigan, C., 339
Bettinger, M. M., 453
Bialo, E. R., 202
Biddle, B. J., 438, 442
Biklen, D., 339, 469
Binkard, B., 157, 166
Birch, J. W., 79, 345, 346, 347, 352, 369, 377, 378, 381, 382, 384, 387, 401, 402, 406
Bishop, K., 161, 286
Blackhurst, A. E., 10, 326, 354
Blake, K. A., 271
Blankenship, C., 44, 140, 380, 381, 387
Bliss, E. C., 191
Blum, I. M., 468
Boning, R. A., 249
Bonjean, L. M., 453
Bonvechio, L. R., 372
Bormuth, J. R., 241
Bos, C. S., 339, 343, 431
Bossert, S. T., 183
Bost, J. M., 149
Boston, J. 158
Bott, D. A., 165
Bowen, E., 442
Bower, E. M., 67, 68
Braaten, B., 469
Braaten, S., 469

Brackett, D., 384
Brady, M. P., 152
Brain Injury Association, 345
Bransford, J. D., 256
Brigance, A. H., 273, 274
Brinker, R. P., 286
Brolin, D. E., 277, 283, 285
Brooks-Gunn, J., 452, 453
Brophy, J. E., 90, 183, 468
Brown, A. L., 249
Brown, F., 157
Brown, G., 167
Brown, L., 301, 475
Brown, V. L., 328
Bruininks, R. H., 70, 271, 273
Bruno, J., 459
Bryan, J. H., 66, 148
Bryan, T., 66, 149
Bryan, T. H., 66, 148
Bryen, D. N., 426
Bulgren, J. A., 98
Burron, A., 241
Bush, D., 79
Butler, O. B., 438, 439, 443
Buttery, T. J., 355
Byrne, C. E., 348
Byrom, C. E., 345

Calculator, S. N., 339, 344
Caldwell, M. L., 281, 283, 292
Calhoun, M. L., 137
California Association for Neurologically Handicapped Children, 235
California Governor's Committee for Employment of Disabled Persons, 22
California Teachers of English to Speakers of other Languages, 431
Callahan, C. M., 397
Campbell, N. J., 149
Campbell, P. H., 161
Capuzzi, D., 448
Carey, D. M., 149, 150
Carlberg, C., 468
Carlson, N. A., 93
Carlson, N., 160
Carnine, D. W., 91
Carta, J. J., 98
Cartledge, G., 119, 151, 152, 153, 163, 164

SUBJECT INDEX